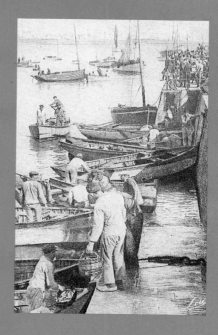

"Notre-Dame-de-Penhors is our own special chapel; the great Pardons held there are the most important moments of our lives." Pierre Jakez-Hélias

Main photograph: Notre-Dame de La Joie; 1954.
Inset: Châteaulin, Chapel of Notre-Dame; 19th century.

“BLACK, COPPER GREEN, COBALT,
REDDISH-BROWN, THE SIXTY BISQUINES
ALL PAINTED IN DEEP,
STRONG COLORS
PLOUGHED THROUGH
THE WAVES.”
ROGER VERCEL

Main picture: St-Malo, Cancale bisquines racing; postcard, early 20th century.

Inset, top: Bisquines at anchor in the port of Cancale; early 20th century.

Inset, bottom: Oyster sorting at Cancale; early 20th century.

EVERYMAN GUIDES

PUBLISHED BY DAVID CAMPBELL PUBLISHERS LTD, LONDON

ISBN 1-85715-841-5

© 1994 David Campbell Publishers Ltd

© 1994 Editions Nouveaux-Loisirs, a subsidiary of Gallimard, Paris.

First published 1994
Second edition revised and updated 1998

NUMEROUS SPECIALISTS AND ACADEMICS HAVE CONTRIBUTED TO THIS GUIDE:
AUTHORS AND EDITORS: Philippe Aballan, Christophe Amiot, Pierre Arzel, Jean Balcou, Nathalie Beaud, Marielle Blanc, Agnès Boubault, Anaïck Bourhis, Jacques Briard, Anne Cabasse, M. Cabot, Mme Chouteau, Yves Cosson, Alain Croix, Françoise Daniel, Dominique Dantec, M. Dao, DASTUM, Henry Decaëns, Denise Delouche, Michel Denis, Madeleine Dervaux, Christelle Drouard, Philippe Dubois, Jean-Pierre Ducouret, Nicole Faucherre, Henri Fermin, Roland Flatresses, Jean-Marie Fonteneau, Patrice Forget, Carole Gaborit, Mme Gargadennec, Claudine Glot, Philippe Henwood, Jean Herisset, Guy Joncour, Yann-Fanch Kemener, Donatien Laurent, Michèle Le Brozec, Jean-Claude Le Dro, Catherine Le Floc'h, Yves Le Gall La Salle, Roger-Henri Le Page, Olivier Le Moign, Gwenhaelle Le Roy, Laurence Lesage, Philippe Le Sturm, Patrick Le Tiec, Jean-Louis Malroux, Claude Marcel, Gaby Marcon, Yves-Marie Maquet, Marie-Dominique Menant, Jean-Yves Monnat, Simone Morand, Francis Muel, Yves-Marie Paulet, Florence Picquot, Jean-Claude Pierre, Edmond Rébillé, Jean-Jacques Rioult, Robin Rolland, Jean-Yves Ruaux, Guy de Sallier-Dupin, Jean-François Simon, Mme Toulet, Riccardo Tremori.

ILLUSTRATORS: J.-P. Arcile, Philippe Biard, Frédéric Bony, A. Bravard, Philippe Candé, Jean Chevallier, Denis Clavreuil, Nicolas Christitch, François Desbordes, Dominique Duplantier, P. Duris, Claire Felloni, Nicolas Gilles, Jean-François Guével, Jean-Marie Guillou, Jean-Benoît Héron, Gilbert Houbre, Catherine Lachaux, Marc Lagarde, Bruno Lenormand, Aubin Leray, Guy Michel, Gilbert Morel, Sylvaine Perols, François Place, Eric Prigent, Olivier Racquois, Pascal Robin, Frédérique Schwebel, John Wilkinson.

PHOTOGRAPHERS: Agene Nature, Gilles Bentz, Jean Chevallier, Eric Guillemot, Flageul, Jean-Louis Lemoigne, Alain Le Toquin.

WE WOULD LIKE TO GIVE SPECIAL THANKS TO:
Maurice Dilasser, Jean-Pierre Gestin, René Le Bihan, Jean-Claude Le Dro, Bernard Le Nail, Jean-Claude Pierre.

TRANSLATED BY CLIVE UNGER-HAMILTON;
EDITED AND TYPESET BY BOOK CREATION SERVICES, LONDON.
PRINTED IN ITALY BY EDITORIALE LIBRARIA.

EVERYMAN GUIDES
79 BERWICK STREET
LONDON W1V 3PF

BRITTANY

EVERYMAN GUIDES

CONTENTS

BRITTANY

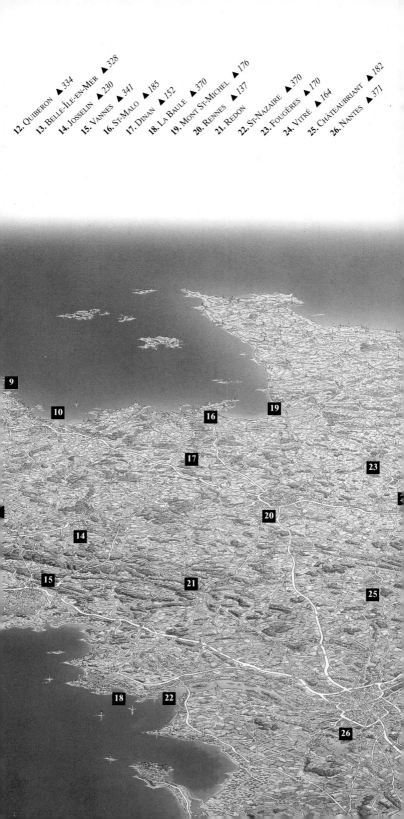

HOW TO USE THIS GUIDE
(Sample page shown from the guide to Venice)

The symbols at the top of each page refer to the different parts of the guide.

- ■ NATURAL ENVIRONMENT
- ● KEYS TO UNDERSTANDING
- ▲ ITINERARIES
- ◆ PRACTICAL INFORMATION

The itinerary map shows the main points of interest along the way and is intended to help you find your bearings.

The mini-map locates the particular itinerary within the wider area covered by the guide.

★ The star symbol signifies that a particular site has been singled out by the publishers for its special beauty, atmosphere or cultural interest.

●▲■◆
The symbols alongside a title or within the text itself provide cross-references to a theme or place dealt with elsewhere in the guide.

At the beginning of each itinerary, the suggested means of transport to be used and the time it will take to cover the area are indicated:
- ⇌ By boat
- ⻊ On foot
- ⚲ By bicycle
- ⏱ Duration

THE GATEWAY TO VENICE ★

PONTE DELLA LIBERTÀ. Built by the Austrians 50 years after the Treaty of Campo Formio in 1797 ● *34,* to link Venice with Milan. The bridge ended the thousand-year separation from the mainland and shook the city's economy to its roots as Venice, already in the throes of the industrial revolution, saw

⻊ Half a day

BRIDGES TO VENICE

NATURE

■ SEA MARKS

The Jardin lighthouse, which marks the reef at the entrance to St-Malo harbor.

Lighthouses, buoys and beacons are immensely important to anyone in charge of a boat. Fixed and floating marks, beacons and buoys all help sailors to determine their position, fix their course and avoid danger when navigating within sight of the coast. Some marks, such as churches and water towers, as well as lighthouses, are on land; these are indicated on navigation charts.

SEAMARKS AROUND CERTAIN COASTAL AREAS. They are used to mark bathing areas, which are closed to navigation.

Such zones are broken by channels that allow light and shallow-bottomed

craft, as well as windsurfers, access to the beach.

LANDMARKS
By taking a compass bearing on a landmark or lining up two such marks, navigators can to calculate their position or plot a course between hazards. Fixed beacons can be used in the same way.

MARKING A CHANNEL
Beacons and buoys are placed each side of a channel to indicate a safe passage for boats. The marks, which can vary in appearance, may be fixed in shallow water or be floating where the water is deeper. As you sail inland toward a harbor, or safe haven, one key rule applies:

keep green marks to starboard (right)

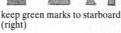

and red marks to port.

When a channel divides, the markers continue to indicate the main channel,

but with a stripe of the opposing color to show their position as markers for the secondary channel.

WHEN THE TIDE IS HIGH, THE MARK IS LOW.
WHEN THE TIDE IS LOW, THE MARK IS HIGH.

MARKS INDICATING THE CARDINAL POINTS
From left to right: north, east, south and west.

SAFE-WATER MARKS
These are placed outside a harbor to show that boats no longer have to follow specific channels.

ISOLATED DANGER
Marks are placed on or just above the hazard.

These special marks are not for navigation but to indicate zones where craft are not permitted.

17

GEOLOGY

Armorican sandstone: the Tas de Pois rocks at Camaret in south Finistère.

The Armorican massif is made up of granite, schist and sandstone. Its geological formation was virtually complete by the end of the Primary era. The Hercynian folds which shaped the formations are responsible for the shape of the peninsula and its coastline. From the start of the Secondary era the Hercynian mountains suffered intense erosion and the massif gradually emerged. Granites, gneiss and sandstone shaped its outline, while schist occurred in the large basins. During the Tertiary era the sea formed bays here and there, notably the Faluns Sea, which flooded the Rennes basin. The plateau was elevated and broken up, and during the Quaternary era subsequent changes in sea level and a periglacial climate put the finishing touches to the shape of the landscape as we know it today.

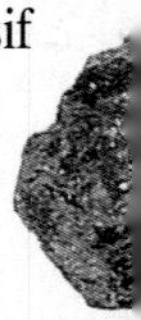

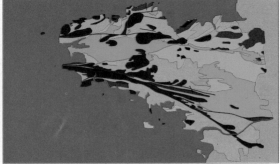

- Brioverian
- Paleozoic lower and middle
- Quaternary
- Other granitic
- Hercynian Leucogranitic
- Microgranitic
- Granitic
- Metamorphic formations
- Carboniferous

Around the coast, the levels of pebbles at the foot of the cliffs indicate the sea level in prehistoric times, which was many feet higher than it is today. One size of stone tends to predominate on a beach.

ARMORICAN SANDSTONE AT THE CAP DE LA CHÈVRE. Thick seams of hard-wearing white quartzic sandstone helped to shape the Brittany landscape in the Primary formations.

Metamorphic schist from Guerphales has been commercially exploited as refractory rock.

SHAPING A SLATE
The splitter forms two sheets of slate with two deft blows of his beetle. His oversized wooden shoes are designed to break the slate's fall, after which the craftsman squares up the edges and smooths them off.

STAUROLITE
This locally abundant mineral often occurs in curious shapes, which are prized as good luck charms.

Plœmeur in the Morbihan is the principal French source of kaolin or china clay, which is used in the manufacture of paper, porcelain and toothpaste.

The pink granite of Ploumanac'h is famous all over France.

Cap Fréhel's high cliffs of red sandstone show a number of successive horizontal layers broken away in places to form a series of tiers.

1. GARNET-RED MICA SCHIST AND GLAUCOPHANE (Île de Groix)
2. SHARK'S TOOTH
A few fossils from the Tertiary era are still to be found in shelly sand.
3. ORDOVICIAN SCHIST

The sea has stripped the rocks of their coating, forming small bodies of diorite.

Limestone is rare in Brittany, and in former times was burned to manufacture quicklime in an oven such as this one from the Loire-Atlantique region.

4. GRANITE
Gray, blue, red or white granite is a ubiquitous feature of Brittany, its color varying according to the minerals it contains.
5. KERSANTITE
6. ANDALUSITE SCHIST
7. RED SCHIST
8. SCHIST WITH TRILOBITES
Fossils are common in sedimentary deposits from the Primary era. Trilobites and arthropods are the most frequently encountered.

Kersanton granite is easy to carve and used for statues in the parish closes, (below Lampaul-Guïmiliau, in north Finistère).

Schist folds caused by Hercynian pressure.

MOLÈNE ARCHIPELAGO

DOLPHINS
A permanent colony of dolphins lives south of the archipelago.

A dozen small islands and low-lying islets are scattered over the treacherous seas between Le Conquet and Ouessant. Around them are the finest beds of seaweed in all France and also some of the most important bird and marine mammal reserves in the country. It was for these reasons that in 1980 Unesco singled out this magnificent unspoilt archipelago and designated it a "biosphere".

SEA-KALE
Flourishes among the pebbles.

1

2

3

Three of the five species of tern found in Brittany: common tern (1), little tern (2) and sandwich tern (3).

GREY SEAL
This was the first place in France where it was observed to breed. The small colony probably maintains its numbers by the influx of young seals from Britain.

ROSEATE TERN
The most endangered seabird in Europe now nests only occasionally in the Molène archipelago.

The 19th-century naturalist from Nantes, Louis Bureau, was the first to draw attention to the islands. Three of them were made into a wildlife reserve in the 1960's: Banneg, Balaneg and Trielen.

LESSER BLACK-BACKED GULL
About 10 % of the European breeding stock nests on the archipelago.

STORM PETREL
Nests underground. Nearly all French petrels nest on Banneg.

OYSTER CATCHER
They nest on the island coasts.

RINGED PLOVER
Lays its eggs on the pebbles.

Great black-backed gull

Lesser black-backed gull

Herring gull

Sheldrake

Storm petrel

Certain seabirds are more common on cliffs and low-lying islets. The key factor favoring this environment for birds is the absence of predators and of man.

Tern

Puffin

Manx shearwater

Ringed plover

MANX SHEARWATER
Like the storm petrel, it is nocturnal and nests in a hole in the ground. Numbers are small but on the increase.

STONY BELT
A coastal strip of pebbles where some plants grow and storm petrels nests.

BROOM PLANTS
growing beside the sea are small
and often clustered near the
ground.

ROCK PIPIT

The cliffs, rising up from the
swirling foam of the sea, are
crowned with windblown grassy
heathland. In between is a sheer
wall of inhospitable, barren rock
where leafy plants are few but
lichens many and various. For
sea birds this is a safe haven
where they can lay their eggs and
raise their broods undisturbed
by terrestrial predators.

SEA THRIFT
In May the rocks
are covered in its
pink flowers.

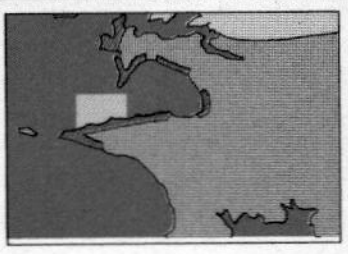

The cliffs of Finistère
are the wildest in
Brittany. At Cap
Sizun they are
granite and at
Crozon the rock
is sedimentary.

PARMELIA
One of the most
common of the 140
lichens to be found
on Brittany rocks.

COASTAL HEATHLAND
In spring it is a
sparkling mixture of
gorse, sea thrift and
campion.

The rock is never
entirely bare. Lichens
form bands of color,
from grey at the top,
then yellow, to black
at the bottom. They
grow lower down or
higher up depending
on their resistance to
the sea.

CHOUGH
A small and delightful member of the crow family, with a bright red beak. The chough lives in mountains and, with increasing rarity, on sea cliffs.

RAVEN

Cap Sizun ravens steal the eggs and chicks of kittiwakes. Fewer than one hundred pairs remain in Brittany.

HERRING GULL

These familiar sea birds scavenge on beaches and garbage dumps, and eat mussels and worms. Cliffs can be suitable nesting places providing there is a wide enough ledge.

GREAT BLACK-BACKED GULL
Along with the gannet, this is the largest French sea bird and a fierce predator of gulls and young cormorants. Nests are often on top of lone rocks.

FULMAR
These increasingly common birds are distinguishable in flight from gulls by their outstretched wings. Outside the breeding season, they live on the open sea.

KITTIWAKE
The name evokes the birds' peculiar cry. Their black wingtips are distinctive.

RAZORBILL
The rarest of all French sea birds (only forty pairs remain). Making no nest, they lay a single egg on the bare rock.

They build nests of grass and earth attached to the vertical rock face. There are nine hundred pairs in the Goulien nature reserve. Late in August the birds leave for the open sea and return in January.

Colonies of sea birds can be densely packed and have complex systems of communication.

COMMON GUILLEMOT OR MURRE
The use of transparent fishing nets has undoubtedly contributed to the decline of this species, but there are still forty breeding pairs at Goulien.

SHAG
The lesser cormorant is ever more common on rocky coasts. It dives to catch whiting-pout, or bib, a fish with an inflatable membrane on its head.

23

Colony of gannets

Puffins and shearwaters

The Sept-Îles nature reserve ▲ 223, established in 1912 in response to the continuous slaughter of puffins, is the oldest in France. Of all the islands in the reserve, Rouzic has the richest variety of wildlife. The reserve is administered by the French society for the protection of birds, and is one of the jewels of the Breton coastline. The Île Rouzic is home to colonies of eighteen different species of sea birds native to the Atlantic coast of France (some of which nest nowhere else in the world), and a small population of grey seals that live here all the year round and breed in the winter months.

GANNET
The gannet is the largest native European sea bird. It eats only live fish, generally mackerel, which it spots from the air and dives to catch – sometimes many feet beneath the surface. It likes to nest on precipitous ledges, using grasses and seaweed, and lays a single blue egg in spring.

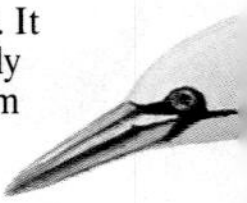

GANNET
The Île Rouzic has the only colony of gannets on the French coast. They returned here in 1939, since when the colony has continually increased: today there are no fewer than six thousand nesting pairs.

The white patch is the colony of gannets, clearly visible from a distance of several miles.

MANX SHEARWATER
A small number of these handsome birds have been established on Rouzic for some fifteen years. On land they are nocturnal birds and like puffins they prefer to nest in burrows, sometimes using rabbit holes.

Puffin colony

Fulmar

PUFFIN
It nests in a burrow whenever possible, which it lines with grass and feathers.

PUFFIN
Some 220 breeding pairs are established on the Sept-Îles. Sadly, numbers are decreasing. They nest in colonies and begin to lay in May, each pair producing a single egg.

COMMON GUILLEMOT
Its numbers diminished in the wake of the *Amoco Cadiz* disaster.

RAZORBILL
This is the rarest French sea bird: twenty of the forty pairs in France nest here.

SHAG
It nests on a ledge, under cover if it can.

GREY SEAL
Some rare white examples of the breed have been born here.

■ DUNES

SEA HOLLY. This spiny plant resembles a thistle, though it actually belongs to the same family as the carrot, coriander, parsley and hemlock and the water parsnips.

Dunes are inland extensions of beaches. They were formed gradually over several thousands of years as the sea retreated. As such they are natural fossil formations but are now threatened by the rising sea level and the incursion of man. Dunes are a fairly rare habitat, particularly in Brittany, where there is relatively little chalk or limestone. They consist largely of shelly sand, a favorable environment for plant and animal life that thrives in warmth and calcareous surroundings. From their salt-bleached fronts across their windblown summits to the damp landward areas, dunes host a microcosm of countless natural wonders, as the interested observer will discover.

SEA GRASS ON THE DUNES
Sand swept up from the lower beach begins to form dunes.

SAND MARTIN
This is the smallest of the swallow family.

Pairs of birds excavate deep horizontal galleries to nest in the dunes.

KENTISH PLOVER
An elegant bird that carefully lays three eggs in the seaward expanses of the dunes. But as the beaches grow in

popularity, the bird is becoming rarer.

Urbanization, extraction, erosion and general exploitation by industrialized society are all contributing to the dunes' decline. Shoring them up with fences offers the best protection.

SEA GRASS
Also known as sea bent or marram grass. It has a highly developed root system to fix itself in the sand.

EVERLASTING FLOWER
This is essentially a southern plant, with a pleasant and distinctive scent. In Brittany it is not found beyond Finistère.

BEE ORCHID
A tiny plant that is patterned to resemble the rear end of a bumble-bee visiting the flower.

ORCHIDS
Orchids thrive in the calcareous sands of the dunes.

LAPWING
In Brittany it lives in dunes and coastal marshes.

Behind the dunes is a delicate structure of flora that helps to consolidate its fragile surface.

SEA BINDWEED
It helps to hold the dunes together.

SAND SNAIL

SKYLARK
Open stretches of land are its ideal environment.

NATTERJACK TOAD
The natterjack, a nocturnal creature, has a distinctive yellow stripe down its back.

TREE FROG
It hides in the foliage.

MUSKRAT
A large aquatic rodent that nests in marshes.

JOINT PINE
A tiny ligneous undershrub with green twigs and fleshy red fruit. In Brittany it is only found on south-facing dunes.

SHOVELER DUCK
It is distinguishable by its large spatulate bill and lives in wet ground behind dunes.

COOT
These excitable, noisy little fowl are on the increase in Brittany, where they flourish in coastal lakes.

The wetlands behind the dunes are richly populated with all kinds of wildlife.

THE SEASHORE

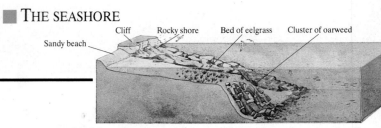

Sandy beach — Cliff — Rocky shore — Bed of eelgrass — Cluster of oarweed

As waves and tides die down at the water's edge, they gradually deposit sediment and detritus the sea has gathered elsewhere, and this forms beaches. Seaweed does not grow readily in such a relatively unstable environment, but these conditions are favorable to planktonic organisms which are filtered out from the water or collected from the surface of the sand by a variety of animals. Predominant among these are worms and bivalves, which densely colonize the sandy deposits on the shore. Then in their turn these creatures fall prey to crabs, fish and birds.

HERMIT CRAB
It clears the beach of waste material.

SHRIMP
Brittany shrimps are highly prized for their flavor.

SAND-MASON WORM
Squiggly coils of sand dotted about the beach are made by these worms, who feed on particles of vegetable matter.

BED OF EELGRASS
These marine herbs have creeping rhizomes and grow in dense beds on the sands, offering an ideal habitat for a wide variety of animal life.

SOLE
Some medium-sized sole swim quite close to the beach and can be caught in the shallow water of the low spring tides.

HERRING GULL
Adult birds have silver-grey upper parts (above) and pink legs.

LESSER BLACK-BACKED GULL
Dark grey back, yellow legs.

GREAT BLACK-BACKED GULL. Largest of the gulls, with dark back and pink legs.

TURNSTONE
This tame and sturdy bird pokes among stones and seaweed in search of food.

RINGED PLOVER
It makes runs along the sand, pausing to pick up food.

OYSTERCATCHER
It feeds on molluscs, which it stabs or hammers open.

FISHING FOR COCKLES
A special little rake is used to separate out small molluscs, such as cockles, buried in the sand.

RAY EGG
Washed up by the tide, these are a common sight on beaches.

SANDHOPPER

F. Desbordes

SHORE CRAB
The crab, a common scavenger on beaches, hides in small crevices when disturbed.

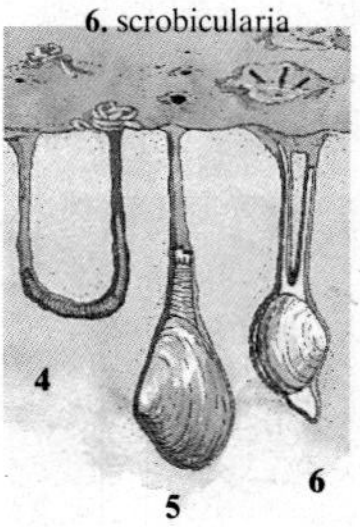

CORYSTES
An animal that lives buried in fine sand.

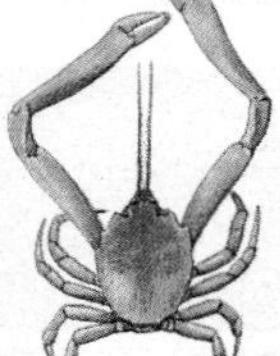

COCKLE (1)
A bivalve mollusc about 1 inch across. The two identical shells each have twenty-six ribs.

DONAX
Found on fine sandy beaches.

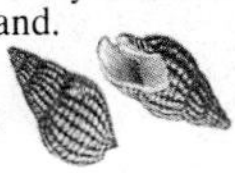

CLAM (5)
It likes to live in pebbly sand. Where the sand is muddy, the shells are darker.

VENUS CLAM (2)
Found at low tide, usually in coarse sand.

NETTED DOG WHELK
A relative of the winkle that likes to feed on dead animals.

RAZOR CLAM (3)
At low tide they bury themselves vertically in the sand, leaving a small hole at the surface.

4. arenicola
6. scrobicularia

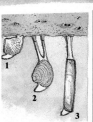

29

ROCKY COASTLINE

Several days a month receding spring tides may leave beds of oarweed exposed.

Man has gathered limpets since time immemorial.

Twice a day the ebbing tide uncovers large stretches of sand and rocks that conceal enormous colonies of diverse marine life in a bewildering variety of shapes and colors. While plants and animals living at the extreme edge of the shore are only briefly exposed, those higher up may have to wait twelve hours for the sea to return, moistening and feeding them. From top to bottom the beach is a series of strips inhabited by creatures that differ according to the amount of immersion each requires.

From this self-contained little microcosm man has sought out the forms of life most useful to him: fish, crustaceans and shellfish for food, and seaweeds to fertilize the food he grows on land.

Colonial ascidium

Yellow sponge
Red sponge
White sponge

The upper sides of stones on the seabed are generally covered with algae-like growths. For lack of light, the undersides are usually bare and serve as protective covering for all kinds of animal life. Many of these organisms will die if the stones they live under are not carefully replaced.

BOTRYLLUS
These little star-shaped creatures live on rocks and seaweeds. They exist in a variety of colors and belong to the family of ascidia.

Carrageen moss (*Chondrus crispus*)

VELVET CRAB
This little animal, also known as the swimming crab, is very agile.

CALCAREOUS ALGAE
Rock pools and stones are often coated with a skin of pink calcareous algae. The dark discs are the winter form of large brown algae.

CONGER EEL
The conger, which inhabits rock crevices, is the largest fish commonly caught at the water's edge.

PRAWN
About 2 inches long, these are often found in rock pools and are eagerly sought as a delicacy.

ROCKLING

ORMER
Now rarely found on the seashore, living permanently under water below low-tide level.

LIMPET
At high tide the limpet feeds by scraping a film of microscopic algae from the rock on which it lives. As the tide ebbs, the animal settles back into its place on the rock, which its shell has grown to fit.

Lichen

High spring tidemark

TROCHUS

High neap tidemark

BLADDER WRACK
The air-filled sacs after which it is named make it buoyant. It is the most conspicuous brown seaweed.

CONCH

Bladder wrack

MUSSELS AND DOG WHELKS
Mussel beds flourish on rocky surfaces, and tend to favor the mid-tide level. The dog whelk is the mussel's chief predator.

Sea wrack

WINKLE   **SEA LACE**

Low spring tidemark

Thong weed

Low neap tidemark

Certain seaweeds, fish, anemones and other organisms that cannot exist away from water can live quite far up the rocks in rock pools.

FEATHER STAR

SAND STAR

CHITON

ANEMONES COMMON (1,2) RED (3), STRAWBERRY (4)
They feed on incautious small creatures and also filter out algae and plankton from the water.

1

2

3

4

31

Mussels, flat and cupped oysters, and clams are four main types of shellfish commercially farmed on the Brittany coast. The cultivation of mussels once called for large areas that would be uncovered at low tide, such as the bays at Mont-St-Michel and St-Brieuc or the Vilaine estuary. But in recent years mussels have been bred on lines in shallow water. As the result of diseases that have decimated the flat oyster population, oyster farming has undergone radical changes over the last thirty years. The Japanese cupped oyster is now the dominant variety everywhere. Breeding clams commercially, using a variety imported from the Pacific, is a relatively recent practise.

Mussels live in a fixed position, feeding by creating a current of water that directs micro-algae to their gills.

Mussel farming began in the Charente in the 17th century. The use of stakes is an ingenious way of increasing the yield, and it also reduces the workload.

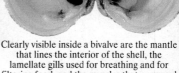

Muscle

Gills

Foot

STAKES AND CATCHMENT LINES
Mussels are farmed on stakes planted on hurdles or in beds in such a way that they are uncovered at low tide.

Clearly visible inside a bivalve are the mantle that lines the interior of the shell, the lamellate gills used for breathing and for filtering food, and the muscles that open and close the shells.

CASES OF MUSSELS
Before dispatch, mussels are stored in boxes placed high up on the beach.

The young mussels are attached to horizontal lines, which are wound in spirals around wooden stakes.

COCKLES
These are not actually [far]med, though spats are [re]moved to convenient locations.

MUSSEL
They reach commercial size in under two years.

CUPPED OYSTER
Originally Portuguese, but Japanese since 1970.

FLAT OYSTER
Flat Brittany oysters are known as *belons*, and taste of iodine.

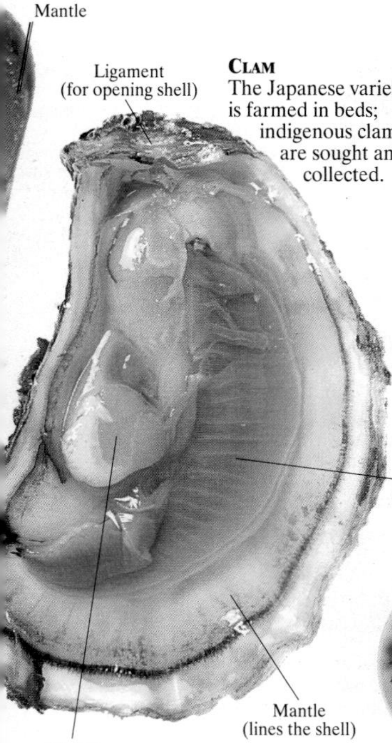

Mantle

Ligament
(for opening shell)

CLAM
The Japanese variety is farmed in beds; indigenous clams are sought and collected.

LARVA AND SPAT
The cupped oyster larva is planktonic, while that of the flat oyster grows within its mother's shell. At three to four weeks the larva metamorphoses and becomes fixed.

CULTIVATION
Cupped oysters are attached to tiles and reared some distance from the shore before being transferred to fattening beds.

Gills
(for feeding and breathing)

Mantle
(lines the shell)

Muscle
(for closing shell)

MOULES MARINIÈRES
A favorite summer dish, made when mussels are at their best, with the maximum sugar accumulated in their mantles.

MATURING
Maturing takes place at the river mouth. Sweet and salt water combine to fatten the oyster's liver and make it juicy.

[O]PENING AN OYSTER
[I]ntroduce the [b]lade of a strong [k]nife between the [s]hells, twist open [a]nd sever the [m]uscle.

SORTING, GRADING AND PACKAGING

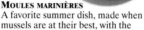

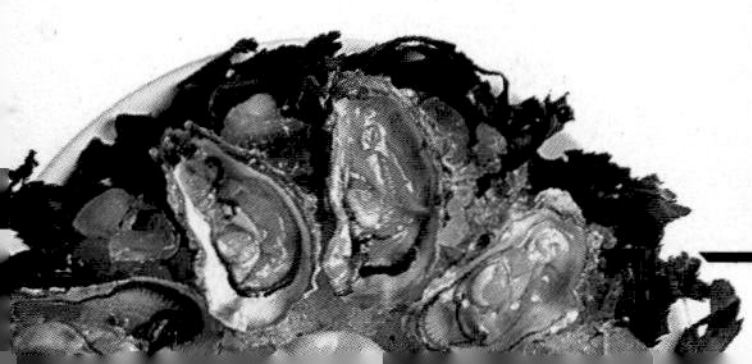

CRUSTACEANS

Traditional woven willow "pots" are fast becoming obsolete.

Spider crabs and edible crabs are the most commonly fished crustaceans. They are caught all round the Brittany coastline, especially in the north and west of the province, where nets have largely supplanted pots for catching spider crabs. Langoustines are generally caught either fairly close inshore or in British waters, and are a specialty of southern Brittany, particularly the Bigouden region around Pont l'Abbé. Other crustaceans are less important economically, although the rocky coast of Brittany has an eminently exploitable lobster population.

EDIBLE CRAB
As the crabs grow, they make for deep water.

LANGOUSTINE
These creatures soon die when removed from the water, and are usually sold cooked

LOBSTER
Lives on the rocky bottom close to shore. Overfishing has made the lobster scarce.

SPINY LOBSTER
They may be distinguished from the lobster by the absence of claws, and are now scarce throughout Brittany.

GALATHEA
Also known as squat lobster. It is a local delicacy.

Pots come in different shapes and are made of different materials. Plastic has all but replaced wickerwork. Lured by the bait, the animal climbs in through the narrow entrance and is trapped.

The boats can sink up to eight hundred pots strung on several lines. A watertight tank in the hold keeps the crustaceans alive while the boat remains at sea.

The net hangs vertically on the ocean bed, trapping the spider crabs when they move.

SPIDER CRAB
They reach maturity at two years old and cease to molt. The male has strong pincers.

SETTING THE POTS
Lines of baited pots are lowered over the side of the boat.

Crustaceans are still a great delicacy, and a valuable cash crop.

In warm weather sardines were once caught off the southern ports from Douarnenez to Croisic. But as sardine stocks have declined Breton fishing grounds have changed radically in recent decades. Hake is now caught around the coast and has become a specialty of Lorient. Since the war the number of trawlers has greatly increased, and during the 1980's nets became much stronger. The wide variety of fishing methods on very varied seabed formations has increased the different types of fish caught. Scores of different kinds of fish are now landed every day in the innumerable ports that line the Breton coast.

LING
A member of the cod family. It is generally caught by trawler and sold cut into fillets.

HAKE
A mild-flavored fish; much in demand as it has few bones.

YELLOW POLLACK
Caught with lines or nets. It is almost olive in color, with a silver or golden underside. Its flesh has a finer taste than black pollack, whose meat is an unappetizing grey.

SARDINE. A small fish of the herring family with fine-flavored but oily flesh. In summer they achieve maximum size and are known as pilchards.

Inshore fishing is generally done in boats from 20 to 50 feet long, and the methods used vary according to season.

TRAWLER
The net is dragged along the sea bed (at depths of up to half a mile). The mouth is held open by two "otter boards". The shoals of fish are disturbed by the motion on the sea bed and take refuge in the net bag at the end of the trawl.

MONKFISH
The head is cut off before the fish is sold, and the flesh is highly prized.

SKATE
Triangular pieces are cut from the wings.

MACKEREL
A fine metallic green, the fish turns blue when caught.

WHITING
Caught with a trawler and usually cut into fillets.

CONGER EEL
This carnivore has vicious jaws and lives in crevices in the rocks. Conger can grow to well over six feet long, and the meat is a popular ingredient in fish soups and stews.

BASS
Also called sea perch, it is a ruthless predator and a prized delicacy.

SOLE
Its first year is spent on the sandy seabed around the coastline.

DOGFISH
Actually a small shark, it has delicate pink flesh when freshly caught.

In most ports the daily catch is sold on the quayside.

BOTTOM (1) AND SURFACE (2) LINES
These can be anchored on the seabed or at mid-depth, according to the fish being caught. The hooks are attached all along the main line.

TANGLE NET
It is left on the sea bed for a period varying from a few hours to several days. Fish are caught by the gills.

TRIPLE MESH NET
Several hundred yards long and made up of three layers of netting, it is generally put out at night.

LIEU DORÉ DU MALAMOCK

■ SEAWEED

Breton améliorant, a seaweed rich in lime, is used to reduce the acidity of the granitic soil in the province.

Seaweed is formed from a single tissue and as such is a primitive plant. Its nutritive organs are distributed all over its surface and, rather than a root, it has a foot that serves as a fixing device. South Finistère and the Côtes d'Armor have exceptionally rich crops of seaweed and at least 670 species. The Laminaria and Fucales account for upward of 80 percent of this biomass, which man has long put to a variety of uses. It first became a commercial crop around the 17th century. When burned it produces soda and iodine. Factories now process more than 60,000 tons of seaweed annually, making colloids and other gelling agents used mainly in the food industry. It seems probable that in the future seaweed will increasingly become part of our diet.

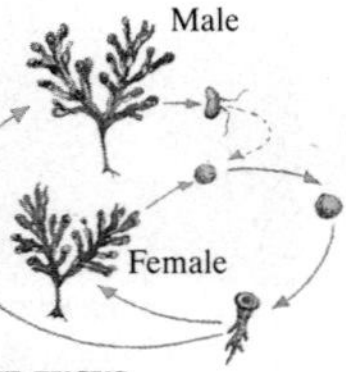

Male

Female

THE FUCUS CYCLE
Male and female gametes come together in the open sea.

PALMARIA PALMATA

CHONDRUS CRISPUS

ULVA LACTUCA

PELVETIA CANALICULATA

FUCUS SPIRALIS

SECTION EXPOSED TO SWELL

SHELTERED SECTION

FUCUS VESICULOSUS

HIGH WATER, SPRING TIDE

Fucus spiralis

Pelvetia canaliculata

Ascophyllum nodosum

HIGH WATER, NEAP TIDE

Fucus vesiculosus

Himanthalia elongata

HALF-TIDE

Fucus serratus

LOW WATER, NEAP TIDE

Palmaria palmata

Bifurcaria bifurcata

LOW WATER, SPRING TIDE

Alaria esculenta

ASCOPHYLLUM NODOSUM

Chondrus crispus

Saccorhiza polyschides

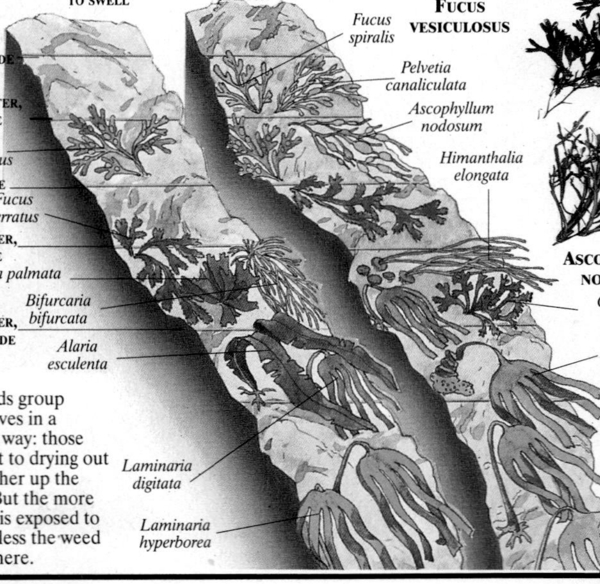

Seaweeds group themselves in a definite way: those resistant to drying out live further up the shore. But the more the site is exposed to air, the less the weed grows there.

Laminaria digitata

Laminaria hyperborea

Laminaria hyperborea

Foot

Until twenty years ago seaweed was gathered after every storm.

Frond. Protects the reproductive organs.

Shore weed was cut with a sickle, while submerged weed was gathered from boats with long hooks called *guillotines*. Both activities have long been strictly controlled.

Once dried, *Laminaria* was burned in low stone ovens to produce blocks of soda for the chemical industry. Shore varieties of seaweed were used as a fertilizer.

The seaweed gatherers used to raise their loads up the cliff by means of rudimentary winches.

SEAWEED OVEN

Wakame is an edible seaweed now cultivated on ropes in northern Brittany (around Ouessant and Pleubian, for example). There is a rapidly developing market for it.

BLOCKS OF SODA

Flexible stem that can survive even the worst storms.

For the last twenty years *Laminaria* has been harvested from boats equipped with a rotating hook, which could be over 11 feet long, known as as "skoubidou". This tears the weed from its mooring up to a depth of 10 feet.

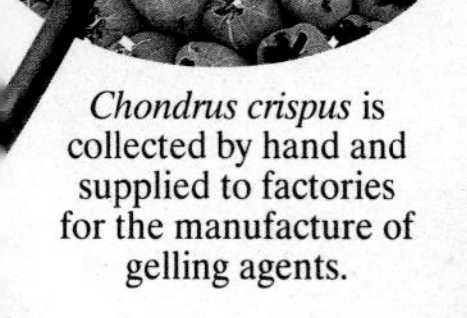

Chondrus crispus is collected by hand and supplied to factories for the manufacture of gelling agents.

In packaged foods E 407 indicates *Chondrus crispus*. E 400 and E 404 indicate Laminaria, *Fucus* and *Ascophyllum*.

These estuaries where the tide reaches far inland are known locally as *rias*, or in Breton as *abers*. *Slikke*, vast expanses of bare mud uncovered as the sea ebbs, are separated from the *schorre* by rudimentary cliffs. The land consists of salt marshes broken up by watery channels and pools, and covered with dense low-growing vegetation. The water is alternately fresh, at low tide, and salty, at high tide. The environment does not suit a wide variety of plants and animals but those that can adapt to it breed abundantly.

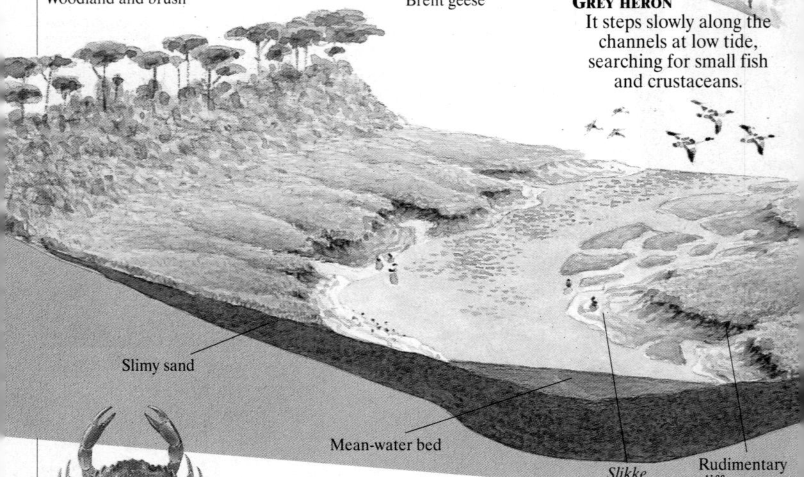

Woodland and brush

Brent geese

GREY HERON
It steps slowly along the channels at low tide, searching for small fish and crustaceans.

Slimy sand

Mean-water bed

Slikke

Rudimentary cliff

SHORE CRAB
It is also known as the green crab, after its color, and is about 2 inches across.

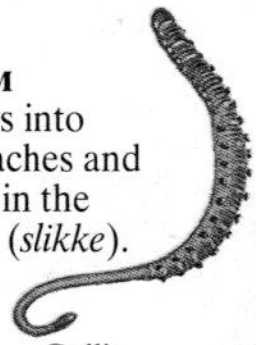

LOBWORM
It burrows into sandy beaches and also lives in the mud flats (*slikke*).

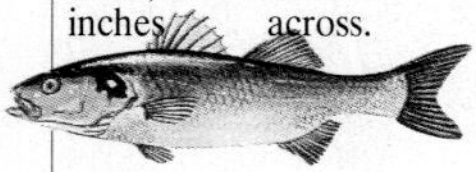

Mud accumulates around the green algae.

Gull's footprints

Lobworm cast

Oxidized exterior

GREY MULLET
Its small toothless mouth distinguishes this fish from the bass. It feeds on microscopic algae, lives around the mudbanks and sometimes swims upriver.

Hole made by scrobicularia

Nereid marks

SCROBICULARIA
It lives deeply embedded, extracting its food from the mud.

NEREID
A marine worm is often used as bait by fishermen.

Sea lavender

MARSH SAMPHIRE AND SPARTINA
These plants colonize the banks of the *slikke*, helping to hold the mud together and encouraging the deposit of further layers of mud.

Marsh samphire

Spartina

Sea aster

SEA LAVENDER
In summer the *schorre* is pale mauve, carpeted with this short perennial and with sea asters. The sea covers it only at spring tides.

OBIONE. It can cover enormous stretches of the *schorre*. Its fleshy leaves are a good example of adjustment to a saline habitat.

HIGH AND LOW TIDES
At high tide the mud flats look like a miniature fjord, but when the tide is out the river dwindles to a small channel.

Schorre

Cormorant (winter plumage)

SHELDRAKE
It nests in burrows, sometimes far from the water.

BRENT GOOSE
A small goose that visits bays and estuaries from October to April. It loves eelgrass.

LITTLE GREBE
An energetic diver, also known as the dabchick.

CURLEW
Its long curved beak searches out small creatures buried deep in the mud, and it also eats shore crabs.

REDSHANK
A wader frequently seen on mud flats and marshes.

DUNLIN
Also known as the red-backed sandpiper. This common wader walks round mud flats looking for worms, crustaceans and small molluscs.

CORMORANT
Feeding on flatfish and eels, they are most commonly seen in estuaries from the fall through the end of winter.

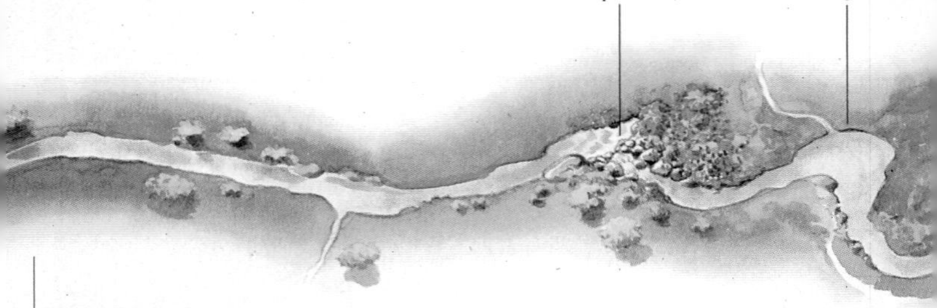

RIVERS AND TORRENTS

Steep slope causes
rapid flow

Meander has slow-
moving water

The majority of Breton rivers are short and, flowing down
from the heights of the Argoat, change suddenly from
rushing torrents to muddy tidal streams. For virtually
their entire length they are classified as prime-
category rivers, well stocked with salmon. Many
of the rivers are now under threat from
agricultural pollution, and are kept under close
observation by Breton water and river authorities.

ALDER
Grows by still and fast-
flowing water.

Caddis fly
larva

WATER SHREW
It searches for small fish and
tadpoles in streams and rivers.
The female burrows into the
bank to make a nest.

Leafy covering

The river is flowing from left to right. Fast-flowing and calm stretches alternate, and each harbors different forms of wildlife.

Calm stretch

American mink

MINK
By a rapid increase in its numbers American mink, escaped from captivity, is threatening the rare European mink.

European mink

Fast-flowing and well oxygenated water is favorable to salmon.

KINGFISHER
It nests in a horizontal burrow high on the river bank.

POLECAT
Though much less at home in the water than the otter, it may be seen swimming to catch fish and small animals at the water's edge.

GREY WAGTAIL
An elegant bird that is frequently seen beside streams in Brittany.

Cleaning the river to allow light to filter through the water.

OTTER
This lithe aquatic hunter is increasingly rare, but can be found in Breton rivers.

WATER VOLE
It is the largest of the voles, and is often called the water rat.

Light and oxygen are both essential to support life.

ATLANTIC SALMON
Its presence and continued return means that the water is clean. It is still found in many Breton rivers and streams.

LOACH
It lives on the river bed.

EEL
The eel hatches in the Sargasso Sea and spends at least five years in fresh water before returning to the sea.

TROUT EXHIBITING COURTSHIP DISPLAY
Eggs are laid in place in the late fall.
TROUT
A member of the salmon family, needing clean, well-oxygenated water. It eats insect larvae, small crustaceans and tiny fish.

BULLHEAD

GUDGEON

MINNOW

43

■ WOODLAND

GROUND BEETLE
One species dwelling in the ancient forests of Brittany has a coppery sheen.

At times Breton woodland takes on a mysterious appearance.

Brittany is in fact one of the least thickly forested regions of France, though numerous copses and patches of woodland sometimes give it a dense appearance. The acidity of the soil and the Atlantic climate combine to give its wooded areas a distinctive appearance: they consist mostly of oak and beech trees, with very little hornbeam, and the widespread presence of that relic of ancient forests, the yew. Wildlife is not limited to trees, deer or mushrooms: from the ground up to the topmost foliage a whole host of animals and plants each play a part in keeping the woodland alive.

POLYPOD Small fern commonly found on mossy tree trunks.

BILBERRY
It flourishes in the acid Breton soil.

POLYTRICHUM
One of numerous mosses found in the woods.

Wild daffodil

Wood spurge

Solomon's seal

Many woodland plants flower in early spring, before the new leaves on the trees deprive them of light.

BADGER
Their many-chambered earths are impressive, reaching many feet down into the ground.

BANK VOLE
It searches for insects and seeds among the fallen leaves.

WOODCOCK
A rare but regular visitor.

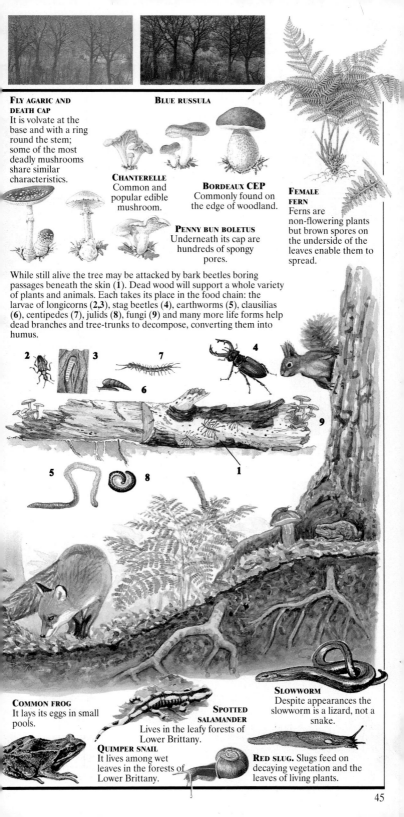

FLY AGARIC AND DEATH CAP
It is volvate at the base and with a ring round the stem; some of the most deadly mushrooms share similar characteristics.

BLUE RUSSULA

CHANTERELLE
Common and popular edible mushroom.

BORDEAUX CEP
Commonly found on the edge of woodland.

PENNY BUN BOLETUS
Underneath its cap are hundreds of spongy pores.

FEMALE FERN
Ferns are non-flowering plants but brown spores on the underside of the leaves enable them to spread.

While still alive the tree may be attacked by bark beetles boring passages beneath the skin (**1**). Dead wood will support a whole variety of plants and animals. Each takes its place in the food chain: the larvae of longicorns (**2,3**), stag beetles (**4**), earthworms (**5**), clausilias (**6**), centipedes (**7**), julids (**8**), fungi (**9**) and many more life forms help dead branches and tree-trunks to decompose, converting them into humus.

COMMON FROG
It lays its eggs in small pools.

SPOTTED SALAMANDER
Lives in the leafy forests of Lower Brittany.

QUIMPER SNAIL
It lives among wet leaves in the forests of Lower Brittany.

SLOWWORM
Despite appearances the slowworm is a lizard, not a snake.

RED SLUG. Slugs feed on decaying vegetation and the leaves of living plants.

45

TREES

The trees that grow best in Brittany are those that enjoy a certain degree of humidity and an acid soil. Species sensitive to cold, such as the sea pine, are able to adapt thanks to the mild climate. Common and peduncular oaks, Norway pines and chestnut trees are often seen. Oak is highly valued and still a favorite building material, while the smaller chestnut provides wood of inferior quality, used for making casks and as firewood. It has the advantage of being easy to split, and tannin from the bark is used to process leather. Beech is used for charcoal. Elm and ash are the traditional woods for making carts and wagons.

Curved timbers for ship building came from trees that were artificially bent.

In the past, two thousand oaks were needed to build a ship of the line.

OAK
Its hard long-lasting wood has many uses. Its fine color and grain make it ideal for traditional furniture and for carving.

Stout and solid trunks of oak or sometimes chestnut are necessary for making traditional timber frames.

Sawyers cut the wood into planks for use by carpenters.

Cladding exterior walls with chestnut tiles protects them against the weather.

TURNED WOOD
Rounded lengths make handles as well as arms and legs for furniture.

HORSE CHESTNUT
Like the sweet chestnut, its wood is easy to split, has an even grain and takes a high polish.

YEW. Its slow growth produces a hard, close-grained flexible wood that was used to make longbows.

COMMON ELM
Most have now fallen victim to Dutch Elm Disease, borne by a spore carried by the scolytid, an insect whose larvae feed on the wood.

BEECH
The moist climate suits it perfectly. Its wood is easy to work and is often used to make furniture.

CLOGMAKER
Having roughed out the shape he needs, the craftsman next hollows out the block of beech with a gouge.

ASH
This large tree grows rapidly in cool ground. Its strong elastic wood is used for shafts, poles and oars.

Eels were once caught with bundles of chestnut sticks. The same wood was used for making lobster pots.

BARRELS
Coopers make barrels from staves of oak bound with iron hoops, or from staves of chestnut bound with boughs of the same wood.

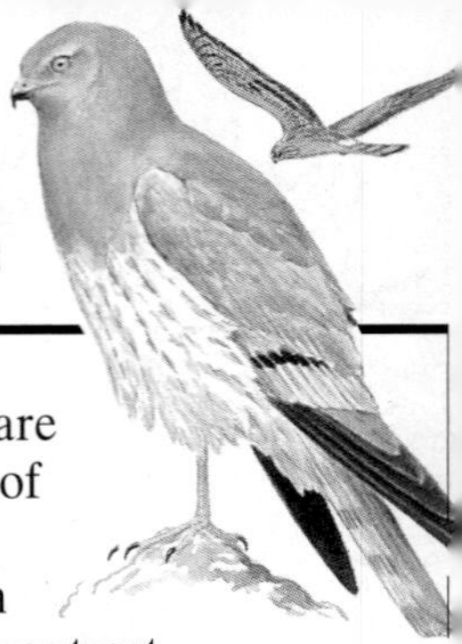

HEATHLAND

The heathlands of Brittany differ dramatically according to their situation. Bare expanses sweep away from the windy coast of Cap Fréhel and up the ridges of the Monts d'Arrée, while the Lanveau heath is uneven and scrubby. At Paimpol the land is dry, in contrast to the peaty slopes of the Black Mountains (*Montagnes noires*) which are wet and boggy. But these apparently diverse environments are fundamentally quite similar. They are covered mainly with heather and gorse, which are indigenous to the cliffs and hilltops of Brittany. Heathland has always been a familiar part of the landscape as well as a key element in the rural economy.

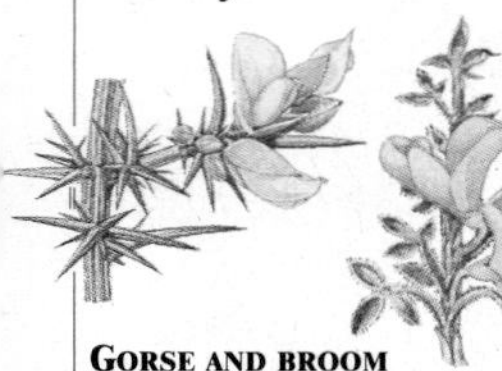

GORSE AND BROOM
Gorse has prickly spines rather than leaves.

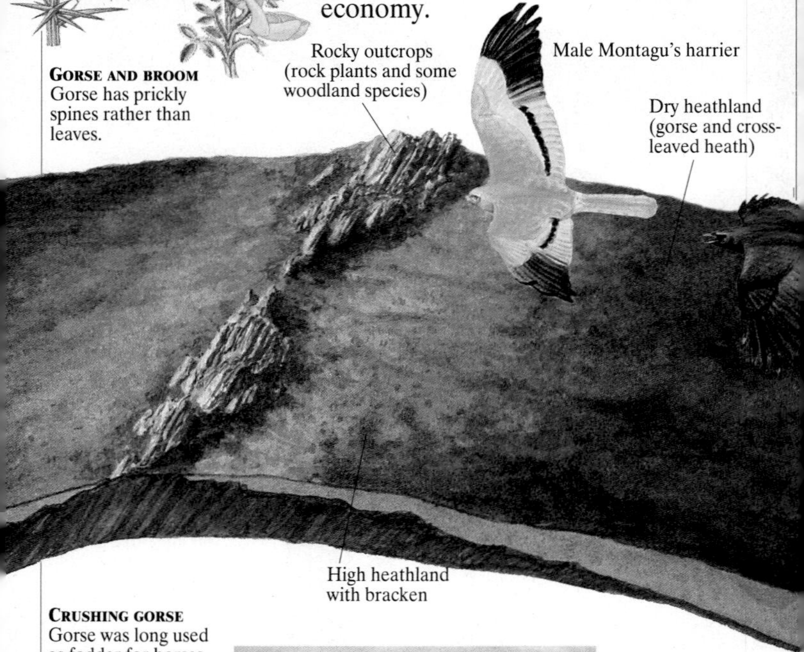

Rocky outcrops (rock plants and some woodland species)

Male Montagu's harrier

Dry heathland (gorse and cross-leaved heath)

High heathland with bracken

CRUSHING GORSE
Gorse was long used as fodder for horses, and was often grown especially for the purpose.

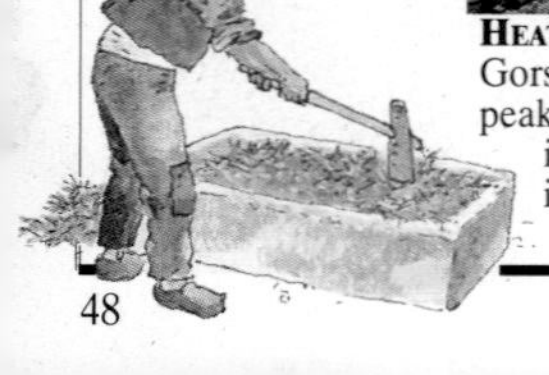

HEATHLAND FLOWERS
Gorse flowers all year round but reaches a peak in spring, when the heath is covered by its bright yellow flowers and suffused with its delicate almond scent.

GORSE
Heathland is characterized by an abundance of gorse. It is a spiny evergreen growing up to 6 feet high, and a member of the pea family.

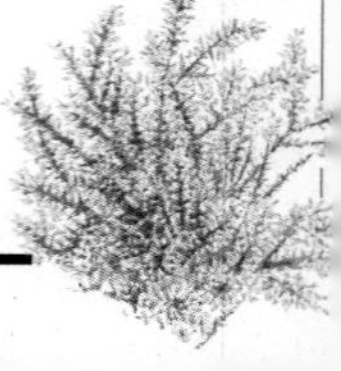

GREENFINCH
Prefers the highest heathland for its nest.

HEATHER

DORSET HEATH

CROSS-LEAVED HEATH

Cross-leaved heath tends to be found on high, dry heathland, while the Dorset heath prefers moist ground. Heather thrives in both situations. Irish heath is happiest in wet moors and bogs.

Female   Male

LINNET
A charming heathland bird that arrives from Spain and Morocco in April.

KESTREL
Preys on small mammals and large insects.

1

DARTFORD WARBLER
One of the few birds that are equally at home in wild areas of the Mediterranean and on the Breton heaths.

YELLOWHAMMER
Likes to nest on the fringes of woodland.

MEADOW PIPIT (1)
STONECHAT (2)
Nest on bare heathland.

Wet heathland (gorse, Dorset heath, flying bent)

Stream and boggy heathland

2

TRAP-DOOR SPIDER
Its heathland home is a silk-lined hole in the ground.

WEASEL
Can attack rabbits but usually preys on small rodents and birds.

WOOD MOUSE
Lives wherever there are seeds for it to eat.

WILD RABBIT
Rabbits dig extensive burrows in the slopes of Breton heathland.

49

HEDGEROW

Protects crops and soil from the wind, conserves moisture and provides shelter for livestock.

"Leave your fields open to the wild beasts and rough sea wind, and there won't be enough left in it to fill a poet's purse", runs an old Breton adage noted down in 1835 by a scholar traveling in the province. Much has been written on the advantages of banked hedgerows to the farmer and the environment, but this saying sums up the importance of the traditional method of fencing off the land. In Finistère alone, there were once 90,000 miles of raised hedgerows, enough to go three times round the Earth, a remarkable amount of hedging that compensates for the lack of forests in Brittany.

The bank is not merely heaped-up earth, but a proper construction.

POLLARDED OAK

BROWN HARE
Most hunters agree that the local hare population should now be given a chance to recolonize Brittany, for alien stock artificially introduced would not adapt well.

HEDGEHOG
This friendly beast is useful as a predator of slugs and insects.

SHORT-TAILED VOLE
It is a valuable source of food for owls.

PRIMROSES
Many hedgerow plants are native to woodland.

MOLE
Its little hills are not nests, but excavated earth.

AGILE FROG

BLACKBIRD
Originally a woodland bird, now also inhabiting hedgerows and gardens.

STARLING
Easily distinguishable from the blackbird by its shorter tail and mottled appearance. It has bred abundantly in Brittany for many years. Migratory flocks can also be a major nuisance in the province.

SONG THRUSH
It has dark arrow-shaped spots.

BARN OWL
It preys mainly on field mice, voles and other small rodents.

ROBIN

CHIFF-CHAFF

LITTLE OWL
Small and squat, with a flat head and round yellow eyes. It is now becoming scarce.

JAY. Acorns make up much of its diet in the fall.

SPARROW-HAWK
In Brittany the population of this bird of prey has steadily declined since the 1970's.

BULLFINCH AND GREAT TIT

MAGPIE AND CARRION CROW. The most common members of the Corvidae family in Brittany.

PINE MARTEN
Another forest creature that has learned to coexist with man. It lives in empty buildings, steals fruit and fowls, and kills rats.

Brimstone butterfly   Ragged robin

CORN BUTTERCUP
Its yellow flowers on unfurrowed stalks have spreading sepals.

EARLY PURPLE ORCHID
It flowers in May in uncultivated grassland.

Ribgrass

Ox-eye daisy

Red campion

51

■ URBAN FLORA AND FAUNA

MARTEN
Often inhabiting barn or cottage roofs, the marten lives close to its diet of chickens, fruit and tiny rodents.

From small hamlet to great city, the built-up areas of Brittany retain an abundance of wildlife. As well as the more familiar wild animals and plants – both indigenous and introduced – human settlements are often host to a variety of unexpected visitors, such as foxes in the suburbs of Brest, brown owls in the middle of Rennes and civet cats scavenging in the dustbins of Nantes.

LONG-EARED BAT

PIPISTRELLE

BATS
Old barns and under cottage roofs are ideal environments for bats to live and breed.

HYDRANGEA
Every village throughout Brittany seems to have a house with hydrangeas growing in the garden. They originally came from China and Japan.

BARN OWL
Though it sometimes nests in a barn, this elegant predator prefers undisturbed countryside.

SWALLOW
Brittany is one of the regions where swallows still nest in chimneys.

COLLARED TURTLE-DOVE
Since it first settled in Rennes in 1958, the bird has spread to towns all over Brittany.

BLACK REDSTART
Buildings of all kinds in towns and villages have innumerable cracks and crevices where redstarts nest.

SWIFT
Their careering flight at dusk, accompanied by shrill screams, fills the evening air in spring and summertime.

WHITE WAGTAIL
In winter they busily search streets and car-parks for tiny insects.

HOUSE SPARROW
As its name suggests, this cheeky bird is rarely found far from human habitation.

HISTORY AND LANGUAGE

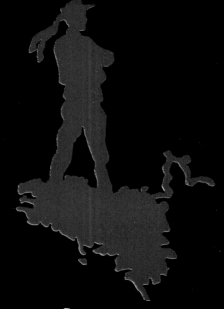

PREHISTORY

3500 BC
Writing invented in Mesopotamia.

2700–2300 BC
Pyramids of Cheops, Chephren and Mykerinos built in Egypt.

1500 BC
Trojan War. Reign of Rameses II in Egypt.

8000 BC. ARMORICA was first populated in Paleolithic times, by sparse bands of hunter-gatherers whose quarry was stags and mammoths. Between 3000 and 1800 BC this way of life gradually gave way to farming and agriculture, and a Megalithic civilization evolved. Scattered tribes, each based

around the shelter of a fortified camp, developed the skill of raising huge stones to stand vertically, and they had a sophisticated system of burial rites. A vast number of menhirs weighing up to 100 tons, cairns up to 80 yards long and dolmens made of stones that weighed 20 tons can still be found all over Brittany. The end of this era was marked by communication with the outside world, through seafaring and along the Loire valley.

1800 TO 600 BC. IN THE BRONZE AGE Armorica became a highly developed civilization, trading with northern countries like Germany and Scandinavia and with the Iberian peninsula to the south. Artefacts such as double-headed axes and swords were manufactured to highly original designs. The sheer quantity of Bronze Age objects that have been found bear witness to the unusual prosperity of Brittany at this period.

ANTIQUITY

500 BC
Temple of Apollo built at Corinth.

Darius I conquers Persia.

31 BC
Defeat of Antony and Cleopatra at Actium.

Roman Empire reaches its apogee.

500 BC. THE CELTS, who had mastered the art of ironworking, settled in Armorica and revolutionized its economy. They had a wide variety of practical skills, and they organized the indigenous population into the region's first cities. There were five principal tribes: the Veneti in the Morbihan, and others at Finistère, Côtes-d'Armor and in the northeast of the peninsula. It was they who called the region Armor (*ar* = on, *mor* = sea). Their society was highly ordered, and their workshops produced exquisitely wrought artifacts in gold and silver.

57 BC. THE ROMANS were intent upon the complete subjugation of Gaul. They were fiercely resisted by the Veneti, who were excellent sailors, and who rose against their oppressors in the winter of 57 BC only to suffer a decisive maritime defeat the following year. Armorica became a Gallo-Roman province, and the two cultures quickly learned to live equably side by side without losing their sense of national identity. The land was intensively farmed and trade flourished. A complex system of roads, marked out with milestones at regular intervals, was also built throughout the region.

5TH CENTURY. THE BRITONS arrive. Roman influence weakened between 235 and 400 AD, and hordes of barbarians from central Europe overran many provinces. Armorica too fell prey to these invasions, which increased in intensity until the region's economy lay in ruins. Then a second wave of Celts arrived from Britain, seeking in the Armorican

peninsula refuge from the Saxon invaders of their islands. They brought the Christian religion, founded monasteries and built the first churches.

400 TO 938. THE BIRTH OF BRITTANY. In 751 AD there began a period of unrest between the Celts and the Frankish peoples, particularly the Carolingians. It was finally resolved some eighty years later when Louis the Pious, third son of Charlemagne, put his imperial envoy Nominoë in charge of Brittany. This Breton nobleman maintained peace in the province, but after Louis' death in 840 he resolved to free himself from the yoke of the French kings. In 845 he completely defeated the Franks at Ballon, forcing King Charles the Bald to recognize the independence of Brittany. Nominoë extended Brittany's frontiers to the east, seized Nantes and Rennes and invaded Maine. He died suddenly in 851 at Vendôme and was succeeded as Duke of Brittany by his son Erispoë, who followed in his father's footsteps by inflicting another crushing defeat on the Franks. Erispoë was murdered by his cousin Salomon (Salaun), who then extended the territories to include the Cherbourg peninsula, and who in turn perished at the hands of jealous kinsmen. The years that followed were unsettled, until in 938 Norse invaders were finally driven away under the leadership of Count Alan Barbe-Torte and prevented from establishing a second Normandy on the Loire. Alan became Duke of Brittany, and established a feudal system which he ruled from his capital at Nantes. The Breton language was spoken west of a line from Dol, through Rennes and to St-Nazaire in the south.

200–300
Mongol invasions.

5TH CENTURY
Beginning of Mayan civilization.

500
Vikings reach America.

571–632
Mahommed.

6TH CENTURY
Arab invasions.

800
Charlemagne crowned Emperor in St-Peter's, Rome.

962
Foundation of the Holy Roman Empire.

THE MIDDLE AGES

982
Viking explorer Eric the Red discovers Greenland.

1099
Jerusalem falls to the Christians.

1271
Marco Polo's first voyage.

1325
Aztecs found Tenochtitlan (Mexico City).

938 TO 1213. DUCAL BRITTANY. The period that followed was fraught with disagreement and revolt. Rival claimants to the duchy plotted and counterplotted. Only the marriage of Alix, daughter of Conan of Rennes, to the Capetian prince Peter I of Dreux prevented Brittany becoming part of the Plantagenêt (Angevin) empire. Peter (known as Pierre Mauclerc) was a strong ruler who imposed order on his dominions, established an efficient bureaucracy, developed seaborne trade and forged an alliance with England. His successors continued his good work, but this period of peace and prosperity was short-lived.

1341. THE WAR OF SUCCESSION. On the death of the childless duke, Jean III, in 1341 there were two rivals to the throne of Brittany: Jean de Montfort (Jean III's half-brother), and Charles de Blois (husband of John III's niece Jeanne de Penthièvre). Jean de Montfort had the support of the English king, Edward III, already deeply involved in the Hundred Years' War. The War of Succession dragged on until 1364, when Charles was defeated and killed at Auray, and the following year the French king, Charles V, recognized Jean as Duke Jean IV of Brittany. He was for a time dethroned for allying himself with the English, but the conflict was finally resolved in 1381 when Jean paid homage to the King of France. After Jean's death, the reign of his son as Jean V (1399–1442) marked a golden age in Breton history.

1348
The Black Death.

MODERN HISTORY

1440
Gutenberg begins printing.

1453
Fall of Constantinople.

1492
Christopher Columbus discovers America.

1488. ANNE OF BRITTANY. When Duke Francis died without a son in 1488, his eleven-year-old daughter succeeded to the throne and married by proxy Archduke Maximilian of Hapsburg. This provoked the young King Charles VIII of France to send troops into Brittany and capture several towns. Trapped and surrounded by the French, Anne abandoned her proxy husband and agreed to marry King Charles. The wedding took place at the château of Langeais in 1491. When her husband died seven years later, Anne lost no time in establishing her own supremacy and then marrying his successor, the Orleanist king Louis XII, in January 1499 at Nantes. Anne worked tirelessly for the good of her duchy, restoring much of its former peace and prosperity. She was also deeply religious

and a dedicated patron of the arts. When she died at Blois on January 9, 1514, Anne's name had become synonymous with Brittany for her sorrowing subjects. Her daughter Claude brought Brittany as a dowry to her husband, the future king, François I of France. An important treaty was signed on September 21, 1532 that irrevocably placed Brittany within the kingdom of France, though it retained many local privileges, such as its own parliament.

1600. THE ANCIEN RÉGIME. From this time on, Brittany was administered largely by the centralized French system of government and received the benefit of substantial economic aid. It was a time of prosperity, with industry and seaborne trade flourishing. The population began to grow rapidly. In 1561 Rennes became the seat of the Breton Parliament, unfortunately for Nantes, which was further away from Paris. As a court of justice it had authority over other courts in the province. In 1588 the Duc de Mercoeur, governor of the province, attempted to revive Brittany's independence at the head of the Catholic League. Many religious partisans rallied

to his cause, but he was finally defeated by the Protestant Henri VI in 1598. There were bandits too, such as the notorious La Fontenelle, who put all who stood in their way to fire and the sword. At the beginning of the reign of Louis XIV, taxes levied on stamped paper (used for official documents), tobacco and domestic tinware provoked the famous "Stamped Paper Revolt" of 1675 in the towns of Upper Brittany and among the disaffected "bonnets rouges" in the countryside of Lower Brittany. The revolt was fiercely put down, leaving Brittany crippled by repressive measures that stifled its trade – in particular a levy raised by Colbert on cloth exported to England.

1789. THE TOWNSFOLK OF RENNES were very much in tune with the fashionable anti-aristocratic notions of the age, which escalated into open conflict when the

Breton Parliament assembled in January 1789. The skirmishes of the 26th and 27th claimed three lives, the very first victims of the French Revolution. But the Bretons were quick to step back from the brink: the populace, of whom 90 percent were peasants, at first feared what the bourgeois might do if their Revolution became a reality; and they were to react strongly against the oaths of allegiance to the Revolution that the clergy were obliged to swear (and which 80 percent of them refused to do). The proclamation of obligatory conscription

1497
Vasco da Gama finds route to India round the Cape of Good Hope.

1517
Lutheran Reformation.

BONNETS
ROUGES
ET
PAPIER
TIMBRÉ

1520–66
Reign of Suleyman the Magnificent: apogee of the Ottoman Empire.

1588
Defeat of the Spanish Armada, and the end of Spanish maritime supremacy.

1602
Foundation of the Dutch East India Company.

1762–96
Reign of Empress Catherine II of Russia.

1787
American Constitution adopted on September 17.

57

by lottery of 300,000 men was the final straw: the first counter-revolutionary riot broke out at Cholet on March 2, 1793. When the Vendée rose up against the new Republic, it was followed by the first outbreak of *chouannerie* ● 62 in Brittany. At first this was limited to parts of Morbihan and the north coast, and to the districts where the old Gallo dialect was spoken. The rest of Brittany, however, soon rallied to the cause.

19TH AND 20TH CENTURIES

1869
Suez Canal opened.

1917
Russian Revolution.

1918
United States of America become leading world power.

1922
Italian Fascists march on Rome.

1927
Charles Lindbergh makes first solo non-stop transatlantic flight.

1933
Hitler becomes Chancellor of Germany.

Like the Revolution before it, the Empire drained what was left of Brittany's economy, and reduced the peasants and working classes to penury. The land was ripe to receive the seeds of Christian Socialism and, after 1884 (the year they were legalized), for the growth of trade unions. This resulted in a number of strikes and violent clashes in all five *départements* of Brittany. At the same time a strong feeling of Breton nationalism was developing, resulting in the formation of many local political and cultural associations such as the *Gorsedd*, the *Bleun Brug* founded by the priest Yann-Vari Perrot, the Breton Nationalist Party and many others, most of them doomed to extinction in the wake of World War One.

1914. WORLD WAR ONE. Brittany made a particularly grim sacrifice to the nation during World War One, with at least 125,000 dead, perhaps double that number, as the cenotaph erected at Sainte-Anne-d'Auray in 1932 bears tragic witness. The terrible slaughter, whose toll is recorded like so many litanies on the war memorials of Brittany, gave birth to a new wave of social unrest, and political movements sprang up that were federalist or sometimes fiercely nationalist in feeling. Most famous among them was *Breiz Atao*, founded in 1918 by Morvan Marchal (the man who designed the Breton flag). He was a committed federalist and pacifist whose ideas soon collided with those of Olier Mordrel, editor of the Party newspaper, who left the movement in 1924. More signs of disaffection were to be seen in the journal *Gwalarn*, in the Federal League of Brittany founded by Marchal and Debeauvais, in Mordrel's National Breton Party, the secret society *Gwenn ha du*, the *Bleun Brug*, and finally the *Adao* founded by a priest named Madec. Cultural movements such as *Ar Falz*, founded by Yann Sohier, and Roparz Hemon's *Gwalarn* sought to revive Breton language and culture, while at the same time introducing new artistic currents to the region.

1939. WORLD WAR TWO. In June 1940 hundreds of young Bretons left France to join De Gaulle. Fighting side by side with the Allies, they were to take part in the North African and French campaigns. Others set themselves to organizing underground resistance movements, which played a key role in the eventual liberation of Brittany by American troops. Last of all were those who for the most part had participated in the nationalist movements in the interwar years, and who saw in the German occupation an unhoped for opportunity to realize their ideals. They collaborated openly with the enemy, which made all indigenous cultural movements deeply suspect for a while after. In June 1941 the Vichy government separated the lower Loire (now the Loire-Atlantique) from Brittany. St-Nazaire, Lorient and Brest, where the occupying forces had built submarine bases, and St-Malo were wrecked in bombardments by the Allied forces.

1950. THE POSTWAR YEARS. The CELIB (Committee of Breton Studies) was founded in 1951 under the directorship of Joseph Martray and, helped by militant Celtic associations, trade unions, peasants and industrial workers, strengthened the feelings of a separate national identity. But the majority of the electorate remained moderate and conservative. Traditional farming methods gave way to new systems that replaced wheat with vegetables. Giant cooperatives sprang up and farming gradually developed into an industry. The policy of industrial decentralization brought the Citroen factories to Rennes, and that of the CNET to Lannion. Roads, ports and railways were improved and expanded, and in the space of sixteen years between 1951 and 1967 (the year the tidal power station on the estuary of the Rance was opened), Brittany emerged from its former isolation. But Breton nationalism still had its militant extremists, and there were clandestine organizations such as the ARB (Breton Revolutionary Army) and FLB (Breton Liberation Front). They came to public attention through numerous bombing incidents, including that of the television transmitting station at Roc'h Tredudon in the monts d'Arrée, but these outrages were soon brought under control. In 1965 the Breton language became an approved subject for the Baccalauréat examination in schools, Celtic festivals became increasingly popular; and in 1977 the first Diwan school was founded, which offered a bilingual education. In 1977 the petrol tanker *Amoco-Cadiz* ran aground off Portsall, and 230,000 tons of oil polluted more than 700 miles of coastline. Finding the proposed indemnity against those responsible to be grossly inadequate, no less than seventy-six communities jointly took the Amoco corporation to court and finally won their case in May 1992.

1945
Yalta Conference between Roosevelt, Churchill and Stalin, February 4–11.

1945
Hiroshima destroyed by atomic bomb on August 6.

1947
India gains independence.

1948
Assassination of Mahatma Gandhi.

1963
Assassination of John F. Kennedy.

1969
First man on the Moon.

1975
Reunification of Vietnam after thirty years of war.

1989
Destruction of Berlin Wall (November).

1991
Foundation of CIS (Confederation of Independent States).

"FIRST THEY BURY ME IN EARTH AND THEN THEY PULL ME OUT; NEXT THEY COVER ME WITH WATER AND THEN THEY PULL ME OUT;

From the 16th to the 18th centuries the production of linen, hemp and canvas was an industry that contributed greatly to the prosperity of Brittany. Manufactured goods were exported to Britain, Spain and even the American colonies.

The work of making linen began in mid-July when the flax plants were pulled up by the roots, and then left to soak in a stream or in stone troughs. They were left to steep for several days, for the water to dissolve the gummy substances in the fibers. Next the flax was ginned with a steel comb, and the stems laid out in small bunches. Sometimes the flax was ginned before being soaked.

The seeds could be used to sow the next crop, or might be pressed to make linseed oil. Then came the process of scutching, in which the fibers were scraped with a sharp-edged piece of glass or metal to remove impurities. Short fibers were used to make tow for caulking the hulls of boats, or else mixed with oil to stopper wine bottles when real cork was not available.

Skilled workmen would go from farm to farm, preparing the

fibers on wooden frames. In the fields or round the fireplace, the womenfolk would spin the thread on large bobbins either by hand or with a pedal-operated spinning wheel. The bobbins (spindles) were then placed end to end on a reeling machine to wind the thread into skeins, which were next dispatched to the weaver, who made up the cloth. Each region had its own special cloth: at Merdrignac they made "les Oléronnes", in

Rennes "les Noyales", in Locronan they made "les Olonnes", "les Crées" at Le Léon, while in the Trégor between St-Brieux and Pontivy they made "les Bretagnes légitimes".

The production of linen continued up to the 1950's in the Trégor district, but was eventually superseded by the cheaper cloth produced in the north of France.

Peasants formed themselves into bands of guerillas at the time of the ill-fated uprising in the Vendée, and revolted against taxes levied for the French wars, the introduction of paper money and the outrageous punishment inflicted on renegade priests. These heroic Chouans took their name from Jean Cotterau and his followers, leading insurgents in the Maine region, whose secret call imitated that of the brown owl (in French *chat-huant*). Other notorious guerrilla chiefs included Boisguy and Boulainvillier in the Ille-et-Vilaine, Boishardy in the Côtes-d'Armor and Cadoudal in the Morbihan.

THE FIRST UPRISING
This lasted from the autumn of 1793 to spring 1795. The Chouans were few in number, half-starved and badly clothed, and at first only carried out small raids and ambushes. In October 1793 they were joined by refugees from the Vendée army. From the beginning of 1794 they became an organized force, thanks to the addition of former salt smugglers and to a few brave exiled noblemen who returned to fight. Joseph de la Puisaye, an aristocrat who had fled to London, convinced the English that he could organize an uprising in Brittany and persuaded them to make a foray. With the death of Robespierre in July 1794, the revolutionary government offered an amnesty to the insurgents, which was signed with General Hoche in the spring of 1795. The ensuing peace gave the disaffected insurgents a chance to rearm.

ARMAND TUFFIN, MARQUIS DE LA ROUËRIE
Tuffin suggested to Louis XVI's brothers in 1791 that they should organize a counter-revolution in Brittany. But the plot was foiled the following May, and the Marquis died in January 1793 at the Château de la Guyomarais, just after the King's execution.

THE SECOND UPRISING

A group of émigrés were landed at Quiberon on June 16, 1795 by an English naval squadron, to be met by a force of almost 20,000 Chouans. General Hoche, who commanded the republican army, defeated them decisively. He hunted the Chouans down relentlessly, reducing support for them among the Breton peasants by a policy of religious toleration. By June 1796 most of the remaining Chouans had abandoned the struggle.

GEORGES CADOUDAL (1771–1804)

Born into a prosperous peasant family near Auray, Cadoudal was a lawyer's clerk before he espoused the royalist cause in 1791 and fought with the Vendéens in 1793. He became leader of the Morbihan Chouans and took part in the Quiberon landings of 1795. His forces made a stand against Hoche the following year, but capitulated only to take up the fight again in 1798. The future (though already self-styled) King Louis XVIII put him in command of the Brittany forces. He made two attempts to assassinate Napoleon (in 1800 and 1804), but was finally captured and guillotined.

ANTOINE DE LA TREMOILLE, PRINCE DE TALMONT

He was involved in La Rouërie's plot, and executed in the Château de Fougères. after the defeat of Savenay in 1793.

THE THIRD UPRISING

With the renewal of religious persecution, fighting broke out again in 1797. Two years later a law was passed permitting the families of wanted men to be taken as well as the partisans themselves; and this, together with the excessive conscription demanded by the Government, caused a fresh outbreak of hostilities. Finally in 1800 Bonaparte reinstated religious freedom, and abolished conscription in exchange for the Chouans' surrender.

●THE BRETON LANGUAGE

> "Have you lost your way?
> Is it far to town?
> Yerss.
> How do I get there, kind sir?
> Along with you! I've told
> you all I know."

ORIGINS

For centuries, Brittany has been divided into two separate linguistic regions. The western region of Lower Brittany has been the home of the Breton language, while in Upper Brittany in the east the Gallo dialect has traditionally been spoken. Before French became the common language, these two regions were virtually incapable of communicating. Gallo is a dialect variant of the Oïl language of northern France, itself one of the Romane languages; Breton, or Brezhoneg, by contrast, has distinct Celtic origins and belongs to the same family as the Gaelic spoken in Ireland and Scotland. The Brythonic language on the other hand includes Welsh, and old Cornish, which was spoken in Cornwall, England, up to the 18th century. Breton is predominantly a Brythonic importation: around the 5th century the Bretons who arrived from Devon, Cornwall and Wales transformed and enriched the Gallic language spoken in Armorica.

EXPANSION AND RECESSION

When in the latter half of the 6th century Saint Gregory of Tours gave the name Britannia to the land where the Bretons lived, the River Vilaine was the eastern boundary between their country and the Frankish territories. The Breton language stayed firmly west of this frontier until the middle of the 9th century. It appears to have reached a peak around 1050. At that time it was spoken from the bay of Mont-St-Michel right down to the region of St-Nazaire. The Gallo dialect was predominant in the eastern regions of Brittany, while in the center it coexisted with Breton. From the 9th to the 11th centuries Breton was a relatively homogeneous language. During the Middle Ages French advanced westward into Brittany. By the end of the 16th century spoken Breton had all but disappeared in the east of the province, as the diagram (opposite) shows, and where the divide between Upper and Lower Brittany first became apparent. This demarcation line was at first variable, but settled into its present position around 1886.

FRENCH SUPREMACY

Thanks to its prestige in the literary, legal and mercantile spheres, from the 13th century onward French took over from Latin throughout Brittany as the official language of diplomacy. Townspeople in Lower Brittany became bilingual, and

Breton itself began increasingly to borrow and adopt words from French. It was above all the language of poor country folk, and those who could speak no French became increasingly isolated. In addition Breton had broken up into four separate dialects, which can be divided into two groups: KLT (the dialects of Cornouaille, Trégor and the Léon regions), and the Vannes dialects (the Breton spoken at Batz-sur-Mer and in the Loire-Atlantique, which finally disappeared in the 1960's). Despite the efforts of several scholars, spoken Breton proved an impossible language to stabilize, each little community gradually evolving its own particular idioms and constructions. The clergy were virtually the only people who knew how to write it, and their own idiosyncrasies exacerbated the problem. One of the pioneers in classifying the language was a scholar from the Trégor named Jehan Lagadeuc, who was born in 1464. He compiled the first known French dictionary, a trilingual one in Breton, French and Latin called the *Catholicon*. Aimed at the impoverished clerics of the province, it set out to teach them French and Latin.

A DIMINISHING FRONTIER
The ever-shrinking area of Breton as a spoken language, from the 9th century to the present day.

Ablamour m'en deus
KOMZET BREZONEG!
(Parce qu'il a parlé breton!)

A LANGUAGE REBORN

At the beginning of the 19th century a reaction set in. Sweeping away all words "borrowed" from French, the brilliant grammarian and lexicographer Le Gonidec set about standardizing Breton grammar and orthography. His first attempts failed, being too purist and dogmatic. Nonetheless he sparked off something of a literary renaissance, inspiring the publication in 1839 of *Barzaz-Breiz* or *Popular Songs of Brittany* by Hersart de Villemarqué. Breton literature now became increasingly secular and the number of books appearing in the vernacular steadily increased. Eventually Breton was taught in schools once more. The educational authorities, which had formerly banned the language, readopted it in 1977. The first Diwan schools were opened and Breton was taught from nursery level onward, the study of French not beginning until some years later. By 1991 there were twenty-seven Diwan schools, though the future of Breton as a living language is uncertain. In spite of its demographic spread, its actual use is diminishing. The Gallo dialect is likewise at risk. At present there are 300,000 speakers of Breton in Lower Brittany, and 600,000 people who understand it.

KAN AR BOBL

THE BRETON LANGUAGE

Breton weavers' stamps, dating from 1720.

BRETON ROAD SIGNS
In 1985 the département of the Côtes d'Armor was the first to introduce a policy of bilingual road signs. Signs marking towns, villages and hamlets are paid for by the local authorities concerned.

PLACE NAMES

Place names make the linguistic divide in Brittany immediately visible to the visitor. More than half the towns and villages in the province have names of Breton origin, while the remainder are a mixture of Gaelic, Gallo-Roman, Low Latin and French. Among Breton names that antedate the 10th century is *ploe* (from the Latin *plebem*, meaning a parish or community of the faithful), which still exists in various forms such as *plou-*, *plo-*, *plu-*, *plueu-*, *ple-*, *pli-*, and even *poul-*. It signifies the site of an early Christian settlement from as far back as the 6th or 7th century. It is usually followed by the name of a medieval saint, as also is the prefix *lann*, meaning a hermitage or monastery. In Breton names from the 11th to the 14th centuries, it is important to remember *ker* (a farm or village), which in early Breton is written *caer*. This is the commonest word in use, occurring in some form in more than 18,000 place names.

NAMES OF PEOPLE

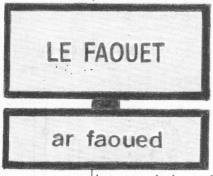

Le Bihan (small); Le Coant (pretty); Le Coz (old); Le Treut (skinny); Le Guen (white, pale); Pennec (having a large head); Pensec (broad-bottomed); Le Fur (wise); Queffelec (silly); Le Guevel (a twin); Le Henaff (elder or eldest); Person (parish priest). These informal and affectionate nicknames are typical of Breton humor. They became increasingly common after the 10th century and gradually became hereditary. But it was not until the Renaissance that they were adopted as official surnames, when the keeping of state registers became obligatory in 1539. These and others are still among the most common names today.

ARTS AND TRADITIONS

● FURNITURE

The basic items of Breton furniture vary little throughout the province but regional differences in decoration are marked. A wide choice of local wood, including cherry, chestnut and oak, and imported timbers such as Brazilian rosewood were used. These woods were carved with detailed and imaginative decoration.

CHEST-BENCHES
They were first made in the Loire-Atlantique region and were carved using a technique known as *à l'ongle* ("fingernail work"), by which the surface was covered with semicircular or triangular notches.

A VARIETY OF MOTIFS
Floral bouquets, birds, plants and religious images were used to decorate Cornouaille furniture.

BRANTHOME STYLE
This style of furniture first appeared in Rostronen. It is inspired mainly by the neo-Regency decorative style of the Second Empire, and by 18th- and 19th-century Rennes furniture. Rosettes, roundels and plant motifs are the most frequently recurring decorative devices.

LÉON CHESTS
Widely used until the 16th and 17th centuries, they served various purposes: grain storage, linen chests ...

BOX-BED FRONT
In the Auray region cupboards and box-beds were stained red with ox blood or a mixture of tannin and sorrel. Their most attractive feature was often their turned boxwood bars.

A cherub on an oak chest from Léon.
Oak was easy to carve and was often
darkened with a walnut stain.

BRETON INTERIOR
This late 19th-century scene shows a typical
Breton room with some of the most common
features: a frieze of turned wooden bars along
the top of the box-bed, a chest serving as a
step to climb into it, and the simple straight
lines of the capacious chestnut wardrobe.

18TH-CENTURY WARDROBES
They were large, had plain doors often
decorated with brass fittings, and could
be dismantled. St-Malo shipowners had
a particular liking for these pieces of
furniture and often had them
made in exotic woods.

BOX-BEDS
These beds increased
in popular after the
16th century. There
were three types: *en
carosse*, the front and
sides of turned wood;
others had plain
wooden boards on all
sides; the *lit d'angle*
was built to fit into a
corner.

The front of the box-
bed had two fixed
uprights set either
side of the door, or
doors, either carved
or pierced with an
openwork design. In
the Léon region beds
had only one door
(right). This
design continued
to be used well
into the 20th century.

69

● TRADITIONAL DRESS

Dinard women wore a headdress that stood up like a crest and was known as a "cock's comb" ▲ 201.

During the 18th century the farming community prospered and the number of local costumes multiplied. Brittany was so cut off from the rest of the world that differences of dress between villages, towns and regions assumed a singular importance both as a means of self-assertion and for easy identification. The Cornouaille region, far from courtly influences, had the most varied costumes.

THE "FISEL" STYLE
In Carhaix and Rostronen men wore a buttonless jacket of black cloth over a waistcoat with a double row of buttons.

MALE ATTIRE IN PLOUGASTEL-DAOULAS
The cloth could be green, blue, red or rich purple, set off with brightly embroidered ribbons.

THE "GIZ FOEN"
The style worn around Rosporden, decorated with fluttering ribbons.

THE BIGOUDEN HEADDRESS
Until the 1920's the headdress, set on a *koef-bleo* (coiffed hair), had an extra pointed piece on top, the *beg*. Hence the name "bigouden".

"BRAGOU BRAZ"
Baggy knee-breeches (left) worn with an embroidered velvet waistcoat (above) in the Cornouaille region.

THE LARGE LÉON SHAWL.
This was made of coarse muslin and could be black, beige, grey or pale green.

EMBROIDERIES
The most popular motifs were the peacock feather (symbol of pride) and the ram's horn (courage), as well as the fish and the chain of life.

EMBROIDERERS
Bigouden costumes were traditionally embroidered by men. The last of this proud fraternity of craftsmen disappeared around 1960.

THE BAUD REGION
Here the women could choose between several different styles: the "capot", the "raie" and the "kornek".

CHATEAULIN WOMAN
(1846, right).

PONTIVY DRESS
Color was strictly limited to pockets and buttons on the "moutons blancs" (white sheep), men's jackets made of pale imported wool that appeared in the 19th century.

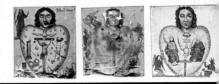

FESTIVALS AND PARDONS

VOTIVE OFFERINGS
Gifts presented to the saint in thanks for prayers answered.

A pardon is a day of worship dedicated to a local patron saint. It is an annual event gathering the people of the parish and the faithful from nearby villages. After a solemn mass there is a procession, with the congregation chanting canticles and carrying banners, relics, statues, and crosses. This is followed by a secular celebration with music, dancing, and traditional entertainment.

DIVINE PROTECTION
Like votive offerings, stained glass windows illustrating the terrible dangers of the sea were also pleas for intercession. In this detail from the chapel of Clis (below), Saint Jacques listens to a fisherman's prayer (the man is kneeling in the next window, not shown here).

BLESSING OF THE BOATS
Fishermen were deeply religious: these ceremonies had enormous importance for Breton people, who attended in large numbers.

DEATH, THE FELLOW TRAVELER
The Ankou (above) is the most familiar image of death in Brittany.

CASKETS
Nobles and other worthies were buried inside the church, but if there was no room left their skulls would be kept in boxes, which were often placed above the porch.

"THE BANNERS' GREETING"
(Olivier Perrin). The banners of neighboring parishes had to touch in fraternal greeting. The priest insisted on this "kiss of peace" to dispel any rivalries.

THE "TAOLENNOU" OF SAINTE-ANNE-D'AURAY
Paintings representing the Christian conscience, used by priests when teaching the faith.

"PROCESSION OF THE VIRGIN OF THE SEA"
Detail from a triptych by Charles Cottet showing a scene probably set in Landudec, in the Bigouden region.

HEALING SAINTS
The figures are in the chapel of Notre-Dame-du-Haut near Moncontour. A complex ritual was attached to seeking their traditional cures.

● MUSIC AND DANCE

Dancing in the church square at Carantec at the turn of the century.

A linguistic divide running across Brittany from north to south separates the country into two distinct cultural entities. Bagpipes, clarinet and *kan ha diskan* (singing with descant) characterize the musical tradition of central Brittany and north Finistère. In the east around St-Malo and Cancale instruments such as the hurdy-gurdy, violin and button accordion are used to accompany traditional dances. Modern musicians and dancers have now largely abandoned traditional dress, but music still plays a key role in all public festivities.

BOMBARD
A wooden wind instrument with a conical bore and double reed like an oboe. It has six finger-holes and is popular in the Vannes region.

WEDDING AT PLOUGASTEL-DAOULAS
"Dance was the expression of the community's collective spirit, forged and strengthened by working together and by the important alliances that were celebrated at village weddings."
Pierre-Jakez Héliaz

DETAILS OF A TYPICAL BOMBARD
Above, two keys and an example of metal inlay on an instrument.

CLARINETIST
In Haute-Cornouaille the clarinet is known as *treujeun gaol* (literally "cabbage stalk"). It arrived in Brittany in the 19th century, making its way across the Monts d'Arrée into Upper Brittany, Trégor and the southern extremities of the Côtes d'Armor. Early instruments like the one shown on the right had only five keys.

DANCE TROUPE FROM KERFEUNTEUN
More than a hundred Celtic groups in Brittany perform the old dances in traditional costume. The gavotte can be danced in open or closed formation.

BUTTON ACCORDION
Unlike the more modern piano accordion, this is a diatonic instrument. It came into fashion in Upper Brittany in the 19th century.

BAGPIPER
The ancient traditional *biniou kozh*, which has a piercing sound, has only a single drone, as opposed to the larger *biniou gras*. Pipes and bombard are the most popular musical combination in southern Brittany.

For centuries the galette, a pancake made from buckwheat flour, was the staple of the Breton peasants' diet. In Upper Brittany this simple food was usually eaten with sardines or an egg. Nowadays it is often accompanied by ham or sausages. The galette would be cut into pieces and dipped in buttermilk, called *lait ribot*, or in soup. In Lower Brittany the batter is finer and lighter and galettes are eaten plain with butter.

1. Put the buckwheat flour and salt into a large bowl and mix thoroughly.

2. Add water a little at a time, stirring continuously until the batter is creamy but not too thick.

5. Ladle a little of the mixture on to the hot griddle.

6. Spread the batter evenly with a light wooden implement called a *rouable*.

9. To make a "filled" galette, put a slice of ham on top.

10. Break an egg over the ham and allow it to cook.

Buckwheat flour came originally from Central Asia and was introduced into Europe at the time of the Crusades. It is also known as Saracen corn, *sarrasin* in French. Buckwheat is still grown in Brittany, though now it is no longer a staple food. It is used to make the galettes of both Upper and Lower Brittany, but the flour is milled in different ways in each region.

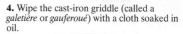

INGREDIENTS: 1lb buckwheat flour, pinch of salt, a little water, butter.

3. Do not leave batter to stand.

4. Wipe the cast-iron griddle (called a *galetière* or *gauferoué*) with a cloth soaked in oil.

7. When the surface of the batter dulls, loosen and turn with a palette knife.

8. Let it cook for just a second or two before placing a knob of butter in the center.

11. Scatter some grated gruyère cheese on top and fold the sides of the galette over.

Les Galette de PLEYBEN

TRAOU MAD DE PONT-AVEN
AU BEURRE FIN DE BRETAGNE

CRÊPES À DENTELLES
"LES DÉLICIEUSES"
TANGUY, QUIMPER

CAKES AND BISCUITS MADE WITH SALTED BUTTER: *crêpes dentelles* invented in the early 20th century by Marie-Catherine Cornic, *Kouign-Amann* from Douarnenez, *Traou-Mad* from Pont-Aven and Pleyben *galettes*.

CIDER (from Fouesnant) and *Chouchenn*, made from fermented honey.

QUIMPER POTTERY
▲ *302*

The faïence industry is still flourishing, though prices are high for these souvenirs.

SARDINES
from Quiberon or Étel.

PÂTÉ. The little round tins of Henaff pâté are famous all over the world, and have proved especially practical for use at sea.

BUTTER. Farm butter from Brittany is of exceptionally high quality. The *Paysan breton* brand is churned by Coopagri at Landerneau, the largest industrial company in Finistère.

WHEATEN CRÊPES AND BUCKWHEAT GALETTES. The thin crêpes are usually sugared and eaten as dessert, while the coarser galettes can have endless combinations of succulent savory fillings.

ARCHITECTURE

There are an enormous number of megaliths in Brittany. These menhirs (standing stones) and dolmens (like huge stone tables) were erected between 5000 and 2000 BC and mark burial sites or places of worship.

Some menhirs, standing alone or set in lines or circles, date back to the Neolithic period.

DOLMENS are tombs that have a complex structure: a long corridor leads to one or more chambers formed by huge slabs of stone and sometimes roofed with smaller stones. The tomb, which usually contained communal graves, was either constructed above ground and then covered by a mound of earth (tumulus), or dug out beneath the ground, sometimes into a hillside. The monument would be enclosed by a line of stones or a dry masonry façade.

After the Neolithic period, standing stones were destroyed or given Christian significance. On the Saint-Uzec menhir (Côtes d'Armor) the symbols of the Passion were carved above a painted figure of Christ, now worn away.

These monuments can be dated from the carvings that they bear. Fine carvings such as broken lines, snakes, axes and crooks first appeared around 5000 BC. By 3000 BC stones were carved in relief with daggers, oars, axes and breasts decorated with necklaces. Female idols placed in pairs indicate Near Eastern influence.

Druids singing on the dolmen of Kenac'h-Laëron, near Gouarec (Côtes d'Armor).

ALIGNMENTS. Monuments built around 3500 BC, in the Neolithic period, consisting of long lines of menhirs ending in circles or semicircles of stones. The stones were placed according to precise astronomical calculations, and were oriented toward the solstice. The alignments had important significance in the seasonal round of the farming year.

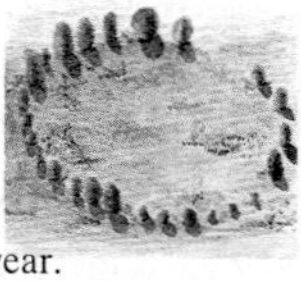

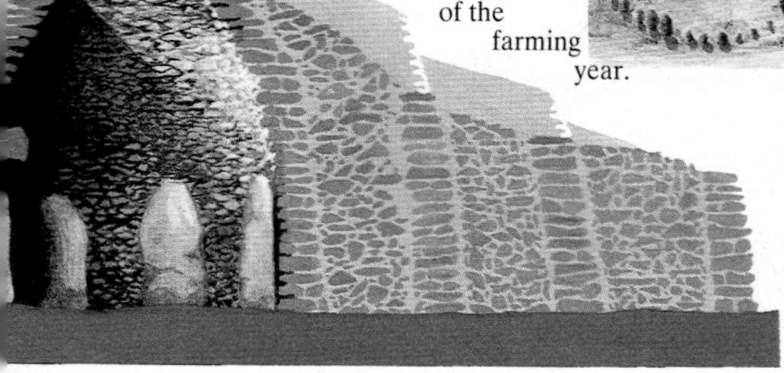

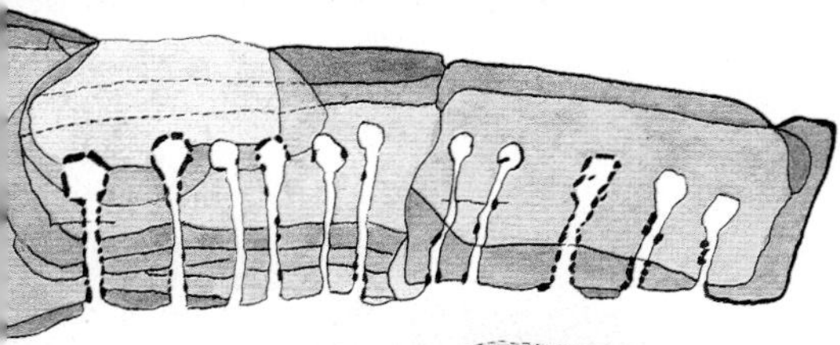

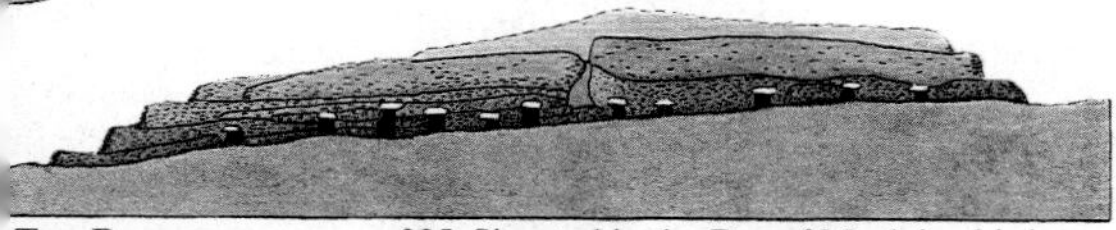

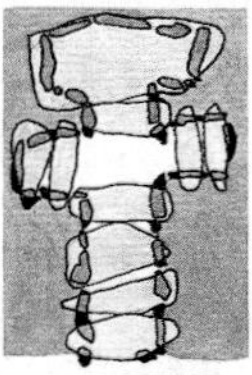

TRANSEPT DOLMEN

ELBOW DOLMEN

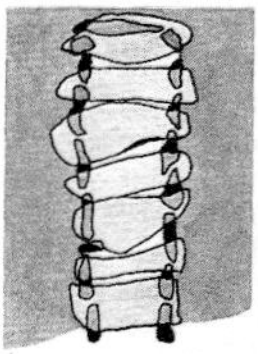

ALLÉE COUVERTE

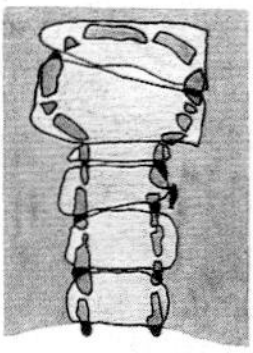

CORRIDOR DOLMEN

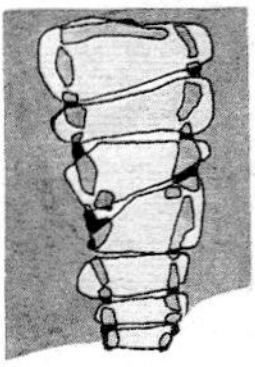

THE BARNENEZ CAIRN ▲ *225.* Situated in the Bay of Morlaix, this is a necropolis of eleven dolmens within an arrangement of carefully positioned stones.

FUNNEL DOLMEN

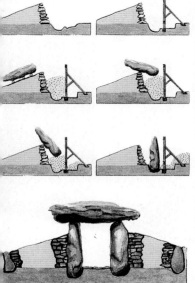

HOW A DOLMEN WAS BUILT. Enormous slabs of stone were pushed up a slope, with logs as rollers. From the top of the slope they were tipped over into a ditch, their fall broken by sand or brushwood. Then the roof stone was eased into position. The structure was reinforced with stones packed behind the upright slabs, and a mound which in the case of a dolmen would cover the entire structure, but reached only as far as the roof stone on an *allée couverte*.

In the 14th century Breton military architecture consisted mainly of massive fortified towers of complex design. A century later castles were built along the coast and the eastern borders facing France. The slender outlines of the early castles gave way after 1450 to more functional and compact structures, designed to withstand the onslaught of artillery.

THE MEDIEVAL MOTTE
The leader's fortified residence was based on the "motte and bailey" principle: a central mound (motte) with a wooden tower on top and an enclosure (bailey) below. Around the year 1000 these flimsy structures began to be replaced by square or rectangular stone keeps. Two hundred years later round towers began to be built, giving better protection from the new cannons and making it possible to ward off attack from all directions.

FORTIFIED GATEHOUSE
Fortified gateway, with entrance protected by drawbrige, housing part of the garrison.

1. DRAWBRIDGE
A bridge raised and lowered by means of a counterweight. It could be operated by just one man.

2. BARTIZAN
A turret corbelled out above the drawbridge to enhance its defensive capabilities.

3. ASSOMMOIRS
Openings above the gateway from which soldiers could drop stones or pour hot pitch.

4. GUARDROOM
Chamber directly above the gateway from which the portcullis was operated.

CROSS-SECTION OF GATEHOUSE

6. LOOPHOLES OR ARROW LOOPS
A narrow slit in the the wall for the use of archers. Sometimes they were wider, to permit the use of cannon.

7. CURTAIN
Stone rampart between two bastions.

5. POSTERN GATE
Soldiers caught outside the castle at the moment of attack could enter by this hidden door even when the drawbridge was raised.

The fortifications of Brest ▲ 274.

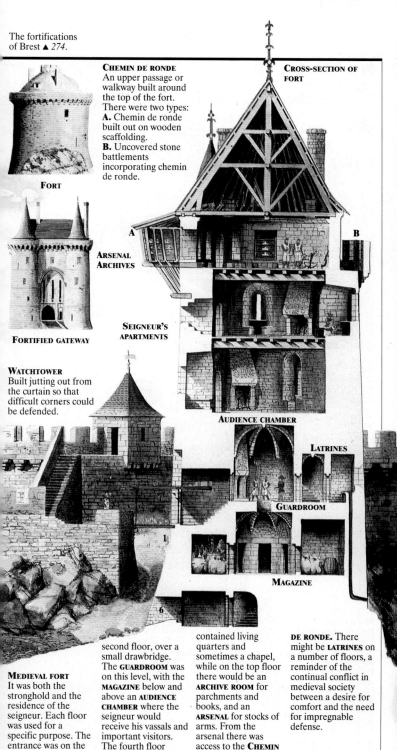

FORT

FORTIFIED GATEWAY

CHEMIN DE RONDE
An upper passage or walkway built around the top of the fort. There were two types:
A. Chemin de ronde built out on wooden scaffolding.
B. Uncovered stone battlements incorporating chemin de ronde.

CROSS-SECTION OF FORT

ARSENAL ARCHIVES

SEIGNEUR'S APARTMENTS

WATCHTOWER
Built jutting out from the curtain so that difficult corners could be defended.

A

B

AUDIENCE CHAMBER

LATRINES

GUARDROOM

1

MAGAZINE

6

MEDIEVAL FORT
It was both the stronghold and the residence of the seigneur. Each floor was used for a specific purpose. The entrance was on the second floor, over a small drawbridge. The **GUARDROOM** was on this level, with the **MAGAZINE** below and above an **AUDIENCE CHAMBER** where the seigneur would receive his vassals and important visitors. The fourth floor contained living quarters and sometimes a chapel, while on the top floor there would be an **ARCHIVE ROOM** for parchments and books, and an **ARSENAL** for stocks of arms. From the arsenal there was access to the **CHEMIN DE RONDE.** There might be **LATRINES** on a number of floors, a reminder of the continual conflict in medieval society between a desire for comfort and the need for impregnable defense.

● COASTAL FORTIFICATIONS

1. CURTAIN
Section of rampart between two bastions.

2. BASTION
A fortification jutting out from the external wall to catch attackers in cross-fire.

3. MOAT

4. ARSENAL
A storehouse and repair workshop for weapons.

5. TERREPLEIN
A raised flat space on the ramparts where guns were mounted.

More modern defensive structures in Brittany were concentrated on the coast and offshore islands that might be taken by the enemy as bases. On the landward side the forts were built in a star shape so that they could be defended by cross-fire from across the moat. On the seaward side they were rounded, which made it possible to fire in all directions.

FROM FORTS TO FORTIFIED HARBORS
Late in the 16th century, the Duc de Mercoeur built forts at strategic points such as Nantes, Suscinio ▲ 362, Port-Louis ▲ 332 and Brest. In the next century Colbert built fortified harbors at Brest ▲ 276 and Lorient ▲ 320 and set up defenses around St-Malo ▲ 186. By then other defenses were springing up around the huge bays of Morlaix and Cancale. They were kept in good repair until changes in weaponry around 1870 made them obsolete.

THE CITADEL OF BELLE-ILE-EN-MER (AT LE PALAIS) ▲ 328
The island fortress was built as a vital outpost to the ports of Lorient and St-Nazaire. It was begun in 1572 and underwent many later improvements. At the center is a star fort; another defensive wall was added in Napoleonic times. Low towers and gun emplacements guard all possible landing points.

6. COUNTERSCARP Outer wall of the moat.
7. FLANK Side wall of the bastion designed to permit raking fire.

8. SCARP Inner wall of the moat.
9. POWDER MAGAZINE
10. RAMPART BARRACKS Troops' quarters built

in the defensive wall.
11. DEMILUNE Triangular outwork protecting the curtain.
12. GLACIS Landscaped terrain

beyond the moat to permit grazing fire.
13. CLOSE WAY Divided into sections with obstacles to prevent it suddenly being overrun.

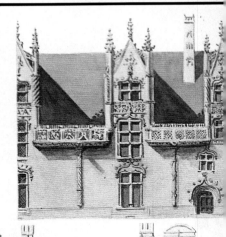

Château de
Kéruzoret at
St-Vougay.

Breton châteaux long
continued to be built on
Gothic models, until they
came under the influence
of the more austere style
of the late Renaissance
architecture. In the 17th
and 18th centuries the
nobles built themselves
large and comfortable
residences whose
appearance was strongly
influenced by French
classical architecture of
the period.

RENAISSANCE WINDOW

The window has a
stone mullion and
transom, and is
framed by pilasters on
either side, with an
architrave above.

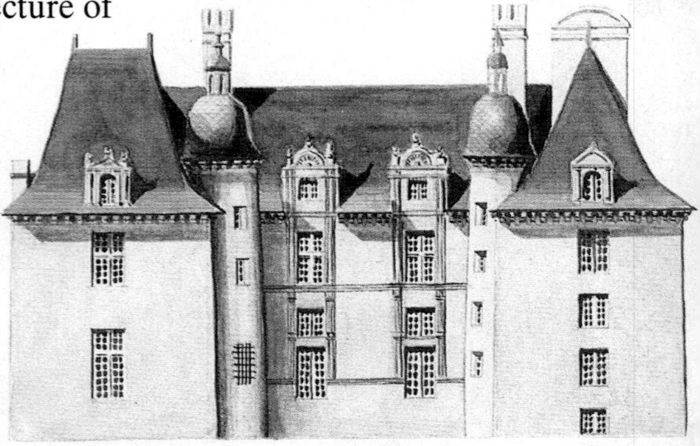

A RENAISSANCE CHÂTEAU, LA CHAPELLE-CHAUSSÉE (ILLE-ET-VILAINE)
A small château near
Rennes exemplifying
the Renaissance style
of architecture that
appeared toward the
end of the 16th
century. The overall
structure is
symmetrical. The
central portion of the
building is set back,
and the impression of
regularity is
reinforced by the
squared pattern of
horizontal string-
courses and vertical
pilasters.

17TH-CENTURY WINDOW

The window has a
wooden mullion and
transom, and a plain
stone lintel decorated
with a mask.

A 17TH-CENTURY CHÂTEAU, LE ROCHER-PORTAIL (ILLE-ET-VILAINE)

Le Rocher-Portail
▲ 176, built in 1617, is
impressive rather
than beautiful. Like
the château of
Kerjean (1580) in the
Finistère, its buildings
are set around a
square courtyard,
with wings set at an
angle and galleries
supported by arcades.

Classical French garden design.

GOTHIC WINDOW

The window has a stone mullion and transoms and is framed by carved moldings with a sculpted ogee arch above.

A GOTHIC CHÂTEAU, JOSSELIN (MORBIHAN) ▲ 231

Jean II of Rohan built the château between 1490 and 1505, against the walls of a 13th-century fortress. Josselin is typical of the residences built by Breton noblemen up to the middle of the 16th century. The layout is simple and elongated, with one room leading on to another, and the style is still the Flamboyant Gothic of the medieval manor house. The ornamental false battlements and extravagantly decorated upper windows show the influence of the Loire Valley châteaux.

TYPICAL FEATURES OF A NOBLE DWELLING

From the 16th century onward it became customary to build a chapel (**2**) at one corner of the courtyard in front of the château. In the following century this was often balanced by a dovecot (**1**), which only noblemen were allowed to possess. A grand entrance (**3**) with two or three arches would be built between the two, topped by a pediment carved with the family crest.

ROOF SHAPES

Steeply pitched roofs (**A**) continued to be built in Brittany much later than elsewhere. They were either hipped or finished at each end by a horizontal gable end. Slowly, however, architects adopted the mansard roof (**B**). This roof design, dating from the mid-17th century, had two distinct slopes, the lower steeper than the upper. It meant that rooms with straight walls could be built under the eaves.

18TH-CENTURY WINDOW

With limestone tufa surround. The mullion has been abandoned and improvements in glass-making have made possible larger window panes.

18TH-CENTURY MILITARY STYLE, KERANROUX (FINISTÈRE)

In the 18th century military engineers introduced a severe style of architecture. These buildings had a projecting central section, pitched roof and segmental arches over the windows. Decoration was more or less limited to the triangular pediment.

MANOR HOUSES

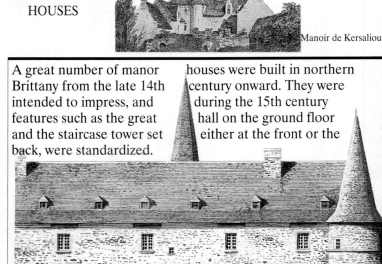

Manoir de Kersaliou

A great number of manor houses were built in northern Brittany from the late 14th century onward. They were intended to impress, and during the 15th century features such as the great hall on the ground floor and the staircase tower set either at the front or the back, were standardized.

Renaissance influence did not reach Brittany until around 1560. It brought in symmetrical façades, new styles of chimney decoration and straight staircases. The wars of the League interrupted these developments. By the 17th century, noblemen no longer wanted manor houses but châteaux.

BOISSORCANT, NOYAL-SUR-VILAINE (ILLE-ET-VILAINE)
The home of one of Duchess Anne's financiers. The removal of four dormer windows in the 19th century has spoilt the superb balance of the façade of this 15th-century manor house, but the interior is perfectly preserved.

LA CHÂTAIGNERAIE, ST-NICOLAS-DU-TERTRE-(MORBIHAN)
A manor house built in 1634 that was late to adopt Renaissance features. The cultural revolution of the 16th century was extremely slow to penetrate Brittany. It reached the rich nobility first, then slowly filtered down through the social strata to influence more popular architecture.

OCULUS from the Kerligonan manor house at Kergloff.

INSIGNIA FROM CHÂTEAU DE ROCHEFORT-EN-TERRE (MORBIHAN)
Many dwellings are decorated with the symbols of nobility: in the 18th century 1 percent of Bretons were noble.

LE GOLLEDIC, LANRIVAIN (CÔTES D'ARMOR)
A 17th-century manor house. The Renaissance passion for symmetry became standard, with the main doorway always in the center. The double gateway was also a common feature, one entrance for carriages and a narrower one for those on foot.

COATCOURAVAL, GLOMEL (CÔTES D'ARMOR)
The archetypal Breton manor. It was built by the Boutevilles in the mid-15th century and stands in isolation, surrounded by woodland. The staircase tower, topped by an upper room, rises behind it.

COAT OF ARMS FROM THE MANOIR DE KERIAR, PLONEVEZ-PORZAY (FINISTÈRE)

KERPONNER, NOYAL-PONTIVY (MORBIHAN)
Even modest manors were designed to stand out from humble dwellings. Here the plain façade is crowned by a dormer window with ornate pediment and along the top are rows of *boulins* (decorated earthenware pigeon holes that denoted nobility, since only nobles were permitted to keep pigeons).

GOTHIC DOOR FROM THE MANOIR DE KERIAR

RENAISSANCE STONE BASIN FROM THE MANOIR DE TRONJOLY
▲ *263*
The Italian fashion for fountains reached Brittany in the 16th century.

TRONJOLY, CLÉDER (FINISTÈRE)
Around 1540 a staircase tower and new wing were added to the 15th-century manor. In the 18th century the main door and gable window were moved to restore balance to the whole.

● MALOUINIÈRES

Having made their fortunes with the French East India Company and by privateering, the shipowners of St-Malo built themselves elegant residences in the surrounding countryside. These dwellings were of military design in the style introduced by Marshal Vauban's architects. At least 112 of these houses, or *malouinières*, have been recorded in the Clos-Poulet region around St-Malo.

Malouinières varied greatly in size, but they were first and foremost family houses. They were all very similar in appearance, with white rendered façades broken by the granite door and window surrounds, horizontal string-courses and quoins (corners). The steeply sloping roofs had necessarily tall chimneys and were often surmounted by ornamental lead or earthenware finials.

The stone dormers emphasized the symmetry of the façade, being set at intervals into the roof, a common 18th-century practice. This

formal design contrasted strongly with the ornate follies erected by the decadent nobility in Paris and elsewhere in France.

Elevated cross-section of the Malouinière du Bos ▲ *160*, at St-Jouan-des-Guérets, the only one currently open to the public.

The Malouinière du Mur Blanc at St-Meloir-des-Ondes (below) was built around 1730.

Inside, these houses were often lavishly decorated. Furniture and floors were made from exotic woods brought back from distant voyages for the wealthy shipowners. There was porcelain from the Orient, and marble from Italy to make imposing fireplaces. Rooms were often wood paneled. The garden was laid out after the classic French style with formal geometric flowerbeds.

The port of Morlaix.

The earliest Breton townhouses were timber-framed, but many of them were subsequently destroyed by fire. In the 17th century they began to be replaced by stone buildings, and their design was simplified in the 18th century under the influence of strategic military architecture.

OLD HOUSE IN DINAN (CÔTES D'ARMOR) ▲ *152*
A typical early timber-frame house (15th century), elegantly styled and crafted, and without ornamentation.

HOUSES IN RUE DE LA VICTOIRE, ST-MALO (ILLE-ET-VILAINE)
Following a series of great fires, it became obligatory to build in stone. As walled towns were becoming constricted and overcrowded, houses were built higher and with larger windows.

CORNER NICHE
Late 17th century, St-Malo.

HOUSE WITH TWO CONVEX COLUMNS, LAMBALLE (CÔTES D'ARMOR).
Toward the end of the 16th century different architectural features evolved in different regions. In the Penthièvre houses had columns and, in the Trégor, unbroken rows of windows.

HOUSE OF DUCHESS ANNE, MORLAIX (FINISTÈRE)
From 1500 onward Gothic houses often had carved decoration.

WINDOWED HOUSE IN RUE PÉLICOT, ST-MALO ▲ 192
Houses like this began to appear in the region in the late 16th century.

SHINGLED HOUSE, RUE KÉRÉON ▲ 300, QUIMPER (FINISTÈRE)
Shingling with slate or wooden tiles gave good protection against bad weather.

HÔTEL HARDY, VITRÉ (ILLE-ET-VILAINE)
Vitré was among the first Breton towns to have stone-built houses. They date from late in the 16th century, and this is the only town with large Renaissance townhouses.

HÔTEL DE LIMUR, VANNES (MORBIHAN)
In the 17th century large stone-built townhouses were uncommon and usually belonged to the aristocracy.

HÔTEL DE CHÂTEAUGIRON, c. 1730, RENNES (ILLE-ET-VILAINE)
In the 18th century the royal engineers inspired an austere, functional style of architecture.

HÔTEL DU QUAI BRANCAS, NANTES (LOIRE-ATLANTIQUE)
The severe military design was applied to buildings of every kind. Apartment blocks, factories and private dwellings, all constructed in this functional but elegant style, were virtually indistinguishable.

A wide variety of building styles can be seen in the Breton countryside. Many regional characteristics are markedly different between one area and another, and also demonstrate how isolated and resistant to change Brittany remained until after World War Two.

Houses in Brittany are by no means all built of granite. They can be of sandstone, schist and cob. Often several materials are combined. Roofs slope steeply and since the last century slate tiles from Angers have replaced the traditional thatch, which was considered too dangerous. The range of dwellings is enormous: there are low farmhouses with living space for both men and animals, weavers' cottages, craftsmen's workshop homes, village shops and the houses of the clergy. Styles differed according to region. In northern Finistère houses tended to be built with an overhanging roof, while in eastern Morbihan they were particularly low. Cob was much used in the Rennes basin.

HOUSE DATED 1567, ST-BRICE-EN-COGLES (ILLE-ET-VILAINE)
There is a remarkable concentration of well-preserved 16th-century dwellings in the region of Coglès, north of Fougères. This building served as house, stable and barn.

THE LATE 16TH-CENTURY LE FRESNAY HOUSE, MELESSE (ILLE-ET-VILAINE)
Built in stone and timber. This combination was restricted to the countryside around Rennes.

DECORATIVE LIGNOLET SLATES
A 19th-century feature in the Finistère regions of Commana and Sizun.

BREAD OVEN, TREGUNC (FINISTÈRE)
The stone vault might be covered with earth

PLAQUE FROM A FISHERMAN'S HOUSE
A ship's anchor follows the date (Côtes d'Armor).

HOUSE DATED 1622, CAULNES (CÔTES D'ARMOR)
The two floors incorporate a living-room, stable and storage loft. The stone and earth walls have a mellow tone that is much warmer than granite. These materials are typical of the Caulnes, Evran and Bécherel regions.

Extraordinary ridge tiles carved from Lignolet slate, from a house in the village of Ruffiac, Morbihan.

17TH-CENTURY HOUSE, ST-RIVOAL (FINISTÈRE)
A house with overhang (*kuz-taol*) and an extension enclosing the front staircase. It is typical of the Monts d'Arrée region.

DIVIDED DOOR
A stable-type door; the top could be opened while the lower half was shut to keep animals out.

17TH-CENTURY HOUSE, PLEUMEUR-BODOU (CÔTES D'ARMOR)
A tall dwelling built of fine dressed granite, with a room and a loft above.

CARVED LINTEL, 1722, KERGRIST (MORBIHAN)
The chalice indicated a priest's house.

WELL, GUERN (MORBIHAN)
The decoration of the crosspiece is characteristic of the area.

HOUSE DATED 1858, CLÉDEN CAP SIZUN (MORBIHAN) Houses near the sea were often rendered for extra protection against the weather.

16TH- AND 17TH-CENTURY FARMHOUSE, ST-NICOLAS-DU-PELEM (CÔTES D'ARMOR)
A five-roomed house: three for the farmer and family, one stable and a storage loft. A priest lived in the upper room, reached by the exterior staircase.

17TH-CENTURY FARMHOUSE, BRANDIVY (MORBIHAN)
A long structure with a loft running above, and holes in the wall for pigeons to roost. Many thatched roofs have survived in the Morbihan.

● Tidal mills

The concept of a tidal mill seems a novel idea at first. But the tides in north Brittany have an exceptionally high rise and fall: it is small wonder that the resourceful inhabitants devised a profitable way to exploit the immense power of the sea. Such mills were not designed by professional engineers: they were conceived and built by peasants, who understood the tides. Most of these marine mills were in the Morbihan, and a number remained in operation until the 1960's.

PEN CASTEL MILL
Not many mills retain the outward signs of their original function, having by now either fallen into ruin or been converted into holiday homes. The 17th-century Pen Castel mill is an exception. It has been meticulously restored and now houses a restaurant.

THE MECHANISM
The wooden exterior wheel (**1**) is connected by a drive-shaft to a smaller angle wheel (**2**) inside, made of cast iron and with wooden cogs. This turns a smaller cast-iron cog attached to a vertical shaft (**3**), which sets the grinding wheel, or wheels, in motion. Above is a wooden frame (**4**) supporting a trough (**6**) into which grain is fed from a hopper (**5**). It gradually releases its contents, which is ground between the running and the fixed millstones beneath. The flour produced is collected in a bin (**7**).

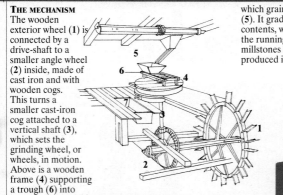

PALUDEN MILL
The mill is built on a dyke across a small bay, and powered by water. A hinged flap is pushed open by the rising sea, but falls tightly shut at the ebb.

KERVILIO MILL
The last mill in the Morbihan to remain in perfect working order. Its wheel is blocked until gradually released by the ebbing tide. Then a little flap at the rear of the mill is opened to free the water from the millpond above, which sets the wheel turning.

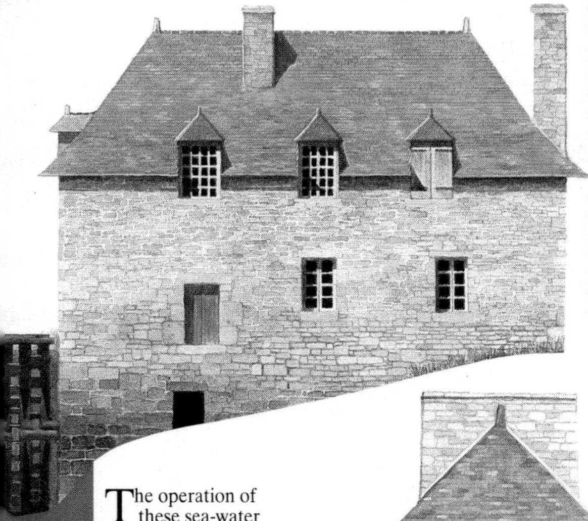

The operation of these sea-water mills was governed by the tide. At certain times of year the tides lack the energy to power the mechanism. Then the mill would stand idle, and the miller would carry out maintenance work on the mechanism. The channels on the stone wheels whose grooved surfaces crushed the grain as finely as possible, needed to be recut from time to time. Often a miller would own a wind-powered mill on a nearby hill as well, which would keep his business turning over.

 Between 1450 and 1650 an enormous number of devotional shrines were erected along the roadsides of Lower Brittany. These open-air chapels were for the most part the work of anonymous artists and craftsmen. They were cherished and embellished over the centuries, monuments to Brittany's ardent Catholic allegiance. Crucifixion is the dominant theme, but there are also other scenes from the life of Christ, and local saints were sometimes featured too.

CRUCIFIXION AT ST-NOYALE (MORBIHAN)
The oldest shrines (c.1450) stand at Kerbreudeur, in St-Hernin, and at Tronoën. Shrine building reached its artistic peak around the middle of the 16th century with the monuments at Plougonven (1554), Pleyben (c. 1550), Quilinen and St-Sebastien (1547), followed later by those at Cléden Poher (1575) and Guimiliau (1581–8). The calvary at Plougonven was signed by two craftsmen, Bastien and Henry Prigent, but generally the work was anonymous. The appearance and position of shrines was often altered. That of Pleyben was begun around 1550, was moved away in 1650 to be completed elsewhere, and was restored to its original position in 1738.

A COMPLETE SCENE
The exploded view below shows the elements of the west face of the calvary at Cleden Poher, Finistère (1575).

1. **CHRIST**

2. **ANGELS**

3. **THE VIRGIN**

4. **SAINT JOHN**

5. **PENITENT THIEF**
6. **IMPENITENT THIEF**

7. **PEDESTAL**

CALVARY CARVED IN RELIEF, MAURE-DE-BRETAGNE (ILLE-ET-VILAINE).
The shrine dates from the 15th or 16th century. Its west face is shown above left.

8. **COLUMN SHAFT**

9. **KNIGHT**

10. **PIETÀ**

11. **MARIE-MADELEINE**

12. **BASE**

13. **ALTAR**

Three carved blocks from the north face of the Tronoën ▲ *307* shrine depicting the Nativity. Joseph sleeps exhausted, resting on his pilgrim staff. The Virgin lies bare-breasted in bed while the young Jesus, already grown to boyhood, stands holding the globe. The Magi, representing the homage of the nations, bring gifts of gold, frankincense and myrrh.

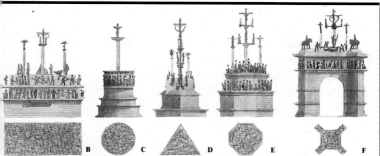

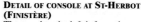

THE CROSSES ARE SET ON VARIOUSLY SHAPED BASES

The figurative scenes were sculpted out of "Kersanton" granite, a soft, fine-grained stone, but the base was always of local granite. It might be square, as at Coëtlogon (**A**), rectangular as at Tronoën (**B**), round as at Pleubian (**C**), triangular as at Quilinen (**D**), octagonal as at Plougonven (**E**), or cruciform as at Pleyben (**F**).

DETAIL OF CONSOLE AT ST-HERBOT (FINISTÈRE)
The angel to the left is from the upper part of a scene of the *Crucifixion*. In one hand he holds a hammer and in the other three nails: the implements used to fix Christ to the cross.

CRUCIFIXION AND TRIUMPHANT RESURRECTION AT GUIMILIAU ▲ *253* (FINISTÈRE), 1581
The base of the monument is cruciform, as at Pleyben. The structure is complicated since it also served as a pulpit for occasions such as the traditional Breton pardons. The upper section shows Baroque influence in its remarkably expressive and dramatic sculpture. Christ has risen and stands tall above two sleeping soldiers, while the figures to his left and right seem to be pushed back by the power of his presence.

TWIN STATUES
Roland Doré sculpted this pair, representing Saint Yves back to back with a woman, in 1630. Their appearance suggests that shrines were once painted.

SAINT SEBASTIAN AT ST-SEGAL (FINISTÈRE)
In Crucifixion scenes the cross always faced west. For other scenes, such as Christ in Glory, or the Martyrdom of Saint Sebastian above, the cross would be turned toward the east.

● BELL TOWERS

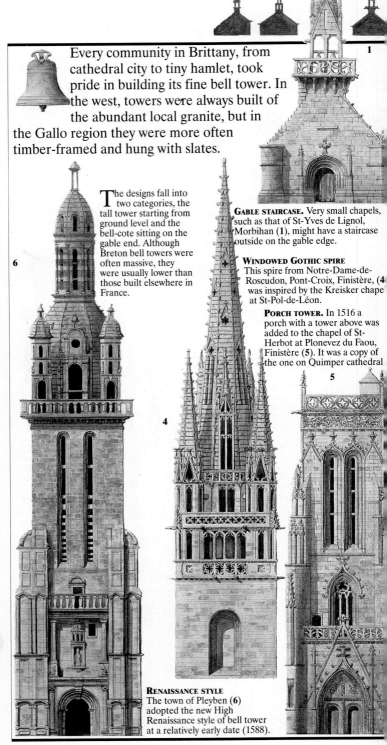

Every community in Brittany, from cathedral city to tiny hamlet, took pride in building its fine bell tower. In the west, towers were always built of the abundant local granite, but in the Gallo region they were more often timber-framed and hung with slates.

The designs fall into two categories, the tall tower starting from ground level and the bell-cote sitting on the gable end. Although Breton bell towers were often massive, they were usually lower than those built elsewhere in France.

GABLE STAIRCASE. Very small chapels, such as that of St-Yves de Lignol, Morbihan (**1**), might have a staircase outside on the gable edge.

WINDOWED GOTHIC SPIRE
This spire from Notre-Dame-de-Roscudon, Pont-Croix, Finistère, (**4**) was inspired by the Kreisker chapel at St-Pol-de-Léon.

PORCH TOWER. In 1516 a porch with a tower above was added to the chapel of St-Herbot at Plonevez du Faou, Finistère (**5**). It was a copy of the one on Quimper cathedral

RENAISSANCE STYLE
The town of Pleyben (**6**) adopted the new High Renaissance style of bell tower at a relatively early date (1588).

COMBINED BELL-COTE AND PORCH TOWER

In the Trégor the style is slightly different. The bell tower was supported by buttresses and a staircase tower. The church at Trédez, Côtes d'Armor (**2**) introduced the concept of a porch below.

2

MAIN FAÇADE

At the chapel of St-Fiacre du Faouët in the Morbihan (**3**) is a principal bell tower with a decorated open gallery below, supported on corbeling and extended over arches to link it to two secondary bell towers, one with a spiral staircase.

3

8

9

TIMBER-FRAMED BELL TOWERS

In Upper Brittany bell towers were built of wood. The 15th-century church of Chavagne in the Ille-et-Vilaine (**7**) is a beautifully simple example of the polygonal spire. For the church at St-Etienne de Rennes, Ille-et-Vilaine (**8**), also 15th-century, the carpenters created a timber dome and lantern, which in other parts of France would have been roofed with lead. A marvelous variety of shapes and designs can be seen in many other fine timber-framed bell towers, such as the one on the church at Faouët, in the Morbihan (**9**).

PROUD BELL TOWERS

Brittany's proud bell towers reach up towards the sky, fashioned in the distant past, to praise the Lord most high. Immutable, eternal, keeping watch o'er house and farm, Over men who gave their lives to keep these churches from all harm." Théodore Botrel

CHURCH INTERIORS

The décor and furniture inside Breton churches have always been inspired by a mix of popular belief and official doctrine. Much was produced by local craftsmen, but there are also many sophisticated features paid for by local aristocrats or by the wealthy parishes themselves.

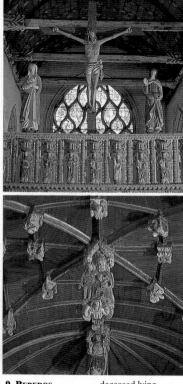

1. HIGH ALTAR
A consecrated table set in the chancel at which the priest celebrates Mass.

2. TABERNACLE
Small cupboard set on the high altar in which the Eucharist is kept.

3. SIDE ALTAR
Usually dedicated to a particular saint.

4. ROOD BEAM
Often decorated with scenes from the Bible, and separating the chancel from the nave. On it was a cross, often with Mary and Saint John on either side.

5. LECTERN
Stand on which the Bible or other text is placed, for reading or chanting.

6. ROOD SCREEN
A tall partition between chancel and nave topped by a throne reached by a rood stair.

7. DECORATED STRINGER

A beam running lengthwise, often carved with scenes from the Bible or visions of Hell.

8. VOTIVE OFFERINGS
Symbolic gifts brought in thanks for some Divine intercession. Among local people so closely bound up with the sea, they would often be in the form of boats.

9. REREDOS
Painting, carving or decoration behind or above an altar. From Quimper to Morlaix they were of wood. Around Rennes, Vitré, Vannes and Pontivy they were made out of marble or tufa by architects from Laval.

10. LAVABO
A kind of sink set into a niche with a shelf on which the altar-cruets stand.

11. RECUMBENT FIGURE
Carved effigy of the deceased lying serenely on his or her tomb.

12. PROCESSIONAL BANNER
The symbol of a parish or brotherhood carried in open-air processions in such ceremonies as pardons.

13. PULPIT
A raised and enclosed platform from which the priest delivers the sermon to the assembled faithful.

14. STOUP
Basin for holy water.

15. PROCESSIONAL STATUES
Breton statues were made from a wide variety of materials: wood, different granites, marble, limestone. Their themes were often traditional (the life of Christ, the Virgin and Child, the Apostles), but with the reform of the Catholic

church new ones, like the rosary and Saint Joseph, were also adopted. There were always many popular saints.

16. BOSS
An ornamental projection placed at the intersection of the ribs of a vault.

17. TIE-BEAM
Horizontal beam spanning the church and supporting the sloping roof timbers. At each end are gargoyles.

18. FONT
A vessel usually of stone and set on a base, containing the water for baptism. It sometimes has a canopy.

19. TOMB RECESS
An elongated niche, often framed with elegant carving, in which a funerary monument is set.

20. LEDGER
Large flat stone with inscription laid over a tomb.

BRITTANY
AS SEEN
BY PAINTERS

DENISE DELOUCHE

Cancale first became a favorite haunt of artists during the 1860's. *Landing Oysters at Cancale* (**1**) was painted by August Flameng in 1888. *Easter Convoy* (**3**) by Marin Marie (**2**) dates from the 1930's. Over the years the same themes predominate, largely centered around oysters, still a cottage industry in the 19th century. Other artists specialized in portraits of the local peasants and fisher-folk, though their

interpretation of these themes tends to sweeten and idealize. With his brother, Auguste Feyen-Perrin was a frequent visitor to Cancale in the 1870's. He chose graceful fair-haired models for his pictures. *Cancale Girl Knitting* (**4**) is a sentimental and nostalgic vision far removed from the harsh realities of life. The young American John Singer Sargent (1856–1925) paid a brief visit to Cancale in 1877 and painted *The Oyster Gatherers* (**5**), a composition filled with light that strongly recalls the Impressionist paintings of the period.

> **"THE SEA IS ENGAGED IN BREAKING UP THE CLIFFS – HAS BEEN FOR SOME TIME – EVEN AS THE CLIFFS IMAGINE THEY ARE SPLINTERING THE SEA."**
>
> ROBERT DALEY

The endless variety of the Brittany coastline and the fathomless blue of the sea exercised a profound influence on painters who came here. At Ploumanac'h

in 1913 Henri Le Fauconnier, a recent convert to Cubism, came face to face with the strange rock formations here and used these shapes in his *Houses among the Rocks* (**1**). In 1888, Émile Bernard had developed a new approach to landscape at St Briac on the Côte d'Émeraude, using simplified shapes, strong colors and flat surfaces. This was the style of the Pont-Aven school (**2**). In 1861 J.M. Whistler (1834–1903; **4**) had come to convalesce in Brittany, and he painted a stretch of the deserted coast (**3**) with bare sand and jagged rocks where a young girl has come to grieve in solitude alone with the breaking waves. Maurice Denis (**6**) used the granite rocks of Ploumanac'h, where he had a house, as the setting for his remarkable Saint George fighting the Dragon (**5**). Its subject recalls Gauguin's famous

Vision after the Sermon which featured Jacob wrestling with the Angel. Like Gauguin, Maurice Denis placed ancient legend in a contemporary setting, though the Bretons pictured here fleeing from the combat have a different function from those in Gauguin's abstract red meadow. Denis had no need to construct an imaginary setting; he simply used the fantastic coastline of Ploumanac'h.

The traditional costumes worn on the Plougastel peninsula held a fascination for many painters. In the 1860's, when Eugène Boudin was painting here, the elaborate headdress had two wings that jutted out

behind, but were later folded on top of the head, as when Charles Cottet (1) made them the subject of a painting (2). In this picture a procession of snowy-capped profiles trips across the canvas, interrupted only by the dazzling crimson of a girl's bonnet and jabot at the center: the black velvet dresses, pink complexions, white bonnets and sky-blue ribbons form a satisfying chorus of colorful contrasts. Eugène Boudin (1824–98) had plenty of time to study local costume when he spent his summers at Hanvec, near Faou, in the 1860's. His wife came from this region, and Boudin

was fascinated by the fairs and pardons he went to see. He also visited Passage, on the banks of the Elorn. Before the bridge was built women used to wait there for the ferry to go to Brest; Boudin made sketches of the squat figures of the women of Kerhor (3) with their outsize headdresses, and of their graceful compatriots from Plougastelen (4 and 5). A few strokes of pencil or brush conjured up the way their headdresses were blown about by the wind. In *Interior of the Church at Hanvec* (6) Boudin experimented with

seemingly random dashes of white against a spare austere background to suggest groups of women standing or kneeling in shadow, evoking an atmosphere of peace and prayer. This marvelous work was merely a sketch as far as Boudin was concerned, remaining unfinished in his studio.

"NOWHERE DOES THE PAST SEEM SO VIVIDLY ALIVE AS AT VITRÉ, WHERE SCENES FROM PAST CENTURIES SPRING TO MIND WITH AN EFFORTLESS FLICK OF THE IMAGINATION."

L. GALLOUEDEC

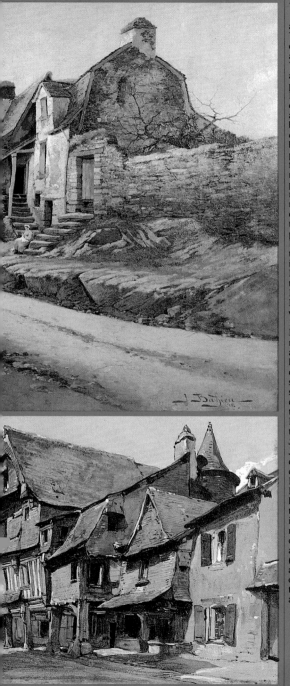

Unlike Fougères, which held little appeal for artists, Vitré features in countless drawings and paintings. Visitors were at first attracted by the presence nearby of Mme de Sévigné's chateau at Rochers, and were captivated by the architectural delights of the town beside it. In 1887 painter Jules Bahieu, for whom scenes of mean and squalid poverty held a strong romantic appeal, made the poor quarter of the town the subject of his picture *Petit Rachapt, Vitré* (1), a throwback to the troubled imaginings of Kaspar David Friedrich and the Byronic agony. Rumanian painter Nicolas Grigoresco was in Vitré between 1876 and 1886. Instead of taking a realist or romantic approach to the town, he captured dramatic effects of light and shade by using rich, subtle, thickly laid colors suggestive of the contemporary Impressionists, as in this detail from his *Street in Vitré* (2). Judging by the large collection of water-colors left by Eugène Isabey (now in the Louvre), he must have worked hard there during his stay in 1850. He made many studies of the old houses there, and, as in *Street in Vitré* (3), he paid close attention to the play of light and shade on the covered sidewalks and timeworn roofs.

1	
2	3

SAINTE-NOYALE

In this painting by Pierre Cadre the unusual bell tower of the chapel of Ste Noyale near Pontivy dominates the composition, soaring above the figures of pilgrims in traditional dress just arrived on horseback for the annual June pardon.

BRITTANY
AS SEEN BY WRITERS

The Sea

Dangerous Terrain

Chaucer's "Canterbury Tales", begun in 1387, include what is perhaps the earliest recorded description of Brittany. In "The Franklin's Tale", the beautiful Dorigen pines for her absent husband Arveragus, and contemplates the forbidding black rocks and foaming seas of coastal Armorica.

❝But, Lord, thise grisly feendly rokkes blake,   *fiendish*
That semen rather a foul confusion
Of werk than any fair creation
Of swich a parfit wys God and a stable,
Why han ye wroght this werk unresonable?
For by this werk, south, north, ne west, ne eest,
Ther nys yfostred man, ne bryd, ne beest;   *sustained*
It dooth no good, to my wit, but anoyeth,
Se ye nat, Lord, how mankynde it destroyeth?
An hundred thousand bodyes of mankynde
Han rokkes slayn, al be they nat in mynde,
Which mankynde is so fair part of thy werk
That thou it madest lyk to thyn owene merk.   *in; image*
Thanne semed it ye hadde a greet chiertee   *love*
Toward mankynde; but how thanne may it bee
That ye swiche meenes make it to destroyen   *means*
Whiche meenes do no good, but
everye anoyen?   *do harm*

GEOFFREY CHAUCER,
CANTERBURY TALES,
PUB. EVERYMAN'S LIBRARY, 1992

Wrecked off Molène Island

The writer of the following passage was one of three to be saved from a total of 253 when the liner "Drummond Castle", en route from Cape Town to London, struck the Pierres Vertes off Molène Island on June 16, 1896.

❝When you have the finest ship that man can build under your feet, the most skilful and experienced of captains, the best of officers, and are making a voyage which has been made safely thousands of times before, you take it for granted that all will be well with you, and that you will reach port. Such was the conviction of every soul on board the *Drummond Castle* when she left Cape Town for London on what proved to be her last voyage.

The *Drummond Castle* was not a very big steamboat, even for that period – Cape liners have grown enormously since then – but she was as stout a craft as you could wish to have; big enough and stout enough to stand any weather.

By the time we got into the Bay of Biscay, people had got to know one another, and were thankful the end of the voyage was so near. Already there were those who were preparing to go ashore, joyful at the thought of meeting friends and relatives from whom they had been parted, perhaps for years. The whole ship was full of happy people, and by way of celebrating the successful passage a concert was given in the saloon.

That was on the night of June 16. The weather was not what you would call bad, but the air was pretty thick, and there was a nasty drizzle. It was my watch . . . I was busy at my task – which in the darkness was not a very easy one, but simple enough compared with some of the duties of seamen in less favoured vessels – when I felt a slight jar; that was all – just the sort of thing I had often felt when a steamboat was being made fast alongside a quay. But in such a place and at such a time a sailor instantly sets his wits to work to find the reason why a jar or shock is felt . . .

Yet there was no sign of sailing-vessel or steamboat anywhere, no further grinding which could indicate the presence of a rock. We were still wondering and bewildered in the gloom and drizzle when we heard a quiet, steady voice from the bridge: "Clear away the boats!"

It was clear that the ship had struck . . . and the *Drummond Castle* was making water fast. At the same time stewards and passengers rushed up from below, crying that water was pouring into the ship. The order to lower the boats was given. Discipline prevailed – I have told you that, and there was no panic; but is it necessary to describe the heartrending scenes into which we were plunged? The passengers, who but a few moments before had been enjoying themselves at the concert, had rushed on deck; the crew had hurried up, too, and everywhere men, women and children were clamouring for salvation. Husbands and wives clung to each other, mothers clasped their children in agonies of terror.

While I was busy at my fall, four passengers rushed up and tried to get into the boat. I warned them that if they interfered at such a crisis there would be no chance of saving them. Even as I spoke the words there was an overwhelming rush of sea, and I and all about me were swept away. In that short space of time, literally before we realised that she was badly damaged, the *Drummond Castle* had plunged into deep water. The very bottom of her must have been torn off by the awful force with which she had struck.

At that terrible moment such a cry went up as I hope I may never hear again. It was the united voices of the doomed, who in the darkness found themselves hurled into the water. Some went down with the ship, those who were not drawn into the vortex were struggling for life, and from the gloomy sea there came the most piteous appeal for the help which no man could give. Few were there who could even make shift to save their own lives.

The vessel had disappeared bodily, taking the boats with her before they could be so much got out and lowered. In an instant I was carried off my feet, and hurled by the press of water across the boat-deck . . . as I was borne resistlessly overboard, unable to help or save myself, I saw the captain and one of the officers standing side by side . . .

The disaster was so swift and complete that until I found myself floating about I did not realise what had happened. I knew, however, too thoroughly when I was struggling for my life, and when all around me there rose the most dreadful cries for help, mingled with the more terrible shrieks of those who sank to rise no more. Some of these poor creatures were just near me, struggling fiercely.

I could do nothing to help them – that was not humanly possible; yet I have never ceased to regret that I had not the chance at least to try to get some girl or child or woman on to a bit of floating wreckage . . . In my frenzy and despair I clutched wildly about me and, as luck would have it, managed to grip a floating hatch . . .

Night in June is very brief, but it seemed long indeed before the dawn broke. By that time there was a deathly stillness about me. Not a cry was heard, not a soul seemed to be left of all the *Drummond Castle*'s people except myself, but suddenly I heard groans very near me.

'Who's that?' I called, feebly enough, for I was becoming exhausted and was numb with cold. 'It's Wood,' a voice replied, and I knew that this was one of my shipmates, a quarter-master . . .

Nine full hours had passed since I was hurled into the water – nine hours of agony which was almost unrelieved by hope. I lived and Wood lived – that was all. Despair had entered my soul and I had ceased to hope when I saw a sight which instantly filled my chilled blood with fire – the sight of fishermen stealing to sea from the shelter of the land.

We were seen, and three Breton fishermen in their little boat bore down and took us off our raft. We were more dead than living, and if it had not been for the care and kindness of our friends we could not have survived. They got us ashore and stripped and warmed and rubbed us. They took off their own dry, warm clothes and put them on to us. We had landed, we learnt, at Molène, at about eleven o'clock in the morning, nearly twelve hours after the loss of our ship. **99**

W. J. GODBOLT, QUOTED IN *SURVIVORS' TALES OF FAMOUS SHIPWRECKS*, PUB. WALTER WOOD, 1932, REPR. E. P. PUBLISHING, WAKEFIELD, 1974

DEPARTURE AND RETURN

Pierre Loti (1850–1923), an officer in the French navy, discovered Brittany in 1867. He spent two years there, and the region inspired two novels, "An Iceland Fisherman", his first great literary success, and "My Brother Yves: A Tale of Brittany". Despite his intimate knowledge of the people and the place, a sense of strangeness and exoticism pervades his description of life on the Breton coast.

66The vessel was called Marie; her captain was Guerneur. Every year, on a fishing expedition, she made the trip to those cold and dangerous regions, where the summers no longer have nights.

Like her patron saint, the clay Virgin, she was very ancient. Her massive sides, with their oaken ribs, were scarred and seamed and impregnated with moisture and brine. But she was still rugged and seaworthy, exhaling an invigorating odor of tar. While at anchor, her heavy framework made her appear cumbersome, but when the strong westerly gales were blowing she quickly recovered her sprightly vigor, like seagulls awakened by the wind, and in a manner all her own she bounded lightly over the billows, more briskly, in fact, than many a younger craft wrought with modern finesse.

As for her crew, the six men and the cabin boy, they were Icelanders (a sturdy race of sailors, scattered mainly over Paimpol and Tréguier, who from father to son were all devoted to the sea).

They rarely saw the summer of France. Towards the end of each winter, in the port of Paimpol, they received, along with the other fishermen, the parting benedictions. In honor of the day an altar was erected on the wharf. It was built in imitation of a rocky grotto; enthroned among trophies of anchors, oars and nets was their patron saint, the sweet impassive Virgin, taken for this occasion from the church. For generation after generation she gazed with the same lifeless eyes, upon those fortunate ones for whom the season held good promises and upon others who were doomed never to return.

The holy sacrament was followed by a procession of wives and mothers, fiancees and sisters, who slowly wound their way about the harbor, where all the flag-bedecked ships bound for Iceland saluted as they passed. The priest paused before each one, uttering the words and making the significant gestures of benediction. After which, in a fleet, they all departed, leaving the country also destitute of husbands, lovers and sons. As the boats glided out into the distance, the men sang, in vibrant full-throated voices, the canticles of Marie, Star-of-the-Sea.

Each year saw renewed the same parting ceremonies, the same adieux.

Then again would begin the life of the open sea, three or four rugged companions isolated on moving planks in the midst of the icy arctic waters.

Until now they had always come safely back – Marie, Star-of-the-Sea, had protected the boat that bore her name.

They usually timed their return for the end of August. But the *Marie* followed the custom of most Icelanders, merely touching Paimpol in passing and continuing on down the Gulf of Gascogne where their fish could be sold at a greater profit, and from there to the sandy islands and salt marshes where they bought their salt supply for the next expedition.

The men, thirsting for pleasure, lingered a few days in these sunny southern ports. They were intoxicated by this bit of summer, by the warm air, by the earth and by the women.

With the coming of the first autumnal fogs they returned to their firesides in Paimpol or else to the huts scattered about the district of Goilo, and there, for a time, they occupied themselves with affairs of family, of love, or marriage and of birth. Almost always they found little newborn babes awaiting godfathers, that they might receive the holy baptism: they had need of many children, this race of fishermen that Iceland devours. 99

PIERRE LOTI, *AN ICELAND FISHERMAN*,
TRANS. YNGVE BERG,
STOCKHOLM, 1931

FIN-DE-SIÈCLE VERSE

In his short unhappy life English poet Ernest Dowson (1867–1900) was hardly prolific, but his verse has a sincerity that mannered contemporaries such as Oscar Wilde freely acknowledged. He spent much of his youth in France and traveled extensively in Brittany. The lyric below is less well known than his famous refrains "I have been faithful to thee, Cynara, in my fashion," and "They are not long, these days of wine and roses", but it has a direct and touching simplicity.

IN A BRETON CEMETERY

66They sleep well here,
These fisher-folk who passed their anxious days
In fierce Atlantic ways;
And found not there,
Beneath the long curled wave,
So quiet a grave.

And they sleep well
These peasant-folk, who told their lives away,
From day to market-day,
As one should tell,
With patient industry,
Some sad old rosary.

And now night falls,
Me, tempest-tost, and driven from pillar to post,
A poor worn ghost,
This quiet pasture calls;
And dear dead people with pale hands
Beckon me to their lands. 99

ERNEST DOWSON, *COMPLETE LYRICS*,
PUB. PETER PAUPER PRESS, MOUNT VERNON, 1938

HISTORY

CONFLICT

In an age when almost half the population of Europe and western Asia was wiped out by the Black Death, it is extraordinary that so many marvels – Europe's great cathedrals, the universities of Oxford and the Sorbonne, the tales of Boccaccio and Geoffrey Chaucer, for example – date from the 14th century. American historian Barbara Buchman's study "A Distant Mirror: the Calamitous 14th Century", from which this extract is taken, is a fascinating book and full of surprises.

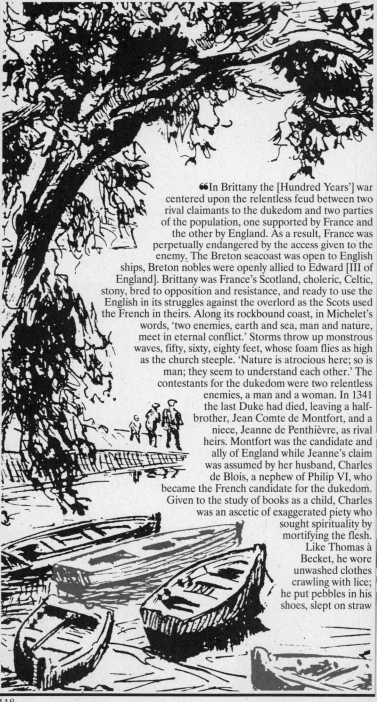

❝In Brittany the [Hundred Years'] war centered upon the relentless feud between two rival claimants to the dukedom and two parties of the population, one supported by France and the other by England. As a result, France was perpetually endangered by the access given to the enemy. The Breton seacoast was open to English ships, Breton nobles were openly allied to Edward [III of England]. Brittany was France's Scotland, choleric, Celtic, stony, bred to opposition and resistance, and ready to use the English in its struggles against the overlord as the Scots used the French in theirs. Along its rockbound coast, in Michelet's words, 'two enemies, earth and sea, man and nature, meet in eternal conflict.' Storms throw up monstrous waves, fifty, sixty, eighty feet, whose foam flies as high as the church steeple. 'Nature is atrocious here; so is man; they seem to understand each other.' The contestants for the dukedom were two relentless enemies, a man and a woman. In 1341 the last Duke had died, leaving a half-brother, Jean Comte de Montfort, and a niece, Jeanne de Penthièvre, as rival heirs. Montfort was the candidate and ally of England while Jeanne's claim was assumed by her husband, Charles de Blois, a nephew of Philip VI, who became the French candidate for the dukedom. Given to the study of books as a child, Charles was an ascetic of exaggerated piety who sought spirituality by mortifying the flesh. Like Thomas à Becket, he wore unwashed clothes crawling with lice; he put pebbles in his shoes, slept on straw on the floor next to his wife's bed, and after his death was found to have worn a coarse shirt of horsehair under his armor, and cords wound so tightly around his body that the knots dug into his flesh. By these practices a seeker of holiness expressed contempt for the world, self-abasement, and humility, although he often found himself guilty of a perverse pride in his excesses. Charles confessed every night so that he might not go to sleep in a state of sin. He fathered a bastard son called Jehan de Blois, but sins of the flesh did not have to be eschewed, only repented. He treated the humble with deference, it was said, met the complaints of the poor with goodness and justice, and refrained from too heavy taxes. Such was his reputation for saintliness that when he undertook to walk barefoot in the snow to a Breton shrine, the people covered his path with straw and blankets, but he took another way at a cost of bleeding and frozen feet, so that for weeks afterward he was unable to walk. **99**

BARBARA W. TUCHMAN,
A DISTANT MIRROR,
PUB. ALFRED A. KNOPF, 1978

ROUGH JUSTICE

The Chouan uprising in the west of France at the end of the 18th century is an ugly page in French history. Politically anti-republican and pro-Catholic, its most prominent features were the same arrogance, greed and cruelty that had characterized the Terror before it. The young Balzac (1799–1850) used it as the theme of the first novel in his epic sequence "La Comédie Humaine", and at the time he was writing of events well within living memory. In this excerpt the peasant Galope-chopine is wrongfully accused by two fellow-Chouans, Pille-miche and Marche-à-terre, of passing information to the military (the Blues). The scene takes place in Galope-chopine's cottage just outside Fougères.

66The two Chouans appeared in the little yard, looking with their dark faces and well-worn wide hats like the figures engravers place in their landscapes.

'Good day, Galope-chopine,' said Marche-à-terre gravely.

'Good day, Monsieur Marche-à-terre,' humbly replied Barbette's husband. 'Will you come in and drink a few *pichés*? I have cold buckwheat cake and fresh-made butter.'

'That's not to be turned down, Cousin,' said Pille-miche. The two Chouans entered the house. There was nothing in this first approach to alarm the master of the house; and he hastened to his big cask to fill three *pichés*, while Marche-à-terre and Pille-miche, sitting on each side of the long table on the gleaming benches, cut buckwheat cakes for themselves and spread them with rich yellow butter oozing droplets of milk under the knife. Galope-chopine placed the *pichés* of foaming cider before his guests and the three Chouans began their meal. But the host cast a sidelong look at Marche-à-terre from time to time as he busied himself satisfying his guests' thirst.

'Give me your snuff-horn,' Marche-à-terre said to Pille-miche.

And when he had vigorously shaken several pinches into the palm of his hand, the Breton sniffed his tobacco like a man preparing for serious business.

'It's cold,' said Pille-miche rising and going to close the upper leaf of the door.

The mist-darkened daylight now entered the room only through the little window, and shed a very dim light on the table and two benches, but the surfaces gleamed with red reflections from the fire. Galope-chopine finished replenishing his guests' *pichés* for the second time and set them before them; but they refused to drink, threw aside their wide-brimmed hats, and suddenly adopted a solemn air. Their movements and the look they exchanged as though consulting each other made Galope-chopine quake, and he thought he saw blood under the red woollen caps they were wearing.

'Bring us your chopper,' said Marche-à-terre.

'But, Monsieur Marche-à-terre, what do you want with that?'

'Come, Cousin, you know very well,' said Pille-miche, putting away the snuff-horn that Marche-à-terre returned to him. 'You're sentenced.'

The two Chouans rose simultaneously, seizing their guns.

'Monsieur Marche-à-terre, I said *naught* about the Gars . . .'

'I told you to fetch your chopper,' the Chouan answered.

The unhappy Galope-chopine stumbled against his son's clumsy wooden crib, and three hundred-sou coins rolled out on the floor. Pille-miche picked them up.

'Oho! So the Blues gave you new coins,' exclaimed Marche-à-terre.

'As true as that's Saint Labre up there, I said *naught*,' protested Galope-chopine. 'Barbette took the Counter-Chouans for *gars* from Saint-Georges, that's all.'

'Why do you talk to your wife about business?' Marche-à-terre said sternly. 'Besides, Cousin, we're not asking for excuses, only your chopper. You're sentenced.'

At a sign from Marche-à-terre, the two men seized their victim. Finding himself in the Chouans' hands, Galope-chopine lost all powers of resistance, fell on his knees and held out despairing hands towards his executioners.

'Good friends, Cousin, what would become of my little boy?' he said.

'I'll take care of him,' said Marche-à-terre.

'Dear comrades,' said Galope-chopine, ghastly pale, 'I'm not in a fit state to die. Would you let me go without confession? You have the right to take my life, but not to make me lose the eternal blessedness.'

'That's true,' said Marche-à-terre, looking at Pille-miche.

The two Chouans stood there for a moment greatly embarrassed, unable to find a way of resolving this problem of conscience. Galope-chopine listened to the faintest sounds caused by the wind as if he still retained some hope. The noise of the drop of cider falling at regular intervals made him throw a mechanical look at it and sigh sadly. Suddenly Pille-miche pulled the condemned man by one arm into a corner and said, 'Confess all your sins to me. I'll repeat them to a priest of the true Church and he'll give you absolution; and if there's penance to do, I'll do it for you.'

Galope-chopine's circumstantial account of his sins gained him some respite; but numerous and fully detailed though they were, he came to the end of his recital at last.

'Wrong it may be, Cousin,' he said in conclusion, 'but after all, as I'm talking to you like it was my confessor, I tell you by God's holy name that I've nothing much to blame myself for, except for having a few pickings here and there and buttering my bread a bit too freely, and I call Saint Labre above the chimney-piece there to vouch for me that I said *naught* about the Gars. No, good friends, I'm no traitor.'

'Come, that's all right, Cousin, get up. You can settle with God about that, all in good time.'

'But let me have a moment to say a word of good-bye to Barbe . . .'

'Come on,' answered Marche-à-terre; 'if you don't want to be blamed more than you have to be, behave like a Breton and make a proper end.'

The two Chouans took hold of Galope-chopine again and laid him along the bench, where he made no more sign of resistance now than the convulsive movements of animal instinct. Finally he uttered one or two mindless howls, ended abruptly at the heavy thud of the cleaver. The head was struck off at one blow.

Marche-à-terre lifted the head by a lock of hair and went outside the cottage. He searched in the roughly-made doorposts for a large nail, and when he had found one twisted the fistful of hair he held round it and left the bloody head to hang there, not even closing the eyes. **99**

HONORÉ DE BALZAC, *THE CHOUANS*,
PUB. PENGUIN, HARMONSWORTH, 1972

LIFE IN BRITTANY

A PUBLIC HOUSE AT ST-JUVAT

In 1839 Thomas Adolphus Trollope (1815–82) steamed from Southampton to Le Havre to explore the remote and isolated land that Brittany then still was. Capturing the sombre and romantic character of the country, the author filled two volumes with a "full-length portrait of the Breton peasant in all his different varieties, and marked by all those peculiarities". Having walked from Evran on an all but empty stomach, Trollope and his companion stop for sustenance in St-Juvat.

❝We were agreeably surprised . . . on entering the door of what looked like a farm-house, but was marked as a place of public entertainment by the withered bush hanging over the door, with a bottle suspended in the midst of it, to find every promise of the means of satisfactorily supplying the deficiencies of the Evran breakfast.

We found ourselves in a large but low kitchen, which derived at least as much of the light it enjoyed from the huge fire blazing on the hearth, as from the one small and dirty window. A very satisfactory scent saluted our noses as they first entered the hospitable mansion; and our eyes soon discovered that our arrival was most opportune. For the mid-day meal was on the point of being placed upon the table, and our proposition of joining the company who were about to partake of it having been graciously heard by the landlady, we had before we fell to a few moments of leisure to observe the scene around us.

Though the room was large, and the style of its accommodations rather better than those of most of the road-side 'cabarets' we had seen, it was still evidently nothing but a village drinking-shop; and doubtless we should not have found so fair a promise of good cheer, had it not been that there were four or five rustics, travellers from another part of the country, and bound to a neighbouring cattle-fair, who had chanced to halt there.

Over the chimney were ranged in a goodly row the wife's pots and pans, shining as brilliantly as well scoured brass could make them. On one side of the ample fire-place was the invariable box bedstead. This is 'de rigueur' in a Breton cottage. On the side of the fire-place farthest from the door there invariably stands a huge dark oaken piece of furniture, which would have the exact appearance of a clothes-press, were it not that in the side next to the fire there is a square aperture, which discloses a pile of mattresses reaching nearly to the top of the machine. This is the bed of the master and mistress.

Very frequently a similar box on the opposite side, but exhibiting a less monstrous pile of bedding, is the resting-place of the maid, or any other member of the family. The aperture, which is left as the sole means of access to the interior of this retreat, is furnished with sliding doors, generally – as well, indeed, as the whole of the front of the bed – handsomely carved. So that the occupant may, if he so please, shut himself in. This is termed a 'lit clos', for which I should think 'a close bed' must be a very appropropriate translation. Indeed it is marvellous how the owner of a hansomely furnished 'lit clos' can breathe in it, or even get into it at all, so great a proportion of the enclosed space is occupied by mattresses and beds, piled one on another. I have seen in the cottage of a labourer, where no furniture, and scarcely the utensils necessary to cook a meal, were to be found, a pile of bedding four feet high!

It may easily be conceived how far such a mass, never moved, and surrounded by filth of all kinds, is likely to conduce to health and cleanliness. The only water which a

● BRITTANY AS SEEN BY WRITERS

Breton peasant much cares to use is holy water; and of this a little 'benitier' full, surmounted by a cross, is invariably attached to his portentous bedstead.

In front of this bedstead is seen, almost as invariably as itself, a large oaken chest, the same length as the bed, about twenty inches high, and as much broad. This is always the seat of honour, and serves also as a step to assist mine hostess in mounting to her exalted couch.

The seat of honour . . . was occupied . . . by two cattle-drivers from the Méné hills, while another [was] lighting his 'brule-gul' [pipe] with a morsel of burning wood from the fire. The two sisters, who kept the house, were both 'on hospitable cares intent,' the one taking up a roast quarter of veal from the fire, and the other mincing meat and herbs together for the production of some delicacy intended for the second course.

Opposite to her sat, apart from the rest, being apparently not one of their party, a perfect picture of an old man, with the most beautiful streaming, silvery locks, a charming old-world cocked hat on his head, and the most picturesquely patched coat conceivable. Immediately in front of him, as if it had been placed there as his share of the coming repast, was one of those gigantic pats of butter in a lordly dish, which constitute the wealth and glory of a Breton farm-house. The mass in question might have weighed some thirty pounds, and was probably destined to be sent on the following day to Dinan market.

To complete the detail of this somewhat lengthy inventory of the parts of the chamber and its contents, it must be added that the floor was of clay, and, notwithstanding the refuse of vegetables and the poultry [pecking about under the sisters' feet] was cleaner and in better order than the generality of those we saw; and that from the ceiling was suspended the most heterogeneous collection of every sort of thing conceivable. Sausages, shoes, hams, candles, onions, bladders full of lard, tin pots, and earthenware pipkins, sabots, crucifixes, horseshoes, bottles, and cart-harness, were hung up side by side, jostling each other in most admirable confusion. **99**

THOMAS ADOLPHUS TROLLOPE,
A SUMMER IN BRITTANY
PUB. HENRY COLBURN,
LONDON 1840

COLETTE AND THE CANCALE COAST

Inspired by several visits to Roz-en-Ven, near Cancale, Colette (1873–1954) wrote a serialized story for "Le Matin" in 1922, called "The Ripening Corn". It is based on Colette's minute, close and penetrating observations of her daughter, Bel-Gazou, and the sons of her husband, Henri de Jouvenel. The writer paints a wonderfully sensitive picture of the sensibilities of two adolescents who are just beginning to discover love.

66Philippe was the first to reach the road – two ruts in the dry shifting-sand, mobile as a wave, with a median ridge of sparse salt-bitten grass – down which the carts went to gather sea-wrack after the neap tides. He leaned on the two poles of the shrimping-nets and had a couple of creels slung over his shoulder, having left Vinca to carry the two slender gaffs baited with raw fish, and his fishing blazer – a precious relic, with amputated sleeves. He was treating himself to a well-earned rest and condescended to wait for his fanatical little friend, whom he had abandoned in the desert of rocks and pools and seaweed left uncovered by the August high tide. He tried to pick her out far below before he let himself slide down into the road bed. Beyond the sandy declivity, among the scintillating sparks set off by the sun's rays striking a hundred little mirrors of water, a blue woollen beret, faded to the tint of sea-holly, marked the spot where Vinca was still hunting determinedly for shrimps and edible crabs.

'Ah, well, if it amuses her!' he said under his breath.

Then he let himself go, his bare back extracting a delicious thrill from contact with the cool sand as he slid along the track. Close to his ear he could hear, issuing from the creels, the moist susurrus of a fistful of shrimps and the sharp scraping of a large crab's claw against the lid.

Phil sighed, overcome by a sense of vague unclouded happiness, in which his agreeable fatigue, the twitch of muscles still tensed after rock-climbing, and the warmth and colour of a Breton afternoon suffused with vaporised saline, each severally played its part. He sat down, dazzled from staring at the milky sea, and was surprised to see the new bronze texture of his arms and legs – the arms and legs of a sixteen-year-old – slender, yet fully moulded over taut, unobtrusive muscles, which could have been as much the pride of a girl in her teens as of a growing boy. He had grazed his ankle and it was bleeding. After wiping the abrasion with his hand, he licked his fingers and tasted the mingled saltiness of blood and brine.

An off-shore breeze wafted the scent of the new-mown after-crop, farmyard smells, and the fragrance of bruised mint: little by little, along the level of the sea, a dusty pink was usurping the domain of blue unchallenged since the early morning. Philippe did not know how to express such a thought as: 'All too few are the occasions in life when, with mind content, eyes surfeited with beauty, heart light, retentive, and almost empty, there comes a moment for the senses to be filled to overflowing: I shall remember this as just such a moment.' Yet the bleat of a goat and the tinkle of the cracked bell round its neck were enough to make the corners of his mouth quiver with anguish and his eyes fill with tears of pleasure. He did not let his eyes linger on the dripping rocks where Vinca was roaming, did not even breathe her name when experiencing his pure emotion: at the crisis of such unheralded delights, a child of sixteen would not know how to call for succour to another child, herself perhaps in a similar predicament . . . **99**

COLETTE, *THE RIPENING SEED*,
FARRAR, STRAUS AND CUDAHY, NEW YORK, 1955

AN EYE FOR DETAIL

'We good Americans," wrote Henry James (1843–1916) *"are too apt to think that France is Paris, just as we are accused of being too apt to think that Paris is the celestial city."* To rectify this state of affairs, in the fall of 1882 he set out on a substantial tour that took him through Tours, Bordeaux, Carcassonne, Arles and Avignon, though he only touched briefly on Brittany. His experiences were on the whole undramatic: what pleases most is his unerring eye for the tiny detail that exposes the whole.

❝If I spent two nights at Nantes, it was for reasons of convenience rather than of sentiment; though, indeed, I spent them in a big circular room which had a stately, lofty, last-century look – a look that consoled me a little for the whole place being dirty. The high, old-fashioned inn (it had a huge, windy *porte-cochère*, and you climbed a vast black stone staircase to get to your room) looked out on a dull square, surrounded with other tall houses, and occupied on one side by the theatre, a pompous building, decorated with columns and statues of the muses. Nantes belongs to the class of towns which are always spoken of as 'fine', and its position near the mouth of the Loire gives it, I believe, much commercial movement. It is a spacious, rather regular city, looking, in the parts that I traversed, neither very fresh nor very venerable. It derives its principal character from the handsome quays on the Loire, which are overhung with tall eighteenth-century houses (very numerous, too, in the other streets) – houses with big *entresols* marked by arched

windows, classic pediments, balcony-rails of fine old iron work. These features exist in still better form at Bordeaux; but, putting Bordeaux aside, Nantes is quite architectural. The view up and down the quays has the cool neutral tone of colour that one finds so often in French waterside places – the bright grayness which is the tone of French landscape art. The whole city has a rather grand, or at least an eminently well-established air. During a day passed in it of course I had time to go to the Musée; the more so that I have a weakness for provincial museums – a sentiment that depends but little on the quality of the collection. The pictures may be bad, but the place is often curious; and, indeed, from bad pictures, in certain moods of the mind, there is a degree of entertainment to be derived. If they are tolerably old, they are aften touching; but they must have a relative antiquity, for I confess I can do nothing with works of art of which the badness is of recent origin. The cool, still, empty chambers in which indifferent collections are apt to be preserved, the red brick tiles, the diffused light, the musty odour, the memento around you of dead fashions, the snuffy custodian in a black skull cap, who pulls aside a faded curtain to show you the lustreless gem of the museum – these things have a mild historical quality, and the sallow canvases after all illustrate something. Many of those in the museum of Nantes illustrate the taste of a successful warrior, having been bequeathed to the city by Napoleon's marshal, Clarke (created Duc de Feltre). In addition to these there is the usual number of specimens of the contemporary French school, culled from the annual Salons and presented to the museum by the State. Wherever the traveller goes, in France, he is reminded of this very honourable practice – the purchase by the Government of a certain number of 'pictures of the year', which are presently distributed in the provinces. Governments succeed each other and bid for success by different devices; but the 'patronage of art' is a plank, as we should say here, in every platform. The works of art are often ill-selected – there is an official taste which you immediately recognize – but the custom is essentially liberal, and a government which should neglect it would be felt to be painfully common. The only thing in this particular Musée that I remember is a fine portrait of a woman, by Ingres – very flat and Chinese, but with an interest of line and a great deal of style.

There is a castle at Nantes which resembles in some degree that of Angers, but has without, much less of the impressiveness of great size, and, within, much more interest of detail. The court contains the remains of a very fine piece of late Gothic, a tall elegant building of the sixteenth century. The chateau is naturally not wanting in history. It was the residence of the old Dukes of Brittany and was brought, with the rest of the province, by the Duchess Anne, the last representative of that race, as her dowry, to Charles VIII. I read in the excellent handbook of M. Joanne that it has been visited by almost every one of the kings of France, from Louis XI downward; and also that it has served as a place of sojourn less voluntary

on the part of other distinguished persons, from the horrible Maréchal de Retz, who in the fifteenth century was executed at Nantes for the murder of a couple of hundred young children, sacrificed in abominable rites, to the ardent Duchess of Berry, mother of the Count of Chambord, who was confined there for a few hours in 1832, just after her arrest in a neighbouring house. I looked at the house in question – you may see it from the platform in front of the chateau – and tried to figure to myself that embarrassing scene. The duchess, after having unsuccessfully raised the standard of revolt (for the exiled Bourbons) in the legitimist Bretagne, and being 'wanted' as the phrase is, by the police of Louis Philippe, had hidden herself in a small but loyal house at Nantes, where, at the end of five months of seclusion, she was betrayed, for gold, to the austere M. Guizot by one of her servants, an Alsatian Jew named Deutz. For many hours before her capture she had been compressed into an interstice behind a fireplace, and by the time she was drawn forth into the light she had been ominously scorched. The man who showed me the castle indicated also another historic spot, a house with little *tourelles*, in which Henry IV is said to have signed the Edict of Nantes. I am, however, not in a position to answer for this pedigree. **99**

HENRY JAMES,
A LITTLE TOUR IN FRANCE, 1884

A KICK IN THE EYE

American writer Jack Kerouac (1922–69) developed a freewheeling prose style that he named Beat and later became the spokesman for the Beat Generation. "Satori in Paris", written in the same freewheeling prose style that characterized "On the Road", his famous semi-autobiographical novel, recounts ten days Kerouac spent in Paris and Brittany, where he claimed to have located his family's roots.

66Somewhere during my ten days in Paris (and Brittany) I received an illumination of some kind that seems to've changed me again, towards what I suppose'll be my pattern for another seven years or more: in effect, a *satori*: the Japanese word for 'sudden illumination,' 'sudden awakening' or simply 'kick in the eye.' – Whatever, something *did* happen and in my first reveries after the trip and I'm back home regrouping all the confused rich events of those ten days, it seems the satori was handed to me by a taxi driver named Raymond Baillet, other times I think it might've been my paranoiac fear in the foggy streets of Brest Brittany at 3 A.M., other times I think it was Monsieur Casteljaloux and his dazzlingly beautiful secretary (a Bretonne with blue-black hair, green eyes, separated front teeth just right in eatable lips . . .

– My plan being, after five days in Paris, go to that inn on the sea in Finistère and go out at midnight in raincoat, rain hat, with notebook and pencil with large plastic bag to write inside of . . . and write dry, while rain falls on the rest of me, write the sounds of the sea, part two of the poem 'Sea' to be entitled: 'SEA, Part Two, the Sounds of the Atlantic at X, Brittany,' either outside of Carnac, or Concarneau, or Pointe de Penmarch, or Douardenez, or Plouzaimedeau, or Brest, or St. Malo . . .

[At a little Breton inn, on the Rue Victor Hugo in Brest] I pour myself a creamlike head over my beer out of the bottle of Alsatian beer, the best i' in the west, as he watches disgusted, what's this dopey American Canuck hanging him up for and why does this always happen to him? . . .

He said: 'Now eat your good Breton butter.' The butter was in a little clay butter bucket two inches high and so wide and so cute I said: – 'Let me have this butter bucket, my mother will love it and it will be a souvenir for her from Brittany.'

'I'll get you a clean one from the kitchen. Meanwhile you eat your breakfast and I'll go upstairs and make a few beds' so I slup down the rest of the beer, he brings the coffee and rushes upstairs, and I smur (like Van Gogh's butterburls) fresh creamery butter outa that little bucket, almost all crunch, munch, talk about your Fritos, the butter's gone even before Krupp and Remington got up to stick a teaspoon smallsize into a butler-cut-up grapefruit.

Satori there in Victor Hugo Inn?

When he comes down, nothing's left but me and one of those wild powerful Gitane (means Gypsy) cigarettes and smoke all over.

'Feel better?'

'Now that's butter – the bread extraspecial, the coffee strong and exquisite – But now I desire my cognac.'

'Well pay your room bill and go down rue Victor Hugo, on the corner is cognac, go get your valise and settle your affairs and come back here find out if there's a room tonight, beyond that old buddy old Neal Cassady cant go no further. To each his own and I got a wife an kids upstairs so busy playing with flowerpots, if, why if I had a thousand Syrians racking the place in Nominoé's own brown robes, they'd still let me do all the work as it is as you know, a hard-net Keltic sea.' (I ingrained his thought there for your delectation and if you didnt like it, call it beanafaction, in other words I beaned ya with my high hard one.)

I say 'Where's Plouzaimedeau? I wanta write poems by the side of the sea at night.'

'Ah you mean Plouzémédé – Ah, spoff, not my affair – I gotta work now.'

'Okay I'll go'

But as an example of a regular Breton, aye? 99

JACK KEROUAC, *SATORI IN PARIS*
ANDRÉ DEUTSCH
LONDON, 196

A SUMMER STORM

The English novelist and short story writer H. E. Bates (1905–74) is best known for "The Darling Buds of May" (1958). This was the first in a series of comic novels featuring the Larkins, stories centered round the larger-than-life figure of an anarchic scrap dealer and his colorful family. The extract below comes from the second of the Larkin novels, in which the family ventures abroad for the very first time, to enjoy a summer holiday on the coast of Finistère.

66 When Pop drew up the Rolls outside the Hotel Beau Rivage at half-past six in the evening of the last day of August a gale was raging in from the Atlantic that made even the sturdy blue fishing boats in the most sheltered corners of the little port look like a battered wreckage of half-drowned match-stalks. Dancing arches of white spray ran up and down the grey quay walls like raging dinosaurs forty feet high. Rain and spray beat at the windows of the little hotel, crashing pebbles on the shutter-boards. A wind as cold as winter ran ceaselessly round the harbour with unbroken shriekings and occasional whistles like those of Mr Charlton's much-loved, long-distant little train. 'For crying out gently, Charley,' Pop said. 'Where'

his? Where the pipe have we come to? Lapland?' With a sudden feeling of low, cold dismay Mr Charlton stared silently at the Beau Rivage. The hotel seemed altogether so much smaller, so much shabbier, so much more dilapidated and inexclusive than he remembered it being in the last summer before the war. It seemed to have shrunk somehow. He had fondly pictured it as large and gay. Now it looked dismal, dark, and pokey.

Its style of creosoted Tudor looked incredibly flimsy and insecure and now and then the blistered brown shutters sprang violently on their hooks and seemed, like the rest of

the hotel, ready to collapse, disintegrate, and wash away. On the little outside terrace rows of coloured fairy lights, strung necklace fashion between half a dozen plane trees pollarded to the appearance of yellowish skinning skeletons, were swinging wildly about in the wind, one or two of them occasionally crashing on to the concrete below. There was very little Beau about it, Mr Charlton thought, and not much Rivage.

'Well, I suppose we ought to go in,' he said at last and suddenly led the way with an appearance of remarkably enthusiastic alacrity into the hotel, hastily followed by Ma carrying little Oscar, then Primrose and Montgomery submerged under one raincoat, the twins, Victoria and Mariette under one umbrella, and finally Pop carrying two suitcases and a zip canvas bag.

Pop was wearing thin blue linen trousers, a yellow sleeveless shirt, yellow canvas shoes, and his yachting cap in anticipation of a long spell of French hot weather. In the short passage from the car to the hotel he half-rowed, half- paddled through rising lakes of Atlantic rain and spray. Several times he was convinced he was going under. Once he slipped down and one of the suitcases was blown out of his hands and began to wash away along the quayside. He grabbed it, battled on, and a few moments later found himself shipwrecked inside the vestibule of the hotel, where he was at once assailed by a powerful smell of linseed oil, drain-pipes, French cigarettes, and leaking gas. One single electric bulb burned above the reception desk in the gloom of early evening and this was flickering madly up and down.

When Pop was able to get to his feet again he was more than glad to observe that Charley was already in charge of things at the reception desk. Charley, even if he didn't feel it, looked calm, self-possessed, even authoritative. He was speaking in French. Pop liked it when Charley spoke in French. It seemed to ease and resolve the most anxious of situations.

H. E. BATES, *A BREATH OF FRENCH AIR*,
PUB. MICHAEL JOSEPH,
LONDON, 1959

An intellectual romance

The English writer A. S. Byatt was born in 1936. Though principally a novelist, she i
also well known as a broadcaster and critic, and has published studies of Wordsworth
Coleridge and Iris Murdoch. This extract is from a long novel of academic rivalry tha
also includes many historical flashbacks, with poems and extracts from 19th-century
journals, and deals with two scholars on the trail of a Victorian man of letters.

❝The irruption, or interruption, occurred at the Baie des Trépassés. It was one c
Brittany's smiling days. They stood amongst the sand-dunes and watched the wave
crawling in quietly from the Atlantic. The sea wove amber-sandy lights in its grey
green. The air was milk-warm, and smelled of salt, and warm sand, and distan
sharp leaves, heather or juniper or pine. 'Would it be so magical, or sinister
without its name' Maud asked. 'It looks so bland and sunny. 'If you knew about th
currents you might find it dangerous. If you were a sailor.' 'It says in the *Guide Ver*
that its name comes from a corruption of 'boe an aon' (baie du ruisseau) into 'bo
an anaon' (baie des âmes en peine). It says that the City of Is was traditionally i
those marshes at the river-mouth. Trépassés, trespassed, passed, past. Name
accrue meaning. We came because of the name.' Roland touched her hand, whic
took hold of his. They were standing in a fold of the dunes. They heard, fron
beyond the next sandhill, a loud transatlantic cry, rich and strange. 'And that mus
be the Île de Sein, right out there. I've always dreamed of seeing that place, where
the nine terrible virgins lived who were called Seines or Sénas or Sänes after th
island, which is *Sein*, which is a fantastically suggestive and polysemous word
suggesting the divinity of the female body, for the French use *sein* you know to
mean both breasts and womb, the female sexual organs, and from that it has also
come to mean a fishing-net which holds fish and a bellying sa
which holds wind, these women could control tempests, an
attract sailors into their nets like the sirens, and they built thi
funeral temple for the dead druids – a dolmen I suppose it was
another female form, and whilst they

constructed it there were all sorts of taboos about not touching the earth, no
letting the stones fall to the earth, for it was feared the sun or the earth woul
pollute them or be polluted by them, just like the mistletoe, which can only b
gathered without touching the earth. It has often been thought that Dahud Quee
of Is was the child of one of these sorceresses, and when she became Queen of th
Drowned City she became Marie-Morgane, a kind of siren or mermaid who drev
men to their death, and it is thought she was a relic of a matriarchy as the Sene
were, in their floating island. Have you read Christabel's *Drowned City*?' 'No,' sai
a male voice. 'It is an omission I must rectify.'❞

A. S. BYATT, *POSSESSION*
PUB. CHATTO & WINDUS
LONDON, 199

Brittany itineraries

▲ The "Tas de Pois" reefs, Crozon peninsula. The Pointe de la Torche

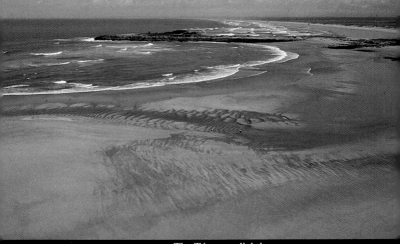

▼ The Tévennec lighthouse.

▲ The Isle of Costaéres off Ploumanac'h.

The Héaux reefs off the Sillon de Talbert.

Porz Bugate, Plougrescant. ▼

▲ Tombelaine Rock and Mont-St-Michel, almost an island.

▼ The Hébihens archipelago ne

St-Malo old town. ▼

St-Jacut-de-la-Mer.

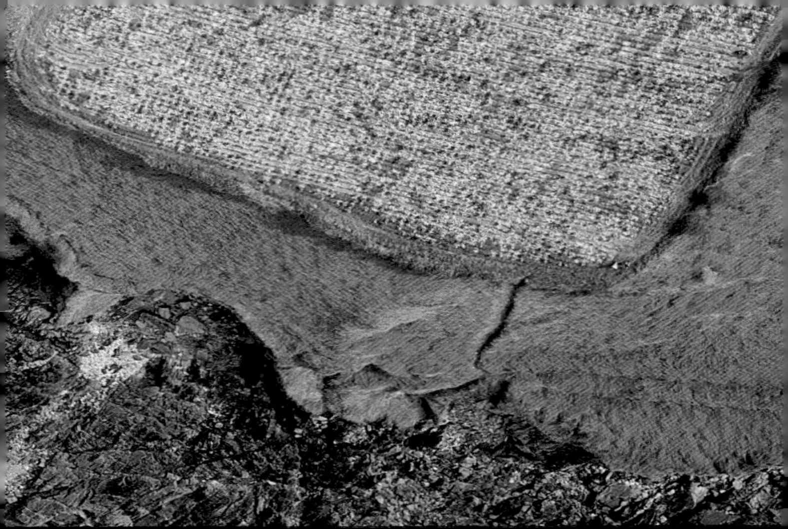

▲ West of Loquirec.
St-Michel-de-Brasparts.

▼ Seagulls near St-Thégonnec.

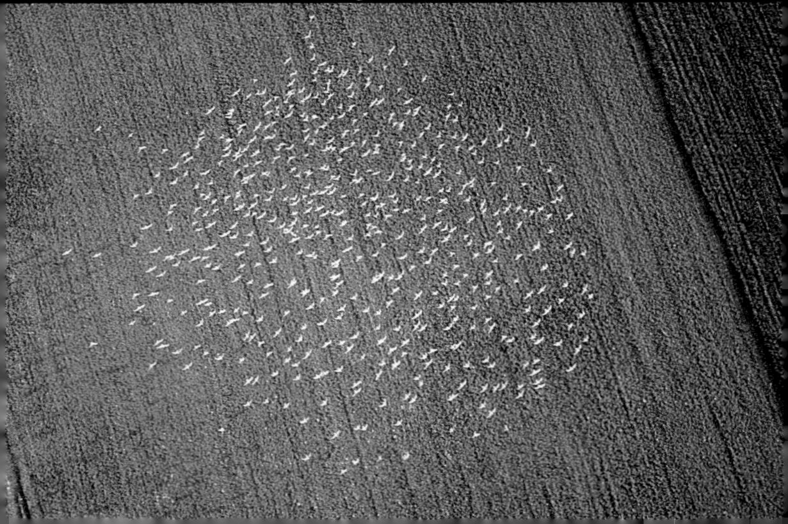

▲ The lake at Chapelle-Erbrée.

▲ The Vilaine river, near Messac.

▲ Kernic cove.   Portsall. ▼

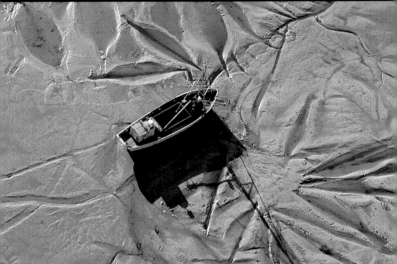

▼ Aber Benoît.

RENNES

THE CITY, *138*

HISTORY

ORIGINS. Rennes has its roots as a Celtic settlement situated on a rocky promontory at the confluence of the Ille and Vilaine rivers. In the 2nd century BC it was the capital of the Gallic tribe of the Redones, and after Julius Caesar had conquered the Gauls it became a prosperous Roman town.

ASSIZE COURT
Now the Law Courts, the Parliament house was home to the Court of Appeal until a fire in 1994.

PARLIAMENT OF BRITTANY ▲ *143*. In the Middle Ages Rennes became the capital of the Duchy of Brittany and Parliament of Brittany was installed here in 1562. Many nobles were drawn to the city, and built fine townhouses. Parliament sat twice a year, and marked the beginning of a contentious relationship between Brittany and central government in Paris. Matters came to a head in 1675 with the introduction of stamp duty. The ensuing "stamped-paper revolt" spread quickly throughout the province and claimed several lives. The Parliament was suspected of collusion with the revolutionaries, and was exiled to Vannes ▲ *342* for fifteen years and the city occupied by four thousand men.

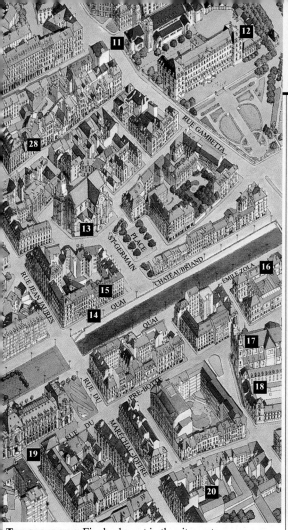

THE GREAT FIRE. Fire broke out in the city center on December 22, 1720. No less than 845 timber-framed houses were destroyed in the blaze, which lasted for seven days. The destruction spared the Parliament House, but much of the rest of Rennes was devastated. The citizens resolved to rebuild and make the city one of the most beautiful in France.

YEARS OF REVOLUTION. The King's attempt to dissolve the Brittany Parliament in May 1788 resulted in riots: the first blood of the Revolution was spilled in Rennes, according to the writer Chateaubriand. When the Revolution came the following year it was regarded at first with a benevolent eye by the citizens. Predominantly republican in sympathy, it was later beset by the Chouan ● *62* royalist rebels. From 1793 to 1800 Rennes was in a state of siege, defended by the forces of General Hoche. After eight years of civil unrest, the Concordat eventually resolved the situation.

THE DREYFUS CASE. Convicted of treason on the skimpiest of evidence in 1894, Captain Alfred Dreyfus was sentenced to hard labor on Devil's Island in French Guyana. Then in

CAPITAL OF THE DUCHY ● *56*
Seat of the bishop, former residence of the counts of Rennes and the dukes of Brittany, this ancient fortified city with narrow streets is the administrative center of the province.

The Great Fire of Rennes burned for a whole week.

1899 a military tribunal in Rennes heard that the evidence against him was forged. But Dreyfus, a Jew, was not declared innocent until 1906: the gallant, persecuted victim went on to distinguish himself in World War One, and was awarded the Légion d'Honneur in 1919.

PLACE DES LICES

In the Middle Ages tournaments were held in this square, which was once outside the city walls. It was enlarged in the 16th century, and surrounding lots were sold as building sites in 1658. Around the square are some fine half-timbered houses and other grand homes built by members of parliament in a mock-medieval style.

HÔTEL DE LA NOUE. This is at no. 26 Place des Lices, a half-timbered building dating from 1658. It has a large and magnificent central staircase, with a wagon-style roof and stylized lanterns.

HÔTEL RACAPE DE LA FEUILLÉE. Like the Hôtel de la Noue, this house, at no. 28, also dates from 1658; it was constructed on a similar plan and covered with a coating of plaster to give protection against fire.

HÔTEL DE MOLANT OR HEVIN. The house at no. 34 dates from 1666. Its wooden staircase is a masterpiece of the carpenter's art. Mme de Sévigné and her companion the Duc de Chaulnes (governor of the province) stayed here in 1689.

HALLES DE MARTENOT. The market buildings, designed by Jean-Baptiste Martenot ▲ *145*, are a fine example of 19th-century ironwork. They were listed as a historical monument in 1990.

CATHEDRAL

St-Pierre de Rennes is built on the site of this ancient city's most important temple. The

TOWNHOUSES IN THE PLACE DES LICES
These were built as homes for members of the Brittany Parliament, and have delightful and elaborate timber-work. Right, the Hôtel de La Noue (no. 26) and Hôtel Racape de La Feuillée (no. 28). Above, three details from these houses. Though built in mock-medieval style they in fact date from 1658.

west façade, parts of which go back to 1540, was completed in 1704 in classical style. In the late 18th and early 19th centuries, the rest of the cathedral was rebuilt in a bourgeois classical style that nevertheless excited the novelist Stendhal: "They have started work on a cathedral here," he wrote, "that is going to have at least as many columns as at Santa Maria Maggiore or St-Paul's Without the Walls in Rome." The gilt and stucco decoration that was added during the Second Empire is rather gaudy.

RUE DU CHAPITRE

HÔTEL DE BLOSSAC. The fine house at no. 6 stands at the western limit of the great fire of 1720. Its design was inspired by the work of architect Jacques Gabriel (1667–1742), and it consists of two separate buildings: in 1728 the huge hôtel built for Louis-Gabriel de La Bourdonnaye de Blossac was grafted onto the original 17th-century house. The façades giving onto the courtyard and garden stand end to end, forming the most beautifully designed house in Rennes, a superb example of a rich man's townhouse, or *hôtel particulier*. After the Revolution, however, it was converted into flats, which ruined much of the interior design. It was acquired by the State in 1982 and since then has undergone extensive restoration.

HÔTEL DE BRIE. In spite of its appearance, the house was only built in 1624. An old alleyway leads to the interior courtyard of the building, which was joined to the Hôtel de Blossac in the 18th century.

HÔTEL DE BLOSSAC
With its superb monumental entrance, this is the most beautiful of Rennes' fine townhouses. The grand staircase (above) has a stylish wrought-iron banister rail; from the top there is a striking view down on to the pink marble columns of the portico and surrounding colonnade.

POLYCHROME HOUSES
These 15th- and 16th-century houses in the Rue du Chapitre have been restored and repainted in their original colors.

TIMBER-FRAMED HOUSES NEAR THE CATHEDRAL OF ST-PIERRE
The medieval tradition of half-timbered houses became largely obsolete after the Renaissance. Grotesquely carved beams and corbeling gave way to façades ornamented with molded foliage, and supporting consoles formally decorated with acanthus leaves, as on the capitals of Corinthian columns.

A hanging inn sign in the Rue St-Sauveur.

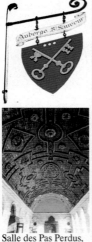

Salle des Pas Perdus, Parliament house.

RUE DES DAMES

The Hôtel de Freslon, at the corner of the Rue Griffon, has a courtyard enclosed by a high wall, with a terrace above that joins the two wings. The granite façade of the HÔTEL DE VAUCLERC at no. 8 is partly 16th century, while at no. 2 the courtyard of the HÔTEL DE LA MONNERAIE DE BOURGNEUF has corbeling supported by carved Louis XV consoles.
CHAPEL OF ST-YVES. The chapel at the corner of Rue St-Yves and Rue Le Bouteiller was completed in 1494. It is all that remains of the ancient St-Ives hospital, and is the most beautiful Gothic building in the city.

RUE DE LA PSALLETTE

The narrow street skirting the chancel of the cathedral contains a mixture of 17th- and 18th-century houses. Its name comes from the MAISON DE LA PSALLETTE at no. 8, the house where the cathedral choristers lived. No. 1 (or Maison du Coin) is an old church property dating from 1609 that has some fine carved wood decoration.

RUE ST-SAUVEUR

At the corner of this street and the Rue du Chapitre is the MAISON DES CHEVALIERS DU ST-ESPRIT, an old house which is half timber-framed and half stone-built. The latter part dates from the 17th century, and forms a corbeled nook. Nos. 5, 6 and 8 together form an ensemble of late 15th- and early 16th-century houses with particularly attractive corbeling. The large prebendary house at no. 6, which dates from the 15th century, has three floors and a typical Rennes-style roof.
CHURCH OF ST-SAUVEUR. When part of St-Sauveur's façade fell down, major rebuilding was begun. It lasted from 1703 to 1764, though work was interrupted by the fire of 1720, which inflicted substantial damage. The graceful Italianate façade dates from 1755 and is the work of architect Forestier.

RUE RALLIER DU BATY

Before its demolition in the 15th century, Rennes castle stood on the site now occupied by the HÔTEL CHEREIL DE LA RIVIÈRE, at no. 7. The building adjoins a section of the old ramparts of the city. The old High Court of Rennes, at the end of the Impasse Rallier du Baty, contained the St-Michel prison. The entrance is flanked by a 15th-century POLYGONAL STAIRCASE TOWER, and the square courtyard still has traces of the walkway that led to the various offices.

RECONSTRUCTION

The disastrous fire that broke out on December 22, 1720 ▲ *139* did extensive damage, particularly to the old timber-

Left, the Hôtel de Brie has an unusual Second Renaissance façade, with three different orders superposed one above the other. Right, a detail from a house at no. 20 Rue du Chapitre.

framed houses. The authorities were faced with a decision: either to rebuild to the former layout, or to redesign the city center completely. They chose the latter, and the architects set to work on a layout that would be both aesthetically satisfying and practical. This time they built higher, leaving more space at ground level. A logical and coherent system of urban squares let more light into the city, and gave it a noble, monumental quality that showed its important buildings, especially the Houses of Parliament, to good effect.

BRITTANY PARLIAMENT

When in 1561 Rennes was chosen as the seat of the Brittany Parliament, the city was faced with the expense of building a palace grand enough to contain such an august institution. Construction lasted from 1618 to 1655: the original plans by Germain Gaultier failed to satisfy the authorities and the work was entrusted to Salomon de Brosse, the architect of the Palais du Luxembourg in Paris. He designed a relatively straightforward palace along Italian lines. The façade was altered in 1726 by Jacques Gabriel (1667–1742), great-nephew of the famous architect François Mansart. Gabriel removed both the interior terrace and the great outside staircase, which consisted of two symmetrical flights of steps. This simple layout gave members a good view over the city and surrounding area.

OSTENTATIOUS DECORATION. The finest painters, sculptors and woodcarvers of the day were called in to work on the interior design of the palace. The paintings on the ceiling of the Grand'Chambre (now the Court of Appeal) are dated 1662 and signed by the young Noël Coypel, who worked under the direction of Charles Errard, court painter and designer to King Louis XIV. The paintings in the Second Civil Chamber are by Ferdinand Elle the Younger; while those in the First Chamber, framed in a sculpted ceiling by François Gillet, are the work of Jean-Baptiste Jouvenet. They depict allegorical figures, predominantly the attributes of Justice such as *Religion*, *Oratory* and *Knowledge*.

PLACE DE LA MAIRIE

The Place de la Mairie (or the Place Neuve) was included by Gabriel in his design and dedicated to Louis XV. It is lighter in feeling than the Place du Palais, to which it was intended as an extension. On its west side stands the immense HÔTEL DE VILLE. The façade, with a concave central section, is most

A MAJOR DISASTER
Having escaped the fire of 1720, the Parliament building was burned on the night of 5–6 February 1994. This historic

monument was a potent symbol of Breton tenacity and power, and its destruction was a grievous loss to the citizens of Rennes. The superb 17th-century timberwork in the roof as well as all the archives were totally destroyed. The Salle des Pas Perdus and the ceiling of the grande salle were both badly damaged. Substantial restoration work is now underway to repair its façade.

The façade of the Parliament building, built by Salomon de Brosse around 1618, was altered by Gabriel in 1726. Latterly it housed the chief Law Courts of Brittany.

The Brittany Museum contains an interesting collection of Rennes faience.

View of the Place de l'Hôtel de Ville.

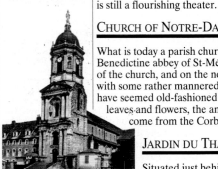

impressive. Work began on the city hall in 1735, the project including the Presidial (local tribunal) and the FINE BELFRY.

THEATER

Facing the Hôtel de Ville across the Place de la Mairie is the 19th-century theater, whose construction involved the demolition of the Place des Arbres, which originally extended the square to the east. The theater replaced the former Salle du Jeu de Paume (tennis court) in the Rue de la Poulaillerie, which offered only scruffy and cramped housing. The city council approved the project in 1831, and the plans were drawn up by a young local architect named Charles Millardet. The theater was inaugurated on March 1, 1836, and the building astonished his contemporaries: it was built in white stone and had a great simplicity of line, with a convex peristyle that corresponded to the concave façade across the square. The auditorium was on the second floor, leaving an open space for a large foyer beneath, which gave onto the two covered walkways around the building. It is one of the few neo-classical buildings to have survived to the present day and is still a flourishing theater.

CHURCH OF NOTRE-DAME-EN-ST-MÉLAINE

What is today a parish church was once the church of the Benedictine abbey of St-Mélaine. The altar is in the east end of the church, and on the north side is a beautiful CLOISTER, with some rather mannered carved figures that must already have seemed old-fashioned in the 17th century. The carved leaves and flowers, the angels, and the surbased arches all come from the Corbineau brothers.

JARDIN DU THABOR

Situated just behind the church of Notre-Dame-en-St-Mélaine, this lovely garden was once the abbey orchard and extends over 25 acres. It was opened to the public in the 18th century, and laid out by landscape designer Denis Bühler, who with his brother Eugène had already designed the Tête d'Or garden in Lyon and the Borély botanical gardens in Marseille. In 1866 he set to work to create a formal French garden, laying great stress on symmetry and the balance between floral beds and pools.

LANDSCAPE GARDEN. "Studied carelessness" was the keynote here, a carefully formed arrangement that followed the natural contours of the land. Sequoias, gingkos, cork-oaks, magnolia and cedar trees are the legacy of a fondness for exotic trees

On top of the belfry is a gilt statue of the Virgin.

GATE AND FENCE OF THE THABOR GARDEN Martenot's design emphasizes the formal elegance of the Thabor.

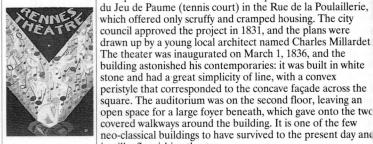

that was widespread in the 19th
century. There is also an
elegant bandstand and an
aviary, both designed by Jean-
Baptiste Martenot.

BOTANICAL GARDEN. No less
than three thousand species of plants are represented here,
each classified by a system of color-labeling: red for medicinal
plants, white for edible plants, yellow for plants with
industrial uses, black for poisonous varieties, and green for
plants with no specific properties.

ROSE GARDEN. This is one of the Thabor's most popular
attractions. The number of varieties is astonishing, a
testament to the passion for roses that goes back for
centuries.

Martenot's bandstand
in the Thabor.

RUE ST-GEORGES

The street, now a pedestrian area, escaped the fire of 1720, as
efforts were made to spare Monsieur de Robien's art
collection, which was located there. The street has some fine
16th-century half-timbered houses and an early Renaissance
building. The passage through the old Hôtel de la Moussaye
runs right through to the Rue Victor Hugo.

QUAYS AND LOWER TOWN

A new cultural center is being built on the site of the old
haulage depot. It will incorporate the Musée de Bretagne, the
library, and the Center for Scientific Culture.

FINE ARTS MUSEUM. The Musée des Beaux Arts dates back to
1794 and exists thanks again to Monsieur de Robien, whose
fabulous collection of drawings is a major part of its holdings.
There is a fine collection of 17th-century pictures, including
Virgin and Child by Georges de La Tour, and works by
Veronese and Rubens. Nineteenth-century art is also well
represented, with works by Sisley and the Pont Aven school.

BRITTANY MUSEUM. The Musée de Bretagne is the best
possible guide to the history and culture of the province, and
should not be missed. It is the result of many years of research
and considered selection, imaginatively presented: the
prehistoric displays are especially good. Its treasures include a
1st-century bronze goddess, and missals with text in old
Breton, and porcelain imported by the Compagnie des Indes
▲ *320*. The emergence of Brittany into modern France late in
the last century is particularly well treated.

PALAIS DU COMMERCE. This impressive block was built from
1886 to 1929 by Jean-Baptiste Martenot, in the
then prevalent academic style. It was big enough
to conceal many of the poorer buildings so
offensive to 19th-century sensibilities.

**JEAN-BAPTISTE
MARTENOT
(1828–1906)**
He was a native of
Burgundy and studied
at the Beaux Arts in
Paris. From 1858 to
1894 he was official
architect to the city of
Rennes and designed
many great urban
projects, including the
Lycée and the
buildings in the
Thabor Garden.

▲ Rennes to St-Malo via Dinan

DINAN DINARD ST-MALO TINTÉNIAC CANCALE CANAL D'ILLE-ET-RANCE DOL-DE-BRETAGNE COMBOURG

RENNES

Château de Caradeuc

CARADEUC
Though the château itself is closed to the public, access to the grounds is permitted.

A double flight of steps leads to the terrace, adorned by two sphinxes and a figure of Cupid. The delicate grace of the landscaped gardens recalls the 18th-century paintings of Boucher, Watteau or Fragonard.

The property, set on a wooded hill, evokes many memories of Monsieur La Chalotais, a member of the Brittany Parliament who lived here. Numerous statues and other artefacts decorate the lawns and avenues, in lively contrast to the formal Regency style of the château. Only the gardens are open to the public.

A PASTORAL WALK. Between 1890 and 1900 the garden was completely redesigned according to the precepts of the great 17th-century landscape gardener Le Nôtre. An explanatory brochure is available at the entrance. The so-called "Gaming Table" or "Diana's Lawn" to the left of the château complete

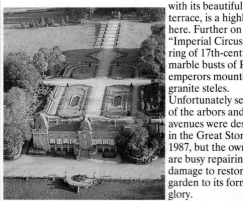

with its beautiful terrace, is a highlight here. Further on is the "Imperial Circus", a ring of 17th-century marble busts of Roman emperors mounted on granite steles. Unfortunately several of the arbors and avenues were destroyed in the Great Storm of 1987, but the owners are busy repairing the damage to restore the garden to its former glory.

Along with these iron cats, the caretaker's lodge at Caradeuc bears the legend: "Friends may open the doors; all others stay outside."

CHÂTEAU DE MONTMURAN ★

In times gone by this was the seat of the important castellany of Tinténiac. The original castle was built in the 11th century at Tinténiac itself. Then in the 13th century another castle was built nearby, which subsequently became home to some of the grandest families in Brittany. The Lavals were the lords of Tinténiac-Montmuran for two centuries. In 1547 the heiress Charlotte de Laval married Gaspard de Coligny, soon to be Admiral of France. On their visit here the lavish banquet held in their honor lasted for three days. The Tinténiac canvas industry flourished with the support of the Lavals until the religious wars of the 16th century. The couple's conversion to Calvinism meant that Gaspard's days were numbered: he was assassinated in Paris on the night of August 24, 1572 during the infamous St Bartholomew's Eve Massacre, after which his body was taken from his home at the Hôtel de Ponthieu and strung up on a nearby gallows. Montmuran remained in the hands of the Coligny family until 1643 when the young, beautiful but extravagant heiress Henriette sold the château. Over the centuries the property passed into the possession of a number of noble families: it currently belongs to the La Villéons. The avenue of trees leading up to the gates was destroyed in the storm of 1987.

BLOODY THURSDAY. During the Hundred Years' War, the widow of a lord of Montmuran named Alain de Tinténiac who had been killed in battle, invited a number of the local nobility to a banquet in honor of Marshal d'Audreheim of France. The latter arrived at the château on Maundy Thursday in 1354, accompanied by a young Breton officer named Bertrand Du Guesclin. At that time Montmuran was hemmed in between two English-held citadels, Bécherel and Hédé. Thinking that the English might well take advantage of the occasion to launch an attack, the young Du Guesclin decided to move first and surprised the enemy just near Bécherel. The slaughter was total: not an Englishman escaped alive, and the road became known as the Bloody Way. Du Guesclin himself was knighted in the chapel at Montmuran, and many years later returned there to marry the young Jeanne de Laval, his second wife.

Below, a miniature of Montmuran taken from a book of hours dating from the 15th century.

Left, portraits of Jean-Baptiste de La Villéon (1740–1820) and his sister.

THE CASTLE ● 82, 86 It consists of two semicircular towers linked by a small curtain wall and a projecting parapet. Portcullis, drawbridge and moat still defend the entrance. The fortress is joined to two other round towers by the west curtain. The mechanism for operating the drawbridge is in the guardroom above the entrance. While the central part of Montmuran was built in the 18th century, the two towers on the north side, with conical roofs, date from the 12th and 13th centuries.

There is a small museum on the first floor.

READING STAINED GLASS
The successive rows of images in the windows read from left to right and from bottom to top.

CHURCH OF ST-OUEN
Above right, an aerial view of the church. Above, details of one of the two bell towers, and gargoyles.

TWO OF THE THREE MAGI
Detail of a stained glass window in the left-hand chapel of the church of St-Ouen. This 16th-century work is signed by a famous master of the art named Michel Bayonne.

LES IFFS

The village of Les Iffs, not far from St-Brieuc-des-Iffs, takes its name from the trees in the Parish Close (*if* means yew).

CHURCH OF ST-OUEN. The church is in the Flamboyant Gothic style of the 14th and 15th centuries: the exterior is particularly beautiful. It was built with the generous assistance of the Laval and Coligny families, and with the support of the local population as well. The porch with three arches was reserved for lepers. The wooden vaulting inside is supported by beams decorated with fabulous beasts.

STAINED GLASS. There are nine superb Renaissance windows, which show the influence of the Italian and Flemish schools. The bright colors have lost none of their vibrancy. The faces

are expressive, the attitudes natural and easy. In a series of twenty panels, the windows in the APSE tell the story of the Passion, from the Entry into Jerusalem to the Entombment of Christ. The tympanum at the top has scenes from the Last Judgment. On the right in the CHAPEL OF ST-YVES a window tells the story of Susanna and the Elders. Falsely accused of adultery by two old and vengeful lechers whose infamous advances she had shunned, Susanna was condemned to death but saved at the last by the prophet Daniel, who exposed the falsity of the charge and ordered the elders to be beheaded. The window was made in Vitré in 1530. On the right is a window depicting the 13th-century Breton Saint Yves, patron saint of lawyers and a model of impartiality, also known throughout the province as "an attorney who was an honest man". He wears a red gown and a white surplice trimmed with ermine. The rich man (François de Coligny, son of Gaspard) sports a violet cloak, and the peasant wears a green doublet. An unidentified battle is being fought to the left of the window. In the CHAPEL on the left (known as the LAVAL or Montmuran chapel), two windows recount the birth and childhood of Jesus (note the grinning devil in the top left-hand corner). The windows in the SOUTH TRANSEPT are devoted to the Transfiguration of Christ and the beheading of John the Baptist. The donor of the windows, one of the Laval family, is also here, together with the armorial bearings of the nearby seigneurie of Montmuran ▲ *147*.

SPRING OF ST-FIACRE. The spring is located 30 yards outside the village, on the right-hand side and set back from the road. Dating from the 15th century it is the only enclosed spring in the region. In time of drought, pilgrims would make their way here to pray for rain. The priest would dip the foot of his crucifix in the miraculous waters, and if the prayers were answered a downpour of rain would fall upon the heads of the assembled crowd.

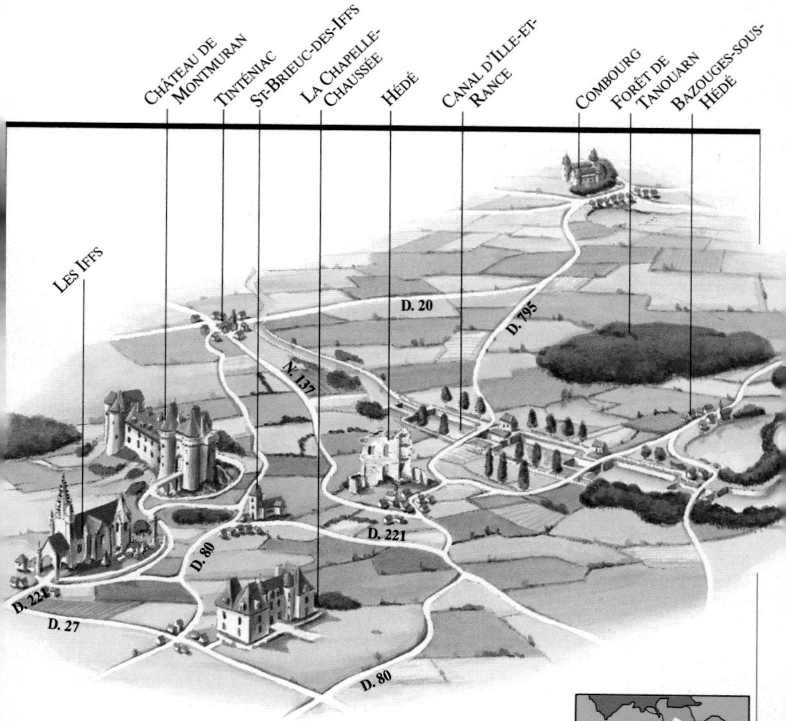

CHÂTEAU DE MONTMURAN   TINTÉNIAC   ST-BRIEUC-DES-IFFS   LA CHAPELLE-CHAUSSÉE   HÉDÉ   CANAL D'ILLE-ET-RANCE   COMBOURG   FORÊT DE TANOUARN   BAZOUGES-SOUS-HÉDÉ

LES IFFS

D. 20

D. 795

N. 137

D. 221

D. 80

D. 222

D. 27

D. 80

THE ILLE ET RANCE CANAL

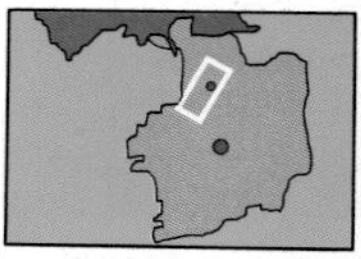

WATERWAY HISTORY. Thanks to the minimal fall of the Vilaine river, in the 16th century flat-bottomed barges ▲ *160* could go right into Rennes. At that time there were only fifteen locks. It was not until the 18th century, when the English dominated the sea, that it seemed a worthwhile plan to build a canal between the Vilaine and the Rance. Under the Ancien Regime the economic advantages of linking the two rivers were already apparent: situated as it was half-way between the two port cities of St-Malo and Redon, Rennes stood to become the very hub of commerce in Brittany. After the Revolution, the English blockade of Continental ports accelerated the construction of this important inland waterway, which had now acquired a strategic importance. The canal would be able to supply both the naval ports, which were constantly under threat from enemy forces, and the French fleet, which was unable to leave harbor.

"THE HÉDÉ STAIRCASE", AND THE WALK ALONG THE LOCKS ★
Coming from Combourg ▲ *150* on the road D 795, take the D 87 on the left before the entrance to Hédé, toward Bazouges sous Hédé. Stop at the Palfrère, Pêchetière and La Sagerie locks, and turning to the right set off on foot or by bicycle along the old towpath (GR 37) as far as the Bazouges basin. This lovely walk passes a staircase of eleven locks (left), which allow craft to descend through a height of 89 feet. The Hédé Staircase is the biggest engineering project on this peaceful canal, lined with pretty gardens tended by the lock-keepers.

149

The La Gromillais lock on the canal.

SLAVE LABOR
The work of cutting the canal, which was dug out with picks and shovels, was so arduous that prisoners of war were used for the job. The cut between the two locks at Ville Morin was dug in 1813 and 1814 by Prussian and Austrian prisoners. If extra labor were needed, convicts from Brest ▲ 276 and deserters from the French army were brought in as reinforcements.

WORK BEGINS. Excavation work on the canal started in 1804. Revictualling the port of St-Malo would become much easier, and the canal (along with the Vilaine) at last provided a strategic link between the northern and southern ports of the peninsula. But work was slowed down by the Napoleonic wars. It was all but complete in 1815 but, when peace was declared, the canal ceased to have any military value.

THE GREAT DAYS. The canal was finally opened in 1832. At first it was used as a means of reclaiming waterlogged land, and for the transport of such goods as wood, wheat, oats, hay, apples, spirits, peat, charcoal and iron ore. Traffic on the canal was busiest between 1860 and 1880, when 40,000 tons of goods were shipped on the canal each year and an average of two thousand boats passed through the locks in each direction.

THE FATAL BLOW. With the arrival of the railroad and the opening of a mainline station at Rennes, the canal's days were numbered. By 1900 the volume of canal traffic had fallen drastically, due largely to the competitive prices offered by the railroad companies. Today the leisure industry has expanded onto the inland waterways, and thousands of holidaymakers make the most of its peaceful 50-mile stretch. At Hédé the Maison du Canal d'Île-et-Rance traces the history of the canal. The museum is also a reception and information center for visitors.

The canal at Tinténiac in the 1930's.

THE COLLECTION IN THE CHÂTEAU DE COMBOURG
The château has a valuable collection of furniture, pictures and other works of art. There are two fine Italian cabinets in Renaissance style, an inlaid Boulle cupboard in ebony and ormolu, pictures from the schools of Raphael and Francke, and works by Bellini and Van Orley.

COMBOURG

THE CASTLE AND ITS ILLUSTRIOUS OWNERS. In 1761 René-Auguste de Chateaubriand, a wealthy shipowner from St-Malo and father of the future author, bought the castle from his uncle the Duc de Duras. Here he settled with his family in 1777, the young François-René being at that time just eight years old. On the death of his father, Jean-Baptiste (the writer's elder brother) inherited the castle, which was looted and confiscated during the Revolution but returned to the family in 1796. Jean-Baptiste's grandson Geoffroy de Chateaubriand undertook major restoration work in 1875. The castle is the home of Geoffroy's great-great grandson.

TOWERS AND RAMPARTS. The castle was built in three distinct phases. The oldest takes in the TOUR DU MORE in the north-east of the castle: it was built in the 13th century and it served as the keep. The remains of the former drawbridge, removed in the 17th century on the orders of Cardinal Richelieu, are plainly visible on the north façade. Richelieu was Louis XIII's Chief Minister, and in a bid to diminish the power of feudal

Below, the Château de Combourg, which dominates the little town, and the lake below where the young Chateaubriand used to sit and dream.

"THE HOUSE IN THE FOREGROUND"
The artist and engraver Albert Robida described this old house in Combourg (left) as follows: "The rest of the picture is unimportant, what matters here is the foreground, a tall and massive house built of grey granite, pierced with loopholes and Renaissance windows with a corbeled watchtower to the rear, and another huge tower to the side with scarcely any other openings than loopholes."

landlords he ordered drawbridges to be demolished and battlements to be roofed over on all castles throughout France. The TOUR SYBIL dates from the 14th century and bears the name of the wife of Geoffroy IV, Baron Chateaubriand. The TOUR DU CHAT, also built in the 1500's, is named after the ghost of a black cat that is said to wander the castle. During restoration work in 1875 the remains of a cat were discovered in one of the walls. The 15th-century FAÇADE, described by Chateaubriand as "grim and unrelenting", consists of a stone curtain wall topped with machicolated battlements and roofed over. It links the Tour du More with the 15th-century TOUR DU CROISÉ.
IN THE WRITER'S FOOTSTEPS. The guided tour of the castle takes about forty-five minutes. It includes many objects associated with Chateaubriand, the exotic and Romantic novelist.

CHÂTEAU DE LA BOURBANSAIS ★

The chateau is one of the loveliest in the Ille et Vilaine. Its almost pyramidal outline, with bell-shaped towers and a landscaped garden, is visible from the main road linking Rennes and St-Malo.
TOUR. The ground floor is open to the public. There are two main reception rooms, one decorated in the style of Louis XIII. The other, known as the BLUE DRAWING-ROOM, is decorated in the style of Louis XV, with beautiful 17th-century paneling and some exquisite 18th-century furniture inlaid with exotic woods. The MUSEUM contains some fascinating family memorabilia, and at the end of the tour visitors pass through a vestibule and dining-room hung with Aubusson tapestries. Other attractions here include a post-chaise (1771) that once belonged to Marie Antoinette's lady-in-waiting, the kennels, gardens, and a small zoo.

GRACE AND MAJESTY
La Bourbansais is a delightful combination of local architectural features and the classic courtly style, particularly apparent in the formal gardens. With its gracious statuary and the wooded ride, the park also reflects a dignified opulence.

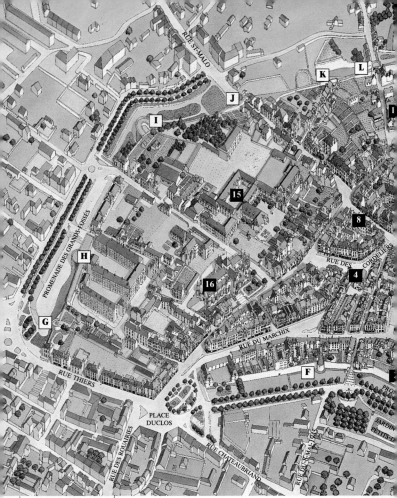

History

Before 1000 AD two important roads met at Dinan, one leading up into Normandy and the other heading southeast to Rennes. It was formerly a highly fortified harbor town, and has a vivid and turbulent history.

AN IMPORTANT STRONGHOLD. By the 11th century Dinan was already a sizeable town with a Benedictine monastery. In the 12th century the town was surrounded by a rough defensive wall. By the 14th century Dinan was busy and prosperous thanks to its trade links with England and the Low Countries. But much of this was to disappear in the ravages of the Hundred Years' War. The town had taken the side of Charles de Blois in the quarrel for the succession to the Dukedom of Brittany, and it was besieged by Jean IV, the future Duc de Montfort. His claim to the Dukedom was supported by the English, who harrassed the town ceaselessly. The knight Du Guesclin, who led the

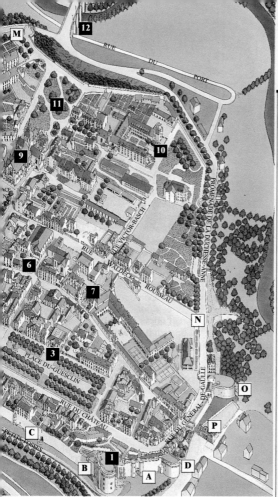

esistance, emerged victorious from his famous duel with Sir Thomas Canterbury. In the 16th century Dinan sided with the Protestant King Henri IV. Economically the town did not recover until the 18th century, when its streets echoed with the clatter of eight hundred looms. Canvas was exported as far afield as the West Indies and South America. Huge fairs at Dinan attracted vast crowds.

DINAN TODAY. Thousands of people visit the town each year: the high point of the season is the annual "FÊTE DES REMPARTS", a medieval fair, complete with tournaments held against the picturesque backdrop of the old town, and with all the citizens decked out in colorful medieval costumes.

AROUND THE CASTLE

KEEP. Fourteenth-century buildings in a good state of preservation are rare in France. Estienne Le Fur, architect of the Solidor Tower ▲ 194 at St-Servan, laid down the plans for the building around 1380 on the orders of Jean V. The keep consists of two linked towers 122 feet high, and formerly had a roof, which was replaced by an artillery platform in the 18th century. It fulfilled the double function of fortress (complete with peepholes and a lookout-post on every floor) and residence, with mullioned windows, huge

THE KEEP AT DINAN CASTLE
Stone carvings on the façade are a reminder that

this was not only a home but a fortress as well.

RENNES TO ST-MALO VIA DINAN

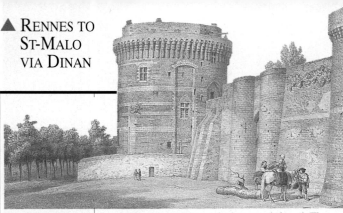

DINAN CASTLE
A colored lithograph by the Béquet brothers from *France in Our Times*, showing, from left to right the keep, the Porte du Guichet and the Coëtquen Tower.

AUGUSTE PAVIE
The house of the famous explorer in the Place St-Sauveur attracts crowds of tourists. Pavie (1847–1925) was born in Dinan and spent much of his career as minister plenipotentiary in South-East Asia. He was among those responsible for forging the strong links between France and Indo-China.

West front and apse of the basilica of St-Sauveur, drawn by Charles Chaussepied in 1898.

fireplaces and an elaborately decorated chapel. The accommodation was probably fairly basic. Today the keep houses the museum.

MUSEUM. Vivid displays here recount in detail Dinan's storm history. There is also a reconstruction of a weaver's workshop featuring original equipment, and a fine collection of headdresses ▲ 70 from all over the region.

TOUR DE COËTQUEN. The Coëtquen Tower was built in the 15th century. It has three floors, with three large vaulted rooms and walls 16 feet thick. The bottom room is a dank and chilly crypt with an uneven floor and seven figures, including Geoffroy Le Voyer, Jean IV's chamberlain, recumbent on their tombs.

PROMENADE DES PETITS-FOSSÉS. This attractive walk running below the ramparts on the west of the town was laid out in the 18th century on an ancient earthwork that protected the base of the walls against cannonballs. It passes beneath the 13th-century TOUR DE BEAUFORT, which was part of the original fortifications, and the 15th-century TOUR DU CONNÉTABLE. In between is a bust of Charles Duclos-Pinot, who created the promenade, sculpted by Jehan Duseigneur in 1842.

PLACE DU-GUESCLIN AND PLACE DU-CHAMP-CLOS. This area was rebuilt in the 18th century. A statue of Bertrand du Guesclin was erected here in 1902 (the original model for it is in the museum). It is the only equestrian statue in the entire Côtes d'Armor, and is the work of Emmanuel Frémiet (1824–1910), who also sculpted the Archangel on top of Mont-St-Michel.

AROUND ST-SAUVEUR

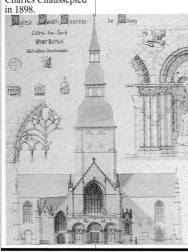

THE BASILICA OF ST-SAUVEUR. In the 12th century a knight from Dinan named Rivallon Le Roux left for the Crusades, having made a vow to build a church if he returned safely. The building shows the influence of Byzantine art: some of the ornamental detail, such as dromedaries, winged lions and sirens, is without parallel in Brittany. In the 15th century the growth in population made it necessary to enlarge the church: the work went on for 150 years and gave the church its present shape, with fourteen side chapels. It became a basilica on May 23, 1954. Inside are some 17th- and 18th-century ALTARPIECES, a 12th-century font in the baptistry, camels and dragons carved on

the capitals of the columns in the inside wall, a lovely alabaster *Virgin,* made in Nottingham, England, and dating from the 15th century, and a CENOTAPH containing the heart of Du Guesclin. The HIGH ALTAR in the chancel, dating from the 17th and 18th centuries, is outstanding, both for its baldacchino and for the lifelike figure of Christ above.

ENGLISH GARDEN. The *Jardin Anglais* is an ancient parish graveyard converted into an English-style garden in the last century. From here, from the 14th-century TOUR CARDINAL – or, even better, from the 13th-century TOUR STE-CATHERINE, a perfect look-out post – is a splendid view over the port, the viaduct and the Rance valley. From here a winding road leads down to the port. In the CHAPEL OF THE CATHERINETTES CONVENT ★ is a trompe l'oeil altarpiece and one of the town's greatest treasures, the *Choeur des Religieuses* (Nuns' Chancel), with a vaulted ceiling decorated with magnificent frescoes.

RUE HAUTE VOIE. At no. 1 is the beautiful turreted HÔTEL BEAUMANOIR, with its imposing Renaissance porch. The building dates from the 16th century and until 1664 it was the Catherinette convent. It was badly burned in 1943, but has since been restored and converted into council flats.

THE APPORT DISTRICT

TOUR DE L'HORLOGE. Every visitor to Dinan should climb the famous clocktower, 197 feet tall. A flight of 160 stone steps leads to a wooden staircase and finally a ladder. The platform at the top was formerly used by a watchman who kept a look-out for fires, and the view down over the city is perfect. The Duchess Anne presented the tower to Dinan, and the clock mechanism by Maître Hamzer of Nantes was made in 1498.

RUE DE L'HORLOGE. The street seems more like an open-air museum of timber-framed houses (outstanding examples are nos. 13, 27, 31 and 33). At the junction with the Rue de l'Apport are some fine old porticoed buildings.

PLACE DES MERCIERS. The square contains the famous restaurant of LA MÈRE POURCEL, a beautiful 15th-century half-timbered building. It is also known as "Saint-Dinan", after the carved figure on one corner. Between the narrow RUE DU PETIT PAIN and the RUE DE LA CORDONNERIE stands the MARKET HALL, set in a passage lined with shops that have stood here for centuries.

RUE DE LA POISSONNERIE. At no. 6 is one of the oldest houses in this picturesque town, with thick granite walls and fine corbelling. An inscription on the façade gives the date of its construction as 1494.

AROUND THE CHURCH OF ST-MALO

CHURCH OF ST-MALO. The first church was in fact built outside the city walls, on the site of the present Chapel of St-Joachim. It was demolished in the 15th century for fear that it would be of strategic use to besiegers. The foundation stone of the new church was laid in 1489, though the building remains unfinished, and still lacks a bell tower. Inside are

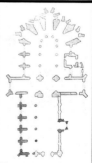

THE BASILICA OF ST-SAUVEUR
The plan above shows the different periods of construction: the 12th-century parts are grey, 15th-century parts mauve, and 16th-century sections pink. Illustrated at the top of the page are three decorative details from the façade.

THE MASON'S HOUSE
A notice on this house in the Rue de l'Horloge announces that a master-carver of monumental tombs once lived here. This particular 14th-century figure came to light during restoration work on the house. These statues, placed on the top of tombs, were carved in advance, the facial features and coat of arms of the deceased being added later.

THE OLD GATES OF DINAN
The Porte de Brest, painted in 1881 by Walsh Jackson.

RUE DU PETIT-FORT
The so-called "Governor's House" at no. 24, above which is a tanner's house (nos. 49–51).

some interesting stained-glass windows from the early 1900's, a stoup borne by a devil bent under the weight of his burden, and a superb ORGAN dated 1889, made by the English builder Alfred Oldknow. The blue and gold painted pipework is extremely rare.

COUVENT DES CORDELIERS. This Franciscan monastery was founded in 1241 by Henri d'Avaugour, a knight of Dinan, on his return from the Crusades, where he had taken a vow to become a monk. The refectory, formerly the chapter house, was sometimes used as a meeting place for the States of Brittany. Today the building is a private school, one of the best-known in the province.

PROMENADE DES GRANDS-FOSSÉS. The wide walk leads along a section of the town walls past the TOUR ST-JULIEN, which was once much taller and had a machicolated gallery and slate roof. During the wars of the League it was used as a powder magazine, and blew up. Further along is the TOUR DE LESQUEN, which was never finished, while near by is the imposing TOUR DE BEAUMANOIR with walls 26 feet thick. From the Rue du Roquet the TOUR DU GOUVERNEUR can be seen; it controlled two entrances to the city, the PORTE ST-MALO and the PORTE DU JERZUAL.

RUE DU JERZUAL AND THE PORT

RUE DU JERZUAL. This steep and delightful little street was the main road into Dinan, before the viaduct was built. In those days it was usually full of carts loaded with skins, bales of canvas, wood and grain going down the hill toward St-Malo. They would return filled with salt from the coast, cod, tea, spices and pottery. The street is much quieter today. It is lined with picturesque old timbered houses, adorned with carvings, that were built by well-to-do merchants from the 15th century onward. At the bottom is the 14th-century TOWER-GATE OF JERZUAL, the subject of a well-known painting by Corot. The actual gate is set in the middle of the tower, an unusual arrangement since gates were usually flanked by two towers. The STONE COAT OF ARMS (half Breton and half French) that was set above the window in 1642 is now on the façade of the Town Hall (Hôtel de Ville). Beyond the Jerzual Gate the road winds down the RUE DU PETIT FORT to the harbor, with some interesting buildings along the way, among them the MAISON DU GOUVERNEUR (Governor's house) at no. 24, dating from the 15th century and in magnificent Renaissance style, and at nos. 49–51 a huge early 17th-century open-work building where skins were dried. There used to be a number of tanneries in the street, the skins being washed in the waters of the Rance near by.

PORT. This was once the center of the city. With the decline of seaborne trade, the harbor has become an attractive mooring for leisure craft and it is a delightful place in which to stroll before enjoying a meal in the shadow of the great viaduct, built in 1852.

WALKS

FONTAINE DES EAUX. The Argentel is a tributary of the Rance, and the valley on its left bank, running from the port at Dinan, is a peaceful haven of greensward. Along the way are several mills that belonged to noblemen and wealthy clerics from St-Malo. The way was once quite busy, for it led to the Fontaine des Eaux, where there used to be a spring whose mineral waters became famous in the 17th century. The building there was destroyed in 1929 during a storm and the spring is little visited now, though the surrounding countryside is still delightful.

"THE MEADOWS OF LÉHON". Another attractive walk, a popular outing for local inhabitants, runs along the right bank of the Rance toward Léhon. Writer Roger Vercel found it an ideal opportunity to meditate upon nature: "The walk

RUE DU JERZUAL AND RUE DU PETIT-FORT
The difference in height from the top of the town down to the harbor is clearly apparent in this illustration. The steep gradient however is one of the little street's most charming features. The climb failed to damp the enthusiasm of Roger Vercel, Professor of Literature at Dinan in 1920: "The steep slope of the hill will get to you just the same whichever way you climb it: whether you toil up the Rue du Jerzual in the shade of the ancient overhanging houses propped up by worn pillars, and through the fine Gothic gateway; or whether you trudge up the winding paths, the climb will wear you out."

through the meadows that link Lehon and Dinan is little more than a mile long. The borders of the Rance are quite perfect. It is the quintessential river, calling up fond memories and dreams, evoked by the matchless harmony between hills, trees, and water."

LÉHON

VIEW OF LÉHON IN THE LAST CENTURY
The illustration on the right shows the ruins of the Priory of St-Magloire in the center, the towers of the castle on the right and, in the distance, the city of Dinan.

A detail from the façade of the church at Léhon. Inside is the tomb of Jean III de Beaumanoir, carved in the 14th century on the orders of his brother Robert, who was unjustly accused of having murdered him.

This pretty village nestles in a curve of the Rance. The narrowing of the river here, together with a steep hill, made it an ideal site for a monastery. It was built near the bridge, and above it the lords of Dinan built a wooden fort. This was replaced in the 12th century by a castle, which survived intact for over three hundred years, although it was besieged on numerous occasions. Its ruins overlook the site of the abbey.

PRIORY OF ST-MAGLOIRE. In the 9th century King Nominoë of Brittany gave the lands of Léhon to a band of six monks for them to build an abbey. So as to secure the protection of the king, the monks set off to rifle the relics of Saint Magloire that were on Sark, in the Channel Islands. Such an act was common practice. The abbey prospered for many years before it finally fell into disuse, to be abandoned and looted. After years of restoration work, the ABBEY CHURCH was reconsecrated in 1897. Entrance is through a beautiful Romanesque portal, and inside are six stone tombs bearing figures of members of the Beaumanoir family. A door on the north side opens onto a CLOISTER, the east side of which has a mansard roof.

CASTLE. The castle was built on a feudal motte in the year 1000 and underwent substantial modifications in the succeeding centuries. It was the scene of numerous battles, and of a deadly combat between the brothers Eudon and Alain, sons of Duke Geoffroy I of Brittany. By the 17th century it was of no strategic importance, and was demolished on Cardinal Richelieu's orders. All that remains now are the ruins of seven towers.

AN EXCURSION ON THE RANCE
From 1838 visitors to the Côte d'Émeraude could go up the Rance as far as Dinan by steamboat. Until that time, however, only the most intrepid tourists had dared to venture out in the little boats that set out from Port Solidor on a round trip lasting over four hours.

BRIDGE. The Pont des Ânes (Bridge of Asses) in the village of Léhon allowed the monks to control the movement of traffic across the Rance and, more significantly, to charge a toll for its use, a practice that continued until 1767.

WALKS. The youth hostel at Dinan has laid out an attractive walk that follows the left bank of the Rance. The circular itinerary covers about 8 miles and its most distant point is in Tressaint woods.

RIGHT BANK OF THE RANCE

The tidal mouth of the river lies in gentle
landscape, which is unusual in Brittany.
Among its aficionados was writer Roger Vercel:
"The estuary sprawls everywhere, a dull mineral
blue like a scarf of watered silk . . . The cliffs are
the color of honey, and the waves spread away
to the south like a rumpled coverlet. Brittany is
fair, almost sensual, here." Those lines are from

his book *The Rance*, which is one of the most poetic
appreciations of the region, together of course with the
writings of Chateaubriand ▲ *151*. An excellent way
to appreciate what Vercel saw and to
understand his feelings would be to take
an excursion on one of the Emerald
Line boats from
St-Malo to Dinan, but to
comprehend fully the
exceptional beauty of this
twelve-mile stretch the
traveler must explore
"all the detail of its tiny
coves and lagoons, for
this is where the sea
merges with the
countryside," according
to Vercel's poetic
description.

**AN ARTIST'S VISION OF
THE RANCE**
Above is one of
twenty gouaches
painted by Jean
Urvoy as illustrations
for Roger Vercel's
book *The Rance*,
which was published
in 1945. At the top of
the page is a
lithograph of Dinan
as seen from Léhon.

**THE RANCE IN FORMER
TIMES.** This was at one
time a busy working river.
Up till World War Two it
operated as the main
thoroughfare for produce coming
from farms and market gardens up to
the maritime port of Dinan. Its banks used
to ring with the cries of boatmen who plied their
way ceaselessly to and fro between St-Malo and Dinan.
Propelled by the current, lines of barges made their way
downstream, riding low in the water as their cargoes of wood
and grain weighed them down. Later they would make their
way back upriver, now loaded with coal or fertilizer. The
barges, designed and constructed so as to fit exactly into the
canal locks, were drawn by horses as far as the lock at
Chatelier, where bargees would take over and with long poles
propel the craft on to Mordreuc. Only there could they finally
hoist sails and relax. In the fall huge coastal sloops like
waterborne lorries, their holds filled with coal from England
or cement from Boulogne, would come upstream along the
right bank and return with cargoes of cider apples. On the
other side boats from Pleudihen ▲ *160* were on their way
downstream to supply the bakeries of St-Malo with wood for
their ovens, crossing paths with the heavy carriers that served
the mills and quarries of Mont-Garrot. "Chippes" ▲ *161*,
boats fishing for eel and plaice, passed them too. Steamboats
first appeared on the Rance in 1838, carrying tourists on
excursions to see the beauties of this exceptionally
picturesque region.

COMMON HERON
This large bird ■ *40*
has grey wings and
upper parts, and a
white abdomen. It
haunts any fresh
water where fish are
to be found, standing
stock still in wait for
its prey.

"LES GABARIERS", THE RANCE BARGEES
These floating dealers were the virtual kings of the river. Their cumbersome craft fitted with large reddish-brown sails carried the vast quantities of wood needed by bakeries in St-Malo.

The Beauchet tidal mill.

The formal gardens of the Malouinière du Bos slope gently down to the Rance. The design of the lawn and of the garden echoes the rounded shape of the façade, a typical 18th-century practice.

ST-HÉLEN

Cross the little town and take the road that leads to the ruined fortress at Coëtquen, on the edge of the forest. In the village a tragic legend is told about this 15th-century fortress. The last Marchioness of Coëtquen is said to have been walled up in a cellar there, for having loved a simple commoner and refused to marry the husband chosen for her. The building was demolished by the Revolutionary government in 1794 to prevent it from being used by the royalist Chouans ● 62 and the remains of the castle were dynamited in 1953.

PLEUDIHEN

CIDER MUSEUM. The valley of the Rance, and in particular the area round Pleudihen, is famous for its varieties of apples and its excellent cider. One of the locals decided to start a cider museum: there is a video introduction, reconstructions of a cooper's and a hoop-maker's workshops, and interesting displays showing all the stages that go into the making of traditional cider. At the end of the tour is an attractive tasting room. As well as the care expended in its pressing and fermentation, cider quality depends above all on fruit of just the right soundness and on the varieties of apple used. Here in the Rance valley varieties with such quaint names as "Chaperonnais", "Jeanne Renard", "Marie Menard" and "Doux Évêque" are the ones most widely used.

ST-SULIAC

THE GARROT. The road to Mont-Garrot was once lined with walls of quartz, which can still be seen on the first stage of the ascent. It led to an ancient monastery, which was replaced by a chapel in the 15th century. A cross and a ruined windmill are all that are left today at the summit of the highest point in the region – just 240 feet above sea level! All the same, there is a grand view from here over the Rance valley, Mont Dol ▲ 181 and the bay of Mont-St-Michel. In good weather it is possible to count no less than thirty-two bell towers. At low tide the stone foundations of a Viking settlement can be seen at the foot of the hill.
MOULIN DU BEAUCHET. Perched on its breakwater, this ancient tidal mill ● 96 is now surrounded by fishponds. The area is also a bird sanctuary where heron, grebes and sheldrake love to forage. Along with those at Quinard, Mordreuc and Plouer, Beauchet is one of the rare surviving historic tidal mills and the last to have continued working, powered by the ceaseless ebb and flow of the sea.

ST-JOUAN-DES-GUÉRETS

MALOUINIÈRE DU BOS. The road from St-Jouan-des-Guérets leads to the only *malouinière* ● 90 open to the public. It was built between 1715 and 1717 on the site of an old 16th-centur manor house by two important families of St-Malo

shipowners. Several features of the former manor house, including two fireplaces and a carved lintel in yellow granite, were incorporated in the outbuildings around it. The design and decoration of the *malouinière* are outstanding: figures of Aeolus and Mercury decorate the entrance, which opens on to the garden where stand statues of the Four Seasons. This elegance is continued inside the house, which has beautiful marble and wooden floors. The Louis XVI paneling in the drawing room is carved with pastoral, musical and military designs; to one side of the large French windows are a straw hat and a set of bagpipes, and on the other a musical score,

symbols of the contrast between folk and formal music. The Regency dining room has carved oak paneling of the kind that was popular with the wealthy merchants. The library, containing at least eight thousand books, is now filled with 19th-century furniture from a château in Maine-et-Loire. This arrangement is a shadow of the décor's former grandeur. There were once six Gobelins tapestries, gleaming copper fountains, upholstery in Russia leather, Chinese porcelain and lacquered cabinets, all opulent trimmings to an essentially plain interior. The round building to the right of the entrance to this magnificent *malouinière* is the only local example of an ice-house: it once contained ice shipped from Norway.

CALE DE LA PASSAGÈRE

FERRY. The name of the quay, *"passagère"*, comes from the ferry that used to carry people across the Rance from here. It was one of the six last ferries over the river, and ceased working in 1959. In early times the only places to cross this unruly river were fords at St-Suliac, Mordreuc, Taden and Léhon. In the Middle Ages monks began to row people across, accepting only token payment, and mooring their boats at the first "charity" ports of Port-St-Jean in the Baie du Prieuré, and at the Cale de la Passagère. Later this became a privilege granted by the king or duke to a particular lord or religious order. Around the 10th century, two bridges, at Léhon and Dinan, were built.

VILLA OF COMMANDANT CHARCOT. Between polar expeditions, the famous explorer liked to relax in his large family house above the Cale de la Passagère. From here he could also keep an eye on construction and repairs to his two ships, at St-Malo and on the Rance.

THE "CHIPPES" OF ST-SULIAC
These long pointed boats (above) were quite unlike any other craft in Brittany. A *chippe* has been reconstructed according to written accounts of them by Jean Le Bot.

"THE FOUR SEASONS"
Four 18th-century Italian statues symbolizing the seasons decorate the Malouinière du Bos. In those days the St-Malo shipowners sold their cod in Genoa, and would bring back marble statues with which to adorn their country houses and the parks of St-Malo.

THE HOUSE OF COMMANDANT CHARCOT
Jean-Baptiste Charcot (1867–1936) led two expeditions to the Antarctic before World War One, and was eventually drowned off Iceland.

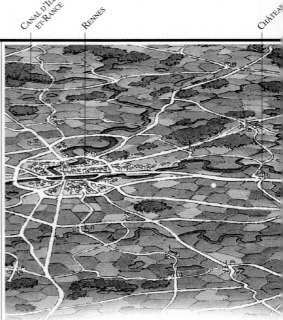

CANAL D'ILLE-ET-RANCE · RENNES · CHÂTEA

THE CLOCKTOWER
The bell in the tower is known as "Henrietta", and was a gift from the Cossé-Brissac family in 1600. Behind it the sturdy keep of the castle of Châteaugiron stands proudly on the frontier of Brittany, keeping invaders at bay.

The belfry of the collegiate church at Champeaux.

CHÂTEAUGIRON

The town, founded in the 11th century, takes its name from Giron, the son of a Norman knight who emigrated to Brittany around 1008 and rebuilt the ancient wooden fortress.
CASTLE. It was built to defend the city of Rennes from invaders, and combines a grim medieval austerity with the graceful balance of its classical façade. The oldest part of the fabric is the CHAPEL OF STE-MADELEINE, which from the 16th to the 19th centuries was the parish church. At either end of the moat are two imposing towers: the TOUR DE L'HORLOGE, which served as a bell tower under the Ancien Régime, and a massive 14th-century keep.
KEEP. The keep is 125 feet high, and dominates the castle. In the late 18th century its huge walls, up to 14 feet thick, were pierced by large windows. It once stood apart from the castle, its entrance defended by a drawbridge and portcullis, whose emplacements are still visible. Opposite the castle is a lake with an artificial beach.

CHAMPEAUX

"There is no holy chapel in France, apart from those founded by the great kings, to stand comparison with it." Those words were written in 1548 and show the regard in which the collegiate church of Champeaux was held. It was originally built as the funerary chapel of the great Franco-Breton family the Espinays.
COLLEGIATE CHURCH. The chapel was built in 1430 on the orders of Robert I d'Espinay. Two years later he obtained permission from the Pope to elevate it to the status of a collegiate church, giving it the right to have canons, chaplains, choristers and a choir school. Around 1440 his grandson (also Robert) rebuilt the CHANCEL in the form it has today. It is larger than the nave; whereas the nave was designed to hold

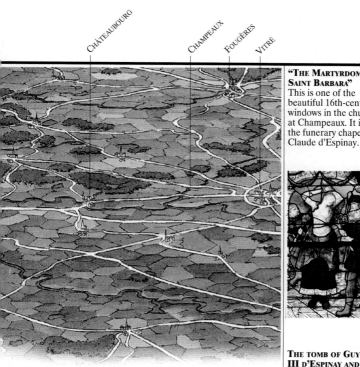

"THE MARTYRDOM OF SAINT BARBARA"
This is one of the beautiful 16th-century windows in the church at Champeaux. It is in the funerary chapel of Claude d'Espinay.

THE TOMB OF GUY III D'ESPINAY AND LOUISE DE GOULAINE
In the middle of the tracery is an epitaph by Charles d'Espinay celebrating the immortal quality of love: *"Fama mortalibus una superstes."*

TREASURES OF CHAMPEAUX
The 16th-century painted wooden reredos in the south chapel shows scenes from the Passion of Christ.

only a small congregation, the chancel had to accommodate not only the the canons but their clerks too. Houses for the canons were built around a courtyard that was called a "cloister": it was closed at sunset, and women were forbidden.
RENAISSANCE DECORATION. The interior décor is more or less intact, and reflects the taste and the wealth of the church's benefactors. The chancel has a double rank of oak CHOIRSTALLS dating from 1540 and exemplifying Renaissance decoration at its purest. Through the GREAT WINDOW IN THE APSE, from the same period, red, green and golden light beams into the chancel: it is the work of Gilles de la Croix-Vallée, and depicts the *Crucifixion.* In the lower part is a representation of the *Death of Mary Magdalene*, framed by portraits of the benefactors, Guy III d'Espinay and his wife Louise de Goulaine.
ESPINAY TOMB. Guy III and Louise's monumental tomb is on the left-hand side. It is in Renaissance style, in white stone decorated with marble of different colors, and was made by the Tours-trained Anjou sculptor Jean de l'Espine. The figure of Louise de Goulaine is now in the upper recess ● *102*, while that of Guy III lies on the surface below, where the couple originally lay together. It is one of the finest tombs of its time, and was inspired by that of Louis XII and Anne of Brittany in the basilica of St-Denis just outside Paris. The chapel on the south side of the nave has a window representing Pentecost, showing the Virgin surrounded by the Apostles.

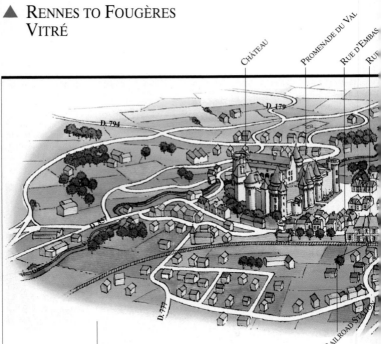

CHÂTEAU · PROMENADE DU VAL · RUE D'EMBAS · RUE · D. 179 · D. 794 · D. 777 · RAILROAD STATION

This watercolor painted in 1930 shows a girl in traditional Vitré costume.

HISTORY

A BRETON BARONY. Vitré first made its mark on history in the 10th century with Riwallon. He was a staunch supporter of the Comte de Rennes, who made him governor of a huge territory and charged him to guard its frontier against Frankish invaders. Riwallon accordingly built wooden forts around the hill of Ste-Croix, marking out the future barony of Vitré, one of Brittany's original nine. A defensive wall around the town was added in the 13th century.

THE GUILD OF MERCHANT ADVENTURERS. The Brotherhood of the Annunciation was founded by merchants from Vitré in 1472. Thanks to the flourishing cloth trade ● *60* these wealthy dealers prospered for more than a century, trading with Flanders, England, the Hanseatic ports, Spain and even South America. In 1600 the population of Vitré stood at 6,000 to 7,000 souls, roughly half that of Rennes, but business went into a decline in the 17th century.

VITRÉ TODAY. The town is set in the middle of a highly developed agricultural region, where dairy farming is a major industry. In the 1970's Vitré successfully expanded its cheese, milk and beef production, and developed a thriving shoe-manufacturing industry.

CHÂTEAU DE VITRÉ

Recent excavations have revealed the foundations of an earlier fortress built in 1060. It was rebuilt in the 13th century and enlarged to its present layout. The town of Laval was taken by the English in the 15th century and the noble family of Laval-Vitré were forced to flee and settle in Vitré. Before they arrived the castle was transformed into a luxuriously comfortable home for its distinguished new guests, and in the following century it was further decorated and modified in full-blown Renaissance style.

COURTLY SPLENDOR. For more than a century the lords of

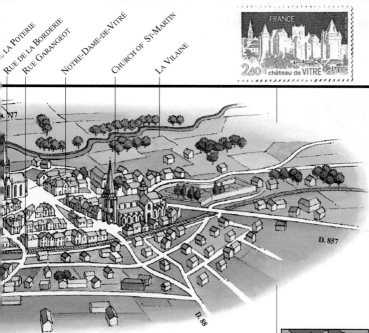

LA POTERIE RUE DE LA BORDERIE RUE GARANGEOT NOTRE-DAME-DE-VITRÉ CHURCH OF ST-MARTIN LA VILAINE

D. 777

D. 857

D. 88

Vitré maintained a costly and resplendent court, were
receptive to all the latest Italian ideas and fashions and
moved in the most illustrious circles. Early in the 16th century
Guy XVI married Charlotte of Argon, daughter of the king of
Naples and lady-in-waiting to the French queen (formerly the
Duchess Anne of Brittany).

YEARS OF NEGLECT. During the wars of the League, Vitré
declared for the Huguenots and withstood a Catholic siege.
But soon afterward it was abandoned and fell into a state of
dilapidation. After its purchase by the local authorities in
1820 it became a prison, and was completely restored between
1875 and 1902.

CASTLE MUSEUM. The museum, which opened in 1876, was
largely the work of historian Arthur de la Borderie. The TOUR
DE L'ARGENTERIE houses an interesting collection of 19th-
century natural history. The museum also presents displays of
decorative and traditional features characteristic of the
region, including a beautiful door from a 16th-century house.
A fireplace dating from 1583 is an interesting example of
domestic decoration of the period. It was built for a local
cloth merchant, whose likeness is carved
on the ornamental front surrounded

**"LES GRANDS
FOSSÉS"**
An illustration from
the 1850's showing a
section of the old
road from Paris to
Brest on the outer
wall of the town's
great ditch. In the
center can be seen
the impressive tower
of Claviers,
demolished in 1894,
whose Vitré
sandstone cladding
was decorated with
bands of blue schist.
On the left is the
elegant Hôtel
Sévigné-Nétumières.

▲ RENNES TO FOUGÈRES
VITRÉ CASTLE

1. MONTAFILANT TOWER
This was probably built in the 13th century. It stands at the northwest corner of the castle and is connected to the Tour de la Madeleine by the north wall (in the background of the illustration), which is set with two square towers.

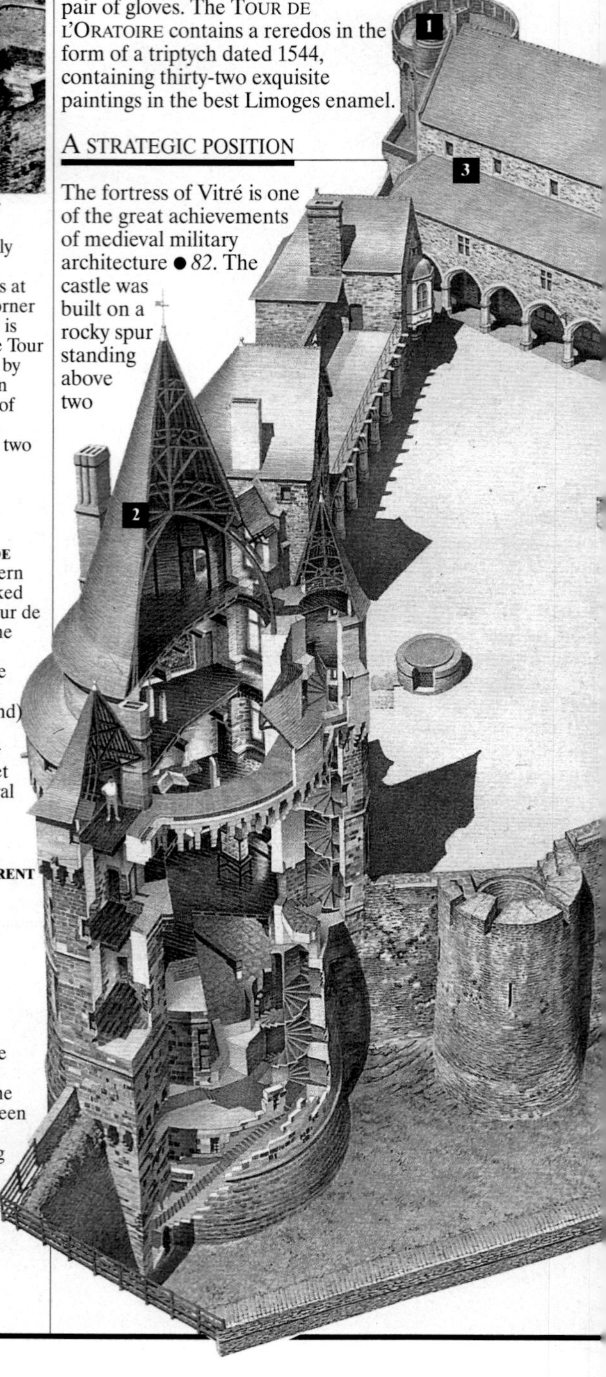

THE WEST FAÇADE
(right) The western elevation is flanked by the square Tour de l'Oratoire and the round Tour de l'Argenterie. The Tour St-Laurent (in the foreground) stands at the southeast corner alongside a turret containing a spiral staircase.

2. TOUR ST-LAURENT

3. ORATORY AND LOGGIAS

THE SOUTHEAST FAÇADE
This connects the keep (Tour St-Laurent) to the gatehouse. Between the two are the remains of a long demolished tower, the Tour du Véel, or Tour du Veau.

by all the trappings of his wealth: his purse bulges with money, and his wife, beside him, wears a pair of gloves. The TOUR DE L'ORATOIRE contains a reredos in the form of a triptych dated 1544, containing thirty-two exquisite paintings in the best Limoges enamel.

A STRATEGIC POSITION

The fortress of Vitré is one of the great achievements of medieval military architecture ● 82. The castle was built on a rocky spur standing above two valleys, where all that was needed to make it impregnable was a deep transversal ditch. The design was altered in the 12th century to form an almost perfect triangle.

TOUR ST-LAURENT. Built in the early 15th century the tower was an early attempt to combine a dwelling with a structure that, with its exceptional four-storey height and gunports, would be proof against the new artillery. The small side turrets allowed a defender to shoot at invaders.

GATEHOUSE. The high towers and machicolation of the gatehouse, built in 1380, controlled

4. THE GATEHOUSE
The fortified gatehouse was added in the 14th century. Two round towers with conical roofs rise over the crenelated battlements. The gatehouse has two separate entrances: a narrow one for those arriving or leaving on foot, and one much larger to let riders or waggons pass in and out. Each entrance was equipped with its own drawbridge.

5. TOUR DE LA MADELEINE

all traffic in and out of the castle

TOUR DE LA MADELEINE. This tower was named after the nearby collegiate church, and was the last to be built (c. 1420). It is of grey-green schist, and the interior designed as a residence. In preparation for the arrival of the Laval-Vitré family, a bathhouse was even installed.

LOGGIAS. Around 1530 Guy XVI added two loggias to the old castle. One, which served as an oratory, was built of white Loire limestone carved in early Renaissance style.

"THE ANNUNCIATION"
A detail from the series of Limoges enamels adorning the reredos in the Tour de

HÔTEL DU BOL D'OR
Its eccentric
silhouette enlivens
the period charm of
the Rue d'Embas.

LES ROCHERS
Mme de Sévigné
settled here as a bride
with her husband in
1644. These were the
happy days of her
short married life: her
husband soon took to
philandering in Paris,
and in 1651 he was
killed in a duel
over "La Belle
Lolo", a lady of
easy virtue.

DISTRICT OF THE MERCHANT ADVENTURERS

Vitré is enormously proud of having kept so many of its little
15th- and 16th-century streets intact, and everywhere there
are mementoes of the great merchant sailors who founded the
fortunes of the town. Their discerning taste is reflected in the
elegant timber-framed houses, with arched doorways,
overhanging gables and slate-clad walls, that they built.

RUE D'EMBAS. The street leads to an ancient fortified gate in
the town wall called the Porte En Bas (Lower Gate), where
one of the towers still remains. The impressive façade of the
house at no. 30 gives a good idea of the status of the
merchants who built it in the 15th and 16th centuries. The
remarkable HÔTEL DU BOL D'OR at no. 10 is a delightful
Gothic-style building with an asymmetrical outline, though
the front section of the house has disappeared.

RUE DE LA BEAUDRAIRIE. This is one of the few old streets in
town to run from north to south. *Baudroier* is an archaic
French word for a leather worker. No. 30, a fine 15th- and
16th-century *hôtel particulier*, is one of the more interesting
buildings on the street. The house at no. 16 has a beautiful
Renaissance doorway, while no. 5 has fleurs-de-lis carved on
its timbers.

RUE DE LA POTERIE. In former times many potters had their
workshops in the street here. The house at no. 27 has a
drafted stone façade of 1623, while the beautiful 15th-
and 16th-century Gothic-style house at no. 33 rises up in
a series of overhanging stories. The latter, which also has
a 19th-century painted wood frontage, is linked to a
house in the courtyard behind by a series of wooden
galleries, a system
that was once
common in Vitré

LES ROCHERS-SÉVIGNÉ

This small château with corner towers and a moat stands on a rocky hillside, which accounts for half of its name. The other comes from the fact that this was the favorite country retreat of Madame de Sévigné (1626–96), the most famous letter writer of her day. The château had been in her husband's family since 1410, and was rebuilt in the 16th century.

GOTHIC INSPIRATION. The château is built in the form of a square and, in its carving and its sweeping vertical lines, imitates the Flamboyant Gothic style. At one corner a polygonal staircase tower of graceful proportions is surmounted by a turret containing another staircase leading up to the roof. The doors, windows and gables of the wings have all been altered and enlarged. In 1671 the CHAPEL was rebuilt by Mme de Sévigné's uncle, the Abbé Coulanges, who kept her company. It is built on an octagonal plan symbolizing the Kingdom of Heaven, and is covered with a wooden cupola beneath a roof with a little belfry in the form of a lantern.

THE LITERARY LIFE. Marie de Sévigné became a widow at the age of twenty-five when her dissolute husband the Marquis was killed in a duel. She never married again, and from 1654 to 1690 spent long periods here at Rochers, from where she wrote many of the great series of letters to her married daughter Françoise de Grignan. These intimate and lively letters detail much of what was going on at her great house in Paris, and as a wealthy widow not yet in middle age she had the utmost freedom in society as well as the social gifts that made her a favorite everywhere. Though she loved Rochers, she had distinct reservations about her fellow countrymen: at one gathering she was surprised to find "that among all these countless Bretons there are actually some men of intelligence". The château MUSEUM contains many family portraits, and the famous GREEN ROOM has a beautiful fireplace decorated with painted initials.

THE MARQUISE DE SÉVIGNÉ
This portrait was painted at the time of her marriage, when she was just eighteen and brought her husband a dowry of 100,000 crowns. The painting is in the Château des Rochers.

PEACE AND QUIET, FAR FROM THE CITY
Though she moved in the highest intellectual and social circles in Paris, Mme de Sévigné also need the seclusion offered by her beloved Brittany home. "When I am away from Paris, I want nothing but the country life," she wrote. "We are in perfect solitude, which suits me very well."

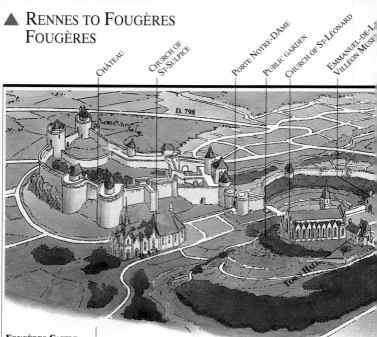

CHÂTEAU

CHURCH OF ST-SULPICE

PORTE NOTRE-DAME

PUBLIC GARDEN

CHURCH OF ST-LÉONARD

EMMANUEL-DE-LA VILLÉON MUSE

D. 798

TOWN HALL

FOUGÈRES CASTLE
Raoul II's fortress looked impregnable, with its three huge concentric encircling walls and the keep at the center. The Gobelin and Mélusine towers were added toward the end of the 12th century. A hundred years later, machicolation was built on at strategic points of the wall, the better to repel invaders. Finally, in the 15th century two new towers, the

Françoise and the Tourasse, were added onto the south rampart.

HISTORY

Fougères grew up in the 11th century at the foot of a castle built to defend the northeast frontier of the Duchy of Brittany. In 1307 Philip IV ("the Fair") confiscated the barony of Fougères; from then on the town belonged to a succession of absentee landlords. Its future lay in the hands of its citizens who made a success of it. In a new district, the Bourg Neuf ("New Town") which grew up outside the old town center, they built a bell tower and a town hall as symbols of their power and responsibility. The weavers in the 14th century, the dyers and cloth merchants ● *60* in the 15th century, and the linen manufacturers in the 16th century brought the town wealth and renown. In 1793 Fougères was the scene of some bloody fighting between the Republican forces and Catholic royalists. In the 19th century the town became industrialized; and in 1944 it was badly damaged under German occupation.

CASTLE

The first building to be razed to the ground by the English king Henry II in 1166. It was rebuilt soon afterward, Fougères being strategically very important. The present fortress is largely the work of Baron Raoul II. It ceased to play a military role toward the end of the 15th century, when Brittany lost its independence ● *57*.
CHURCH OF ST-SULPICE. The church was founded in the 11th century and rebuilt in the 1600's in Flamboyant Gothic style. Inside are two of the last surviving medieval Breton ALTARPIECES, and the wooden statue of Notre-Dame-des-Marais, which is still the object of a fervent cult. The church also has some lovely 16th-century WINDOWS made by Fougères artist Pierre Symon.

BEFFROI · RUE NATIONAL · LE NANÇON · RUE DE LA PINTERIE · CONVENT OF THE URBANISTES

RÉPUBLIQUE FRANÇAISE · POSTES · 0.30 · CHÂTEAU DE FOUGÈRES

THE BELL TOWER
The oldest bell tower in Brittany lives on as a symbol of the power of the bourgeoisie who ran the textile industry that formed the basis of the town's prosperity between the 14th and 16th centuries.

RAILROAD STATION

THE BOURG NEUF

This old quarter has been the real heart of the town since the Middle Ages.
THEATER. It was designed by Fougères architect Jean-Marie Laloy and opened on September 24, 1886. It is an Italianate building, with a monumental façade decorated with the masks of Tragedy and Comedy. The mayor of the time wanted to provide the workers with a place of respectable entertainment; seats were cheap and sold well. The theater was closed in 1970, for safety reasons.

BELL TOWER

The bell tower's silhouette has dominated the skyline of the Bourg Neuf since 1397. It once represented the increased power of the merchant classes. It is a high tower of dressed stone, square at the base and then octagonal. Its balustrade, in the Flamboyant Gothic style, is a later addition, and the sculptures that decorate it date from the 15th century.
CLOCK. The bell in the tower has been striking the hours for the citizens of Fougères since the end of the 14th century. Despite the noise of motor-cars in the town today, the bell can still be heard when the wind blows from the west, even in the outermost suburbs. Its very presence explains why none of the other churches in the town have a clock. Dinan and Fougères are in fact the only towns in the province to have retained their traditional bell

At no. 14 Rue Nationale, this stylish horseshoe-shaped staircase is virtually the only decorative feature in an architectural scheme that seems to be reduced to bare essentials.

towers, which had the additional function of alerting the populace in the event of danger.

RUE NATIONALE

The street is also known as Rue du Bourg Neuf or Grand-Rue. It was formerly the main commercial street of the upper town, and still has some lovely 18th-century buildings.

A NEW ARCHITECTURE ● 92. The town was ravaged by fire in 1710 and again in 1751, the flames spreading rapidly on each occasion through the old timber-framed houses. For the work of rebuilding stone was selected, for it was less dangerous, and the old medieval streets were completely refashioned. The new buildings were of granite, with arcades at ground level, and were designed by the royal architect Jacques Gabriel. They completely altered the face of the town. The houses had little in the way of ornamentation. Such decoration as there was concentrated on details like wrought-iron balconies and paneled doors.

HÔTEL DANJOU DE LA GARENNE. Situated at no. 30 Rue Nationale, this was built on the site of Annibal de Farcy's house. The carved medallions on the exterior are the work of Rennes artist Jean-Baptiste Barre, who also designed the interior. Upstairs is a beautifully preserved parquet floor laid out in a star pattern. Also in the street is the birthplace of Admiral de Guichen (1712–90), who distinguished himself in several engagements with the English fleet, and that of Aimé Picquet de Boisguy (1776–1839) who led the royalist insurrection in the Fougères region.

HOUSE WITH A PORCH Such houses were formerly widely distributed throughout Upper Brittany, though this example, at no. 51 Rue Nationale, is the last one of its kind in Fougères. Built in the 17th century, today it houses the museum of late Impressionist painter Emmanuel de la Villéon.

EMMANUEL-DE-LA-VILLÉON MUSEUM

This is in a superb old porched house in the Rue Nationale.
WOODLAND SCENES. A native of Fougères, Villéon (1858–1944) was a prolific painter. He was primarily a landscape artist, was passionately fond of nature and was one of the last Impressionists. The MUSEUM contains around a hundred of his most representative works, from his first canvas, painted at the age of seventeen, up to one of his last pictures, painted in 1944.

PUBLIC GARDENS

The gardens, also known as the Place des Arbres, were laid out on two levels with lovely views over the valley of the Nancon, the lower town, the castle and the ramparts.

These lovely gardens became dear to Victor Hugo and Honoré de Balzac, who stayed in Fougères and used them as a setting for his novel *Les Chouans*, preserving them for ever within the pages of Romantic literature.

FOUGÈRES GLASSWARE

The influx of Italian glass blowers here in the 16th and 17th centuries stimulated an industry that was already established in the region. There was sand (the base material of glass), there were abundant ferns (*fougères*, rich in soda), and unlimited supplies of wood for the furnaces. In 1646 a glassworks had been established just outside the town.
THE "NOUVELLE CRISTALLERIE DE HAUTE BRETAGNE". Traditional glassmaking is still carried on in this factory, the last one in the region. The giant industrial glassworks have led the company to specialize in high-quality tableware, traditional glasses and luxury scent bottles using techniques largely unchanged since the last century, including mouth-blown glass. The workshops may be visited by appointment.

SHOEMAKERS

From 1870 until World War One Fougères was considered the world capital for feminine footwear. Long before the 19th century, craftsmen were already making clogs, lisle stockings, and woollen or felt slippers with leather soles. In 1868 a native of Fougères named Hyacinthe Cordier (1825–95) modernized this cottage industry by introducing American technology. Success was almost instantaneous, and the town's fortunes prospered: the population grew from 11,000 in 1872 to reach 22,000 by 1906. Even by 1870 twenty-seven shoe factories were employing a large proportion of the town's workforce, and by the 1920's the number had passed one hundred. But between 1946 and 1968 competition forced at least half of them to close.

THE FOUGÈRES CRYSTAL WORKS
Today the factory specializes in goods for the luxury market, such as bottles for the famous perfume houses.

A lady's high-heeled boot decorated with the Fougères coat of arms.

DIFFICULT YEARS
The prosperity of the region in the early years of this century could fluctuate, with serious results. Industrial workers might have to endure long periods of unemployment. Working life was also liable to interruption by strikes: that of 1932 was particularly serious. Below, the cutting-room in the factory of Cordier et Fils.

Fougères castle was built on the site of a wooden fort destroyed by the English in 1166. The massive structure was designed according to a clear strategic plan, begun in the 12th century and repeatedly enlarged until the 15th century. The outworks, the main enclosure and the redoubt form three distinct sections illustrating the medieval defensive plan of progressive withdrawal to the highly fortified keep.

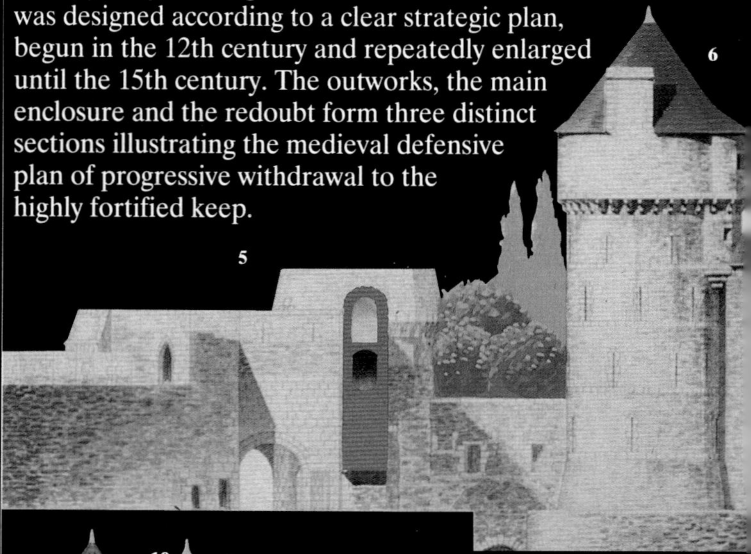

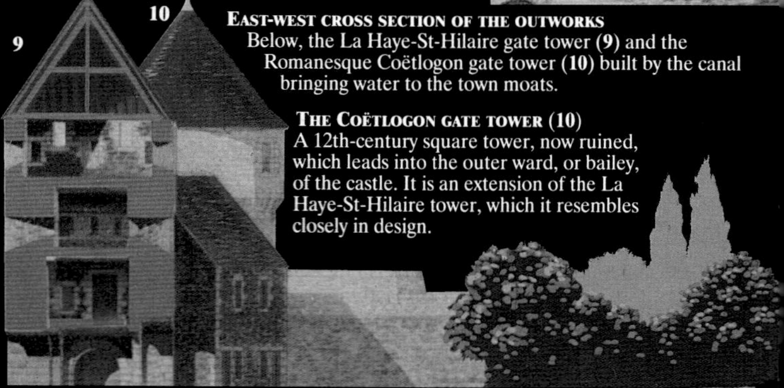

EAST-WEST CROSS SECTION OF THE OUTWORKS
Below, the La Haye-St-Hilaire gate tower (**9**) and the Romanesque Coëtlogon gate tower (**10**) built by the canal bringing water to the town moats.

THE COËTLOGON GATE TOWER (10)
A 12th-century square tower, now ruined, which leads into the outer ward, or bailey, of the castle. It is an extension of the La Haye-St-Hilaire tower, which it resembles closely in design.

Detail of the combination of brackets and arcatures on the machicolation of the Coigny tower.

EASTERN ELEVATION OF THE OUTWORKS
Left, the exterior of the La Haye-St-Hilaire gate tower (**2**) flanked by the 13th-century Plesguen (**1**) and Guémadeuc (**3**) towers. Lower down, the Notre-Dame gate (**4**) is shown from the outside, looking toward the town. The gateway was rebuilt in 1477 with battlements for artillery.

WESTERN ELEVATION OF THE OUTWORKS
The interior façade of the La Haye-St-Hilaire gate tower (**7**), with the Plesguen (**8**) and Guémadeuc (**6**) towers, and the Notre-Dame gate (**5**) shown from within.

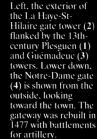

Gorge façade of the Raoul tower (above), with outside steps and door leading to upper floors.

SOUTHERN ELEVATION OF THE KEEP (12)
Left, the postern gate (**11**) led via a drawbridge to the Couarde rock (removed during quarrying in the 19th century). On the left is the Gobelin tower, and on the right the Mélusine tower.

ST-MALO   CANCALE   DOL-DE-BRETAGNE   MONT-ST-MI

CHÂTEAU DU ROCHER-PORTAIL   ● 8

The magnificent château manor house stands just outside
St-Brice-en-Coglès. Construction began in 1617; it is steeply
roofed and handsomely proportioned with a central portion
flanked by wings standing at right angles. Along one side of
the central courtyard a Renaissance arcade with fluted
pilasters leads to a chapel with loophole windows. The other
wing has a large central door and was used as store-rooms.
This is just one of three residences built by Gilles Ruellan,
the commoner turned lord of the manor. He was a
man of humble birth who started out as carter
to a linen merchant and made his fortune by
trading initially in weapons and then in salt.
He invested in land and, as a reward for his
loyalty, Henri IV made him a knight in
1604, and then gave him two baronies. His
fortune was such that he was able to marry his
daughters into the most aristocratic Breton
families and buy his sons seats in the Brittany Parliament

**CHÂTEAU DE LA
MOTTE OR ST-BRICE**
A handsome country
house near to St-
Brice-
en-
Coglès.
Judging by the
elegant chapel and
splendid orangeries,
it was obviously once
extremely grand.

MONT-ST-MICHEL

A BREATHTAKING SIGHT. Approached from Pontorson, the
Mont-St-Michel does not come into view
until the road actually reaches the wide
causeway leading across the bay to its
entrance. The original Mont Tombe was a
tiny granulite islet: two others can still be
seen, one at Tombelaine and one at Dol.
But Mont-St-Michel is an incredible sight,
crowded with houses on its lower slope
and crowned with the monastery buildings
and church. It measures less than a mile in
circumference and rises to a height of 260
feet high. The causeway that links the
mount to the mainland was built in 1880.
ONLY JUST AN ISLAND. Environmental
threats to the bay have attracted a great
deal of concern, particularly about its
gradual silting up. Little by little Mont-
St-Michel is ceasing to be an island as only
very high tides encircle it completely. The
causeway is preventing tides from
sweeping away mud and sand deposits, so

Chemins de Fer de l'État

Le Mont Saint·Michel

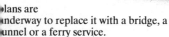

lans are
underway to replace it with a bridge, a
tunnel or a ferry service.

HISTORY

SAINT AUBERT'S DREAM. A 10th-century manuscript tells how,
one night in the year 708, Saint Michael appeared to Aubert,
Bishop of Avranches, in a dream and asked him to build a
church on the Mont Tombe. A small oratory was constructed
and the shrine, now called Mont-St-Michel, was soon drawing
pilgrims who arrived from all over Europe to pay homage to
the warrior Archangel Michael, "Captain of the heavenly
host". It rapidly became one of the most important centers of
pilgrimage in the Christian world.

ZENITH. In 966 a Benedictine monastery was founded. It
received revenue from lands presented by noblemen as well
as a token sum from each pilgrim and soon became a wealthy
establishment. It was both a place of intense spirituality and a
center of learning. The scriptorium, which was already in
existence in the 11th century, reached a peak of activity under
Robert de Torigni, abbot from 1154 to 1186, by whose efforts
so many manuscripts were produced in the monastery that it
became known as the "City of Books".

GOTHIC CONSTRUCTION. In 1204 Breton soldiers set fire to
Mont-St-Michel, destroying parts of the Romanesque
monastery. They had been acting on behalf of the king of
France, Philippe Auguste, who was trying
to expand his kingdom. However, to
atone this act the king gave the
monastery large sums of money which
were used to build new monastic
buildings around the abbey
church. Soaring upward from
the rock, they came to be
known as *La Merveille* (The
Marvel). At the end of
the Hundred Years'
War the English
made
frequent
attacks on

This north-south cross-
section is by the
architect Édouard
Corroyer, who restored
the Mont-St-Michel
between 1872 and 1888.

Saint Michael slaying
the dragon.

**SAINT AUBERT'S
SKULL**
A relic preserved in
the church of St
Gervais d'Avranches.

The famous bay is gradually
becoming silted up with sand.
Over the years land
reclamation has involved the
rerouting of rivers whose
waters used to run into the bay
and wash the sand out to sea.

Architect Paul Gout's reconstruction of the decoration of the 12th-century chapel of St-Étienne.

the mount, which had been fortified from the 13th century. They were unsuccessful, but did manage to make the chancel of the church collapse in 1421. Donations from pilgrims paid for its reconstruction.

DECLINE. From the early 16th century onward monastic activity on the mount dwindled. By the 18th century only about ten monks were still living there. The last few were expelled during the Revolution, when the buildings were taken over as a prison. In 1873 the abbey was handed over to Monuments Historiques, France's institution for the protection of historic buildings.

THE VILLAGE

RAMPARTS. These date from the 15th century and are the most interesting feature of the village. The best way to see them is from below, walking around the rock at low tide. There are seven towers joined by curtain walls all of the same height, and with a *chemin de ronde* linking each one to the next. Starting at the south, these are the TOUR DU ROI, THE TOUR DE L'ARCADE (the only one to have kept its roof), the TOUR BÉATRIX (or *Liberté*), the TOUR BASSE, the TOUR CHOLLET (or *Demi-Lune*) the TOUR BOUCLE, and the TOUR DU NORD. Further on around the mount, the site of St-Aubert's Well is clearly visible, a miraculous spring that was long the only source of fresh water for the monks on the rock.

RAMPART GATES. A series of gateways was constructed to defend the entrance to the village; the outer one, the PORTE DE L'AVANCÉE, was added in the 16th century. The inner Porte du Roy (King's Gate) once had a drawbridge.

GRANDE RUE. Just a handful of the 15th- and 16th-century houses on this stret have escaped conversion into commercial premises in the 20th century. Some are built of stone, like the house that was once the communal bakehouse, with a façade

THE GRANDE RUE
From the gates guarding the entrance to the mount a narrow street curves up the steep slope to the abbey. The many shops and restaurants have been here since the 19th century, though from earliest times pedlars were always ready to ply pilgrims with souvenirs.

A plan for the restoration of the church, in a watercolor of 1848.

supported by two granite arcades. Others are half-timbered:
one of the more remarkable of these is the MAISON DE
L'ARCADE which backs on to the tower of the same name and
spans the staircase leading to the chemin de ronde.

ABBEY

The abbey consists of a densely packed mass of buildings
dating from the 10th to the 16th centuries. They include two
churches and a number of monastic buildings, some in
Romanesque and some in Gothic style. The shape of the
original rock made it impossible to lay the monastery out
according to a standard Benedictine design set around a
cloister. Instead,
the buildings
cling
round
the
steep sides of the
rock, set one above the
other on three levels that
lead up to the abbey church
standing on the summit.

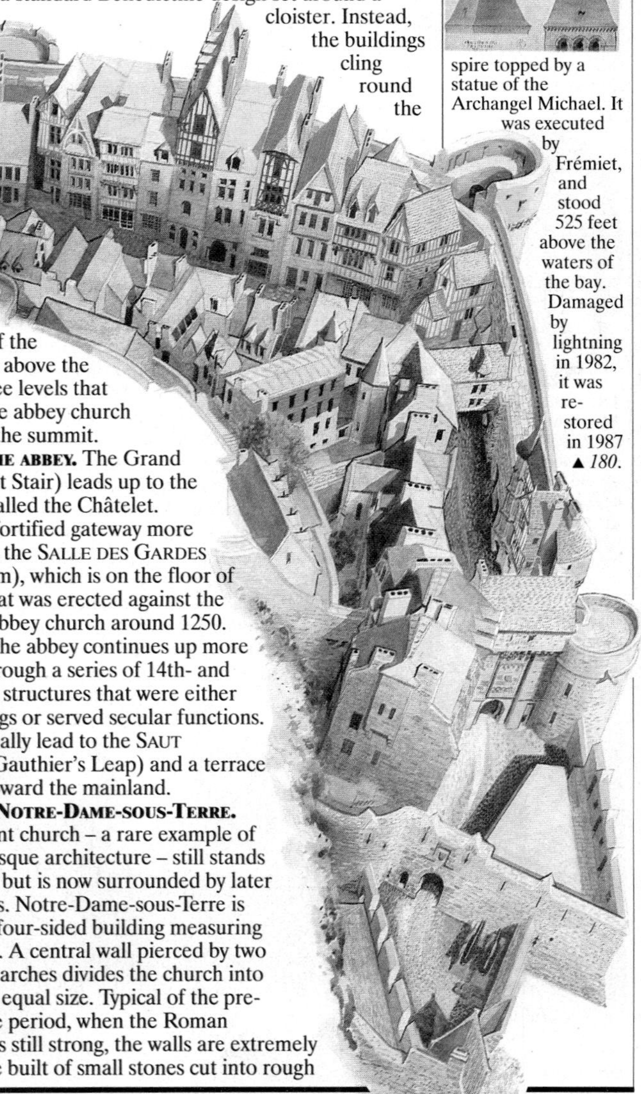

ENTERING THE ABBEY. The Grand
Degré (Great Stair) leads up to the
gatehouse, called the Châtelet.
Beyond the fortified gateway more
stairs lead to the SALLE DES GARDES
(Guard Room), which is on the floor of
a building that was erected against the
apse of the abbey church around 1250.
The tour of the abbey continues up more
stairs and through a series of 14th- and
16th-century structures that were either
abbey lodgings or served secular functions.
The steps finally lead to the SAUT
GAUTHIER (Gauthier's Leap) and a terrace
with views toward the mainland.

CHURCH OF NOTRE-DAME-SOUS-TERRE.
A very ancient church – a rare example of
pre-Romanesque architecture – still stands
on the Mont but is now surrounded by later
constructions. Notre-Dame-sous-Terre is
an irregular four-sided building measuring
36 by 42 feet. A central wall pierced by two
semicircular arches divides the church into
two naves of equal size. Typical of the pre-
Romanesque period, when the Roman
influence was still strong, the walls are extremely
thick and are built of small stones cut into rough

THE SPIRE
In 1894 Victor
Petitgrand submitted
a plan for a 100-foot

spire topped by a
statue of the
Archangel Michael. It
was executed
by
Frémiet,
and
stood
525 feet
above the
waters of
the bay.
Damaged
by
lightning
in 1982,
it was
re-
stored
in 1987
▲ *180*.

179

THE REFECTORY
The embrasured windows along the walls let in a gentle light and also give an impression of increased depth to this beautiful hall, as shown in this drawing.

THE CLOISTER
The robust Caen stone in the spandrels of the colonnade is carved into floral designs, which make the most of the strong light that shines down into this elevated spot to create remarkable effects of light and shade. Inside the cloister is a small garden, and the granite outer walls feature blind arcades and carved trefoils.

squares. When it was put up in the 10th century the church stood in the open, set below the rock's summit to the south and built on a platform between two overhanging rocks. When the abbey church was begun, late in the 11th century, the west end of Notre-Dame-sous-Terre was extended to support part of the nave.

ABBEY CHURCH. The monks built the main church in the 11th century. Today it is one of the oldest sizeable Romanesque buildings to survive in the region. As was the custom for shrines dedicated to Saint Michael, it was built on a rock (in his battles with the devil the saint would bound from rock to rock). Building a cruciform structure nearly 250 feet long on a point was no easy matter. As well as reinforcing and extending the old church to support the first four bays of the nave, three crypts were built up from the steep rocky sides of the mount to create building platforms. In fact only the last three bays of the nave and the crossing sit directly on the rock itself. St-Martin's Crypt forms the foundation of the south transept. Its plainness exemplifies the simple beauty of very early Romanesque structures. The walls are enormously thick, built to take the weight of a barrel-vaulted ceiling that is reinforced by a massive transverse rib in the center. The CRYPT OF NOTRE-DAME-DES-TRENTE-CIERGES, which supports the north transept, is not entirely symmetrical since it was modified in the 13th century during the construction of the Merveille. The NAVE was altered at the end of the 18th century and damaged by fire in 1834, but it is still remarkable. It has a wooden ceiling, and vaulted ceilings over the side aisles only. The CHANCEL had to be reconstructed after it was damaged in the early 15th century. It is in Flamboyant Gothic style, entirely different from the nave and marking the great spiritual and aesthetic changes that had taken place. It is also higher than the nave and transept and is built over the sturdy Crypt des Gros Piliers. One of the chapels on the right in the chancel has a door leading to the ESCALIER DE DENTELLE (Lace Staircase), with exquisite carved stone balustrades. It climbs up over a flying buttress to an open-air gallery with a superb view over the bay.

INTRICATE CARVING
A carving in a spandrel (right) from the
13th-century cloister, showing someone
picking grapes. Left, the statue of the
Archangel that stands high over the abbey.

THE ROMANESQUE ABBEY. The 11th- and 12th-century
buildings that remain below the abbey church, set
around the church of Notre-Dame-sous-Terre, give an
idea of the life led by monks and pilgrims at this time. To
the north, the largest structure has the SALLE DE
L'AQUILON on its lower floor, which served as a
hospitum, or hall where the poor were given shelter.
Sturdy columns, their massive capitals carved with
simple designs, bisect the room. Above it is the
PROMENOIR, a covered walkway that is longer than the
hall below, since the shape of the rock made it possible
to extend the building by two extra bays at the eastern
end. It is also divided in two and its ceiling is an early example
of ribbed vaulting. The DORMITORY on the top floor was partly
destroyed in the late 18th century. From here there is a door
to the church. On the western side are ABBOT ROBERT DE
TORIGNI'S APARTMENTS, built in the second half of the 12th
century. They consist of twin cells, a porter's lodge and the
abbot's living quarters. Torigni also built the funerary CHAPEL
OF ST-ÉTIENNE, which has a connecting door to the infirmary
and another opening into the little graveyard on the east side.
THE GOTHIC ABBEY. Just as Romanesque buildings are set in a
semicircle around Notre-Dame-sous-Terre, so the Gothic
buildings sit in an opposing semicircle around the apse of the
abbey church. Among them is a group of buildings known as
LA MERVEILLE, contained by tall outer walls that rise from the
rocks, reinforced by twenty buttresses. This, one of the finest
examples of 13th-century monastic architecture, consists of
two continuous buildings erected between 1211 and 1228. The
rooms within reflect the hierarchy that dominated their age. It
was a society divided into three classes: commoners, nobles
and clergy. The older of the buildings faces east and on its
lowest floor is the AUMONERIE (*hospitum*) for the poor. Above
lies a hall where the abbot would receive visitors, while at the
top is a REFECTORY divided down the center by columns. At
the bottom of the second building is the CELLAR and above it
the SALLE DES CHEVALIERS (Knights'
Hall) where the monks worked. It is well
proportioned, with a vaulted ceiling
supported by three rows of pillars. On
the third level is an enchanting
CLOISTER.

THE KNIGHTS' HALL
Three rows of short,
broad columns
supporting a
relatively low vaulted
ceiling divide the
wide hall
longitudinally into
four. The carved
capitals and the
strongly defined
molding that outlines
the arches of the vault
are typical of the
Normandy Gothic
style.

DOL-DE-BRETAGNE

ARCHBISHOPRIC. In the 6th century Saint
Samson came from Wales to bring
Christianity to this marshy land. He
founded a monastery and in the 9th
century King Nominoë ● 55 created an
archsee here to free the Breton clergy
from the authority of the archbishop of
Tours. This autonomy lasted only until
1199, but the town of Dol-de-Bretagne
retained its bishop until 1789. In 1793 it
was the scene of one of the most bloody
battles with the Chouans ● 62.
CATHEDRAL. A sturdy structure
reinforced by massive buttresses, the

BISQUINE REGATTAS
The races reached a high point between 1900 and 1905 when spectators came from the holiday resorts of the Côte d'Émeraude. In 1990 a regatta was held to revive the old tradition.

Dol cathedral

A HARD LIFE
Shipowners paid only a small advance to men sailing for Newfoundland. It was not enough to feed a family and women had to do piecework or sell fish to make ends meet.

cathedral looks rather like a fortress. An earlier Romanesque building was burnt down by the English king John Lackland in 1203. Today's cathedral is for the most part a good example of early Normandy Gothic. The SOUTH TOWER was begun in the 12th century and completed in the 17th, while the NORTH TOWER was begun in 1520 and never finished at all. The south front has a marvelous 16th-century porch with intricate stone carvings. In the APSE a magnificent STAINED-GLASS WINDOW dating from the late 12th century illustrates stories from the life of Saint Margaret, Abraham, Saint Samson, the first bishops of Dol and Christ himself. Eighty fine oak STALLS from the early 14th century are carved with leaf motifs and the heads of men and animals. On the left side of the transept lies the TOMB OF BISHOP THOMAS JAMES. The monument was carved in the early 16th century by two Florentine sculptors, and it is one of the first examples of Renaissance art in Brittany. Other interesting features of the cathedral include a modern high altar dating from 1980, a painted wooden figure of the Virgin and Child above the old high altar, and a carved and gilded wooden crook dating from the 16th century.
OLD STREET. A visit to Dol-de-Bretagne should include a stroll along such streets as the GRANDE RUE DES STUARTS, the RUE CEINTE and the RUE LEJAMPTEL. There are some lovely houses to be seen, some dating back to the Romanesque period (e.g. MAISON DES PETITS PALETS, no. 17 Grande Rue des Stuarts) and others going right up to the handsome HÔTELS of the 18th century.

ST-BENOÎT-DES-ONDES

DIGUE DE LA DUCHESSE ANNE. A dike runs alongside the D 155 road from the oyster beds at Nielles as far as the chapel of St-Anne on the other side of Cherrueix, a distance of almost 14 miles. It makes a lovely walk (footpath GR 34), with views over the salt marshes, and punctuated by several 18th-century WINDMILLS. Allow about seven hours.

CANCALE

Today Cancale is a town famous for one thing: its oysters. In the little streets around the port of La Houle, where simple fishermens' cottages stand as a reminder of an isolated existence, the atmosphere of old Cancale is still tangible.

WOMEN OF CANCALE. Until recently life in Cancale was quite unlike life in the rest of France. Business was conducted according to local traditions, religion followed its own pattern, and the people spoke a patois of their own. The men earned their living by fishing so the women came to the fore for six to eight months. They were a formidable though jolly bunch, with predominantly dark brown hair that was said to come from Portuguese ancestors shipwrecked on the coast in the distant past. Certain unusual customs resulted from this matriarchal society. A Cancalaise woman would propose to her man, and after marriage she would continue to use her maiden name. Very often a sailor went off to sea leaving his wife to discover she was expecting a baby. These pregnancies were both frequent and unwanted, and once the boats had sailed for Newfoundland the women would ask one another: "Have you saved yourself this year?"

LA HOULE

CANCALE'S PORT. For centuries the port of La Houle was virtually cut off from the rest of the world. Until 1831 it was joined to the town of Cancale by no more than a path and the sea frequently destroyed the houses of fishermen in the lower part of the town. In 1838 the inhabitants began to replace the dilapidated and inefficient sea wall, erected by the Brittany government in 1773, and put up a new wall and a jetty (below, right) sturdy enough to protect their boats and homes.

FISHING SMACK RESTORED. Since 1987 a real bisquine, the traditional local fishing boat, goes out on fishing trips just like in the old days. *La Cancalaise* has been renovated by a local association of enthusiasts, and is a good example of the style of Normandy boat adopted by Cancale fishermen in the early 19th century. The boats had a large amount of rigging and

OYSTERS AND MUSSELS ■ *32*. Cancale's year-old oyster spat (spawn) now come from Arcachon or the Charente coast, further south. They are raised in protective wire-mesh containers set on raised boards and take three or four years to grow. The town of Vivier sur Mer is known for its special *de bouchot* mussels, which have been farmed since 1954. They are grown clinging to oak posts over an area of 120 square miles.

WATERSIDE AT LA HOULE

Men who fished Newfoundland waters once lived in the cottages that line the quay. They have now been converted into restaurants.

OLD SLIPWAY
The inhabitants of La Houle built the jetty in a large semicircle

to protect their boats from the battering wind and seas. One or two fishing boats are still to be seen in the harbor.

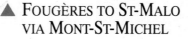

GUNNER FROM THE REIGN OF LOUIS XV
Militiamen (right) were recruited on the spot to defend the coast from enemy attack.

Cancale's famous rock.

COLETTE AT ROZ VEN
A road marked *Blé en Herbe* leads to La Touesse beach, where Colette spent her holidays between 1911 and 1926.

could be used for many purposes: trawling, line fishing and also dredging for oysters.

OYSTER BEDS. Along the coast huge expanses of greyish beach are criss-crossed with Cancale's oyster beds, nine hundred acres of tidal land split into 95 lots and divided from one another by streams. As a result of over-exploitation and increasing pollution, the gathering of wild oysters ceased in the 1920's, and they are now farmed. Modern farming techniques were pioneered here in 1858 by a naval commissaire called Bon who managed to catch oyster larvae using homemade equipment. However, the tides around Cancale proved too strong and the water temperature too variable for the raising of larvae. Nowadays seed oysters are bought in from elsewhere.

VISIT TO AN OYSTER FARM. On Aurore beach the Parcs Kerber oyster farm has set up an excellent little MUSEUM of oyster farming.

CANCALE COAST

From Cancale it is possible to walk to St-Malo along the coast following footpath GR 34 along the coast. The journey can also be made by car along the scenic D 201. The coast path between St-Benoît-des-Ondes and the POINTE DE LA VARDE has long been used by coastguards, and leads past old look-out points and military emplacements, including an 18th-century fort.

POINTE DU GROUIN. This rocky headland has marvelous views over the bay of Mont-St-Michel, the Chausey islands and the Normandy coast. It is worth walking on from the signal station to the end of the point. The headland is well known by ornithologists too, and telescopes have been set up to give a close-up view of the nature reserve on the ÎLE DES LANDES. At the tip of the land a steep path leads down (check the tides) to a CAVE. From here there is an unforgettable view of the HERPIN LIGHTHOUSE out to sea.

ROTHÉNEUF

SCULPTED ROCKS. A bizarre work of art, combined with nature, created by the Abbé Fouré (1839–1910). For twenty-five years the priest chiseled at the rocks near Rothéneuf, carving over three hundred weird figures, grimacing faces and strange sea monsters now known by names such as Gargantua, the Egyptian, High-Tail and Lucifer.

St-Malo

The city, *186*

St-Servan, *193*
Coastal forts, *196*
The privateers, *198*

**JACQUES CARTIER
(1494–1557)**
In 1534 François I
commissioned Cartier
to find a northwest
passage through
Newfoundland to
China. Failing that, he
should search for
gold. He first
explored the mouth
of the St-Lawrence
river. In 1535 he
reached Montreal,
where he was snowed
in for the winter.
A third mission in
1541 proved
unproductive.

ST-MALO AND LE CLOS-POULET

The region of St-Malo derives its name from *Pagus Aleti*, the
ancient Gallo-Roman capital that was built on the site of what
is now St-Servan ▲ *193*. In the mid-12th century it became
the seat of the Archbishop, and was under the rule of a
bishop, who was nominally its overlord, together with a board
of canons. There were many political differences with the
feudal Duke, which escalated into open defiance of Duke
Jean IV between 1379 and 1394, when the city declared for
the King. It became a separate French province in miniature
for twenty years. In 1590 the population rebelled against the
governor, who supported the Protestant king Henri IV, and
proclaimed itself an independent republic.

A CITY OF SHIPOWNERS

By the 16th century St-Malo was a key international port, its
wealth founded on the fishing-grounds in Newfoundland, on
the export of Brittany canvas and linen ● *60*, and on maritime
trade with Spain. An influential class of seagoing shipowners
emerged. In 1688 France entered the European war as an
important maritime power, with St-Malo as an ideal target for

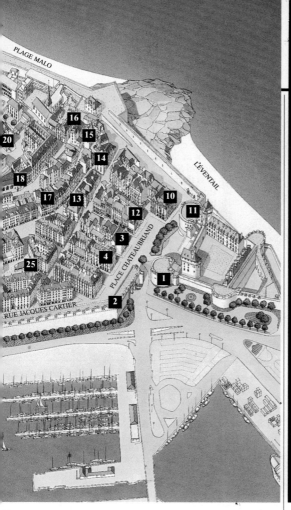

the English fleet, which attacked it in 1693 and 1696. Fortresses sprang up all round the city ▲ *196*, and its seagoing workforce became pirates in all but name. In 1698 they opened up the sea route round Cape Horn to win over the Spanish colonies of Chile and Peru, and exploited the potential offered by the South Seas trade. In 1713 the Treaty of Utrecht put an end to these years of glory: St-Malo lost the monopoly over trade with India and was slow to exploit trade with the West Indies. Even the coming of the railway in the reign of Napoleon III failed to turn its fortunes around. St-Malo was a key feature of the Atlantic defenses in 1944, and most of the city was destroyed by American bombardment.

A WALK IN THE FOOTSTEPS OF KINGS

The best way to discover St-Malo is to begin with a tour of the ancient walls. The view from the old ramparts gives the best idea of the city as it used to be. The ocean, the changing colors of the sky and the impressive ancient buildings combine to suggest the image of a vast stone ship about to weigh anchor and sail away.

LE CLOS-POULET
The citadel of Aleth ▲ *193* has the best views over St-Malo, as shown in this 1930 oil painting by the Le Havre artist Othon Friesz (1879–1949). Aleth and Le Clos-Poulet, the region around St-Malo, both derive their names from *Pagus Aleti*, the Gallo-Roman

settlement later known as Plou d'Alet.

PORTE ST-VINCENT

La Porte Saint-Vincent. – St. Vincent Gate

THE GATE. It was built in 1708 to ease the passage of traffic and is still the main entrance to the city. Two wooden shields bearing the arms of St-Malo and of Brittany, with the legend *Semper Fidelis*, are clearly visible as you pass through. On the pedestrian passage through the gate is the little PORTE DU BIDORET, behind which is a small chamber where tardy travelers who missed the 10 o'clock curfew were confined for the night. The curfew remained in force from the Middle Ages until 1770.

ARMORIAL BEARINGS OF THE CITY
Sailors from St-Malo proudly gave the name of their city to "Las Malvinas", today the British colony of the Falkland Islands. The arms of the city have undergone changes since they were first devised in the 14th century, and were redesigned in 1949. They are clearly visible on the St-Vincent Gate (above), one of the town's two principal entrances situated near the cathedral of the same name.

THE PLACE CHATEAUBRIAND AND ITS 18TH-CENTURY TOWNHOUSES. The square is a fine example of military architecture, which permeated St-Malo when the king's engineers arrived and began to redevelop the city. These stone buildings, up to seven stories high, needed heavily reinforced foundations because of the sandy soil. Elegant arcades at street level housed shops and craftsmen's premises, and the wealthy shipowners of St-Malo lived above.

THE GREAT GATE

THE GATE. It was once the main entrance to the city and is an outstanding example of early 15th-century military architecture, designed to ensure the port's security in the event of attack.

STATUE OF NOTRE-DAME-DE-BON-SECOURS. The statue, in painted limestone, dates from the 15th century and dominates the main gate. It was thought to have miraculous powers, and to have been responsible for quenching flames of the great fire of 1661, which destroyed more than 287 wooden houses. After this disaster, it became obligatory to build houses in stone on the harbor front.

THE GREAT GATE
Its two massive towers were built in the 15th century to defend the harbor. Now they look down on hordes of little sailing-boats moored at the quayside.

PORTE ST-LOUIS

HÔTEL TRUBLET DE NERMONT (1724) This is now a branch of the Banque de France. Its façade has been disfigured by modern additions, but it still has a fine projecting front and mansard roof with double incline.

HÔTEL MAGON DE LA LANDE. The building originally had vaulted cellars, shops on the first floor and three upper stories divided into apartments. The rear elevation of the house facing the garden can be seen from the ramparts: there is a double flight of exterior stairs, and running along the side of the Rue de Toulouse are the stables, having a flat terraced roof overlooking the harbor. Between the third and fourth windows on the right is a mezzanine room. This was a typical feature in old houses of the region and was known as a *tréhory*; it gave directly on to the kitchen and functioned as the servants' living-quarters.

BASTION ST-LOUIS

The bastion was built to replace the earlier buttress wall built in the late 16th century by the Duc de Mercoeur (1558–1602). The building work took place from 1716 to 1721, in two stages. The watchtower in the corner, and the iron rings to which the cannons were affixed to limit their recoil can still be seen. Together with the fortress of Naye opposite, the bastion was intended to defend the harbor basin. The flight of steps leading down to the city is known as the "Red Staircase": during the Revolution executions were carried out in the Place Chateaubriand, and when not in use the guillotine was probably kept in one of the street-level storerooms. Since 1973 a copy of a statue of the St-Malo pirate DUGUAY-TROUIN originally cast in the 18th century overlooks the CALE DE LA BOURSE and the sliding bridge (1986), which leads to the HARBOR DEPOT, an impressive structure in glass, granite and metal.

PORTE DE DINAN

THE GATE. It was formerly known as the Marine Gate, and from 1714 it was through this entrance that the inhabitants of Dinan entered the city, having sailed down the Rance. From the Dinan quay visitors can take a trip to Dinard in a small motorboat and enjoy fine views of the bay, which can be crossed in just 15 minutes.

BASTION ST-PHILIPPE. The ramparts here command magnificent views, with (from left to right) the Rance estuary, Dinard, the Pointe du Décollé, and in fine weather Cap Fréhel and the small ISLAND OF HARBOUR ▲ *197*. Further over is Le Petit Bé, with the island of Cézembre and the FORT OF LA CONCHÉE ▲ *196* in the background. It lies just over 2 miles north of the city, and is considered one of Marshal Vauban's finest designs. It was one of the first fortifications ever to be built on a submerged rock, and construction, which took place from 1692 to 1695, was beset with difficulties. There were not only the problems offered by the site to contend with but the English as well, who in 1693 set fire to the scaffolding and kidnapped the workforce. The fort is awaiting

Plage de l'Éventail beneath the castle walls.

THE BEACH BENEATH THE RAMPARTS
At the foot of its ancient city walls, St-Malo has pleasant beaches at low tide. The beaches of Bon-Secours (below) and the Mole (access through the Estrées gate) are excellent for walking, as is the

BÉS GATE
The gate, built in 1871, leads to Bon-Secours beach, and beyond (tides permitting) to the islets of Petit and Grand Bé ▲ *197*.

ST-MALO

ST-MALO CASTLE
Sections and elevations of parts of the castle from Regnault's *Atlas of Military Buildings* (1857). Below: a storm on the Chaussée du Sillon, December 2, 1862.

THE LEGEND OF SAINT MALO
Having left Wales with a band of followers, Malo arrived in the region of Aleth in the late 6th century. He stopped at the island of Cézembre, where he greeted the monk Festivus and banished a dragon. He finally settled at Saintes, where he died and from where in the 8th century a religious procession set out for Aleth carrying the head and the hand of its first bishop.

restoration, and landing there is forbidden. In the summer trips to the ISLAND OF CÉZEMBRE leave from the quay. The beach is the whitest in the whole bay but the rest of the island is out of bounds, due to persisting danger of German mines.

BASTION DE LA HOLLANDE

Built to keep English ships out of the bay, this bastion also housed the kennels of the watchdogs that patrolled the shore. On the rampart is a STATUE of the great Renaissance navigator JACQUES CARTIER, a native of St-Malo. The bronze was cast in 1905 by Bareau, financed by subscribers from Canada, the country that Cartier had claimed for François I in 1534.

AROUND THE CASTLE

PLACE CHATEAUBRIAND. The very heart of the city, where people relax in one or another of three famous St-Malo cafés. The BRASSERIE DES VOYAGEURS boasts two enormous paintings by Gustave Alaux, one of them a view of the harbor in the 17th century. The CAFÉ DE L'UNIVERS still has the elegant décor of its former life as the St-Malo Yacht Club, with turtle shells, diving gear, and models and photographs of old racing craft. Legend has it that the famous oceanographer Jean Charcot had his final drink here in 1936 before setting out on the voyage from which he never returned. The CAFÉ CHATEAUBRIAND has a splendidly preserved *fin-de-siècle* interior.

THE CASTLE. Set a little to one side of the city, the castle has always been a potent symbol of ducal and then of royal power to the inhabitants of St-Malo (the Malouins). It owes its present appearance to Marshal Vauban (1633–1707). The castle is joined to the TOUR QUIC-EN-GROIGNE, and incorporates part of the original battlements. The horseshoe-

haped keep, the GROS DONJON, is 112 feet high and was built
o stand guard over what was then the main entrance to the
ity, the St-Thomas Gate. Today it houses the town's museum
f history. In 1475 the Pope gave Duke François II a piece of
and next to the Gros Donjon on which to build a tower to aid
im in his struggle against the king of France. This is the
OUR GÉNÉRALE. Its walls are 23 feet thick in places, and
nside is the Museum of Ethnography of the Malouin Region.

T-MALO MUSEUM OF HISTORY. The museum is largely
evoted to the history of the pirates ▲ *198* of the region,
xplained through a collection of objects, curios, models and
aintings. Among the items on display are the famous portrait
f the writer Chateaubriand, and an extraordinary picture of
he room in which he was born, made out of the author's hair
y his barber. One of the strongest images in the museum is
he gigantic figurehead of an old sailing-ship, and there is a
ine collection of miscellanea collected by the great sailor
Robert Surcouf (1773–1827), who fought valiantly against the
English in the Napoleonic wars.

MUSEUM OF ETHNOGRAPHY OF THE MALOUIN REGION. The
hrilling story of the Newfoundland fishermen from St-Malo,
nd daily life in the region in former times are documented in
his small museum.

QUIC-EN-GROIGNE GALLERY. This private museum,
ounded in 1947, recreates great moments in the town's
istory, with models of the great and famous who lived
ere, and backdrops of painted scenery.

RUE CHATEAUBRIAND. There are several elegant stone
ownhouses in this street that are typical of the 17th
entury. They are built of granite from the island of
Chausey and of schist from nearby St-Cast. At no. 3 is
he HÔTEL DE GICQUELAIS (1640), which was the
irthplace of Chateaubriand and is in fact two separate
ouses. No. 4 is the HÔTEL DE LA BLINAIS (1670), the
ypical home of a wealthy shipowner in the late 17th

**FRANÇOIS-RENÉ DE
CHATEAUBRIAND**
(1768–1848) St-
Malo's most famous
son was born near the
Quic-en-Groigne
tower, in poor
but genteel
circumstances, the
tenth and last child of
impoverished parents.
Unwilling to enter the
church or the law as a
career, he joined the
army and left for
Paris in 1786 at the
age of eighteen. Later
he lived for a while in
both America and
England, and wrote
perceptively about his
experiences. At his
own request he was
buried on the islet of
Grand Bé, off
St-Malo.

THE HOUSE OF DUCHESS ANNE
This superb late medieval building has been meticulously

restored. The architectural style of the main building and the tower is typical of the pre-Renaissance period. Today (above) it appears just as it did in the late 15th century; two extra stories, visible before restoration (above right), have been removed.

ST-MALO IN RUINS
The photograph shows all that remained of the area round the castle after the terrible bombardment by American forces in 1944.

century. Inside the courtyard at no. 11 are elegant glazed galleries, and a small staircase, the work of some long-dead ship's carpenter.

OLD ST-MALO ● 9:

DUCHESSE ANNE. At no. 2 stands the building known as the HOUSE OF DUCHESS ANNE, a beautiful turreted edifice dating from the 15th century. Like the Hôtel Beaumanoir at Dinan ▲ 153, it is a perfect example of a great late medieval townhouse. That this was actually the home of Duchess Anne is pure fabrication, although wealthy and influential people

certainly did live here in the early 16th century. At no. 10 is a magnificent private house dating from 1673, with fine interior décor and a coffered ceiling painted with a trompe l'oeil design by Rennes craftsmen. Paneled beams and moldings define its three bays, and in the center are three medallions with allegorical and mythological figures such as Peace, Fame and Providence. Other equally magnificent interiors existed in the 1670's. The paneling in the mayor's apartments, which must have come from a long-vanished noble house, is another example.

RUE DU PÉLICOT. The small turreted house at no. 1 is an excellent example of a 16th-century country house. Those at nos. 3 and 5 have a first floor built of stone and a gallery above, typical of the early 17th century.

RUE MAHÉ DE LA BOURDONNAIS. Of interest at no. 2 are the Renaissance patterns on the imposing PORTAL, part of which is 16th century, although the house itself was built in 1652. It was the birthplace of the naval commander Bertrand François de la Bourdonnais (1699–1753), who was to harry the English fleet so successfully off the coast of India.

RUE DU COLLÈGE. At no. 2 the HÔTEL DE PLOUËR (1698–1700) shows the stylistic transition between the bourgeois townhouses of the 17th century and the military architecture of the following years. It was built on the site of an old cemetery by a wealthy Malouin shipowner called Pierre de la Haye, Comte de Plouër. It has an imposing monumental gateway and was one of the first houses to have a courtyard large enough to admit carriages.

ST-MALO REBUILT

On August 14, 1944, after a week of American bombardment designed to drive the German garrison out of the town, 80 percent of St-Malo lay in ruins. Rebuilding and restoration work were carried out according to strict guidelines The large old hipped roofs and stately chimneys were meticulously restored: only features such as lintels, cornices and coping stones were prefabricated in cement for reasons of speed and economy. The enormous task of rebuilding began in 1948 and was

FORT D'ALET · VESTIGES OF THE RAMPARTS · CATHEDRAL RUINS · SOLIDOR TOWER · COVE OF ST-PÈRE · ST-MALO INTRA-MUROS · SABLONS LIGHTHOUSE · CHURCH OF SAINTE-CROIX · LE VAL-MARIN · ENGLISH CEMETERY

ompleted in
953. Today the
estoration of St-Malo
 proudly regarded as an
utstanding success.

HE CITADEL OF ALETH

n this rocky promontory there once stood a Coriosolite
ettlement that formed the capital of the region in the
st century BC. The settlement's harbor was the cove of
olidor, which was well protected from the sea, and there was
 great deal of trade with the Channel Islands and the south
 oast of Britain.

HE GALLO-ROMAN TOWN. The Romans moved the capital
 land to Corseul, leaving only the harbor at Aleth. A
 UMPING STATION that replenished the fresh-water supply of
 oored ships has been discovered in the harbor. Aleth
 ecame an important place once again in the 3rd century AD,
 hen the Romans moved back, and the citadel became a
 ace of refuge from the privateers that abounded in the
 egion. It was surrounded by stout RAMPARTS, and around the
 ar 350 a CASTELLUM was built to house the Roman legion.
 he BASTION WALLS and the base of the eastern tower are all
 at remain of the enclosure. Having regained its status as a
 apital city, it became a cathedral town in the 6th century,
 ith St-Malo as its first bishop. From the arrival of Briton
 efugees at the end of the 5th century until the Norman
 vasion of 1066, the city developed further and became an
 nportant religious center. But the rising tides worked
 elentlessly on the face of the land. The removal of the
 shop's seat to the town of St-Malo in 1146 set the official
 al of decline on Aleth.

HE FORT AND THE CAMPING SITE. The CAMPING SITE at the
 astern end of the peninsula enjoys unrivaled views over St-
 alo. A walk down the PROMENADE DE LA CORNICHE shows
 e old shipping roads, while in the northeast are the ruins of
 fort built in 1758 by the English after the occupation of St-
 ervan. During World War Two the promontory was heavily
 ortified by the Germans: fuel tanks and electrical systems
 ere concealed in underground bunkers. Now open to the
 ublic, it houses the 1939–45 Memorial on several levels.

MINTING
The ancient
Coriosolite capital of
the 1st century BC has
left its mark on the
promontory of Aleth.
The local center of
regional archeology
has been digging in
the area for twenty
years, and in summer
there are guided tours
of the excavations.
The Coriosolite coin
below was found on
the site: staters and
quarter-staters were
minted in an alloy of
copper and silver.

193

TOUR SOLIDOR

The three joined towers of the fortress which Théophile Briant aptly likened to an ace of clubs, stand high above the estuary. The original Breton name was *steir dor*, "gate of the river"; there is now a 750-yard wide tidal power station across the entrance to the Rance. There are numerous drawings, plans, and elevations of the Tour Solidor. They are kept in the Direction du Patrimoine library (above) and also in the Archives de Vincennes.

(Left, the 1697 Garangeau plans). From the top of the tower there is a view up the Rance, which François-René de Chateaubriand described as "an endless stretch of rocks and greenery, sandy spits, wooded banks, creeks, and tiny riverside villages".

Port Solidor

Tour Solidor. This 14th-century fortress dominating the Rance estuary is 90 feet high. Since 1970 it has housed the Museum of Cape Horn Sailing Ships. It stands on the site of a Roman *castellum* and consists of three towers linked by stone curtains. From the time of the Revolution until 1811 it was a prison for French soldiers and for English prisoners-of-war, as graffiti carved in the wall shows. In 1985 a cross was erected in front of the tower in memory of Jacques Cartier, who set out from this spot on his second voyage in 1535 ▲ *186*.

The International Museum of Cape Horn Sailing Ships Anyone interested in the history of sail will be delighted by this tiny museum. Three rooms deal with the discovery of Cape Horn, while the rest of the collection shows life aboard the long-distance sailing vessels. The items range from charts and ships' instruments to objects made by sailors on their lengthy voyages, and a huge stuffed albatross.

AN EXHAUSTING LIFE
Ships could all too easily get stuck in Antarctic ice, as shown in this 1909 picture by Mohrmann. The sailor below, seen putting a model ship in a bottle, is not yet thirty years old. Voyages of eight to twelve months' duration had a tendency to accelerate the ageing process.

ROUND THE HORN
The crew of the *Thiers*, a square-rigged three-master

St-Malo and Cape Horn

Officially, the first Frenchman to sail round Cape Horn into the Pacific was a Malouin named Gouin de Beauchesnes. In 1698, hoping to establish peaceful and profitable relations with Peru and Chile, he embarked on the 13,000-mile voyage from St-Malo to Callao stopping only at the Canaries and the Cape Verde Islands. Before long, other intrepid sailors began to follow his example. Because of the high risks of such a voyage which took 20 to 28 months to complete, the rewards were substantial. The traders also dealt in costly luxury goods; the finest-quality linen and silk were exchanged for silver ingots from Potosí. The high cost of the voyages was met by capital raised all over France and by ship-owners floating shares to be traded in all the French centers of commerce. From 1778 the Cape was also a center of the whaling industry. In 1850 the discovery of the Californian goldfields became a further incentive to make the perilous voyage round Cape Horn, and also marked the start of the industrial exploitation of the Pacific. Once the supply of gold dried up, the cargo was replaced by guano (birdlime, highly prized as a fertilizer) from Chile and the Chincha Islands off Peru. The Cape Horn ships brought wool from Sydney, corn from California and Oregon, nitrates from Chile and coal from New South Wales. But from 1880 the supremacy of the great sailing vessels was threatened by the new steamships. This, together with the opening of the Panama Canal in 1914 and World War One, heralded the end of the golden age of the great ships.

THE PORT OF BAS SABLONS. There are 1,200 moorings in this marina, opened in 1976 to popularize sailing as a leisure industry. It is one of the four busiest in Brittany.

of 3,450 tons launched in 1901. The captain wears a cloth cap, while the shipowners have bowler hats.

195

In the 17th century St-Malo was the forem
commercial port of France, but rapid
advances in artillery were making it
vulnerable to attack by the English. In 1
Vauban began work on a vast defensive
plan. His strategy was to build a series of coastal fo
reaching from the Pointe de la Varde to Cap Fréhel.

FORT DE LA VARDE
The fort dates from 1758 and was built on the site of the Vauban battery. It marks the eastern end of the St-Malo coastal defenses. In 1898 a modern gun position was set at the tip of the headland, later to be fortified by the Germans in World War Two. It is now listed as an historic monument.

LA CONCHÉE
The fort covers the entire surface of a submerged rock lying 22 miles north of St-Malo and 1 mile east of the island of Cézembre. Its purpose was to defend the "passe aux Normands", a sea passage that was beyond the reach of the cannons of La Varde and Cézembre. The fort is shown as it is today.

MODEL AND PLAN
Right, raised relief model of La Conchée made in 1700. Bottom right, opposite page, plan of the fort drawn up in 1694 by Siméon de Garangeau, the King's engineer. Garangeau's arrival in St-Malo was to have important influences on military and civil architecture in the town. He was responsible for the construction of Vauban's most brilliant defenses.

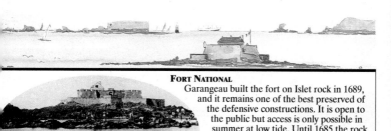

FORT NATIONAL

Garangeau built the fort on Islet rock in 1689, and it remains one of the best preserved of the defensive constructions. It is open to the public but access is only possible in summer at low tide. Until 1685 the rock was a place of execution, with four gibbets and a stake.

THE ISLAND OF HARBOURG

Although once attached to the mainland, the island is now out at sea, opposite Dinard and the Rance estuary. St-Malo is said to have visited the hermit Aaron of Brittany on the rock, on his way over from Britain. In 1697 Garangeau built a fort and barracks that covered the entire rock surface. It is now an historic monument.

LE PETIT BÉ

The fort, guarding the entrance to the Rance, was built by Garangeau between 1689 and 1693 on the site of a smaller fort dating from 1667. It is a tremendous construction of dressed stone, with firing points covering every direction. The main gate was never finished; it opens into thin air, still awaiting a drawbridge.

The shipowners of St-Malo became known as *corsaires*, or privateers. In times of war they were extremely successful in the skill of "la course", an institution dating back to the 13th century but given official sanction by Louis XIV's minister Colbert. Private ships were licensed to assist the navy by giving chase to enemy ships and boarding them. The spoils quickly made St-Malo rich.

ROBERT SURCOUF
He was one of the last St-Malo privateers, engaging in "la course" until 1809. His plundering of English ships made him a hero.

Privateer's ax and powder barrel.

Surcouf's tomb Rocabey cemeter St-Malo. Opposi page, boarding an enemy ship.

THE TAKING OF THE "KENT"
Surcouf's greatest exploit: the *Kent* belonged to the British East India Company.

THE "RENARD"
A privateer's cutter (right) built in 1813 and equipped by Surcouf the following year. A replica, now in St-Malo, was launched in April 1991.

RENÉ DUGUAY-TROUIN
(1673–1736). He was
born into a
shipowning family
and sailed as a
volunteer with a
privateer at the
age of fifteen.
Later he became
a *corsaire* himself
and took over
three hundred
merchant vessels,
twenty warships, and
the city of Rio de
Janeiro in 1711. He was
given a title and a place on
the board of the Compagnie des Indes ▲ *320*,
and ended his career as a naval commander.

PRIVATEERS, NOT PIRATES.
Privateers were legally permitted to pursue
enemy ships. They also had to share the
proceeds with the State. While Colbert
brought in laws controlling privateering in
1681, Vauban encouraged it as "the cheapest
way for the country to wage war". The
practice was abolished in 1856.

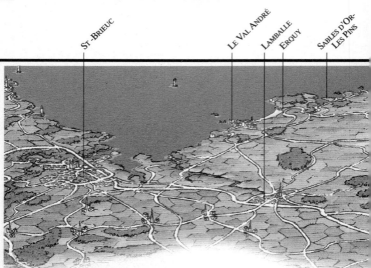

ST-BRIEUC   LE VAL ANDRÉ   LAMBALLE ERQUY   SABLES D'OR-LES PINS

THE RANCE ESTUARY
The tidal power station closes off the estuary (see aerial view, above). On the rock of Bizeux stands a statue of the Virgin by Caravinier. Its unveiling on October 24, 1897 was marked by tragedy. The priest had just finished blessing the statue from a steam launch when a nearby boat foundered and sank, with the loss of several lives.

THE MOUTH OF THE RANCE

TIDAL POWER STATION. The local inhabitants are very proud of their power station (virtually the only one of its kind outside the former USSR), which harnesses the energy of the rising and falling tides. The Rance estuary was chosen as the site on account of the exceptional height of its tide, which at 44 feet is one of the largest in the world. Twenty-five years of research were followed by six years of construction, and on November 26, 1966 the power station was opened by General de Gaulle. It works on a similar principle to that of a tidal mill ● 96, though sophisticated technology allows the turbines to operate while the tide rises and falls, so that energy is produced both during the filling and the emptying of the basin. The huge complex includes a lock, a MACHINE ROOM (open to the public), a dam 400 feet wide and a moving barrage with six sluices. The station produces almost one quarter as much power as a typical nuclear equivalent. Power is transmitted first to Nantes and then to the national grid.

DINARD

A SEASIDE RESORT. Until the middle of the 19th century Dinard was nothing more than a small fishing village, most of whose boats went out on the Newfoundland run. It owes its first popularity as a resort to an English lady by the name of Faber. Mrs Faber found the climate agreeable and the village delightful: in 1852 she rented the Villa Beauregard, and then built the Villa Sainte-Catherine, which was completed in 1858. A rich American gentleman called Coppinger then

The cove of Dinard, illustration of 1886.

settled in Dinard. The village soon became fashionable and attracted large numbers of English tourists who until then had tended to stay at Dinan, Avranches or Pau. Soon Parisian gentlefolk started to visit Dinard, and a local politician called Paul

TRADITIONAL DRESS
Dinard women wore
a headdress with a
crest called a "cock's
comb" ● *70*

Féart,
who had enjoyed his
summer holiday there, decided
to promote Dinard as a tourist resort.

Buildings sprang up to accommodate the summer visitors.
The arrival of wealthy Lebanese count, Joseph Rachaïd Dada,
was an important feather in Dinard's cap. He purchased land,
and built a villa, Deux-Rives, on the Pointe de Moulinet.
COSMOPOLITAN ARCHITECTURE. High spirits and fashion were
the keynotes of Dinard's architecture, an unconventional
mixture of opulent fantasy in a frivolous variety of styles.
Traditional beams, turrets, exotic glasswork, clapboard,
verandas, granite and stucco might all be seen on the same
façade. A style known as "maritime" came into vogue around
1892, but it was ridiculed for enabling its occupants "to see
and to be seen":
perhaps the first
example of this
endearing nonsense was
the VILLA CRISTAL on
the Plage de l'Écluse. In
the inter-war years the
Vicomté district was
developed and a new
architectural trend
emerged, exemplified by
the HÔTEL GRANVILLE,
with its extraordinary
cupola, and the so-
called "Gallic" building
inspired by colonial
architecture. The stock

A VILLAGE TRANSFORMED
A few notable visitors
made Dinard famous
after its discovery by
the Englishwoman
Mrs Faber in 1852.
The British film
festival testifies to the
continuing English
presence in Dinard.

market crash of 1929 sounded the death knell of the *Belle
Époque*: newly impoverished Americans no longer ventured
abroad while the English were frustrated by a law preventing
them from spending money abroad. The first wave of paid
holidays for factory workers in 1936 finally ended the idea of
Dinard as a resort for the well-to-do, who fled to the Riviera.
MARINE MUSEUM AND AQUARIUM. Architect Yves Hemar, one
of the inventors of the style known as neo-Breton, designed
this ingenious rotunda, which now houses an attractive small
museum, together with an aquarium and the Dinard Maritime
Laboratory. In the museum are memorabilia of Commandant
Jean Charcot ▲ *190*.

The Bay of St-Enogat (detail, opposite). Watercolor on yellow paper by Eugène Isabey (1803–86).

Landscape between Dinard and St-Enogat, by Eugène Isabey.

The Villa de la Garde (top) on the Pointe du Moulinet, built in the 19th century by the Hennessy family. Above, the coastal path that leads from the Pointe de la Malouine.

JUDITH GAUTIER AT ST-ENOGAT
Théophile Gautier's daughter entertained such figures as Claude Debussy at her seaside villa.

COASTAL WALKS

One of the delights of Dinard is exploring its coastline and seeing the enormous villas perched on top of the cliffs. It is possible to walk directly from the Pointe de la Vicomté as far as St-Lunaire (approximately three hours) along three successive coastal paths.

PROMENADE DU CLAIR DE LUNE. Ignoring the suggestion of moonlight in its name, it is best to take this delightful walk in the morning or around midday so as to enjoy maximum sunshine. On top of the steep cliffs are a number of delightful villas: this part of Dinard is known as Bric-à-Brac. The lane leads to the YACHT CLUB, which was built in 1879, destroyed and then rebuilt in 1932.

POINTE DU MOULINET. Take the Promenade Robert Surcouf, and then the Chemin de Ronde du Moulinet. This route passes the VILLA DE LA GARDE, built in the last century for the Hennessy family, the cognac millionaires. The family first had demolished another superb villa on the site built around 1860 by the wealthy American John Camac. The "palace" that they constructed is quite fantastic; it has crenelated walls built out of the living rock, bow windows and corner turrets with pointed roofs. Leaving the Villa de la Garde, descend to the Palais des Congrès by the Rue Coppinger, passing the VILLA ST-GERMAIN (this is immediately identifiable by its medieval gateway salvaged from a local ruin) and the VILLA LA ROCHE PENDANTE, with its neo-Gothic windows. A little further on the right-hand side is the opulent VILLA DES DEUX RIVES, once the home of the Lebanese count Joseph Rachaïd Dada but now converted into apartments. From the tip of the Pointe du Moulinet you can enjoy a spectacular view of the bay of St-Malo.

PROMENADE DE LA MALOUINE. The walk begins at the Plage de l'Écluse and goes right along to the Pointe de la Malouine. An esplanade lines the beach, on which stands the CASINO PALAIS D'ÉMERAUDE. The POINTE DE LA MALOUINE derives its name from the villa named La Malouine, built in 1866 by the Duc d'Audiffret-Pasquier, who, out hunting, discovered and fell in love with the spot. It was but a passing passion, however, for Monsieur le Duc sold the property in 1880 to a Captain Poussineau, who immediately divided the estate into lots. The Pointe, which once had only six villas, developed into a lively residential quarter with some of the most outlandish holiday homes in the area.

ST-LUNAIRE

AN ANCIENT HERITAGE. The settlement established here by St-Lunaire in the 6th century developed over the centuries into a flourishing agricultural and fishing community famous for the beauty of its womenfolk. Toward the end of the last century it became a seaside resort thanks to a wealthy Haitian banker named Scylla Laraque. As part of his plan to put St-Lunaire on the map, he built a granite esplanade opposite the beach, and here he built the GRAND HÔTEL and the casino. Domestic life revolved around the Pointe du Décollé, where Laraque had built twenty villas. Fashionable society soon came to spend their holidays at St-Lunaire. Among them was painter Henri Rivière (1866–1951), who in 1891 made ten wood engravings after the Japanese style of the Pointe du Décollé. Others included writer Émile Bergerat (1845–1923), winner of the coveted Prix Goncourt and son-in-law of France's great poet Théophile Gautier, and actress Eve Lavallière, from the Théâtre des Variétés in Paris.

GRAND HÔTEL, ST-LUNAIRE

THE POINTE DU DÉCOLLÉ. During the *Belle Époque* this wooded area was the residential district of St-Lunaire. Its delightful 19th-century villas are set along the BOULEVARD DES ROCHERS and the BOULEVARD DU DÉCOLLÉ. Two fine neo-Gothic examples are the VILLA STE-ANNE and the VILLA LE REVENANT at nos. 55 and 65, Boulevard du Décollé. Look out also for the colonial style VILLA STE-HÉLÈNE (32 Boulevard des Rochers), and the Scottish baronial Manoir KILMALIEU (152 Boulevard des Rochers). From the tip of the Pointe there is an excellent view over St-Lunaire. A GRANITE CROSS was erected here in 1880 to protect the fishermen: sixty men and forty horses were needed to drag it up to the summit.

An early 20th-century postcard showing the sumptuous Grand Hôtel, which overlooks the beach of this fashionable resort.

ST-BRIAC-SUR-MER

A RESORT FOR ARTISTS. Following in the footsteps of St-Malo and Dinard, St-Briac began to develop itself as a tourist resort in the late 19th century. Like Pont-Aven in south Finistère ▲ 312, its remarkable scenery soon made it the haunt of painters. Between 1884 and 1891 Auguste Renoir, Émile Bernard and Paul Signac were among the artists who stayed there.

DINARD GOLF-COURSE. There can be few golf courses anywhere with such a superb setting, overlooking the sea. It was laid out in 1887 on the Plage de Longchamp, backed by a group of Englishmen together with a local banker named Jules Boutin. It was enlarged in 1892.

THE BAY OF LA FRESNAYE
The large expanse of mud flats ■ 40 is seen here at low tide. They are an ideal environment for mussel and oyster beds.

BAIE DE LA FRESNAYE

The bay, basically a tidal reservoir ■ 40 (known locally as a *slikke*), is just under 4 miles long, and a little over 1 mile wide between the fort of La Latte to the west

and the Pointe de St-Cast in the east. Two thirds of the bay are uncovered at low tide, which makes it ideal for angling but especially for bracing walks from St-Cast to neighboring beaches and around the bay. The wealth of marine fauna and flora in the bay has favored the establishment of mussel and oyster beds ■ *32*. The rocky coastline is home to around eight hundred varieties of brown, red and blue seaweed, and about ninety separate species of mollusc. A BEACON at the entrance to the bay recalls the tragedy of the frigate *Laplace*: in 1950 she had just anchored off Fréhel to take part in celebrations for the opening of two locks at St-Malo when she struck a German mine laid during World War Two.

CHÂTEAU VAURG

MONTBRAN TOWER

CHAPEL OF ST-SÉBASTIEN

HENRI RIVIÈRE (1864–1951) Rivière met artist Paul Signac at school in Paris when they were both nine years old. At eighteen the famous cabaret impresario Rodolphe Salis gave him a job editing a weekly magazine, and Rivière soon became a Montmartre personality. Signac later introduced him to St-Briac at a time when he was interested in wood engraving; the result was *Brittany Landscapes*, forty plates inspired by his stay there.

Fort La Latte

The fort of La Latte stands high above the sea, set on a rocky peninsula with access only possible by a drawbridge, and surrounded by walls of local pink sandstone. The first fortress was built here in 937 by a Breton noble named Goyon to protect the region from Norse pirates. The present structure dates from the 14th century and is known locally as "la Roche Goyon". The fort was unsuccessfully besieged first by the English in 1490 and then by the rebellious League in 1597. In May 1694 Marshal Vauban undertook modifications to the place and noted its run-down condition: "The officer commanding the fort is Captain Hoquincourt, who has served in Ireland. He has been here for three years without spending one sou of his allowance. He broke a leg eighteen months ago which still does not appear to have healed . . . his gunnery officer has only one arm: in fact the garrison's two officers between them have only half the requisite number of arms and legs!" In 1815 royalists seized the fort, but were soon dislodged. In 1890 it was sold, passing into private hands, and in 1925 was listed as an historic monument.

TOUR OF THE FORT. The gateway, the platform guarding the entrance and the curtain walls underwent radical alteration in the 17th and 18th centuries. Beyond the drawbridge is the courtyard, enclosed by the guardroom, governor's quarters, water cistern and the chapel. Beyond the so-called "cannon-proof" wall is the WATCHTOWER, dating from the 15th century, and the KEEP, built in 1341. The top of the tower and the battlements command fine views over the Côte d'Émeraude.

AN IMPREGNABLE FORTRESS Although privately owned, the fort is open to the public. The craftsmanship of its construction, no less than the massive strength of its walls and keep, show why it managed to resist all attempts at conquest.

Cap Fréhel

A PLACE OF LEGEND. The high cliffs of schist and pink sandstone overhanging the deep green water are an unforgettable sight. The colors certainly caught popular imagination: according to a legend recounted by local historian Pierre Amiot, they were the result of a miracle. An

D. 34   D. 16   D. 786   GR. 34   D. 13   D. 19   D. 14

ish missionary saint who had
anded here to preach the Gospel one day gathered the
population together opposite the little island of St-Michel and
poke at length of the Archangel. When his sermon was over
local overlord put this question to him, not without irony:
Saint Michael was a messenger of God. You told us that
hen his foot touched the rock, the rock turned red. If you
oo are a messenger of God, can you not turn this cliff red?"
When he heard this the saint turned toward the cliff, made a
ut in his finger and let fall a drop of blood, whereupon the
iffs all round the cape immediately turned red. Spellbound
y this miracle, the entire crowd is said to have undergone
nmediate conversion. The cliffs were also supposed to
ave been haunted by the jolly giant Gargantua, a
egendary figure who often appears in Breton
nythology. At Cap Fréhel it was while he was getting
eady to take a mighty leap that would carry him to Jersey
nat he left his mark. "Preparing to leave . . . he felt a soreness
n his foot, and feeling in his shoe he pulled out a rock.
There's the little pebble that was causing the trouble,' he
ried, throwing it over his shoulder; the spot where it landed
s now the Amas du Cap. Bending down to drink some water,
e jabbed his stick into the ground near the fort of La Latte,
aying: 'So long as the world keeps rolling, as long shall my
ick stay here'. This is now the famous Gargantua's Finger,
so known as his Needle." (Paul Sébillot: *Gargantua in
opular Mythology*.)

RÉHEL LIGHTHOUSE. The present lighthouse stands 338 feet
bove sea level, and its beam can be seen from a distance of
) miles. It was built in 1950 to replace an earlier one dating
om 1847, and destroyed by the Germans during World War
wo. From the top there is a superb view from the top,
xtending from the Pointe de Paimpol in the west to the
ointe de Grouin in the east. On a clear night it is possible to

ON LOCATION
Several epic movies
have been shot at La
Latte fort. Richard
Fleischer's *Vikings*
was made there in
1957, as was Philippe
de Broca's *Chouans,*
some years later.

**THE LEGEND OF
GARGANTUA**
Painter and
ethnologist Paul
Sébillot was
fascinated by French
folklore, and made a
detailed study of the
legendary good-
humored giant
immortalized by
Rabelais. He claimed
that Gargantua
originated in Celtic
myth, and was later
identified by the
Romans with
Hercules.

see the beam of the lighthouse at La Corbière on the southwest tip of Jersey, 30 miles away.

THE OLD LIGHTHOUSE (OR TOUR VAUBAN). It was built of Chausey granite in the reign of Louis XIV to designs by Simon Garengeau, and was powered initially by coal. Later the lamp was adapted to burn fish oil, until rapeseed oil came into common use.

The old lighthouse stood 40 yards from the Vauban tower and was electrified in 1886.

BIRD SANCTUARY ■ *22*. There are almost 4 miles of promontories and islets with steep cliffs around Cap Fréhel, home to some seven or eight hundred pairs of nesting birds. A hazardous rocky path, on which great caution is advised, offers fine views of the birds soaring round the cliffs. Two islets, LA PETITE AND LA GRANDE FAUCONNIÈRE (formerly the breeding-ground of peregrine falcons) to the east of the cape, are home to a colony of guillemots, auks, oyster-catchers, shags, kittiwakes, great and lesser black-backed gulls, and in spring and summer a few pairs of gannet from the Sept Îles. The POINTE DU JAS to the west of the Cape has a colony of petrels. From the path leading to it, birds of another sanctuary can be seen in the distance, on the cliffs of the AMAS DU CAP opposite. The Society for the Protection of Wild Life in Brittany (SEPNB) sometimes organizes guided visits.

RAVEN
A few pairs of ravens inhabit the islets of La Petite and La Grande Fauconnière. They are protected birds because they are now extremely rare: there are estimated to be only ninety nesting pairs in the whole of Brittany. The bird has black plumage, a powerful beak and points on its wingtips.

HEATHLAND (LA LANDE) ■ *48*. To the south and southeast of Cap Fréhel are more than 1,000 acres of heathland (one of the biggest in western Europe) where, according to season, various heathers, thyme, sea-pink, hyacinth, many different mosses and lichens, and even flowering fern, can be found, making it a treasure trove for the botanist. Its bleak, uninviting appearance in winter gives way in spring through fall to a riot of color, the purple heather blending with the brilliant gold of gorse. The heathland used to be carefully tended by the local inhabitants. Every ten or twelve years the vegetation would be cut closely back and the tiny gorse seeds gathered at the beginning of summer resown. There are still about half a million acres of heathland in Brittany, forming an ideal environment for rabbits, foxes and many other small mammals and an impressive variety of birds.

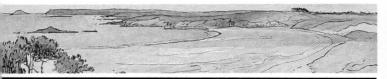

SÉVIGNÉ COVE. To reach the fort of La Latte on foot take footpath no. GR 34, which runs along the cliffs surrounding Sévigné cove. The cove is famous in folklore for the TEIGNOUSE GROTTO, where a fairy is said to have lived. Many folk tales of the Fréhel region were collected by Paul Sébillot.

SABLES D'OR-LES PINS

A SEASIDE RESORT IN THE MAKING. With its immense beach of fine sand, the best in all Brittany, Sables d'Or-Les Pins is in a class by itself. The resort was created between 1922 and 1924 by two entrepreneurs, Roland Brouard and Bernard Launay. They chose the beach at Minieu, where dunes, sea and woodland formed a perfect setting. "I tried to blend architecture with nature," said Brouard in 1934, "by creating carefully planned contours that formed an agreeable landscape in which to build a small town without slums or squalor." In under ten years this idealistic visionary built a holiday resort with spacious avenues, flower gardens and romantic walks. By 1924, seven miles of avenues had been laid out, with leveled building plots ready for sale and fresh spring water piped everywhere. Publicity bills and a program of entertainments sang the praises of this new "Golden Horn" in the west. In 1923, Brouard turned the publicity generated by the first crossing of the Sahara (in caterpillar tractors, organized by the Citroën company) to his own advantage, bringing in two of the vehicles to clamber up and down the dunes.

ARCHITECTURE 1924–30. The two architects chiefly responsible for this development were Yves Hémard and Pol Abraham (1891–1966), whose attempts to popularize the Art Deco style found little favor. Social, sporting and cultural life reached a peak here in the years 1924–28. But inept management and the crash of 1929 put paid to Brouard's plans, and further work on the project was halted. The uncompleted Hôtel des Arcades was repossessed and sold by creditors in 1932. Financially ruined, alone and ill, Brouard lived to see his dreams shattered. He died in January 1934.

SABLES D'OR TODAY. Its magnificent setting, broad graceful avenues and charming architectural design still work their spell on visitors. At first glance it becomes obvious that the town is unfinished. A stroll around Sables d'Or, along the few short promenades that were created, is a profoundly nostalgic experience: the VALLÉE DE DIANE with its open-air theater is now deserted, just like the southern beach at the southwest entrance to this beautiful broken dream.

ERQUY

The origin of this unusual name is uncertain. It may derive from the Breton words *er* and *gwick* ("eagle" and "mountain"), from *c'herregi* ("the rocks"), or most probably from *ar cae* ("entrenchment"), a reference to the trenches of Catuelan and the Pleine Garenne that were on the Cap d'Erquy.

"THE BEACH AT ERQUY"
Ink and watercolor on paper, painted by FRANCIS AUBERTIN in 1897.

GOOD PUBLICITY
"For a wonderful holiday, come to Sables d'Or-Les Pins in beautiful Brittany, where man and nature between them have created a resort unique in the world. All our guests have a happy and healthy stay, whatever their special tastes or requirements." This alluring offer comes from a poster that first appeared in 1935.

THE SCALLOP
The scallop is the symbol of St James the Apostle. It is a bivalve mollusc with a flat base and convex upper shell.

JEAN RICHEPIN
(1849–1926)
The poet is buried in the graveyard at Pléneuf. He was born in Algeria and after graduation joined a mercenary regiment, leading a hard life between 1871 and 1875. He next appeared in the Latin Quarter of Paris, where he was feared for his quick temper. A book of poems, *The Beggar's Song* (1876), was widely condemned for immorality, and Richepin moved away to Val-André. There, the Côte d'Émeraude provided inspiration for another collection of poems, *The Sea* (1886).

The Port of Dahouët, by Albert Robida.

SCALLOPS. Erquy jealously guards its reputation as the foremost scallop-fishing ground in France. At least 10 percent of the three thousand inhabitants are fishermen. Its golden age was the decade between 1965 and 1975, when production accounted for 95 percent of the national output. The season lasts from November to March and is strictly controlled. The scallops are brought up by dredging. Since the 1980's the supremacy of Erquy scallops has faced competition from cheaper imported shellfish.

AROUND PLÉNEUF-VAL-ANDRÉ

CHÂTEAU OF BIENASSIS. This impressive moated castle with walls of pink Erquy granite could once be reached only by a drawbridge. The present 17th- and 18th-century building is essentially residential, but the original castle built by Geoffroy du Quélénec early in the 15th century was a late medieval fortified construction. One tower still stands to the rear of the present house, containing a spiral staircase of megalithic proportions. On the south side the surviving building dates from 1650–60, and 1690–1700 on the north. The château is lived in, but may be visited.

PLANGUENOUAL. This beautiful dovecote with four turrets is unique in Europe. It was saved from ruin and restored by enthusiasts between 1980 and 1984. Originally it belonged to the manor of Vaujoyeux, which no longer exists. There is an interesting four-hour walk, which passes the dovecote and takes in several chateaux nearby, including the romantic MANOIR DE LA PETITE HERVÉ.

PLÉNEUF-VAL-ANDRÉ

The village was first settled in the Paleolithic period. It became a Christian settlement in the 5th century under the guidance of Saint Symphorian, who is commemorated in a small chapel where the villagers would invoke his name in times of drought. But their traditional way of life was wrecked forever in 1882 when the village of Val André sold land on the Pointe de Pléneuf to developers, to be divided into building sites. Pléneuf became another seaside resort. The cultural touch was added by poet Jean Richepin, who lived here until his death in 1926, but Pléneuf's best years came when paid holidays became legally compulsory in 1936.

BEACH OF VAL-ANDRÉ. One of the finest on the north coast of Brittany. A promenade leads up to the Pointe de Pléneuf, with marvelous views of Erquy and the bay of St-Brieuc.

THE PORT OF DAHOUËT. A tiny harbor on the estuary of the river Flora, safely protected from the fierce tides, Dahouët fishing-boats went out in search of cod as far as Iceland until the beginning of the present century. In 1509 its fishermen were the first to cross the Atlantic and exploit the fishing-grounds of Newfoundland.

St-Brieuc

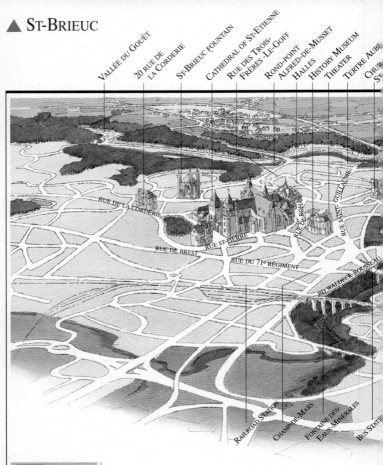

VALLÉE DU GOUËT · 20 RUE DE LA CORDERIE · ST-BRIEUC FOUNTAIN · CATHEDRAL OF ST-ÉTIENNE · RUE DES TROIS-FRÈRES-LE-GOFF · ROND-POINT ALFRED-DE-MUSSET · HALLES · HISTORY MUSEUM · THEATER · TERTRE AUBÉ · CHUR S

RUE DE LA CORDERIE · RUE DE BREST · RUE ST-PIERRE · RUE DU 71e RÉGIMENT · RUE DE ROHAN · RUE SAINT-GUILLAUME · BD WALDECK-ROUSSEAU

RAILROAD STATION · CHAMP-DE-MARS · FONTAINE DES EAUX-MINÉRALES · BUS STATION

A poster from between the wars promoting the port of Légué, now in the Musée de la Publicité in Paris.

MAX SAUER BRUSH FACTORY
Seventy percent of the brushes used by French artists are made here. Exported brands include Raphaël, Berge et Joris, and Isabey et Renaissance.

HISTORY

CATHEDRAL CITY. The early history of St-Brieuc centers almost entirely around religion. It is today the capital city of the *département* of the Côtes d'Armor, but until the Revolution it had little importance but for its bishopric. Saint Brieuc, one of the seven holy founders of the Breton sees, was born in Wales in the late 6th century. He seems to have pursued his mission in southwest Britain before crossing over to Brittany and founding a monastery near the town of Tréguier. Later he moved west to the place that now bears his name and where his successors established the bishopric around 848. A wooden cathedral was probably built here, but the town had neither castle nor ramparts and in the 13th century it was replaced by a fortified church.

CHANGE OF DIRECTION. In 1790 the Constitutional Assembly made St-Brieuc the departmental capital. With 6,400 inhabitants, it was far smaller than Quintin but it had the advantage of a more central location. Industrial expansion followed the arrival of the railroad in 1862 and the city began to grow on the landward side, spreading over the plateaus to the south and southwest. Heavy industry came to St-Brieuc in 1873 with the creation of iron and steel works, along with the accompanying rolling-mills. Brushmaking emerged as another St-Brieuc activity. In 1925 the family business of Max Sauer opened a factory. The firm has been making paintbrushes in Paris since 1793, and is still a leading producer today.

Labels on map:
GRANDES PROMENADES
ROND-POINT-HUGUIN
LE GOUËT
VALLÉE DU GOUËDIC
GRAND SÉMINAIRE
PORT DE COMMERCE
TOUR DE CESSON

AV. CORNEILLE

FONTAINE-AUX-LOUPS

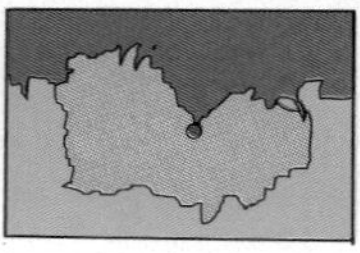

CITY EMBLEM
St-Brieuc has a gryphon as its symbol, a mythical beast half eagle and half lion. It can be seen in a stylized version, as above, or in classic

flamboyant pose on flags and coats of arms. The gryphon also features on street signs in the city.

UNCERTAIN IDENTITY. St-Brieuc has a strong radical tradition and a history of freemasonry, but the military influence due to the large barracks in the city also dates back a long way, and religion too has continued to hold an important place. Since World War One city planning had produced a number of interesting developments such as the pedestrian area, the Îlot du Chai and the Îlot St-Vincent, but there have also been some deplored mistakes, in particular the new Halles. Apart from the cathedral St-Brieuc is a city with few outstanding features. There is a lively population of young artists and a new center for contemporary art has just been built. But these initiatives, along with the setting up of the world's first "zoopole" at Ploufragan, and the development of an up-to-date food processing industry have failed to prevent the population from dropping by four thousand in less than ten years.

A 19th-century colored engraving of St-Brieuc, which has developed from a thriving market town into a busy industrial city and is today the capital of the Côtes d'Armor *département*.

AROUND THE CATHEDRAL

ST-ÉTIENNE. The original wooden cathedral burned down not long after 848, but another was built in stone around 970. The relics of the patron saint, which had been temporarily transferred to Angers, were then brought back to St-Brieuc. They are reputed to have trembled with joy on their return. But in 1346 the English invaded, pillaging the city and

destroying the Romanesque cathedral. Today only its foundations remain. The new cathedral was completed under Duke Jean IV, who had besieged the city in 1375. He pronounced it "most heartily strong" but in 1592 it was pillaged by forces of the League. During the Revolution it was first appropriated by the "Cult of Reason and the Supreme Being", and was later used for making saltpeter, then became a cannon store and finally a stable. The statues and decorative woodwork were used as firewood.

FORTRESS-LIKE APPEARANCE. On the eastern side are the nave, rebuilt between 1712 and 1715, and two massive towers. Inside the cathedral, on the south side of the nave, is the CHAPEL OF THE ANNUNCIATION, a masterpiece of expert craftsmanship. Note the bishop's coat of arms held by two angels, carved above the little turret door that once led to the old library. The CHANCEL, with its polygonal apse, shows a strong Anglo-Norman influence.

FURNISHINGS. Although much was destroyed during the Revolution, certain treasures survive. Among them are the handsome paneled organ-chest, which dates from 1540, and the chapel of the Annunciation, which contains one of the finest wooden altarpieces of any church in the Côtes d'Armor, from the workshop of Yves Corlay.

YVES CORLAY'S MASTERPIECE
The wooden altarpiece ● *102* dates from 1745 and is considered the finest surviving work by Trégor sculptor Yves Corlay.

CATHEDRAL TOWERS
The massive Tour Brieuc and Tour du Midi (14th and 15th centuries) are plain and unadorned apart from their loophole windows.

The south transept is lit by a superb stained glass window depicting the symbols of the Eucharist. In the chancel stands a beautiful 14th-century statue of Saint Stephen, the church's patron saint.

OLD ST-BRIEUC. The French novelist Louis Guilloux, who wrote *Sang Noir* (1935) and *Jeu de patience* (1949), was born in the center of St-Brieuc in 1899. He described his birthplace in these words: "Behind the cathedral, dark narrow streets had to force their way between the old wooden houses. This was the lowest part of town, home to shopkeepers, junk merchants and workers." The little streets around the cathedral survive today, as do many of St-Brieuc's ancient HALF-TIMBERED HOUSES, each busy façade a story in itself. Those set on corners are easy to see. Others, standing half-hidden in the shadows of Rue Fardel and the Place au Lin, or packed tightly around the Place du Martray beneath overhanging roofs, must be sought out. There are some very picturesque examples on the Place Louis-Guilloux and also at no. 4, Rue Notre-Dame and no. 4, Rue Quinquaine (HÔTEL DES DUCS DE BRETAGNE). Among the very oldest houses are a number with unusual herring-bone or crossed patterns on their façades, some picked out in bright colors. St-Brieuc's fine old houses also feature sturdy columns, often with capitals decorated with leaves. Other carvings, including anchors, crosses and hearts, can also occasionally be seen on the house fronts. More fine stone houses can be seen along the winding streets and in the small squares. In the Rue Henri Servain, near the cathedral itself, stands the HÔTEL DE BELLESCIZE, an 18th-century residence named after the last bishop of St-Brieuc under the Ancien Régime. It has an oval design and a beautiful curved flight of steps. The inns and taverns that once filled the neighborhood have disappeared but their memory lingers in the names of the streets where they once stood: L'Écu de France, Le Croissant d'Or, La Couronne, and L'Hermine.

FONTAINE ST-BRIEUC. Take the Rue Notre-Dame and then the Rue Ruffet to see the lovely 15th-century St-Brieuc fountain. It stands beneath an ogival porch said to mark the spot where St Brieuc built his first chapel. The settlement spread outward from this spot set between the steep valleys of the rivers Gouët and Gouëdic. As a result the city has a complicated and unusual lay-out. The rivers are spanned by a number of bridges, the oldest being the 17th- and 18th-century PONT DU GOUËDIC, but the two

HALF-TIMBERED HOUSES
Some of the finest examples are around the cathedral, at nos. 6 and 9 Rue Quinquaine, no. 32 Rue Fardel, and a little house at the corner of Rue Quinquaine and Rue Notre Dame.

Le Ribeault is one of the most intricately decorated houses.

most spectacular are the railroad viaduct built in 1862, and the Harel-de-la-Noë bridge, which was erected in the early 20th century. A flight of two hundred steps leads from the Pont du Gouët to the Tertre Notre-Dame, a little hill overlooking the old town. As a child Louis Guilloux was enthralled by the view: "From high up here we could see the ocean and we would spend ages watching the slow progress of a fishing boat out to sea."

RUE DE LA CORDERIE. An amazing mosaic decorates the façade of a house at no. 20 (above): it is covered with shells of

ever-increasing size, spreading upward in a fan design. At no. 24, also in Rue de la Corderie, stands a house with another striking and original façade stuck with broken glass tiles in all shades of blue. Both houses were decorated between 1928 and 1930 to designs by Isidore Odorico, a Rennes artist of Italian origin. He also created the reinforced concrete façade of the Grand Séminaire chapel.

THE COMMERCIAL CENTER

SHELL MOSAIC
The mosaic façade in Rue de la Corderie was produced by the Odorico family workshops, mosaic artists from Rennes. The detail shows the colored circles that decorate the length of the cornice.

CHAMP-DE-MARS. A barracks and a convent once stood on this large open space. Later it was used for sporting events. Nowadays a busy flea market fills the Champ-de-Mars on Sundays, and every year at Michaelmas, around September 29, a three-day regional trade fair is held there.

PEDESTRIAN AREA. Before the Pont d'Armor was built the PLACE DU GUESCLIN stood at the entrance to the city. In the 1920's well-to-do visitors would stay at the Hôtel d'Angleterre and local men would drink at the Café du Commerce. Women liked to wander around the Nouvelles Galeries department store, a 19th-century shoppers' paradise in baroque white stucco, but recently closed. A pedestrian precinct full of busy shops and offices leads from the Place Du Guesclin.

MUSEUM OF HISTORY. The museum, housed in a former police barracks, opened in 1986. It traces the recent social, economic and cultural history of the Côtes d'Armor and is full of interesting exhibits, well displayed and lit. Along with costumes and furniture there are also some clever

FOIRE ST-MICHEL
This three-day regional fair is also known locally as the *foire aux puces*. It is held each year around September 9.

reconstructions of homes and workshops, and marvelous scale models. They all contribute to a detailed picture of the domestic and working lives of the farmers, sailors and craftsmen of St-Brieuc and the surrounding region. Most of the scale models were made by Roland Gestin, a native of Finistère, who was born in Landerneau and who studied at the École des Beaux Arts in Paris and with sculptor Zadkine.

A WALK AROUND THE CITY

THE "GRANDES PROMENADES". One of the finest features of St-Brieuc is the municipal garden, the Grandes Promenades, laid out in the 19th century on part of the old ramparts. A pretty path runs along the top edge of the green river valley, following the Gouëdic for well over a mile. Also in the park are a number of statues by the city's famous sculptors. These include *La Forme se dégageant de la matière* (Form emerging from Matter) by Paul Le Goff, a monument by Élie Le Goff dedicated to writer Villiers de l'Isle-Adam (born in St-Brieuc in 1838), and *La Bretonne du Goëlo* (Breton woman from Goëlo), a powerful sculpture by Francis Renaud, who also made the winged and helmeted figure on St-Brieuc's war memorial. The gardens have some fine floral displays, magnificent trees, a lake and an open-air theater built of lovely pink granite and sadly unused. In fine weather the park is filled with enthusiastic boules players.

CHAPELLE DU GRAND SÉMINAIRE. The chapel was designed in Art Deco style by Isidore Odorico in 1927. In the chapel, Odorico tried to foster a sense of space, balanced by geometrical designs. The carpet has Celtic-style spirals and crosses, while the patterns on the pillars and their mosaic capitals might be described as "neo-Norman". The backdrop to the chancel is a huge openwork design in concrete. The high altar, constructed from pink granite, is encrusted with pieces of glass and mother-of-pearl, and surmounted by a painted altarpiece.

PLACE ST-MICHEL. Set in the old part of town, Place St-Michel is the only square in St-Brieuc that is laid out to a deliberate plan. A columned church, much like a basilica, stands at the western side. Inside the church are some Italianate paintings, the most interesting of which shows the death of Saint Anne, an event seldom depicted.

MASTERS OF MOSAIC
The Odoricos came to Rennes from northern Italy in 1882. The father made a name for himself with his mosaic shop front designs. His son Isidore (1893–1944) studied at the École des Beaux Arts in Rennes, but the 1925 Universal Exhibition inspired his love of the decorative arts. His most original work is seen in the "Maison Bleue", Rue de la Corderie.

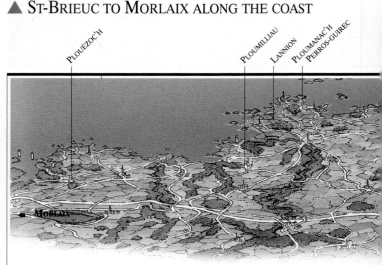

PLOUÉZOC'H

PLOUMILLIAU

LANNION

PLOUMANAC'H
PERROS-GUIREC

◀ MORLAIX

POINTE DU ROSELIER
The cliff rises 230 feet above the sea with a view over the bay of St-Brieuc from Cap d'Erquy to the Bréhat island. The Douaniers footpath leads on from here. Look out for a path leading to a *four à boulets*, a furnace where, in the 18th century, cannonballs were heated before being fired at enemy ships.

POINTE DE PLOUHA
The cliffs along this coast rise nearly 350 feet above the sea and are the highest in Brittany. Along the top runs the Gwin Zégal footpath, starting at the village of La Trinité.

BINIC

Since the early 17th century boats from Binic had been fishing for cod off the coast of Newfoundland. By 1845 the port was the most active in France. Reminders of this past prosperity include the town houses built by wealthy shipowners that stand along the QUAI JEAN BART, and the fine old AUBERGE DU CHEVAL BLANC, which also dates from the 17th century. Today the town makes its living from sailing and tourism.

ST-QUAY-PORTRIEUX

The Irish missionary Saint Ke is said to have landed here in the 5th or 6th century. Later the town became a fishing port, and deep-sea fishing boats were built. The harbor at St-Quay is being enlarged so as to attract more yachts. The town, a seaside resort since 1841, is popular for its fine sandy beaches.

PLOUHA

A SLICE OF HISTORY. The port of Gwin Zégal, a simple mooring with a wooden jetty is (with the one at Mazou-en-

Porspoder in Finistère) the last of its kind in Brittany, and an important relic of the ancient seafaring tradition.

...ANTIC

CHAPELLE DE NOTRE-DAME-DE-LA-COUR. The chapel still has two beautiful 15th-century stained glass windows. The one in the transept, showing scenes from the life of Mary and Jesus, is the work of Olivier Lecoq and Jean Lavenant, two master-craftsmen from Tréguier. The window in the chancel illustrates the legends of Saint Bernardine of Siena and Saint Nicholas of Tolentino.

CHAPELLE DE KERMARIA-AN-ISKUIT-EN-PLOUHA

The original chapel was built by Henry d'Avagour on his return from the Crusades in 1240. Only four bays in the nave and the side aisles remain.

PORCH. This is one of the finest in Brittany. It has an ogival bay supported by columns on either side, and contains statues of the twelve Apostles.

DANCE OF DEATH. The chapel is famous for its 15th-century frescoes, and especially for the *danse macabre*, which might have inspired Saint-Saëns' popular composition. At the time it was painted (possibly after an outbreak of the plague) themes of mortality, fate and death as the great leveler were uppermost in people's minds.

ABBAYE DE BEAUPORT ★

The abbey was built by Premonstrant monks and completed around 1250, with the exception of the refectory, which is a slightly later addition.
AN IMPORTANT INSTITUTION. The abbey was frequently used as a stopping-place by pilgrims on the road to Compostela, and was visited by monks from Ireland, Scotland and Cornwall. It came under the direct authority of the Pope, and its abbot had the privilege of wearing a miter, which

FINE STATUARY
A Virgin and child from the chapel of Kermaria. The infant is refusing the breast, emphasizing the fact that his nourishment has a spiritual source.

217

Only seven murals representing a *Danse macabre* have survived in France. One at the church of Notre-Dame-du-Roncier at Josselin in Brittany was destroyed around

1860, although a watercolor sketch of the mural still exists. The one in the Chapel of Kermaria is quite well preserved, and its different scenes are painted above the arches of the nave. Forty-seven figures (dead as well as living) are individually depicted in painted arcades. The *Danse* begins on the south side, near the chancel, and ends on the opposite side to the north. The fresco was painted some time between 1488 and 1500 and for years lay hidden beneath a coating of plaster, to be rediscovered in 1856.

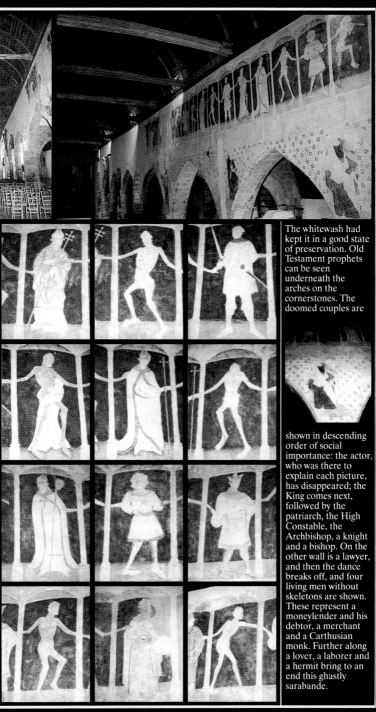

"AS I AM NOW, SO SHALL YE BE: DEAD, NAKED, ROTTING, STINKING. POWER AND RICHES ARE AS NAUGHT, SO BETHINK YE OF THE LOATHSOME END THAT WAITS FOR THEE."

The whitewash had kept it in a good state of preservation. Old Testament prophets can be seen underneath the arches on the cornerstones. The doomed couples are shown in descending order of social importance: the actor, who was there to explain each picture, has disappeared; the King comes next, followed by the patriarch, the High Constable, the Archbishop, a knight and a bishop. On the other wall is a lawyer, and then the dance breaks off, and four living men without skeletons are shown. These represent a moneylender and his debtor, a merchant and a Carthusian monk. Further along a lover, a laborer and a hermit bring to an end this ghastly sarabande.

The pleasing architectural harmony of the Beauport Abbey buildings (right).

POINTE DE GUILBEN
The headland is a striking mix of black basaltic rock and pink granite. The climate is particularly mild, encouraging the growth of myrtle, mulberry and fig trees, cypresses, fennel and garlic, and wild bees make their nests in the rocks. Cars must be parked nearly half a mile away from the point. The walk there and back takes about one hour, allowing plenty of time to admire the view over the bay of Paimpol.

THE YACHTING FRATERNITY
The port of Paimpol has less than ten thousand inhabitants,

raised his status to a level equal to that of the Bishop of St-Brieuc. Until the middle of the 17th century the abbey was responsible for administering justice in over thirteen parishes. It was closed in 1791, in the aftermath of the Revolution, and was sold to raise money for the State. When the library was transported by sea to St-Brieuc many of its two thousand volumes were lost in transit.

TOUR OF THE ABBEY. Inside are rooms such as the almonry, pressing-house, the great cellars, guest house and refectory. The CLOISTER contains a niche with a stone basin where the abbot would wash the feet of his guests. Spectacular views of the ancient buildings can be seen from a FOOTPATH that runs from the south side of the abbey along the marsh.

PAIMPOL

COD FISHING. Right from the beginning the monks levied taxes on trade in Paimpol, particularly on fish, salt and corn. From the 16th century schooners sailed from here to the cod-fishing grounds off Newfoundland. Cod fishing reached its peak in the 19th century, when shipowners abandoned Newfoundland for Icelandic waters. In 1895 the town had a fleet of more than eighty schooners. The last great fishing season was in 1935. Today these intrepid boats have been replaced by pleasure craft.

LITERARY RENOWN. The town owes most of its fame to Pierre Loti (1850–1923), an officer in the French navy and a prolific writer; his successful novel *Pêcheur d'Islande* (1886), dealt with the cod fishers of Iceland and Newfoundland. There was the composer Théodore Botrel too, whose song *La Paimpolaise* (1895) was inspired by Loti's novel: both novel and song glorify a dreadful and dangerous life. If cod brought prosperity to the town, fishing for it cost countless lives,

bringing destitution to thousands of homes left fatherless. Only the shipowners (whose motto was "All for Cod") grew rich on the lives of their fishermen.

MARITIME MUSEUM. With the aid maps, models, photographs, costumes, ships' logs and all kinds of memorabilia, the Musée de la Mer traces the existence of these brave sailors. A look around here could be followed by a visit to the Mad Atao, a *Dundee* ▲ *326* built at Camaret, which was listed as an historic monument in 1983.

but the population swells dramatically in the holiday season. Today Paimpol's quays are lined with all kinds of sailing boats and pleasure craft: the nearby Bréhat archipelago and the estuaries of the rivers Trieux and Jaudy make it a popular mooring.

POINTE DE L'ARCOUEST

The headland commands one of the most spectacular views of GOËLO, a little coastal region between St-Brieuc and Paimpol. It overlooks Bréhat and the host of little islands around it. In clear weather, to the west of Bréhat can be seen the island of St-Maudez, the shingled spit of Talbert and the Héaux lighthouse. Left of the road leading to the departure point for Bréhat is a monument to Irène Joliot-Curie (daughter of Pierre and Marie Curie) and her husband; both famous French physicists used to spend their holidays at Arcouest.

ISLAND OF BRÉHAT ★

Boats leave for Bréhat from the Pointe de l'Arcouest. The island is a lovely place the whole year round. It has been the haunt of artists and a favorite with tourists for many years. Less than one nautical mile from the mainland, the scenery of the archipelago is varied and relatively unspoilt, and its climate is agreeably warm thanks to the proximity of the Gulf Stream. Cars are banned but the island can be explored on foot or by bicycle, and there are also boat tours of the "*Île aux Fleurs*", which leave from Port Clos, on the archipelago.

THE ISLAND OF FLOWERS. The sheer abundance and variety of flowers is remarkable: all species common to the Brittany coastline are to be found here, together with a whole host of specimens brought back from all over the world by Bréhat sailors.

BIRDLIFE ■ *24.* There are around 120 different species of

birds to be found on the island, and an observant visitor might catch a glimpse of a rare warbler or hear the clear ticking call of a Lapland bunting. The large and varied population of woodland birds prefers the southern part of the island, where vegetation is thickest, while at the wilder northern end some small predatory species make their nests amid the pines and bracken. Cormorants, gulls, terns and gannets can be seen all around the coast.

ISLAND WALKS. Just over two miles long and less than one mile wide, the island of Bréhat is so small that it is best to explore it on foot. Even the most unpractised walker will find it quite easy, and will be rewarded by some magnificent landscapes and seascapes. The southern section of the island is more densely populated, lively and cheerful. The village of Le Bourg has a 16th-century church that has undergone much alteration. The northern part, reached by the little Pont-ar-Prat, a bridge built by Vauban, is a much more desolate stretch of heathland and pink granite rocks. At its tip is the Paon lighthouse.

LOGUIVY-DE-LA-MER

A charming port set in a narrow river inlet. Lenin came here for his holidays in 1902. The town has a fair number of busy lobster boats, which provide its main income. Loguivy became part of Breton folk culture because of a melancholy song by Francois Budet about the passing of the great days of the Brittany fishing fleets. The refrain nostalgically laments: "Loguivy-de-la-Mer, Loguivy-de-la-Mer, your sailors brave and true are dying. Loguivy-de-la-Mer, the hulks now rot in our harbor."

KESTREL
A small bird of prey that can be seen

hovering above the northern heathlands of the island of Bréhat, a habitat shared with larks, buntings and wheatears.

CROIX ST-MICHEL
The cross stands high above the granite landscape, looking out toward the island of Grouezen. The view extends to the islands of Beniguet and Maudez, and to the Sillon de Talbert.

THE ISLE OF COSTAÉRES (right)
On it stands an eccentric pink granite
château built in the 1890's.

SILLON DE TALBERT

An unusual spit of sand and pebbles projects nearly 2 miles
into the sea, just north of Pleubian. The pebbles are pieces
broken from the rocky coast during the Ice Age and rolled
smooth by the sea. The spit makes a bracing walk, but do not
be tempted to go too far at low tide as you could get cut off
when the waters rise. To get a good general view of the Sillon
de Talbert go to the old signal
station of Crec'h Maout, about
half a mile west of the spit.

TRÉGUIER

HISTORY. Tréguier stands
at the head of the Jaudy
estuary. The town grew up
around an old abbey and by
the 14th century it had begun
to gain a wide reputation as a
city of religion and culture. Many
talented artists and craftsmen were
drawn here, contributing to the intense
artistic and intellectual activity that was
developing. There was a great interest in printing
and a flourishing trade in grain and wine kept the port busy.
The wars of religion triggered the decline of the city and the
League's ● 57 internal bickerings dealt a temporary blow to
Tréguier's prosperity. During the Revolution the town was
pillaged, but later another prosperous period began, based on
the linen industry ● 60 and the production of spring
vegetables. But religion continued to be the driving force in
Tréguier. The well-respected historian and philologist Ernest
Renan felt its influence strongly. Born here in 1823, he
trained for the church and left for Paris when he was fifteen.
The city is still an important religious center today, but it
relies mostly on its tourist trade.

THE CATHEDRAL. St-Tugdual, a Gothic cathedral built in the
early 12th century, is one of the finest in Brittany. The three
entrance PORCHES – of the Lepers (*Ladres*), the Bells
(*Cloches*) and the People (*Peuple*) – have exquisitely detailed
carvings. In the vast, sixty-foot-high nave with seven bays is
the tomb of Saint Yves. There is also a lovely pulpit decorated
with floral motifs, and at the far end is an enormous 18th-
century organ, restored in 1989. The CHANCEL contains forty
stalls carved with an enchanting array of animals
constituting an entire medieval bestiary! THE CLOISTERS,
built between 1450 and 1458, are as impressive as the
cathedral itself.

A tower of boulders
on the Sillon de
Talbert still stands
firm, defying the wild
Atlantic seas that
break against it.

SAINT YVES
"Give a poor man the
benefit of the doubt."
Saint Yves, the most
popular saint in
Brittany, was born
near Tréguier in 1253.
He studied law and
became a judge. He
later turned to the
priesthood and was
revered for his
fairness and his great
concern for the poor.

LE GRAND PARDON
● 72. One of the most
important pardon
ceremonies is held in
Tréguier on May 19,
the day of the death
of Saint Yves. People
come from
surrounding parishes
to join the procession
to the cathedral,
where mass is
celebrated.

A view of Tréguier
from around 1900.

TOWN CENTER. Tréguier is full of lovely old houses. Medieval dwellings are interspersed with handsome stone buildings dating mostly from the 18th century. There are also a number of 17th-century half-timbered houses, the majority of which are in the Place des Artisans.

PLOUGRESCANT

CHAPELLE DE ST-GONÉRY. Among many lovely things to see in this little church is a series of small naive paintings dating from the late 15th century. They include a number of scenes from the Book of Genesis and episodes from the life of Christ.

SEPT-ÎLES NATURE RESERVE

Off the coast at Perros-Guirec is a nature reserve and bird sanctuary consisting of seven islands and islets: Rouzic, Malban, Bono, the ÎLE AUX MOINES, Le Cerf Les Costans, and Île Plate. They cover about 100 acres at high tide, but nearer to 700 when the tide is out. Visits are made only to the Île aux Moines: boats leave from Trestraou and there is an information center at Pleumeur-Bodou, the ornithological station on the Île Grande.

THE RESERVE ■ 24. The group of islands was officially made into a wildlife sanctuary in 1976 for the protection of birds. With thirteen species nesting here and an estimated minimum of twelve thousand pairs, it is the most important nesting site for seabirds in France. It is also the only place in France where puffins rear their young. The various birds include a number of coastal species. There is also a small colony of grey seals, and a pair of ravens that nest regularly on Bono.

PLOUMANAC'H

THE PINK GRANITE COAST. The stretch of coast between Perros-Guirec and Trébeurden, beginning officially at RANOLIEN-PLAGE, is known as the *côte de granite rose*. Huge boulders litter the moorland beside the ocean, and along the water's edge massive piles of rocks, often grotesquely shaped and balanced in spectacular positions, rise out of the water.

GANNET
This is only one of many breeds that nest on the Sept-Îles.

LIGHTHOUSE AND SENTIER DES DOUANIERS ★
The Douaniers (excisemen) footpath dates back to 1907 and leads around the Pointe de Ploumanac'h, a headland that is one of Brittany's sites of outstanding natural beauty. It is best to begin the walk, which takes a morning or afternoon, from above the landing stage at Trestaou. There are plenty of interesting features along the way: the remains of 17th-century coastal

defenses including a fort and powder magazine, a lookout used by the excisemen, a lifeboat with slipway, and the lighthouse (above), which was rebuilt after the war.

CHÂTEAU DE TONQUÉDEC
A fort has stood here since the 13th century, the first destroyed in 1395 and a new castle begun in

1406. This was a four-sided structure with a semicircular tower at each corner, and modifications continued until well into the 16th century. Richelieu had the castle demolished in 1622.

CHURCH OF PLOUZÉLAMBRE
The 16th-century church is

dedicated to Saint Zélambre.

A model of the Barnenez cairn made for an archeological exhibition at the Grand Palais in Paris in 1989.

Their unusual forms were caused by the sea eroding the granite over millions of years to expose a layer of porous volcanic magma. The waters then wore deep crevices into it. There are little coves along the coast with hidden and relatively peaceful beaches. Thousands of visitors come each year to see these 12 miles of pink rocks set against the changing colors of the moorland: yellow with gorse in spring, then scattered with purple and pink heather from early summer onward.

ÎLE GRANDE

The island could once be reached from the mainland by fording shallow water, but is now connected by a small bridge. A path will take you about three-quarters of the way round the coast. The sheltered southern side has a natural winter harbor and stretches of low-lying pasture land that are covered by the sea when tides are particularly high. The west and east coast are sandy and well sheltered too. It is only the northern edge of the island that has been battered by the open sea into a series of extended headlands and deep pebbly coves. The CENTER FOR ORNITHOLOGY has an information point in an old quarry building on the island.

LANNION

The town of Lannion has grown enormously in recent years. In the 1960's it was selected for the creation of a national institute for telecommunications research (CNET), and it has since become a center of expertise in this field. Resulting prosperity has also enabled the ancient buildings of the town to be preserved and well restored: the most beautiful old houses are on the Place du Général Leclerc and there is a fine view of the town from the 12th-century church of Brélévenez.

CHÂTEAU DE TONQUÉDEC

The Château de Tonquédec is perched on a rocky spur above the river Leguer, south of Lannion. A drawbridge leads to a gateway with separate entrances for carriages and pedestrians. The castle was virtually impregnable, with a deep moat, portcullis, sturdy doors, gunports and cruciform apertures for soldiers to return fire and further defenses within. The living apartments were on the west of the main courtyard: in peacetime the seigneur and his family lived here with their servants and men-at-arms. When attacked they took refuge in the keep. The church in Tonquédec village has a superb stained-glass window.

PLOUMILLIAU

CHURCH OF ST-MILLIAU. The chancel of the church has sixteen remarkable carved and painted panels showing scenes from the Passion. Other features include early 16th-century baptismal fonts, a gracious Pietà, a statue of Saint Milliau and a wooden image of the Ankou.

THE ANKOU. There were originally two Ankous which would be placed on either side of the coffin during burial services. The Ankou takes the form of a skeleton carrying a spade and a scythe. The legend is that one Christmas Eve an honest blacksmith called Fanch ar Floch continued to work while his wife and children went to midnight mass at Ploumilliau church. His wife warned him not to be working when the bell rang for the elevation of the Host but, engrossed in his work, he labored on. A man in a wide-rimmed hat appeared carrying a scythe with a bent handle and Fanch agreed to straighten it for him. The stranger then warned him, "Go to bed, and when your wife comes back tell her to fetch a priest. The work you have just done for me is your last." And when the cock crowed next morning Fanch ar Floch departed this life, having worked during the elevation of the Host.

CHURCH OF ST-JEAN-DU-DOIGT

On the coast north of Morlaix is the village of St Jean du Doigt, so named because Saint John the Baptist's finger (*doigt*) has been kept in its church since the 15th century. The church is a well-proportioned Gothic edifice with a high-vaulted nave. The parish close is one of the most interesting in the region, and the monumental fountain in the graveyard is called the Fontaine du Doigt.

PLOUÉZOC'H

BARNENEZ CAIRN ● 81. Only the efforts of archeologist Giot saved this ancient megalithic monument from destruction. From 1955 to 1968, he directed excavations at this spectacular site overlooking the sea. It is a double cairn, built in two stages, and with eleven dolmens. The first part, to the east, is a trapezoid tumulus with five corridor dolmens. To the west is a second granite mound with another six dolmens. Because of their unusual corbeled roof structure, they are known as "Armorican corridor dolmens", the oldest known megaliths. Their great antiquity has been confirmed by flint tools and carbon 14 dating carried out on pottery discovered at the site, which have dated the construction of Barnenez to about 5000 BC. The design of the tomb is unusually sophisticated, and pillars in its vaulted antechamber are carved with ax signs.

THE ANKOU, IMAGE OF DEATH ● 70. Wooden statue of the Ankou to be seen in the south aisle of Ploumilliau church.

THE "BRETON PARTHENON" André Malraux described the Barnenez cairn as the Breton Parthenon. At 230 feet long and 82 feet wide at its western end, its size is astonishing.

CARNAC ROSTRENEN LANNION GUÉMÉNÉ-SUR-SCORFF LAC DE GUERLÉDAN GUINGAMP AURAY LOCMARIAQUER PONTIVY MUR-DE-BRETAGNE SAINT-GILDAS-DE-RHUYS QUINTIN LOCMINÉ SAINT-BRIEUC LOUDÉAC ROHAN VANNES GOLFE DU MORBIHAN JOSSELIN LAMBALLE

SPINNING WHEELS
At the outbreak of the Revolution there were over nine hundred spinners working at home. They produced the fine linen thread for Quintin cloth, used to make headdresses, collars and cuffs ● 72.

QUINTIN

Quintin is typical of those small Breton cities of feudal origin that grew rich on the linen industry during the 17th and 18th centuries. Fine architectural features from the period survive.
A CITY OF WEAVERS AND MERCHANTS. The first Brittany cloth ● 62 produced here was coarse and rough, but it was soon refined and exported to the Spanish colonies as "Quintin" cloth. The linen that was processed in this area came from the Trégor and Léon regions. Quintin was also an important seat of regional justice and was dominated by a number of municipal magistrates from the wealthy merchant classes. In 1789 the Revolution overturned this social structure, and all attempts to revive the linen trade in the 19th century ended in failure. By then the market was firmly in the grip of English and Prussian manufacturers, and competition from cotton was growing stronger all the time. Although the weaver's shuttle still features on the town's coat of arms, the industry is long dead. Sadly the main events that marked the importance of Quintin as a regional center, in particular the cattle market and the traditional St-Thurian Fair, are also gone.
FINE CRAFTSMANSHIP. Quintin still has a thriving market each Tuesday, with many stalls selling goods and varied produce. More unusual is the presence of some highly skilled craftsmen including cabinetmakers, stone engravers, potters and clockmakers. There are also two stained glass artists: Jean-

Michel Baladi, who restored the church of St-Magloire de Châtelaudren, and the workshop of Hubert de Sainte-Marie, which undertook the repair of windows in the parish close church of La Martyre ▲ 256 and at Dol Cathedral.

UNFINISHED CHÂTEAU. Seen from the Champ de Foire the château is a magnificent sight. It was designed for Henriette de La Tour d'Auvergne by architect Gabriel Androuet du Cerceau and its buildings were to be set around a square central courtyard. It was begun around 1640 but the work was never completed.

Details of the Logis des Chanoines and the tympanum of the basilica.

LATER ADDITIONS. When the castle subsequently passed to Guy de Durfort he converted the stables into living apartments and added two towers along with the orangeries. Today part of the first floor has been made into exhibition rooms with displays illustrating the history of Quintin. Valuable collections of locally made fans, gold and silverware, and porcelain are also housed here and a temporary exhibition on a different theme is mounted each year.

MANNERIST INFLUENCE
A rejected plan for the château at Quintin by Gabriel Androuet du Cerceau (1640).

BASILICA OF NOTRE-DAME

The basilica, an imposing neo-Gothic structure nearly 250 feet high, stands on the site of an earlier collegiate church at the top of Rue Notre-Dame. The LOGIS DES CHANOINES, at no. 7, was once the residence of the senior clergy. The basilica of Notre-Dame is dedicated more specifically to Our Lady of Deliverance. This was a cult introduced to the region in the 15th century by Isabeau de Montauban, wife of the then lord of Quintin. She had obtained a fragment of the Virgin's belt, a holy treasure formerly worshipped at Puy-Notre-Dame, a town in Anjou. The basilica was long known locally as the *Vierge à la quenouille* (Virgin of the distaff), because it was a tradition for apprentice spinners to bring an offering of the linen spun from their first distaff (the cleft stick on which the flax was wound for spinning). The baptismal fonts date from the late 14th century and come from the original collegiate church. The lettering and patterns that decorate them are clearly influenced by Celtic designs from the other side of the channel.

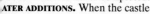

SACRED BELT
To convince Saint Thomas of the reality of the Assumption, the Virgin tossed her belt down to him from heaven. In 1600 fire destroyed the church treasury, where the fragment of the belt was kept, but the holy relic survived.

THE OLD QUARTER OF QUINTIN

PLACE 1830. It is well worth taking the time to wander around Quintin, explore its steeply sloping streets and view the fine old houses. The prettiest part of town is around the Place 1830 where the *cohue*, or market hall, used to stand. There are some ancient half-timbered houses, including an unusually long two-storied dwelling on the corner of the Rue au Lait and the Rue Belle-Étoile (no.2).

The Grande-Rue in Quintin still has many lovely old beamed houses.

Pontivy is
charming town, fu
of rich decorativ
detail (right

In 1895 Beaumanoir
was restored and
"cleaned up" with all
the unquestioning
confidence of the late
Victorian age.

**LES FORGES DES
SALLES ★**
The great furnace of
the ironworks is
surrounded by a
cluster of buildings.
There are sheds for
storing coal, opening
directly onto the
furnace, and others
where the iron was
worked. There are
also houses for the
workers, a church and
school, along with a
café and
public

garden. The village,
now being restored, is
all built in the same
schist stone.

**ÉTANG DE
BOSMÉLÉAC**
A delightful hour or
two can be spent
strolling around the
shady banks of this
attractive lake. Its
prettily landscaped
slopes are crossed
with paths that wind
among the trees.
There are beaches
from which it is
possible to bathe in
the brownish-red

It has a corbeled overhang and two charming corner turrets
decorated with intricate carving. A human face grimacing
from the façade of a house on the corner of the Place 1830
(no.6) and the Rue au Lait is known as the "*Papa au Lait*" or
the "*Bonhomme Quintin*". The gabled AUBERGE DE LA PORTI
À LA ROSE at no. 5 is a well-preserved 15th-century building.

CHÂTEAU DE BEAUMANOIR AU LESLAY

The château of Beaumanoir lies a few miles northwest of
Quintin in landscaped grounds of lakes and woodland. It is
here that Roman Polanski chose to film *Tess* in 1979. Two
wings were added to the main building, one in the 16th
century and one in 1895. The well-preserved corner tower
houses a spiral staircase dating back to the 15th century and
the time of the Eder family, first lords of the manor.
PRIVATE COLLECTION. There is now a collection of modern ar
on show in the Château de Beaumanoir. The works displaye
in fine paneled rooms include portraits of the
owners by Hans Bellmer, sculptures by César
and Niki de Saint-Phalle, and paintings by
many other contemporary artists such as
Olivier Debré, Robert Combas, Eugène de
Kermadec, Jean Degottex and Jacques Villon

FORÊT DE LORGE

A few miles to the other side of Quintin is the great Lorge
forest, which covers 6,000 acres. It is privately owned and run
on model lines. Walkers may enjoy the estate but picking or
collecting anything in the forest is strictly forbidden. Rare
plants include types of asperula and asphodel, and virtually a
varieties of fern, lichen and moss known in Brittany are to be
found here. The forest is also home to salamanders, rare
species of frog and beetle and a protected species of snail, th
élone de Quimper. On its northwest edge at La Pas an
ironworks dating from the early 19th century can be seen; ore
was smelted here until 1978.

BOSMÉLÉAC RESERVOIR

DAM AND WATERFALL. At Bosméléac, southwest of the forest,
lies a long man-made stretch of water retained by a dam. In
1832 the river Oust, a tributary of the Vilaine, was dammed i

...rder to supply water to the Nantes-Brest canal via the ...ilvern drainage channel. The sturdy, rustic construction, ...ith four huge buttresses, and the fine waterfall it creates ...ave made the reservoir a popular spot for visitors. It ...ontinues to serve the important purpose of controlling the ...aters of the Oust.

GORGES DU DAOULAS

...ontinue to Corlay and then head southwest for ...aniscat. From here the little D44 leads south ...hrough spectacular scenery. Rocks bristle from the ...eep sides of the valley as the road runs between ...eep cliffs cut by the river aeons ago. A number of ...ck-climbing schools are based here.

ABBAYE DE BON-REPOS. The ancient abbey of Bon-Repos was ...unded in 1184 by Alain III de Rohan for an order of ...istercian monks. Most of the buildings that remain today ...ate from the 13th century and were restored five hundred ...ears later. During the Revolution the abbey was used as a ...eaving mill, then fell into disuse and disrepair. It is still ...eing restored, and an archeological dig is in progress. There ...re pleasant gardens and a lovely Romanesque cloister, as ...ell as a tourist information center and an inn.

MÛR-DE-BRETAGNE

ATURE UNDISTURBED. Near the town of Mûr, around the ...uerlédan lake, the countryside has remained unspoilt. Apart ...om the lake itself there are flourishing woods of beech, oak ...nd chestnut interspersed with pines and firs. North of the ...ke are stretches of moorland. The river gorges of Daoulas ...nd Poulancre provide a quite different natural environment, ...s do small ponds created for the iron-smelting industry at the ...llage of Forges des Salles, and there are also areas of ...etland and peat bogs.

ROND-POINT DU LAC". Just over a mile west of Mûr-de-...retagne is an excellent view overlooking the whole of ...e LAC DE GUERLÉDAN. The lake lies at the foot of an ...d slate works now overgrown with oak trees. Steep paths and flights of steps lead down to the water's edge.

DAM AND LAKE
The huge dam, 660 feet wide and 160 feet high, was built in 1930 and created a lake over 7 miles long. It is well loved by walkers and

birdwatchers, and much in demand as a venue for all kinds of water sports.

THE ROHANS' CASTLE
● 82. The huge square structure, 295 feet by 250 feet, is built upon the rock, with massive walls 16 feet thick. At each corner stood a round tower with turret roof, joined by outer walls 65 feet high. Only the front two remain standing today, a *chemin de ronde* on machicolated support running between.

PONTIVY

The Rohan family ruled the region of Pontivy, at the very heart of inland Brittany, for centuries. The many well-preserved chapels, manors and farmhouses dating from the 15th to the 18th centuries are proof of an unusual long-term political stability. Pontivy is at the junction of the Nantes-Brest canal and the river Blavet, which bestowed much importance on the town. Today its industry is mainly concerned with the production of food.

THE CHÂTEAU. This is one of the best surviving examples of late medieval military architecture in the region. Over the centuries the castle was converted into a residence, and was opened to the public in 1953. Today it is used for concerts and exhibitions, particularly during the *Été musical*, Brittany's biggest festival of classical music. Near the castle is the old quarter of town, which also retains a strong medieval flavor.

ANCIENT STREETS. A number of houses in the Rue du Pont have corbeling on one or two floors. The eighty-five workshops that once lined the RUE DU FIL (Thread Street) supplied the canvas and linen industry ● *60* that once made Pontivy a wealthy town. The PLACE DU MARTRAY has many façades that date mostly from the 17th century, and a busy market is held here each Monday.

THIMADEUC ABBEY

The Cistercian abbey was founded by Father La Trappe, a native of the Morbihan, on the site of the castle of the Lords of Thimadeuc. In 1841 he bought the land, including a dilapidated 16th-century manor house; a large-scale building project began, and the church was consecrated in 1846. The monastic complex was completed a few years later. In 1859 the

monastery already had fifty-three monks, and at the request of the Breton bishops it became an abbey. By 1895 another church had to be built. Today it hosts spiritual retreats. The monks live by farming the estate and making "La Trappe" cheese and fruit candy. Thimadeuc Abbey is not open to the public, but it is possible to attend religious services; the monastic liturgy is in French, with Gregorian chant. There is good view from the hill behind the abbey buildings.

JOSSELIN

HISTORY. Josselin is a delightful little medieval town set at the heart of the Porhoët region. It is built on a hillside

overlooking the river Oust, and the walls and turrets of the castle are dramatically reflected in the water below. In the early 11th century Guéthénoc, lord of Porhoët, had a chapel built here and then a castle: the latter was sacked by the English, but rebuilt in the 12th century. The town was named after his son Josselin.

OLIVIER DE CLISSON. In the mid-14th century Olivier de Clisson acquired the castle and moved in with his wife, Marguerite de Rohan. From the prime strategic location of the Château de Josselin De Clisson was able to direct both his estates and his resistance to the Duke of Brittany. When Du Guesclin died in 1380 De Clisson became the High Constable of France and one of the most important men in the kingdom.

THE ROHANS. Around 1120 Alain, a descendant of the lords of Porhoët, settled in Rohan and founded the dynasty. In the 15th century Alain VIII of Rohan married one of Olivier de Clisson's daughters and became lord of Josselin. But in 1488 the conflict between the Rohans and the dukes of Brittany came to a head and the castle was destroyed. Only the outer façade survived. It was restored in 1490 and 1510

with help from the king, Charles VIII, in gratitude for the Rohans' loyalty. The magnificent courtyard façade dates from this period. A century later the château was destroyed once again when it was knocked down on Richelieu's orders to punish Henri de Rohan for supporting the Huguenots. During the 17th and 18th centuries the château stood in ruins, but in the 19th century, encouraged by the Duchesse de Berry, the Rohan family began restoration.

THE CASTLE ● 87

Ever since the 15th century the property has remained in the possession of the Rohans (later the Rohan-Chabots). Such a long line of inheritance is extremely rare. The soaring medieval ramparts of the fortress, famous throughout Brittany, are best viewed from the Pont Sainte-Croix. The brown schist walls extend upward from the cliffs above the Oust. Three towers nearly 200 feet tall are joined by a massive curtain wall. The carved granite inner façade, erected by Jean II de Rohan, is quite different, being in highly decorated Flamboyant Gothic style. Prosper Mérimée, official Inspector of Buildings and author of *Carmen*, was not greatly impressed by the castle; however, he did consider the openwork balustrade a "masterpiece of delicacy and attention to detail". The residential part of the château was rebuilt in the 19th century in neo-Gothic style. It contains various items relating to the Rohan family, some portraits, and an equestrian statue of Oliver de Clisson by Emmanuel Frémiet, dating from 1892.

DOLL MUSEUM. In one of the castle's old stable buildings is a delightful collection of some five hundred dolls. It was begun nearly a century ago and the dolls, made mostly of wax or wood, date from the 17th and 18th centuries. Below the museum lies the Place St-Nicolas from which a little road leads to a holy well, the Fontaine Notre-Dame-du-Roncier.

PROUD TOWERS
The tall towers and curtain wall (above) that rise so impressively above the canal are all that remain of the old castle of the Rohans. Behind it are buildings of much more recent origin.

THE INNER FACE
The carved granite dates from the 15th century, the time of Jean II de Rohan. He came back from the wars in Italy bringing sculptors to work. The Rohan motto *A plus* is carved above the fireplace in the great hall.

OLIVIER DE CLISSON
Emmanuel Frémiet's equestrian statue.

THE TOWN AND ITS OLD HOUSES

The half-timbered houses with their lovely decorations and ancient carvings illustrate Josselin's long history.

RUE ST-NICOLAS
A watercolor by Albert Robida on display in the Rennes museum, showing the street in about 1880.

THE TOWN

Josselin was formerly a walled town, and sections of the ramparts are still to be seen around the old town center. The walls gave Josselin great strategic importance as a stronghold right up until the 18th century, and particularly during the Revolution. In the 16th century the town was famed for the quality of its linen. Josselin cloth was white and edged with two thin bands of blue, and in those days there was a special place in town known as the *Camp des Drapiers* (Drapers' Field) where cloth makers would meet to talk business and sell their goods. With the coming of the Industrial Revolution, weaving on such a small scale was no longer viable and the population of Josselin declined. Today the town's fortunes have improved and the population has expanded once again, mainly through growth in the food-production sector and the development of tourism. Josselin has lovely houses dating from the 15th to the 18th centuries, many half-timbered and some decorated with ornate carvings. Most of them are in Place Notre-Dame, Rue des Vierges, Rue Olivier-de-Clisson and Rue des Trente. The latter street commemorates a battle, known as the War of the Thirty, that took place in 1352 between the French garrison at Josselin and the English at Ploërmel. Thirty unmounted knights from each side joined combat to settle their long-standing rivalry. Victory went to the French.

CHURCH OF NOTRE-DAME-DU-RONCIER. The church was founded in the 11th century but has since undergone many alterations. Flamboyant Gothic is the dominant style, although the bell tower was actually put up in the present century. The origin of the

church's name, Our Lady of the Thorn-bush, comes from the story of a peasant who found a statue of the Virgin here in some brambles and took it home. The statue soon found its way back to the bush, and this being taken as a sign, a chapel was built on the site. The statue was burned in 1793, but a fragment is conserved in a reliquary. Of the original shrine, only three pillars remain, to the left of the chancel, which has 12th-century ogival vaulting. The nave dates from the 15th century and contains an unusual cast-iron pulpit, locally made. In a chapel on the right is a marble cenotaph with the figures of Olivier de Clisson and Marguerite de Rohan. It dates from the early 15th century, though it was restored in 1856. The costumes are typical of the period; De Clisson is clad in his armor and Marguerite de Rohan has a square hairstyle, flowing dress and surcoat lined with ermine. The organ chest is 17th-century. The exterior of the church has a number of eye-catching gargoyles and, on the west side, a 15th-century *Virgin and Child*. There is a good view over the castle courtyard from the bell tower.

PARDON FOR EPILEPTICS. On September 8 every year processions are held through the streets of Josselin and along the banks of the river Oust, for the cult of Notre-Dame-du-Roncier. The ceremony is also dedicated to the cure of epilepsy. According to legend, the Virgin appeared one day in the town disguised as a beggar. She asked some washerwomen to give her a drink but they chased her off, setting the dogs on her. The Virgin punished the women by condemning them and their descendants to "bark like mad dogs at a certain time of year".

SAINTE-CROIX. On the other side of the Oust stands the CHAPEL OF SAINTE-CROIX, built up against the hillside. Its 11th-century nave was altered in the 14th and 17th centuries. The rest of the chapel seems to date from the 12th century. There is a good view of Josselin from the cemetery.

GUÉHENNO CALVARY ● 98

The shrine, built around 1550, was all but lost when Revolutionaries demolished it in 1794. The desecration, and the subsequent efforts of a priest and curate to rebuild the shrine, have added to its mystique. Although so unskilfully restored, the Calvary remains a powerful monument.

KERGUÉHENNEC

The château of Kerguéhennec and its 400-acre estate receive twenty thousand visitors every year. There are lakeside botanical gardens and a sculpture park in the grounds, and the elegant 18th-century château is now a center for contemporary art.

THE CHÂTEAU. The estate was acquired in the early 18th century by Daniel and Laurent Hogguer, two Swiss bankers based in Paris. They called in Olivier Delourme, an architect from Vannes, to design them a château of harmonious, classical proportions. In 1872 the Comte de Lanjuinais bought

Above, the château of Kerguéhennec.

THE GUÉHENNO CALVARY
This is the only monument of its kind in the Morbihan.

CENTER FOR CONTEMPORARY ART

Modern sculpture in a rural setting encourages visitors to consider the relationship between art and nature. *The Phoenix*, above, is by Carel Visser.

233

FRAISES DE COLPO
LA FERME FRUITIÈRE

the property. He had the fabric restored and the interior redecorated.

CENTER FOR CONTEMPORARY ART. Since 1985 sculptors from all over the world have been invited to come here and work. The sculptures are then set up in the park. They already include some fine pieces such as *Floating sculptures* by Martha Pan, *Names on Plaques, Names on Trees* by Ian Hamilton Finlay and *Mimi* by Markus Raetz. The center also organizes temporary exhibitions.

BIGNAN

Pierre Guillemot (1759–1805) was born in Bignan. He was a lieutenant under the Chouan leader Cadoudal, and known locally as "King of Bignan". The memory of the Chouannerie ● *62*, the royalist revolt in the Vendée and Brittany against the excesses of the Revolution, was revived in 1902 by Father Buléon, rector of Bignan from 1900 to 1906, in an attempt to put down the movement toward the separation of Church and State. To reinforce his sermons and commemorate the exemplary conduct of the people of Bignan during the Revolution, he commissioned two paintings from illustrator Théophile Busnel: *Clandestine Mass at the Calvary of Kervidogan* (1902) and *The King of Bignan* (1905). The paintings hang in the presbytery.

COLPO

Colpo owes its fame to the Princess Elisa Napoleone Bacciochi (1806–69), niece and goddaughter of Napoleon I and cousin of Napoleon III. The Italian princess, whose only son had committed suicide, was desperately searching for a new purpose in her life. In 1857 she made a journey to Brittany and came to visit Colpo. Soon after she bought 1,300 acres of land to farm. On it she also built a château, church, presbytery, town hall, school and hospital. She encouraged the creation of the first cultivated oyster beds in the river Auray, she planted trees on the Quiberon peninsula and she paid for the building of Créac'h lighthouse on Ouessant ▲ *278*. She also came to the aid of the islanders of Molène, struck by a cholera epidemic, and instituted local agricultural shows. She died in her château on February 3, 1869, and more than fifteen thousand people attended her funeral. Mixed agriculture continues in Colpo.

AVENUE DE LA PRINCESSE. Colpo's main street was renamed on July 31, 1969, the centenary of the death of Princess Elisa Bacciochi. Sadly the magnificent lime trees that once lined the street, and whose shade was so welcome on hot summer days, had to be cut down in 1989.

CHURCH OF NOTRE-DAME-DE-L'ASSOMPTION. The Princess is buried in Colpo church. Her tomb is granite, carved with Imperial bees and is similar in shape to the tomb of Napoleon at Les Invalides in Paris. The church façade is decorated with the Imperial crown and eagle, and the family coat of arms.

KORN-ER-HOUËT. From the road, heading south toward Vannes, a château in Louis XIII style can be seen standing in picturesque grounds. Korn-er-Houët château has now been converted into an old people's home.

"KING OF BIGNAN"
The Chouan leader Pierre Guillemot was executed in Vannes in 1805.

TOMB OF ELISA NAPOLEONE BACCHIOCHI
The mausoleum of the tireless benefactress who adopted Colpo as her home is in the church that she built as part of a model village for her estate workers.

MORLAIX

Morlaix added a lion and
a leopard to its arms
after it successfully
resisted an English
attack in 1522.

CHURCH OF ST-MARTIN

TOBACCO FACTORY

VOTIVE OFFERING
This anonymous
painting dates from the
16th century, after the
demolition of Morlaix
castle. The castle is
seen in the background
however. The offering
comes from the
collegiate church of
Notre-Dame-du-Mur,
and is now in the
Jacobin Museum
▲ 239. It was offered
to the Virgin in thanks
for saving a child from
drowning, and is the
only known depiction
of the castle.

HISTORY

One half in Léon and the other in the
Trégor, Morlaix clings to the banks of
the Jarlot and the Queffleut, two small
rivers that meet and flow down to the
Channel. Writer Anatole Le Braz
saw Morlaix as a caravanserai,
describing it as "Nestling in the
hollow of a spectacular estuary
among the foot-hills of the
Monts d'Arée, where wagons
coming down from the hills
met ships from far-off lands."
The early Gauls built a
fortified settlement on the site
of the present Square du
Château, taking advantage of the
rocky ground where the rivers
met. The Romans then built a camp
here called the *Castrum Mons
Relaxus*, before expatriate Britons from
across the Channel came in to occupy the
region. Much later, around 1000 AD, the Lord
of Tréguier built a castle there. The main
occupations in Morlaix at that time
were fishing, craft and trade. It soon
became a busy town, developing on both
sides of the river, and early in the 12th
century it became the property of the
Comte de Léon. To defend it from
possible attack, the town was
surrounded by a wall, and for many
years it continued to thrive thanks
largely to its fishing fleet and the sale of
dried fish. In 1187, however, the town
was taken by Henry II, the English king,
on behalf of the young Duke Arthur of
Brittany, whose guardian he was. Above all it was linen ▲ *60*
that was to make Morlaix's fortune: it was grown in the
surrounding area and woven into finest quality white cloth
called *creas nuevas*. In 1452 the Duc Pierre II decreed that all
cloth woven within a radius of 18 leagues should be sold only
at Morlaix Cloth Market before export. Spain and Portugal
were especially privileged customers.
ARMED CONFLICTS AND PRIVATEERS. In 1522, in reprisal for
raids on Bristol by Morlaix pirates under Jehan de
Coëtanlem, the English sacked the town; and to prevent such
a disaster happening again the Château du Taureau ▲ *259*
was built at the entrance to the bay. It is said to be this
incident that gave rise to the town's famous saying, "If they
bite you, bite them back!" Morlaix, a strong supporter of the
Catholic League ● *57*, was entrusted to the care of the
partisan Seigneur de Rosampoul during the Duc de
Mercoeur's struggle against the Protestant King Henri IV.
The king successfully besieged the town in 1594, and the
castle was demolished. In the following years Morlaix's
fortunes continued to prosper, however: from the 15th to the
18th centuries its harbor was one of the most important on

COINS
Until the 15th century
Morlaix minted its
own coins in the Tour
d'Argent, which no
longer exists.

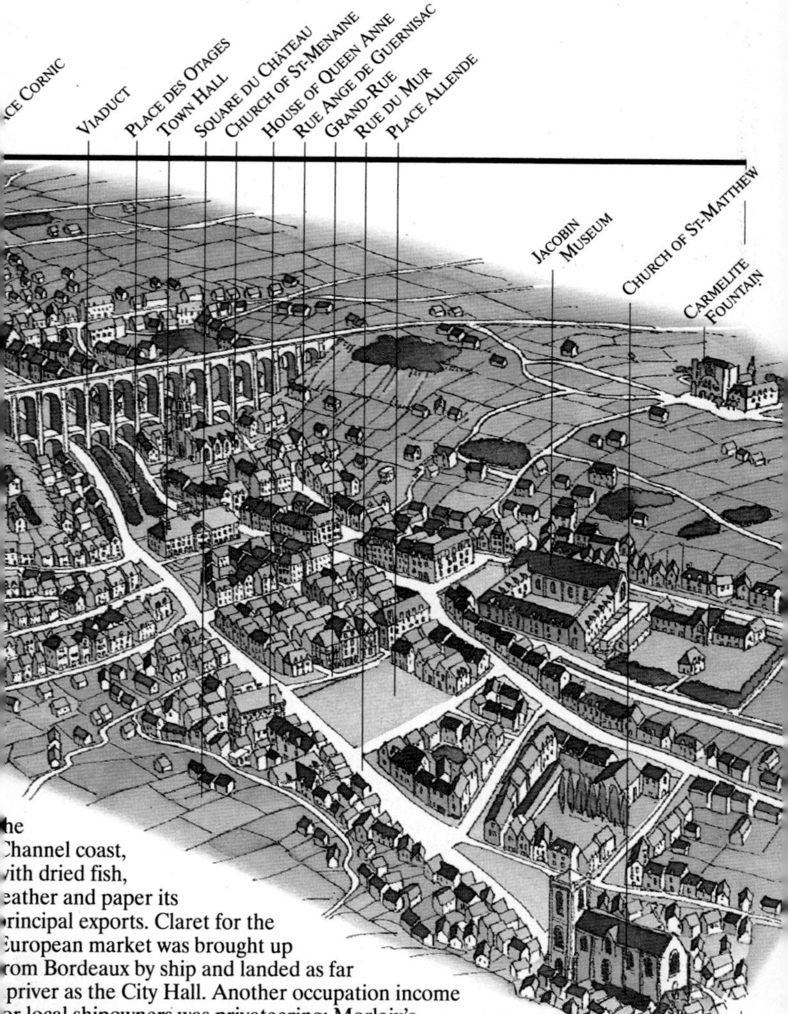

(top panoramic illustration with labels)

CE CORNIC VIADUCT PLACE DES OTAGES TOWN HALL SQUARE DU CHÂTEAU CHURCH OF ST-MENAINE HOUSE OF QUEEN ANNE RUE ANGE DE GUERNISAC GRAND-RUE RUE DU MUR PLACE ALLENDE

JACOBIN MUSEUM CHURCH OF ST-MATTHEW CARMELITE FOUNTAIN

...he
...Channel coast,
...with dried fish,
...leather and paper its
...principal exports. Claret for the
...European market was brought up
...from Bordeaux by ship and landed as far
...upriver as the City Hall. Another occupation income
...for local shipowners was privateering: Morlaix's
...prosperity at this time was reflected
...in its architecture, notably its
..."lantern" style houses.

INDUSTRIAL MORLAIX. Morlaix
became an industrial town in the
18th century. From 1736 there was a
tobacco factory on the Quai de Léon,
which at the end of the last century
had expanded to employ 1,800
workers (today there are 250). The
viaduct was built in the 19th century

THE "CORDELIÈRE"
The flagship of the
Franco-Breton fleet
was built at Morlaix
between 1496 and
1498. It was involved
in privateering, and in
the crusade against
the Turks. In 1512 it
sank in a battle with
the *Regent*, an English
ship.

to facilitate the construction of a rail link between Paris and
Brest, though this engineering triumph narrowly escaped
destruction in the British bombardments of August 1943.
Road-widening schemes and residential redevelopment have
drastically altered the face of Morlaix in recent years, the
fishing industry has declined and much of it is now carried on
by outsiders. Surviving industries include cask-making
(cooperage), the carving of wooden shoes, tanning and the
manufacture of candles. But even at a brief glance the visitor
will see that Morlaix's greatest asset is its past and its greatest
industry is tourism.

237

AROUND THE PLACE ALLENDE

The most important surviving examples of 16th- and 17th-century architecture in Morlaix are between the Grand-Rue and the Rue du Mur. Beams carved with grotesque faces or likenesses of saints, and other features of the peroid transport the visitor back to the Renaissance.

GRAND-RUE. The Cloth Market, which made Morlaix's fortune in the 14th century, was once held here. The street leads to the Pavé, once the center of the old town, but largely

destroyed during the construction of an arterial roadway linking Paris to Brest. The wooden STATUE OF A PIPER at the corner of Rue Carnot and Rue du Pont-Notre-Dame is the sole vestige of its former splendor. At the corner of the Place des Halles, the statue of the *Bonhomme de Morlaix* bears the legend: "Bowed down with work, crippled with taxes, robbed, looted, ill-used by the Duke's and the King's men . . . here he stands outside this house . . . waiting in hope for the hour of his release."

RUE DU MUR. Formerly the Rue des Nobles, where the nobility lived until the Revolution. The HOUSE OF QUEEN ANNE at no. 9 is a classic example, though the Queen never spent time here. She merely passed through the town in 1505 on a pilgrimage to Folgoët in the hope of obtaining a miraculous cure for her husband King Louis XII. The House of Queen Anne is the only "lantern" house open to the public. Its façade is decorated with carvings: on the second floor is a group of the *Annunciation*, with the saints James, Lawrence, Nicholas and Barbara on the story above.

THE DISTRICT AND CHURCH OF ST-MATTHEW.
The Priory of St-Matthew dates from the 11th century. A Norman church outside the town was rebuilt between 1498 and 1505 in the Gothic style, and remodeled in 1824 as a neoclassical building. The tower, begun in 1548, is an early example of the Renaissance style in Brittany. The interior contains the large 16th-century FIGURE OF CHRIST, the CHOIR WINDOW

depicting the Church together with Saint Matthew, and the "VIERGE OUVRANTE". This 15th-century statue, formerly in the collegiate church of Notre Dame du Mur, is a typical piece from the Cologne workshops in Westphalia: closed, it represents the Virgin and child, and opened shows the Holy Trinity. The district of St-Matthew is the oldest in Morlaix: the Venelle aux Archers, Place au Lait, Rue aux Bouchers and the Place du Marc'hallah (market) all evoke the busy commerce that once enlivened this area.

NOTRE-DAME-DU-MUR. The RUE DES VIEILLES MURAILLES leads to the site where the collegiate church was built. Duc Jean II laid the foundation stone of the chapel in 1295. For centuries its 280-foot high octagonal tower

THE "PAVÉ"
This painting by local artist Edmond Puyo shows Morlaix as it was in 1815. It is now in the Jacobin Museum.

STATUE OF ANKOU
The museum has a fine collection of sculpture dating from the 15th to the 18th centuries. This grotesque figure of *Ankou* was carved in the 17th century.

erved as a landmark ■ *16* for sailors. It was deconsecrated during the Revolution and its bells melted down. Then it was old to a developer, who demolished the nave for its stone: in 806 the bell tower collapsed, killing five people.

THE CASTLE. It was built around the year 1000 on the orders of the Lord of Tréguier, and soon passed into the hands of the Comte de Léon. Supporters of the Catholic League ● *57* who pposed the King took refuge here in the late 1700's, and it was demolished after their surrender to the royal troops. Only rees now mark the spot where it once stood, dominating the own at the confluence of the two rivers. The only surviving ikeness of it is a painting, much later and probably imaginary, n a votive offering ▲ *236* in the Jacobin Museum.

AROUND THE JACOBIN MUSEUM

MUSÉE DES JACOBINS. The town museum is housed in the hurch of the Jacobin monastery. It was founded by the Dominicans when Saint Dominic came in 1213, and Jacobin 10nks lived there up until the time of the Revolution. Its reputation (particularly hat of its library) attracted visitors such s the Duchess Anne of Brittany, Mary Queen of Scots, and the learned monk lbertus Magnus, who wrote his *Lives of 1e Saints* here. The museum was opened 1 1887: it contains pictures of the Italian, 'lemish and French schools from the 16th the 19th centuries together with a ollection of Impressionist and Post-mpressionist paintings. Works by Rodin, 3oudin, Couture, Courbet, Monet, Bonnard and Raffaelli ang side by side with those of painters who worked in Brittany. In 1985 the museum was enlarged to accommodate arge temporary exhibitions as well.

PLACE DES VIARMES. A house once stood here, flanked by the our d'Argent where up until the 15th century coins were ninted ▲ *236*. From the square one can still see where ne River Jarlot used to run.

VENELLES. The Venelles lead to the CARMEL, a part of ne town situated on a hilltop, and enclose a residential istrict containing many religious institutions. From ne museum take the Venelle des Fontaines and then ne Rue Ste-Marthe, walk down the Rue Créac'h Joly eside the Ursuline convent and turn into the Rue des 'ignes. The high walls of the houses enclose terraced gardens ith up to four levels, sometimes rising so steeply up the illside that the top of the garden is higher than the house.

NOTRE-DAME-DU-MUR
The old collegiate church on the outskirts of town, seen from the site of the castle in the 18th century.

MUSEUM IN A CHURCH
Left, a painting by Jules Noël. Right, the beautiful rose window in the apse.

THE VENELLES
They are steeply sloping and often have flights of steps with gutters carved into them.

LANTERN HOUSES ★. There are still about ten of these unique buildings in Morlaix, in the Grand-Rue, the Rue du Mur and Rue Ange de Guernisac.

3

"FINE GENTLEMEN INHABITED SPANISH-STYLE HOUSES WITH ELEGANT GLASS-ROOFED PATIOS THAT LINKED THE REAR QUARTERS WITH FRONT ROOMS OVERLOOKING THE BUSY STREET."

FRANÇOIS MENEZ

"The town had so much more character when it was full of medieval houses with their jutting corbels and upper floors leaning out over the streets!"

Louis Le Guennec

MONUMENTAL FIREPLACE
The street side of the house had a corbeled façade, often decorated with statues, and the ground floor was a shop. In the central room there was a massive carved fireplace that heated the whole house. The owners generally belonged to the wealthy bourgeois class of weavers, shipowners or brokers.

Houses like these were built from the 15th to the early 18th century. All had the same basic design as the HOUSE OF QUEEN ANNE, the only one open to the public. The houses are two or three stories high and built in two halves, one facing the street, the other the courtyard. These are joined by an interior ratio lit by a "lantern" window in the roof. From this central room a spiral staircase leads directly to the upper floors on the street side. The rooms at the rear of the house are reached ver carved wooden walk-ways, *ponts d'allée* or *pond alez*. The ewel post supporting the staircase was often topped by a atue of the owners' patron saint.

"LOBSTER TAIL"
The Morlaix headdress is
known as a *queue de homard*.

MORLAIX BEER
Bretons enjoy *Coreff*, the local brew, which is only available in cafés that have the right conditions and equipment to serve it properly.

CHAPELLE DE NOTRE-DAME-DE-LA-FONTAINE. The chapel was built around 1390 and presented to the Carmelites in 1624. All that remains is the rose window, and at its foot a fountain in the Flamboyant Gothic style of the 15th century. Its spring was an important place of pilgrimage in the Middle Ages.

THE BREWERY "DES DEUX RIVIÈRES". An establishment on the outskirts of town as the land rises up into the Trégor. Since 1985 the brewery has specialized in a barley beer known as *Coreff* or *Cervoise*, which is fermented naturally, and has a pleasantly bitter and malty flavor not unlike that of traditional British ales. It is not widely available, but highly prized locally. There are frequent guided tours, which include tastings of the delicious beer!

AN IMPRESSIVE EDIFICE
The viaduct was built to designs by the engineer Fenoux. It is 190 feet high and 958 feet long, supported by fourteen semicircular arches. Nine smaller arches support the first story, which is open to pedestrians in summer.

"LANCES"
Houses on the harbor front once had a projecting second floor supported on pillars that formed a shelter beneath, known as a *lance*. They protected unshipped goods as they were loaded into cellars. The demolition of houses of this type began with the building of the viaduct, and gradually continued.

AROUND ST-MARTIN

THE VIADUCT. It was built between 1861 and 1863 in local granite, and was a vital link on the railroad from Paris to Brest. The Western Railway Company (Compagnie des Chemins de Fer de l'Ouest) built it to avoid the steep valleys of the North Brittany coast: their franchise on the route was responsible for several expensive marvels of engineering.

VENELLE DE LA ROCHE. Here there is a magnificent view over Morlaix. The chapel of Notre-Dame-des-Anges was built in memory of the children and teacher of a nursery school,

victims of British bombing in 1943. **CHURCH OF ST-MARTIN.** It was destroyed by lightning in the famous storm of 1771 and later rebuilt. Inside are two marble angels taken from a Genoese ship by Morlaix privateers.

VENELLE DE LA FONTAINE COLOBERT. Fine stairways flanked by walls enclosing private gardens, lead to an ancient WASH HOUSE, which has been restored and is partially covered by a slate roof.

RUE LONGUE. Until the Rue de la Villeneuve was opened in 1744 this was the main road to Brest. It was fashionable residential district in the 16th century, as the columned façades of its fine old houses still testify. In later years workers in the tobacco factories settled here, while today the Rue Longue has been taken over by professional men and women. The curiously named MAISON DU TEMPS PERDU was formerly the city hall.

AROUND ST-MELAINE

THE CHURCH OF ST-MELAINE. This was originally a Norman priory, founded in 1150 by the Lord of Morlaix, Guyomarc'h III. In 1489 it was rebuilt in Batz granite in Flamboyant Gothic style. The south side chapels, with their altarpieces and funerary niches, are in an excellent state of preservation. The north side had to be rebuilt after the bombings of 1943. Among the carving on the beams is an ermine decorated with the Benedictines' motto "A ma vie".

RUE ANGE DE GUERNISAC. Access is by the VENELLE AU SON or the VENELLE DU FOUR ST-MELAINE, where the parish oven (*four*) once stood. The street is now largely given over to boutiques and restaurants. The neighboring streets are narrow and have attractive slate-hung houses. At the top of the Rampe de Créou or the Venelle aux Prêtres are the old QUARTIER DU CALVAIRE and the ESPLANADE DE L'ANCIENNE CITÉ D'AUMONT. From here, as the land falls away steeply down to the town, one looks down on to the Place Cornic, the harbor and factories. Freebooter Jehan de Coëtanlem ▲ 236 (who became Admiral

of the Portuguese fleet) lived in the Manoir de Penanru. The center of Morlaix changed radically when for health reasons the rivers Jarlot and Queffleut were covered over. It certainly smelled better! Until then boats would come up as far as the present city hall. Unfortunately, when the railroad viaduct was built, the oldest overhanging "lance"-style houses had to be demolished, and the remainder gradually followed in their wake. In the late 19th and early 20th century, buildings rapidly sprang up on the land created by these works, tightly packed against the cliffs of schist. The bandstand in the PLACE DES OTAGES (hostages), where the German army held a macabre lottery in 1943, is a particularly gruesome reminder of the Occupation.

THE PORT

THE TOBACCO FACTORY. It was built between 1736 and 1740 by the famous royal architect Blondel, who also built the Porte St-Denis in Paris. The factory superseded an earlier one situated at the Manoir de Penanru, which was not ideal as a

The church of St-Melaine and the long flight of steps leading up to it.

OLD MORLAIX
This 1940 woodcut by Félicie Herr shows the Venelle au Son, a winding footway between old houses hung with slates.

Old cigar boxes from the Morlaix tobacco factory.

THE TOBACCO FACTORY
This fine early 18th-century industrial complex was built on the harbor frontage of the Quai du Léon.

"THE SNUFF-TAKER"
Oil on canvas (1841), now in the St Malo Museum ▲ 191. "Morlaix" has been a popular variety of snuff since the 18th century.

site for a factory, access being difficult. This is the oldest building belonging to the French national tobacco company (SEITA). Before the introduction of machinery around 1870, cigars, cheroots, cigarettes and even snuff were all made here by hand. By 1879 about two thousand workers, mostly women and girls, were employed here. But over the years production gradually dwindled, and the workforce is now greatly diminished.

PLACE CORNIC. The square is named after the freebooter Charles Cornic known as "Duchesne" who until 1778 served in the king's navy fighting the English, and who later went to sea again in the service of the Revolutionary navy. He laid out the defenses in the bay of Morlaix. Cornic never aspired to the higher echelons of the navy, however, and was content to serve as a middle-ranking officer. Around the side of the Place Cornic are the last surviving "lance"-style houses ▲ 242.

THE HARBOR. From the 12th to the 18th centuries, the harbor, tucked away in the corner of a tidal estuary, was large enough to rival Nantes and St-Malo. Its fortune was based on linen ● 60. Boats loaded with cloth set sail for the Iberian peninsula, returning with cargoes of citrus fruit, wine and iron ore. From here local produce such as grain, dried fish, leather and paper left for northern Europe, to return with timber for masts, steel and tar. Morlaix was also a depot for wine from Bordeaux and salt from Guérande, while from the Channel Islands came commodities such as wool, zinc, tobacco and gold coins. Then came the great age of privateering: the port suffered under finance minister Colbert's protectionist policies, and the English responded by reserving the monopoly on imports for their own ships. Wars with Holland (1672) and the Augsburg League (1689) hastened the port's decline, though privateering was still profitable, especially for the shipowners. Seized goods were sold or bartered on the stone quays. These date from the late 16th century, and the names "Quai de Téguier" and "Quai du Léon" emphasize the town's position in between the two regions. Too small to accommodate the tonnage of today's ships, the harbor is now only used by pleasure craft.

PARISH CLOSES

Brittany's most remarkable parish closes are on the southern and lower slopes of the Elorn valley in Léon, in Trégor and in Cornouaille. They are an architectural phenomenon closely bound up with important religious processions. All have very similar design, buildings and monuments, and a décor that returns time and again to the central episodes of the Christian faith: the suffering of Christ on the cross and his resurrection. Of course parish closes represent only one aspect of Breton Christianity. Abbeys, cathedrals, churches and great shrines all

bear witness to an unusually high-minded and introspective religious spirit. But from one parish close to the next in rural Brittany, church missions proclaimed the triumph of the Christian faith with uncompromising fervor.

1. BAPTISTRY
It stands at the entrance to the church, and in Finistère is often crowned by a wooden canopy with ornate twisted columns.

2. OSSUARY
Until the 18th century the dead were buried inside the church. When there was no more room, their bones were moved here.

3. BARRIER
Entrances are blocked by a step topped with a flat stone set on edge. This keeps out farm animals, and marks the divide between sacred and unconsecrated ground.

4. SOUTH PORCH
A vestibule where the faithful wait before mass while contemplating the Biblical scenes carved or painted on the arches of the colonnade.

5. STAINED GLASS
"Passion" windows, many of which date from the 16th century, tell the story of the Crucifixion in much the same way as calvaries. Each small section of a window illustrates a different episode.

6. ALTARPIECES
The Passion story was again taken as the central theme when in the 17th century altarpieces began to replace stained glass. The detailed panels and surrounds are richly ornamented.

7. PLACÎTRE AND CEMETERY
The *placître*, specific to Brittany, is the holy ground around the church. At one time the dead were buried here, but the cemetery is now separate.

8. CALVARY
It stands to the right of the south porch and was the only cross in the cemetery until, in the 19th century, one was put on every grave. Calvaries were decorated with scenes from the New Testament and are often very elaborate.

9. TRIUMPHAL ARCH
The grand entrance may have two or four supporting pillars. Every procession, whether baptismal, nuptial or funeral, passes beneath its central arch.

FROM RELIQUARY TO CHAPEL

In the 16th and 17th centuries the close ceased to function as a cemetery and people were buried inside the church. Ossuaries had to be built to make more room for the remains. Later these became funerary chapels. The façade and wall facing into the close were lined with narrow arcades or a honeycomb pattern of recesses, with holes into which remains could be placed and blessed.

OSSUARIES built adjoining the church were attached to the west side of the south porch, while chapel-ossuaries were placed on the southwest side of the enclosure. In both cases the openings would be on the same one or two sides. Below, the St-Thégonnec ossuary ▲ *252*.

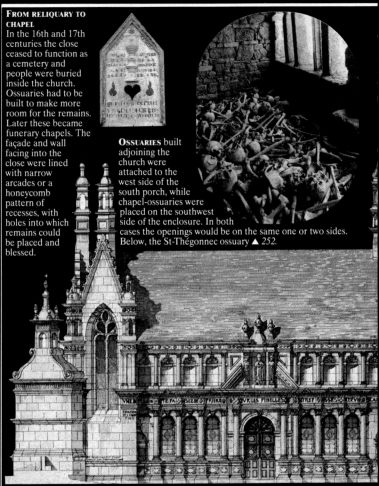

PLACÎTRE AND CEMETERY

The *placître*, the holy ground around the church, was gradually taken up with tombs when the dead were no longer buried in church, and the ossuaries had changed to become chapels. Below, the church of La Roche-Maurice and its cemetery.

La Roche-Maurice ossuary.

Guimiliau ossuary.

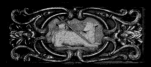

A lean-to chapel erected over the hermitage (*penity* in Breton) of the founding saint, sheltering the recumbent figure.

INTERIOR EMBELLISHMENT

A decree of 1758 made burial in a cemetery obligatory. Ossuaries were therefore redundant; they became funerary chapels and were adorned with baroque altars and altarpieces, often richly ornamented. Above, detail of a column from the Dirinon ossuary.

MEMENTO MORI

Inscriptions in Latin, Breton and French invite the reader to prepare himself for the inevitable approach of death. These warnings are backed up by striking carvings of skull and crossed bones and the figure of the Ankou himself, a skeleton carrying a scythe. Some chapels also contain small wooden reliquaries in the shape of miniature houses.

Adam and Eve before and after eating the apple: detail of the Rosary altarpieces in St-Thégonnec.

BAROQUE ALTARPIECES

Altarpieces began to appear in Breton churches during the 17th century. Above, the St Joseph altarpiece in Guimiliau ▲ *253*, and the Rosary in Commana ▲ *255*. Whether painted or carved, they created a sumptuous and animated backdrop to each altar. In Finistère they were always made of wood.

THEMES

The most popular subjects were those involving Christ and the Virgin Mary, the Apostles, John the Baptist, local saints, healers and protectors of animals, the dead, and Purgatory.

THE ROSARY ALTARPIECE

A common theme, with the Virgin in the center presenting a triple rosary to Saint Dominic and Saint Catherine of Siena. Depicted around them are the great Mysteries of the faith. Such an altarpiece indicates the existence of a brotherhood that once gathered here to recite the rosary.

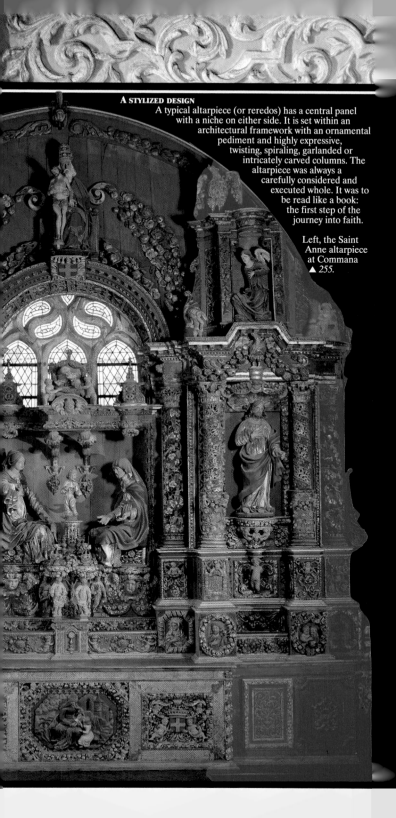

A STYLIZED DESIGN

A typical altarpiece (or reredos) has a central panel with a niche on either side. It is set within an architectural framework with an ornamental pediment and highly expressive, twisting, spiraling, garlanded or intricately carved columns. The altarpiece was always a carefully considered and executed whole. It was to be read like a book: the first step of the journey into faith.

Left, the Saint Anne altarpiece at Commana ▲ 255.

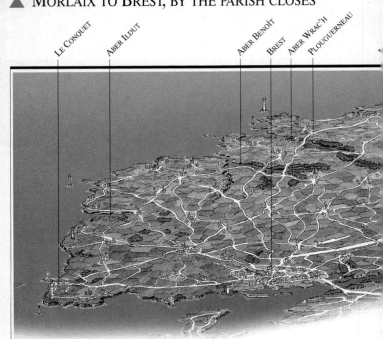

LE CONQUET ABER ILDUT ABER BENOÎT BREST ABER WRAC'H PLOUGUERNEAU

REREDOS IN THE ROSARY CHAPEL (1697) The exquisite poychrome carving of the *Virgin and Child* (detail below) in the beautiful church of

St-Thégonnec was the work of Palmay and Lespaignol, two craftsmen from Morlay.

COMPETITIVE RELIGION. The parish closes (*enclos paroissaux*) ▲ *245* of Brittany were designed to reflect the eternal themes sacred to the Catholic faith: the death and Resurrection of Christ, and the fate of man's soul. In the 16th and 17th centuries Bretons became passionate and fiercely competitive builders of these walled churches, each village trying to outdo the others in opulence and skill. Success at sea and in the cloth trade ● *60* had made this period Brittany's Golden Age and the Bretons' great prosperity was reflected in their parish closes.

ST-THÉGONNEC

This village was the home of a special caste of peasants called Julots, who made their fortune out of trading in linen and breeding Breton horses. Keen to have the finest religious buildings in the area, they brought in artists and craftsmen whom they commissioned to realize such substantial projects as their parish close. **PARISH CLOSE.** Although almost excessively ostentatious, the arrangement at St-Thégonnec is typical of many closes. The entrance, a triumphal arch built in 1587, consists of four massive pillars topped with lanterns and delicate aedicules. The CALVARY, which dates from 1610, was the last one to be given a storied base. The depth of feeling in these three crosses gives the Calvary a monumental quality. The OSSUARY (1676–82) is the finest of its kind, built when the vogue for such charnel houses was coming to an end. **CHURCH OF NOTRE-DAME.** The church has been lavishly restored. Of the former building, which dated from 1563, only

a bell
tower and steeple
remained. The new one had
to be taller, so between 1599 and 1610
a tower was built that would rival the one at
Pleyben. The same competitive spirit is also apparent in
the church furnishings. The sumptuous REREDOS IN THE
ROSARY CHAPEL (1697) is the work of Palmay and Lespaignol.
The REREDOS ON THE HIGH ALTAR, carved by Carquain in
1662, shows a *Nativity*. The Adoration of the Holy Sacrament
is an 18th-century addition. Two more altarpieces complete
the interior balance of the chancel. The PULPIT which stands
in the nave is an outstanding piece of workmanship, carved in
1683 by Lerrel de Landivisiau. The restoration of the ORGAN
was completed in 1978.

**ALTARPIECE OF SAINT
JOSEPH, GUIMILIAU**
Joseph, at the center,
has charge of the
young Jesus. Saint
Anne and Saint
Elizabeth occupy
niches, while the
pediment features
Saint Lawrence.

The 17th-century
pulpit at Guimiliau.

GUIMILIAU

This finely proportioned architectural group shows the love of
exuberant ornamentation characteristic of the wealthy
peasant community for whom it was built.

PARISH CLOSE. The triumphal arch with Baroque pediment is
a relatively modest example of its kind. But the
remaining buildings in the enclosure are
more extravagant. The OSSUARY is set to
the west of the portico in keeping with
tradition, and is complemented here by
the FUNERARY CHAPEL on the eastern
side. The most remarkable feature of the
chapel is the PULPIT set between two
pillars and provided with a sounding-
board: it was used for funeral orations. The
powerful CALVARY rises from its base to a
cross, on which are carved the dates 1581 and 1588 and which
has the figures of Mary, Saint John, Saint Peter and Saint
Yves carved on the horizontal beam. The whole Calvary
swarms with figures arranged on two levels. Twenty-five
scenes, including a superb representation of the *Entombment
of Christ*, form a fascinating though chronologically inaccurate
sequence.

CHURCH OF ST-MILIAU. There is a belfry from the
Beaumanoir workshops in Tréguier; and the tower, flanked by
a spiral staircase, has an ornate gallery around the bell. The

The banner of the Brotherhood of the Rosary (1658) at Guimiliau.

PORCH, built between 1606 and 1617, has a semicircular arch with decorated keystone between two imposing corner buttresses. Above is a classical pediment supported by two ringed and fluted pillars. In niches on the porch canopy are figures of the twelve Apostles (six of them in stone), which probably came from the workshops of Roland Doré. Inside the church light pours into the nave and transepts, with their perpendicular vaulting, and sets the three 17th-century ALTARPIECES aglow. There is an imposing BAPTISTRY, with fonts (1675) covered by a carved wood canopy. Finally there are two banners displayed in the church: one belongs to the parish, which depicts the Crucifixion and Saint Miliau, and the other is the banner of the Brotherhood of the Rosary.

LAMPAUL-GUIMILIAU

The *lan* (monastery) of Paul Aurélien, Lampaul-Guimiliau honors the memory of the first Bishop of Léon and his travels Originally part of the *trève* (church land) of Guimiliau, Lampaul-Guimiliau was established as a parish after the Concordat and was quick to rival its more important neighbor. The finest craftsmen and materials were brought in to build a magnificent close: triumphal arch, Calvary and ossuary around a large and costly church.

THE BAPTISTRY AT GUIMILIAU
It shows John the Baptist baptizing Jesus, surrounded by the twelve Apostles.

LOCMÉLAR
Remote and secluded, the little village has a parish close of moving simplicity. The Calvary is shown below.

PARISH CLOSE. The 16th-century CALVARY, which bears the two thieves on its crosspiece attempts to equal that 2 miles away at Guimiliau, which tells the story of the life and death of Christ. On the TRIUMPHAL ARCH at the western side stands another Crucifixion, with two gibbets and the pleading figure of Mary Magdalene. The OSSUARY is dated 1667 and is now a chapel dedicated to the Holy Trinity. It is a stately building: inside is a marvelous 17th-century ALTARPIECE glorifying the Holy Trinity and invoking Saint Roch and Saint Sebastian, protectors against plague.

CHURCH OF NOTRE-DAME. At first sight the most impressive feature of the church is its tower, with a spire that once reached a height of 230 feet above the ground. It is somewhat truncated now, having been struck by lightning in 1809. With its galleries and turrets, the tower encapsulates a style of Breton design that was at once traditional and innovative: if the larger design elements are Gothic, the decoration is wholly Renaissance. Inside, the colors glow like gemstones upon woodwork, altarpieces and baptistry, gleam through the stained glass windows and shine quietly on the organ pipes. The 16th-century ROOD BEAM (above), which carries a carved Crucifixion, tells the story of Christ's passion in bright polychrome. The PASSION REREDOS, to the left of the choir, is a 16th-century work from Antwerp attributed to Robert Moreau. Eight panels decorated with figures and set between pillars illustrate scenes from the Last Supper and Blessed Sacrament. To the right of the choir is a REREDOS OF SAINT JOHN THE BAPTIST. An ALTARPIECE depicting SAINT ANNE is in the right-hand side aisle, and on the RETABLE dedicated to him, Saint Lawrence holds a heart in one hand, and a book

ROOD BEAM
A carving in the church of Notre Dame de Lampaul-Guimiliau featuring an impressive Crucifixion and scenes from the Passion (detail, right).

...nd his martyr's gridiron in the other. The retable opposite, ...edicated to St Margaret, presents a striking contrast between ...he elegant young woman with oval face, slender neck, supple ...igure and hands joined in prayer, and the monster from ...vhich she has just been delivered. Beyond that is a ...epresentation of the ENTOMBMENT OF CHRIST (1676), which ...vas carved in the naval dockyards at Brest and is signed ...Antoine fecit". The face of Christ stands out from those of ...he other figures. Mary is supported by John the Baptist, her ...orrowing expression suffused with sweetness. On the south ...ide opposite are the BAPTISMAL FONTS. The octagonal granite ...asin dates from 1651 and the canopy from 1650. Further ...long in the side aisle is a holy-water stoup whose most ...emarkable feature is not the depiction of Christ's baptism ...ut the demons writhing in agony in the water.

Altarpiece of Saint Anne at the church of Saint Derrien, Commana. Below, the statue of the pregnant Mary.

COMMANA

PARISH CLOSE. A somewhat austere monumental gate with ...wo turrets gives access to the enclosure, which also has a ...emetery and rather plain ossuary (completed in 1687).
CHURCH OF ST DERRIEN ★. Work on the church began at the ...nd of the 16th century and continued well into the 17th ...entury. The interior is in total contrast to the general ...mpression of severity outside. Inside, the furnishings ● *102* ...re exuberantly Baroque, and the finest pieces are found in ...he baptistry. The SAINT ANNE ALTARPIECE is a magnificent ...nsemble. It was offered to the church by the parishioners in ...tonement for having lynched the priest: they thought he had ...heltered the excise-men, which was a serious offense against ...heir moral code. The altarpiece was installed in ...682, and depicts Saint Anne with Jesus and Mary. ...he balustraded BAPTISTRY dates from the 17th ...entury, and the baptism of Christ is depicted on the ...anopy above. The ROSARY ALTARPIECE is also of great ...rtistic interest, dominated by the figure of God; ...urrounded by angels, He holds the world in His left ...and and gives a blessing with His right. The FIVE ...WOUNDS ALTARPIECE, also known as "The altarpiece of ...Christ", was donated by a brotherhood devoted to ...neditating on Christ the Redeemer and praying for ...he afflicted. This unusual reredos, predominantly ...vhite and gold, comes from the naval dockyards at ...3rest. The sculptors have imbued the panel with ...incerity: it is full of life, and highly decorated. At ...he center two bare-breasted angels with flowing ...air are crowning Christ as He displays his wounds. ...There are numerous statues around the church, ...otably a beautiful sculpture of the VIRGIN painted ...n delicate colors, and another late 15th-century ...vooden one painted in polychrome, showing MARY ...GREAT WITH CHILD.
ALLÉE COUVERTE AT MOUGAU ● *80*. At the western ...nd of the village of nearby Mougau Bihan is a ...negalithic monument, an *allée couverte* 46 feet long ...vhich may be a communal tomb from the Neolithic ...eriod (c. 2000 BC). Some of the supporting stones ...ave lines carved in them, which would represent ...oreasts, axes with handles or long-shafted spears. The

THE "LIGNOLETS"
These decorative carvings are
worked into the ridged slates

KÉROUAT MILLS
The two mills of the
Monts d'Arrée
ecomuseum

are powered by the
river Stain at the point
where it enters the
lake.

CARYATID
In the passageway
around the Church
of La Martyre stands
this caryatid, its hair
plaited, half-naked, a
vacant expression on
its face and its legs in
chains.

ensemble, called *mougeo* (Breton for "grotto") or "the Giants' grave" has given its name to the village.

KÉROUAT MILLS. This is the name of the MONTS-D'ARRÉE ECOMUSEUM, opened in 1975 on the site of a deserted village and made up of about ten different buildings. The UPPERMOST MILL is one of the most important, built around 1610 or 1618 and formerly equipped with a horizontal wheel. Water from the Stain, a stream which flows into the mill pond, ran beneath the building. Other interesting buildings include the DWELLING HOUSE (1777) of the miller and his family, the BAKEHOUSE (1822) complete with kneading-trough and surrounded by stables and barns, and a second cottage containing a *lit-clos* (boxed-in-bed).

SIZUN

PARISH CLOSE. Sizun has the most remarkable entrance gate of all the closes. Its magnificent TRIPLE ARCH is framed by four Corinthian columns which open on to a vast enclosure. While the latter may lack the unity of the closes at Guimiliau or St-Thegonnec, its spaciousness has allowed an elegant arrangement of the monuments put up between the 15th and 18th centuries. The OSSUARY is most unusual and its façade, which dates from 1585, is decorated with a procession of apostles.

CHURCH. This was rebuilt in the 17th century, though its Gothic porch was preserved, now stripped of its carved apostles and with strange sculptures in their place. The bell tower is 18th century. All the indecipherable carvings lend the church a unique atmosphere. The interior is strikingly unusual: the eye is repeatedly drawn toward the chancel, which is of an impressive size and has three elevated RETABLES. The small 17th-century RETABLE ON THE HIGH ALTAR is richly decorated, with columns and statues of the four Evangelists in turreted niches. The magnificent ORGAN CHEST, made between 1683 and 1686, completes this impressive interior that seems to encapsulate the religious spirit of the Counter-Reformation.

"MAISON DE LA RIVIÈRE, DE L'EAU ET DE LA PÊCHE". Housed in an old mill at Vargraon-en-Sizun, this center is open to all, and will be of particular interest to anglers. There are aquariums, exhibitions, and guided visits to the River Elorn.

LA MARTYRE

The derivation of this small village's name is shrouded in mystery. It is situated on a plateau, and is best-known for its famous Paris Clos. A large fair used to be held here every year in July. It lasted for eight days, and attracted itinerant tradesmen from Tours, Angers, Normandy and even from overseas who came to deal in cloth, horses and cattle. Such a prosperous state of affairs was bound to arouse envy so the wealthy tradesmen of Landerneau,

with the support of the Rohans, attempted to do him harm in any way they could.

PARISH CLOSE. Access is by a TRIUMPHAL ARCH, a copy of which was on display at the Paris Universal Exhibition in 1900. It has a triple entrance, the main arch surmounted by a CALVARY set on a large console and dominated by the figure of Christ in Judgment. The figure of the crucified Christ is back to back with the image of Christ resurrected, supported by two angels. The GOTHIC PORCH is decorated with the Joyful Mysteries set around a NATIVITY on the tympanum (right). It is remarkably similar to the porch at Folgoët.

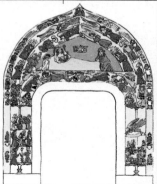

CHURCH. Built between the 14th and the 17th centuries. In the 15th century the church benefited from the patronage of Duke Jean V (1399–1442), who paid for enlargement and rebuilding, specially of the porch. The OSSUARY dates from 1619.

STAINED GLASS AND FURNISHINGS. The windows behind the high altar were made in 1535 and bear the signature "Jost". Their cartoons served as models for the Quimper workshops throughout the 16th century. The main window has a fine Crucifixion, while on the north side a window with sections shows scenes from the Passion, as well as likenesses of patrons: René de Rohan is depicted with his wife Isabeau d'Albret. There are fine STATUES, a beautifully decorated BAPTISTRY with canopy dated 1635, and ornamented holy water stoups. From the stoup inside the porch, the figure of Ankou (Death) rises up, carrying the head of a child. The stoups inside the entrance are less melodramatic: one, dating from 1601, has an angel with an aspergillum, and another, of 1681, offers life and salvation through holy water.

CHURCH OF LA MARTYRE
This reconstruction of the polychrome tympanum was made by the architect Fons de Kort.

LANDERNEAU

BRIDGE OF ROHAN. A total of twenty-nine towns in Europe have bridges with buildings on them, thirty-five in all. But only six, two of which are in France, at Landerneau and Narbonne, are permanently inhabited. Whereas everywhere else, whether in Florence, Nuremberg, Lucerne, Ronda (Spain) or Ambleside (England), the bridges are in the middle of town, the famous Pont de Rohan at Landerneau is unique in being washed by the sea. The original bridge at Landerneau was probably wooden, built by the Romans over a

"THE HOUSE OF DUCHESS ANNE"
Also known as the *Maison de la Sénéchaussée*. It was built in 1664 and, unusually, one façade is built of stone while the other is half-timbered.

A general view of the western façade of the Pont de Rohan.

HENVIC   ÎLE CALLOT   CARANTEC   TAULÉ   PENN-AL-LANN PENINSULA   ÎLE LOUËT   CHÂTEAU DU TAUREAU   LOCQUÉNOLÉ   ST-FRANÇOIS DE CUBURIEN

D. 173   D. 73   D. 58   D. 58   D. 73   D. 769   D. 58   N. 12   D. 712

over a ford. The present bridge was completed in 1510 by that indefatigable builder Jean, Vicomte de Rohan.

THE PENN AL LANN PENINSULA
A footpath goes round the peninsula from Carantec.

From the north the Château du Taureau (top) is clearly visible.

FROM MORLAIX TO THE SEA

Leave town by the road that follows the left bank of the river down to the Bay of Morlaix, and that, according to one writer "snakes along the river's length, faithfully mirroring its every bend. The houses on the opposite bank, without being ostentatious like those beside the Odet, are attractive enough especially those that overlook the sea." (Christian Frochen, *Finistère and Léon*.)

CHÂTEAU DE LANNUGUY. The château stands above the Donant estuary, on a cape formed by a stream that meets the river here. Before the Revolution it belonged to the De Villemarqué family, one of whom was the compiler of the *Barzaz-Breiz* ● 65.

PENN-AL-LANN PENINSULA

The little peninsula lies east of Carantec, ending in a string of islets of which the most important is the Île Louët. The peninsula, edged with beaches and small coves, is largely covered with pine forest where mimosa and eucalyptus grow. There are also many holiday villas, but a coastal path allows the visitor to walk round it in little more than one hour from the PLAGE DU KÉLENN at Carantec. From the path there are good views of the Trégor coast, the islets in the estuary, the famous fortified Château du Taureau and the Île Callot. The latter is reachable on foot at low tide by means of a sandy spit linking it to the mainland.

Château du Taureau. After Morlaix was sacked by the English fleet in 1522, the inhabitants decided to build a fortress at the mouth of the river. The castle was completed in 1552, but its upkeep was prohibitive. Louis XIV took charge of it in 1661, and entrusted the task of modernization to Marshal Vauban. In the 18th century it became a state prison, and later was for a while a yachting school. Currently it is awaiting restoration.

Bay of Morlaix

Bird sanctuary. With a superb natural environment, the bird sanctuary has made the Bay of Morlaix unique in Europe. The Île aux Dames and the Îlot Petit Ricard house a magnificent colony of terns, with more than a thousand nesting pairs of three different species: common terns, sandwich terns and black-beaked roseate terns ■ *20*. Naturalist Jean-Jules Duchesne de la Motte first noted the presence of the latter on the Île aux Dames in 1824. Entrance is strictly limited.

The Île Louët. Close inshore, the Île Louët (*Enez Louët*, meaning "the grey island", in Breton) is easily identifiable by its lighthouse and its single house. It faces Tahiti beach on Penn-al-Lann.

Carantec

The town stands at the edge of a rocky plateau that dominates the bay of St-Pol-de-Léon. Its beaches and lake, sheltered from the fierce northwesterly winds, attract large numbers of tourists.

"La Chaise du curé". The so-called "Priest's seat" is a rocky platform to the north of Carantec, overlooking the entire bay of St-Pol-de-Léon. The views from here are magnificent.

St-Pol-de-Léon

Paul Aurélien. In the 6th century this Celtic monk, who had retired for a time to the Île de Batz, returned to the mainland to preach the Gospel in a Gallo-Roman settlement called *Castellum Leonense Pagus*, and a barbaric and degenerate place he found it. He became its temporal as well as spiritual leader, and strove to revive its fortunes. He was the first bishop of Léon, and gave his name to this town.

Above, the Pointe de Carantec with the Île Callot (far left).

Château du Taureau It covers the whole of the rocky island.

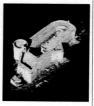

Carantec This has been a popular family resort since the turn of the century. It is an ideal spot for dinghy sailing and windsurfing, and there is diving too at the Plage du Kélenn, Carantec's only beach.

Phila... The Kre... tw... d...

CHOIR STALLS
Two rows of oak seats are carved with a wealth of fascinating detail. One carving

depicts a duck playing a tune on a pipe.

KREISKER CHAPEL
"You can imagine nothing lighter or more elegant than this superb tower, which far surpasses anything I have seen in all my travels. Its marvelous steeple blots out from my mind the famous spire of St Louis on the little island in Paris. Even those who have seen the bell towers of Flanders and Malines admit that there is nothing anywhere so fine as this."

Jacques Cambry,
Catalogue of objects that have escaped destruction in Finistère.

THE CATHEDRAL

Building work on the cathedral, which was erected on the site of a Norman basilica founded in the 12th century, lasted from the 13th century until the middle of the 16th century. Among the cathedral's many treasures mention should be made of a 15th-century figure of CHRIST in the south transept, the sixty-six STALLS dating from the 16th century and carved with a wide variety of motifs, the 17th-century ORGAN built by the Englishman Robert Dallam, and the 18th-century high altar in black marble surmounted by a decorative palm tree whose foliage forms a ciborium (canopy). But the most unusual feature is the ENFEU DES CRÂNES or "niche of skulls", thirty-five in all arranged in the shape of a chapel. They were formerly housed in the choir, and after restoration were removed to the sacristy, where they can be seen as part of the guided tour of the cathedral.

THE TOWNHOUSES OF ST-POL

Many noble families once had houses in the town. Two examples are the 16th-century HÔTEL DE KÉROULAS in the Rue du Petit Collège, and the HÔTEL DE KERMENGUY in the Rue du Général-Leclerc.
RUE DU GÉNÉRAL-LECLERC. The street, formerly known as the Grand' Rue, has retained many great traditional town houses, including one timbered building in medieval style. The MAISON DU PILORI, with its Renaissance entrance, recalls a time long ago when condemned men were forced to undergo public disgrace. Old granite houses with mullioned windows and massive wooden doors studded with iron nails line the RUE CROIX AU LIN, the RUE AUX EAUX, the RUE DES CARMES and the RUE DE LA PSALLETTE.

NOTRE-DAME DU KREISKER

This "waterfall of lace in stone", with a slender spire pierced with more than eighty openings, is built on four rectangular piles and stands nearly 260 feet

... cathedral ch?
... sker che?
... o jewels
...-Léon
... on this
... (left)

defying the laws of gravity. "It is a wonder of balance and bold design," commented Marshal Vauban.

THE CHURCH AND ITS LEGEND. A poor woman was struck down and paralyzed for having worked on the feast-day of the Blessed Virgin, runs the story. Stricken with remorse, she begged the Virgin to pardon her and promised to build a chapel in her honor. The chapel, first destroyed by the Normans, was rebuilt in 1345 only to be demolished again by the English thirty years later. It was rebuilt in the 15th century by Bishop Guillaume Ferron, whose arms decorate the keystone of the vault. Intrepid visitors who make the ascent of the BELL TOWER ● *100* (163 steps) are rewarded with a spectacular VIEW: the Pointe de Trégastel, the cape of Primel, the Château du Taureau, Roscoff, the Île de Batz all stretch out below, with the Monts d'Arrée on the opposite side.

LA CEINTURE DORÉE

The so-called "Golden Belt" is the prime producer of early vegetables in the region around St-Pol-de-Léon. The climate is favorable, enjoying the lowest range of temperature fluctuation recorded in France. The land is extremely fertile, supplying France with three-quarters of its cauliflowers, artichokes and shallots.

ROSCOFF

In Roman times, Roscoff (*Rosk o Gozen* in Breton) was a fishing village. It was laid waste by the English in 1375. During the Revolution it was a smuggler's stronghold, running illicit tea, brandy and gin across to England. It was "A hornets' nest of pirates and privateers", according to the cynical young Morlaix poet Tristan Corbière (1845–75). With its mild climate, thanks to the Gulf Stream, Roscoff was able to open the first French center for thalassotherapy in 1899. Today it continues to enjoy a wide reputation for seawater treatment. The town's fame as a fishing port is international too: its shellfish are known the world over. There are also regular ferry services to England and Ireland from the nearby Port de Bloscon, and fresh vegetables from the Golden Belt are exported from here.

SHIPOWNERS' HOUSES. These elegant granite mansions with decorative gables are evidence of Roscoff's prosperity in the Renaissance, when shipowners and privateers built themselves comfortable houses near the church and the harbor. The RUE ARMAND ROUSSEAU (formerly the Rue des Perles) contains several, and there are more in the church square. The finest of them, in the Rue Amiral-Réveillère, is known as the Maison de MARIE STUART.

INSTITUTE OF BIOLOGY AND AQUARIUM. This is behind the church square facing the sea. In high season it has fascinating displays of marine fauna and flora.

CHURCH OF NOTRE-DAME DE KROAZ-BRAZ. The church

"THE POTATO PICKERS"
Colored wood engraving by Henri Rivière.

ARTICHOKES
Artichokes, which originated in Sicily, were once thought to be aphrodisiac. Catherine de' Medici encouraged their cultivation in France.

The port and church of Roscoff, seen from the chapel of Ste-Barbe.

Place Lacaze-Duthiers.

MARY STUART IN ROSCOFF
The visit of François II's bride-to-be in 1548 was a great occasion in Roscoff's history. In the early 19th century two houseowners in the Rue Amiral-Réveillère claimed that the princess had lodged at their property, though the episcopal archives showed that these houses were not even built at the time!

ÎLE DE BATZ
The northwest of the island is harsh and rugged, while the south side, where the harbor is located, is where most of the inhabitants live. In the north are fine sandy beaches, where until recently horses were used to gather seaweed. The longest beach is the one known as the Grève Blanche.

square, or PLACE LACAZE-DUTHIERS, is especially fine, and the beautiful church at its center is a marvelous example of 16th-century Flamboyant Gothic. The maritime community that built it left their mark on the fabric in the form of carved CARAVELS. The church took more than a hundred years to complete. There are two OSSUARIES in the square. The one on the north side has been classified as an historical monument, and the other has openings on two floors where the bones of the dead were thrown.

ÎLE DE BATZ

Landing here is not easy, for at low tide the island doubles in size. The land is exceptionally fertile: there are palm trees, agapanthus and even samphire, thanks to a micro-climate which allows spring vegetables to mature one month earlier than in Léon just opposite.
COLONIAL GARDEN. This was opened in 1902 on Penn-ar-Chéguer point: it is planted with palms and a wide variety of tropical plants.
LIGHTHOUSE. The granite tower situated on the west of the island was built in 1836. It is 141 feet tall and stands 236 feet above sea level. The tiring climb (210 steps) is well worth the effort in clear weather, for the VIEW is grand.

CHÂTEAU DE KÉROUZÉRÉ ★

CASTLE TOWERS
The Château de Kérouzéré once had four towers. But after alterations in the 16th century, the one in the southwest corner was not rebuilt, being almost in ruins. Above, a plan of 1882 showing the parts of the original castle.

Construction of this impressive fortress began in 1425 on the orders of the lord of the manor, Jehan de Kérouzéré. He had lived at court, as did his son after him, and the castle only livened up in the following century. In 1590 it belonged to Pierre de Boiséon, the royalist governor of Morlaix. It was besieged by the Leaguers ● 57 on the orders of the Duc de Mercoeur, and once the exterior defenses were destroyed the castle was forced to surrender. It was looted by the local peasantry, and was only repaired once peace had been restored. The NORTH FAÇADE is the one that has changed the least. On the south side the building seems half military and half unfortified. The castle is in private hands, but is open to the public.

PLOUESCAT

The town center of this little seaside resort has fortunately

retained its COVERED MARKET. It is an impressive 16th-century wooden structure that once belonged to the lords of Kérouzéré, who exacted a levy on goods sold there.

CHÂTEAU DE KERJEAN

The château is at St-Vougay. Built between 1550 and 1590, it is one of the finest Renaissance buildings in the region. The house is surrounded by a massive fortified wall, recalling the defenses put up at the time of the wars of the League. In the 17th century, when the title that went with the property became that of marquis, the château drew this comment from King Louis XIII: "So beautiful and noble a house should be added to our possessions, it being one of the fairest in our kingdom." The château was looted during the Revolution and the owner, Mme de Coëtanscourt, was guillotined at Brest in 1794. The remaining contents were auctioned. Kerjean is now a cultural center where exhibitions are held, and there is an interesting son et lumière.

KERJEAN MUSEUM. Inside the castle are models, costumed figures, photographic displays and all kinds of curios. Upstairs there is a collection of traditional Léon furniture, including chests, heavy cupboards, two boxed-in beds and a linen press dated 1615.

THE PARK. The park covers a total area of around 25 acres, complete with Renaissance fountain and dovecote, and is beautifully laid out. After the fashion of the 17th and 18th centuries, the garden was designed as a relatively informal area meant for peaceful walks and contemplation.

KÉREMMA

THE DUNES. This is one of the most interesting areas of the region. Behind 5 miles of beach that is now a bird sanctuary, is an enormous inland area of sand dunes covering almost 500 acres ■ 26. THE MAISON DES DUNES (open in summer) holds exhibitions, and organizes fascinating nature walks to discover the fauna (Kéremma is a stopover for thousands of migratory birds) and the flora (about six hundred different species) of the area.

PLOUGUERNEAU

This pretty little seaside resort has one of the largest seaweed industries in Brittany. It was also the birthplace of the priest Michel Le Nobletz (1577–1652), who invented the *taolennou* ● 71, naive paintings that served as a visual aid in religious instruction.

LIZ KOZ. The evocative ruins of the church at Tréménac'h

THE FRONT PORTICO
This watercolor of 1905 by Charles Chaussepied shows the view from the courtyard. Kerjean has the traditional enclosed courtyard, but with added Renaissance decoration.

THE MANOIR DE TRONJOLY ● 89
This 16th-century stately home, refined by two centuries of elegant decoration, is not far from Kérouzéré. The polygonal structure at the corner contains a splendid monumental spiral staircase.

In the 1870's an artistic circle existed at Kéremma, centered around Armand Rousseau, owner of the manor. Cultured friends and relations were given a warm welcome. In 1988 the museum at Morlaix held an exhibition of work by members of the group.

known as *Iliz Koz* ("the old church") were unearthed in 1970. Around 1720, after a series of storms that moved the coastal dunes inland, Tréménac'h disappeared, along with its presbytery and graveyard. It was abandoned around 1726.

Île Vierge lighthouse. It was built between 1897 and 1902, in granite, and at 253 feet high is the tallest lighthouse in Europe. In clear conditions its beam is visible from a distance of more than 30 miles. The lighthouse is open to the public.

Aber Wrac'h

The black tide
On March 16, 1978 the supertanker *Amoco Cadiz* ran on to rocks at Men

Goulven with a crew of fifty-two. It was more than a mile offshore, and the spillage of 230,000 tons of oil polluted 250 miles of coastline from St-Mathieu to Brehat, causing catastrophic ecological damage.

The Breton word *Aber* signifies a valley that has been invaded by the sea. The largest of three "abers" on the Côte des Légendes is a delightful little port, though it is difficult to enter from the seaward side because of the rocks and the narrowness of its three channels. It is also a popular place for pleasure craft and there are excellent sandy beaches.

Aber Ildut

This is the smallest of the three abers on the northwest coast of Finistère (the middle one is Aber Benoît), and the largest center of the seaweed industry in France ■ *38*. From mid-May to mid-October the seaweed boats are continually busy discharging their cargos on the rising tide. The weed is then taken away to be processed at Lannion or Landerneau.

Le Conquet

"Landscape at Le Conquet"
This anonymous 19th-century oil painting of the Maison des Seigneurs hangs in the Jacobin Museum at Morlaix ▲ *239*.

This busy fishing port has a fleet of some forty boats, and lands huge quantities of edible crab as well as a wide variety of fish. It is also the place to catch ferries to Ouessant (Ushant) ▲ *278* and the islands of Molène.

Pointe Ste-Barbe. At sunset in clear weather the view from Pointe Ste-Barbe is magical, as all the lights of the sea – lighthouses, ships' lights and marker-buoys ■ *16* – begin to appear. Starting from the left, one can see the Pointe St-Mathieu, then the Vieille lighthouse, the Île de Sein ▲ *304* the Ar Men lighthouse, Molène, the Lieu, the Grande Vinotière; next is the Kermorvan peninsula, the La Jument lighthouse, Nividic, the lighthouses of Créac'h and Stiff on Ouessant ▲ *278*, with the Four lighthouse away to the north.

> **"**WHAT COULD BE MORE . . . AWE-INSPIRING THAN THE COAST AROUND BREST, THE FURTHEST OUTPOST OF AN ANCIENT WORLD . . SPRAY FROM THE SEA IS DASHED AGAINST THE CHURCH TOWER, WHILE INSIDE THE NUNS KNEEL IN PRAYER.**"**   JULES MICHELET

POINTE ST-MATHIEU

ABBEY OF ST-MATHIEU. The large Benedictine abbey church of St-Mathieu-Fin-de-Terre (*Loc Mazé Penn ar Bed*), founded in the 6th century, lies in ruins. It was abandoned during the Revolution, then looted and demolished for the price of the stone. Legend has it that the body of Saint Matthew the Apostle was brought here from Ethiopia for burial.

ST-MATHIEU LIGHTHOUSE. The lighthouse, which is open to the public, is 82 feet tall and stands 177 feet above sea level. It was built in 1835 and its beam has a radius of some 30 miles.

THE PIERRES NOIRES LIGHTHOUSE
This stands 7 miles out to sea, on the treacherous Black Rocks. It is easily identified from the shore by its bold red and white coloring. The hazardous job of construction was completed in 1871.

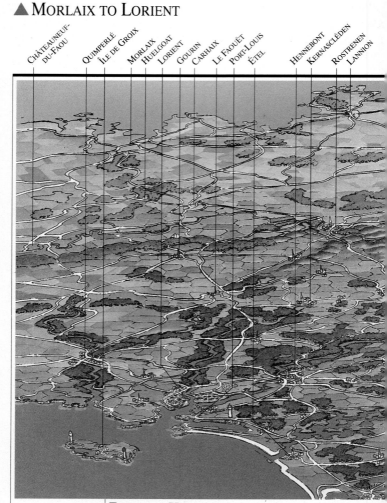

CHÂTEAUNEUF-DU-FAOU · QUIMPERLÉ · ÎLE DE GROIX · MORLAIX · HUELGOAT · LORIENT · GOURIN · CARHAIX · LE FAOUËT · PORT-LOUIS · ÉTEL · HENNEBONT · KERNASCLÉDEN · ROSTRENEN · LANNION

FOREST OF HUELGOAT

"Twenty years ago, frustrated by all these useless stones around them, they decided rather ingeniously to use them to build something and with no further reflection they began to saw them up."
Victor Segalen, *Diary.*

With its rocky, primeval landscape, the forest north and east of Huelgoat village has inspired countless legends. Though many of its trees were destroyed in the Great Storm of 1987, it is easy for the visitor to imagine himself in a kingdom of elves and giants.

THE "CHAOS DU MOULIN". At one end of the lake, the river Fao (known locally as the *rivière d'Argent* because of its silver-bearing lead mines, now been exhausted) on its way down from the La Feuillée mountain, falls 66 feet to lose itself in the Chaos du Moulin, "a jumble of haphazard rounded rocks, the greatest wonder of this wonderful place", according to writer Louis Le Guennec. The stones have been broken up under the constant battering of the waterfall and then rolled down the slope. Some, like the so-called ROCHE CINTRÉE, have come to rest precariously balanced. According to legend Gargantua the giant was so angered by being given just a bowl of buckwheat porridge to eat in Huelgoat that in

his rage he hurled all the rocks down here by way of reprisal. According to another story, when God was mixing granite it went into lumps and he tipped them out here.

TROU DU DIABLE. The Devil's Grotto was said to be the gateway of the road to Hell, lined with ninety-nine taverns where the wine was served by barmaids who became more desirable every minute. Those who arrived sober were allowed to make their way back. Drunkards, however, were made to drink a potion made of the blood of toads and snakes, and were condemned to eternal damnation.

ROCHE TREMBLANTE. Weighing over 100 tons, this "Rocking stone" can be made to wobble if pushed in the right place.

MÉNAGE DE LA VIERGE. Another famous rock mass was called the Virgin Mary's first home: her bed, her cooking pot, umbrella and Jesus's cradle can still be made out.

GROTTE D'ARTHUR. The Forest of Paimpont in the Ille-et-Vilaine is still probably better known in France as one of the sites of Arthurian legend ▲ *357*, though it has a persuasive counterpart here. Arthur's Grotto is said to have been the king's home in this region. His bed is a hollowed-out stone set high against the intrusion.

ARTHUR'S CAMP. This is a Gallic hill fort of importance, complete with *murus Gallicus* (a rampart and double ditch with stone defenses) forming an ellipse almost 900 feet long, 380 feet wide and in places more than 33 feet high.

RIVER ARGENT. Leaving the *Ménage de la Vierge* take the Allée Violette, which follows the course of the river to join the Carhaix road. Steps lead down into an impressive gorge where the river falls from a height of more than 30 feet. At times the rocks stain the water the color of blood.

LES MONTAGNES NOIRES

The Black Mountains range 37 miles from Menez Hom in the east to Gourin in the west ▲ *269*, roughly parallel to the Monts d'Arrée. The highest peak rises 1,070 feet above sea level. The southern half is of Armorican sandstone, while blackish schist predominates in the north.

CHÂTEAUNEUF-DU-FAOU

The name comes from the castle built on a rocky spur overlooking the valley of the Aulne (and which has all but disappeared today), and from the Breton *fau* or *fhao*, meaning "beech". There is a grand view over the Black Mountains from the ruined castle. The baptismal chapel in the 19th-century church at Châteauneuf was decorated by Paul Sérusier.

THE LEGEND OF ARTHUR
Son of Uther Pendragon and Queen Ygerna (Ygaerne), he was educated by the magician Merlin and became king of Brittany (or Britain) when he pulled out the sword Excalibur from its magic stone, and founded the Knights of the Round Table. One seat was left empty, reserved for he who should find the Holy Grail.

"THE SILVER RIVER"
The river Fao, home to the fairies of the Huelgoat forest, takes its romantic nickname to a former lead mine near by. Its ore contained a relatively high percentage of this valuable metal, which was extracted by smelting.

The house of painter Paul Sérusier at Châteauneuf-du-Faou.

A pencil sketch of Paul Sérusier by Georges Lacombe, drawn around 1900.

PAUL SÉRUSIER ▲ *316.* The famous painter Paul Sérusier (1864–1927) was born in Paris and came to live at Châteauneuf du Faou at the beginning of the century. His house was large, and he was frequently visited by friends from the school of Pont-Aven ▲ *312,* such as Pierre Bonnard, Armand Seguin and Maurice Denis. His was a profoundly spiritual nature, and he had already spent time at the Benedictine monastery of Beuron in the Black Forest, south Germany, where he was deeply impressed by the simple shapes and colors of the medieval murals. The style of his own religious frescoes was affected by the austerity of these works.

SACRED AND PROFANE DECORATION. In 1904, in preparation for decorating the church in Châteauneuf, Sérusier painted a number of wooden panels, such as *The Adoration of the Magi, The Annunciation* and *The Burning Bush.* They were never installed, however, though he decorated the walls of the baptistry some years later. As a painter he was unusually consistent, with a fondness for grey tones and geometric forms. He decorated his house with friezes illustrating the signs of the zodiac, and painted the walls with scenes from everyday life, together with some religious pictures and a representation of the jolly giant Gargantua. The dining-room fireplace was flanked by two ceramic statues: one, a monk, was a likeness of Sérusier himself, while the other was of the nun who founded the Augustinian convent that later became Beuron monastery. The house belongs to an artist who has hardly altered it at all.

TRÉVAREZ

THE CHÂTEAU DE TRÉVAREZ
It was requisitioned for use as a convalescent home by the Germans during World War Two. The château was severely bombed by the Allies in 1944 but has been meticulously restored to its original condition.

With its huge clumps of rhododendrons, camellias and azaleas, the extensive gardens of Trévarez, covering almost 400 acres, belong to the Province of Brittany and are the most beautiful in the region. Its château, of granite and red brick, was built between 1894 and 1906 on a headland overlooking a valley of the Aulne. The floors were served by an elevator, a luxury at the period. The stable-block is used for exhibitions.

SPEZET ★

NOTRE-DAME-DU-CRANN. The original chapel here was founded in 1248 by a crusader in thanks for recovery from the plague. It was rebuilt in 1540 and a Calvary was added in the 18th century. The stained glass, perhaps the most beautiful in all Brittany, is spectacular. Eight windows depict the Nativity, the Baptism of Christ, the Passion, Saint Eligius (Eloi), Saint Lawrence and Saint James, and the Dormition of the Virgin.

Opposite, frescoes painted by
Paul Sérusier in the church of
Châteauneuf-du-Faou.

GOURIN

Beginning in the late 19th century, emigration from Brittany
to North America changed the region a great deal. The first
to go was a tailor from Roudouallec named Nicolas Le
Grand, who attracted a lot of attention when he returned to
France after having made his fortune. By 1927 an average of
fifteen emigrants per month was recorded in Gourin and
Roudouallec. About five thousand people from Gourin
currently live in the United States. Some have come back, and
built houses resembling those of the eastern seaboard of the
United States.

THE FAOUËT REGION

The Faouët region, set between Cornouaille and
Morbihan, is an isolated area. It is a rugged,
almost mountainous place whose name comes
from its beech-covered hills. Descending from
the Black Mountains, the rivers Inam and Ellé
are steely blue in the distance and meander
through steep gorges. Gorse shines yellow in
the valleys, and the beeches glow red in the fall.
The Ellé is a good salmon-fishing river, and on its
right bank is the quiet little town of Le Faouët,
spread around the church and market square. The
manor houses and religious buildings give a good
idea of the region's prosperity in the 16th and
17th centuries. At the beginning of the 20th
century painters were attracted to the
wild unspoiled countryside here, which
seemed to encapsulate the true Brittany. "Inside a rough
rectangle with its corners at Le Faouët, Langonnet,
Ploërdut and Kernascléden, Breton art is seen at its
best and most varied . . . [there are] the Norman
churches of Langonnet, Priziac and Ploërdut;
while Saint Fiacre near Le Faouët has the finest
rood screen in the province, with another
beautiful Renaissance example at St-Nicolas-de-
Priziac. Le Faouët has the best market hall in
Brittany; there is the spectacular setting of Sainte
Barbe, and lastly the murals at Kernascléden."
(Jean-Marc Huitorel, *Kernascléden and
Pont-Callec*).

LE FAOUËT

The little town, nicknamed "Far West",
stretches out in a line from east to west,
with a fortified castle, church and then
the market place.
MARKET HALL. The superb covered
market stands alone in the Place
Bellanger. It is 174 feet long by 62 feet
wide and has a large double-pitched,
hipped slate roof supported by
magnificent oak and pine beams sitting on
granite pillars ranged along a low stone wall.
The central section, topped off with an

GOURIN
Set on the edges of
Cornouaille and the
Vannes region,
Gourin, capital of the
Black Mountains, is
now included as a
part of the Morbihan.
It was once the
largest parish of
Cornouaille and the
center of a flourishing
slate industry, though
it is now
predominantly a
community of peasant
farmers.

**THE OSSUARY AT LE
FAOUËT**
In here is the skull of
Louis Le Ravallec,
who was murdered on
April 13, 1732 on
his way back from
a pardon ● 70 at
Saint Fiacre.

269

CARVINGS IN SAINT FIACRE
Some of the figures are
grotesquely vivid, like the man
squatting on a beam (right),
and the drunkard pictured
vomiting a fox (below).

An ink and wash
drawing of 1915
showing Le Faouët's
market hall.

octagonal belfry, consists of fifteen bays with side aisles
separated by a virtual forest of wooden posts. There are four
entrances with porch roofs. The market hall was built in 1542,
and restored several times in the 19th century.

THE PAINTERS OF LE FAOUËT. The Ursuline that stands at the
southwest corner of the convent was founded in 1658. Today it
houses the MUSEUM OF ART OF THE LE FAOUËT SCHOOL
(Musée des Peintures de l'École du Faouët), "A group of
artists dedicated to capturing on canvas as faithfully as
possible everyday life in this remote backwater". In the early
20th century it was hardly touched by the industrial
revolution, with unspoiled countryside and old-fashioned
peasants whose pious womenfolk filled the splendid Gothic
chapels of Saint Fiacre and Saint Barbe. There was the busy
market hall, livelier than ever when there were fairs. The
work of the school of Le Fouët was for decades
considered to consist of anecdotal paintings of
little intrinsic interest; however,
connoisseurs and the public revised
their judgment when the Musée
d'Orsay in Paris opened in 1986,
admitting the school's work to the
annals of 19th and early 20th century
art." (Claude Arz, Musée du Faouët).

CHAPELLE DE ST-FIACRE ★

This baronial chapel is famous for its
rood screen (which divides the chancel
from the nave). It is a unique

**"A FAIR AT LE
FAOUËT"**
This canvas, painted
around 1930 by
Arthur Midy,
captures the
atmosphere
brilliantly. The hall's
16th-century slate
roof is supported by
columns of wood and
stone, and has been
beautifully restored.

masterpiece of Gothic art that includes pagan as well as
Christian images. It was begun around 1450, and took several
decades to complete. It was paid for by the Boutteville
(Montmorency) family, wealthy rivals of the munificent
Rohans, who patronized the church at Kernascléden ▲ *272*.
Local craftsmen spared no effort on the superb church
furnishings, which included altars, stoups, niches and statuary.

**THE ROOD SCREEN AT
ST-FIACRE**
A magnificent screen
in carved wood
executed in 1480 by
Olivier Le Loergan
with exquisite
delicacy. The two
thieves on either side
of the crucified Christ
are shown contorted
with agony. Saint
John and the Virgin
keep their vigil at
Christ's feet, while
nearby are the
humiliated figures of
Adam and Eve, as
well as the Archangel
Gabriel.

LIFELIKE SCULPTURE. The richly decorated interior has a wealth of paneling. At the center of the transept, the arches and keystone are ornamented with angels, animals and fabulous beasts, men carved in strange twisted posture, a mixture of both pagan and Christian symbols.

THE WINDOWS. In the 16th century the stained-glass workshops of Brittany were flourishing. Here are some of the most inspired examples of their art. The eight panes of the south window illustrating the life of Saint Fiacre (patron saint of gardeners, and traditionally invoked by sufferers from hemorrhoids) are sublime. They bear the date 1552 and the signature of P. Androuet. Other windows bearing the arms of the Boutteville family illustrate scenes from the life of Christ.

CHAPELLE DE STE-BARBE

"Set among rocks against a wall of granite, here is a nest of turtle doves high above the ravine and the river," run the words of an old hymn. The chapel is built on a narrow ledge overlooking beech trees that cling to the side of a dizzy ravine. It plunges down to the valley, from which rises the distant rumble of the river Ellé.

THE CHAPEL'S ORIGINS. An inscription below a statue in the south transept is carved with the date July 6, 1489, when work on the building began. Inside, a stained-glass window recounts the chapel's history: the knight Jean de Toulbodou was out hunting on the lands of the lord of Le Faouët when he was surprised by a sudden storm. The rocks above were struck by lightning and began to tumble down around him, and the knight made a vow to build a chapel here if his life were spared. He kept his word, choosing a site a little upstream. But mysteriously the building work was regularly demolished each night, until the knight agreed to erect the chapel in the exact spot where his vow was made. It was completed in twenty-four years.

BELL TOWER. The imposing tower stands high above the flight of steps leading to the chapel. Each visitor is traditionally meant to ring the bell to announce his arrival. The STEPS themselves are on

the grand scale, with Louis XIII-style balustrade and a landing below, which joins the little bridge leading to the ORATORY OF SAINT MICHEL.

THE CHAPEL. It is long and narrow after the Gothic style, and has a transept but no nave, and a chancel with a three-sided apse. Two exquisitely carved doorways have double doors with pierced spandrels. A number of votive offerings demonstrate the fervor with which the saint's blessing was invoked.

SAINT BARBE
A stained-glass window with sailors rescued from a storm.

Saint Barbe's aid is invoked against fire, gunpowder and (consequently) sudden death! The powder magazine on board a ship of the line used to be known as the "Saint Barbara".

SAINT BARBE
This pagan girl, born in Turkey into a wealthy family, became a Christian. Refusing to renounce her faith, she was put to death by her own father in 235.

The château of Pont-Callec.

Set in the Scorff valley, this romantic

forest is crossed by numerous paths. Squirrels, foxes and roe deer are a common sight, and there is a wide variety of birds. A nature walk helps visitors identify such trees as beech, chestnut, mountain ash and yew ● *46.*

THE POURLET REGION
The district is centered around Guéméné-sur-Scorff. The ink and wash drawings below are signed Charpentier and dated 1825. They depict two Pourlet peasants, and are on show in the Musée Breton at Quimper ▲ *299.*

ST BARBE. Three stained-glass windows illustrate the life of this patron saint of sailors, gunners, miners, firemen and many others, and whose aid is often invoked against lightning. There is one in the chancel (19th century) and one in the north transept (16th century). A third, behind the high altar (16th century), is dedicated to the martydom of St Barbe.

CHÂTEAU DE PONT-CALLEC. This has a remarkable history, though the present château dates only from 1882. The original moat of Pont-Callec was dug in 1291, and in 1298 the feudal stronghold became Pont-Callec castle, part of the ducal territory. It passed into the hands of the Du Guesclins and the Malestroits, then to the Guer family, whose head was raised to the rank of marquis in 1657. The castle was an important stronghold in the wars of the League. Between 1718 and 1720 it was the center of the "Pont-Callec Conspiracy", a doomed plot hatched by Breton aristocracy (with the support of Spain) against French supremacy.

KERNASCLÉDEN ★

A BRIGHT JEWEL. Historian Arthur de La Borderie described Kernascléden in the following terms: "The queen of all chapels in Brittany blooms like a rose in the plains of Vannes." The church was commissioned in the mid-15th century by the Rohan dynasty ▲ *231,* lords of Pontivy and Josselin. It stands in an elegant setting at the center of the village and was probably built by the architects of St-Fiacre ▲ *270;* the clarity of its outline and its glorious decoration make it one of the architectural gems of Brittany. The chancel is as long as the nave, in esthetically satisfying proportions. The two porches on the south side are separated by a rose window with eight sections and are richly ornamented; the east door was the men's and the west door the women's entrance. The large number of turrets is typical of the Flamboyant Gothic style.

THE DANCE OF DEATH. The chapel has 15th-century paintings on the stone vaulting, a rare feature in Brittany. In the south transept there is a most unusual representation of the DANSE MACABRE, the only one of its kind in Morbihan. It depicts a ghoulish scene with cauldrons, stakes, claws, hooks and other forms of torture warning medieval sinners against the horrors of Hell. By way of contrast, in the chancel among angels playing musical instruments and scenes from the life of Jesus and Mary, is a delicate Annunciation.

LES ROCHES DU DIABLE

At the foot of a jumble of granite set among tangled undergrowth, the Ellé rushes in a torrent reputed to be an image of the Devil. This was once a part of his kingdom, so the story goes, until Saint Winwaloe (Guénolé) chased him away and founded a hermitage on the spot. The waters then lost their immense power.

BREST

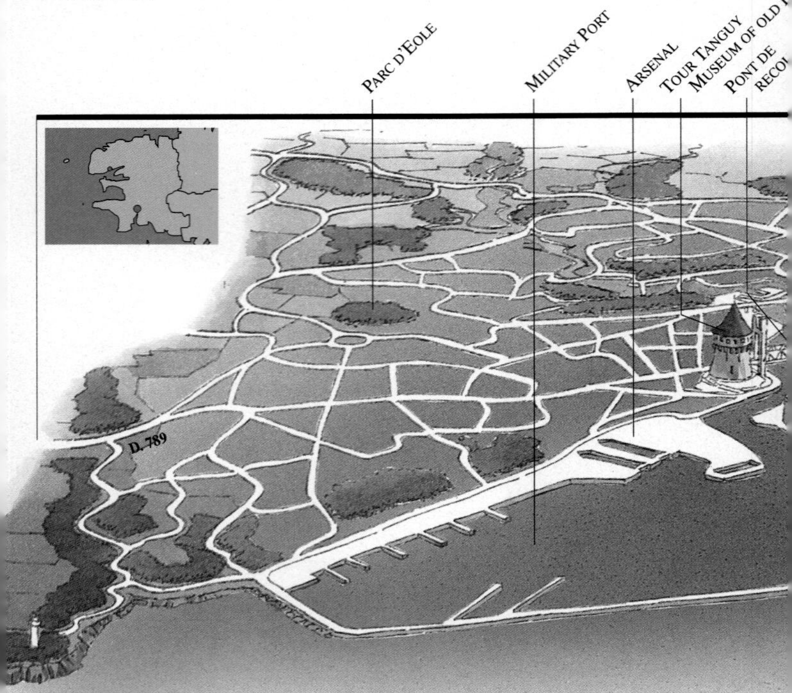

▲ BREST

PARC D'EOLE

MILITARY PORT

ARSENAL

TOUR TANGUY

MUSEUM OF OLD B

PONT DE
RECO

D. 789

A WAR-TORN TOWN
The Tour Rose was
built on the Cours
Dajot to
commemorate the
American landings
here in 1917. It was
demolished by the
occupying Germans
in 1941, but was
reconstructed down
to the last detail after
the war.

THE PORT OF BREST
An oil painting by
Louis Garneray,
dating from the
beginning of the 19th
century. It shows the
naval harbor, with the
munitions store in the
foreground.

HISTORY

Brest lies on the north bank of a natural harbor (the Rade de
Brest) extending over some 80 square miles and reached by a
narrow channel (the Goulet of Brest), which is lined with
cliffs about 100 feet high. It is fed by two rivers, the Aulne and
the Élorn. Brest's position at the westernmost tip of Europe
gives it its strategic importance. In the 3rd century the
Romans built a *castrum* on the left bank of Penfeld river
where it meets the sea. In the 12th century the counts of Léon
built a castle here, which passed into the hands of the Dukes
of Brittany in the 13th century. When Louis XIII built and
based the French fleet here, the modest settlement became a
substantial town. It was laid out by Vauban. As today, the
entire town revolved around the navy base there (with the
Arsenal ▲ 276 at its center).
DESTRUCTION. Brest, once a town of quaint streets, paid
dearly for the presence of a German submarine base in its
harbor: from 1940 to 1944 it was subjected to a continuous
onslaught of bombs and shells. Of its 16,500 buildings, 7,000
were destroyed and 5,000 had to be demolished. The rest

AU DE BREST
MUSÉE NAVAL
CHURCH OF ST-LOUIS
RUE DE SIAM
LE QUARTZ
TOWN HALL
PORT DE COMMERCE
CONSERVATOIRE BOTANIQUE
OCÉANOPOLIS
MARINA

N. 12

were damaged in some way. The center was rebuilt over ten years to designs by architect and town planner J.-B. Mathon. The University of West Brittany was opened in 1960: it currently has 20,000 students, many specializing in oceanography, agricultural research, and the study of Breton and Celtic civilization.

Tonnerre de Brest!...

TOWN CENTER

CASTLE ● 84. This trapezoid fortress was built between the 15th and 17th centuries and covers about 3 acres. The naval headquarters are here, commanding the entire Atlantic fleet.

MUSÉE DE LA MARINE. The maritime museum contains some superb figureheads carved in cedar of Lebanon by the craftsmen of the Arsenal.

RUE DE SIAM. Thanks to the French war poem *Barbara* by Jacques Prévert, the Rue de Siam is the town's most famous street. It was formerly a narrow thoroughfare, and is now a long avenue, straight and very wide. Its name dates back to June 1686, when three ambassadors of the King of Siam paraded through the town in their exotic robes.

PLACE DE LA LIBERTÉ. In the heart of the city, this square was completely restructured by architect Bernard Huet in 1996. It has a computer-programmed fountain that is at its best when the square is lit up in the evening.

THE QUARTZ. This ultramodern cultural center has a 1,500-seat multifunctional auditorium.

COURS DAJOT. Almost half a mile long, this promenade runs from beneath the ramparts to the Square Beautemps-Beaupré. It was built in 1769 by convicts from the local prison and is a good spot for viewing commercial ships on the Rade.

MUSÉE DES BEAUX-ARTS. The museum has on display more than three hundred paintings from the 16th century to the 19th century, in particular many from the symbolist movement, including works by the Pont-Aven group ▲ *312.*

RUE DE SIAM
The winding street sheltered from the fierce Atlantic gales fell victim to the terrible destruction of World War Two.

Convicts in the Recouvrance prison wore uniforms like those shown in the engraving above.

Quai du Commandant Malbert. Here are the head offices that control the lighthouses and beacons of Finistère, seven hundred maritime signal stations and sea marks ■ *16* that together account for one sixth of all those in France. Here too is the commercial port, marked by a hundred brightly colored buoys, at the foot of the Cours Dajot. At the quayside stands the *Georges-de-Joly*, built in Germany in 1929 and the oldest French merchant ship still in service; the *Abeille-Flandres*, one of the five most powerful tugboats in the world, whose duty was to protect the safety of shipping off the island of Ouessant; and the *Recouvrance*, launched in 1992 as a replica of a superb six-gun fighting schooner dating from 1817.

Arsenal

Richelieu then Colbert laid out Brest as a military stronghold and built its naval dockyards. Engineer Choquet de Lindu built the original Arsenal between 1746 and 1784, and its grim and forbidding façade remained but little changed up to World War Two. Today it extends more than 2 miles, from the submarine base at Lannion to the left bank of the Penfeld, where it meets the commercial port. It is still an important center of shipbuilding and repair: the French navy employs more than twenty thousand people here, just under one third of the town's workforce. The Arsenal may only be visited by French citizens.

Prison. It extends up river from Recouvrance, on the left bank of the Penfeld, and was built in 1750 to hold around three thousand convicts. By the time that it was closed in 1858, seventy thousand prisoners had served their sentences here. Most famous was François-Eugène Vidocq, imprisoned here in 1797 before becoming chief of police. It was demolished in 1947.

Recouvrance district

Beyond the Pont de Recouvrance, one of the largest bridges in Europe (it has straddled the Penfeld since 1954 and its huge concrete towers support the moving span), is a bustling, populous

Masting shears A large hoisting machine, shown in this 19th-century detail from an engraving of *The Port of Brest* by Gilbert.

Glass and concrete Marine architect Jacques Rougerie designed this amazing building. Inside are study areas with lecture theater, an oustanding multimedia library of the sea, and even a gift shop.

district that is the center of
Brest for much of the town's workforce. Before the
bridge was built Brest and Recouvrance were separate, and
the crossing could be made only by ferry.

TOUR MOTTE-TANGUY. Known locally as the Tour Tanguy. It
stands below the bridge overlooking the castle. It was
formerly the fortress of Quilbignon and belonged to the lords
of Chastel, who administered feudal justice from here. This
great cylinder of granite and gneiss was restored in 1970.
Inside is a massive central pillar 12 feet in circumference that
supports the topmost story.

MUSEUM OF OLD BREST. Housed in the Tour Tanguy. It
contains photographic records and fascinating dioramas
showing the development of the town over the centuries.

MARINA

The marina is situated at Moulin Blanc, at the extreme
eastern edge of the town in the direction of Quimper. With
mooring for 1,325 craft, it is the biggest marina in Brittany.

OCÉANOPOLIS. Océanopolis, which is situated close to the
marina, is a scientific, technical, and industrial center
dedicated to the sea. It is a white concrete and glass structure
built in the form of a crab, and was opened in 1990. It has
around 30,000 square feet of exhibition space and 13 large
open-air seawater aquariums, three of which are very big
indeed. One aquarium is devoted to grey seals. Films and
special effects assist an understanding of this fascinating
subject. There is also a department dedicated to the care of
marine mammals, and a lecture theater. Each year about
300,000 visitors come to Océanopolis.

CONSERVATOIRE BOTANIQUE NATIONAL.
The botanical gardens are in the Stang
Alar valley, just over a mile north of
Moulin Blanc. It is dedicated to the
preservation of over 1,200 endangered
plant species, in particular those of the
Armorican *massif*, the Atlantic coast and
outlying islands. In 1989 the Conservatoire succeeded in re-establishing
Lysimachia minoricensis in the Balearic
Islands, its native habitat, where it had been extinct since
1926. The gardens, open to the public, cover almost 40 acres.
Plants native to the five continents are grouped as far as
possible in their natural environment: after Kew
Gardens in London, it is the institution
with the largest collection of
rare species in the
world.

**THE RECOUVRANCE
PRISON**
The prison wall, 850
feet long, was
equipped with a
walkway enabling the
guards to keep a close
watch on their
charges. The young
Vidocq (below)
escaped twice during
his imprisonment.

**FRANÇOIS-EUGÈNE
VIDOCQ** (1775–1857)
Careful observation
of criminals while he
was himself a prisoner
here made Vidocq
France's greatest
detective.

RARE SPECIES
The Brest botanical
gardens are a treat
for lovers of wildlife.
There is an
astonishing variety of
rare plants, many of
which have now
totally vanished from
their original native
environments. As
well as cultivating
these species in a
carefully created
habitat, the
Conservatoire
preserves stocks of
seeds in freezers prior
to reintroducing them
into areas where they
once grew wild. One
example is *Echinium
pinana*, native to the
Canary Islands.

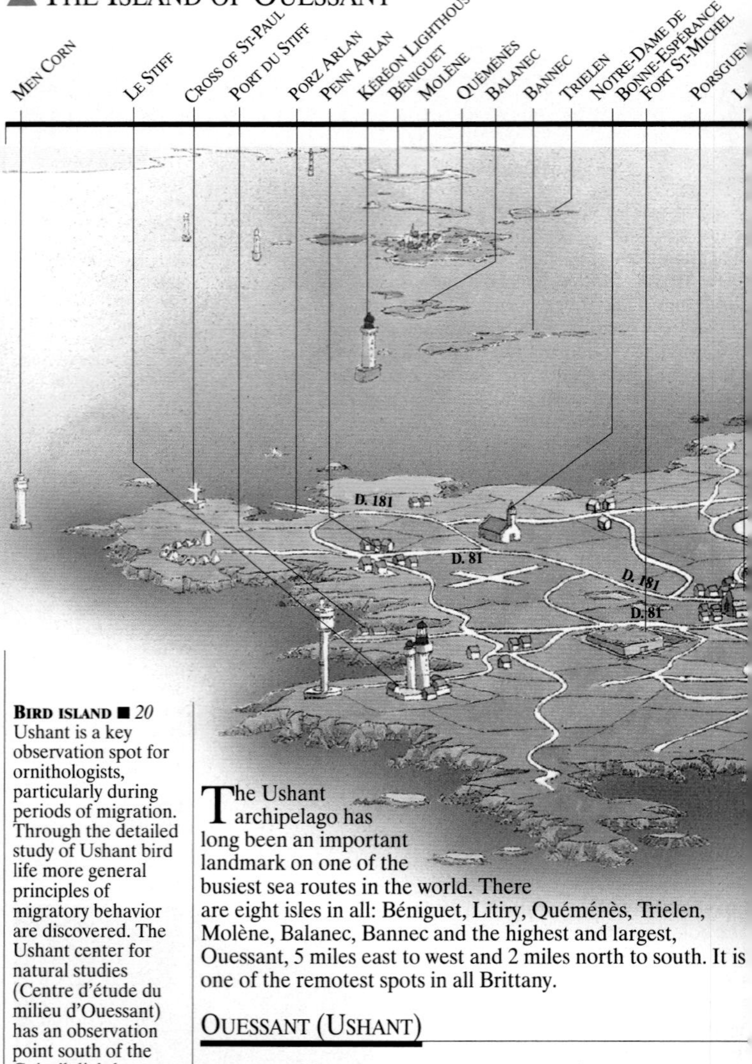

MEN CORN · LE STIFF · CROSS OF ST-PAUL · PORT DU STIFF · PORZ ARLAN · PENN ARLAN · KÉRÉON LIGHTHOUSE · BÉNIGUET · MOLÈNE · QUÉMÉNÈS · BALANEC · BANNEC · TRIELEN · NOTRE-DAME DE BONNE-ESPÉRANCE · FORT ST-MICHEL · PORSGUEN · L...

D. 181
D. 81
D. 181
D. 81

BIRD ISLAND ■ 20
Ushant is a key observation spot for ornithologists, particularly during periods of migration. Through the detailed study of Ushant bird life more general principles of migratory behavior are discovered. The Ushant center for natural studies (Centre d'étude du milieu d'Ouessant) has an observation point south of the Créac'h lighthouse.

POINTE DE PERN
The point and its rocks have been classed as a site of outstanding natural beauty. One rock is painted white on the south side as a landmark for sailors.

The Ushant archipelago has long been an important landmark on one of the busiest sea routes in the world. There are eight isles in all: Béniguet, Litiry, Quéménès, Trielen, Molène, Balanec, Bannec and the highest and largest, Ouessant, 5 miles east to west and 2 miles north to south. It is one of the remotest spots in all Brittany.

OUESSANT (USHANT)

MUSEUM OF USHANT TRADITIONAL LIFE. The NIOU-UHELLA ECOMUSEUM was the first of its kind in France. The Ecomuseum is certainly the best place to begin a visit to the island. Most interesting is the island cottage as it would have been in the mid-19th century, with its simple kitchen, massive table and box beds, one for the parents and the other for the children.
WOMEN IN CONTROL. Ushant had no natural sheltered harbor, so fishing was not possible and the men had to go as sailors on merchant vessels. This meant long voyages and months, maybe years, away from home. Island society adapted: the women farmed the land and it was the girls who proposed marriage.
PERN POINT. A rocky point which at low tide leads down to a long causeway. At the end stands a ruin, known locally as the "villa des Tempêtes" (House of Storms).
CREAC'H LIGHTHOUSE. The black and white striped tower

Maurice Utrillo, *The Rocks of Ushant* (1912).

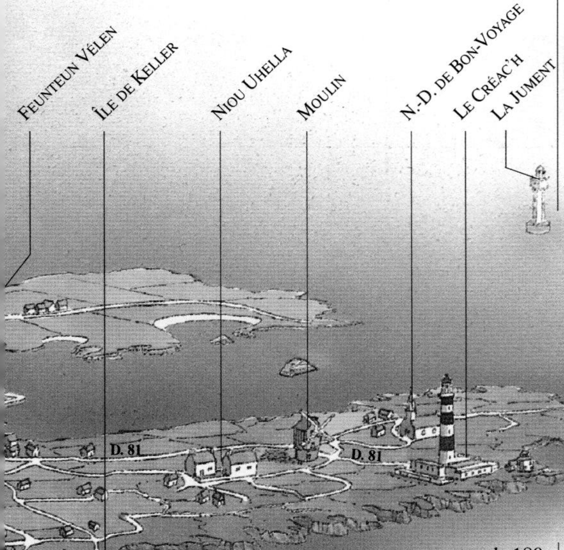

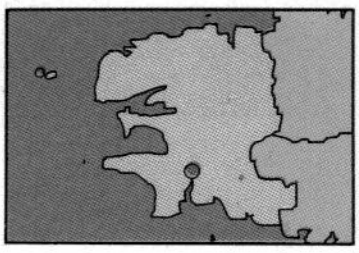

FEUTEUN VÉLEN   ÎLE DE KELLER   NIOU UHELLA   MOULIN   N.-D. DE BON-VOYAGE   LE CRÉAC'H   LA JUMENT

D. 81   D. 81

POINTE DE PERN   NIVIDIC

stands 180 feet tall. The beacon was first lit in 1863 and for many years remained the most powerful in the world. In 1971 its beam swept a radius of 33 nautical miles (37.5 miles), and it remains a vital landmark for the two hundred or more merchant vessels entering or leaving the western end of the English Channel. The Créac'h is not open to visitors.

LIGHTHOUSE AND BEACON MUSEUM ■ *16*. The museum was opened in 1988 with a display based on exhibits collected for the 1878 Universal Exhibition and kept in storage ever since. Technical details are explained and the life and work of the lighthousemen are described.

STIFF RADAR STATION. The high concrete tower standing some 100 yards south of the STIFF LIGHTHOUSE dates from 1700 and is one of the oldest in France. Inside is a radar station keeping watch on the busy maritime traffic. It is one of a number of safety measures set up after the terrible *Amoco Cadiz* disaster ▲ *264*.

THE PROELLA MEMORIAL. A monument standing in the graveyard of the church in Lampaul, the main village of Ushant. It is a reminder of the many islanders who lost their lives at sea. A drowned sailor could not be buried in consecrated ground, and his body was symbolized by a small wax cross. The *proella* was the name of the cross and the ceremony.

Porsgwenn sheep fair.

JUMENT LIGHTHOUSE
The strong currents here meant that the lighthouse was built at tremendous risk. The difficult task of constructing a tower on a rock that was uncovered only for a few hours each day was begun in 1904 and completed in 1911. New reinforcements that were needed were finished around 1940. The 138-foot-high light has been operated automatically since 1991.

POINTE DU RAZ POINTE DU VAN CAMARET AUDIERNE MORGAT

ALBERT LOUPPE BRIDGE
The bridge spanning the Elorn, designed by engineer Freycinet, opened in 1930. It ended the extreme isolation of the Plougastel peninsula. The prestressed concrete structure with its three great arches is over half a mile long. Today it is reserved for pedestrians and cyclists: a new bridge carries road traffic.

STRAWBERRIES
This fruit seems to have been introduced from South America in the late 18th century by the botanist Frézier. Strawberries began to be grown around Plougastel in the late 19th century, reviving

the town's fortunes and making it famous. They were exported to England in ships owned by companies that specialized in the trade. Nowadays strawberry production has dwindled.

PLOUGASTEL-DAOULAS PENINSULA

The peninsula juts out into the Rade de Brest, Brest's immense natural harbor. With its gentle hills, sheltered coves and headlands, it is very different to the flat plateau of Léon to the north and the more dramatic Monts d'Arrée eastward.

THE "GARDEN OF BREST". Plougastel enjoys a mild climate and the land is good, apart from on the rocky northern coast. It is a fertile area. At the end of the 19th century, when flax was no longer wanted for the linen industry ● *60*, strawberries earned farmers an extremely good living. By 1870 there were 500 acres already under cultivation, and by 1937 this had risen over 3,000. Today only 600 tons are grown a year, a dramatic reduction from the 6,000 tons that were produced annually in the 1950's. Since 1970 the farmers of Plougastel have successfully redeployed their assets and now grow top grade tomatoes, flowers and shallots under glass.

RICHES FROM THE SEA. In the present century the fishing of scallops in the bay has become big business. But between 1960 and 1965 the catch diminished drastically. It has now dropped from a peak of 2,000 tons a year to a mere 300. In winter the

fishermen also drag for clams and other shellfish. In summer they go out line-fishing for mackerel and bass. There are oyster and cocklebeds in suitable spots along the shores of the peninsula.

PARDON OF SAINT JEAN
A pardon held on the last Sunday in June at the chapel of St-Jean. It was believed to be especially good for healing the sick and was popular with the people of Brest and the region of Léon, who would arrive by steamboat.

Women from Kerhuon returning from collecting shellfish.

CHAPEL OF ST-JEAN. In the 12th century the Knights of St John built a leper-house here on the banks of the Elorn. A 15th-century chapel which was remodeled in the 17th century now stands on the site, with another one next to it.

PLOUGASTEL-DAOULAS

The town has many fine historical features. The Calvary is among the most interesting in Brittany ▲ *282*, and there are also eight chapels, each with its own cross and fountain.

HERITAGE MUSEUM (MUSÉE DU PATRIMOINE). The museum was opened in 1991 and its collection of old furniture and objects of local origin provides a colorful introduction to the region and its history. Exhibits illustrate its agricultural and maritime past, its traditions and costumes. The rich, exuberant clothes of the people of Plougastel and the women's unique headdresses are radically different from the more sober and restrained dress of their neighbors to the north of Léon.

THE CHAPEL OF ST-JEAN
The bell bears an inscription in English, "The Fame of Noshields", and the date 1795. It was no doubt looted from an English ship.

281

Following an outbreak of Plague in 1598 the local population decided to build a monument in the hope that it would protect them. Everybody agreed to share the cost and work began as soon as possible. The base was ready by 1602 and the Calvary was completed two years later. It is a magnificent piece of work but it is unsigned and the craftsman responsible remains unknown. It was badly damaged by bombardments in August 1944 but, with the help of the J. D. Skilton Foundation in America, it was skilfully restored by the sculptor Millet in 1948–9.

CHRIST ON THE CROSS
The tall base of cross is carved bumps repres Plague buboes was tradition practise, ofte where a Cross erected after epidemic. At end of the cross a small angel in adoration.

Dis
rep
thic

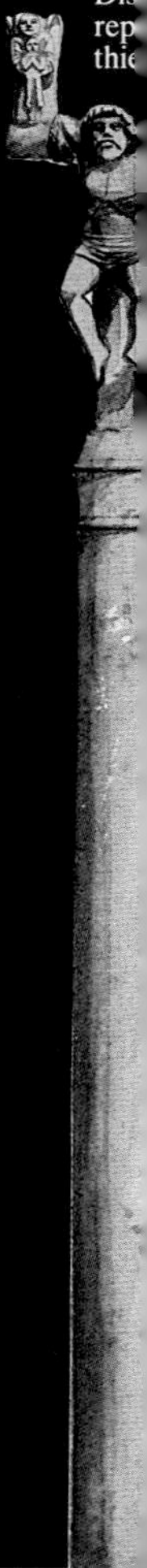

DOUBLE TRIO. The representation of three figures was a popular theme in Celtic mythology. Here, it is doubled in the figures on either side of the Virgin Mary. Carved back to back with Marie Salomé is Saint Peter holding the keys of Paradise, while Saint John is back to back of Mary Magdalene. They stand each side of Christ in blessing, making a double trio of holy figures.

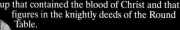
Feast Day at Plougastel-Daoulas, a painting by Charles Cottet.

THE CHALICE. Beneath Christ's feet two angels catch his blood in a chalice. Originally, on two other brackets two more angels collected the blood from his hands and side. Such figures are often seen in Breton Calvaries and are the origin of the legend of the Holy Grail, the fabulous cup that contained the blood of Christ and that figures in the knightly deeds of the Round Table.

Longinus

Stephaton

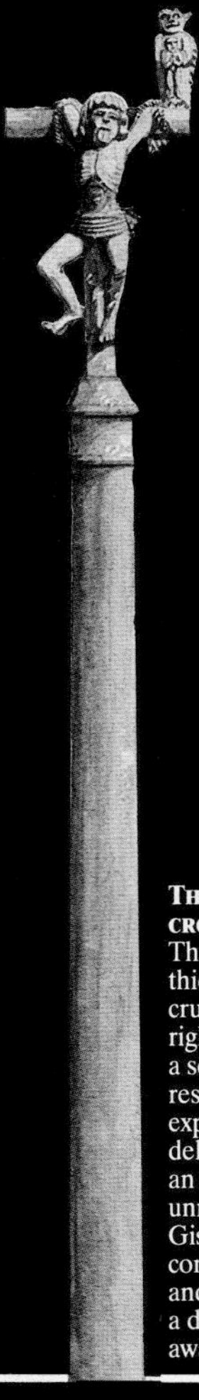

Gismas, the unrepentant thief.

THE PIETÀ
On the second crosspiece below is the group of Our Lady of the Sorrows: Marie Salomé, a holy woman; the Virgin Mary kneeling in contemplation of the martyred body of her son, the central figure in this powerful Pietà; and Mary Magdalene, with braided hair, carrying the traditional jar of ointment.

THE RIDERS
Two riders, Longinus and Stephaton, stand on the first crosspiece below Christ. Longinus, the only original carving in his group, holds his hand to his eye, a reference to the legend that he received a drop of Christ's blood in his eye, which opened his eyes to the truth.

THE THIEVES' CROSS
The repentant thief Dismas, crucified to the right of Christ, has a serene and resigned expression as he delivers his soul to an angel. The unrepentant thief, Gismas, by contrast, protests and blasphemes as a demon carries away his soul.

283

One feature that sets this Calvary apart from the others is the use of two contrasting materials: yellow Logonna stone for the base, and grey Kersanton granite for the characters in the drama. The 181 carved figures tracing the story of the life of Christ were formerly painted, and are arranged in groups in formal hieratical poses. The figures on the upper part are quite different from those beneath.

UPPER SECTION: EAST FAÇADE. BAPTISM OF JESUS. John the Baptist wets the head of Jesus with water from the Jordan, while an angel carries his robe.

NORTH FAÇADE: THE FLAGELLATION. Christ is tied to a pillar and cruelly beaten by two soldiers. Nearby stand two more soldiers waiting to take their turn.

CROWN OF THORNS. Three executioners force the crown of thorns onto Christ's head with a stick. In front an old soldier puts out his tongue at the victim and strikes him with a reed.

WEST FAÇADE: THE DEVIL TEMPTS JESUS. "Are you a king?" Pilate asks Jesus, to which he replies, "You say that I am a king." Then the Devil tempts Jesus by offering him the world to rule.

RESURRECTION. Christ in Glory raises his right hand in blessing as he rises from the tomb, while the guards on either side fast asleep.

SOUTH FAÇADE: THE WAY OF THE CROSS. There are fourteen figures in this procession: Veronica displays the handkerchief with which she mopped Christ's face and which

carries the imprint of his features; John supports Mary; some soldiers try to make the Cross heavier by leaning upon it, while in the center Jesus

ENTOMBMENT. Eight figures stand around the body of Christ: among them the Virgin Mary supported by the apostle John, Mary Magdalene bearing her jar of ointment and Saint Nicodemus.

JESUS BEFORE ANNAS. With hands bound and surrounded by guards, Jesus appears before the high priest, who is seated and wears a miter.

JESUS BEFORE PILATE. Christ is shown to the crowd, while the seated Pilate prepares to wash his hands in water brought by a servant.

SCOURGING OF CHRIST. Blindfolded and with hands bound, Jesus is repeatedly struck and forced to guess where each blow came from.

JESUS AMONG THE SCRIBES. The young boy disputes and debates with the astonished scribes, shown carrying their scrolls.

DESCENT INTO LIMBO. Christ rises from the dead and returns from Hell, bringing salvation to two sufferers whose hands he holds. The gate of Hell is depicted as a dragon's mouth with Satan enthroned above, while demons torment the damned.

receives discreet help from Simon of Cyrene. The procession follows some musicians with a drummer and a self-important official on horseback.

UPPER SECTION. EAST FAÇADE. ANNUNCIATION. The Virgin Mary kneels on a *prie-dieu*, with the angel Gabriel at the extreme right. **VISITATION.** Great with child, Mary visits her cousin Elizabeth who is also expecting a baby. **MARRIAGE.** A priest holds Mary and Joseph by the hand to unite them in holy matrimony. **BIRTH.** Jesus lies between Joseph and

NORTH FAÇADE. MOUNT OF OLIVES. Remarkable for its unusual height, the tall figure of Jesus speaks surrounded by three drowsy disciples, Peter, James and John. **ARREST OF JESUS.** Saint Peter prepares to draw his sword, restrained by Jesus. Judas has just kissed Jesus and clutches a purse, while a soldier tumbles backward.

WEST FAÇADE. ENTRY INTO JERUSALEM. The city is represented by a small crenelated tower, which Christ prepares to enter accompanied by John and four other disciples. **ARCH.** Saint Peter bears his keys and wears the Papal crown; Saint Roch shows the marks of the plague which afflicts him.

SOUTH FAÇADE. THE LAST SUPPER. In this composition the apostles are represented by three groups of four figures surrounding their beloved Master. Some of them appear to be in animated discussion: the gesture of crossing fingers is supposed to represent settling a decisive point. Saint John rests his head on Christ's breast, a pose which allowed the

Mary. A little angel kneels beside Joseph. **Circumcision.** The high priest performs the operation in front of Joseph and Mary. **Flight into Egypt.** Fleeing from the wrath of Herod, Joseph leads the donkey bearing Mary in whose arms rests the infant Jesus. Saint Mark is seen on the projecting corner.

Jesus before Caiaphas. Held by three soldiers, his hands tied, Christ is brought before a nobleman wearing a crown and carrying a scepter. This is probably the high priest Caiaphas, although it could be King Herod. To his right is a bishop. On the right of the staircase is Saint John together with his symbol of the eagle.

Adoration of the Magi. Jesus holds out his hand for one of the gifts of the Three Kings. On the projecting corner stands Luke the Evangelist with a bull at his feet.

sculptor to preserve the balance of the ensemble. **Washing of the feet.** On his knees Jesus washes the feet of Peter. The apostles stand in three groups behind them, as in the preceding scene. The Evangelist Matthew is carved on the projecting corner, leaning on a desk supported by an angel.

PEN-HIR POINT
The tip of the Crozon peninsula falls away dramatically. Extending out into the ocean are a series of rocks: the "Tas de Pois". There are views over the Cap Sizun and in clear weather as far as Ouessant.

Exhibitions in the former abbey of Daoulas are very popular in the region.

Landévennec: a view of the abbey in 1655.

DAOULAS

The harbor town of Daoulas, standing on the river Mignonne, was once of great importance in the region. This was due to its abbey; to its port, navigable at high tide; and to its possessions which extended over nine parishes. Justice was administered from here, fairs and markets were held, and feudal life revolved around the town, making it busy and prosperous. The port flourished in the 15th and 16th centuries, exporting cannon-balls made of local stone.

DAOULAS ABBEY. Augustinians occupied the abbey until 1789. The gaunt abbey church was built between 1167 and 1173. Its Romanesque chancel and the transept were rebuilt in the 16th century, but the chancel and its contents were irreparably damaged during the Revolution. There is a Gothic porch leading to the cemetery. The cloister is unique in Brittany: the carved pillars and columns with capitals are typically Romanesque in style. The cultural center now housed in the old abbey attracts many visitors.

ABBAYE DE LANDÉVENNEC ★

A SAD FATE. The ruins of this abbey, in their setting at the innermost point of the Rade de Brest, attract many visitors, tourists and pilgrims. This is the most famous and oldest holy place in Brittany. It was probably founded in 485, and in 913 it was burned down by Norsemen. Later it was pillaged by the League ● 57, and at the Revolution the library was ransacked and over two thousand works were lost.

SITE MUSEUM. An exhibition illustrating the history of the abbey with a fine display of archeological finds.

CROZON PENINSULA

A cross-shaped peninsula forming the southern side of south of the Rade de Brest, and covered in gorse and bracken.

IS GOLDEN TOWER
Marshall Vauban called his
fort (right) "ma tour dorée":
the walls have a mellow glow
in the evening sun.

Much of its coastline consists of
steep cliffs, but there are hidden
and secluded beaches. The shape
of the peninsula is due to its
geological formation. The sea has
worn away the soft rock and come
up against the hard sandstone
plateau, whose cliffs drop to the sea.

CAMARET

Camaret or *Kamelet*, "port of the curved wake", seems
to have been founded by Saint Roch when he
established a hermitage in the 4th century. Before
steam vessels, its sheltered cove was a
haven for boats unable to navigate the
into the harbor of Brest. From the
8th century onward, the main
occupation of the inhabitants was sardine fishing. When these
fish disappeared early in the 20th century, the men were
forced to fish crawfish off the coasts of Mauritius and Brazil.
This too came to an end in 1980's. Today the pretty port of
Camaret makes its living principally from tourism.

NOTRE-DAME DE ROCAMADOUR. The chapel stands on the
Sillon, a natural shingly spit that protects the harbor. It is an
impressive structure, over 80 feet long and 40 wide. Inside,
the nave is flanked by aisles, with four arcades on either side.
Many visit the chapel to see the fine old wooden statues, but
its most fascinating and moving feature is the collection of
votive offerings that have accumulated over the years,
brought by sailors in thanks for narrow escapes at sea. In 1910
the chapel suffered terrible damage in a fire.

VAUBAN'S TOWER. Vauban, the superintendent of fortifications
under Louis XIV, saw Camaret as "Brest's antechamber" and
built a fort on Sillon point in 1689. It soon proved its worth,
repulsing an attempted landing by the Anglo-Dutch fleet in
1694. For this victory Camaret was awarded the title of *Custos
orae aremoricae* (Guardian of the Armorican coast). The
tower now houses an exhibition devoted to the life and work
of the military engineer, and a museum is being considered.

AN ARTISTS' COLONY

TRENDSETTERS. Artists and writers have been coming to
Camaret since 1870. Eugène Boudin was the first to spend
time here. He used to stay at the Hôtel de la Marine and
made about sixty paintings in all, the best-known being of the
harbor. In 1886 he introduced a writer friend to the town, and
Gustave Toudouze's famous novel *Perished at Sea* made the
region famous. Many others, including the painters Charles
Cottet, Marcel Sauvaige, George Lacombe, Pierre Vailland
and the poet Saint-Pol Roux, were to follow in their wake.

SAINT-POL ROUX. The poet, born in Marseilles in 1861, was
an extraordinary character. The Surrealists saw him as the
founder of modern poetry. He published his masterpiece,
Woman with a Scythe, in 1899. It was not well received by the
Paris *literati* and Roux buried himself in the countryside. He
designed a weird house called "Coecilian", and invited friends
such as Max Jacob, Paul Eluard and Pierre MacOrlan to stay.

**THE VAUBAN
TOWER**
Section and
elevation by the
engineer
Traverse (1696).

ROSALIE DORSO
The landlady of the
Hôtel de la Marine
was the doyenne of
the local community
and welcomed the
artists who began to
visit Camaret around
1870. "She was loved
and respected for
miles around for her
sound advice,
common sense and
warm heart. She

would
tell us about Camaret
as it used to be," said
writer Toudouze.
Saint-Pol Roux ended
his oration at her
funeral: "She knew
things that are not
written in books,
things it takes many
long years to
understand."

THE CHURCH OF CROZON. A large crowd attending the annual pardon in the early years of the present century.

REREDOS IN ST PIERRE DE CROZON The carved and painted wooden altarpiece dates from the early 17th century. In twenty-nine pictures featuring over four hundred figures it illustrates an episode from the Golden Legend: the martyrdom of ten thousand members of the Theban Legion, crucified for their conversion to Christianity. The piece is extraordinarily rich and full of life.

CROZON

THE CHURCH OF ST-PIERRE. Only the 16th-century main door and the altarpiece "of a thousand martyrs" survived when the church was rebuilt in 1900.

DINAN POINT. In rough weather the sea hurls itself against the rocky mass known as the "Château", spurting up against the crags and seething in the hollows of the cliffs.

MORGAT

In 1885 Louis Richard, a commercial traveler, paid a visit to the little town of Morgat. With industrialist Armand Peugeot he set up a company to exploit its tourist potential. Peugeot sent executives from his company on holiday

CAP DE LA CHÈVRE The access road runs along the cliffs, which can rise as high as 300 feet above the sea and are rich in mineral deposits. A cliff path starting about 500 yards from the lighthouse leads to the wild Cap de la Chèvre itself.

The port of Morgat.

there and built hotels, such as the Grand Hôtel de la Mer. Fine villas soon followed, among them the Villa Demarets, a portable construction that was later exhibited at the Universal Exhibition in Paris in 1889.

THE GROTTOES. Over the years the sea has enlarged fissures in the schist cliffs. The erosion has created many grottoes, some of them so large that the can be visited by boat. The largest is the GROTTE DE L'AUTEL, with a cathedral-like interior 300 feet long and 33 feet high and brightly colored walls.

LOCRONAN

SAINT RONAN. The Irish monk Saint Ronan arrived in the region of Léon in the 11th century. He took up residence in the Forest of Névet, near Locronan ("Ronan's place"). He died not far from Lamballe and his body was brought back to be buried on the spot where the church now stands.

PROSPERITY AND STAGNATION. In the 16th and 17th centuries Locronan lived almost exclusively off the thriving linen and canvas industries ● *60*. Its canvas was considered the toughest and best in the diocese, and six thousand lengths were made a year. The cloth found markets all over Europe, from Spain to Scotland, shipped out from the nearby port of Pouldavid. The town's fortunes slowly declined, however: clients such as the French East India Company disappeared and the market gradually collapsed.

AT THE MERCY OF WOLVES. In the early 19th century wolves were still a serious problem in the country around Locronan. They lived in the huge tracts of dense forest, and the peasants

THE MAIN SQUARE OF LOCRONAN
A dramatic aerial view of the handsome square with its dark granite-built church, houses and ancient well.

Charles Daniélou was elected mayor of Locronan in 1912, and with the help of the townspeople he set about preserving and restoring its fine old buildings.

were unable to defend themselves as they lacked the necessary weapons. It was not until the middle of the century that concerted efforts managed to bring these predators under control.

FAR-SIGHTED MAYOR. Locronan gradually emerged as a tourist center, thanks in great part to the work of Charles Daniélou.

LA GRAND'PLACE ★. The whole of this magnificent old square is now classified as an historic monument. It has fine 17th- and 18th-century townhouses built of granite. These were the homes of town dignitaries, officials in the service of the king and merchants who had done well out of the cloth trade. At the lower end of the square stood the headquarters of the French East India Company ▲ *320*, founded in the 18th century by Louis XIV's minister of finance, Colbert. It traded in spices and luxury goods. The town's only source of drinking water was the well sunk in the center of the square. Each year it had to be cleaned. Volunteers would descend to a niche marking the lowest level of water and set to work: when the job was completed there would be a big party in the square.

CHURCH OF ST-RONAN. This was built in the Grand' Place between 1424 and 1480 with funds supplied by three Dukes of Brittany: Jean V, Pierre II and François II. They each came here on a pilgrimage "to increase the fruit of their line", for pagan superstition traditionally associated St-Ronan's with fertility. The church is one of the most beautiful examples of 15th-century Flamboyant Gothic. Its spire, which was struck by lightning on three occasions, was finally demolished in 1808 and replaced by a turret. The interior furnishings are also outstanding, with a fine altarpiece, statues of Saint Corentin (first bishop of Quimper) and Saint Ronan.

THE "GRANDE TROMÉNIE"

Once every six years, at the end of July, the procession of the Grande Troménie follows a path that was first set out in the 11th century by Alain Canhiart, Comte de Cornouaille. He fervently wished to keep the cult of Saint Ronan alive and every week he walked the same route, barefoot and fasting.

Carved medallions on a ceremonial seat in the church of St Ronan, illustrating the life of the saint.

OPEN-AIR RELIGION Bearers would take turns to carry the banners spread out at intervals along the pardon processions ● *70*. Strong winds often made the job extremely difficult.

This ceremony has not been transformed into a secular occasion.

TWELVE KILOMETERS AND TWELVE STATIONS. The completion of one Grande Troménie is enough to open the doors of Paradise. It takes three of the "ordinary" ones to secure the same redemption; these are held each year along a shorter route. "He who has never done the Troménie, will have to do it when he's dead, advancing but his coffin's length each day." The old and infirm could pay alms to a pauper who would walk the route in their place. The unusual feature of this procession is the *tro minihi* ("monastery tower"), a lesson from the Gospel read at each of the twelve stations of the Cross that stand along the way. The Troménie can be begun at any point, as long as it is walked following the sun and with the church of Locronan on the right ▲ *291*, and that it is followed full circle. It used to be forbidden to turn round or to talk. Only prayer was permitted, or the singing in Breton of the canticle that tells the legend of Saint Ronan.

DOUARNENEZ

The bay of Douarnenez is lined by fine sandy beaches and tall cliffs, and dominated by Mount Menez-Hom, one side of which has been eroded by wind and water. In 1794 the bay was described by Cambry in a book *Journey through Finistère* as "one of the finest expanses of water to be seen in all Europe".

A BUSY PORT. In the 1st century AD Douarnenez was already an important Gallo-Roman settlement with an economy based on the production of *garum* (a pungent fish sauce used in a great variety of Roman dishes). By the early Middle Ages it had become a busy fishing port, part of the estates of the Duke of Brittany. In later centuries linen produced in the Porzay was shipped from the port. By 1900 the canning industry had developed on a huge scale, employing several thousand people. Today, however, Douarnenez depends increasingly on tourism for its survival.

PORT-RHU. In 1992 a barrier was built across the river mouth at Port-Rhu to create the largest floating museum in Europe. On the town side is the BOAT MUSEUM and the Enfer boatyards, where craftsmen specialize in the repair of traditional wooden craft.

PORT MUSEUM. The museum, which exists thanks to the efforts of a group of enthusiasts who wanted to preserve the maritime heritage of the town and save its old working boats, was opened in 1992.

PLAN OF THE MUSEUM
1. Boat museum
2. Traditional boatyard
3. Village of l'Enfer
4. Traditional fishing harbor
5. Fish market
6. Coasters' harbor
7. Yacht harbor
8. Mess
9. Tall ships
10. Aquarium
11. Barrage and walkway
12. Sail-making
13. Landing stage
14. Shellfish tanks

ENFER WORKSHOPS
This is a training center for boat-building, maritime carpentry, and sailmaking. Here one can learn how to build a boat the old way.

FETCHING IN THE HARVEST
A painting by Georges Clairin (*Gathering Kelp on the Pointe du Raz*) ■ *38*, showing how seaweed was hauled up the steep cliff by means of a primitive winch.

Tins from the Douarnenez cannery.

At night, with the beacons of its two lighthouses beaming their intermittent signals through the darkness, the Pointe du Raz is a marvelous sight. **"**The coast was extraordinarily rugged, the sea green and mauve seething over the rocks. It made my heart lurch.**"**
Simone de Beauvoir

There are now more than a hundred craft, both French and foreign, to be seen. Some are afloat in the artificial basin of Port-Rhu, while others are displayed out of the water in an old cannery building.

POINTE DU VAN

The cape looks out due west over the Baie des Trépassés. The scenery of high cliffs topped with rough heather and rocky lichen-covered outcrops is wild and magnificent. Patches of vivid-yellow gorse shine out: "a golden flower that seems to hold and reflect the light unlike any other" (Louis Guilloux, *Bretagne que j'aime*, 1973).

ST-THEY CHAPEL. It stands perched high above the sea looking west toward the horizon, a last stop before setting out on the "great journey". In good weather the Île de Sein ▲ *304* can be seen silhouetted against the sky. There is a steep path down to the MOUILLAGE DE VORLENN, an ancient mooring on the south side of the point. This path can be very dangerous when the wind is from the west.

BAIE DES TRÉPASSÉS. The origin of the name, which means "Bay of the Dead", is uncertain. Many theories, both linguistic and romantic, have been put forward. The most popular legend is that the mythical town of Ys, submerged by vengeful Providence, may lie beneath the waters near by.

POINTE DU RAZ

The Pointe du Raz is at the end of Cap Sizun, and is a popular site in Brittany. Stormy weather attracts a particularly intrepid kind of sea-lover. Over the next few years costly improvements will be made to the site. Classed as a "Grand Site National", its future now seems assured. In front of the lonely signal station stands an impressive statue of the Virgin, Godebsky's *Notre-Dame-des-Naufragés* (*Our Lady of the Shipwrecked*), unveiled during the pardon of 1904.

QUIMPER

BRETON COSTUME

Two figures, painted by Christophe-Paul de Robien, are from an 18th-century map of Quimper. This is one of the earliest illustrations showing Bretons in traditional costume.

HISTORY OF THE CITY

AQUILONIA. In the 1st century BC Roman legions built a town on the left bank of the river Odet. This was Aquilonia, located downstream from the present center of Quimper, on the site of the Locmaria district at the foot of Mont Frugy ▲ *302*. Ships came up with the tide to unload their cargoes here. The town continued to flourish until the fall of the Roman Empire at the beginning of the 5th century.

LEGENDARY ORIGINS. According to myth, the legendary town of Ys was swallowed up by the waters as the result of the misconduct of Dahut, daughter of King Gradlon, a Briton chief who had fled his native land to escape the Saxon invaders. He abandoned his town to the rising waters and moved on to stop at the river Odet at its confluence with the river Steir. Here he founded the town of *Kemper* (Confluence), which became the capital of southern Cornouaille.

THE MEDIEVAL RAMPARTS. In 1209 the Duke of Brittany built a castle on the right bank of the river in an attempt to check the power of the bishop, temporal as well as

QUIMPER ▲

1. **FINE ARTS MUSEUM**
2. **CATHEDRAL OF ST-CORENTIN**
3. **BRITTANY MUSEUM**
4. **CAFÉ DE L'ÉPÉE**
5. **LES HALLES**
6. **CAFÉ DE BRETAGNE**
7. **CHURCH OF ST-MATTHEW**
8. **PRÉFECTURE**
9. **CAR PARK**
10. **MONT FRUGY**

FIGHTING FOR THE CROWN

Rivalry between Léon and Cornouaille, as to whether Landerneau or Quimper should be the regional capital, flared up in 1789. Quimper was initially chosen by the ruling Girondins, but in 1793 the Convention changed to Landerneau, accusing Quimper of political incorrectness. One year later, however, Quimper regained its title.

spiritual ruler of the city, who also bore the title Comte de Cornouaille. Around the year 1230 the bishop enclosed the 40 acres of the city with a long wall set with ten towers and six fortified gates.

SIEGES AND RELIGIOUS WARS. In 1344 Charles of Blois sacked Quimper and routed the English troops under the command of Jean de Montfort. Twenty years and numerous sieges later Montfort's son Jean IV recaptured the city, and kept control of it until the knight Du Guesclin delivered it to the king of France. Intermittent religious conflict raged around Quimper into the 16th century. The Catholic League ● 57 at first resisted the advance of the forces of the Protestant king Henri IV until Marshal d'Aumont finally triumphed in 1594, when the king's troops bombarded and took the city. Some years later a notorious brigand named Guy Eder de Beaumanoir made three vain attempts to conquer Quimper.

"THE ASSASSINATION OF BISHOP AUDREIN"
In 1800 the Chouans ● 62 captured and shot the regicidal bishop of Finistère outside Quimper. The incident inspired this painting by Maurice Bertheaux.

297

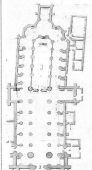

EARLY GOTHIC
St-Corentin was one
of the earliest Gothic
cathedrals in Brittany.
Musical angels adorn
its south door. Inside
is a magnificent
gilded high altar
dating from the 19th
century, as well as
some fine 15th-
century stained glass.

THE 19TH AND 20TH CENTURIES. The 19th century brought
prosperity to Quimper. Its population doubled, and in 1863
the opening of the railroad transformed its economy. Many
streets were rebuilt and widened, and much of the old city
wall was demolished. The Odet was canalized, and new
bridges across it diminished the size of the harbor. In 1960
Quimper officially absorbed some of the outlying villages such
as Penhars and Kerfeunteun: within a few years the
population had grown from 17,000 to 60,000.

CATHEDRAL OF ST-CORENTIN

It took three centuries to complete the cathedral. Work began
in the 13th century with the construction of the chancel,
which incorporated an ancient chapel dedicated to the Virgin.
The towers and nave were added in the 15th century
following the Wars of Succession, which had severely
disrupted the Duchy of Brittany. The impressive stone spires
that dominate the city were added around
1856: to pay for them the diocese imposed a
levy of one sou per year from each
parishioner.

A FAÇADE IN THE ENGLISH STYLE. Though
the two square towers, each 250 feet high
and with galleries at the top, were in
traditional Breton style, the west front
with its single porch and two great
windows above recalls English Gothic.
Among the carvings round the
entrance can be seen the lion of the
Montfort family and the armorial
bearings of nobles who lived nearby.
Between the towers stands the
EQUESTRIAN STATUE of the
legendary KING GRADLON. It was
unveiled in 1858 to replace an earlier
statue destroyed by lightning, once
the focal point of a ceremony that
took place annually on July 26. On
that day a mounted herald offered
Gradlon a goblet of wine,
wiped his mouth, emptied the
cup and threw it to the crowd
below. Whoever caught it
without it breaking was to be
rewarded with one hundred
gold coins, though no-one
ever won the prize.

AN ECCENTRIC AXIS. Inside,
visitors immediately notice
the eccentric alignment of the
nave and chancel. The
builders appear to have used
the foundations of two earlier
buildings. The 13th-century
chancel (magnificently
restored) was built on the
remains of an ancient
chapel containing the

tomb of Alain Caniard, who conquered the Normans in the 11th century. The nave was built in the 15th century on the site of an 11th-century Norman church. The paucity of decoration inside is the result of the so-called "Saints' bonfire" held in the present Place de la Résistance in 1793, at the height of the Revolution, "to rid the city of all its feudal trappings". Two 17th-century statues have survived: one of *Saint Anne teaching the Virgin to read*; and the other of *Santik Du*, a monk who nursed victims of the Black Death before succumbing to it himself in 1349 and who is still revered by the inhabitants of Quimper. The chapels in the nave and transept are decorated with frescoes signed by Yann Dargent, a 19th-century artist. Parishioners banned from the cathedral for one reason or another worshipped from behind the window-grille of the Penitential Chamber.

BRITTANY MUSEUM. It was opened in 1846 by the Archeological Society of Finistère and since 1911 it has been housed in the former Bishop's Palace at Quimper. This remarkable building stands just south of the Cathedral and consists of two perpendicular wings enclosing the house of the Rohans (below right). The wing fronting the river was altered in 1866 by Joseph Bigot. This tireless architect, a native of Quimper, also designed the cathedral spires and the cloister in the episcopal garden: it is said that Bigot never took so much as a day's holiday in all his life. This was the first museum of its kind to be opened in Brittany and it has gradually focused more and more on social history and local customs. The regions dealt with include Léon, Cornouaille and Petit-Trégor, and its collections of traditional costumes, furniture and local pottery are unique ▲ *302*. There are prehistoric displays as well, and some fine statues such as a 14th-century *Saint Anne*, and 17th- and 18th-century Baroque pieces.

FINE ARTS MUSEUM. In 1864 Jean-Marie de Silguy bequeathed a substantial collection of paintings and drawings to the city of Quimper on condition that a museum was built to house it. The museum, which finally opened in 1872, is one of the finest in Brittany, with Old Masters of the Dutch, Flemish, Italian and French schools, including works by Rubens, Boucher, Fragonard and Corot. There are many historical and allegorical paintings, and seascapes. Paintings of the Pont-

KING MARC'H
This striking granite figure was carved in the Middle Ages, and is on show in the Brittany Museum.

THE HOUSE OF THE ROHANS
The building bears the name of the bishop for whom it was built during the Renaissance. The foundation stone was laid in 1505. It is a remarkable house, with a massive spiral staircase and two

extensive wings. The one overlooking the Rue Gradlon was demolished in the late 16th century but rebuilt less than a century later. The other wing, which borders the river Odet, was an 18th-century addition, modified by Bigot in 1866. The building, whose first-floor rooms have intersecting semicircular arches, now houses the Brittany Museum.

Aven school ▲ *312*, linked with the Nabis and Symbolist movements, constitute another highly prized collection. Paintings firmly rooted in the styles of the early 20th century lead to rooms dedicated to the work of Quimper-born poet and painter Max Jacob (1876–1944) and his friends. Contemporary art is also represented, notably by the paintings by Pierre Jacob, "Tal Coat".

THE OLD DISTRICTS. Developers have not left to posterity much of the noble old city and its majestic walls. After the disastrous fire of 1762 that destroyed the ancient quarter of town round the cathedral, construction of old-style houses was forbidden. The traditional timber-framed buildings with cob filling were replaced by stone. Existing houses were left untouched for the time being, though many were demolished in the following century in a drive to straighten out the old winding streets. The Rue

THE RUE KÉRÉON
This colorful street is now a pedestrian area. Traditional headdresses are still to be seen here, especially on market days. Look in front of the cathedral to see Bigouden women selling hand-crafted lace gloves and table linen.

Kéréon was one notable victim: its old overhanging houses were replaced by buildings with strict straight lines faced with stone cladding or plaster rendering. The medieval walls of the episcopal city were knocked down, and new façades were built in dressed timber, marble and granite, in the latest style. But the passion for modernism has somehow failed to destroy the medieval atmosphere of the old city center, whose delightful old-world flavor remains.

RUE KÉRÉON. Shoemakers' shops were concentrated in this street. It extends west from the cathedral, and the view along it is particularly attractive. The street reaches the old ramparts at the PLACE MÉDARD, from where the Pont Médard bridges the Steir. This was once a drawbridge and the western entrance to the city. The HÔTEL DU HAFFOND in the square is a fine example of the severe 18th-century style that predominated in the province. Nobles, well-to-do merchants, lawyers and churchmen once lived in the Rue Kéréon. Their opulent houses were timber-framed, with stone corbels at street level. Some of them have survived: the finest, dating from the 16th century, stands at the corner of the Rue Kéréon and the RUE DES BOUCHERIES. As its name implies, in the Middle Ages butchers were obliged to have their premises in the latter street, and could not "sell or display their goods elsewhere". They also had to keep all their marrowbones for the lord of Cludou, who in his turn, whenever a new bishop was proclaimed in Quimper, had to escort him from the chapel of Penity to the cathedral.

The street signs are the work of well-known artists.

RUE FRÉRON. The street is named after Élie-Catherine Fréron, a man of letters who was bitterly opposed to the *Encyclopédistes*. He was born in Quimper in 1718 and died in Paris in 1776. Voltaire was constantly teasing and taunting him in print: "The other day when Jean Fréron was out for a walk he was bitten by a snake, and what do you think happened next? Why, the snake died!" In its time the Rue Fréron has had many changes of name, but the locals still call

At the turn of the century Quimper's 20,000 inhabitants had a choice of no fewer than 127 cafés.

it the "Rue Obscure" (dark street), a name that harks back to the time when it was just a constricted alleyway.

THE QUAYS

With flower-decked footbridges spanning the Odet, the theater, the Bishop's palace and the ramparts, the quays are the heart of Quimper and a microcosm of its history. The ramparts still stand along the BOULEVARD DE KERGUÉLEN.

THEATER. It was built on the site of the former orchard of Couchouren, near the Rue du Pont Firmin. But there was a problem, for Urbain Couchouren had left this land to the city on condition that it was used to build an old people's home. It took six years of wrangling between the civic authorities and the minister responsible to arrive at a compromise. Eventually the theater and a garden were constructed in Couchouren's orchard, while the old people's home was built as an annex to an existing hospital.

PRÉFECTURE. Redevelopment of the site where St-Catherine's Hospital formerly stood began in the early part of the present century. The neo-Gothic building that fronts on to the quayside was opened in 1909.

PALAIS DE JUSTICE. The law courts are housed in an impressive neo-classical building dating from 1829. The famous Breton engineer Charles Freminville, however, condemned it as "niggardly and sham".

People from the Bigouden region frequented the cafés along the Rue Bourg-les-Bourgs and Rue Pont l'Abbé, while those from Ergué-Armel drank in the Rue Neuve. Fashionable society met on the boulevard, either at the Café de Bretagne or the Café de l'Epée, where the guest book includes the signatures of Paul Sérusier, Max Jacob and General de Gaulle. The murals painted for the café by Lemordant have been removed to the Fine Arts museum ▲ 299.

THE QUAYSIDES OF THE TOWN
People stroll up and down the quays and over the little footbridges, watching the bustle of everyday life. Writers and artists have often used the quays as a setting or a model for their work. This painting by Caveng captures the cheerful atmosphere of the lively quaysides.

DECORATION
The craftsman's brushes, which he usually makes himself, are of hair from a cow's ear (used for outlining and filling in) or from a grey squirrel (ideal for *touche* brushstrokes). The patterns are first drawn on paper, and then outlined with pinpricks before being rubbed over with a charcoal-filled pounce to transfer the design on to the ceramic surface to be decorated. The pattern thus remained consistent, but the decoration was entirely hand-painted.

MONT FRUGY. There is a car park and a tourist office at the foot of this wooded hill (233 feet high). The two-hundred-year-old trees that lined the avenue were flattened in Great Storm of 1987, but the narrow way up to the summit has lovely views over the city and river below.

THREE HUNDRED YEARS OF QUIMPER POTTERY

EARLY YEARS. In 1690 a potter from Provence named Jean-Baptiste Bousquet settled at Quimper, in the suburb of Locmaria. He opened a faience workshop there (which finally changed its name to HB in 1928). Bousquet's business soon prospered: deposits of clay at Toulven on the banks of the Odet were perfect for his needs, and there was no shortage of wood to fire the kilns. Quimper's geographical situation was another bonus, since it was a port and was also at the center of a network of roads leading to all the important towns of Lower Brittany. In 1749 a potter from Rouen by the name of Pierre-Clément Caussy married Bousquet's granddaughter and set out to reproduce in Quimper the popular faience of Rouen. Two more potteries soon opened. The first, called Eloury-Porquier-Beau (PB), was opened in 1772 by François Eloury, who had formerly worked for Caussy as a thrower. The second, called Henriot (HR), was founded in 1791. Until the middle of the 19th century these establishments produced crockery and other pots in glazed earthenware and stoneware. In addition, religious figures became a Quimper specialty and an important part of the market.

DECORATIVE FAIENCE. By the end of the 19th century particular styles and techniques had evolved that characterized the faience of Quimper. Everything was decorated by hand, most often in the style known as "*à la touche*" with tear-shaped brushstrokes forming flowers and foliage. The most famous of the decorations, called "*du petit Breton*", first appeared around 1850 and features a peasant in traditional costume pictured in profile between two clumps of vegetation.

NEW DESIGNS. Around 1870 something of a revolution took place in

local faience decoration, instigated by the design director of the Porquier Pottery, Alfred Beau. His designs, drawing on scenes of everyday life in the province, were imaginative little images of beggars, dances, weddings, markets and even the pardon celebrations. By the end of the century, at a time when Brittany and its colorful traditions were all the rage, and when artists were coming from all over France to paint there, Alfred Beau's decorations (quickly taken up by the HB and Henriot workshops) were an enormous success. The great Paris Universal Exhibition of 1878 was an important marketplace for Quimper faience: from this time on the skill of the Locmaria decorators was acclaimed the world over.

Design for a plate by Georges Renaud (1931).

Head of a Congolese Woman, exhibited by the Henriot workshops at the 1931 Colonial Exhibition.

TRADITION AND INNOVATION. Soon after World War One a new trend using contemporary art as the basis for new designs evolved in the HB and Henriot workshops. Quimper faience was featured at the Universal Exhibitions of 1925, 1931 and 1937. The well-known illustrator and decorative artist Mathurin Méheut was appointed artistic director of the Henriot factory, while the sculptor René Quillivic was put in charge of design at HB. Around eighty painters and sculptors were commissioned to design pieces in faience and stoneware that were sold as limited editions; these talented artists included Bouchard, Bachelet, Léonardi, Bazin, Nam, Giot, Bar, Hagemans, Brisson, Quincaud, Monier, Broquet and Renaud. The young artists of the group known as *Seiz Breur* (Breton for "seven brothers", in homage to the founding saints of Brittany) found Quimper an ideal place to work. Under the name "Odetta" HB marketed a range of stoneware with abstract geometric designs in the Art Deco style fashionable at the time. At the same time the Quimper faience factories continued to produce costly luxury items using Rouen-style decoration and the designs of Alfred Beau, as well as everyday crockery featuring traditional motifs such as the rooster, the flower basket and the famous "*Petit Breton*". In 1946 Victor Lucas opened another pottery called Kéraluc ("house of Luc"), and brought in such talented young artists as Toulhoat, Yvain, Le Corre, L'Helguen, Quéré and Krebs to design his stoneware, which became widely popular.

Bigouden Boy, stoneware figure by René Quillivic (1930) from the HB Pottery, which recalls a design first used in 1909.

"Odetta" vase (1930) in enameled stoneware.

Vase decorated with Breton women by Louis Garin (HB, c. 1930).

CONTINUED EXPANSION. The faience industry is still thriving in Quimper. The two most important factories in Locmaria, HB-Henriot and Kéraluc, continue to uphold the tradition first established in the shadow of the old Norman church by Jean-Baptiste Bousquet three hundred years ago.

The harbor at Sein in the early 20th century.

FOUR FEET WIDE

A municipal by-law controlled the width of the streets. Space between houses on Sein had to be sufficient to allow a barrel to be rolled.

FOR A FAVORABLE WIND

The statue of the patron saint in the chapel of St-Corentin guaranteed favorable winds to secure a good catch. All you had to do was turn his crozier in the direction required!

ÎLE DE SEIN

The extraordinary small island of Sein is a flat raft of rocks and sand 5 miles off the Pointe du Raz ▲ *294*. There is a daily ferry service from Audierne. Sein is little more than a mile long and half a mile wide, and its highest point is 20 feet above sea level. The island is lashed by storms and gales all the year round, and is home to about 250 people known as Senans. The community has had an eventful history: in 1756 the Duc d'Aiguillon, Governor of Brittany, offered money to Sein's inhabitants to enable them to move elsewhere. They refused to budge, but were willing to have the construction of dikes subsidized. They were exempted from paying regional taxes by decree of Louis XIV: "To tax Sein and Molène, already sorely taxed by wind and weather, would be like taxing the rocks and the ocean," he remarked.

MISSIONARIES. Sein was converted to Christianity in the 17th century, first by the monk Michel Le Nobletz and then by the Jesuit father Julien Maunoir. Conversion radically altered the Senans' way of life: from carrying on a notorious lifestyle as wreckers, they became skilled and courageous lifeboatmen. In 1940 the island put itself at the service of the French Resistance. After the historic call-to-arms on June 18 (which did not reach the island until

Labels on the map:
SAUVETAGE STATION
CHURCH OF SAINT-GUENOLE
SÉNANS LIBRES MONUMENT
CHAPEL OF ST-CORENTIN
LIGHTHOUSE

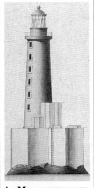

AR MEN LIGHTHOUSE
This illustration gives some idea of the immense difficulties faced by engineers and workmen on this daunting project, which involved building a huge tower on a surface that was uncovered only at low tide. In 1923 a keeper by the name of Fouquet was marooned for 101 days without provisions, because of severe weather conditions.

June 22), about 250 men, all the able-bodied inhabitants of Sein, left to join up with the Free French forces in London. They accounted for a quarter of the first wave of Resistance volunteers to rally to De Gaulle. This prompted his saying, still proudly remembered on the island: "The Île de Sein is one quarter of France."

FOOD FROM THE SEA. The inhabitants cannot live off the land, but they use their thorough knowledge of the sea to seek out skate, conger-eels and bass ■ *36*. Increasingly, however, the island derives a livelihood from summer visitors: tourism has become a vital part of its economy.

SEIN LIGHTHOUSE. The original lighthouse, built in 1838, was destroyed by the Germans in World War Two. The present building was constructed in 1945: it is 160 feet high, with 249 steps leading up to the top, and stands facing the reefs known as the Chaussée de Sein.

AR MEN LIGHTHOUSE. France's most famous lighthouse was a triumph of engineering. The problems of building a 115-foot stone tower in the middle of the ocean on a small rock made of unstable granite schist seemed at first insurmountable. Work started in 1867, though during the first year the boats carrying workmen and materials could only make nine landings. After fourteen years of desperately hard work, the light was finally illuminated at midnight on August 31, 1880. Today the lighthouse is operated by remote control.

"DIEU A BESOIN DES HOMMES"
Jean Delannoy's excellent film "God Has Need of Men" (1950), was partially shot on the Île de Sein.

305

POINTE DE PENMARC'H LE GUILVINEC PONT-L'ABBÉ QUIMPER BÉNODET CONCARNEAU

The Bigouden country

BIGOUDEN HEADDRESSES
These are sometimes known as "sugarloaves" or even "Eckmühl lighthouses".

Heb Ken ("We alone") is the motto of the Bigouden country, a region immediately identifiable by the tall headdresses of its womenfolk, whom Guy de Maupassant described as "tall, beautiful and fair-skinned". On the north the region is bounded by the village of Pors Poulhan, and to the east by the right bank of the Odet. In the late Middle Ages the port of Kérity fitted out a fleet of more than two hundred merchant ships and obtained the monopoly on transporting wine out of Bordeaux. But eventually this monopoly was broken, and this together with the problems brought by the religious wars of the late 16th century put an end to Bigouden's prosperity. Fishing and tourism are its industries now, and the region has four fishing ports: Le Guilvinec Léchiagat, St-Guénolé, Lesconil and Loctudy.

Pont-l'Abbé

AN ILLUSTRATED CATECHISM
The Tronoën Calvary can be "read" in an anticlockwise direction beginning with *the Annunciation*, the last tableau on the eastern side.

The historic capital of the area. Its name derives from the monks of Loctudy who built the first bridge across the river, inland from the estuary, called *Pons Abbatis*.
BIGOUDEN MUSEUM. A collection housed in the 13th-century castle keep. It includes traditional costumes and headdresses, traditional furniture and exquisitely crafted model boats. A visit here is complemented by a trip to the MAISON DU PAYS BIGOUDEN, an ecomuseum situated in the Kervazégan farm, just over a mile away on the road to Loctudy. This restored

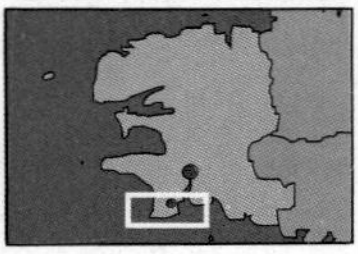

Bigouden farm has a
courtyard, a well, stables,
cowsheds and living quarters.

TRONOËN   ● 99

TRONOËN CALVARY ★. The oldest of the large Breton roadside
shrines seems to be sinking under the weight of its saints.
Nineteen scenes from the life of Christ carved in stone on two
levels have stood here since 1450, when the shrine was built.
Some figures are carved in relief, others in the round. In spite
of much erosion over the centuries much of the detail remains
visible, as in the *Confinement of the Virgin* where Mary,
stretched out and half-undressed, welcomes the three Magi.

BAIE D'AUDIERNE

POINTE DE LA TORCHE. This rocky spur is at the
southernmost point of the Bay of Audierne, with a fine
panoramic view. Its Breton name *Beg an dorchenn*
means "Cape with a little hill", for the Pointe is also an
archeological site ● *80* with a tumulus surmounted by a
dolmen. The bay is a favorite spot for windsurfing.

LE GUILVINEC

With its busy naval dockyards, canneries and fishing
fleet, this is the fourth largest port in Brittany. It
attracts many tourists, and in the afternoon crowds
gather to watch the return of the local fishing boats.

PENMARC'H

POINTE DE PENMARC'H. The cape is notorious for its
treacherous reefs and spectacular storms. "Thick
clouds of soaking vapor whirled around my head,
it was impossible to tell where the sky ended and
the sea began. All that could be seen through the
thick mist were huge blobs of sea spray thrown
here and there by the violent wind; the
sound was deafening," noted one visitor
in the 19th century.

❝Frozen in stone, [the
holy figures] play out
their parts in this
dramatic ritual, with
no audience save the
spirit of God moving
over the face of the
waters.❞
                    Yves Le Gallo

**WHERE THERE'S
A WILL . . .**
The Marquise de
Blocqueville was
the daughter of
General Davout,
Prince of
Eckmühl. When
she died in Paris
in 1892, she left
300,000 francs for
the construction
of a lighthouse on
this dangerous
part of the
Breton coastline.
It was to be
named after
her father.

A COMPETITION, c. 1920
The contest to build the best model of a fishing boat took place at the Sailors' Rest in Guilvinec.

A ceramic map of Bénodet, designed and made by Crédel and Piclet around 1960.

"Bénodet, a name but loosely moored, as if the river would drag it down to the weedy depths below," was Marcel Proust's enigmatic verdict in 1919. Before him Emile Zola, Sarah Bernhardt and Guillaume Apollinaire came here in search of peace and quiet.

ECKMÜHL LIGHTHOUSE. A temporary light was first installed in an old tower on the point in 1831, and was replaced by a more powerful paraffin lamp in 1835. But its efficiency was seriously impaired by its lack of height, and a new one was finally built in 1897, thanks to a gift by the Marquise de Blocqueville. It is 213 feet tall, built entirely of Kersanton granite, and open to the public. A climb up 307 steps is rewarded by marvelous views.

SAINTE-MARINE ★

The Brest writer and traveler Victor Segalen (1878–1919) was charmed by this little port when he visited it in 1899: "Smart and shining, the village is lined with crisp young pine trees set against rose-colored cottages and the lighthouses of Bénodet in the distance, all as fresh as an artist's canvas." A Sailors' Rest and a little chapel stand beside some friendly cafés.
THE SAILORS' REST. Jacques de Thézac was born in 1862, and because of his delicate health as a boy was sent to the Charente coast. He grew to love the sea, married a Breton girl in 1888 and settled at Sainte-Marine. Under the influence of Pierre Loti's novel *My Brother Yves*, which painted a harsh picture of alcoholism among the seafaring population, De Thézac decided to fight this curse, and acquired plots of land to begin to realize his ideal. His first Sailors' Rest opened in 1900 at Guilvinec, to be followed by a dozen others along the Brittany coast to care for retired seamen, but the last of them finally closed in the 1960's.

BÉNODET

In the Middle Ages ships from Bénodet carried dried and salted fish to Nantes and Royan, returning laden with cargoes of salt and wine. Today the little port is an attractive seaside resort, whose reputation has been enhanced by writers and painters who come to stay.

CONCARNEAU

Konk-Kerné means "inlet of Cornouaille" in Breton. From the bridge spanning the Moros, the wide estuary with a large fishing harbor and a marina suddenly comes into sight.

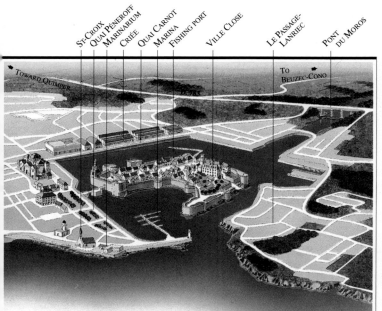

St-Croix · Quai Péneroff · Marinarium · Criée · Quai Carnot · Marina · Fishing Port · Ville Close · Le Passage-Lanriec · Pont du Moros

Toward Quimper

To Beuzec-Cono

Between them on a rocky island reached
by a drawbridge is the Ville Close, the old walled
town of which Gustave Flaubert said in 1847: "The town is
surrounded by a wall whose base is battered by waves at high
tide. The machicolation is still intact, exactly as it was in
Queen Anne's day, and the line of carved stones which runs
along the ramparts rises
up through the mist."
Though small, this
fortification was the
cradle of Concarneau's
early history.
**THE CONCARNEAU
GROUP.** From 1870 to
1950 many artists came
to paint here, and at the
instigation of Alfred

Guillou formed themselves into a committed group. Their
efforts saved the ramparts from the auctioneer's hammer;
they were listed as an historic monument in 1899. Some artists
settled here. Others, such as Gauguin, stayed only briefly: his
visit in 1894 ended in a quayside fight.
FISHING PORT. The inner harbor was opened in 1925 and has
been growing ever since. It is the third largest fishing port
after Boulogne and Lorient and also boasts the biggest
catches of tuna in France.
THE "VILLE CLOSE" ★. The little island,
400 yards long and 120 yards wide,
housed nothing but a small priory until
the 10th century. It was next encircled by
earthworks and a stockade as a
defensive refuge in case of attack. By the
14th century it had become a fortress,
and was the object of much attention
during the Hundred Years' War. In 1694
the defenses were improved by the

**THE FÊTE DES FILETS
BLEUS**
The annual Festival
of Blue Nets (the
ones used for sardine
fishing) held on the
penultimate Sunday
in August has been a
popular event, with
music and dancing,
for more than eighty
years. Below, an early
20th-century poster
from the studio of
Mathurin Janssaud.

309

indefatigable Marshal Vauban, with the addition of two great towers. The island has been carefully restored in recent years. The FISHERY MUSEUM has displays explaining the various techniques of fishing, with some intriguing models. In the Place St-Guénolé stands a MONUMENTAL FOUNTAIN.

PONT-AVEN

"PONT-AVEN HAS FOURTEEN MILLS AND FIFTEEN HOUSES", runs an old saying. It is an exceptionally lovely place. The mills are perched on rocky escarpments on both banks, while the Aven bounds from rock to rock below.

FLOUR MILLS AND BISCUIT FACTORIES. Long before it became an artists' settlement where painters came in search of local color in the 19th century, Pont-Aven was a lively town. The river Aven broadens out here into a long tidal estuary along which boats carried corn, cider and dressed stone. The mills from which the town derives its name were kept busy: peasant farmers sometimes had to wait several days for their corn to be ground, though the only one to carry on the tradition today is at Pénanros. The Pont-Aven biscuit factories, particularly the Traou Mad factory, are famous throughout France. The ancient Place Royale on the right bank has beautiful houses that were once the homes of wealthy merchants, mill owners and royal officials, all witness to the town's former prosperity. The plaque and medallion on the wall of the bookshop in the Place Gauguin mark the site of a former inn belonging to Marie-Jeanne Gloanec, the haunt of painters of the Pont-Aven school.

ARTISTS IN PONT-AVEN ▲ *312*. From 1860 the railway began to open up Brittany. Artists from Paris and abroad were quick to enjoy this new easy way to travel, and writers, such as Victor Hugo, Chateaubriand, Flaubert and Prosper Merimée, also came to escape industrial urban squalor. To them Pont-Aven was a haven of tranquility and unbroken tradition. They all needed lodgings, so attics and lofts around the town were converted into studios to rent. In 1886, two years before the creation of the Pont-Aven school, Paul Gauguin arrived. He was the leader of the group known as "Impressionists", who lodged at the Gloanec establishment, while the so-called "Academics" lived at the Hôtel Julia. Even after 1894, the year of Gauguin's last visit, painters continued to come, making this an important outpost of 20th-century art.

MUSEUM. The museum is located in the town hall. It presents a display of the history of the Pont-Aven school, and regular exhibitions of the work of Gauguin and his friends.

THE BOIS D'AMOUR. The inhabitants of Pont-Aven love to stroll in this wood, and many local artists have put up their easels there. Cross the footbridges and follow the jumble of rocks: on the left bank is the impressive Roche-Forme, also known as Gargantua's Shoe.

CHAPELLE DE TRÉMALO. Avenues of oak and beech lead to the 16th-century chapel of Trémalo, situated above the gardens of the BOIS D'AMOUR. The chapel is dominated by its bell tower and the north slope of the asymmetrical roof reaches almost to the ground. Inside is a 17th-century figure of CHRIST, carved in wood and painted in polychrome, which became famous when Gauguin used it as the model for his painting *Le Christ jaune* (Yellow Christ).

RIEC-SUR-BELON

The small town stands between the estuaries of the Aven and the Belon. Many artists were drawn here, attracted by its delightful landscapes – and by the superb cooking of Mélanie Rouat at the inn. Riec has long been renowned for its excellent cuisine, such as the local oysters known as *belons*.

WALKS. Each of the estuaries has its own port, and both are well worth a visit. There is ROSBRAS on the Aven, and BELON on the Belon. The tourist office has useful information about the "Cornouaille" painters and about the local footpaths too. A splendid walk starting at Belon follows the river as far as the Pointe de Penquernéo and thence to the rivers' mouth. A battery of five cannons here once protected the entrance against attack by the English, who several times occupied the islands of Glénan. The left bank of the Belon provides another interesting walk. It is muddy at low tide and the locality echoes with the cries of a wide variety of birds.

311

la galerie de Pont-Aven

Somewhere along the bank of the Aven in September 1888, Gauguin was giving a lesson to the young Paul Sérusier: "Do you see that blue shadow? Paint it with the most beautiful blue on your palette . . . Don't copy nature too faithfully, just look at it and dream." This was Synthetism, which set out to remove all encumbrances between an artist's vision and the canvas, and it was to open the way to abstract painting. The effect of Brittany on these artists was also considerable: its friendly inns and marvelous stained glass windows, its landscapes and its people. There were also the lessons to be drawn from Japanese engravings, and above all the dissatisfaction these young men felt with an art that consisted simply of realistic representation. The chief protagonists were the youthful Émile Bernard and Gauguin, who painted a number of works here such as *The Vision after the Sermon* and *The Yellow Christ*.

Dissatisfied with self-righteous artistic pundits, and there were plenty at Pont-Aven, the group soon moved to Pouldu in search of solitude. In 1889 an exhibition in Paris put all the innovations developed in Brittany on public view, and the group known as *Nabis* (from the Hebrew word for "prophet") was born. One of them, Maurice Denis, became the theoretician of the movement, which set out to take art back to basics, while the young critic Albert Aurier hailed Gauguin as the father of Symbolism. Many artists from France and abroad made the journey to Pont-Aven, but the movement's life there was short: the band of friends soon dispersed to pursue their own ideals elsewhere.

Paul Sérusier made many sketches of life at Pont-Aven. Paul Gauguin is plainly visible here on the right of the boat.

An earthenware vase made by Gauguin in 1886, one of the first in a long series. Breton peasants are its decorative theme.

Paul Gauguin in 1891, during a short stay in Copenhagen.

Marie-Jeanne Gloanec was the proud proprietor of the inn beside the bridge. She offered unbeatable prices, good meals and a warm welcome. In exchange she received many pictures from he impoverished guests. A group of them is seen here gathered around the dominant figure of Paul Gauguin. But the group soon moved to Pouldu, to be free of outside influences.

When the young idealistic group of painters first discovered Pont-Aven, it must have seemed like the Garden of Eden. "As soon as my clogs struck the hard granite cobblestones, I knew that this was the rough earthy sound I wanted to capture in my painting," wrote Paul Gauguin.

Paul Sérusier, Paul Gauguin and Émile Bernard were the founders of the movement known as Synthetism. Its manifesto was Gauguin's *The Vision after the Sermon* (1), painted in 1888. In it some dreaming Bretons see the fight between Jacob and the Angel, in which Gauguin was inspired by Hokusai's illustration of two wrestlers (2). The painting represents a break with both Impressionism and realism, and

introduced a new creative approach. In his *Beating the Apple Trees* (3) of 1890, Émile Bernard (4) experiments with a quasi-Japanese arrangement of the figures, and with traditional balance within a picture. The

colors are strong and flat, just as vivid in the distance as in the foreground. Gauguin gave his picture *Breton Peasants* (5) a distinct Tahitian flavor.

The Bois d'Amour at Pont-Aven, with its rock-strewn floor (**3**), and the banks of the Aven were the favorite haunts of these painters. Here, in

September 1888, the young Paul Sérusier received his famous painting lesson from Paul Gauguin. The result was "a landscape without form, synthetically produced"; this was *The Talisman* (**2**), a picture enthusiastically acclaimed in Paris by Maurice Denis (**1**) and the

future Nabis painters. Maurice Denis defined the new artistic movement in terms of "a flat surface overlaid with colors in a distinctive characteristic arrangement", which swept away the traditions of realism and contained the seeds of abstract art. At Huelgoat, Sérusier ▲ *268* went on to explore the ideas he had learned in his lessons with Gauguin.

The peasant girl who sits musing in *Solitude* (**4**) in the middle of a jumble of rocks is defined by the landscape around her: her head is round like the rocks in the picture, and her coloring is drawn from theirs. The descending lines echo the sadness in her expression, and the entire painting suggests melancholy surrounded by the oppressive forces of nature. Maurice Denis was Synthetism's first theorist, and he too applied Gauguin's esthetic standards to his work. In the painting of a pardon entitled *The Bowl of Cider* (**5** and **6**, details), he simplifies or dismisses the figures, defines their shapes by a simple outline, and rejects the effects of perspective.

Yet he preferred subtle and subdued tones to primary colors: the white of the headdresses becomes a delicate blue to suggest the shadow thrown by the trees.

1	2	4
		5
	3	6

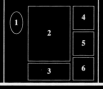

Irishman Roderic O'Connor (1860–1940) worked extensively in France and met Gauguin in 1894, or perhaps earlier. His work became simplified under Gauguin's influence though its rich brushwork endowed it with a unique spirit and passion, as in his *Breton Pastures* (**1**).

Pole Wladislaw Slewinski accompanied Gauguin to Pont-Aven in 1890, and frequently came back before settling at Doélan. A picture he painted in 1897, entitled *Two Breton Girls with a Basket of Apples* (**2**) employs a distinctive subdued palette, though the shapes are straightforward.

Cuno Amiet was Swiss, and stayed at Mme Gloanec's pension in 1892 and 1893.There he painted this *Breton Girl in Profile* (**3**) in which the colors are heightened in places to produce a powerful and poetic effect.

LORIENT

▲ LORIENT

SUBMARINE BASE

FISHING PORT

RUE MADAME-
DE-SÉVIGNÉ

TOW

A WHALING STATION
For four years in the
18th century Lorient
specialized in
catching sperm
whales. After the War
of Independence,
shipowners from
Nantucket (a small
island south of Cape
Cod on the
Massachusetts coast)
lost their English
markets. William
Rotch, one of the
shipowners
concerned, decided to
accept Louis XVI's
offer of asylum. His
son François settled
at Port-Louis and had
six whalers fitted out
at Lorient, though
few Bretons were
among his crews. The
war between France
and England soon
drove him back to
America.

"Lorient is not a
large town. . . . but
trade is flourishing.
The nobility live in
Port-Louis but the
merchants, the fine
silks and muslins, the
silver and the pretty
girls are all to be
found in Lorient."
Bernardin de Saint-
Pierre (1768)

HISTORY

TRADE WITH THE EAST. In 1664, on the advice of his astute
minister Jean-Baptiste Colbert, Louis XIV set up the
Compagnie des Indes to promote commerce with Asia and
profit from the lucrative spice trade. The new company was
located on the Blavet estuary, and in June 1666 opened for
business beneath the citadel at Port-Louis. Boatyards were
opened at Faouëdic, on the other side of the water. Two new
frigates were quickly built for the trade, along with a 1000-ton
ship, the *Soleil d'Orient*. During construction it came to be
known as L'Orient, and the town that sprang up around the
works took the same name, *An Oriant* in Breton. The spices,
tea, silks and other cloths, the lacquered goods and chinaware
from the East Indies that passed through the town made the
Compagnie des Indes rich. But the War of the League of
Augsburg and the Wars of the Spanish Succession disrupted
this maritime trade, and in the early 18th century the
company collapsed.   In 1719 a financier named Law
founded a new one   called the Compagnie Perpétuelle
                        des Indes and this took
                        over the trade

monopoly between France and its colonies in the West Indies and Louisiana, as well as Africa, the Indian Ocean and the China Seas. As the new company prospered so did the little town of L'Orient, which in 1738 became a city and organized Europe's biggest trade exhibition.

NAVAL L'ORIENT. The loss of the French colonies in 1763 resulted in the demise of the Compagnie Perpétuelle des Indes six years later. The king bought back the shipyards at L'Orient in 1770 and it became a naval port with a royal arsenal. In 1783 it was made a free port on the signing of a treaty between France and the U.S. From the Revolution, when the name was changed to Lorient, hopes of renewed international trade faded away. In the early 19th century the fishing industry began to expand. And here, later in the century, the first armored ships were built.

GERMAN RESISTANCE. The port was occupied by the Germans late in 1940 and under Allied bombing 95 percent of the old town was destroyed. The Normandy landings to liberate France took place in June 1944, but the German resistance in Lorient did not surrender until the signing of the Armistice on May 8, 1945.

THE TOWN TODAY. Lorient was rebuilt in the 1950's. Its fishing port on the Keroman estuary currently lands the second biggest catch in France, and the most valuable in the country.

St-Louis Church and Kerentrech Church and bridge.

321

▲ LORIENT

Design for an apparatus
to mast ships at the port
of Lorient (1825).

MADAME DE SÉVIGNÉ VISITS LORIENT
During a stay at Port-Louis in 1689 Mme de Sévigné made a trip to Lorient. The future town was then just a muddle of hurriedly built huts. She liked the busy atmosphere of the docks and the profusion of merchandise, and was impressed by its porcelain and cloth. At Kerentrech a road lined with houses featuring colorful ceramic decoration on their façades (1928) is named after her.

The naval base continues to support 45,000 people. Lorient is entirely different in character from its neighbor, the medieval and conservative-natured city of Vannes ▲ *342*. The old buildings of Lorient have gone, but the people have proud memories of their long industrial history and their ancestors on whose labor it was built.

THE TOWN CENTER

THE MERVILLE DISTRICT. A flourishing feature of this part of the town is a market known as *les Halles Rondes*, which is famous for its superb fish ■ *36*. The area also has a number of fine Art Nouveau and Art Deco houses. The former date from the turn of the century and have delightful curving lines and colorful decoration. The latter are spare and geometric in design.

PLACE ALSACE-LORRAINE. This vast square marks the center of the modern town. Notre-Dame-des-Victoires, a church constructed from granite and reinforced concrete, was built in 1954 on the site of Saint-Louis church. Also on this square is an underground shelter from World War II, which is open to the public and has been chosen as the site of the MEMORIAL.

THE FIVE PORTS

Right at the heart of the city, between the Quai de Rohan and the Quai des Indes, lies the pretty SAILING MARINA OF KERNEVEL , whose dock, which is overlooked by some elegant 18th-century town houses, has remained miraculously unscathed. However, thanks to its strategic position and to its hard-working populace, Lorient has become home to a number of other important marine activities, military as well as industrial.

The huge electric crane in use at the Arsenal early this century.

PASSENGER BOATS. Not far from the Maison de la Mer, on Boulevard Auguste Pierre, boats leave for the island of Groix ▲ *324*, Port-Louis and Locmiquélic and also make trips up the river Blavet.

LORIENT-KERGROISE. The port's tall cranes and storage silos, set between the Quai de l'Estacade and the huge icehouse of the fishing port, stand out against the sky. Ships moor to unload sand, wood, wine and various oil products, but mostly to deliver soya, manioc, peanuts and fish meal, ingredients for the manufacture of animal feed. Kergroise is the second busiest commercial port in Brittany after Brest, handling 2 million tons of goods a year.

LORIENT-KEROMAN. To reach Keroman's harbor complex, take the Avenue de la Perrière

and then the Boulevard Nail. The fishing port was opened in 1927, and its eight docks extend over 180 acres. The yards where boats are built and repaired, the canneries, the fileting stations and the ice-manufacturing units cover another 90 acres. The port of Keroman can handle 120,000 tons of fish per year and employs about 4,500 people.

OCEAN TO TABLE. The boats come into port after dark and around midnight one can see them at the far end of the Grand Bassin (the main dock). The catch is brought up in baskets out of the trawler's hold and tipped on to a conveyor belt to be taken off and sold. It is sorted by hand and put into containers that are then carried by dockers to the auction room, called the Pan Coupé. Auctions take place from 4.30 to 7.30 in the morning. Once sold, the fish is cleaned and packed, and at 11am the refrigerated trucks arrive

at the loading bays to take it away. The last trucks leave Lorient at around 6pm bound for the huge national and international food market at Rungis, south of Paris, where the fish is sold early the next morning to retailers and restaurants.

SUBMARINE BASE. The 900,000 tons of reinforced concrete laid down by the Germans now form the core of the Ingénieur général Stosskopf submarine base, used today by French nuclear submarines. They lie between the Pointe de Keroman and the mouth of the river Ter. The first two U-boat pens, 425 feet long and 60 feet high, were built in 1941, while the third, 550 feet long and over 30 feet high, was not completed until 1943. Between them they could harbor over forty submarines. The base is named after an Alsatian officer in the Naval Engineering Corps who was shot by the Germans in 1944 for having given the Allies secrets about the U-boats.

AROUND THE ARSENAL

BIBLIOTHÈQUE HISTORIQUE DE LA MARINE. A library specializing in naval history and set in the Enclos de l'Amirauté gardens. It holds many original archives as well as a collection of 150,000 volumes, all of which can be consulted by the public.

ARSENAL DE LA ROYALE. The sinister machines of war that surrounded the Arsenal were Lorient's prime attraction in the opinion of Lorient poet Auguste Brizeux (1803–58): "Its black cannons, chain-shot and explosive devices, the countless engines of destruction death loves so well." These naval dockyards, open

only to visitors who hold a French passport, are exclusively involved with the building of surface craft. The entrance is at the Porte Gabriel, at the end of Rue Cale Ory. The most interesting work here involves research into composite materials. The laboratories lead the world in developing techniques for the construction of demagnetized ships.

ART NOUVEAU AND ART DECO
The Hôtel Terminus, opposite the station, has a typical 1930's façade. It is decorated with geometric designs and the upper corners of the windows are angled. Villas of the period feature many unusual choices of material for gables, porches and staircases, resulting in an abundance of colors. Their painted plaster rendering can be equally varied in texture and appearance: smooth, roughened, pebble-dashed or with more elaborate designs such as latticework or inset medallions.

INTERCELTIC FESTIVAL
The Festival des Cornemuses, first held in 1971 and taking place annually between August 4 and 13, draws some 4,500 Celtic artists and sportsmen from Brittany, Wales, Scotland, Ireland, Cornwall and Galicia (northern Spain). It attracts huge audiences.

323

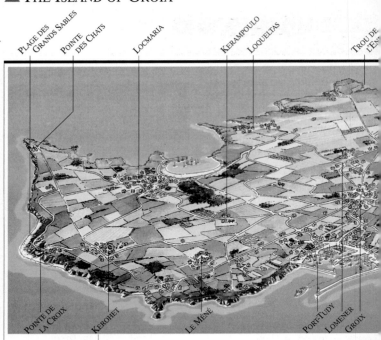

PLAGE DES GRANDS SABLES   POINTE DES CHATS   LOCMARIA   KERAMPOULO   LOQUELTAS   TROU DE L'EN⸱

POINTE DE LA CROIX   KEROHET   LE MENE   PORT-TUDY   LOMENER   GROIX

MINERALOGISTS' PARADISE ■ *18*
The rich variety of minerals and geological features concentrated in the cliffs of the island of Groix make it a key spot for the study of the geological history of the Armorican peninsula.

TUNA FISHING
Tuna was caught using lines attached to two long mobile chestnut booms set either side of the mast. At first the fish

were kept on the deck, partially sheltered by the bulwarks. Later they were hung from a frame. Eventually, motorized and refrigerated trawlers took over.

GROIX

It takes 45 minutes to cross from Lorient ▲ *320* to Groix, an island with a mild micro-climate much envied by Sein and Ouessant further west. It is best to explore the island by bicycle or on foot. The distances are short, since Groix is only 5 miles long and 2½ miles wide, and there is a signed coastal path all around that can be walked in two sections, one taking three hours and the other four. Groix is scattered with tiny hamlets, now depopulated as most of the 2,500 inhabitants are concentrated in the larger villages of Groix, Port-Tudy and Locmaria.

TUNA. The island has survived by fishing and sea trade ever since it came under the domination of the Rohans ▲ *231* in the 14th century. But its history has been marked by two periods of particular prosperity. The first was due to the activities of Colbert's Compagnie des Indes ▲ *320*. The second began in the 19th century, when methods of canning fish were perfected. Groix became the major tuna fishing port in France, its harbor packed with hundreds of boats. With the coming of motorized trawlers in the 1940's Groix lost its ascendancy: entire families were forced to leave the island for Lorient.

THE FISHERMEN OF GROIX. In the early 19th century albacore tuna was fished from the ports of Saint-Jean-de-Luz, the Île d'Yeu, and the Île de Ré. Around 1840 the Groisillons (inhabitants of Groix), who had until then been sardine fishermen using open longboats, took to fishing tuna. The season lasted from June to October. The albacore tuna lives in temperate waters south of a line running from the Azores

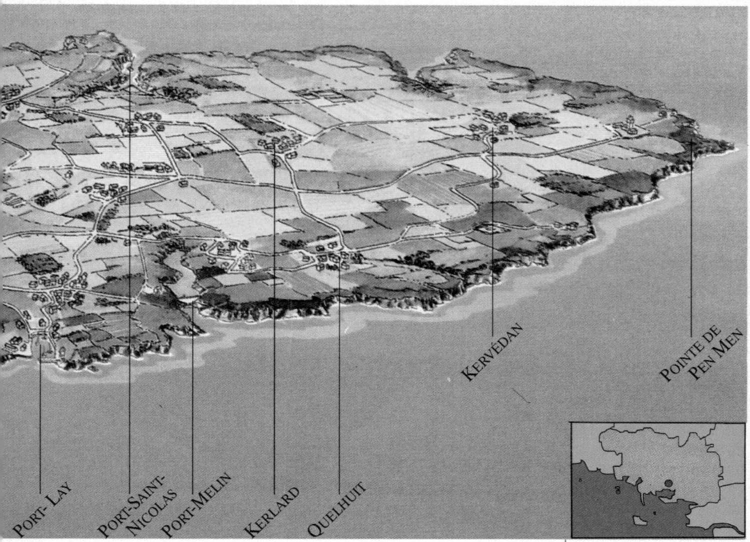

PORT-LAY PORT-SAINT-NICOLAS PORT-MELIN KERLARD QUELHUIT KERVÉDAN POINTE DE PEN MEN

to the Gulf of Gascony, but it also follows the Gulf Stream further north, and so is found off the west coasts of Brittany and Ireland. The Groix tuna-fishing industry grew rapidly in the 1880's: by 1900 there were 198 boats going out from its little harbor, out of the total of 268 Brittany craft involved in the trade. In 1911, 1,638 people – a quarter of the island's population – made their living from tuna.

THE GROIX ECOMUSEUM. The museum, housed in an old cannery, was set up by the islanders in 1984. The exhibits illustrate the island's abundant plantlife and wildlife, and its interesting rock formations. The history of Groix is told through old photographs and paintings, and through documents revealing much about the life of the people. Exhibits go back to the Mesolithic and Neolithic periods. As well as a Bronze Age tomb and an incinerated Viking craft, exhibits include objects from the more recent past and objects of interest saved from the canneries, such as sardine presses. A genuine 1950's lifeboat is the focal point of the section on the still-active island service. The ecomuseum also has a *sentier de*

Among objects on display at the Groix Ecomuseum is this sailor's outfit, worn in the early 19th century.

UNUSUAL FAÇADES
Apart from tilling the fields and mending the nets, Groix women used to make blocks of fuel for winter heating from cow-dung. They would stack it against the cottage walls so that it would dry and become combustible.

325

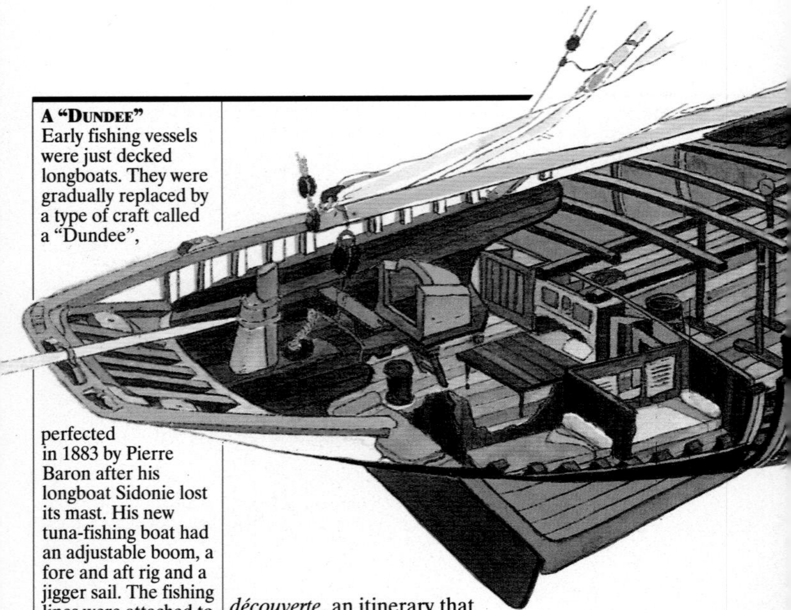

A "DUNDEE"
Early fishing vessels were just decked longboats. They were gradually replaced by a type of craft called a "Dundee", perfected in 1883 by Pierre Baron after his longboat Sidonie lost its mast. His new tuna-fishing boat had an adjustable boom, a fore and aft rig and a jigger sail. The fishing lines were attached to the ends of booms. Its only fault proved to be a certain instability when running before a strong wind.

SINKING OF THE EXCISEMEN'S BOAT
A votive offering from 1826 kept in the chapel of Notre-Dame de Placemanec, in Locmaria.

découverte, an itinerary that leads around the island.

POINTE DE LA CROIX

GRANDS SABLES BEACH. A stretch of beach that is convex in shape, which is most unusual in Europe, and curves around the headland. It has wonderfully fine sand.
RED SAND. At the southern end of the beach are a number of small coves where garnets have colored the sand red.

LOCMARIA ★

The village faces out across heathland to the ocean. Its winding streets are lined with pretty houses rendered in different colors. They were built in the early 20th century, along with their wash houses and fountains, by once-

NAUFRAGE DE LA CHALOUPE DES DOUANES DE GROIX ENTRE LES HÉRENTS, ET CAVRE, DANS LA NUIT DU QUATRE DÉCEMBRE 1825, EN REPORTANT AU PORT-LOUIS M⁻ LE DOCTEUR LESTROHAN, MÉDECIN DES EPIDÉMIES DE L'ARRONDISSEMENT, APPELÉ DANS L'ILE POUR LE TRAITEMENT D'UNE MALADIE CONTAGIEUSE. EQUIPAGE: J. M. STEPHANNO; PATRON: J⁻ M. TONNERE; PIERRE EVEN; E. SIMON. PASSAGERS A⁻ LESTROHAN, C. BARON, MARIE=ANNE LE LIVEC; THÉRÈSE BERNARD.

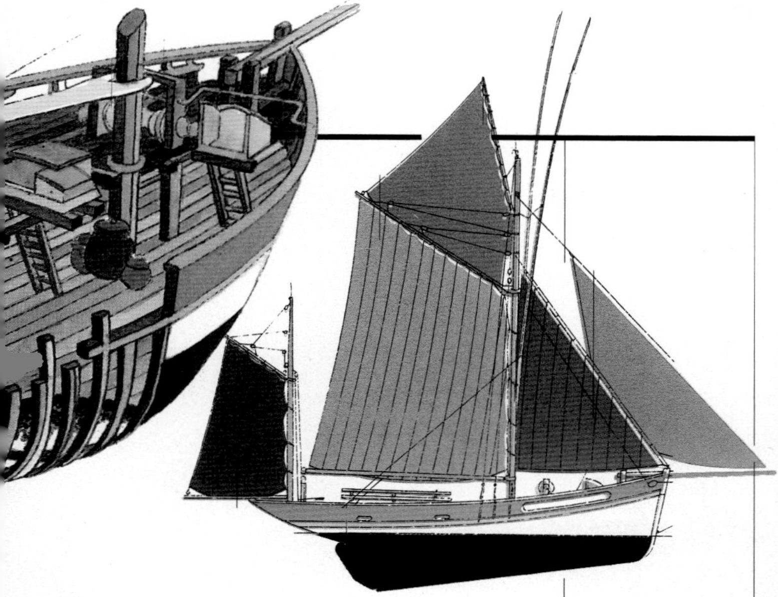

prosperous fishermen and boat-owners. The harbor is created by a single jetty built out into the little bay, behind which craft can moor in relative safety. In 1906 the remains of a Viking ship were discovered between the village and jetty. It dates from the 10th century and had been incinerated as part of a burial rite common in Scandinavia. The find confirmed the theory that Vikings came to Groix.

NOTRE-DAME DE PLACEMANEC. The church in the center of the village has an interesting 19th-century votive offering. It was given by excise men after the sinking of their boat.

THE FRANÇOIS-LE-BAIL RESERVE. In 1983 a nature reserve covering two areas of Groix was created. It is named after François Le Bail (1903–79), a mineralogist who dedicated his life to the study of the Armorican Peninsula.

MOUSTACHIOED HORSE. In the 19th century Groix horses were used for transport, ploughing and treading out the corn. They commonly sported moustaches, possibly evolved as a means of protection since prickly gorse was a major part of their diet.

THE TOWN OF GROIX

The low slate-roofed houses of the island's capital cluster protectively around the church. It has a half-domed apse flanked by chapels and spiral staircases leading up to galleries on either side. The Route des Plages leads to the cemetery where a granite monument commemorates the many sailors who were lost in the terrible storm of 1930.

POINTE DE PEN MEN. The rocky headland looking out over the Morbihan coast from the Pointe du Talud to Port-Manech is the most westerly point on the island. Pieces of decorated pottery found here date back to the 3rd millenium BC. Further south is the Côte Sauvage.

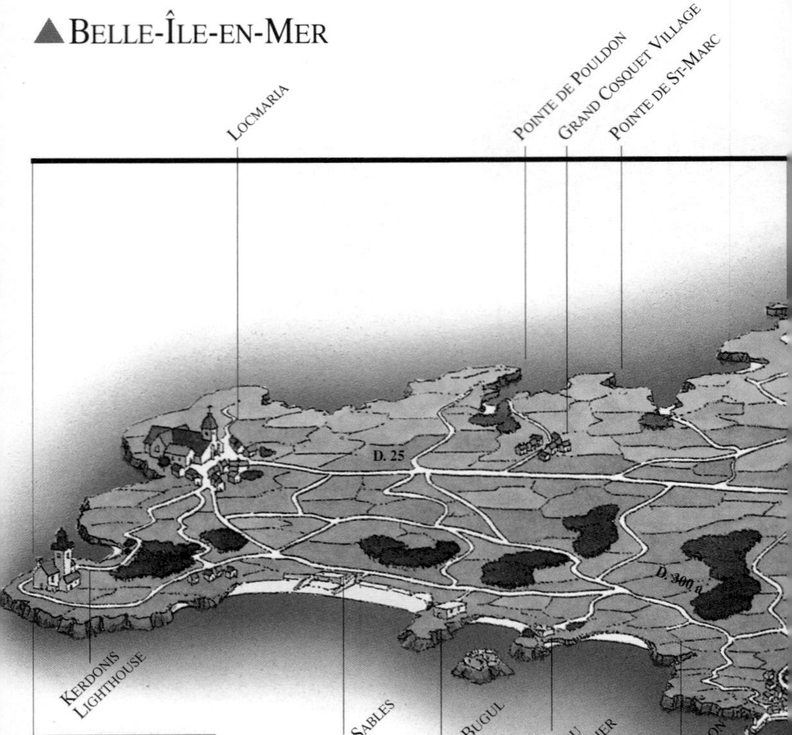

LOCMARIA

POINTE DE POULDON

GRAND COSQUET VILLAGE

POINTE DE ST-MARC

D. 25

D. 300 a

KERDONIS LIGHTHOUSE

GRANDS-SABLES BEACH

POINTE DU BUGUL

POINTE DU GROS-ROCHER

FORT LARRON

According to legend Belle-Île, the largest island in Brittany, is a new Atlantis risen from the waves. Some fairies, chased out of the Forest of Broceliande, cried so many tears that it formed the Gulf of Morbihan. They threw their floral crowns into the gulf, to become its 365 islands. Three crowns floated as far as the ocean. Two formed the islands of Houat and Hoëdic, and the Fairy Queen became Belle-Île.

LE PALAIS

The first place to visit is the little capital of Le Palais and its citadel. The town's name comes from *pallae*, a derivation from the Celtic word *ballé*, which simply means town.
THE CITADEL ● *84*. The star-shaped fort was built by Vauban in the early 18th century on older foundations. It was thought to be invulnerable but the English took it in 1761. The

EVA JOUAN
The poetess of Belle-Île was born in Le Palais in 1857. In a poem from her collection *De la Grève* (1896), she coined a phrase now used as a slogan for the island: "Belle-Île la bien nommée" ("Belle Île, the aptly named").

The spectacular rocks of Port Coton (right) stretching out to sea.

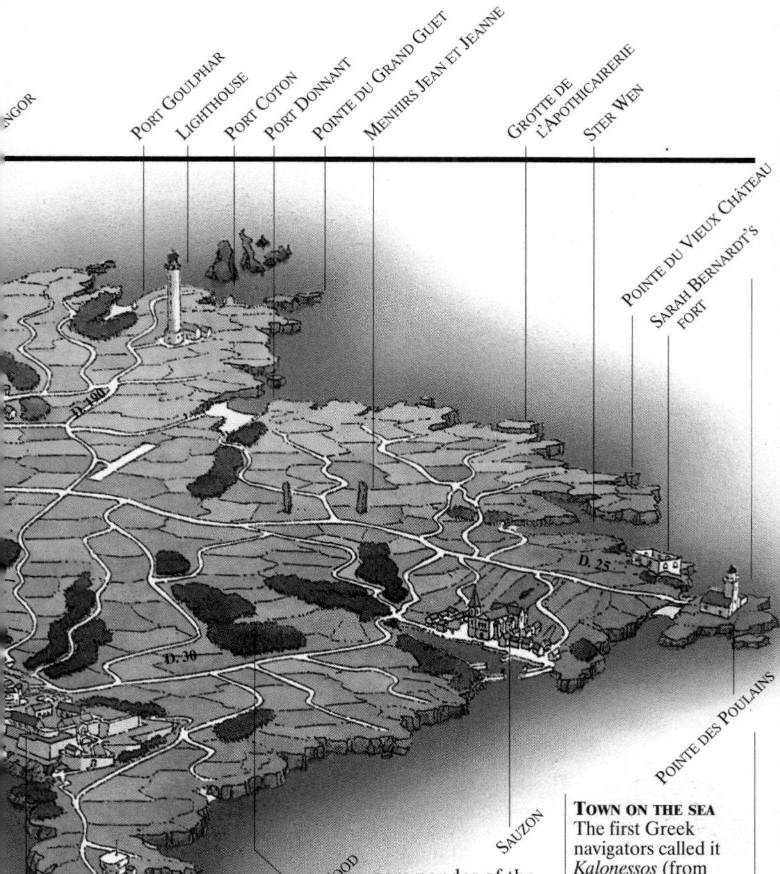

...NGOR
PORT GOULPHAR
LIGHTHOUSE
PORT COTON
PORT DONNANT
POINTE DU GRAND GUET
MENHIRS JEAN ET JEANNE
GROTTE DE L'APOTHICAIRERIE
STER WEN
POINTE DU VIEUX CHÂTEAU
SARAH BERNARDT'S FORT
D. 190
D. 25
D. 30
POINTE DES POULAINS
SAUZON
TROCHU WOOD
POINTE DE TAILLEFER
LE PALAIS

commander of the fort, Saint Croix, held out for thirty-eight days and agreed honorable conditions of surrender.

HISTORY MUSEUM. The fort has a museum showing the history of the island. It also tells of the famous people who have spent spent time on Belle-Île. Some came because they loved the place; others were there under duress. There is also a RELIEF MODEL (1704) of the fortress itself, a copy of the original kept at Les Invalides in Paris.

BASTION DU GOUVERNEUR. One of the bastions of the central fortified structure is now a garden with an exceptional view. Below, fishing boats and yachts slip gently past and the mail boat from Quiberon chugs in and out of the harbor. Visible in the distance are the tiny islands of Houat and Hoëdic.

THE OFFICERS' QUARTERS. The building dates from 1680. In 1802 Placide Toussaint-Louverture, son of the famous Haitian general who led the 1796 to 1802 uprisings in Santo Domingo, was imprisoned here. He was exiled with his family on the orders of Napoleon, and stayed for two years.

BASTION DE LA MER. From here there is a splendid view over the Coureau, the stretch of water between Belle-Île and the mainland. In 1832, Dom Pedro I, having just abdicated as Emperor of Brazil, rallied a fleet of allies to help him regain the throne of Portugal. Forty-two ships with 7,500 men aboard remained moored at Belle-Île for two long months before setting sail to accomplish their mission.

TOWN ON THE SEA
The first Greek navigators called it *Kalonessos* (from *kallos*, beauty, and *nessos*, island). On a ducal chart dated 1006 it is marked as *Guedel*, but the meaning is always the same: "Belle Île" (Beautiful Island). Bretons themselves call it *Guerveur Ihuel*, or "the town on the sea".

A superb model of the *Joséphine* in the historical museum at Le Palais.

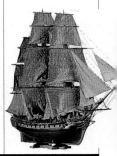

a. *Brèche à la face du B.^{ion} du Gouverneur* .   d. *Face du Bon Dauphin dont les deffenses sont ruine*
c. *Brèche de l'envelope* . K.*Trou de mineur* .   e. *Cavalier* .

BELLE-ÎLE'S DISTINCTIVE LIGHT
Claude Monet, shown (above) in a portrait by Renoir, painted non-stop during his stay at Kervilahouen in 1886. The landscape below, from this period, is on show in the Jacobin museum at Morlaix ▲ *239*.

THE INTERIOR COASTLINE

The Route des Défenses Côtières leads from Le Palais to Locmaria, sticking close to what is known as the "en dedans" (inside) coast, a low-lying seaboard with several beaches looking toward the mainland. In the 17th century it was fortified along its whole length and many traces of these old defences are still to be seen.

KERDONIS LIGHTHOUSE. This was the scene of dramatic events on the night of April 11, 1911. The lighthouse keeper dropped dead unexpectedly and his children Marie Matelot, fourteen, and her brother Charles, twelve, kept the lantern turning, pushing it round by hand from 8 o'clock in the evening until 5.15 the following morning. The postcards illustrating the children's bravery, are now valuable collectors' items.

PLAGE DES GRANDS SABLES. Between Le Palais and Kerdonis head lies the biggest beach on the island, nearly 2,000 yards long. In June 1674 Dutch troops landed here and in April 1761 the English chose Port Andro beach (*porz* meaning "cove" in Breton) as a strategic landing point.

BANGOR

Bangor is a peaceful inland village set among fields.

THE CHURCH. Although the church dates back only to the mid-19th century, the presbytery is far older and has had an eventful past. In August 1654 Cardinal de Retz took shelter here after his escape from Nantes prison. He had been locked up for instigating the 1648 Fronde uprising against Mazarin. The presbytery was also used as headquarters by the English invaders in 1761. In Bangor graveyard is the tomb of Maria Antonietta Mattiocci, wife of the Australian painter John Peter Russell. She was a model for a number of well-known sculptors, including Auguste Rodin (1840–1917) and she lived in Bangor for twenty-three years.

CLAUDE MONET. A short distance west of Bangor lies the hamlet of Kervilahouen. Memories linger here of Claude Monet (1840–1926). From September 15 to November 25, 1896 he painted the same stretch of wild coast thirty-six times, in all weathers. To find the spots that inspired him, walk from the Pointe du Talut to the Pointe du Grand Guet, keeping close to the sea. Monet also painted the village of Cosquet in the rain, and honored his easel carrier, a fisherman called Poly, with a portrait. The painting was stolen from the Musée Marmottan in Paris on November

bréche prise fur la ligne , E, F, du plan .

illon d'officiers rétabli par les Anglois .   h. Ruines de la maison du gouverneur et du

tie du grand quartier rétabli par les Anglois .   Pavillon du Lieutenant de Roy .

27, 1985, but recovered in Corsica in December 1990.

THE GRAND PHARE. From Kervilahouen a road leads to the island's tall southern lighthouse, the Grand Phare, built between 1826 and 1835 to plans by engineer Augustin Fresnel. It rises 300 feet above the sea and its light flashes out over an immense distance of 60 nautical miles.

PORT GOULPHAR AND PORT COTON. The stretch of coast surrounding the Grand Phare is the most spectacular on the whole island. The coastal path, thrilling in stormy weather, leads to the pretty, sandy beach of Port Donnant (dangerous for swimming). The cliffs are fiercely weather-beaten and at a spot called LE TROU DE WAZEN water and sea spray can be seen spurting high up into the air through holes in the heather- and gorse-covered heath.

SAUZON

GROTTE DE L'APOTHICAIRERIE. A colony of cormorants used to nest here, their bottle-shaped bodies lining the vertical sides of the cavern like the rows of jars in an old-fashioned chemist's shop. It was a stopping place for visitors on their way to the Pointe du Vieux Château: the emerald, sapphire and amethyst colors of the sea water within made it one of the most wonderful sights in Brittany. Rockfalls, serious injuries and deaths have caused the cave and steep path down to be closed.

POINTE DES POULAINS. The memory of Sarah Bernhardt lingers at the Pointe des Poulains. The famous actress was spellbound when she first came to this wild, romantic headland. In 1894 she bought the small abandoned fort, along with land around it. Except for the years of the Great War she went there regularly until 1922. Many friends from her theatrical and artistic circle came to stay, among them writers Edmond Rostand (author of *Cyrano de Bergerac*) and Tristan Bernard, composer Reynaldo Hahn and painter Georges Clairin. Nothing remains of Sarah Bernhardt's five houses or her garden, destroyed in the last war, and only the skeleton of the little fort and a few outhouses are left. The few souvenirs of the actress's time on the island that do still exist are a hat-box painted by Clairin, a fan, a parasol and some photographs, in the Citadel museum at Le Palais.

PORT DE SAUZON. Sauzon comes from "saxon", the name that the Bretons came to give the English. From the 4th century the Saxons had made this port a stronghold for pirates. Many artists have been attracted by the clear, bright colors of Sauzon and surrounding landscape. Among them are painter Marcel Gromaire, and Victor Vasarely, originator of Op Art.

THE CITADEL ● *84*
The *chemin de ronde* runs around the central fortifications set upon massive terrassed outer defenses and protected by four bastions. The curtain that links these four is surmounted by triangular blocks against assault, and overlooks a steep drop into a wide moat.

Rocks near the Grotte de l'Apothicairerie.

A RARE DELICACY
The *pouce-pied*, a much sought-after shellfish, is found on Belle-Île. It has six feet, or tentacles, one of which it attaches to a rock and from which the shell then grows. The harvest of these creatures is strictly controlled to prevent depletion of the stock.

331

QUIMPERLÉ
ÎLE DE GROIX
LORIENT
PORT-LOUIS
HENNEBONT
ÉTEL
QUIBERON
CARN

PORT-LOUIS CITADEL
● *84*
It resembles a great stone ship, watching over the town. The troops of Philip II of Spain built the fort in 1590, calling it *Fuerte del Aguila* (Fort of the Eagle). The structure that surmounts Porte Royale, the main gate, and the two spade-shaped

bastions are typically Spanish and were the work of Cristobal de Rojas. The other bastions were designed by Jacques Corbineau, Marshal de Brissac's architect.

PORT-LOUIS

The port was known as *Blabia* in Caesar's time, and by the Middle Ages it had become Port Blavet. It was renamed Port Louis in honor of Louis XIII. During the uprisings of the League ● *57* the Spaniards, who had come to lend support to the Catholic Duc de Mercoeur, improved the port's defenses and built a fortress. This they surrendered to the French in 1598. Under Louis XIV the town became the busiest trading post in Brittany. The first directors of the Compagnie des Indes took up residence there, but in 1666 they moved to Lorient. In the 19th century the fishing industry regained importance. From the Esplanade des Platos a gate in the ramparts leads to the PLAGE DES GRANDS SABLES. This beach, with its casino, is very busy in summer.

CITADEL. A bridge leads to the raised exterior defenses and the demilune (1636), which protected the access to the PORTE ROYALE, the main gate. Above the gate is a dungeon and on either side are bastions built by the Spanish. Inside the gate are the governor's quarters and those of the king's officers. Beyond is the PARADE GROUND, surrounded by barracks built in the reign of Louis XIII and Louis XIV. There is a rear courtyard with the arsenal, powder room and magazine.

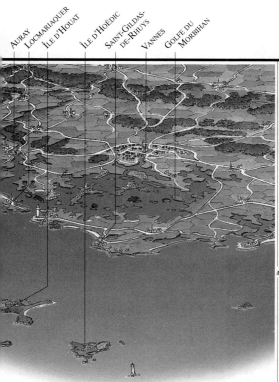

ORIENTAL PORCELAIN
▲ 320
A figure on show in the museum at Port-Louis, from the collection devoted to the history of the Compagnie des Indes.

CHEQUERED HISTORY OF THE PONT LOROIS
Building a bridge over the *ria* ■ 40 of the Étel estuary was an ambitious project, but the work was completed in 1840. The bridge served for over half a century

MUSEUMS. There are four separate collections to be visited in the citadel. The MUSÉE DU PORT LOUIS ET DE LA CITADELLE traces the maritime history of the town. The MUSÉE DE L'ARSENAL displays a large number of model ships. The MUSÉE DES ARMES NAVALES has a collection of naval weaponry dating from the 17th to the 20th centuries. Lastly, the MUSÉE DE LA COMPAGNIE DES INDES is devoted to the the French East India Company. There are models of the ships, maps of routes they took, descriptions of the distant ports they visited, records of their crews and descriptions of the rich cargoes.

THE RIVER ÉTEL

The river penetrates only ten miles inland but the total length of its banks must add up to at least seventy. Countless little roads and lanes go down to the river, coming to an end at the water's edge, perhaps leading to oyster beds or just to some corner of this last truly wild and deserted area." Michel de Galzain so described the Étel in 1984. The wide river is dotted with an intricate pattern of islands and peninsulas. Oak and beech, gorse, heather, broom and foxgloves grow along its banks, and a series of villages with chapels and fountains are set along its course.

A TIDAL ESTUARY. The Étel is a "bottleneck" *ria*: it flows into the ocean through a narrow mouth. The tides cause strong currents in the estuary and the river runs rapidly down on to the dangerous bar of rocks and sand where it meets the sea.

and was destroyed by a storm in 1894. It was rebuilt and reinforced, only to be bombed by the Allies in 1944 in a bid to cut off Germans holding out at Lorient. It was repaired once again in 1954. It is now possible to cross on foot: worth it for the view.

ST-CADO CALVARY
The monument was erected in 1832, close to the chapel. Three sets of wide stone steps with low balustrades lead up to the Cross. The entire village of St-Cado is listed as an historical monument.

POINTE DU MAT FENOUX. Because of the bar, it is difficult and dangerous to take a boat into the river Étel. Mme Josiane Péné, who lives on the western headland at the river mouth by the lighthouse and signal station, helps craft to negotiate the bar. She is on duty when the waters make the sandbanks invisible, from three hours before high tide to two hours after.

SAINT-CADO. This strangely beautiful village, with a Romanesque chapel, is best visited on foot. It is set on an island joined to land by a granite causeway built on low arches, under which traditional flat-bottomed boats still pass. The little harbor, quite important in the 17th century, still operates on a small scale.

St-Cado on its isle.

CHAPEL. Built by Benedictine monks from Quimperlé in the 11th century. It has undergone numerous repairs and alterations but the nave, side aisles and chancel are Romanesque. Note the wooden vaulted ceiling, stone altar, stained-glass window of Saint Cado and the touching 16th-century *Pietà*. A stone staircase leads up to a fine wooden Gothic gallery. The processional boat is carried during the pardon on the third Sunday in September. The 19th-century south chapel contains the stone bed of Saint Cado on which the deaf would lie, hoping to be cured.

ÉTEL. The name Étel comes from "ételle" (big wave). The port does not have a long history; it grew into a sizeable village in the 19th century because of its busy fishing harbor. Initially the catch was sardines, but later the fishermen turned to deep-sea tuna fishing. In the early 20th century Étel had one of the finest fishing fleets of the entire French Atlantic coast, but this is no longer true. The name of the ECOMUSEUM is apt: Autrefois Étel ("Étel as it was").

ISLAND OR PENINSULA?
With variations in sea level over the centuries, there have been periods when Quiberon has been cut off from the mainland by water. This will probably happen again, as the waters are rising by

about one inch a year and the spit of land that joins the town to the mainland is alarmingly narrow in places.

QUIBERON PENINSULA

Quiberon lies at the end of a spit of land extending south into the sea for nearly 9 miles. This is the Isthmus of Penthièvre, a sandy belt, known as a *tombolo*, that links Quiberon to the mainland. It is 42 miles across at its widest point and little more than 100 feet at its narrowest. The fine sandy beaches on the sheltered eastern side lie on the peaceful Bay of Quiberon, while the rugged western coast, justly known as the CÔTE SAUVAGE (Wild Coast), is battered by relentless winds and seas that have worn the land into jagged cliffs ringed with fierce-toothed rocks, and formed countless little coves and caves. Quiberon itself has an extremely mild climate and is busy all year round partly because ferries leave from here to the islands of Belle-Île, Houat and Hoëdic.

"ÉMIGRÉ" INVASION. Early in 1795 the Revolutionary government did its best to calm the wave of insurrection that was creating a ghastly bloodbath in the west of France. But hot-headed *émigrés* decided to rally the rebellious factions under a single command, and persuaded the English to lend their support. On June 27 a small joint force of Englishmen and émigrés landed in the Bay of Carnac, under the command of the Comte de Puisaye and the Comte d'Hervilly. The two Royalist leaders lost so much time in disagreement that the Republican forces were able to crush the invasion. Over seven hundred aristocrats were put to death but the peasants were released.

PENTHIÈVRE BEACH. An unspoiled beach over 10 miles long backed by impressive dunes ■ *26*. It is a favorite place for surfing and sand yachting.

CÔTE SAUVAGE. The rugged western side of the peninsula is not only wild but can be extremely dangerous, with slippery rocks, ground swell and sudden unexpected squalls. When the wind is from the west the ocean hurls itself against the cliffs, throwing up spouts of foam and water. A number of serious accidents have prompted stern official safety warnings. Visitors to the coast will find that certain coves and headlands can only be approached on foot.

CARNAC

A most remarkable concentration of megaliths ● *80* has given its name to Carnac, which means "the place where there are piles of stones".

CHURCH OF ST-CORNÉLY. Few Renaissance-style buildings in the Morbihan match this 17th-century church in Carnac. It was built in the shape of a Latin cross, on the site of a Roman building. Later the church was enlarged and given three parallel naves. The side porch is surmounted by a beautiful 19th-century baldachin, a stone canopy with an openwork design and carved volutes.

THE MEGALITHS. Few other places in the world have inspired so many conflicting theories as to their origin and purpose. Suggestions as to how, between 5000 and 2000 BC, men in the Neolithic period raised the megaliths at Carnac, and as to what they were for, range from plausible scientific explanations to the most arrant nonsense.

PIONEERS. Local Morbihan scholars and historians began to take an interest in the ancient history of their region relatively early. They explored its major tumuli: first Tumiac ▲ *364* at Arzon in 1853, followed closely by Saint Michel, the Moustoir at Carnac and the Mané Lud and the Mané er Hroeg ▲ *339* at Locmariaquer. During these early digs magnificent polished ax heads were found, made of jadeite (a hard green stone) and fibrolite (a flecked white stone found as pebbles

Carved steles from the Luffang dolmen (3000 BC), now in the Miln-Le Rouzic Museum, Carnac.

A large number of engravings of the Breton alignments were made in the 19th century. They were regarded with awe and wonder, which explains their exaggerated size in the print below.

along the waters' edge in Morbihan and Finistère). Beads made of *callaite* (a rare green stone related to turquoise) were also found. All these are now on display in the museums at Vannes and Carnac.

FIRST THEORIES. The suggestion put forward by the navigator Garcie Ferrande in 1521, that the stones were set up as leading marks ■ *16* for sailors, was believed at first. Celtic scholars tried to claim them as a part of their heritage but the clergy were quick to condemn the pagan rites that took place at the stones. Théophile La Tour d'Auvergne, the grenadier and national hero, wrote about Breton antiquities and was the first to bring the words "dolmen" and "menhir" into common usage in 1792. Jacques Cambry, founder of the Académie Celtique, suggested in 1794 that the alignments of stones might be early astronomical observatories. Many other theories were put forward: the stones were anything from a Roman camp to detritus from the Flood.

ASTRONOMICAL COMPLEXITIES. The idea that the stones were set up as an astronomical table has continued to gain support. Captain Alfred Devoir developed this theory, suggesting that the main alignments are positioned according to solar solstice and equinox. The stones therefore formed an open-air calendar, permitting important dates to be identified through the rising of the sun and the agricultural life of the community to be regulated. The French scholar René Merlet and Alexander Thom from Oxford have both advanced theories that suggest that the tumuli and larger menhirs formed part of a complex system of reckoning centered around the Grand Menhir at Locmariaquer ▲ *339*.

RECENT DISCOVERIES. Important excavations are currently going on at the coastal site of Le Petit-Mont at Arzon and inland at Colpo. But the most spectacular recent results have come from Gavrinis ▲ *350* and the *Table des Marchands* at Locmariaquer. These two dolmens contained burial chambers covered by two fragments of the broken Grand Menhir at Locmariaquer. Recent work has added a great deal to our understanding of Neolithic funeral rites.

THE MILN-LE ROUZIC MUSEUM. On his death in 1881 James Miln, a wealthy Scots amateur archeologist who lived at Carnac, bequeathed his collection to the town. His assistant Zacharie Le Rouzic later donated his own finds as well. The museum opened in 1985 and boasts the most comprehensive collection of objects of the period in the world. There are over half a million, from more than 130 archeological sites.

TUMULUS OF ST-MICHEL

This man-made hill of earth and stones is an astonishing 417 feet long by 197 feet wide. Beneath the central *galgal* (tumulus containing a burial chamber), a network of passages leads to some lateral chambers that were probably also burial chambers. Fifteen stone coffins were unearthed here.

THE ALIGNMENTS ● *80*

It is essential to take the alignments at Kerlescan into account when examining the arrangement at Ménec: here the alignment along a northeast to southwest axis would seem to follow the movement of the sun, and may have dictated the way the stones were laid out.

ALIGNMENTS AT KERLESCAN. Take the D 781 road from Carnac to Locmariaquer; at Kérisper turn off on the D 186, which leads to Kerlescan. The lines here run from east to west. The Petit Ménec, which is the first group on the eastern side, stands apart from the other lines whose course runs from the little village itself. They too are oriented in an east-west axis. There are no fewer than 555, arranged in thirteen lines on an area 960 yards long and 152 yards wide. This open colonnade ends in a semicircle of thirty-nine menhirs. The largest *cromlec'h* known to exist stands to the north, a 908-foot-long arc of forty-three menhirs, seven of which are still standing. Further on there is a complex *allée couverte* containing two separate inner compartments. Beyond this again stand two menhirs.

THE MANIO GIANT. Just beyond the last semicircle north of Kerlescan, take the first lane on the right and then the second on the left, ending up in a field. Turn right to come upon a group of small menhirs forming a RECTANGULAR ENCLOSURE. Within stands the Giant, 19 feet high.

THE KERMARIO ALIGNMENTS. The lane meanders on among pine trees

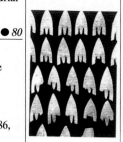

NEOLITHIC PERIOD AND BRONZE AGE

A battleax dating from the late Neolithic period, and Bronze Age flint arrowheads found at Elven.

337

The entrance to the "Trou des Grisons" near Kerlescan.

"ARCHÉOSCOPE" AT MÉNEC
An informative addition to the site that was installed in 1991. Display panels and films explain some of the current theories on the origin of the megaliths and the purpose they served.

ERIC TABARLY
The famous sailor from Nantes, best known for his solo crossing of the Pacific aboard *Pen-Duick V* in 1969. He was also the winner of solo transatlantic races in 1964 and 1976.

POINTE DE KERPENHIR
From this promontory at the neck of the Golfe du Morbihan ▲ *348* where it meets the sea, the view across to Port-Navalo is splendid. The waters are little more than 2 miles across, and the point of confluence between river and sea can be dangerous.

for about 400 yards. Just a short way beyond, 1,029 menhirs in ten lines each 1200 yards long come into sight. These are the best-preserved stones remaining in Carnac, and include a 21-foot-long menhir, now lying on its side. The first stones stand on an elongated mound, identifiable by a menhir that, 10 feet tall, stands higher than the others.

THE MÉNEC ALIGNMENTS. Today these are fenced off, but a platform has been built giving a good view of the largest group of stones at Carnac. No fewer than 1,099 menhirs set in eleven lines are spread over an area 110 yards wide and 1,300 yards long! The alignments come to an end at the hamlet of Ménec with a semicircle of seventy standing stones.

LA TRINITÉ-SUR-MER

Until 1860 the village of La Trinité-sur-Mer was the port of Carnac. Today it survives by catering for ocean-going yachts and is one of the four largest marinas in Brittany. Extending upward from the harbor, the town stretches out along the estuary of the river Crach. Explore some of the narrow streets above the port to glimpse the charm of such little quarters as Kervouden, Kervilhen, Kerbihan and Kerhino.

LOCMARIAQUER

HISTORY. The Roman town of Dariorigum, large enough to have its own theater and with good roads leading off in several directions, once stood looking out to sea on the site where Locmariaquer stands today. Some Gallo-Roman remains, such as those of the aqueduct which brought fresh water to the town, are still visible. The port's strategic position has long been exploited. The Veneti used it as a base for a large fleet of boats; in the 19th century Ferdinand de Lesseps, builder of the Suez canal, wanted to make it the best equipped port in the world; and General Eisenhower planned to use it as a safe haven should the forces that landed in Normandy in June 1944 be forced to withdraw. Today Locmariaquer's small port chiefly deals in oysters, and it offers good beaches, megalithic sites, exploration of the Golfe du Morbihan and trips to the islands of Belle-Île, Houat and Hoëdic.

THE GRAND MENHIR. On the right just beyond the cemetery lies the largest menhir in the world. It is 67 feet long, but is broken into four pieces. The Romans called it the "northern column" and it was used as a leading mark for ships entering the port. The menhir seems to have been knocked over during the Neolithic period. Worn traces of an ax sign cut into the stone are obviously part of the same carving as that found on fragments covering the *Table des Marchands* and Gavrinis burial chambers ▲ *350.*

TABLE DES MARCHANDS. Also at Locmariaquer is a famous Neolithic corridor dolmen concealed beneath a cairn. It dates

from about 3500 BC and was probably the collective tomb of a nearby agricultural community. The covering slab has an ax sign and part of an ox-cart carved on it, and appears to be a fragment broken from the Grand Menhir. At the same site is the TUMULUS D'ER VINGLE (or *Er Crac'h*), which is more than 550 feet long and dates from 4000 BC.

NOTRE-DAME DE KERDRO. Standing on the town square is an 11th-century church, a rare example of Romanesque style in the region. The floor has caved in several times, and the lovely ceiling has now dropped to 4 feet below its original height. The finest features include some elegant carved capitals and a lovely arch at the front of the chancel. Just beyond the town on the right lies the tumulus of *Er Hroeg*, which was excavated at the turn of the century.

AURAY

The pretty countryside of the Auray region (*Bro an Alre*) is extremely popular with tourists. This area is also one of the most deeply religious in Brittany. Auray itself is a busy commercial town making its living mainly from tourism and oysters, its port lying on the estuary of the river Le Loch. It is one of nine Breton towns to have been given the title *ville d'art et d'histoire* ("city of art and history"). The feature that earned Auray this honor is its distinctive domestic architecture, notably some fine 16th-century patrician houses both in the town center and near the port, St-Goustan.

TOWN CENTER. The City Hall is in the Place de la République, opposite three timber-framed houses dating from the 16th century. In the Rue Barré, which by the 17th century was already the busiest trading street in the town, stands the fine old HÔTEL DIEU, dating from 1650.

CHURCH OF ST-GILDAS. A Renaissance porch leads into the large nave where a vaulted ceiling was installed in the 19th century to improve the acoustics. The church is plainly decorated and the high altar has a striking marble REREDOS made by Olivier Martinet in 1657.

ST-GOUSTAN. Over the river from the town center lies the harbor district of St-Goustan, reached by a four-arched bridge with protruding stone piers, rebuilt in the 14th century. At that time whaling boats would be seen in the port and there was cod fishing in the Bay of Audierne. The river was canalized in 1614 and the Quai Neuf, which runs along the Route de Vannes, was built in 1749. During the 16th and 17th centuries Auray was the third largest port in Brittany. Cargoes of grain arriving there would be sent inland to Nantes, and there was also a profitable trade in wine. The railroad sent the port into decline.

BRIDGING THE RIVER. At first the crossing to the port was made over a ford at low tide, and at high tide by ferry. When a stone bridge was built in 1295 it proved unable to withstand the force of the tides. Several attempts were made to rebuild it before the design was perfected.

When Napoleon became First Consul he offered Chouans a compromise, but Cadoudal fled to England. Returning to Paris he joined a plot against Napoleon, was recognized, and guillotined on June 23, 1804.

ANCIENT HARBOR
In St-Goustan, once Auray's busy port, 15th-century stone and half-timbered houses still stand on the cobbled Place Saint-Sauveur, overlooking the old landing-stage.

The bridge at Auray.

A 15th-century house in Auray.

SAINTE-ANNE-D'AURAY

THE MIRACULOUS STATUE. In August 1623 a devout peasant from Ker Anna called Yves Nicolazic had a strange experience. He was awoken by a blinding light, which then disappeared to be replaced by a white lady bearing a flaming torch. The same thing happened several times during the next months, until one day he got up and followed her to a field, Bocenno, where he dug up a painted wooden statue. He was so confident this was a miracle that he convinced everyone around him. In July 1625 the Bishop of Vannes laid the first stone of a shrine dedicated to Saint Anne, Mother of the Virgin. The Carmelites took charge of the shrine, building a monastery and cloister. Since then Bretons have flocked to pay homage to Saint Anne and climb the Scala Sancta on their knees. The first pardon of the year is on March 7 and parish pilgrimages take place from Easter until the first Sunday in October.

BASILICA. The late 19th-century mock-Renaissance basilica was built to replace a church dating from 1645 that was burnt down in 1790. The apse leads through to the old Carmelite monastery with a 17th-century CLOISTER: the roof on the eastern side is all that remains of the original shrine completed in 1628. Inside the basilica the huge bare nave contrasts with the richly decorated chapels in the transept. Stained-glass windows recount the life of Saint Anne and the story of Nicolazic, whose remains lie in the first chapel to the right of the nave.

COSTUME MUSEUM. The museum opened in 1920 and the 150 traditional Breton costumes displayed there were made by parishioners between 1920 and 1940.

TREASURY. In the cloister is a poignant and miscellaneous collection of offerings made to Saint Anne by supplicatory or grateful pilgrims.

FOLK ART. There is a gallery with around one hundred statues carved and painted in polychrome by local craftsmen between the 15th and 19th centuries.

FONTAINE DE SAINTE-ANNE, AURAY
In front of the basilica stands a three-tiered granite fountain surmounted by a statue of Saint Anne to whom the shrine is

dedicated. She was made patron saint of Brittany in 1914.

MONSTRANCE
Set with precious stones and ornately decorated with the Mysteries of the Rosary and scenes from the life of Saint Anne and Saint Joachim, the Virgin Mary's parents. It is one of the treasures of the shrine at Auray.

THE CHARTREUSE D'AURAY

An old collegiate building founded by Jean de Montfort in 1482 was later rebuilt by Carthusian monks and became the Charterhouse of Auray. The existing buildings date from the 17th and 18th centuries. In 1968 the church (dated 1770) and the 19th-century funerary chapel were both badly damaged by fire, but later repaired. A marble mausoleum stands above a burial vault containing the bones of Royalists shot after their counter-Revolutionary invasion failed in 1795 ▲ *335*.

VANNES

CHOCOLAT GUÉRIN-BOUTRON

ARMES DES VILLES DE FRANCE

VANNES

La Cathédrale et les Remparts à Vannes

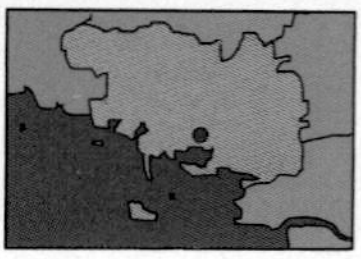

At the top portion is a map with labels:

MAURICE MARCHAIS

RUE THIERS

RUE SALOMON

PLACE DE LA RÉPUBLIQUE

PLACE LUCIEN-LAROCHE

PLACE DES LICES

RUE THIERS

PLACE GAMBETTA

RUE A. PONTOIS

RUE FR

Markers: 1, 2, 3, 5, 8, A, B, C, D, E, F, G

At the turn of the century Vannes (from the Breton *Gwenea*, literally "place of the Veneti") was popularly known as "the biggest village in France" because life there was leisurely and agreeable, and the inhabitants failed to realize the unique beauty of their unspoiled town. Their way of life altered only with the arrival of settlers from beyond Brittany, and with the restoration of the city's old quarters.

HISTORY

A TRADITIONAL SIGN
Old Vannes and his wife are the local mascots.

EARLY YEARS. In the beginning Vannes was probably a thoroughfare between two hills, situated just beyond the reach of the waters of the Gulf of Morbihan. The Veneti's settlement of Dariorigum is now the quarter of St-Patern. Long after Julius Caesar defeated the Veneti in 56 BC ▲ *364*, the town continued to grow, becoming a major Roman outpost. Expansion continued into the 3rd century AD, when Viking and Barbarian invasions started.
A CELTIC CENTER. The Celts arrived from across the Channel in the 4th century. Under the leadership of Waroc'h they seized the town, shifted it to a more strategic position and

MONUMENTS

1. HÔTEL DE VILLE
2. HÔTEL DE LIMUR
3. COHUE
4. CATHEDRAL OF
ST-PIERRE
5. CHÂTEAU GAÍLLARD
6. CHURCH OF
ST-PATERN
7. PRÉFECTURE
8. HARBOR

RAMPARTS

A. PORTE PRISON
B. TOUR POUDRIÈRE
C. TOUR DU
CONNÉTABLE
D. PORTE POTERNE
E. CHÂTEAU DE
L'HERMINE
F. TOUR DE CALMONT
G. TOUR TROMPETTE
H. PORTE
ST-VINCENT

strengthened its defenses. But trade continued to flourish under these difficult conditions, and by the 11th century Vannes was one of the most important cities in the Duchy of Brittany. Between the 15th and 17th centuries, three key events took place that increased its religious and political importance: the arrival of the missionary Saint Vincent Ferrier in 1418 ▲ *345*; the union of Brittany with France in 1532; and the removal there from Rennes in 1675 of the Breton Parliament.

RECENT YEARS. Vannes proved of only limited strategic importance in World War Two, and was consequently spared much of the damage suffered by other cities. Today it is a thriving commercial center and a city of exceptional beauty. Its fine architectural heritage and proximity to the Gulf of Morbihan have made it a popular tourist resort.

ARCHEOLOGICAL MUSEUM
This is housed in the beautiful Renaissance Château Gaillard, and contains some magnificent displays of objects found in the Morbihan. There are Neolithic, Bronze-Age and Iron-Age jewelry, weapons and pottery; Gallo-Roman coins and pottery; and devotional objects from the Middle Ages and the Renaissance. Left, a coin minted by the Veneti, and a bas relief.

Below, the ornate entrance to the cathedral of St-Vincent, on the Rue des Chanoines.

A WALK AROUND THE STREETS

Place Henri-IV.

PLACE GAMBETTA A popular meeting place for the locals, this has now been restored. It acquired its half-moon shape in the 19th century. Old houses surround St-Vincent's Gate, once the entrance to the city.

A polychrome statue on view in the museum at the Cohue.

PLACE DES LICES. The French word *lice* refers to the ancient days of chivalry, when knights entered the lists and fought tournaments here. François I was present at the great celebrations held here in 1532 to mark Brittany's union with France. This is also where Saint Vincent Ferrier came to preach in the last year of his life.

CHÂTEAU GAILLARD. The Rue Noé, which runs down to the FISH MARKET, is especially busy on Saturdays. It contains a beautiful 15th-century building that is now the ARCHEOLOGICAL MUSEUM. This building houses one of the most important mixed collections of prehistoric artefacts in the world.

PLACE HENRI-IV. This is just off the north-west corner of the cathedral square, and was probably the center of the old Gallo-Roman town. It is lined with delightful gabled and half-timbered houses, some of which date back to the 15th century. One of the most attractive of all is at the corner of the Place and Rue des Chanoines.

CATHEDRAL OF ST-PIERRE. The 15th-century high-vaulted nave is bordered with chapels. The CHAPEL OF THE HOLY SACRAMENT is a masterpiece of Italian Renaissance style, and is on two levels. The rotunda (1537) is one of the earliest in Brittany: the tomb and a reliquary of Saint Vincent Ferrier are here. A tapestry on the wall illustrates some miracles performed by the saint. The TREASURE is on view in the chapter house: there are chalices, pyxes, volumes of illuminated manuscripts and a 12th-century wedding chest in vellum-covered decorated wood.

THE COHUE

The word cohue literally means "crowd". This unusual building, which is situated opposite the cathedral, is one of the oldest in Vannes. Enlarged and altered over the centuries, the Cohue has been by turns a market, a courthouse and a theater: the Breton Parliament sat there too. The Cohue currently houses the MUSÉE DES BEAUX ARTS. Formerly it belonged to the Duke, who raised a levy on all activities that took place there.

THE BUILDING. The Cohue has been civic property since 1813. Its central nave dates from the 13th century, and was later

enlarged by the addition of two side naves. The Haute Salle was another later addition, built initially in wood then later rebuilt in stone. The staircase was added in the 19th century.

MUSÉE DES BEAUX ARTS. When it opened the Fine Arts Museum had already received a number of bequests from the State. The most famous of these is a *Crucifixion* by Eugène Delacroix, painted in 1835. More recently the collection has had the good fortune to acquire engravings by Corot, Millet, Goya and Delacroix, as well as works by well-known local artists such as Frelaut and Dubreuil. Contemporary art is also represented, with pictures by Soulages, Tal Coat and others. There is also a valuable collection of polychrome wooden statues from the 14th to the 16th centuries, which come from chapels in the region and illustrate the traditional style of Breton woodcarving. Another section of the museum is dedicated to the Gulf of Morbihan: its geographical features, natural resources, and occupations such as fishing and oyster farming, are featured and explained.

RUE ST-GWENAËL. This medieval street retains much of its ancient character, so that the colorful bustle and noise that filled it hundreds of years ago is quite easy to imagine.

HÔTEL DES TROIS DUCHESSES. One of the city's finest medieval houses is at no. 3 Rue de la Bienfaisance. Three duchesses, including Françoise d'Amboise and Catherine of Luxemburg, lived here in the late 16th century. The beautiful house opposite was built in 1680 to accommodate the members of the Breton Parliament.

PORTE PRISON. The St-Patern Gate changed its name when it became a prison. After the royalist uprising at Quiberon in 1795 ▲ *335*, the captured émigrés were confined here before their execution. Among them were the Bishop of Dol and Charles de Sombreuil.

A rooftop view of Vannes.

THE OLD WASH-HOUSES
They were built in the 19th century beside the river Marle, which runs along the foot of the ramparts and are proof that timber-framed houses continued to be built up until recent times.

SAINT VINCENT FERRIER
This Spanish Dominican monk came to Vannes in 1418, at the behest of Duc Jean V de Montfort, who had become concerned about the profanity of the populace. For two months people came from all over Brittany to hear him preach. He died here the following year and was canonized in 1455.

THE PRISON GATE
The importance given to the preservation of old buildings is a recent phenomenon: this medieval gateway, which has long been a central part of the city's heritage, was partly demolished in 1886. It was originally flanked by the two identical towers shown in this 1840 lithograph. Today only one of them remains.

▲ VANNES

A MEDIEVAL SETTING
The ancient ramparts and the gardens below provide a colorful backdrop for celebrations here in Vannes.

THE HARBOR
The port at Vannes was at its busiest between the 14th and the 17th centuries. Until the end of the 17th century boats came right up and beached at the foot of the ramparts. New quays were built with stones from the Château de l'Hermine. Pleasure craft and racing yachts moor there.

THE RAMPARTS

From the Porte Prison to the Porte St-Vincent, the ramparts of Vannes are among the best preserved in all France. The main tower, the proud emblem of the city, is the 15th-century TOUR DU CONNÉTABLE. The river La Marle follows the same course as the ramparts, past the old city washhouses, the PORTE POTERNE and the CHÂTEAU DE L'HERMINE. The latter, which today houses a law school, was built by a wealthy local caterer in the 18th century on the site of a 14th-century castle, formerly the home of the dukes of Brittany. A walk along the ramparts finishes at the foot of the truncated TOUR DE CALMONT and the 15th-century TOUR TROMPETTE, whose guardian was once the city herald.

THE RABINE

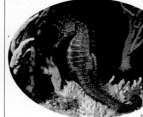

From the marina there is a delightful walk along the Rabine as far as the Conleau peninsula, a distance of 22 miles. The walk passes in front of the former Carmelite convent which has been a school of music since 1979, and takes in the Pont Vert, where multihulled boats are launched.

AQUARIUM. The Aquarium, which opened in 1984, contains more than six hundred species of Atlantic and tropical fish in fifty tanks. There are boatyards further along the channel.

CONLEAU PENINSULA. This is joined to the mainland by an isthmus hardly wider than the road itself, and lined on either side with brightly painted boats. The ferry goes from here to the island of Arz ▲ 350 and Port-Anna, near Séné. The coastal authorities have been trying to preserve the banks of the river Vincin around the peninsula, an important nesting site of some 150 acres with a coastal path running around it.

THE AQUARIUM
Octopuses, piranhas, electric eels, sharks, displays of living coral, and even a crocodile found in the Paris sewers combine to make this aquarium one of the best in Europe.

UNCERTAIN ORIGINS
Some experts claim the Sinagot is descended from the galley of the Veneti, even though the shape of the galley's hull is radically different. However, the Celtic missionary saints who landed in Armorica may well have crossed from Britain in Sinagots.

SÉNÉ

The village and the peninsula of Séné are on the left bank of the river Marle, reached by taking the D 199 road. To the east of the little town is the RÉSERVE BIOLOGIQUE DE FALGUÉREC-SÉNÉ, a wildlife sanctuary with an abundance of marshland birds ● 40. To the south the POINTE DE MOUSTÉRIAN has a beautiful view of the Gulf of Morbihan.

PORT-ANNA. Fishing boats and pleasure craft moor in this little harbor, once the working base for dozens of Sinagots.

> "THERE ARE THE LIVING,
> THERE ARE THE DEAD,
> AND THERE ARE THOSE WHO GO TO SEA."

PLATO

SINAGOTS

Sinagots, literally the inhabitants of Séné, have lent their name to a type of boat used for dredging oysters in difficult and shallow places such as the Gulf of Morbihan, the Bay of Quiberon, and the rivers Crac'h and Pénerf. They were built of oak and rigged with two unbraced masts each having a rectangular sail. They carried enough sail to pull the dredging equipment and were heavy enough to carry the square-footage of sail. The V-shaped hull contained stones or slag as ballast.

THE FISHERMAN'S LOT. A Sinagot generally carried a crew of two, the owner and his mate. The poorer fishermen might even live on board with their families. So as not to deplete stocks, fishing was controlled, sometimes being confined to the month of March, and took place under the watchful eye of a coastguard. A cannon shot at around 8am would signal the time to set sail and the Sinagots would fish until 6 o'clock in the evening. To the women fell the equally arduous job of going from village to village, hawking the catch.

THE LAST SINAGOTS. These boats died out with motorization and with the increasing number of oyster beds in the postwar years. The last real Sinagot finally ceased working in 1961. An association, *"Les Amis des Sinagots"*, is trying to revive the old craft, of which the Solveig (now listed as an historical monument) and the Vainqueur-des-Jaloux, together with a handful of others, are surviving examples.

REGATTAS
These were keenly fought and often spectacular competitions. All manner of tricks were played, and boats

frequently capsized. Around 1900, twenty or thirty Sinagots took part. The prize money offered (100 francs) was a great attraction, though the kudos of winning was important too. The last regatta was held in 1951.

347

▲ GULF OF MORBIHAN

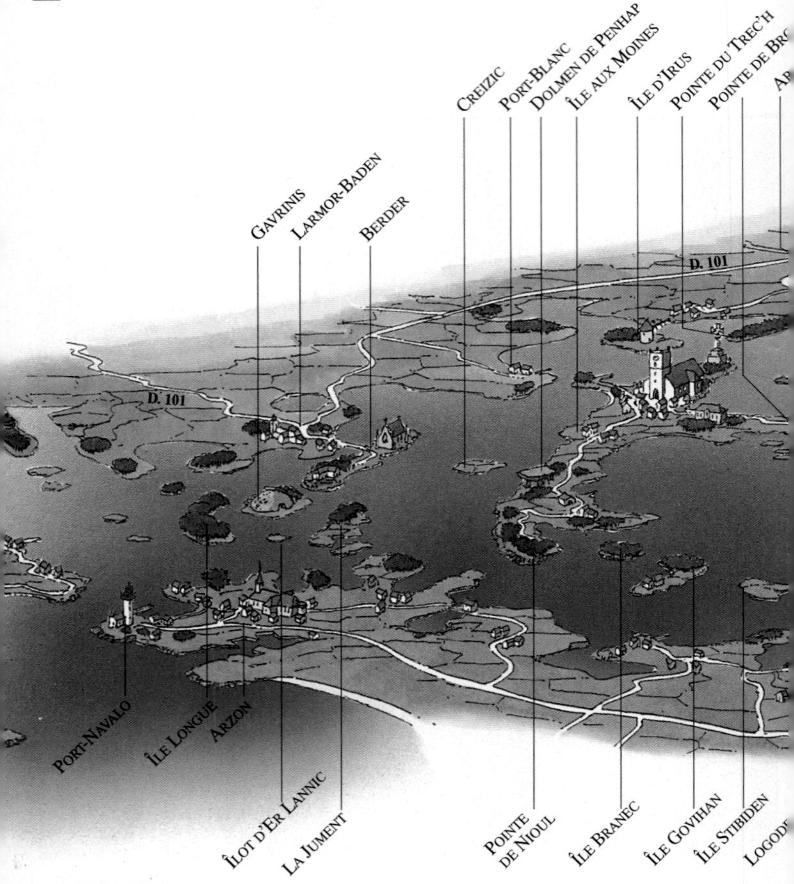

GAVRINIS LARMOR-BADEN BERDER CREIZIC PORT-BLANC DOLMEN DE PENHAP ÎLE AUX MOINES ÎLE D'IRUS POINTE DU TREC'H POINTE DE BR... A...

D. 101

D. 101

PORT-NAVALO ÎLE LONGUE ARZON ÎLOT D'ER LANNIC LA JUMENT POINTE DE NIOUL ÎLE BRANEC ÎLE GOVIHAN ÎLE STIBIDEN LOGOD...

THE GULF

Woman from the Île aux Moines, from a 1930 ad for a Nantes biscuit factory.

The Gulf is scattered with small islands, bare or patched with gorse and heather, that look particularly striking when bathed in the rich colors of a Brittany sunset. Two islands stand out from the rest as altogether more substantial: Arz and the Île aux Moines. Both are the tops of ancient hills that became partly submerged when the Gulf (or "little sea", as it is known in Breton) was formed. The tide flows in through a dangerous channel a little over half a mile wide. The Gulf has been inhabited since Neolithic times: long ago it was home to a mysterious people who built the giant barrow on Gavrinis ▲ *350*, and then to the proud Veneti, who were defeated by Julius Caesar in 56 BC.

AROUND THE GULF BY BOAT. The intricate pattern of inlets and

ÎLES DRONEC · **ÎLE D'ARZ** · **ÎLE DE BOÉDIC** · **ÎLE CONLEAU** · **PORT-ANNA** · **VANNES** · **ÎLE DE BOED** · **SÉNÉ** · **MARAIS DE FALGUEREC** · **MONTSARRAC**

D. 199 · N. 165 · D. 780

POINTE DE LIOUSE · **ÎLE D'HURIC** · **ÎLE D'HUR** · **BILHERVÉ** · **SARZEAU** · **BAILLERON** · **ÎLE TASCON** · **ST-COLOMBIER** · **LE PASSAGE** · **ST-ARMEL**

islets is a fantastic sight from the air: Vannes and Quiberon both have flying clubs, with planes available for sightseeing. But the most popular way of touring the islands is by boat. Motorboat trips leave from Vannes, Larmor Baden, Port Navalo, Locmariaquer and Auray, and craft are also available for charter hire. Best of all is to board a Sinagot (one of the traditional oyster-fishing boats) ▲ *347* at Séné and go out for a day trip.

THE ÎLE AUX MOINES ★

In his *Dictionary* of 1780 the geographer Ogée sang the praises of this fishermen's island (*Izenah* in Breton). It enjoys a gentle climate, the air is scented with gorse, pines and mimosa and there is even a miniature olive grove. Less than 4 miles long, the island is the largest in the Gulf, and derives its living from tourism and oysters.

MEGALITHS. At the center of the hamlet of Kergonan stand twenty-four standing stones that are among the most remarkable Neolithic monuments in Brittany. To the south are the DOLMEN OF PEN HAP and the DOLMEN OF NIOUL, with fine views out over the Gulf.

CHURCH OF ST-MICHAEL
The plain appearance of the interior of this church was relieved in 1930 by the addition of Art Deco windows and mosaics from the Mauméjean workshops in Paris.

Opposite, crowds of spectators watching a regatta on the Island of Arz at the turn of the century.

THE GAVRINIS CARVINGS
It is still a matter of keen debate as to whether or not the great corridor dolmen on Gavrinis was originally painted. The intricate carving (especially of the curved concentric lines, which probably represent an earth goddess) is quite exceptional, and must have required enormous skill and patience on the part of the artists.

A hypothetical reconstruction, based on discoveries made during excavations over the last century, of how such a Neolithic tumulus was built using only the most basic tools and equipment.

ISLAND OF ARZ ★

Arz is just under 2 miles long and has a jagged coastline. On it are preserved a number of 17th-century houses with attractive gabled roofs. Being set further from the mainland coast and the tourist areas, it is quieter than Île aux Moines. It is, however, a busy center of the oyster industry ■ *32,* and several sailing schools are based there.

THE VILLAGE. Its charming old-fashioned streets and lanes are centered round the CHURCH OF NOTRE-DAME, which stands surrounded by a little graveyard. To the south, the beach at Brouel is a good place for a walk: this is the wilder side of the island, with views across to the Île aux Moines.

ISLAND OF GAVRINIS

Gavrinis, consisting of over 30 acres of granite covered by a thin layer of vegetation, boasts one of the wonders of the megalithic world. A 15-minute boat trip from Larmor Baden takes the visitor to the most magnificent of all corridor dolmens, thought to be around five thousand years old. The cairn (a heap of stones covering a burial chamber) of Gavrinis stands in a marvelous setting. The island, once farmland, also had a monastery belonging to the Templars, and from the 15th century the hillock was a well-known landmark ■ *16* for sailors. In 1832 a rockfall revealed the presence of a dolmen inside.

SUBTERRANEAN WONDERS. A corridor 45 feet long leads to a small, almost square chamber situated right at the center of the cairn. The floor is paved with stones, and twenty-three of the twenty-nine supporting pillars are carved with various symbols such as curves, parallel lines, whorls and spirals combined in numerous ways. (Though spirals are a familiar form of decoration on Irish megaliths, this is the only known example of them in Brittany.) The motifs are all clearly visible, despite having endured the touch of thousands of tourists. The most elaborate symbols, such as spirals, hooks and even

> **"THERE ARE VILLAGES OUT HERE ALONG THE CLIFFS ... WHERE THERE ARE VILLAGES THAT MEANS A BEACH BELOW. IMMENSE FLAT BEACHES DOWN THERE, BUT ALMOST DESERTED."**
>
> ROBERT DALEY

serpents, are carved into exceptionally hard granite, which, with only simple quartz and flint cutting tools, would have been a difficult material to work. The paving stones have been cut to the right size and are carefully dressed. In 1980–1 excavations revealed further carvings on the exterior of the corridor and burial chamber. The covering stone was recognized as part of an immense decorated stele, other fragments of which were used to cover the *Table des Marchands* ▲ *338* and the Tumulus d'Er Grah at Locmariaquer. The carving of oxen pulling a cart fits with the one on the *Table des Marchands*! The slab must have been brought from Locmariaquer to Gavrinis on a huge raft. About sixty tree trunks would have been needed to float it over a distance of nearly 3 miles, along a channel which has now been subsumed by the waters of the Gulf. The building at Gavrinis called for about 10,000 tons of material and represents about three years' work for a hundred men. The tumulus must have been abandoned: between 3500 and 3000 BC the timber that stood at the entrance was burned, and soon afterward the façade was closed off behind piles of stones as if to conceal the dolmen inside.

ISLAND OF BERDER. The island, close to Gavrinis, can be reached on foot at low tide from Larmor Baden. An attractive coastal path runs round it.

THE ÎLOT D'ER LANNIC

From the boat to Gavrinis, a double *cromlec'h* in the shape of a figure-of-eight is visible, though partly submerged. This is a rare example of menhir circles in Brittany. It is also the only proof that there has been a change in sea level since Neolithic times, early man being considered unlikely to have built a *cromlec'h* in the water! Hearths and pottery around 5,000 years old have been discovered here.

A GIGANTIC JIGSAW
As excavations have conclusively proved, the slabs covering the burial chambers of the cairns in the *Table des Marchands* at Locmariaquer (top) and Gavrinis (above) have the same origin: both once formed part of the Grand Menhir ▲ *338* at Locmariaquer. The carving on the latter clearly links up with that on the two other pieces of rock.

THE "CROMLEC'H" OF ER LANNIC ● *80*
Because of the bird sanctuary there, landing on the islet is not allowed. It is possible to see the two stone circles, one on the island and the other half-submerged. According to one theory, they are the remains of a kind of astronomical calendar.

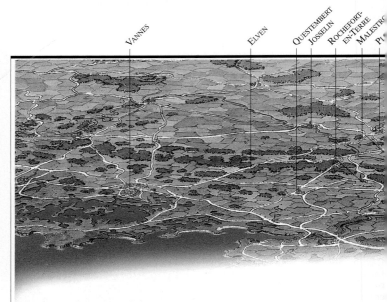

VANNES · ELVEN · QUESTEMBERT · JOSSELIN · ROCHEFORT-EN-TERRE · MALESTROIT · PL...

FORTRESS OF LARGOËT

Although now a ruin, the fortress is still an awe-inspiring sight. It is private property but is open to visitors and can be reached by a half-mile long avenue through the forest. There is an impressive keep in the shape of an irregular octagon; it has five floors, with 184 steps to the top, and is 144 feet high.

The future English king Henry VII was once a prisoner here. The other important surviving feature is a three-story circular building known as the North-West Tower. The rest of the castle is in poor condition but includes a fortified gatehouse and defensive wall, and the entrance to a tunnel that led all the way to Elven, almost 2 miles away. In addition there are moats, now dry but more than 40 feet deep in places. The fortress was begun in the 13th century, and before long envious warlords were eyeing it covetously. It was attacked in the War of Succession, whose opposing leaders were Charles de Blois and Jean de Montfort, at which time it was supported by the English forces. "The assault continued within and without until evening fell," wrote chronicler Froissart. "Ditches were filled with wood and straw, the besiegers made holes in the walls almost a fathom in depth through which they forced an entrance and killed all whom they found."

So finely dressed are the rows of granite stones that this magnificent octagon looks almost like one solid rock, carved by giant chisels and weathered by wind and rain.

THE TOWERS OF ELVEN
The remains of the castle's keep and round tower (above). Right, the ruins as seen in an illustration from a comic book of 1883, *La Diligence de Ploërmel*.

LATER YEARS. In 1839 writer Prosper Mérimée (official Inspector of Historic Monuments) was concerned about the increasing delapidation of the castle's fabric, though restoration of the ruins did not begin until the 1870's. In summer the lake below the castle becomes the setting of an historically dubious son et lumière. At the entrance to the 400-acre park is the caretaker's house, a former hunting lodge with decorations of carved hares.

LA VRAIE-CROIX

The Chapelle de la Vraie-Croix owes its name to the mythical adventures of a Breton knight just back from the Crusades. After his return he wished to kiss the fragment of the True Cross that he had brought back with him. The holy relic had disappeared, but retracing his steps he discovered it in a magpie's nest at the top of a hawthorn tree. In gratitude he built a chapel nearby (now the parish church) and had the holy relic placed inside it, but soon it had disappeared once more. The knight searched again in the magpie's nest, and when he found it he took this as a sign from God that He wished the chapel to be built exactly where the tree stood. Accordingly he built the Chapel of Notre-Dame-de-Secours, a church without a congregation. The chapel is reached by two flights of steps forming a quarter-circle. The fragment of the True Cross is said to be in the reliquary cross there, which dates from the 13th century.

QUESTEMBERT

Known for its excellent cuisine, Questembert is also the economic center of the region. Its name comes from the Breton word for chestnut, *kist*, a common local foodstuff.

LES HALLES ★. The 17th-century timber-framed market hall has three aisles, and is a work of art in itself. The surrounding houses bear witness to the former prosperity of the town. At the edge of the cemetery stands the lovely CHAPEL OF ST-MICHEL, and in the Rue St-Martin is a 16th-century fountain.

THE CHAPEL OF THE TRUE CROSS
At ground level are two open naves exposed to the elements and separated by a paved walkway.

THE MARKET HALL AT QUESTEMBERT
It was built in 1552 then entirely rebuilt in 1675 by Étienne Charpentier. It is one of the oldest covered markets in France. It measures 180 feet long by 50 feet wide, and is 33 feet high. More than 200 cubic yards of oak were used in its construction. The hall became the property of the town in 1845 and is now listed as a historic monument.

Left, the chapel of St-Michel.

ROCHEFORT-EN-TERRE

The site, an outcrop of schist above the valley of the Gueuzon, which is a tributary of the river Arz, was already occupied in the Paleolithic period. Its name is derived from the Rochefort family, who built a castle here in the 12th century to defend the road from Malestroit to La Roche Bernard. The Rocheforts continued to rule until 1374, when heiress Jeanne de Rochefort married Jean II of Rieux. The marriage contract specified that the groom's name and armorial bearings should be combined with the bride's, so the

Rieux-Rochefort dynasty became the next rulers. The dynasty lasted until 1567, when Renée, daughter of Claude I, died without issue. She had taken the name of Guyonne XVIII, and her conduct was by all accounts so outrageous that she was known locally as "Guyonne the Mad".

AN ILL-FATED CASTLE. The medieval castle was wrecked for the first time in 1488, after the battle of St-Aubin-du-Cormier, when the French king Charles VIII beat the Breton forces under Duc François II. Rochefort, Rieux and Elven were razed to the ground. There is a gentle irony in the fact that the king soon after married the orphan Anne of Brittany and offered her tutor, Jean IV of Rieux, a sum of money to rebuild the castle on an even more majestic scale. In 1594 that too was burned down by the Governor of Redon during the religious wars. It was rebuilt, though without the fortifications, in the latter half of the 17th century. Then between April and June 1793 the entire castle was finally dismantled stone by stone.

THE CHÂTEAU OF ALFRED KLOTS. In 1908 the ruins were purchased by an American painter named Alfred Klots, who set to work on the offices and outbuildings that had escaped demolition during the Revolution, transforming them into the current manor. Parts of it, such as doors, turrets and gable windows, were brought from the château of Keralio, near Muzillac. Klots also developed the tourist industry at Rochefort. In 1911 he instigated a competition for the most beautiful floral house façade in the village; this

became an annual event and attracted hordes of visitors in the 1930's. On the death of Klots' son Trafford in 1976 the property was sold to the Morbihan District Council, who opened one of the wings to the public. Inside are paintings, furniture and other works of art.

A PICTURESQUE VILLAGE. Rochefort-en-Terre is one of the prettiest villages in Brittany. The buildings have been restored with the utmost care; television aerials are concealed and electric cables buried underground. Gaudy advertisement hoardings have been replaced by smaller, discreet signs, and most of the streets are cobbled. As well as the castle, Rochefort boasts some splendid 16TH- AND 17TH-CENTURY HOUSES, particularly in the Rue Haute-Candré, the Rue des Douves and the Place du Puits. In the latter square is a charming flower-covered building, which is the courthouse. Most of the houses are still covered with flowers in spring and summer: the municipality has provided greenhouses for the care of delicate plants during the winter, so that in season they may decorate the plain granite walls of the village.

CHURCH OF NOTRE-DAME-DE-LA-TRONCHAYE. It was built in the 12th century and became a collegiate church in 1498 (i.e. endowed for chapter though without a see). Inside is a fine GALLERY incorporating carvings from the ancient rood screen. The church has had some eventful moments in its history: in 1532 François I came here to pray at the tomb of Claude, son of Jean IV of Rieux. During the Revolution, the church had a brave and stubborn priest who was hidden from the bloodthirsty authorities, but who was nonetheless taken and put to death at Lorient. The CALVARY that stands outside the church dates from the early 16th century. It is an unusual example, known as the "Poor Man's Bible" since it was used as a stone *raolennou* ● 72, or visual aid for teaching the Catechism.

MALESTROIT ★

"THE PEARL OF THE WEST". The pretty village is a popular tourist center. There are many attractive old houses, some with gables and overhanging upper stories, and others carved with grotesque gargoyles. The PLACE BOUFFAY in particular has two exceptionally fine 17th-century stone houses and a 15th-century merchant establishment. The Rue du Général-de-Gaulle also has some outstanding stone-built houses, and a delightful timber-framed house at no. 7.

CHURCH OF ST-GILLES. An unusual juxtaposition of styles is apparent in this church. It was built in the 12th century, and was partially rebuilt and enlarged in the 16th century following a fire. The chancel and the south arm of the transept are relics of the original Norman building, and the south doorway has a buttress carved like the ox of Saint Hervé. The handsome PULPIT in the nave, decorated with two sirens, dates from the 17th century.

A 19th-century engraving of the Breton king Judicaël.

TREASURES OF THE ABBEY AT PAIMPONT

This painted wooden figure of the Virgin in the abbey church was for centuries the object of popular devotion. The sacristy houses two notable pieces: an ivory figure of Christ dating from the 12th century, and a 15th-century reliquary containing the radius of Judicaël.

PAIMPONT

This is the largest parish in the Ille-et-Vilaine, and almost all of it is covered by forest. Its name comes from the Breton *pen ponthi*, meaning "end of the bridge". The village is set round a lake, which with a surface area of 120 acres is the second largest in the forest. There is also an impressive abbey, which was a favorite place of eccentric Surrealist writer André Breton.

FOUNDATION OF THE ABBEY. The first monastery to be established here was founded in the 7th century by a monk of royal lineage named Judicaël, who eventually succeeded to the throne of Domnone in Brittany and took up arms to defend his kingdom against Dagobert I, king of the Franks. Peace was soon made however, and Dagobert sent his chief minister Saint Eligius (Éloi) to Brittany. With his kingdom saved, Judicaël returned to his monastery at Saint-Méen having founded a hermitage here at Paimpont. The hermitage became a monastery late in the 12th century, and only fell into disuse during the Revolution.

THE ABBEY CHURCH. Its beautiful Gothic doorway dates from the 13th century. The two doors are surmounted by trefoil arches and a lovely *Virgin and Child* in sandstone. Inside, the Romanesque vaulting in the nave is wooden (it was restored in 1962), while the Gothic vaulting of the chancel and south transept is of stone.

LES FORGES

At the entrance to the village on the right-hand side is the recently restored complex of FORGES D'EN BAS. Iron smelting and related crafts and industries have indelibly marked the countryside around Forges. The village consists largely of squat 18th-century mauve stone houses, formerly the homes of workers in the iron industry. The roadway round the LAKE (which covers about 40 acres) is an agreeable walk.

THE IRON INDUSTRY. Thanks to rich surface deposits of iron ore, Paimpont became the center of a thriving industry, of which many traces remain. In the 15th and 16th centuries a group of blacksmiths specializing in the manufacture of shafted weapons such as spears, pikes and halberds set up in business at Gué Plélan. They sold their goods at Rennes, Vitré and Nantes, and the industry prospered

"THERE WERE WOODCRAFT FOLK IN THE FOREST: LUMBERJACKS, CHARCOAL BURNERS, SMITHS, CLOGMAKERS, BODGERS AND BARK STRIPPERS."

CLAUDE ARZ

The entire forest is a tangle of myth and legend woven around the spirits of the immortals who dwelt there such as King Arthur, the magician Merlin and the fairy Melusine.

THE RUINS OF A BLAST FURNACE
A local society of

until the beginning of the 19th century. Paimpont's forges rivaled the best in Europe, including those of Spain and Sweden. The weaponry they made served both local outlets, supplying tools for farming and nails for building, and furnished the arsenals of Rennes, Brest, Lorient and Nantes.

DECLINE. Around 1820 the town embarked on a huge modernization program, brought about by rapid advances made by the iron and steel industry in England. Rolling mills were installed and two blast furnaces were built. The old foundries were replaced by puddling furnaces fueled by coke imported from England. But despite this costly investment, Paimpont's output eventually proved unable to compete successfully either with English-made goods or with products from northern and eastern France. The factory finally closed in 1884.

LEGENDS OF THE PAIMPONT FOREST

The forest is reputed to be the mythical Brocéliande of Arthurian legend, hence the name of the local hotel, the Relais de Brocéliande. The forest stretches away on both sides of the village of Paimpont, the Basse Forêt to the east and the Haute Forêt to the west. It consists of woodland, copses, heathland and peat bog; there are also a great many lakes and streams. The geological nature of the land is a mixture of green schist, and of red schist many millions of years older. Archeologists have dated the oldest MEGALITHS found in this area to around 3000 BC. An air of romantic mystery, which contrasts strangely with Paimpont's former

enthusiasts devote their spare time to studying the history of the old metallurgic industries at Paimpont. In 1991 excavations at Couedouan en Plélan revealed a group of four primitive furnaces dating from the beginning of the Gallo-Roman period or even earlier.

THE WHEEL
Water flows in over the wheel, making it

CROSS-SECTION OF A BLAST FURNACE after engravings in Diderot and d'Alembert's famous *Encyclopédie*.

revolve and thereby creating a current of air that enters the furnace through huge bellows. This creates a powerful draught, which fans the charcoal fire below.

THE FOUNTAIN OF YOUTH

Beliefs associated with this fountain originate in a Celtic myth which tells how a man might achieve eternal youth by passing through the mirrored surface of the water.

THE GRAIL
A cup such as this was used by Christ at the Last Supper, and caught His blood at the Crucifixion.

importance as a center of the iron industry, pervades the forest; monks came to settle here in search of peace and silence. Finally, and most important of all, Brocéliande is the home of a host of legends: the deeds of King Arthur and his knights, whose wooded sanctuary may have been in this very place.

THE KNIGHTS OF THE ROUND TABLE. Arthur was the illegitimate son of Uther Pendragon, king of the Britons, and Ygerna, wife of the Duke of Cornwall. He was brought up in secret by the magician Merlin and at the age of sixteen, in a tournament attended by all the knights of Britain, Arthur proved the only one capable of pulling the magic sword Excalibur from the stone in which it was firmly fixed. Thanks to this feat he became King, married Guinevere and instituted the brotherhood of the Knights of the Round Table. The table could seat 150 knights, and all who sat round it were equal. The Knights took four vows: loyalty to their lord and master, valor in combat, generosity to the poor and fidelity to their ladies.

THE WIZARD MERLIN AND HIS TOMB. Merlin was the son of a demon and a virtuous maiden, and was saved from diabolic harm through baptism. Thanks to his machinations Uther Pendragon was able to enter Tintagel castle in Cornwall and get the Lady Ygerna with child. Merlin later fell in love with the fairy Vivian, the Lady of the Lake, in the heart of the forest of Brocéliande. She persuaded him to tell her the secret of his magic, and then imprisoned him in a tower of air "within nine circles" in Broceliande. He died in captivity. Early writers on the subject differ on the exact location of the prison, though it was supposed to be closed by two rocks of red schist on which stood an ancient holly tree. The remains of an old *allée couverte* are now known as MERLIN'S TOMB, and at the bottom of the field a sunken lane leads to the FOUNTAIN OF YOUTH.

MERLIN'S TOMB
Some slabs of schist that are the remains of an old *allée couverte* are known as Merlin's tomb. According to legend, the secrets of the magician are also buried here.

CHÂTEAU DE COMPER

AN ANCIENT SETTLEMENT. Not far from the castle are several menhirs, showing that the site was inhabited as far back as the Neolithic period. There is a legend that the Germanic prophet and priestess Velléda once dwelt here, and certainly the site was the stronghold of Salomon, the 9th-century lord of Brittany.

This striking bas relief on the façade of the church of St Léry is an allegory of *Mankind being devoured by his Vices*. The sinner is being stabbed by one of seven monsters symbolizing the Seven Deadly Sins.

STORMY YEARS. Comper became part of a wider history with the barons of Gaël-Montfort: the first of the line, named Raoul, fought with William the Conqueror at Hastings and died in the Holy Land in 1099. From the 13th century onward Comper was considered one of the most important strategic defense points in the region, thanks to its moats carved deep into the red schist and to the five lakes that surrounded it. However, it was ravaged by Bertrand Du Guesclin in 1372, but was rebuilt four years later. The curtain walls date from this period, along with the gatehouse and towers, which are still visible today. In the 16th century François de Coligny d'Andelot, brother of the famous Admiral Coligny and a leader of the Protestant cause, turned the castle into a religious center for the Huguenots but in 1595 it fell into the hands of the League ● *57*. Henri IV started to demolish it in 1598: two of the towers and a curtain wall were destroyed, though the great tower known as the "Gaillard" is still standing. The western section of the domestic quarters was burnt out in 1790 by the Revolutionaries, but was rebuilt in the 19th century. In many ways the legend attached to Comper has proved more enduring than actual fact.

THE LADY OF THE LAKE. Once upon a time long ago a lord by the name of Dymas built this castle by the shore of Lake Comper. His daughter Vivian was born here, a strange girl possessed of supernatural powers who would become the Lady of the Lake. She abducted and brought up the young Launcelot, and when he left her to join the court of King Arthur, Vivian captured the magician Merlin and kept him fast inside "nine magic circles". Merlin remained a prisoner in the gloomy forest of Brocéliande for the rest of his life.

ST-LÉRY

CHURCH OF ST-LÉRY. It was built in the 14th century, probably with some of the stones from the hermitage of Éon de l'Étoile, a monk who crops up frequently in legends and local history. In the chapter house are many 15th- and 16th-century statues; Saint Léry stands with the Duchess Anne (benefactress of the parish), Saint Elocan, Saint Judicaël and Saint Wigrial. A BAS RELIEF on the façade depicts a man being stabbed by one of a group of monsters representing the Seven Deadly Sins. Panels on the south doorway are decorated with 16th-century wooden bas reliefs. Inside the church is an imposing RECUMBENT FIGURE OF SAINT LÉRY, as well as a lovely STAINED-GLASS WINDOW donated by the Duchess Anne: it represents Mary and Joseph and is an allegory of the union of Brittany with France.

THE GREAT LAKE AT COMPER CASTLE Legend holds that this lake is the mirror made to conceal the palace built by Merlin for the Lady Vivian. Known as the Lady of the Lake, she was said to have been born in a castle built on the shore of the lake.

GENEVIÈVE ZAEPPFEL "THE WHITE LADY", known also as "the Druidess" and "the Prophetess of Brocéliande", always dressed in white. She spent her childhood in the old-fashioned manor house at Tertre en Paimpont. Before the war thousands of people would come to listen to this famous clairvoyant, who spoke with conviction about the eternal struggle between the Powers of Light and the Powers of Darkness.

FONTAINE DE BARENTON

"From between the stones bubbles a clear water. Heather, blueberries, soft ferns and sprigs of gorse sprout from the cracks between the mossy stones. The upended slab of an ancient dolmen is nearby. Such is the spring at Barenton."
Ardouin-Dumazet, *Travels in France*

FOLLE PENSÉE

The name comes from an ancient college of Druidical healers who attempted to cure the mentally deranged by administering doses of water from nearby Barenton. It is also the last stop on the way to the spring at Barenton, a popular place for aficionados of the legends of Brocéliande.

FONTAINE DE BARENTON

By the 12th century the reputed wonders of Barenton were already widely known. The medieval French poet Chrétien de Troyes wrote of it in his courtly romance *Yvain, ou le Chevalier au Lion*: "The steps of Barenton, washed by the waters of the spring, have the power to unloose a storm and send down a deluge from the heavens."
THE LORD OF MONTFORT. A charter established in 1467 by the lord of Montfort specified in writing the rights of tenants and peasants with regard to grazing, wood gathering etc, and also gave the lord exclusive rights over the miraculous spring there. Barenton never became officially Christian, though until 1835 it was visited by priests who came to pray for rain in times of drought. Whenever gaseous bubbles appeared at the bottom of the basin the spring was said to be "laughing", and granting wishes made by visitors. A short walk from Barenton leads to the mighty HÊTRE DE PONTHUS, an ancient beech tree associated with one of last legends of the Round Table.

TRÉHORENTEUC

This village, one of the smallest in Brittany, became famous

Windows in the church at Tréhorenteuc tell the story of Saint Onenne, who was saved from a fate worse than death by her geese. On the great window, Joseph of Arimathea is depicted kneeling before Christ.

through one of its priests, Henri Gillard, who transformed the parish church of St-Eutrope into a shrine to the Holy Grail. **THE CHURCH.** "*La porte est dedans*" (the door is within): this esoteric legend carved in the porch would seem to advise visitors that the key to the mysteries of Brocéliande lie inside rather than outside the church. Stained-glass windows tell the story of the life of Saint Onenne, the sister of King Judicaël, who took a vow of poverty and went to live at Tréhorenteuc, where she tended geese. When attacked by some soldiers, her intrepid geese preserved her chastity and poultry of one sort or another are usually to be found on windows dedicated to her. Sometimes they accompany religious processions through the village: they appeared miraculously in front of witnesses in 1957! The windows also tell how Onenne received a kiss from the Virgin after stealing some roses from a garden nearby.

THE MYSTERY OF THE GRAIL. It is uncertain which Grail is celebrated here: it is either the Grail that received the blood of Christ and was brought to Brittany (or perhaps to Britain) from the Holy Land by Joseph of Arimathea, or the ancient Celtic goblet that conferred immortality on those who beheld it. The mysterious cup appears for the first time in the medieval romance by Chrétien de Troyes, though it is an incomplete text and fails to specify the Grail. The Abbé Gillard steered between these two courses, attempting a synthesis of both symbols.

THE VALLEY OF NO RETURN. To reach the *Val sans retour* take the way from the MANOIR DE RUE NEUVE, and allow plenty of time to explore the charms of this delightful spot, the legendary home of Morgan Le Fay. Formerly there were four small lakes in the valley, though the only one to remain is that known as the Fairies' Mirror (*Le Miroir aux Fées*).

TRÉCESSON

Leaving Campénéac in the direction of Rennes, take the left-hand fork toward Paimpont. Just over 1 mile further on a Calvary on the right hand side indicates the road to Trécesson, the most beautiful château in Brocéliande.

THE CHÂTEAU. Trécesson (not open to the public) is surrounded by the rocky crests of Coëtquidan, the Tiot hills and the heath of Saint Jean. Its sheer walls and elegant turrets and corbeling are all reflected in the still waters of its deep moat. The fine entrance once had a drawbridge, though the oldest parts of the château date from the 15th century. In the wars of the League and again during the Revolution, Trécesson was left undisturbed. The château is linked to many tales, the saddest of which is the story of *La Dame Blanche*.

THE WHITE LADY. On a dark night in the 18th century a carriage carrying two gentlemen drew up at the gate. In the approach to the château they buried alive a young woman wearing a wedding dress. A poacher who saw the horrible scene ran to the lord of the manor for help, but when they dug the girl up she was dead. Up until the Revolution her bridal veil and garland were preserved in the chapel of the château, and maidens would come to touch it in the hope of finding a husband.

THE ABBÉ GILLARD When he arrived at Tréhorenteuc in 1942 at the age of forty-one, Gillard devoted his life to restoring the church and breathing new life into the parish. He was struck by the spiritual atmosphere of Brocéliande and its myths, and also attempted to reconcile the Arthurian Legend with the Gospels.

Standing by the water's edge are the ruins of the Moulin de la Vallée, built in the 17th century and demolished in 1938.

Ghosts haunt the Château de Trécesson. The walls exude a mysterious and irresistible scent, that more than once has proved fatal to bees.

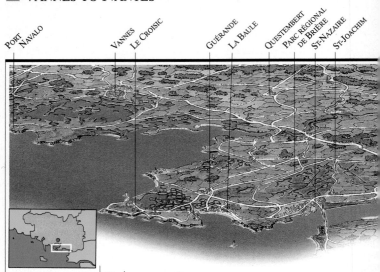

PORT NAVALO · VANNES · LE CROISIC · GUÉRANDE · LA BAULE · QUESTEMBERT · PARC RÉGIONAL DE BRIÈRE · ST-NAZAIRE · ST-JOACHIM

Ground plan of Suscinio castle (12th–15th century), from an engraving made in 1927.

CHÂTEAU DE SUSCINIO ● 84

In the Middle Ages this impressive fortress was one of the favorite residences of the Dukes of Brittany. It has played an important part in the region's turbulent history, and over the centuries its many occupants have made additions and improvements. It is set in a magnificent position on the coast and is one of Brittany's treasures.

THE ORIGINAL MANOR. The name Suscinio appears for the first time on a deed signed by Pierre of Dreux (known as Mauclerc), Duke of Brittany and husband of the Duchess Alix. One of his most illustrious heirs, Arthur III, Earl of Richmond, companion of Joan of Arc and Constable of France, was born here. But before then Suscinio was enlarged by Jean I (Duke of Brittany from 1237 to 1286) and then by Jean II (Duke from 1286 to 1305), who made it his permanent home. Early accounts suggest that he kept a large court, and enjoyed wealth and privilege.

FORTIFICATIONS. After the war of Succession (1341–64), which laid waste to the surrounding countryside and destroyed the chapel at Suscinio, the victorious Monforts, first Jean IV (who reigned from 1365 to 1399) and then Jean V (Duke from 1399 to 1442), transformed the residence into a fortress. In the mid-15th century interest in Suscinio waned. Gradually the fortress

PLEASURES OF THE CHASE
The two stags carved in bas relief above the drawbridge evoke the joys of hunting, one of the main occupations of castle life.

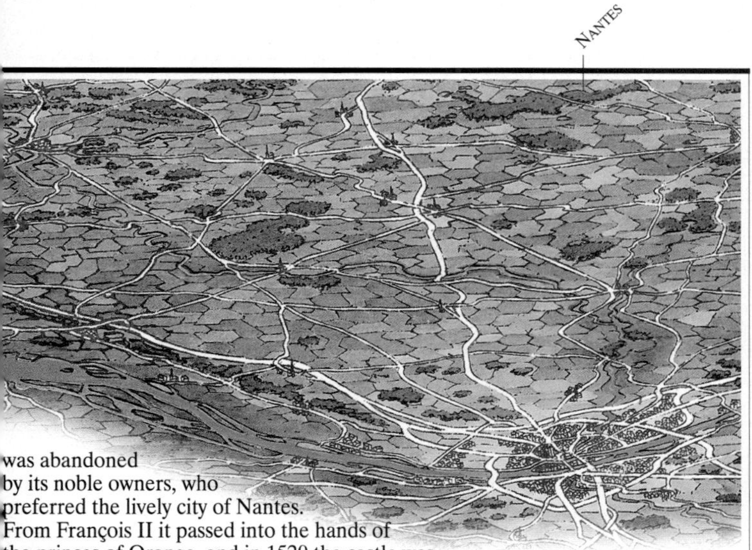

was abandoned
by its noble owners, who
preferred the lively city of Nantes.
From François II it passed into the hands of
the princes of Orange, and in 1520 the castle was
confiscated by the French Crown. As a military stronghold
it sustained substantial damage during the Revolution.
Eventually it was bought by a tradesman who sold the stones
for building material. Today, this once-noble building has lost
much of its dignity.

RESTORATION. At the instigation of Prosper Mérimée, the
famous Inspector of Historical Monuments,   the castle
passed into state ownership in 1840.   In recent
years and with state aid, it has undergone
thorough and meticulous restoration.
In the course of this work, a
remarkable feature was uncovered
near the moat on the south side.
It was a huge mosaic floor, made
up of 33,000 glazed tiles, that
was laid down around 1330.

**A VICTORIOUS
ONSLAUGHT**
The awesome size
and strength of the
fortress failed to
deter various
ambitious attackers in
the course of
Brittany's turbulent
history ● 53. In 1373
the brave knight Du
Guesclin seized the
castle and put to the
sword its English
garrison.

"CAESAR'S HILL"
The tumulus of Tumiac owes its nickname to a tradition that from its summit (top, the view from the hill) Julius Caesar watched the naval engagement that secured victory for the Roman fleet over the Veneti in 56 BC ▲ 342.

VENETI DAGGER

This bronze sheath for a dagger may have belonged to a local chieftain. It was found at Quiberon ▲ 334 and dates from around the 4th century BC.

FOGEO BEACH AT ARZON
In the protected area of Kerjouanno, which is lined with dunes ■ 26, is this superb beach. Along with Kervert, it is one of the finest on the Rhuys peninsula.

MUSEUM OF BRETON HISTORY. Virtually all of the castle, including the outer walls, the six towers and the inner courtyard can be explored by the public. The Musée d'Histoire de la Bretagne, which opened in 1986, is in the state apartments. Exhibits include the mosaics discovered during restoration as well as a bas relief of 1892 entitled *The Constable Olivier de Clisson on Horseback*. The room devoted to the pardon festivities ● 70 reflects the 19th-century obsession with traditional peasant ritual: the strong religious fervor attracted travelers, writers and artists to Brittany. A classic example of this fascination with folk origins is Camille Chazal's large oil-painting *During Vespers, at the Pardon in Notre Dame de la Cour en Lantic* (1873).

TUMULUS OF TUMIAC ● 80

The great tumulus is 66 feet high, has a circumference of almost 1000 feet and is 138 feet in diameter. It has three distinct layers. Mud was laid upon a base of granite shale, which was in turn covered with a coating of earth that tapers away toward the top. When local archeologists excavated the tumulus in 1853, they discovered a burial chamber with carved walls; it contained quantities of highly polished ax-heads and pendants made of precious stones. These are now in the museums at Carnac ▲ 335 and Vannes ▲ 345.
THE VENETI. The tribe after whom the city of Vannes ▲ 342 is named was one of five to colonize Brittany during the millennium preceding the Christian era. They were Celts, who settled the lands and respected local customs, leaving the megaliths untouched and generally integrating quite comfortably with the local population. They were soon skilled craftsmen and were adept in trade, though they had no written language. They were also good farmers, and excelled in the art of making jewelry. In his account of the *Gallic Wars*, Julius Caesar commended their seafaring skill; they built sturdy, fast and sizeable ships with oak hulls and leather sails. They were the first people in Armorica to mint coins. Many of these pieces, made of 18-carat gold, were inspired by the gold staters minted by Philip II of Macedonia (father of Alexander the Great), showing a man with hair depicted in stylized fashion in profile facing to the right. The reverse depicts a horse with a human head being driven by a charioteer.
DEFEAT. In 56 BC, on the pretext of the Veneti's failure to deliver a shipment of corn, the Romans attacked them, launching a seaborne strike as the terrain seemed ill-suited to a land battle. The Celtic sailing ships proved no match for the man-powered Roman galleys, which were lighter and more maneuverable. It is rumored that the decisive battle that confirmed the Roman dominance of Armorica was fought in the Gulf of Morbihan.

ST-GILDAS-DE-RHUYS

The village is the religious capital of the peninsula. It is named after Saint Gildas, a 6th-century monk from Clydeside, Scotland, who is said to have founded the monastery here.

ABELARD. The monastery's most famous abbot was the great theologian Peter Abelard (1079–1142), originally a teacher in the cathedral school at Notre-Dame in Paris. He fell in love with the beautiful seventeen-year-old Héloïse and eloped with her to Brittany, where they were secretly married and where she bore him a son. The girl's outraged uncle, Canon Fulbert of Notre-Dame, caused Abelard to be emasculated, after which he led an unsettled life for a number of years. Ten of these were spent at St-Gildas, of which he wrote to Héloïse: "I live in a land of barbarians whose very language is abhorrent to me: everyone I have to deal with is primitive and brutal. The walks I take are beside a wild, tempestuous sea. The one rule that the monks have here is to have no rules at all. Their doors are decorated with the feet of deer and wolves, and hung with the horrible skins of owls." He left in 1132, and died ten years later on the way to Rome. When Héloïse died in 1164, her remains were laid beside his.

THE ABBEY CHURCH AND ITS TREASURE. The part of the church that houses the sepulchre of Saint Gildas is a rare example of Romanesque architecture in Brittany. The sacristy contains one of the most precious religious treasures in the region: a 16th-century silver-gilt reliquary in the form of a cross ornamented with four emeralds and with winged angels' heads at the ends of the branches. There is also a large casket in chased silver.

COASTAL PATH. It begins at the beach in Port-Maria and finishes less than a mile away at Grand Mont. On a clear day there are views from the Pointe du Croisic to Carnac and Quiberon.

MUZILLAC

PEN MUR PARK. The park is wooded and well tended, and has a fine lake and a mill. It opened in 1962.

PEN MUR MILL. The old mill was converted for traditional paper-milling for the production of traditional hand-crafted paper. It is a living museum, where the actual tools, machines and techniques of the 18th century are used to produce a fine rag paper, which is also on sale here.

PORT-NAVALO
This pretty resort is also a popular mooring for pleasure craft. Perched at the end of the Rhuys peninsula opposite the Pointe de Kerpenhir ▲ *338*, it guards the entrance to the Gulf of Morbihan. Close by the lighthouse, the treacherous currents for which this spot is notorious can easily be seen.

LAKE OF PEN MUR
Long ago a castle stood on the shore of the lake, though all traces of it have vanished. It guarded the road from Nantes to Brest. In 1815 a latter-day company of Chouans ● *62* fought a famous engagement here, celebrated by writer René Bazin in his *Magnificat*.

ST-JOACHIM
An aerial view (above) clearly shows the isolation of this unusual community. Protected by dykes, the inhabitants live round the edges of the little islands. The area in the center is reserved for growing crops.

LE GUERNO

By the 12th century the village was already a halting place for pilgrims on the road to the tomb of Saint James the Apostle at Compostela, in Spain. The village square, with its lovingly restored old houses, is exceptionally pretty.

CHURCH OF NOTRE-DAME. The 16th-century parish church was for many years the property of the Knights Templar and is known locally as the "Templars' Chapel" or sometimes as the "Pepper-pot". The nickname "Pepper-pot" derives from an unusual open-air pulpit, built for use when the number of pilgrims was too great to be accommodated at Mass within the church.

DOMAINE DE BRANFÉRÉ

This is a zoo and botanical garden set in some 80 acres, with six lakes and an elegant 17th-century castle restored in the last century. There are almost two thousand animals in the zoo, some of which are extremely rare and have been brought here and carefully acclimatized to help save them from extinction. Several exotic trees were brought back from abroad and planted here in the 18th century.

GRANDE BRIÈRE REGIONAL NATURE RESERVE

HISTORY. Covering 50,000 acres, this is the largest stretch of marshland in France after the Camargue. It can be divided roughly into two parts: the Donges marsh in the east, with some 20,000 acres of private grazing land; and the GRANDE BRIÈRE MOTIÈRE, another 20,000 acres of continuous swampland that is the communal property of its twenty-one villages, which have joint grazing, turf-cutting, reed gathering, hunting and fishing rights. The earliest documents relating to the region are some letters patent signed by Duke François II of Brittany, dated August 8, 1461. Some later documents of a similar nature dated January 8, 1784 and signed by Louis XVI officially make over the region of La Brière to its inhabitants. During the Revolution the government issued two further decrees confirming this arrangement.

EEL FISHING
A square dipping-net slung between two poles (above) and a fishgig (right) are two essential tools of a Breton eel fisher's trade. When he catches an eel, he pops it into a little box that serves him as a creel.

A SECRET LAND. Over the centuries people have eked out a living for themselves by tending this difficult land and exploiting it to the utmost through hunting and fishing, cutting peat for fuel and reeds for thatch and, most importantly, grazing flocks of sheep, for marshland makes excellent pasture. It would take a lifetime to understand this vast and secret landscape where every little village has its own special character and hidden charm. The marsh is perhaps most beautiful at sunrise, when it is streaked with mist, with flights of teal scurrying across the sky and heron standing

patiently among the wild iris. The area became an official nature reserve in 1970.

RANROUET

A MARSHLAND STRONGHOLD. Ranrouet, a little over a mile northeast of Herbignac, is the last of the feudal castles on the edge of the Brière. Though the oldest surviving parts of it are 13th-century, most of the fabric dates from the 14th and 15th centuries. Standing ominously at the gateway to the Guérande peninsula ▲ *368*, the castle was demolished in 1616 at the request of the Breton parliament, at the same time as the castle of Guérande. It suffered again under the Revolution, but in recent years a group of enthusiasts have started excavations and restoration work.

ST-JOACHIM

This community, at the very heart of the Brière marshes, is an archipelago of granite islands, each with its own village: Aignac, Ménac, Bais, Pandille, Brécun, Mazin and Fédrun. Fédrun is the largest and most visited of the group. Bridges span the canals that surround each settlement, and each of the islands has its own distinct character. The islands are the only available building land, as well as the only ground suitable for cultivation, which is why the houses are grouped together inside the narrow belt of land between the canal and the road that rings round the island. The population density has led to the construction of houses at right angles to the road, each family then also having access to the canal behind, where their barge is moored.

ISLAND OF FÉDRUN ★

Whereas the Briérons once lived exclusively on what could be eaten or sold from the encircling marshes, in recent years a valiant attempt has been made to exploit the Brière as a tourist region and revive its special traditions. There is a TOURIST OFFICE in the center of the island, and two houses, the MAISON DE LA MARIÉE and the CHAUMIÈRE BRIÉRONNE, have been opened to the public. The latter is a typical traditional dwelling, with a thatched roof, limewashed walls and a rustic double door, while inside is a single low-ceilinged room with stairs to the hayloft above. The marsh has lost much of its economic importance to the community.

A CASTLE BY A FORD?
Two ancient Gallic words, *ran*, meaning "land" or "fief", and *rouet*, meaning "ford", may explain the name of the castle in topographical terms.

Thatching a cottage in the Grande Brière.

367

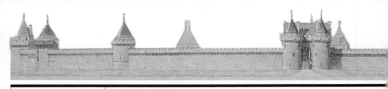

THE RAMPARTS OF GUÉRANDE
A watercolor dated 1878 shows exactly why the town is known as the "Carcassonne of the West".

GUÉRANDE PENINSULA.

Geographically, historically and socially, this little region is an entity in itself, with the fortified town of Guérande as its economic, religious and administrative center. A number of archeological sites, such as Gallic farms and villages, and Gallo-Roman villas, have come to light around the town and prove the importance of Guérande in the surrounding region.

GUÉRANDE AND ITS RAMPARTS. The town was originally defended only by ancient earthen walls. In 1343, after it had been sacked in the Hundred Years' War, the father of Duc Jean IV de Montfort surrounded it with ramparts. Set with ten towers and with gates at the four cardinal points (the VANNETAISE, ST-MICHEL, DE SAILLÉ and BIZIENNE GATES), they are a classic example of medieval Breton military architecture. The distance around them is over a mile. A stretch of moat, running from the Tour Théologale to the Porte Bizienne, still remains, and gives a good idea of what the town looked like in the 14th century.

INSIDE THE WALLS. The so-called *"ville close"* has numerous MEDIEVAL STREETS (Rue St-Esprit, Rue Vannetaise, Rue de Bizienne, Rue du Tricot and Rue Ste-Catherine), many lined with overhanging half-timbered houses that have decorative gables. In the Rue du Pilori are the chapel of Notre-Dame la Blanche and the collegiate church of St-Aubin, a beautiful combination of Romanesque and Flamboyant Gothic, and with a remarkable OPEN-AIR PULPIT.

TRAWLING
The trawl is a net that is dragged along behind a fishing boat. There are two kinds, one that trawls the bottom of the sea, and the "pelagic"

LA TURBALLE

In the 18th century La Turballe was a hamlet of just fifteen houses, battered by the wind and with anchorage for a few sardine boats. There must have been an inn here once, for the name of the hamlet comes from the old French word *triballe*, a wineshop where drinkers took their refreshment standing up.

trawl, which floats much nearer the surface. The bottom trawl catches the kind of fish, such as whiting, hake, red mullet and sole, that is auctioned in the market at La Turballe (above). The pelagic trawl has a wider mouth and catches mainly herring, mackerel, sardines and anchovies.

A MAJOR PORT. The sudden expansion of La Turballe in the 19th century was due to the development of the sardine-fishing industry, which spread along the Brittany coast from the ports of the Vendée. The fish were sent to Nantes in baskets, laid out in neat rows upon layers of fern and covered with salt. In 1824 a local businessman named FRANÇOIS DEFFES opened the first cannery in Nantes: others soon followed, resulting in a greatly expanded sardine market and bringing prosperity to the region. At first the fishing was confined to inshore waters, the fishermen using

a mixture of cod's roe, flour and crushed offcuts of fish as bait. The industry expanded further after World War Two, when trawlers and mackerel boats were brought in. Now, far outstripping Le Croisic in importance, La Turballe has become the leading fishing port of the Loire-Atlantique region.

BATZ-SUR-MER

From the 9th to the 17th centuries the region owed its prosperity to the trade in salt collected from the marshes. **THE SALTMARSH MUSEUM.** Through audio-visual displays, the museum tells the story of life on the saltmarshes, including its technology (salt works and the salt-workers' tools), local life (domestic furniture and other artefacts) and traditional costumes. From April to September there are also organized trips focusing on the flora and fauna of the Blanc Pays region. The salt industry on the peninsula goes back to Roman times, though it was only at the instigation of the Dukes of Brittany in the 15th century that it became economically important. After Brittany became part of the kingdom of France it remained one of the provinces to be exempt from salt tax: when this privilege was taken away in 1789, the industry went into decline.

LE CROISIC

HISTORY. For some time after the fall of the Roman Empire, the region was plagued by Norsemen, who found it a convenient place to provision themselves with salt. In the Middle Ages, Le Croisic was the most important town for the export of salt to Spain, England, the Low Countries and Scandinavia. By the 15th century the little town was a busy harbor, with ships sailing to points far and wide, and a growing population, which resulted in the construction of grand civic buildings and fine houses.
SEA BATHING. Le Croisic was one of the first places to be a seaside resort in the 19th century. Doctors recommended its virtues to their affluent patients, among whom was the successful poet and dramatist Alfred de Musset.
THE HARBOR. The quays are lined with some beautiful old houses. The HÔTEL D'AIGUILLON (town hall) contains an excellent maritime museum. The recently opened OCEARIUM boasts more than five thousand species of shellfish, corals and invertebrates, along with species of fish to be found along the coastline.

SALT WOMEN
The banks of the marshland pools where salt was gathered often proved too soft for wheeling barrows up to the water's edge to collect the salt. Instead women would fill these pots, which they carried on their heads.

Batz and Le Croisic seen from the walls of Guérande, a 19th-century view painted on the lid of a harpsichord.

The casino
at La Baule.

LA BAULE

AN EARLY RESORT. With the arrival of the railroad in 1879 as near as Escoublac, the town was quick to exploit its potential as a holiday resort. That same year the Count of Hennecart and Édouard Darlu formed a company and employed

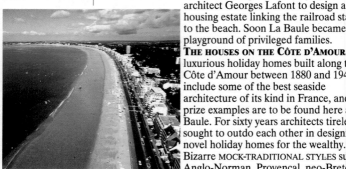

architect Georges Lafont to design a housing estate linking the railroad station to the beach. Soon La Baule became the playground of privileged families.

THE HOUSES ON THE CÔTE D'AMOUR. The luxurious holiday homes built along the Côte d'Amour between 1880 and 1940 include some of the best seaside architecture of its kind in France, and prize examples are to be found here at La Baule. For sixty years architects tirelessly sought to outdo each other in designing novel holiday homes for the wealthy. Bizarre MOCK-TRADITIONAL STYLES such as Anglo-Norman, Provençal, neo-Breton

and Basque produced a host of delightful fantasies. Small-scale Anglo-Norman cottages, which became the fashion at the turn of the century, were half-timbered, with bow windows, verandas and gables. Villas were decorated with mosaics and stained glass, and ornamented further with Art Nouveau and Art Deco motifs.

ST-NAZAIRE

THE ATLANTIC DOCKYARDS. The dockyards go back to the 19th century. The first ship to be built here was the *Empress Eugénie*, in 1864. Vessels of all kinds are built here: cargo boats, warships such as the battleship *Jean Bart*, and some famous liners, among them the *Lafayette*, *Paris*, *Champlain*, *De Grasse*, and the great *Normandie* (launched in October 1932) and the *France* (May 1960).

A GIGANTIC OUTPUT. A total of almost 600 ships, among them 108 passenger vessels, 100 oil tankers, 42 sailing ships, 13 battleships, 11 gas tankers, 10 submarines, 3 aircraft carriers and 23 container ships, have been built in the dockyards. The Penhoët shipyards on the north bank of the estuary have also expanded. The 12 acres of coastline they covered in 1862 had increased to 60 by 1910 and doubled again by 1939. Today they cover a total of 300 acres. The size of the workforce shows a different curve: there were less than 2,000 employees in 1864, 6,000 in 1900 and 8,000 in 1955, but that number is

now reduced to 4,500. Competition has forced the yards into the high-technology sector, building methane tankers and oil rigs. They have also produced luxury liners for the Royal Caribbean Cruise Line.

NANTES

CHEMIN DE FER DE PARIS A ORLEANS

CHÂTEAU DE NANTES
(LE GRAND LOGIS)

A MARITIME CITY
Nantes was originally a settlement on a river spanned by a bridge linking Armorica to France. It developed into a

harbor town that looked resolutely out to the Atlantic. Its strategic position is such that it has never been a city to refuse a challenge.

HISTORY

A STRATEGIC POSITION. Nantes' strategically located site consists of a pattern of islands at the confluence of the Loire and its tributaries the Erdre and the Sèvre Nantaise. Under Julius Caesar it was a mere village but by the 4th century it had become a fortified harbor settlement. In the reign of Charlemagne it was a bastion against Breton invasion until it was captured by Nominoë and made part of Brittany. In 843 the Norsemen sailed upriver and took the town, which they held until 936, when they were conquered by Alain Barbetorte. The city grew with the flourishing trade in corn, Guérande salt and wines from the Loire. Brittany became a province of France in 1532, though during the wars of religion Nantes sided with the League. In 1598 the famous Edict of Nantes was signed here by Henri IV.

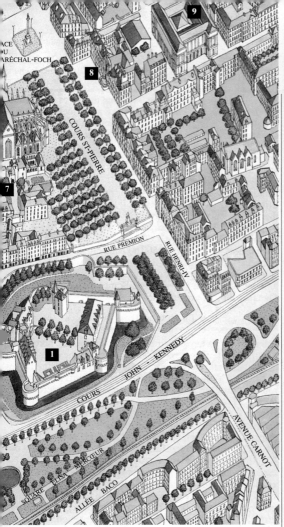

MERCANTILE EXPANSION. In the 17th century Nantes took up international trade on a large scale, for a while rivaling the great ports of Bordeaux and St-Malo. International commerce led in turn to the establishment of naval dockyards and the import of cloth from the East Indies. Nantes also became the center of the French trade in black slaves.

URBAN GROWTH. The profits that busy trade links with Africa, the Americas and the rest of Europe brought to Nantes financed building work in the city. In the 18th century great architectural projects, such as the development of the Île Feydeau (the Négociant district), the construction of the docks, the canalization of the Erdre, the laying out of the Cours St-Pierre and Cours St-André, and the building of the Graslin district, were completed.

RECENT TIMES. Nantes has always been a progressive city, and when Revolution came, it sided with the Republicans. It held out against the counter-revolution of the Vendéens, but its citizens suffered much under the bloody "rule" of Jean-Baptiste Carrier during the Terror. The city's importance waned in the early 19th century with the abolition of the slave trade, the silting up of the Loire and the Continental blockade imposed

INDUSTRIAL GROWTH
Industry expanded rapidly in Nantes at the beginning of the 19th century. Below, the Bergelin brewery.

TREASURES OF THE CASTLE MUSEUM
Right, three designs featuring exotic
animals printed on cloth imported from the
East Indies. The painted wooden figure of a
Chinese mandarin is a figurehead from the
prow of an English merchantman.

The final plan of
Nantes castle (right)
was laid down by
Fournier in 1700.

DRAWBRIDGE
The main entrance to
the castle is between
the Tour du Pied de
Biche and the Tour de
la Boulangerie.

CARDINAL DE RETZ
Jean-François Paul de
Gondi (1614–79),
Cardinal de Retz, was
Archbishop of Paris
when he was
imprisoned here for
his part in the
"Fronde" uprising
against Cardinal
Mazarin. But he soon
escaped and spent
several years
wandering Europe
before Louis XIV
restored him to favor.
Right, a lithograph of
the castle, and the
new railroad, as they
appeared in 1865.

by England. But matters soon improved thanks to industrial
development in areas linked to Nantes' maritime success,
such as sugar refineries, biscuit factories and shipyards for
construction and repair work. In World War Two Nantes
received the distinction of being
made a Compagnon de la Libéra-
ation in recognition of the sacrifice
of fifty hostages and for the
bombardment sustained in 1943.

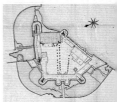

THE PRESENT DAY. Since the war
there has been a marked growth in
population: taking into account its
nearby port of St-Nazaire ▲ *370,*
Nantes now has more than 500,000 inhabitants. From having
been one of the capitals of Brittany, Nantes is now the
préfecture of the Pays de Loire region. Its position at the very
junction of western and southern France makes it much more
than just another provincial city.

CASTLE OF THE DUKES OF BRITTANY

Henri IV first set eyes on the castle when he came here to
sign the Edict of Nantes. "By all the powers!" he exclaimed,
"They're no mean companions our blessed cousins the Dukes
of Brittany!" With its massive walls, battlements and huge
round towers, the ancient ducal fortress, once bordered by the
Loire, has retained its grim appearance.

HISTORY. When Nantes first became a capital city in 937, the
Counts and then the Dukes of Brittany embarked on the
construction of a defensive stronghold. It became a castle in
the 13th century and was further fortified by Duc Jean IV de
Montfort, who added the surrounding towers. In 1440 the
castle was the scene of the trial of Gilles de Rais, marshal of
France, companion-in-arms of Joan of Arc and murderer of
hundreds of children, who was hanged in the city for his
crimes. Duchess Anne of Brittany was born here on January
26, 1477: the present castle dates from this period. Bonnie
Prince Charlie stayed here too while
preparing for his invasion of England
in 1745. In 1800 the

374

powder store in the Tour des Espagnols blew up, destroying the chapel, the archive room and the northwest wing. The castle was acquired by the city in 1915.

TOUR OF THE CASTLE. The building's double function of fortress and palace is immediately apparent. Its forbidding towers and granite walls are in strong contrast to the carved limestone of the residential apartments. The castle's defenses are best seen from outside: the TOUR DU PIED-DE-BICHE, TOUR DE LA BOULANGERIE, TOUR DU PORT, TOUR DE LA RIVIÈRE, the huge TOUR DU FER-À-CHEVAL, and the HALF-BASTION OF ST-PIERRE, all of which (with the exception of the last) date from the 15th century. Beyond the DRAWBRIDGE is the courtyard, containing a WELL with an iron superstructure that represents a seven-pointed star when reflected in the water below. Of the buildings put up in the reign of François II, only the left-hand part of the GREAT GOVERNMENTAL HALL and the lower floors of the state apartments remain. The KING'S RESIDENCE, a small Renaissance building, was visited by all the kings of France from François I (who built it) to Louis XIV. After the renovation visitors will be able to access all the covered ways and view the defensive side of the building and its urban environment.

CASTLE MUSEUMS

The renovation of the castle and the restructuring of its museums is a twelve-year program. The latter, which began several years ago, will focus on the history of Nantes and its surrounds from the time of the castle's construction to the present: the castle of François II and Anne of Brittany (museum of Nantes and its surrounds) will be organized around temporary exhibitions in the Harness Room, the Old Dungeon and the Conciergerie; permanent exhibition rooms devoted to the archeological and factual history of the castle will be opened in the Tour du Fer-à-Cheval; the drawbridge, destroyed in the 19th century, will be reconstructed and the former Loire postern restored; a library/documentation-center will be set up in the Conciergerie, and large reception facilities created on the ground floor of the King's Residence and the Grand Government building.

THE INDIAN VOGUE
In the mid-17th century printed fabrics imported from the East Indies became all the rage in France, where they were swiftly imitated. But the protectionism prevalent at the time forbade their import and their manufacture in 1686. The ban was lifted in 1759, and Nantes became the center of the trade in *"indiennerie"* since it already possessed all the infrastructure necessary for manufacturing the goods. Weaving the fabrics, which were decorated with exotic or nautical patterns, developed into a substantial industry.

Jean-qui-rit and *Jean-qui-pleure*, grotesque faces on the house at no. 12, Place du Pilori.

CONFECTIONERY, A NANTES SPECIALTY Chez Bohu sells its famous "*rigolettes*", pieces of fruit-flavored candy wrapped in paper. Humbugs are another favorite: eccentrically shaped lumps of barley sugar come in all kinds of flavors (though peppermint is perennially popular) and in all colors of the rainbow.

The west front of the cathedral of St-Peter and St-Paul. When the castle arsenal blew up in 1800, the blast shattered the beautiful stained glass.

AROUND THE CASTLE

PLACE DU PILORI ★. The square, formerly known as the PLACE DU PUITS LORY, was rebuilt in 1740 and is lined with a number of fine 18th-century houses. Masks on the house at no. 12 have earned it the name JEAN-QUI-RIT ET JEAN-QUI-PLEURE (Laughing Johnny and Weeping Johnny). Opposite, a building dating from 1732 is decorated with a figure of Neptune.

STE-CROIX DISTRICT. The area around the church of Ste-Croix is an historic and attractive maze of streets such as the RUE STE-CROIX, RUE DE LA BÂCLERIE, RUE DE L'ÉMERY and RUE DE LA JUIVERIE. The last of these was named in memory of the terrible massacre of the Jews following the ducal edict ordering their expulsion in 1240. In later years the Jews of Nantes lived in a ghetto in this street, which was securely locked up at each end each night. There is a beautiful timber-framed house at no. 9, and no. 11 is decorated with unusual bas reliefs.

AROUND THE PLACE DU BOUFFAY. The 10th-century castle of the Counts of Brittany later became the judicial headquarters of the city. The seneschal's court sat here after 1477, and the Revolutionary tribunal from 1793. The castle, demolished in 1843, had a bell tower that is now situated on the church of Ste-Croix.

CHURCH OF STE-CROIX. The church of the Holy Cross built on the site of the castle chapel. It has a classical façade and some interesting 17th-century statuary inside. Its name perpetuates the memory of those who left the city to take part in the First Crusade.

There are also some lovely HALF-TIMBERED HOUSES in the Rue Bossuet, Rue de la Bléterie, Rue des Carmes, Rue de Verdun, Rue de la Juiverie and Rue de la Bâclerie, and others in interior courtyards.

CATHEDRAL

HISTORY. Dignity and grace are the dominant features of this superb cathedral, that is dedicated to SAINT PETER and SAINT PAUL. The present building was by no means the first cathedral in Nantes, however. A cathedral was originally built near the ramparts on the site of an early primitive church, which had been consecrated by Saint Felix, the 6th-century Bishop of Nantes. It was destroyed in the course of Norman assaults on the city, and a Romanesque cathedral was rebuilt on the same site in the 11th century. This was largely destroyed by fire, though the east end survived until the building of a Gothic cathedral, once again in the same place. The foundation stone of the latter was laid by Duke Jean V of Brittany in 1434: the west entrance was the first section to be built. But work progressed slowly, and the cathedral was not finished until 1891, 457 years later!

TOUR OF THE CATHEDRAL. In spite of vandalism during the Revolution, as well as heavy restoration and the bombing of 1943, the west façade, with its two high square towers and five doorways (two of them set at right angles), is still an awesome sight. The CENTRAL DOORWAY, formerly dedicated to the Virgin, has three arches on which are represented the Resurrection of the Dead, Heaven, and Hell. At the foot of the south tower is a badly damaged OPEN-AIR PULPIT. Inside, the tracery in the 15th-century CENTRAL NAVE (which was vaulted in the early 17th century), runs right up to the intersecting ribs: the keystones are higher than those of Notre-Dame in Paris, which is earlier than Nantes cathedral. The 16th-century open-work TRIFORIUM, which runs the length of the nave above the arches, is outstandingly beautiful: illuminated from outside, it throws a soft indirect light into the nave. The vestibule (pronaos) contains an ORGAN LOFT that was built in the 17th century and a fine organ, which was altered at a later date. Here too can be seen the traces of the great window commissioned by the Duchess Anne in 1499. The neo-Gothic chancel was built along 15th-century lines and, like the ambulatory chapels, is lit by modern stained-glass windows, the work of JEAN LE MOAL and ANNE LE CHEVALIER. At the entrance to the ambulatory a staircase leads to two crypts. The 11th-century Romanesque CRYPT houses the cathedral treasure. The second, which leads off the first, is known as the BISHOPS' CRYPT. Beneath the chancel is another crypt housing a permanent exhibition of the cathedral's history.

TOMB OF FRANÇOIS II AND MARGUERITE DE FOIX. The Duchess Anne commissioned Michel Colombe to design the tomb for the bodies of her parents. It was built in the 16th century and was intended for the Carmelite church. After the Revolution it was moved to the cathedral. The monument looks back to the medieval tradition, with

THE FIRE OF 1972
That year, just when the restoration of the cathedral was nearing completion, a huge fire engulfed the nave, devastating the roof and the vaulting. The building was painstakingly restored again.

Details of the entrance.

TOMB OF FRANÇOIS II
"This monument is one of the most brilliant works of the French Renaissance . . . A great table of black marble supports the reclining figures of the duke and duchess, who lie there peacefully and majestically, in their robes and crowns."
Henry James,
A Little Tour in France

"LA PSALLETTE"
This fine 15th-century building stands at the end of the Impasse St-Laurent. It has an elegant square tower, a projecting turret at the corner, and a beautiful spiral staircase.

mourners attending the recumbent figures, but the style is firmly Renaissance; it incorporates motifs taken from antiquity, with Italianate angels at each corner and niches carved in false perspective. The black, white and rose-colored marble of the latter create a particularly striking effect. The faces were originally painted, and highlighted with gold.

FINE ARTS MUSEUM

This is one of fifteen provincial museums founded in 1801 by consular decree. Along with various state bequests, the museum was fortunate to receive the CACAULT COLLECTION in 1810. The collection was assembled in Italy by a diplomat and native of Nantes at the end of the 18th century, and consists mainly of Italian Old Masters and works by Georges de La Tour. The museum also has many 19th-century pictures, some of them state bequests and others purchased by the city,

including works by Delacroix, Ingres, Corot and Courbet. The museum's collection of 20th-century art is particularly well known, and contains paintings by Monet, Gustave Doré, Signac, Kandinsky, Sonia Delaunay and Max Ernst. The entire museum presents a comprehensive overview of western art from the 13th century to the present day.

BOTANICAL GARDEN

The Jardin des Plantes is behind the railroad station, near the Lycée Clémenceau. It was laid out as a park in the English style and was opened to the public in 1865. The authorities here are proud of their long-established camellias and magnolias: some of the latter are nearly two hundred years old. In the elaborately designed greenhouses are numerous rare plants; it was not uncommon for sailors returning from the tropics to bring specimens of exotic plants back with them. The PALMARIUM (1895) is one of the garden's chief attractions; it is a greenhouse of immense proportions planted with trees and other vegetation to form a virtual South American rain forest in miniature.

PLACE VIARME

FINE ARTS MUSEUM
The collection housed here includes many well-known pictures. Above, *Madame de Sennones* (1814) by Jean-Dominique Ingres, and *The Hurdy-Gurdy Player* by Georges de La Tour.

When the Revolution broke out in 1789, ninety percent of the French population were peasants. In the Vendée the latter were persuaded by the nobles (who depended on the peasants for their feudal dues) to condemn the new government, whose edicts included the proscription of 80 percent of the clergy. Worse was to come, when in February 1793 conscription threatened the welfare of countless thousands of families all over France. The Vendée (consisting of a large part of the Maine et Loire province and the northern part of the Deux Sèvres) rebelled. Nantes was attacked by the Vendéens on June 28 and 29, 1793. The assailants were eventually repulsed

Left, the Great Conservatory in the Botanical Garden, drawn in 1895. Below, a lithograph depicting *The Execution of Charette* (1796).

and this was the first significant defeat for the "Blancs", as the rebels were known. after the battle their leader Cathelineau fell mortally wounded in the Place Viarme. That October the new governor, Jean-Baptiste Carrier, arrived from Paris committed to purging the region of all anti-revolutionary sentiment. Nantes became a vision of hell: up to fourteen thousand prisoners were executed, many of them in a variety of cruel ways devised by the people's representative himself. Carrier was recalled to Paris in February 1794, and was guillotined not long afterward.

CHARETTE, THE REBEL LEADER. By 1795 the Republic was working hard on a policy of appeasement and was planning to sign a peace treaty at La Jaunaie, near Nantes, with the elusive Vendéen chief François de Charette. But when he learned of the death of the boy-king Louis XVII in the Temple in Paris, Charette renewed his guerrilla warfare in the Retz region and the Vendée marshland. Hunted down by Republican troops and wounded in a skirmish, Charette was taken prisoner on March 23, 1796. He was tried at Nantes and shot on March 29 in the Place Viarme.

A DECISIVE SETBACK
When royalist forces came to seize Nantes, the death of their leader Cathelineau brought them up short, to the relief of the Republican army. Henceforth Nantes remained a bastion that prevented the Breton Chouans ● *62* from joining up with the Vendéens of Anjou.

GRASLIN DISTRICT

ARTISTIC LIFE. Wealthy entrepreneur Jean-Joseph-Louis Graslin spent his fortune building and developing this quarter. He built the theater, the quaintly shaped PLACE ROYALE, and the PLACE GRASLIN, which was designed to resemble a theater auditorium. Mathurin Crucy undertook much of this work, and two centuries later the Graslin district is still the cultural center of Nantes. Famous English agricultural writer Arthur Young was one of the first to praise the theater, which opened in 1788, while novelist Stendhal compared the new theaters favorably with those in Paris.

PLACE ROYALE. The square was designed by Mathurin Crucy in the late 1900's and represents the emergence of the new urban landscape envisaged by Graslin, from the traditional architecture of the old city. The MONUMENTAL FOUNTAIN in the center is by architect Henri Driollet, and the STATUES are by the 19th-century sculptor Ducommun de Locle.

RUE CRÉBILLON. This busy commercial street, now largely pedestrianized, is a favorite walk of the Nantais.

PLACE GRASLIN AND THE THEATER. Crucy loved the neo-classical style, of which this is a particularly fine example. The square is rectangular with a semicircle added at one end, opposite the THEATER. Its austere façade is fronted by

The auditorium of the Théâtre Graslin, where many great singers performed.

A NEW DEVELOPMENT
Nantes commissioned architect Mathurin Crucy to develop the immense site acquired by entrepreneur Graslin. Below, the Place Graslin and the theater.

LA CIGALE

"LA CIGALE"
In the midst of an area of restrained neo-classical architecture stands the famous late 19th-century brasserie whose exuberant décor includes some beautiful Italian mosaics.

A TOWN WITHIN A TOWN
In the Passage Pommeraye there are three galleries: the

Galerie Santeuil, the Galerie des Statues and the Galerie de la Fosse. Its sixty-six luxury boutiques made it a "temple of commerce" in the 19th century.

eight Corinthian columns, above which are eight Muses clad in classical drapery.

COURS CAMBRONNE. Mathurin Crucy conceived the design for this delightful urban garden, which is protected at either end by elegant iron grilles. It is often compared to the Palais Royal in Paris, whose reconstruction by the Duc d'Orléans is roughly contemporary with the Cours in Nantes. Its precise architectural unity, with identical façades decorated with pilasters and carved stone balustrades, presents a pleasing and harmonious balance. A statue of General Cambronne, carved by Jean de Bay, was placed in the center here in 1848.

MUSEUM OF NATURAL HISTORY. The museum dates from 1810 and in 1958 was listed as a building of outstanding importance. It owes this distinction to its variety and antiquity, and to its collections in the fields of mineralogy, botany, paleontology, ornithology, conchology and entomology. Among prize exhibits are specimens of extinct species such as the great auk, and the egg of an aepyornis (a huge flightless bird from Madagascar). There is also the skin of a flayed man, and the so-called "Rat-king", a litter of rats born joined together at the tail. Last of all are an Egyptian mummy, and the famous meteorite from Rocheservière in the Vendée.

PASSAGE POMMERAYE

"Chinese screens, Turkish sandals and baskets from the Nile ... curios from beyond the seas," enthused Gustave Flaubert of this arcade, which in its day was almost like a real Arab souk. This elegant covered passage was built on the initiative of a lawyer in the reign of Louis-Philippe.

GRAND DESIGN. Intended as a link between the Rue Crébillon and the Rue de la Fosse 30 feet below, the arcade was also meant to decorate the quarter and get rid of all the prostitutes who lived round here. It was financed by a lawyer named Louis Pommeraye, and it ruined him. The architects on the project were Burand and Durand-Gasselin, and the arcade opened in 1843. But if it was a financial disaster, the Passage Pommeraye was an architectural triumph. There is an extraordinary balance between such disparate features as metallic frames, stone columns, glass paneling, medallions of great men and statues of children. The central part has a view over all three levels, while from below the visitor can best examine the superb wooden STAIRCASE and beautifully wrought metal from the Voruz foundries. The original shop-signs have also been preserved.

DEPARTMENTAL MUSEUMS. In local parlance these tend to be grouped together and are collectively referred to as the "Dobrée Museum". They are in fact the ARCHEOLOGICAL MUSEUM and the DOBRÉE MUSEUM itself. Though relatively

Left, the sign from the famous brasserie La Cigale. Below left, portrait of Graslin, the entrepreneur who developed a new quarter of Nantes. Right, the reliquary containing the heart of Anne of Brittany, on display in the Dobrée museum.

eclectic, their collections are of a consistently high quality. Among the treasures here are a SHRINE OF SAINT CALMINIUS in champlevé enamel, and the RELIQUARY designed to hold the HEART of Anne of Brittany. The LIBRARY boasts many precious manuscripts such as the *Chronicles* of Philippe de Commynes, and a number of rare books, including a hundred early printed volumes. The PRINT ROOM contains almost three hundred engravings, with examples by Dürer, Rembrandt and Callot. There is also a wide variety of 16th- and 17th-century furniture, faience, enamelware, tapestries and Oriental porcelain, and two outstanding collections: one of weaponry, and the other of archeological finds.

On reliquary:
…VR DE VERTVS ORNE…
ANCE PETIT VAISSEAU
DE FIN OR DVR ET MVNDE
REPOSE VNG PLVS GRAND CVEV
QVE ONCQVE DAME EVT AV MVND
ANNE FVT LE NOM DE LLE
EN FRANCE DEVX FOIS ROINE
DVCHESSE DES BRETONS
ROYALE ET SOVVERAINE
M V XIII

NÉGOCIANT DISTRICT

ÎLE FEYDEAU. If any quarter of Nantes symbolizes the city's prosperity in the 18th century, it must be the Île Feydeau. In 1720, however, the island was nothing more than a sandbank at the downstream end of an islet in the Loire. But its situation opposite the harbor seemed ideal for commercial development. Accordingly a group of twenty-four merchants (*négociants*) and shipowners decided to develop it, though the site was not finished until 1780. The Île Feydeau was finally joined to the right bank of the river in 1930: at that time the city's numerous canals and river branches were already being filled in, depriving Nantes of much of its watery charm.

RUE KERVÉGAN. This old-fashioned shady street divides the Île Feydeau from east to west. Its overhanging houses and worn stones underfoot recall the old harbor towns of long ago. In the Place de la Petite Hollande is the HÔTEL DE LA VILLESTREUX, at no. 3, which has 108 windows, and at no. 16 Allée Duguay Trouin is the TEMPLE DU GOÛT, which has unusual pot-bellied balconies.

QUAI DE LA FOSSE. In days gone by this was where the big merchant ships loaded and unloaded their cargoes, near the old transporter bridge that has now disappeared. It is easy to imagine how it must have looked in previous centuries, largely thanks to the backcloth of fine old houses, waterside cafés and dark alleyways leading away from the harbor. In the middle of the quayside now is the recent Médiathèque of Nantes, a huge boat replete with glass canopies.

BUTTE STE-ANNE

JULES VERNE MUSEUM. In the cosy setting of a well-to-do 19th-century villa on the side of a hill is the birthplace of Nantes' great writer of science fiction. The house is filled with models, books bound in red and gold leather, letters and other memorabilia. The view from here, overlooking the city, the Loire and the harbor, is exceptional.

MASKS
These carved heads decorating the keystones of arches are one of the distinctive features on houses in the Rue Kervégan and the Place de la Petite Hollande. Many have the faces of mythological characters.

THE VOYAGES OF JULES VERNE
This caricature shows the famous "armchair traveler", the world firmly in the grip of his pen. Verne's vivid novels of imaginary journeys still delight both young and old.

In 1531 Jean de Laval, Governor of Brittany, entrusted the work of building a new château on the ruins of the old fortress to Anjou architect Jean Delespin. That year François I came here to sign deeds relating to Brittany's union with France. After passing into the hands of the Montmorency-Laval and then the Condé families, the château became the property of the Duc d'Aumale, son of Louis Philippe. In 1853 he sold it to the local authorities, who still own the château today.

THE SOUTH GALLERY
Twenty-two arches rest on columns of blue-green schist. Above, the brick gallery has six triangular pediments for seven windows, another unusual feature.

THE MAIN BUILDING
There are two rows of cross-mullioned windows, and gables with carved pediments above. Pilasters divide the façade into decorated panels.

WEAR AND TEAR

Much of the fabric of the château, damaged in the religious wars, deteriorated further in the 18th century, and the west gallery has been demolished. The château was used as a barracks in the Revolution.

THE LAYOUT OF THE NEW CHÂTEAU

The main building is flanked by two houses. In one of them is the grand staircase, with steps made of blue schist, like the terrace overlooking the gardens. Jutting out from the façade, the staircase appears to have served the 15th-century building as well as the 16th-century addition. Upstairs in the North Wing is the guardroom, which has been open to the public since 1988.

A CRIME OF PASSION?

The only apartment in the new building was the bedchamber of Françoise de Foix, reached by a spiral staircase. It was here that Jean de Laval is said to have murdered his faithless wife on October 16, 1537 by having a surgeon bleed her too profusely. Since the only evidence is that the King ordered an enquiry into Françoise's death, the story must remain hypothetical. Even so, Jean de Laval bequeathed everything he owned to the King, the inference being that he was stricken with remorse.

A finely wrought ornamental detail of the château de Goulaine.

Old houses in Châteaubriant, a drawing from the turn of the century.

CHÂTEAUBRIANT

HISTORY. In the 10th century, soon after the Norman invasion, the Counts of Rennes and Nantes each strengthened their defenses. Châteaubriant, in the region of the Mée, was one result of this. Iron smelting was already an active industry here in the Middle Ages, and it was to reach its peak with the blast furnaces of the 17th century. The Revolutionary years were fraught with difficulty, for the Chouans ● *62* waged an intense campaign of guerrilla warfare in the area.

TOUR OF CHÂTEAUBRIANT. The imposing castle standing on

top of a hill consists of a MEDIEVAL FORTRESS ● *82* and a RENAISSANCE CHÂTEAU ▲ *382*. The old town, which extends to the west of the castle, lost most of its ramparts in the 19th century; only the 16th-century PORTE NEUVE remains. The GRANDE RUE, containing the HÔTEL DE LA HOUSSAYE, continues as the Rue de Couéré and was once the main street.

CHURCH OF ST-JEAN DE BÉRÉ. It was built in the 12th century and until the Revolution it was the town's parish church. It is made of sandstone and schist, with ferruginous sandstone dressing, and has an open-air pulpit. The TOWER, dating from the late 19th century, rises up from the crossing. Inside are some lovely altarpieces in limestone and marble.

CHÂTEAU DE GOULAINE

AN UNUSUAL CONSERVATORY
A building in the Château de Goulaine contains hundreds of tropical butterflies, which flutter colorfully around to the delight of visitors.

At first sight Goulaine looks like a typical Loire château; white tufa replaces the ubiquitous Brittany granite, and the watch towers are purely decorative. Beyond the moat, the fortified wall and machicolated gateway (remains of an earlier medieval fortress here), the main courtyard gives access to the principal residence, which was built in the 15th century. The latter is flanked by two polygonal towers and has gables above, carved in the Flamboyant Gothic style with ingeniously interlaced patterns. Two wings of unequal length, which were added in the early 17th century, frame the south façade. The north façade is remarkable for its sobriety and for the asymmetry of the doors and windows.

SPARED BY THE REVOLUTION. The château was fortunate to have preserved its archives, furniture and interior decorations through those lawless years. Remarkably, since the first castle was built here almost a thousand years ago, the estate has remained in the hands of the same family.

Practical information

Brittany is a vast region of France extending west from the north-south divide between Mont-St-Michel and Nantes, the former capital of the province. Both coastal (Armor) and inland (Argoat) areas are renowned for their natural beauty.

Tourism is well provided for and there are numerous ways of reaching Brittany, including direct flights and high-speed trains. The climate is mild and bracing, making it a perfect setting for activity holidays.

FOURTEEN REASONS FOR GOING TO BRITTANY

◆ 1,000 miles of Atlantic and Channel coastline
◆ 106 islets and islands
◆ Its beaches, coves, cliffs and rugged coastline
◆ Countless fishing ports and marinas
◆ 3750 miles of footpaths
◆ 400 miles of navigable waterways
◆ 230 centers for water sports and 120 sailing schools
◆ Its temperate and stimulating climate
◆ 12 thalassotherapy centers
◆ Its granite manor houses, medieval villages and slate-roof houses
◆ Its language, music and Celtic legends
◆ Many festivals and pardons
◆ Chapels and shrines
◆ Mouth-watering regional produce and cuisine

FORMALITIES

EC nationals may spend up to three months in France without a visa.

CUSTOMS

Since the creation of the European Single Market there is no longer any limit to goods bought in France by EC citizens.

WHEN TO GO

If you like wild weather time your visit for the equinox and you may experience a storm on the Pointe du Raz (September or March). Summer is best for swimming and water sports, but the water generally remains pleasantly cool. Spring and autumn are the best times to explore inland areas.

USEFUL NUMBERS BEFORE YOU GO

◆ French Government Tourist Office
178 Piccadilly
London W1V OAL
Tel. 0891 244 123
◆ Brit Air (Gatwick)
Tel. 01293 502 044

◆ Brit Air/ Air France
Tel. 0181 742 66 00
◆ Brittany Ferries
Tel. 0990 36 03 60
◆ Eurostar
Tel. 0345 30 30 30
◆ Hoverspeed
Tel. 0990 24 02 41
◆ Le Shuttle
Tel. 0990 35 35 35
◆ P&O Ferries
Tel. 0990 980 980
◆ SNCF (French Railways), in London
Tel. 0990 30 00 03
PACKAGE HOLIDAYS:
◆ Brittany Direct Holidays
Tel. 0181 641 60 60
◆ Check adverts from private owners in Sunday papers
◆ Vacances Franco-Britanniques
Tel. 01242 240 340

ADDRESSES IN FRANCE

◆ American Embassy
9, avenue Gabriel
75382 Paris Cédex 08
◆ British Embassy
35, rue du Faubourg Saint-Honoré
75383 Paris Cédex 08
Tel. 01 42 66 91 42
◆ British Consulate
9, avenue Hoche
75008 Paris
Tel. 01 42 66 38 10
◆ British Honorary Consul in Brittany
La Hulotte
8, avenue de la Libération
35800 Dinard
Tel. 02 99 46 26 64

ADDRESSES FOR INFORMATION IN FRANCE

◆ MAISON DE LA BRETAGNE
17, rue de l'Arrivée
Centre commercial
Maine-Montparnasse

75015 Paris
Tel. 01 45 38 73 15
Information:
Tel. 02 99 36 15 15

Reservations:
Tel. 02 99 79 07 07
or write to: BP 1006
75737 Paris Cedex 15

MAP SUPPLIERS

◆ Daunt Books
83 Marylebone High Street,
London W1
Tel. 0171 224 2295
◆ Stanford
12–14 Long Acre,
London WC2
Tel. 0171 836 1321

ADVICE ON CLOTHES

Don't forget to take a

windproof, waterproof coat to keep out the wet, gusty winds and ocean spray.

SPRING — March to June

		MARCH 41° 54°
MARCH/APRIL	**QUIMPER FILM CONFERENCE**	
MAY	**PARDON OF NOTRE-DAME DE RUMENGOL**, FINISTÈRE	APRIL 43° 56°
	Procession in traditional costume	
3RD SUNDAY OF MAY	**PARDON OF SAINT-YVES**, TRÉGUIER	
	Lawyers come to celebrate their patron saint	
END OF MAY	**PRINTEMPS DES ARTS**, NANTES	MAY 47° 59°
	Concerts and religious music	
JUNE 26–JULY 1	**INTERNATIONAL FILM FESTIVAL**, LA BAULE	

SUMMER — July to August

		JUNE 52° / 65°
JULY	**FESTIVAL OF BRETON MUSIC** ST-BRIEUC	
JULY 15 TO AUGUST 15	**FESTIVAL OF SACRED MUSIC**, ST-MALO	
	Son et lumière in the castle courtyard	
2ND SUNDAY OF JULY	**EMBROIDERY FESTIVAL**, PONT-L'ABBÉ	
	Singing and dancing in traditional costume	
JULY 22 TO 28	**FESTIVAL OF CORNOUAILLE**, QUIMPER	
	Breton music and dance	JULY 54° / 66°
c. JULY 15	**INTERNATIONAL CONFERENCE OF CELTIC HARP** DINAN	
c. AUGUST 15	**HYDRANGEA FESTIVAL**, PERROS-GUIREC	
	Traditional music and dance	
AUGUST 1 TO 15	**INTERCELTIC FESTIVAL**, LORIENT	
	Festival of international music	
JULY 26	**PARDON OF SAINTE-ANNE D'AURAY**	AUGUST 54° / 68°
JULY/AUGUST	**JAZZ FESTIVAL** VANNES	

AUTUMN — September to November

		SEPTEMBER 52° / 65°	OCTOBER 48° / 59°	NOVEMBER 43° / 54°
SEPTEMBER	**BRITISH FILM FESTIVAL**, DINARD			
END OCT. TO BEG. NOV.	**ART ROCK**, ST-BRIEUC			
	Concerts, exhibitions, performances			
NOVEMBER	**FESTIVAL OF SHORT FILMS**, BREST			
END OF NOV.	**FESTIVAL DES TROIS CONTINENTS**, NANTES			
	AFRICA, ASIA AND SOUTH AMERICA			

WINTER — December to February

		DECEMBER 39° / 48°	JANUARY 39° / 48°	FEBRUARY 37° / 48°
DECEMBER	**TRANSMUSICALES**, RENNES			
	For 15 years, this festival has been at the cutting edge of young rock talent			
ALL YEAR	**LES ILLUMINATIONS DU PORT**, ST-NAZAIRE			

sunny   changeable, cloudy   wet   cold, snow possible

Minimum and maximum monthly temperatures are in degrees Fahrenheit

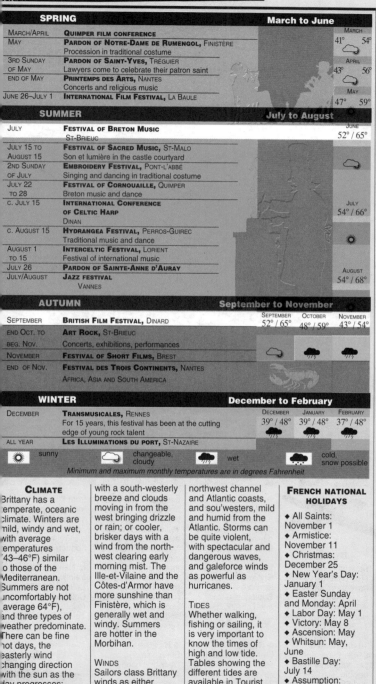

CLIMATE

Brittany has a temperate, oceanic climate. Winters are mild, windy and wet, with average temperatures (43–46°F) similar to those of the Mediterranean. Summers are not uncomfortably hot (average 64°F), and three types of weather predominate. There can be fine hot days, the easterly wind changing direction with the sun as the day progresses; warm, humid weather with a south-westerly breeze and clouds moving in from the west bringing drizzle or rain; or cooler, brisker days with a wind from the north-west clearing early morning mist. The Ille-et-Vilaine and the Côtes-d'Armor have more sunshine than Finistère, which is generally wet and windy. Summers are hotter in the Morbihan.

WINDS

Sailors class Brittany winds as either nor'westers, from the northwest channel and Atlantic coasts, and sou'westers, mild and humid from the Atlantic. Storms can be quite violent, with spectacular and dangerous waves, and galeforce winds as powerful as hurricanes.

TIDES

Whether walking, fishing or sailing, it is very important to know the times of high and low tide. Tables showing the different tides are available in Tourist Information Offices.

FRENCH NATIONAL HOLIDAYS

◆ All Saints: November 1
◆ Armistice: November 11
◆ Christmas: December 25
◆ New Year's Day: January 1
◆ Easter Sunday and Monday: April
◆ Labor Day: May 1
◆ Victory: May 8
◆ Ascension: May
◆ Whitsun: May, June
◆ Bastille Day: July 14
◆ Assumption: August 15

◆ TRAVELING TO BRITTANY

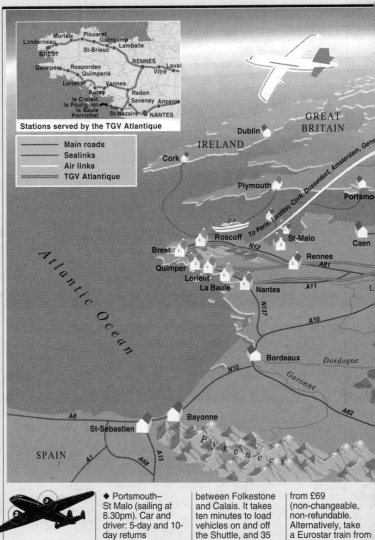

Stations served by the TGV Atlantique

— Main roads
— Sealinks
— Air links
— TGV Atlantique

BY FERRY

Brittany Ferries (Tel. 0990 36 03 60) have three sailings a day from
◆ Plymouth–Roscoff (8am, 2.30pm, 11.30pm). Car and driver: 5-day and 10-day returns £148– £206, and £8 per additional adult; flexible fare £280, and £8 per additional adult.

◆ Portsmouth–St Malo (sailing at 8.30pm). Car and driver: 5-day and 10-day returns £162–£226; flexible fare £300. Prices and times may change. Cheaper still are ferry crossings to Boulogne, Calais and Dunkirk.

VIA THE CHANNEL TUNNEL

◆ BY CAR:
Eurotunnel Shuttle service (Tel. 0990 35 35 35) provides 24 shuttle train services a day

between Folkestone and Calais. It takes ten minutes to load vehicles on and off the Shuttle, and 35 minutes to make the crossing, giving a total journey time of one hour. The prices range from £80–£95 (cars) and £40–£45 (motorbikes). Prices and conditions are subject to change.

◆ BY TRAIN WITH EUROSTAR:
Daily and hourly departures from London Waterloo to Paris Gare du Nord,

from £69 (non-changeable, non-refundable. Alternatively, take a Eurostar train from London to Lille to go direct to Rennes or Nantes. Total train journey time to Brittany 6 to 7 hours. Call Eurostar for reservations, Tel. 0345 30 30 30.

North Sea

Brittany

TGV Atlantique
Bus Air France
OrlyVal
RER Ligne A,B,C
Chatelet-les-Halles
Saint-Michel
Antony

Roissy

Gare du Nord · Gare de l'Est
Gare St Lazare · Gare de Lyon
Gare Montparnasse
Gare d'Austerlitz

Orly

**Arriving in Paris,
leaving to Brittany**

London
Eurotunnel

Amsterdam

A14

NETHERLANDS

A14

Brussels
A4

Dusseldorf

BELGIUM

GERMANY

A13

A26

A1

Paris

A4

A4

Seine

A6

A26

A26

A36

Vosges

N2

Jura

N1

SWITZERLAND

A71

Lyons
A72

A40
A42
A43
A49

A40

Geneva

A40

Clermont
Ferrand

A41

Massif Central

Alps

Rhône

A9

A7

A8

A21

ITALY

A10

gnan

Marseilles

Vintimille

ONCE IN FRANCE
◆ BY CAR:
If coming from
northern or western
France pick up the
"Océane" motorway
at Paris (toll-paying).
It divides into two:
the A11 goes from
Paris to Nantes and
the A81 leads off
at Le Mans toward
Vitré. Motorways
(autoroutes) are
marked on blue
road signs. Tolls:
Paris-Rennes
(217 miles), 135F
for a car, 198F
with caravan; Paris-
Nantes (240 miles),

163F for a car,
246F with a caravan.

◆ BY TRAIN:
The TGV Atlantique
high-speed train
route to Brittany

was opened in 1989,
greatly reducing
journey time from
Paris Montparnasse
station to Nantes
or Rennes to just
two hours. For
information and
reservations:
French Tourist
Office, travel agents,
or SNCF office in
Piccadilly (see
p. 386 for telephone
numbers and
addresses).
Information for
children traveling
alone or handicapped
travelers is also
available here.

Bicycles may be
taken on board
TGV trains provided
they are folded or
put into a cover
(4 by 3 foot
maximum).
Cars can also be
carried on trains
to or from Nantes.
Prices vary according
to the size of the
vehicle and the day
of travel.

389

Destinations in Brittany	Frequencies	Durations
PLANE		
London / Brest	3 flight daily, 2 on weekends	1 h 15
London / Nantes	3 flights daily, 2 on weekends	1 h 15 to 1 h 30
London / Rennes	2 flights a week, 2 on weekends	1 h 15 to 1 h 30
Cork / Quimper	1 flight on Saturday, 09/04 to 10/09	1 h 20
Paris / Orly Ouest / Brest	5 flights daily	55 mn
Paris / Orly Ouest / Lorient	3–4 flights daily, 1–3 on weekends	1 h
Paris / Orly Ouest or Roissy / Rennes	4 flights daily, 1 on weekends	1 h
Paris / Orly Ouest or Roissy / Nantes	8 flights daily, 5 on weekends	55 mn
Paris / Orly Ouest / St-Brieuc	2 flights weekdays	1 h 05
TRAIN		
Paris / Rennes	12 daily TGV	2 h
Paris / Brest	5 daily TGV	4 h
Paris / Nantes	12 daily TGV	2 h
Paris / Quimper	4 daily TGV	5 h
Paris / Lorient	4 daily TGV	3 h 55
FERRY		
Plymouth / Roscoff	1–3 daily crossings (mid-Mar. –mid-Sep.)	6 h
Portsmouth / St-Malo	1 nightly crossing (mid-Mar. –mid-Nov.)	9 h
Cork / Roscoff	1–2 weekly crossings	13–17 h
Cork / St-Malo	1 weekly crossing	18 h

BY PLANE

FROM LONDON GATWICK: Brit Air, in conjunction with Air France, runs regular flights to Brest, Nantes, and Rennes Tel. 0181 742 6600.
◆ Brest: 3 flights Mon.–Sat. (7.45am, 1.30pm, 7.15pm), and 2 flights Sun. (1.30pm, 7.15pm), £202–£472 return.

◆ Nantes: 3 flights Mon.–Sat. (7.45am, 1.30pm, 7.15pm), and 2 flights Sun (1.30pm, 7.15pm), £200–£445 return.
◆ Rennes: 2 flights Mon.–Fri. (8.15am, 7.30pm), 1 flight Sat. (8.15am) and 1 flight Sun. (7.20pm), £200–£470 return. Times and fares are subject to change.
◆ BREST AIRPORT 29450 Guipavas Tel. 02 98 32 01 00
◆ NANTES AIRPORT Château-Bougon 44340 Bouguenais Tel. 02 40 84 80 00
◆ RENNES-ST-JACQUES AIRPORT Av. Joseph-Le-Brix 35136 St-Jacques-de-la-Lande Tel. 02 99 29 60 00.

USEFUL NUMBERS:
AIR FRANCE/ BRIT AIR:
Tel. 0181 742 66 00 (London)
Tel. 02 98 32 01 10 (Brest)
AIR INTER:
Tel. 01 45 46 90 00 and TAT:
Tel. 0 803 805 805 (flights from Jersey, Cork and Dublin)
AIR LITTORAL:
Tel. 02 40 84 83 10 (flights along the French coast)
REGIONAL AIRLINES (Nantes):
Tel. 02 40 13 52 00

TOURIST RECEPTION

TOURIST INFORMATION OFFICES:
There are 196 offices in Brittany, helping three million visitors a year. They are happy to give advice on places to visit, and on travel arrangements. In small towns they tend to be called "syndicats d'initiative", while in larger towns they are "offices de tourisme". Both are indicated by the same signs, which can be the logo of the FNOTSI (Fédération Nationale des Offices de Tourisme et Syndicats d'Initiative) or the

![FNOTSI]

more familiar black "i" for information.

◆ Bretagne Infos 74b, rue de Paris 35069 Rennes Tel. 02 99 36 15 15
◆ Bréhat Tel. 02 96 20 04 15

> ### RESERVING A HOTEL
> ARTUUS interactive information boards, to be found at a number of sites, are extremely helpful for hotel reservations and can be consulted in English, German and French. They have been launched in the département of the Ille-et-Vilaine and will soon be installed in others. There is one at the Erbrée motorway services area, and at the Dinard and St-Malo tourist information offices.

◆ Brest
Tel. 02 98 44 24 96
◆ Concarneau
Tel. 02 98 97 01 44
◆ Dinan
Tel. 02 96 39 75 40
◆ Groix
Tel. 02 97 86 54 96
◆ Île d'Ouessant
Tel. 02 98 48 85 83
◆ La Baule
Tel. 02 40 24 34 44
◆ Lorient
Tel. 02 97 21 07 84
◆ Mont St-Michel
Tel. 02 33 60 14 30
◆ Nantes
Tel. 02 40 20 60 00
◆ Perros-Guirec
Tel. 02 96 23 21 15
◆ Plougastel
Tel. 02 98 40 34 98
◆ Roscoff
Tel. 02 98 61 12 13
◆ Quimper
Tel. 02 98 53 04 05
◆ Rennes
Tel. 02 99 79 01 98
◆ St-Brieuc
Tel. 02 96 33 32 50
◆ St-Malo
Tel. 02 99 56 64 48
◆ Vannes
Tel. 02 97 47 24 34

TOURIST SIGNS

Most sites in Brittany are signposted: the region's two parks (PARC D'ARMORIQUE Tel. 02 98 21 90 69 and PARC DE BRIERE Tel. 02 40 66 85 01), as well as its megaliths, historic monuments, museums and chapels.

ARRIVING IN PORT

When mooring in a port, first go to the harbor master's office to give the boat's nationality. Harbor dues are payable by the night, week or month, and vary according to the size of the craft. Some ports charge by the square meter, others by tonnage. The price of a night's mooring can be anything from around 70F to 200F.

On departure from the port, inform the harbor master of your intended destination, and check your safety gear and flares. Listen to the weather forecasts and be sure to study the charts of your route.

Weather forecast: Tel. 08 36 68 08 08 (recorded information in French).

GETTING TO THE ISLANDS

WESTERN ISLES

The ÎLES DU PONANT, a series of fifteen islands, from the isles of Chausey in the north to Yeu in the south, twelve of which are in Brittany.

◆ BELLE-ÎLE-EN-MER
Flights from Lorient-Lann-Bihoué and Quiberon by Insul'Air (Tel. 02 97 31 41 14). Boats from Lorient and Quiberon. Compagnie Morbihannaise et Nantaise de Navigation (CMNN), (Tel. 02 97 50 06 90).
◆ ÎLE-AUX-MOINES
5 mins from Port-Blanc (Baden). Compagnie Izenah, (Tel. 02 97 26 31 45).
◆ ÎLE D'ARZ
15 mins from Conleau. Compagnie Enez Arz (Tel. 02 97 66 92 06).
◆ ÎLE DE BATZ
15 mins from Roscoff. Vedettes de l'Île de Batz (Tel. 02 98 61 79 66), or Armein (Tel. 02 98 61 77 75).
◆ ÎLE DE BRÉHAT
10 mins from Pointe de l'Arçouest. Vedettes de l'Île de Bréhat (Tel. 02 96 20 00 11 or 02 96 20 03 47).
◆ ÎLE DE CHAUSEY
1½ hours from

St-Malo. Emeraude Lines (Tel. 02 99 40 48 40).
◆ ÎLE DE GROIX
45 mins from Lorient. CMNN (Tel. 02 97 64 77 64).
◆ ÎLE DE SEIN
1 hr 15 mins from Audierne Ste-Evette. Penn ar Bed (Tel. 02 98 70 02 37).

◆ ÎLES DE HOUAT AND HŒDIC
30–60 mins from Quiberon. CMNN (Tel. 02 97 50 06 90).
◆ ÎLES DE MOLENE AND OUESSANT (Ushant): flights to Ouessant from Brest-Guipava (15 mins),

(Tel. 02 98 84 64 87). Boats from Brest (2½ hours) or Le Conquet (1½ hours). Penn ar Bed (Tel. 02 98 80 24 68).
◆ ÎLES DES GLÉNAN from Bénodet, Quimper, Loctudy and Beg-Meil. Vedettes de l'Odet Tel. 02 98 57 00 58).

BRITTANY MARINAS			
Ports	Moorings		Telephone
	a year	visitors	
Arzal-Camoël ★	630	50	02 99 90 05 86
Bénodet ★	496	53	02 98 57 05 78
Binic	400	60	02 96 73 61 86
Brest Moulin Blanc ★	1325	100	02 98 02 20 02
Camaret-sur-Mer	300	70	02 98 27 95 99
Concarneau ★	393	52	02 98 97 57 96
Crozon-Morgat ★	560	50	02 98 27 01 97
Douarnenez Tréboul ★	445	30	02 98 74 02 56
La Trinité-sur-Mer ★	950	60	02 97 55 71 49
Le Croisic	320	28	02 40 23 10 95
Le Pouliguen ★	850	30	02 40 60 37 40
Loctudy ★	530	80	02 98 87 51 36
Lorient, bassin à flot	370	50	02 97 21 10 14
Lorient, Kernével ★	520	60	02 97 65 48 25
Perros-Guirec	680	60	02 96 23 37 82
Pornic ★	919	165	02 40 82 05 40
Pornichet ★	1150	154	02 40 61 03 20
Port Crouesty ★	1000	120	02 97 53 73 33
Port La Forêt ★	1000	100	02 98 56 98 45
Quiberon, Port Haliguen	860	100	02 97 50 20 56
St-Malo, Bas-Sablons ★	1210	60	02 99 81 71 34
St-Malo, Port Vauban	250	100	02 99 56 51 91
St-Quay-Portrieux ★	1030	100	02 96 70 81 30
Sainte-Marine ★	770	70	02 98 56 38 72
Vannes ★	224	40	02 97 54 16 08

Visiting craft can occupy annually leased moorings depending on current availability.
VHF channel 9 and 16 (harbor office hours)

★ FUEL AVAILABLE

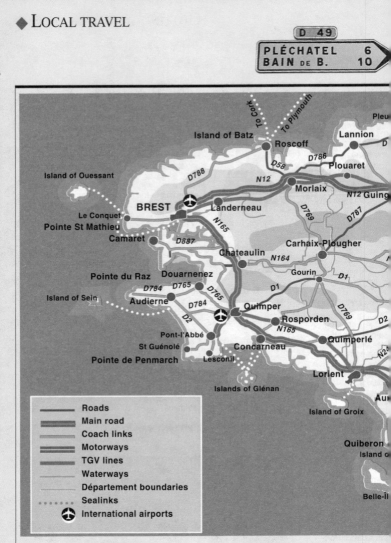

D 49
PLÉCHATEL 6
BAIN DE B. 10

TRAVELING BY CAR

Brittany's road network is good. From the main towns there are more than 500 miles of free dual carriageway roads (speed limit 68 mph/ 110 km/h) around the province: Rennes to Brest, Brest to Nantes, and Nantes to Rennes and St-Malo. On other main roads the speed limit is 55 mph (90 km/h), and in towns and villages it is 30 mph (50 km/h). Town parking is usually charged at 5F per hour, as opposed to 10F per hour in Paris. There are fine coastal roads, which become rather busy in summer but are very pleasant for an unhurried journey. When exploring the islands, do remember that cars are not permitted on many of the islands, including Bréhat, Batz, Ouessant and the islands in the Gulf of Morbihan. However, cars are allowed on Belle-Île-en-Mer, the largest island in Brittany.

RENTING A CAR

Hire cars can be reserved at agencies on arrival in Brittany. Companies like Avis have special rates: "Séjour en France" (1,490F per week for a category A car). Car hire desks can be found at airports and stations, where a vehicle can be obtained on production of a national or international driving licence and a credit card.

◆ AVIS
Brest: 02 98 44 63 02
Nantes: station, north entrance
02 40 74 07 65
south entrance
02 40 89 25 50.
Quimper:
02 98 90 31 34
Rennes:
02 99 51 60 61
◆ HERTZ
St-Brieuc:
02 96 94 25 89
Brest: 02 98 80 11 51
Nantes:
02 40 89 64 04
Quimper:
02 98 53 12 34
Rennes:
02 99 54 26 52
◆ EUROPCAR
Brest: 02 98 44 66 88
Nantes:
02 40 29 05 10
Quimper:
02 98 90 00 68
Rennes:
02 99 50 53 69

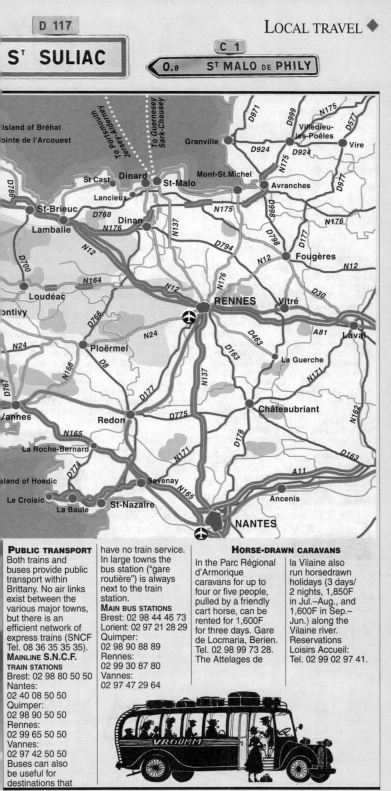

Island of Bréhat
pointe de l'Arcouest

To Portsmouth
Jersey-Alderney

To Guernsey
Sark-Chausey

D971 · D999 · N175

Granville · Villedieu-les-Poêles · Vire

D924 · D924 · N175 · D577 · D977

St Cast · Dinard · St-Malo · Mont-St.Michel · Avranches

Lancieux · N175 · D998 · D177 · N176

St-Brieuc · D768 · Dinan · N176 · D137 · D794 · D798 · D12 · Fougères · N12

Lamballe · N12 · N176 · D30

D700 · N164 · N12 · RENNES · Vitré

Loudéac · D766 · ✈ · A81

Montivy · N24 · Ploërmel · D463 · Laval

N166 · D8 · D163 · La Guerche · N171

D767 · D177 · N137

Vannes · Redon · D775 · Châteaubriant · N162

N165 · La Roche-Bernard · N171 · D178 · D163

Island of Hoedic · D774 · Savenay · A11

Le Croisic · La Baule · St-Nazaire · N165 · Ancenis

✈ · NANTES

PUBLIC TRANSPORT

Both trains and buses provide public transport within Brittany. No air links exist between the various major towns, but there is an efficient network of express trains (SNCF Tel. 08 36 35 35 35).

MAINLINE S.N.C.F.
TRAIN STATIONS
Brest: 02 98 80 50 50
Nantes:
02 40 08 50 50
Quimper:
02 98 90 50 50
Rennes:
02 99 65 50 50
Vannes:
02 97 42 50 50
Buses can also be useful for destinations that

have no train service. In large towns the bus station ("gare routière") is always next to the train station.

MAIN BUS STATIONS
Brest: 02 98 44 46 73
Lorient: 02 97 21 28 29
Quimper:
02 98 90 88 89
Rennes:
02 99 30 87 80
Vannes:
02 97 47 29 64

HORSE-DRAWN CARAVANS

In the Parc Régional d'Armorique caravans for up to four or five people, pulled by a friendly cart horse, can be rented for 1,600F for three days. Gare de Locmaria, Berien. Tel. 02 98 99 73 28. The Attelages de

la Vilaine also run horsedrawn holidays (3 days/ 2 nights, 1,850F in Jul.–Aug., and 1,600F in Sep.– Jun.) along the Vilaine river. Reservations Loisirs Accueil: Tel. 02 99 02 97 41.

VROUMM

Brittany is not a particulary expensive region and an enjoyable stay need not cost a great deal. There are an enormous number of places to stay: 28,000 hotel rooms, 12,000 self-catering units and 850 campsites. The public services in France (post, telephone, transport) are easy to use. There are still many small food shops, despite the growing competition from supermarkets and hypermarkets. The vast hypermarket empire E. Leclerc, with branches all over France, was in fact started in 1953 by a grocer from Landerneau.

MONEY

CURRENCY

100 centimes make 1 franc. The coins currently in use are 20F, 10F, 5F, 2F and 1F pieces, and 50, 20, 10, and 5 centimes pieces. Bills come in 500F, 200F, 100F, 50F and 20F denominations. Bank standard opening hours are 9.30am–noon and 2–4pm Mon.–Fri.

CREDIT CARDS

In France credit cards are accepted

in almost all hotels, restaurants and shops. Almost half of French bank branches have automatic cash dispensers where you can withdraw up to 2,000F per week with an international Visa or Mastercard.

THEFT OR LOSS OF CARD

Advise the company that issued the card of the loss immediately so that the card can be blocked. Declare the theft at the local police station ("commissariat"). Write a registered letter to your bank confirming the loss or theft.
◆ Police
Tel. 17
◆ American Express
Tel. 01 47 77 72 00
◆ Barclaycard
Tel. 01 47 62 75 00
◆ Diner's Club
Tel. 0 800 22 20 73 or 01 47 62 75 50
◆ Eurocard Mastercard:
Tel. 01 45 67 53 53
◆ Visa/Carte Bleue:
Tel. 01 42 77 11 90 or 02 54 42 12 12

TRAVELERS' CHEQUES

Hotel chains, restaurants and shops will only take travelers' cheques in French francs. If you take them in your own currency you will have to change them at a bank or Bureau de Change. There will be a commission (a fixed charge or percentage) which

can vary quite considerably. The Crédit Lyonnais and the Société Générale banks, which have a large number of branches, do not charge a commission.

EUROCHEQUES

Most European countries issue Eurocheques, but always make sure the proprietor accepts Eurocheques before writing one. In France the amount must be written in French francs, and the cheque must be presented with a signed EC guarantee card, proof that it is valid. It is better not to go over 1,400F per cheque and 7,000F altogether, as the payee is not guaranteed payment over this amount.

HEALTH

Make sure you leave the UK with form E111 (available from post-offices or the Department of Health). This will enable you to be reimbursed for medical costs. In France you pay for both medical

consultations and medicines upfront.

ACCOMMODATION

Additional insurance is recommended. All types are available in Brittany: campsite, bed and breakfast (*chambre d'hôte*), rented apartments and houses, hotels, holiday clubs and youth hostels. Beware if you are planning to go to Brittany between

Jul. 15 and Aug. 25 when the whole of France is on holiday. Plan and book well in advance.

HOTELS

There were 1,138 hotels in Brittany in 1992, classed according to the six standardized French categories: from "no star" (*sans étoile*) to "luxury 4 star" (*quatre étoiles luxe*). Many hotels offer a half-board arrangement (with midday or evening meal) that is charged per person. If taking a double room without board the price is for two people. It is best to reserve, particularly during the French summer and Easter school vacations.

SOME HOTEL ASSOCIATIONS:

◆ BALADHÔTEL groups together hotels particularly geared to the needs of ramblers, cyclists and horse riders.
9, rue des Portes-Mordelaises
35000 Rennes,
Tel. 02 99 67 42 22.

◆ RELAIS ET CHÂTEAUX DE BRETAGNE include hotel accommodation in châteaux, manors or other fine buildings and beautiful surroundings.
SIÈGE DES RELAIS BRETONS, Hôtel Castel-Clara, Belle-Île-en-Mer, Tel. 02 97 31 84 21.
Central reservation office:
Tel. 01 45 72 90 00.

RENTED ACCOMMODATION

There are a number of apartments, cottages and houses for holiday rental in Brittany. Estate agencies and private individuals offer accommodation for rent, either directly or through Tourist Information Offices, by the week, fortnight or month. The minimum price for four-bed accommodation is 2,000F. There are many "Gîtes Ruraux" in Brittany. These are cottages in country

surroundings. They are very good value, costing from 1,000F to 1,600F per week, according to comfort category (1 to 3 épis) for 4 to 6 people.
◆ Information:
GÎTES DE FRANCE
178 Piccadilly
London W1,
Tel. 0891 244 123

CAMPING AND CARAVANNING

France is one of the European countries best provided with campsites, both in quantity and quality. There are 850 1- to 4-star campsites in Brittany alone, and many are beside the sea. Prices per day vary according to category, position on the site and available facilities (water, electricity etc.). The great advantage is that there is no need to book. The FÉDÉRATION FRANÇAISE DU CAMPING CARAVANING: 78, rue de Rivoli, 75004 Paris, Tel. 01 42 72 84 08,

publishes the Guide du Camping-Caravaning (76F + postage) and the Guide Officiel des Aires de Services (40F + postage). Also available is the Guide Michelin du Camping-Caravaning en France.

CAMPING-VANS

Brittany attracts 29 percent of all the camping-van tourism in the country. There are a number of roadside servicing areas where camping-vans can be filled up with water, recharged with electricity and pumped out. There are 6 servicing areas in Ille-et-Vilaine, 6 in Côtes-d'Armor, 23 in Finistère, 12 in Morbihan and 13 in Loire-Atlantique. Do not do camp in the wild or on somebody's property without permission.

AVERAGE BUDGET FOR A FORTNIGHT

Brittany is not as expensive as the South of France.
◆ Couple + 2 children in rented four-bed accommodation: minimum 3,500F per fortnight (high season).
Journey by car: based on 625 miles traveling (550F)
+ motorway tolls (300F) = 850F.
Total = 4,350F.
◆ Couple staying in 2-star hotel, half-board: 280F per person per day = 8,400F for 15 nights + journey 850F
Total = 9,250F.
◆ Couple + 2 children on 3-star campsite costing 90 F per night for 2 people (4 people 180F per night): = 2,700F + journey 850F
Total = 3,550F

EATING OUT

Brittany is the land of fish restaurants and crêperies. The latter serve pancakes (crêpes) with savory or sweet fillings, washed down with sweet or dry cider. Restaurants open from 12.30pm to 3pm and 7pm to 10pm in summer. Service is included in the bill.

SOME FRENCH DISHES

◆ A *plateau de fruits de mer* is a selection of shellfish (oysters, mussels, cockles, whelks, clams and winkles) and crustacea (prawns, crab and sea urchins)

◆ *Gigot d'agneau*, or *gigot pré-salé*,

(including strawberries, apples, and pears). Find out when market days are from Tourist Information Offices.

FISH MARKETS

Don't miss the fishing boats

EQUIVALENT MEN'S SIZES	
FRANCE	UK
COATS	
44	35
46	36
48	38
50	39
52	41
54	42/43
56	44
TROUSERS	
44	34
46	35
48	36
50	38
52	40
54	41
56	42
SHOES	
40 ½	44
41	46
42	50
43	54
44	56
45	

EQUIVALENT WOMEN'S SIZES	
FRANCE	UK
DRESSES AND SKIRTS	
34	8
36	10
38	12
40	14
42	16
44/46	18
46/48	20
COATS	
36	10
38	12
40	14
42	16
44/46	18
46/48	20
48/50	22
50	24
52	26
SHOES	
36 ½	4
37	4 ½
37 ½	5
38 ½	5 ½
39	6
39 ½	6 ½
40 ½	7

slices of rare roast lamb often served with green haricot beans and potato gratin.

◆ A *crêpe complète* is a pancake filled with egg, ham and grated Emmental cheese.

MARKETS

France has wonderful open-air markets. Once or twice a week stalls are set up on the town or village square and fresh produce (in particular fish, meat and dairy products) is sold at reasonable prices. There are also local vegetables (such as artichokes, cauliflowers and carrots) and fruits

coming in to port. It is possible to buy fresh fish and live shellfish before they are put into the *criée*, the harbor fish auction. The auctions are generally open to professionals only, although some ports do allow visitors, particularly those in the Cornouaille region. Unloading the catch is a marvelous sight.

◆ Audierne: Tel. 02 98 70 12 00

◆ Douarnenez: Tel. 02 98 92 13 35

◆ Le Guilvinec: Tel. 02 98 58 11 40

◆ Loctudy: Tel. 02 98 87 53 78

TELEPHONE

Nearly all phone boxes now take cards. Cards (for 50 or 120 units, costing 40,60F or 97,50F) can be bought at all post offices and tobacco shops (*bureaux de tabac*). When telephoning

◆ International Directory Enquiries: 00 33 12 + country code, for example, 00 33 12 44 for Great Britain. To call France from abroad dial the code 00 + 33 + area code (dropping the first 0) + the number.

within Brittany or to another region of France, including the capital, dial the 10-figure number. Calls abroad begin with the code 00 + country code + area code (dropping the first 0) + the number.

◆ French Directory Enquiries: 12

POST

The letter tariff for France and EC countries is 3F (card or letter max. 20 gms). For other European countries and Tunisia, Morocco and Algeria the price is 3.80F. It is 4.40F for the USA, Canada and Central Asia. Stamps can be

bought individually or in books of 10 from post offices and bureaux de tabac (tobacco shops).

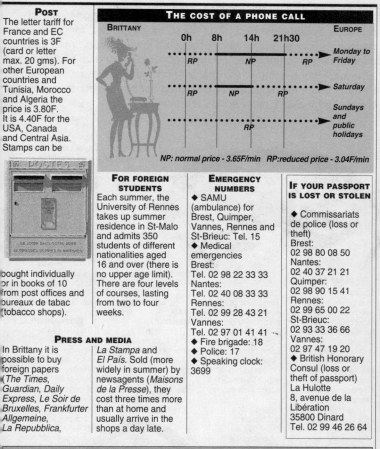

THE COST OF A PHONE CALL

NP: normal price - 3.65F/min   RP:reduced price - 3.04F/min

FOR FOREIGN STUDENTS

Each summer, the University of Rennes takes up summer residence in St-Malo and admits 350 students of different nationalities aged 16 and over (there is no upper age limit). There are four levels of courses, lasting from two to four weeks.

PRESS AND MEDIA

In Brittany it is possible to buy foreign papers (*The Times, Guardian, Daily Express, Le Soir de Bruxelles, Frankfurter Allgemeine, La Repubblica,* *La Stampa* and *El País.* Sold (more widely in summer) by newsagents (*Maisons de la Presse*), they cost three times more than at home and usually arrive in the shops a day late.

EMERGENCY NUMBERS

◆ SAMU (ambulance) for Brest, Quimper, Vannes, Rennes and St-Brieuc: Tel. 15
◆ Medical emergencies
Brest: Tel. 02 98 22 33 33
Nantes: Tel. 02 40 08 33 33
Rennes: Tel. 02 99 28 43 21
Vannes: Tel. 02 97 01 41 41
◆ Fire brigade: 18
◆ Police: 17
◆ Speaking clock: 3699

IF YOUR PASSPORT IS LOST OR STOLEN

◆ Commissariats de police (loss or theft)
Brest: 02 98 80 08 50
Nantes: 02 40 37 21 21
Quimper: 02 98 90 15 41
Rennes: 02 99 65 00 22
St-Brieuc: 02 93 33 36 66
Vannes: 02 97 47 19 20
◆ British Honorary Consul (loss or theft of passport)
La Hulotte
8, avenue de la Libération
35800 Dinard
Tel. 02 99 46 26 64

THE COST OF THINGS

1 BOTTLE OF CIDER: 6F

1 SUGAR CRÊPE: 15F

1 MENU IN A RESTAURANT: FROM 80F

1 NIGHT IN A TWO STARS HOTEL: 300F

1 KG OF LOBSTER: 300F

1 ENTRANCE TO A MUSEUM: 30F

1 HOUR WINDSURF RENTAL: 80F

1 DAY MOUNTAIN BIKE RENTAL: 120F

A stay in Brittany is an opportunity to eat plenty of good fresh fish and local vegetables. Brittany is not so much reputed for its original recipes as for the quality of its produce. Fish, shellfish, fresh and cooked meats (charcuterie), dairy produce, fruit and vegetables are all equally good whether the preparation is elaborate or very simple. Brittany has a few specialities that must not be missed, including crêpes (pancakes), cider and Guérande salt.

SEAFOOD

SOUPS
Practically all Breton restaurants have a fish soup or lobster bisque on the menu, served with *sauce rouille* (mayonnaise with pimento), croûtons and grated Gruyère cheese. *Cotriade* is a Breton mixed fish soup, originally eaten by sailors and made with white fish, onions and potatoes, flavored with thyme and bay.

SHELLFISH
For the fresh flavor of the sea order a *plateau de fruits de mer*, a selection of shellfish and crustacea. Oysters can only be eaten from September to April. The best are found at Cancale (large and horseshoe-shaped, and known as *pieds de cheval*), Riec-sur-Belon (the famous *belons*, smaller and flatter) and those from the Bay of Quiberon. The Côtes d'Armor also has scallops, a specialty of the Bay of Erquy. Good mussels are to be had all over Brittany, often prepared in a white wine (Muscadet) sauce with onions.

COOKED FISH
◆ Lobster or Monkfish *à l'Armoricaine*:
1 large live lobster or pieces of monkfish Sauce, 2 shallots finely chopped, 3 tomatoes peeled and crushed, 1 glass of white wine, 5 oz butter. Melt the butter and fry the pieces of lobster or fish gently. Add the other ingredients and cook for about 30 minutes.
◆ Sea bass *en croûte de sel de Guérande*
Put the sea bass (2–3 lbs) in an ovenproof dish and cover all over with an inch of dough made from Guérande salt mixed with flour and a little water. Cook for 35 minutes, break open the *croûte* (crust): the fish will be perfectly cooked and not at all salty.

LIVESTOCK

MEAT AND CHARCUTERIE
Saltmarsh lamb (*agneau pré-salé*) from Mont-St-Michel bay and the island of Ouessant is a rare gastronomic specialty, usually served roasted with green haricot beans.

The charcuterie is highly flavored: Morlaix ham, tripe sausage (*andouille* or *andouillette*) from Baye, Quimperlé or Guéméné-sur-Scorff. There is wild duck from Rhuys; hens, capons, partridge and hare abound. Frogs' legs are available too. This is a specialty of Brière and a particular delicacy for French visitors.

CHEESE
Brittany is the major French producer of Emmental cheese. The Cistercian monks at Thimadeuc make a cheese called "La Trappe". Other local cheeses include Fougerolles, Saint-Paulin, Caille Rennais and Montauban.

GUÉRANDE SALT

This is a salt particularly high in magnesium and an especially delicious seasoning for fish and grilled meat. It can be bought as Fleur de Sel (fine salt for grills) or as rock salt for cooking in water. In summer the salt gatherers (*paludiers*) can be seen selling their produce along the narrow roads between the salt marshes. It is a strange flat, white landscape, good for cycling if there isn't too much wind.
◆ EXCURSION FLEUR DE SEL: tour of saltmarsh museum at Batz-sur-Mer ▲ 369 and visit to saltworks and the Guérande premises. RESERVATIONS LOISIRS ACCUEIL IN NANTES Tel. 02 451 72 95 31 (145F per person, groups only).

FRUIT AND VEGETABLES

Plougastel strawberries and cherries from Fouesnant in Finistère are both famed for their flavor. Most vegetables are grown on the rich stretch of land between Roscoff and Morlaix, known as the Ceinture Dorée ("golden belt") ▲ 261. New potatoes, carrots, turnips, French beans, cauliflowers, artichokes and asparagus are grown here. Try the markets – Monday in Auray, Concarneau, Vitré; Tuesday: Paimpol, Pont-Aven, St-Malo, La Trinité; Wednesday: Carnac, Tréguier, Vannes; Thursday: Binic, Hennebout, Lannion; Friday: Concarneau, Guincamp, Quimperlé, St-Malo; Saturday: Dinard, Fougères, Josselin, Locmariaquer, Quimper, St-Brieuc, Vannes; Sunday: Cancale, Carnac.

CRÊPES

Breton savory pancakes are made with buckwheat. Buckwheat was brought back from the Holy Land at the time of the Crusades. Buckwheat crêpes are eaten as a main course (*crêpe complète*: ham, cheese, eggs). Sweet pancakes are made with wheat flour and

have various fillings: jam, chocolate sauce, or flambéed with apple or banana.

DRINKS

BRETON CIDER
An alcoholic drink made from fermented apple juice, a perfect accompaniment to crêpes. The best known ciders come from Fouesnant, which is sweet and rich in color, Clohars Carnoët,

which is paler and drier, or the Bigouden region (Pont L'Abbé). Visits and tasting:

◆ MUSÉE DU CIDRE ET CRÊPERIE on an old farm on the road from Brest to Argol (Finistère), Tel. 02 98 27 73 26. History of cider from 5th century to present day, visit to pressing room and tasting. On sale: Vallée d'Aulne cider.

◆ MUSÉE DE LA POMME ET DU CIDRE, La Ville-Hervy, Pleudihen (near Dinan) Tel. 02 96 83 20 78.

NANTES WINES
Brittany has no vineyards, except around Nantes in the Loire Valley. Muscadet is a dry but fruity white wine, good with seafood. There is also the slightly drier Gros Plant, pleasant with oysters.

BEER
An unpasteurized beer, Coreff, is made in Morlaix from hops bought from Alsace and Bavaria.

◆ BRASSERIE DES DEUX RIVIÈRES in Morlaix, Place de la Madeleine, Tel. 02 98 63 41 92. Visits and free tasting.

"CHOUCHEN"
A liqueur of *eau de vie* and honey found mainly in Cornouaille. It is said that if you swallow *couchen* with your head bent backward it is so strong that you will never be able to bend it forward again.

RECIPE FOR CRÊPE BATTER

An easy recipe to make at home with a good heavy-based frying pan.
Ingredients:
1½ cups flour
3 eggs
20 fl oz milk
Mix the eggs and the flour. Gradually add the milk, stirring all the time to avoid lumps. Beat the batter until smooth and creamy. Add a pinch of salt. Leave to rest for half an hour. Heat pan and grease it with an oily cloth. Pour a ladle of batter into it and tip to distribute evenly. Cook until surface is mat, turn and cook other side briefly. Eat immediately.

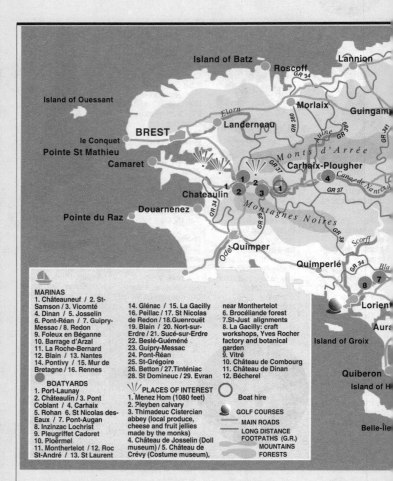

MARINAS
1. Châteauneuf / 2. St-Samson / 3. Vicomté
4. Dinan / 5. Josselin
6. Pont-Réan / 7. Guipry-Messac / 8. Redon
9. Foleux en Béganne
10. Barrage d'Arzal
11. La Roche-Bernard
12. Blain / 13. Nantes
14. Pontivy / 15. Mur de Bretagne / 16. Rennes

14. Glénac / 15. La Gacilly
16. Peillac / 17. St Nicolas de Redon / 18.Guenrouët
19. Blain / 20. Nort-sur-Erdre / 21. Sucé-sur-Erdre
22. Beslé-Guémené
23. Guipry-Messac
24. Pont-Réan
25. St-Grégoire
26. Betton / 27.Tinténiac
28. St Domineuc / 29. Evran

near Monthertelot
6. Brocéliande forest
7.St-Just alignments
8. La Gacilly: craft workshops, Yves Rocher factory and botanical garden
9. Vitré
10. Château de Combourg
11. Château de Dinan
12. Bécherel

BOATYARDS
1. Port-Launay
2. Châteaulin / 3. Pont Coblant / 4. Carhaix
5. Rohan 6. St Nicolas des-Eaux / 7. Pont-Augan
8. Inzinzac Lochrist
9. Pleugriffet Cadoret
10. Ploërmel
11. Monthertelot / 12. Roc St-André / 13. St Laurent

PLACES OF INTEREST
1. Menez Hom (1080 feet)
2. Pleyben calvary
3. Thimadeuc Cistercian abbey (local produce, cheese and fruit jellies made by the monks)
4. Château de Josselin (Doll museum) / 5. Château de Crévy (Costume museum),

○ Boat hire

⛳ GOLF COURSES

— MAIN ROADS

— LONG DISTANCE FOOTPATHS (G.R.)

MOUNTAINS

FORESTS

There is no better way to discover a region and its people than by a leisurely progress along a river or canal. Inland Brittany, so different from the dramatic coastline, can be peacefully explored by taking a boat along shady waterways, with any number of pleasant stopping places. The rivers and canals run through deep countryside and an immense variety of natural landscape: valley, marshland, moor and forest. A good pair of binoculars will reveal abundant wildlife, and there is fishing in both river and nearby lakes. Exploring the Paimpont-Brocéliande forest by waterway adds a new dimension to the discovery of ancient Breton legends and tales of the Knights of the Round Table. Abbeys, lonely chapels and magnificent castles glide past, or can be visited, as at Pontivy or Josselin. And for those keen not to miss out on French cuisine, there are plenty of good restaurants on or near the banks.

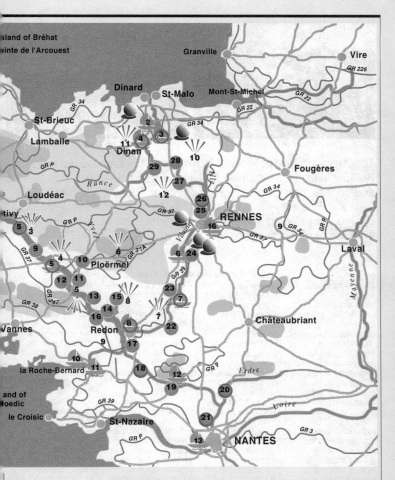

RIVERSIDE RESTAURANTS

On the Nantes–Brest canal, from Port-Launay to Carhaix and from Pontivy to Nantes.
LE GUILLY GLAS
in Port-Launay.
Tel. 02 98 86 29 06
LE BON ACCUEIL
in Châteaulin.
on the quayside.
Tel. 02 98 86 15 77,
RESTAURANT ROBIC
in Pontivy,
2-4, rue Jean-Jaurès, near the Pont de Robic.
Tel. 02 97 25 11 80
LE SUCRIER, in Redon,
39, rue des Douves, very close to the canal.
Tel. 02 99 71 13 42

CRÊPERIE RESTAURANT CHEZ BERNARD
in Saint-Martin-sur-Oust
Rue Gueslin, with canalside terrace.
Tel. 02 99 91 53 84
FERME-AUBERGE LA GRANGE AUX MOINES
near Rochefort-en-Terre, Breton farmhouse meals beside the river Oust. Reservations necessary.
Tel. 02 97 43 54 71

On the Île-et-Rance canal and the Vilaine, between St-Malo and Pénestin.
RESTAURANT LES ROSSIGNOLS, in Dinan.
In the port about 150 yards from the landing stages.

Tel. 02 96 87 92 82
AUBERGE DU HALAGE
in Tinténiac.
At the Pont-à-l'Abbesse, beside the canal.
Tel. 02 99 68 03 64
LA MARINE, in Rennes
2, place de Bretagne. Brasserie about 100 yards from the quay.
Tel. 0299 31 53 84
AUBERGE DU MOULIN DU BOËL, in Pont-Réan
Le Boël, near the lock.
Tel. 02 99 42 27 00

LA BELLE ANGUILLE
in Redon.
Route de Sainte-Marie-de-Redon, on the Vilaine.
Tel. 02 99 72 31 02
LE CARDINAL
in La Roche-Bernard.
On the Quai de la Douane, a gourmet restaurant in the old customs house.
Tel. 02 99 90 79 41
DOMAINE DE ROCHEVILAINE, in Billier.
A gourmet restaurant on the Pointe de Pen-Lan, at the mouth of the Vilaine.
Tel. 02 97 41 61 61

Roc Trévezel (1,200 feet).

Walkers on footpath GR 34.

The Argoat ("Land of Woods" in Breton) is the name given to inland Brittany since Roman times. It is a landscape of valleys, hills, woods and copses, reaching its highest points at Tuchenn Gador (1,260 feet) and Roc Trévezel (1,200 feet) in the Monts d'Arrée. Walking, cycling, horse riding and canal trips are the best ways to discover the secrets of this magnificent area.

THE PATHS OF BRITTANY

Brittany has over 1,550 miles of footpaths out of the total 37,300 miles in France.

LONG AND SHORT DISTANCE PATHS
The GR (*grandes randonnées*) are the long-distance paths. In Brittany some run east-west or north-south, while others are circular (and called *tours*). Each path takes several days to walk and there are ninety *gîtes d'étape*, hostels where walkers, cyclists and riders can stay overnight. The PR (*petites randonnées*) are paths from 2½ to 15 miles long, that can be walked in a day. Each GR path is described in a *Topoguide* which details the route, accommodation and places to get food. A full brochure on Topoguides is available from Comité National des Sentiers de Grande Randonnée 8 ave. Marceau, 75008 Paris Tel. 01 47 23 62 32, else ask for them through a good map

supplier (see p. 386).
◆ Tour of the Monts d'Arrée and parish closes (GR 380, 140 miles): the most famous of the Brittany long-distance paths includes the Léon parish closes of Lampaul, Guimiliau and St-Thégonnec, the Monts d'Arrée and Huelgoat forest. *Topoguide Tour des Monts d'Arrée, ref. 363*, 75F, published by the Fédération Française de Randonnée Pédestre (F.F.R.P.).

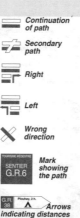

	Continuation of path
	Secondary path
	Right
	Left
	Wrong direction
TOURISME PÉDESTRE SENTIER G.R.6	Mark showing the path
G.R. 38 Plouhay, 2 h. ▲	Arrows indicating distances

◆ Côte d'Émeraude (Emerald Coast), from Mont-St-Michel to St-Brieuc (150 miles): along the coast passing Cancale, St-Malo, Cap Fréhel and the bay of St-Brieuc. *Topoguide GR 34, ref. 310*, 75F, F.F.R.P.
◆ Côte de Granite Rose (Pink Granite Coast), from St-Brieuc to Morlaix (190 miles): following coastal paths through Binic, Paimpol, Tréguier, Perros-Guirrec, Trébeurden and Lannion. *Topoguide GR 34, ref. 346*, 90F, F.F.R.P.
◆ Tour of Brocéliande (100 miles) taking in the legendary sites in the forest of Merlin and Morgan Le Fay. *Topoguide Tour de Brocéliande, Paimpont ▲ 356, Mont-sur-Meu, ref. 062*, 90 F, F.F.R.P.
◆ Tour of the Pays Gallo (210 miles): taking in chapels, chateaux and megalithic sites. *Topoguide Tour du Pays Gallo (GR de Pays), ref. 086*, 90F, F.F.R.P.

ROAD AND CROSS-COUNTRY CYCLING
All the roads in Brittany can by used by cyclists. There are specially signed circuits for cross-country bikes, but bikes are forbidden on certain paths, particularly along the coast and in the Paimpont-Brocéliande forest.
◆ RANDOBALAD 34, 8, rue Louis-d'Or 35200 Rennes Tel. 02 99 30 89 11. Tailored tours with bed-and-breakfast accommodation, and with your luggage transferred ahead.
◆ ASSOCIATION BRETONNE DES RELAIS ET ITINÉRAIRES (ABRI) 9, rue des Portes-Mordelaises 35000 Rennes Information: Tel. 02 99 67 42 20. Reservations: Tel. 02 99 67 42 21

ON HORSEBACK
◆ ASSOCIATION RÉGIONALE POUR LE TOURISME ÉQUESTRE ET L'ÉQUITATION DE LOISIR EN BRETAGNE (A.R.T.E.B). 33, rue Laennec 29710 Ploneis Tel. 02 98 91 02 02

Cycling on the Île aux Moines.

Quai Duquay-Trouin in Redon.

BRITTANY CANALS AND RIVERS

ON THE CANALS

The waterways were once used to transport goods by barge, and total over 400 miles. There are two main routes. One leads from Channel to Atlantic, St-Malo to La Roche-Bernard, by the Ille-et-Rance canal ▲ *149* and the Vilaine. The other is the Nantes–Brest canal (closed between Carhaix and Pontivy), built for military purposes between 1804 and 1842, and begun on the orders of Napoleon I. The two waterways cross at Redon, where companies hire out houseboats and narrowboats, usually supplied with bicycles for excursions along the way. A licence is not necessary to handle a boat and little skill is required for navigation, just patience when negotiating locks. Mooring is permitted anywhere, but it is sensible to use the wooden landing-stages provided at intervals along the banks.

CANOES AND ROWING

Brittany is a canoe and kayak paradise, both on sea and river; there are 70 clubs and 21 rowing clubs. On the canals barges can be moored near *rias* that can only be reached by canoe.
◆ LIGUE RÉGIONALE DE CANOE-KAYAK:
Maison des Sports Rennes
Tel. 02 99 54 67 52
◆ LIGUE DE BRETAGNE D'AVIRON (rowing):
1 bis, rue de la Mairie 29000 Quimper
Tel. 02 98 94 96 24 or 02 98 95 02 17
Clubs in Redon, Rennes and Chateaulin.

AROUND THE CANALS

There are many short paths marked from towns such as Ste-Marie-de-Redon, La Gacilly, Peillac, Rochefort-en-Terre, Malestroit, Guipry-Messac and Langon. For walkers the GR 39 goes from the Channel to the Atlantic. The towpath along the canal from Nantes to Pontivy can make a good long-distance family excursion by bicycle or on foot. It is an easy walk or ride and could be done over a few days, with stops at *gîtes d'étape*. There are many well-signposted cross-country bike routes; one of the best goes from Redon into the Oust valley.
◆ TOURIST INFORMATION OFFICE, REDON
Tel. 02 99 71 06 04. Ask for the *Topoguide VTT en Pays de Redon et de Vilaine*, 80F.

NOT TO BE MISSED

◆ CHÂTEAU DE JOSSELIN
Tel. 02 97 22 22 50
◆ MUSÉE DE LA POUPÉE
Tel. 02 97 22 36 45
The Rohan collection of old dolls.
◆ CHÂTEAU DE CRÉVY, La Chapelle-Caro costume museum, Tel. 02 97 74 91 95.
◆ ESPACE YVES ROCHER (cosmetics made from plants)
◆ MUSÉE DU PARFUM Perfume museum
Tel. 02 99 08 29 29
◆ JARDIN BOTANIQUE at Yves Rocher's factory, 12, rue Antoine-Monteil

CANAL GUIDE

Boat hire: from 3,400 to 8,000F per week, depending on the season, for four-berth boat. Canals closed from October 15 to March 15 for maintenance and improvement. Open every day in season, including public holidays. Speed limit 4 mph on canals and 5–7 mph on rivers. Slight difference in level between upper and lower waters.

LOCKS
Lock-keepers operate the locks and see you through. Open from 8.30am to 12.30pm and 1.30pm to 7.30pm according to the season. Brest to Nantes (closed between Carhaix and Pontivy), 190 miles, 236 locks. Rance barrier to Rennes, 66 miles, 49 locks. Rennes to Redon, 55 miles, 14 locks.

INFORMATION AND RESERVATIONS: Formules Bretagne, Centre Commercial Maine-Montparnasse, 17, rue de l'Arrivée 75015 Paris Tel. 01 42 79 07 07

Anse du Caon, in Douarnenez Bay.

Ocean rescue station.

The Brittany coast stretches 700 miles from Cancale to St-Nazaire. It consists of a ragged succession of cliffs, headlands and bays. The Pink Granite Coast around Trégastel and Perros-Guirec is famous for its strange rocks, worn to fantastic shapes by the wind and sea. The wildest stretch of coast is around the Crozon peninsula, protected as part of the Parc Régional d'Armorique. The Gulf of Morbihan ("little sea" in Breton) stretches like a smooth lagoon, scattered with innumerable tiny islets. And, for many, most lovely of all are the islands of Brittany, each with its own particular charm and character.

THE BEACHES

There are endless bathing spots, from huge sandy beaches to secluded pebbled creeks.

SOME BEAUTIFUL BEACHES
◆ St-Michel-en-Grève (Côtes d'Armor): 3 miles of fine sand sloping gently to the water.
◆ Sables-d'Or-les-Pins (Côtes d'Armor): a vast stretch of dune-lined beach.
◆ Plage de la Palud on the Crozon peninsula: a beautiful spot (dunes) but dangerous for swimming.
◆ Creeks among the pines on the Beg Meil coast (southern Finistère).
◆ La Baule beach: nearly 6 miles long.

WATER TEMPERATURE
The water is cool in Brittany, seldom exceeding 64°F. It is warmer in Morbihan (average temperature July/August at Carnac 62°F) than in Finistère (59°F at Roscoff in July).

SAFETY
At seaside resorts there are always one or two beaches with lifeguard surveillance. Green flag = swimming permitted. Orange flag = swimming dangerous but lifeguard on duty. Red flag = swimming forbidden, no guard. On wild beaches there are often strong waves and dangerous undercurrents. It is possible to have fun in the water, but never get out of your depth.

THE "SENTIERS DE DOUANIERS"

These are paths opened up in 1791 in an attempt to combat smuggling. They enabled customs officers to guard great lengths of coast. The paths were reopened 15 years ago and keen walkers can follow them all the way from Cancale to Brière.

BEST OF THE DOUANIERS PATHS
◆ From Yaudet to St-Michel-en-Grève (3 hrs)
◆ From Fort de la Latte to Cap Fréhel (2 hrs)
◆ From Trestraou beach (Perros-Guirec) to Ploumanac'h, 4 miles (3 hrs)
◆ Plouha cliffs ▲ 216 discovery path: a 2½-mile loop around the Pointe de Plouha and the highest cliffs in Brittany (340 feet)
◆ From Cap de la Chèvre to Morgat, 2 hrs (Crozon peninsula)

◆ Round tour of Belle-Île-en-Mer ▲ 328, 50 miles
◆ From Pouldu to St Maurice abbey, along the Laïta (1 hr)

SEASIDE ACTIVITIES

THALASSOTHERAPY
Seawater therapy (Greek, thalassa: "the sea") was invented in Roscoff in 1899 at the first marine institute. Seawater, rich in oligo elements and mineral salts, can be extremely beneficial in convalescence or after accidents, and for rheumatic conditions, involving such procedures as underwater massage and seaweed therapy. Today there are eleven centers situated between St-Malo and La Baule. Some are simply fitness centers, while others concentrate on rehabilitation or specific problems such as smoking, phlebology or post-natal treatments.

Windsurfing near the beach.

The port of Sauzon, Belle-Île-en-Mer.

NATURISM

On certain beaches nudity is tolerated or officially permitted, but on others a fine of up to 10,000F can be imposed for exhibitionism. Details from the local Tourist Information Office.

GOLF

The best golf course in Brittany is at Dinard. It was opened in 1887 to cater for the British residents. Brittany is an ideal region for the sport, and there are now over 30 good courses throughout the 5 departments. The average price per day is 150F on weekdays, and 300F at the weekend.

SOME SEASIDE GOLF COURSES

◆ GOLF CLUB DES SABLES D'OR-FRÉHEL
22240 Fréhel
Tel. 02 96 41 42 57
A long-established course, designed by a Scots architect in 1925. It then had nine holes, but has since been enlarged to eighteen.

◆ GOLF DE DINARD
54, bd de la Houle
35800 Dinard
Tel. 02 99 88 32 07
Second oldest golf course in France.

◆ GOLF DE ST-CAST-LE-GUILDO
22380 Saint Cast le Guildo
Tel. 02 96 41 91 20

◆ GOLF PLOEMEUR OCÉAN
St-Jude/Kerham
56270 Ploemeur
Tel. 02 97 32 81 82

◆ GOLF DU RHUYS
Domaine de Kerver
56730 St-Gildas-de-Rhuys
Tel. 02 97 45 30 09

◆ GOLF DE BADEN
Kernic
56870 Baden
Tel. 02 97 57 18 96

◆ GOLF DE SAUZON
56360 Belle-Île-en-Mer
Tel. 02 97 31 64 65

ISLAND TRIPS

Some islands, such as Belle-Île-en-Mer and Bréhat, are fashionable. Others have a reputation for sports, such as the Glenan archipelago, where a sailing and diving school started in 1947 has achieved an international reputation. Others, termed the "wild" ones include Ouessant, Sein and the Molène archipelago, lashed by wind and sea. With 504 inhabitants, Sein is Brittany's smallest inhabited island. There are also the many little islets in the Gulf of Morbihan, "one for every day of the year".

PARADISE FOR BIRDS
Gulls, cormorants, gannets and kittiwakes nest on these islands. The Gulf of Morbihan has the greatest concentration of sea birds in the Channel and Atlantic coast (60,000 to 100,000 birds, depending on the time of the year). The best period for birdwatching is in the nesting season, spring until mid-July.

◆ RÉSERVE ORNITHOLOGIQUE DU CAP FRÉHEL
Maison des Deux-Caps (Erquy and Fréhel)
Tel. 02 96 41 50 83

◆ RÉSERVE DE L'ÎLE DES LANDES
(Cancale). The observation point is on the Pointe de Grouin; no visitors are allowed on the island.

◆ RÉSERVE DES SEPT ÎLES (off Ploumanac'h. The oldest bird sanctuary in France: 12,000 nesting pairs of 15 different species. Station ornithologique de l'Île-Grande
Tel. 02 96 91 91 40

◆ RÉSERVE DE KOH-KASTELL EN SAUZON, on Belle-Île-en-Mer. A reserve created in 1962 on a prehistoric site, to protect the southernmost colony on kittiwakes in Europe. Reception point: SEPNB, in the Apothicairerie carpark
Tel. 02 98 49 07 18

◆ RÉSERVE MICHEL-HERVÉ JULIEN at Goulien-Cap-Sizun
Tel. 02 98 70 13 53

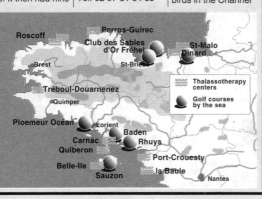

Sail on an old rigger at Bénodet.

Fishing boats on Roscoff harbor.

In Breton, Armor means "land of seas". The Channel and the Atlantic ocean are part of Brittany's beauty and excitement, but they are also dangerous. The seas provide plentiful and delicious fish, as well as the enjoyment of sailing and other water sports. There are 41 marinas and 130 sailing schools around the picturesque and challenging coasts of the province. Before going to sea it is important to know about the winds, currents and tides, and to follow the recommended safety precautions.

THE FISHING FLEETS

Fishing is the main source of income for 6,000 Bretons. The region brings in more fish than any other in France, caught in both coastal and deeper waters.

SPECIALIZED PORTS
Mussels are farmed in St-Brieuc bay and Mont-St-Michel bay. They are raised attached to *bouchots*, oak posts. There is also shrimp fishing in these bays. The region of Erquy is known for its scallops, producing the most in Brittany. Douarnenez and Turballe are important

sardine ports. The picturesque harbors in Cornouaille (Concarneau, Le Guilvinec, St-Guénolé, Loctudy and Lesconil) bring in nearly two-thirds of the national catch of langoustines.

AMATEUR FISHING

If fishing for personal consumption only, no licence is needed. It is forbidden to sell any fish caught, and there are fines for this offence.

ALONG THE SHORE
Anyone with a rake, knife and net can enjoy collecting shellfish and crustacea from flat rocks and beaches at low tide, provided that their harvest is for personal consumption only. Cockles can be found almost anywhere along the Brittany coast. In the Audierne region there are sea urchins, mussels, prawns and crabs. Around the island of Sein there are swimming crabs and winkles, while the

island of Batz is known for its ormers. Don't collect shellfish from the bottom of estuaries, where the water is polluted.

SEA-FISHING TRIPS
Many fishermen are happy to take people out fishing on their boats in summer, and to show how lines are cast, nets brought in and fish landed. The easiest places to arrange such fishing trips are at Concarneau, Douarnenez, Le Guilvinec and Loctudy. Ask at Tourist Information Offices.

UNDERWATER FISHING
Scuba-diving and underwater fishing are very popular along the Breton coast. It is essential to take into account currents and to dive only in slack water. This fishing practice is subject to strict regulations by the various departments. For information contact:
◆ Plongée Bretagne Tel. 02 97 37 51 51

SAILING BRITTANY

Both north and south are marvelous for sailing, although not for the inexperienced. There are currents, choppy seas, difficult winds and treacherous reefs. The tides and currents are stronger in northern Brittany. The southern coast has delightful islands and the Gulf of Morbihan, almost an inland sea, is varied and enjoyable to explore.

LEARNING TO SAIL
Several harbors have been awarded the title "Station Voile" or "Point Passion Plage" to indicate that they are particularly well equipped for sailing. Activities and lessons can be booked by the hour, or in a number of different arrangements at the 130 sailing schools and 250 water sports centers in Brittany. For information contact:
◆ Ligue Bretagne de Voile, in Brest Tel. 02 98 02 49 67

The Pink Granite Coast at Ploumanac'h.

From the top of Cap Fréhel, 230 feet.

WINDSURFING AT ITS BEST

The first windsurfer made his appearance in Brittany at Bénodet in 1970. Since then the number of surfing sports in the region has multiplied: funboards, boogie-boards and surfskis abound, some ridden standing, some sitting and some just for playing about in the breakers.

TOP SPOTS FROM NORTH TO SOUTH
◆ The Sillon beach, 2 miles long, at

St-Malo is perfect for windsurfing and speed-sailing.

◆ Dossen beach, near Roscoff, is good for funboards and boogieboards.

◆ Point du Petit-Minou, between Plougonvelin and Brest, is good for surfing.

◆ Moulin-Blanc beach, west of Brest, is good for windsurfers of all levels.

◆ Crozon peninsula: La Palud beach is recommended for expert surfers only as there are very big waves here, Aber beach for boogieboards, surfskis and speed-sailing.

◆ Baie des Trépassés at Pointe du Raz is recommended for good surfers only.

◆ Pointe de la Torche in Audierne bay (4 miles) is famous for surfing since the World Cup is now held here in October/November.

◆ St-Hugen beach in Audierne bay is ideal for surfing.

◆ Isthmus of Penthièvre (2 miles) at the top of the Quiberon peninsula is very popular for surfskiing and speed-sailing.

◆ La Baule beach (6 miles), set on a calm bay, is perfect for windsurfing.
LIGUE RÉGIONALE DE CHAR À VOILE, Rennes
Tel. 02 99 50 94 28.

AREAS OF OUTSTANDING NATURAL BEAUTY

◆ Mont-St-Michel bay ▲ *176* from Cap Lihou to the Pointe du Grouin. The waters stretch over almost 300 square miles. Mont-St-Michel, "the wonder of the West", is a monument listed by UNESCO. It attracts two million visitors a year.

◆ Cap Fréhel. A protected headland of over 700 acres of protected coastal heathland ▲ *204*.

◆ La Côte de Granite Rose (the Pink Granite Coast) ▲ *223*, from Perros-Guirec to Trébeurden. Spectacular scenery and strangely shaped pink rocks.

◆ The Rade de Brest, one of the most impressive river channels in the world, almost 100 square miles in area ▲ *274*.

◆ Crozon peninsula ▲ *288*. A 15-mile-long cross-shaped promontory with a number of lovely headlands (Pointes des Espagnols, de Pen Hir, du Toulinguet) and the magnificent Cap de la Chèvre.

◆ Pointe du Raz. The furthermost tip of Finistère ▲ *294*, last stop before America. One million visitors come annually to look over the 200 foot cliffs. Steps are now taken to get rid of its unsightly touristic appearance.

◆ Gulf of Morbihan ▲ *348*. *Mor-bihan* means "little sea", as opposed to *mor-braz*, "big sea or ocean". The gulf covers 29,000 acres, scattered with about 50 islands, 15 of which are still inhabited. The largest of the islands are Arz and Île-aux-Moines ▲ *349–50*.

◆ The Côte Sauvage on the Quiberon peninsula is a long succession of cliffs with sea-caves and natural rock arches.

◆ Belle-Île-en-Mer ▲ *328*, the biggest island (10½ miles in length by 5½ miles in width) in Brittany and one of the most beautiful. Not to be missed: the Aiguilles ("needles") at Port Coton, immortalized on canvas by Monet; and the Apothicairerie cave.

SAFETY
The CROSS (rescue services) listen round the clock to channel 16 for distress calls.
CROSS CORSEN: from Mont-St-Michel to the Pointe de Corsen
Tel. 02 98 89 31 31, channel 79.
CROSS ÉTEL: from the Pointe du Raz to Sables d'Olonne
Tel. 02 97 55 35 35, channel 80.
If you see an accident at sea, verify your exact position and immediately alert the CROSS, the local gendarmerie or the nearest ocean rescue station.

PLACE NAMES

◆ AB ◆

ARZH: Arz (Ile d')
ALRE: Auray
AN DRINDED-KARNAG:
  La Trinité-sur-Mer
AN ORIANT: Lorient
AR BAOL: La Baule
AR FAOUED:
  Le Faouët
AR GROAZIG:
  Le Croisic
AR GWERNOU:
  Le Guerno
AR MERZHER:
  La Martyre
BANGOR: Bangor
BENODED: Bénodet
BEGNEN: Bignan
BINIG: Binic
BREST: Brest

◆ D to J ◆

DAOULAZ: Daoulas
DINAN: Dinan
DINARZH: Dinard
DOL: Dol-de-Bretagne
ENEZ-EUSA:
  Ouessant (Ile d')
ENEZ-GAVRINIZ:
  Gavrinis (Ile de)
ENEZ-GROE: Groix
  (Ile de)
ENEZ-SUN: Sein
  (Ile de)
ENEZ-VAZ: Batz
  (Ile de)
ENEZ-VRIAD: Bréhat
  (Ile de):
ERGE-AR-MOR: Erquy

FELGER: Fougères
GELVENEG:
  Le Guilvinec
GERVEUR: Belle-Île-
  en-Mer
GOURIN: Gourin
GWENED: Vannes
GWIMILIO: Guimiliau
GWITREG: Vitré

◆ K ◆

KAMELED: Camaret
KANKAVEN: Cancale
KARANTEG: Carantec
KARNAG: Carnac
KASTELL-BRIANT:
  Châteaubriant
KASTELL-GERON:
  Châteaugiron
KASTELL-NEVEZ-AR-
  FAOU: Châteauneuf-
  du-Faou
KEMPER: Quimper
KIBEREN: Quiberon
KINTIN: Quintin
KISTREBERZH:
  Questembert
KOLPOU: Colpo
KOMMANNA:
  Commana
KOMBORN: Combourg
KONK-KERNE:
  Concarneau
KONK-LEON: Le
  Conquet
KRAOZON: Crozon

◆ L ◆

LANDREGER: Tréguier
LANNIDIG: Lantic
LAMBAOL-GWIMILIO:
  Lampaul-Guimiliau
LANDERNE:
  Landerneau
LOKMARIAKAER:
  Locmariaquer
LOKMARIA: Locmaria
LOKORN: Locronan

◆ MN ◆

MAEN-AR-BOUDIGED:
  La Roche-aux-Fées
MORGAD: Morgat
MONTROULEZ: Morlaix
ENIZENAC'H: Moines
  (Ile aux)
MUR: Mûr-de-
  Bretagne
MUZILHEG: Muzillac
NAONED: Nantes

◆ PR ◆

PEMPOULL: Paimpol
PLENEG-NANTRAEZH:
  Pléneuf-Val André
PONT-AVEN: Pont-
  Aven
PLOUGOUSKANT:
  Plougrescant
PLOUILIO: Ploumilliau
PLOUEZOC'H:
  Plouézoch
PLOUESKAD: Plouescat
PLOUGUERNE:
  Plouguerneau
PLOUGASTELL-

DAOULAZ:
  Plougastel-Daoulas
PONDIVI: Pontivy
PONT-'N-ABAD:
  Pont-l'Abbé
PORSAL: Portsall
PORZH-LOEIZ:
  Port-Louis
RIEG: Riec-sur-Belon
ROAZHON: Rennes
AR ROC'H-KRENV:
  Rochefort-en-Terre
ROC'HAN: Rohan
ROSKO: Roscoff

◆ ST ◆

SANT-TEGONEG: Saint-
  Thégonnec
SANT-VORAN: Ste-
  Marine
SAOZON: Sauzon
SANTEZ-ANNA-WENED:
  Ste-Anne d'Auray
LOKENTAZ: St-Gildas-
  de-Rhuys
SANT-MALOÙ: St-Malo
SANT-BRIEG: St-Brieuc
SANT-KAE-PORZH-
  OLUED: St-Quay-
  Portrieux
SANT-NAZER:
  St-Nazaire
SINE: Séné
SIZUN : Sizun
TINTENIEG: Tinténiac
TREVARE: Trévarez

COMMON WORDS

**EVERYDAY
EXPRESSIONS**
MAC'H PLIJ: please
TRUGAREZ: thank you
DEIZH MAD: hello
NOZVEZ VAD: goodbye
EATING & DRINKING
LOA: spoon
FOURCHETEZ: fork
KONTELL: knife
ASIED: plate
GWERENN: glass
PRED: meal
KOAN: dinner
LEIN: lunch
DIJUNI: breakfast
BOUED: food
FROUEZH: fruit
UI: egg
BARA: bread
DOUR: water
AMANN: butter
SUKR: sugar
KIG: meat
PESK: fish
LEGUMAJ: vegetables
GWIN: wine
SISTR: cider
BIER: beer
GWASTELL: cake
AVAL-DOUAR: potato
THE FAMILY
PAOTR: boy

PLAC'H: girl
GWAZ: man
MAOUEZ: woman
BUGEL: child
TAD: father
MAMM: mother
MAB: son
MERC'H: daughter
BREUR: brother
C'HOAR: sister
TAD-KOZH:
  grandfather
MAMM-GOZH:
  grandmother
MIGNON: friend
VERBS
PRENAN: to buy
KOUSTAN: to cost
LENN: to read
SKRIVAN: to write
KOMPREN: to
  understand
SELLOUT: to look
GWELOUT: to see
DEBRIN: to eat
KOUSKET: to sleep
EXPRESSIONS
PEGEN?: how much?
PESEURT?: what kind
  of?
KALZ: much, many
ALIES: often
E-PAD: during

A-WECHOU:
  sometimes
PEGOULZ?: when?
PEGEIT?: how long?
DIOUZHTU:
  immediately
ADJECTIVES
TOMM: hot
YEN: cold
FRESK: fresh
BRAS: big
BIHAN: small
UHEL: high
IZEL: low
HIR: long, tall
BERR: short
MAD: good
FALL: bad
GWIR: true
FALZ: false
THE HOUSE
TI: house
DAOL: table
GWELE: bed
KADOR: chair
KAMBR: room
ARMEL: cupboard
GEOGRAPHY
MOR: sea
BRO: country
AMZER: weather
HEOL: sun
AVEL: wind

GLAV: rain
OABL: sky
DOUAR: earth, ground
KOUMOUL: clouds
COUNTING
UNAN: one
DAOU: two
TRI: three
PEVAR: four
PEMP: five
C'HWEC'H: six
SEIZH: seven
EIZH: eight
NAV: nine
DEK: ten
DAYS OF THE WEEK
DILUN: Monday
DIMEURZH: Tuesday
DIMERC'HER:
  Wednesday
DIRIAOU: Thursday
DIGWENER: Friday
DISADORN: Saturday
DISUL: Sunday
THE YEAR
BLOAZ: year
MIZ: month
SIZHUN: week
DEIZ: day
NOZ: night
WARC'HOAZH:
  tomorrow
HIZIR: today

◆ CHILDREN'S ACTIVITIES

A sail on the Cancalaise.

Trégor planetarium.

For children a Brittany holiday need not just be swimming and playing on the beach. There are plenty of activities: water sports, leisure parks, animal parks, aquariums, boat museums, boat trips and visits to lighthouses.

BEACHES AND SAILING

During the summer many seaside resorts offer a range of activities at the beach club. Children of three years old upward, of all nationalities, are welcomed, enrolling by the day or half-day. There are organized exercises, trampoline and swings, ball games and contests. Prices are progressively lower according to the number of children in the family and the length of time they stay. Children of six years upward can start learning to sail in "Optimist"-class dinghies, at any of the 130 Brittany sailing schools.

HISTORICAL BOAT TRIPS

Children always enjoy going on boats; a sea excursion on one of Brittany's 250 renovated traditional vessels (fishing boats, clippers and rigged craft) is a particular treat.
◆ Cancale: the *Cancalaise* is a bisquine, once the local 18-meter fishing vessel. Association La Bisquine Cancalaise Tel. 02 99 89 77 87.
◆ St-Malo: the *Renard*, replica of the last boat fitted out by privateer Robert Surcouf, in 1812, Association du Cotre Corsaire Tel. 02 99 40 53 10. Prices per day in high season: adults 350 F, children 16 and under 175 F.
◆ Brest: the schooner *Recouvrance* Tel. 02 98 52 04 80. The Association Gouelia ("hoist the sail" in Breton) represents five old boats: the *Recouvrance* in Brest, the *Belle Angèle* in Pont-Aven, the *Corentin* in Quimper, the *Belle Étoile* in Camaret and the *Dalmate* in Landerneau. Tel. Quimper 02 98 95 32 33.

MARITIME HERITAGE

There are about twenty maritime museums. The largest is the Museum Port in Douarnenez, opened in 1986.
◆ Musée du Bateau Quai du Port-Rhu in Douarnenez ▲ 293 Tel. 02 98 92 67 30 Open every day from 10am to 7pm. One of the richest collections in Europe: two hundred boats from twelve countries. A huge project was begun in 1993 to restore the clipper *Le Paulista*, a boat that carried coffee from Brazil to France in the 19th century. She will be relaunched in the year 2000.

◆ Écomusée du Port de St-Nazaire – submarine base Tel. 02 40 22 35 33. By reservation only: guided visits of the submarine *Espadon*, built 1957 and in service until 1985.
◆ Musée de la Marine in the Château de Brest Tel. 02 98 22 12 39; history of Brest arsenal and the golden days of the great sailing fleets.

SCIENCE
◆ Trégor Planetarium in Pleumeur-Bodou (Côtes-d'Armor) Tel. 02 96 15 80 30. One of the largest in Europe (hemispheric screen nearly 2,000 square feet in area, seats 315).
◆ Usine marémotrice de la Rance ▲ 200 in La Richardais (Ille-et-Vilaine) Tel. 02 99 16 37 14. The Rance tidal power station was opened in 1966. It produces electricity by harnessing the force of the tides, using the same method as the old tidal mills.
◆ Barrage du lac de Guerlédan at St-Aignan (Morbihan) Tel. 02 96 28 51 41 (dam) and 02 97 27 51 39 (museum).

A TRIP AROUND THE LIGHTHOUSES
The Brittany coast is dotted with lighthouses, many of which have been rebuilt over the centuries, standing at key points to signal warning to ships of the dangerous reefs and rocks.
Some lighthouses can be visited:
◆ Phare de l'Île Vierge, the highest in Europe, 252 feet high and 392 steps.
◆ Phare Eckmühl at Penmarc'h, 213 feet high and visible for nearly 34 miles.
◆ Phare de Créac'h on Ouessant, the most powerful in Brittany.
Information from Brest: Tel. 02 98 44 24 96.

Branféré zoological park.

Douarnenez boat museum.

AQUARIUMS

◆ Océanopolis Port de Plaisance du Moulin-Blanc, Brest Tel. 02 98 34 40 40. Open all year. The largest open-air aquarium in Europe, presented with plenty of practical, scientific and technical information.

◆ Aquarium de la Côte de Granite Rose, in Trégastel Tel. 02 96 23 88 67. Open all year, daily in July and August, 9am to 8pm. Twenty-eight aquariums built into the pink granite rocks.

◆ Aquarium de Vannes Tel. 02 97 40 67 40 Aquarium ▲ 346 with several hundred species of fish, many of them tropical, from all over the world.

◆ Le Grand Aquarium La Ville Jouan 35400 St-Malo Tel. 02 99 21 19 02. Circular aquarium open all year and displaying thousands of fish. These include sharks swimming around a sunken vessel.

LEISURE PARKS

◆ Armoripark at Bégard (Côtes-d'Armor) Tel. 02 96 45 36 36. Open April to September on Sundays and during school holidays, and every day from June 20 to September 8. Fifteen acres of park with a covered swimming area, tobogganing, archery, mini-golf, rock-climbing and games.

◆ Village Gaulois at Pleumeur Bodou Tel. 02 96 91 83 95. Open every day except Saturday 1.30pm to 6pm, April to September, and every day 10am–7pm in July and August. The children's aid organization MEEM (Monde des Enfants aux Enfants du Monde) set up an international youth project to build a Gallic and a Togolese village.

◆ Cobac Parc at Lanhélin (Ille-et-Vilaine). Open 10.30am to 6.30pm from April 3 to September 10. Leisure center, pony rides, trains, roundabouts, water slides and bird park.

ZOOS AND ANIMAL PARKS

◆ Parc zoologique de Branféré at Muzillac ▲ 366 (Morbihan) Tel. 02 97 42 94 66. Over 2,000 creatures free to roam in 120 acres of pleasant parkland. Birds predominate (ibis, storks and geese), but there are also monkeys, buffalo, llamas, prairie dogs, Tasmanian kangaroos and Patagonian hares.

◆ Parc zoologique "Moulin de Richard" at Trégomeur (Côtes- d'Armor) Tel. 02 96 79 01 07. Open 2pm to 6pm every day. Animals in an open environment: lions, zebras, gnus, ostriches, yaks, chimpanzees, tigers and wallabies.

◆ Parc zoologique de Pont-Scorff (Morbihan) Tel. 02 97 32 60 86. Open 9.30am to 5pm every day. Bears, bison, giraffes, wildcats and reptiles.

◆ Parc zoologique de la Bourbansais, at Pleugueneuc Tel. 02 99 69 40 07. Open every day. Zoo and games area in the park belonging to the château.

MUSEUMS

◆ Musée Jules Verne ▲ 381 in Nantes Tel. 02 40 69 72 52 Model of the *Nautilus*, flying machines, rockets, illustrated books by Jules Verne, the most widely translated of all French writers, who was born in Nantes.

◆ Dolls and Old Toys Museum ("Musée de la Poupée et des Jouets Anciens") in Nantes Tel. 02 40 69 14 41.

Dolls shown in cases with model furniture of the period (1830–1930).

◆ Pavillon Madeleine Lilas in Nantes Tel. 02 40 71 85 00. Miniature models illustrating the history of the 20th century, from Belle-Époque to May 1968.

Plougastel Calvary.

The Ménec alignments at Carnac.

There are impressive monuments dating from every period in Breton history. The many megalithic sites are mainly concentrated around the Gulf of Morbihan. All over Brittany are calvaries and shrines, parish closes, churches and cathedrals, fortresses and châteaux, dating from the medieval and Renaissance periods. Late in the 19th century this wild region inspired work by some great artists, including Paul Gauguin and Claude Monet.

PREHISTORY

Brittany's megaliths are the remaining signs of a civilization that inhabited Armorica between 3500 and 3000 BC and of which little is known. The monuments can be divided into two main categories: standing stones (*menhirs* in Breton) and stone tables, or dolmens. Dolmens were undoubtedly linked with burial, while menhirs were apparently used for some kind of calculations, astronomical or perhaps more mundane.

There are 4,500 known dolmens and *allées couvertes* (long barrows) in France, 665 of them in the Morbihan and Finistère, and 2,200 menhirs (554 in the same two departments).
◆ Carnac stones ▲ 335. The alignments of 2,935 stones at Carnac are one of the wonders of the prehistoric world. Also at Carnac is the Musée de la Préhistoire J. Miln et Z. Le Rouzic Tel. 02 97 52 22 04
◆ Locmariaquer ▲ 338, an extended site that includes the Table des Marchands (350-ton dolmen with a corridor leading to room with carved dolmen).
◆ St-Just. Standing stones of quartz and schist, circular burial chambers, dolmens, graves. Tel. 02 99 72 60 44
◆ Covered walkway of Roche aux Fées at Essé, 3,000 years BC, 64 feet long, 20 feet wide and 13 feet high: the largest megalithic monument of its kind in Brittany. It consists of forty-one stone slabs, half a dozen of which weigh between 40 and 45 tons.

◆ Cairn de Barnenez at Plouézoc'h ▲ 225 Tel. 02 98 67 24 73 Its size alone makes this the most important tumulus in Europe (236 feet long, from 50 to 80 feet wide and 14 feet high). It contains eleven granite and dolerite megalithic tombs. This immense mausoleum probably contained the bodies of local chieftains, and dates from between 3800 and 3500 BC.

EXCURSIONS
LA ROUTE DES MÉGALITHES
Island of Gavrinis, sites at Carnac and the Table des Marchands at Locmariaquer: 285 F per person.
THE PAYS D'AURAY AND THE CÔTE DES MÉGALITHES
Carnac alignments, St-Michel tumulus, Table des Marchands at Locmariaquer: 190 F per person. Reservations (Vannes) Tel. 02 97 54 06 56

RELIGIOUS ART
1. Calvary of Notre-Dame de Tronoën / 2. Chapel of Notre-Dame-de-bonne-Nouvelle at Locronan / 3. Calvary of Pleyben / 4. Parish close of la Martyre / 5. Parish close of Lampaul-Guimiliau / 6. Parish close of Guimiliau
7. Parish close of Saint-Thégonnec
8. Parish close of Kergrist-Moëlou
9. Chapel of Saint-Fiacre du Faouët
10. Calvary of Nizon

◆ Megaliths

Barnenez cairn

Brest
St-Brieuc
St-Malo
Champ-Dolent menhir

Lagadjar alignments

Quimper

Rennes

Allée couverte de La Roche aux Fées
St-Just alignments

Lorient

Locmariaquer dolmen

Carnac alignments

Gavrinis cairn

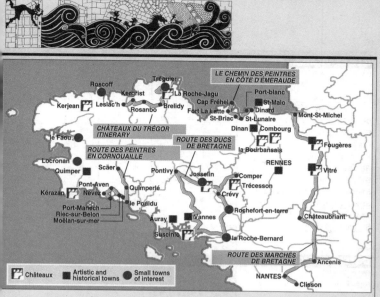

Map showing:

LE CHEMIN DES PEINTRES EN CÔTE D'ÉMERAUDE

Roscoff · Tréguier · Kergrist · La Roche-Jagu · Port-blanc · St-Malo · Leslac'h · Brelidy · Cap Fréhel · Dinard · Kerjean · Rosanbo · Fort La Latte · St-Briac · St-Lunaire · Mont-St-Michel · St-Briac · Dinan · Combourg

CHÂTEAUX DU TRÉGOR ITINERARY

le Faou · ROUTE DES PEINTRES EN CORNOUAILLE · ROUTE DES DUCS DE BRETAGNE · la Bourbansais · Fougères

Locronan · Quimper · Scäer · Pontivy · Josselin · Comper · RENNES · Vitré · Trécesson · Kérazan · Pont-Aven · Quimperlé · Crévy · Névez · Port-Manech · le Pouldu · Riec-sur-Belon · Moëlan-sur-mer · Auray · Vannes · Rochefort-en-terre · Châteaubriant · Suscinie · la Roche-Bernard

ROUTE DES MARCHÉS DE BRETAGNE · Ancenis

NANTES · Clisson

Legend:
🏰 Châteaux ■ Artistic and historical towns ● Small towns of interest

RELIGIOUS BUILDINGS

The most venerated Christian monuments in Brittany are its calvaries. Stone-carved, often from granite, calvaries illustrate the life of the Virgin Mary and Christ (with scenes from the Passion). The oldest one, dating from the late 15th century, is at Tronoën in Cornouaille ▲ 307.

THE PARISH CLOSE ROUTE

For information on the parish closes and Monts d'Arrées, Tel. 02 98 68 48 84. A parish close ▲ 245 is a group of monuments surrounded by a wall

RURAL HERITAGE COMMUNES

Fifteen communes graded according to their heritage value offer discovery tours. For information contact:
Bureau Régional 12-14, rue du Pré-Botté, BP 76032 35000 Rennes Tel. and Fax: 02 99 79 24 20

and containing a church, calvary, funerary chapel or mortuary, a graveyard and a triumphal arch.

BRITTANY CHÂTEAUX

There are 4,000 châteaux, manor houses and other historic dwellings in Brittany, built between the Middle Ages and the 18th century. *Malouinières* are found around St-Malo (as their name implies), while the majority of châteaux are in the Trégor, the Ille-et-Vilaine (*route Chateaubriand*), and on the old frontier of the Duchy of Brittany (*route historique des Marches de Bretagne*).

LA ROUTE CHATEAUBRIAND

This itinerary follows in the steps of the famous French author François-René de Chateaubriand. There are fifteen châteaux to visit, with memorabilia of the writer.
◆ Le Fort La Latte, at Fréhel ▲ 203 Tel. 02 96 41 40 31 This 14th-century fortress dominates Cap Fréhel.

A circular route starting from Morlaix takes the visitor to the closes from St-Thégonnex to Plouneour-Menez.

◆ Château de Combourg Tel. 02 99 73 22 95 A medieval castle where Chateaubriand spent his holidays as a boy.
◆ Château des Rochers-Sévigné ▲ 169 at Vitré Tel. 02 99 96 76 51 Madame de Sévigné retired here after her husband's death, and it was here that she wrote 267 letters to her daughter Mme de Grignan (the famous *Lettres de Madame de Sévigné*).

LA ROUTE HISTORIQUE DES MARCHES DE BRETAGNE

The Marches are the old frontier between the former Duchy of Brittany and the Kingdom of France.
◆ Mont-St-Michel ▲ 176 Tel. 02 33 60 14 14. The world-famous abbey, built on a granite islet.
◆ Château des Ducs de Bretagne ▲ 374, at Nantes. Tel. 40 41 56 56. Several kings, stayed here.

ARTISTS IN BRITTANY

Cornouaille attracted many painters in the latter years of the last century, mainly grouped around Paul Gauguin ▲ 312. The *Route des Peintres en Cornouaille* association has five suggested itineraries that take in the sights and landscapes linked with these artists. Information at the Office de Tourisme in Pont-Aven:
Tel. 02 98 06 04 70
◆ Musée de Pont-Aven ▲ 311 Tel. 02 98 06 14 43 has works by the Pont-Aven School (Gauguin, Sérusier, Émile Bernard).
◆ Maison de Marie Henry at Le Pouldu Tel. 02 98 39 98 51 This is the former Buvette de la Plage rebuilt according to paintings by Gauguin, Meyer, de Haan, Sérusier and Émile Bernard painted in the winter of 1889.
◆ Le Bois d'Amour, on the bank of the Aven with the 16th-century chapel of Trémalo. It contains the wooden figure of Christ that was the model for Gauguin's *Christ jaune*.

TOWN	TELEPHONE (TO: tourist office, SI: syndicat d'initiative, TH: town hall)	▶ ITINERARY	▪ USEFUL ADDRESSES	MUSEUM	PLACE OF INTEREST	SPECIAL
ILLE-ET-VILAINE						
CANCALE (35260)	02 99 89 63 72 (TO)	182	418	●		●
CHÂTEAUGIRON (35410)	02 99 37 41 69 (TH)	162	419		●	●
COMBOURG (35270)	02 99 73 13 93 (TO)	149	419		●	
DINARD (35800)	02 99 46 94 12 (TO)	200	422			●
DOL-DE-BRETAGNE (35120)	02 99 48 15 37 (TO)	181	420			
FOUGÈRES (35300)	02 99 94 12 20 (TO)	170	420	●	● ◆	●
LES IFFS (35630)	02 99 45 83 69 (TH)	148	420		●	●
PAIMPONT (35380)	02 99 07 84 23 (SI)	356	438			●
RENNES (35000)	02 99 79 01 98 (TO)	138	418	●	●	
ST-BRIAC-SUR-MER (35800)	02 99 88 32 47 (TO)	203				
ST-JOUAN-DES-GUÉRETS (35430)	02 99 19 19 00 (TH)	160	421			●
ST-LUNAIRE (35800)	02 99 46 31 09 (TO)	202			●	
ST-MALO (35400)	02 99 56 64 48 (TO)	186	422	●	●	●
ST-SULIAC (35430)	02 99 58 41 22 (TH)	159	421			
TINTÉNIAC (35190)	02 99 68 09 62 (TO)	147		●	●	●
VITRÉ (35500)	02 99 75 04 46 (TO)	164	421	●	●	
CÔTES-D'ARMOR						
BINIC (22520)	02 96 73 60 12 (SI)	216	424	●		
BRÉHAT (ÎLE-DE) (22870)	02 96 20 04 15 (SI)	216	424		●	
DINAN (22100)	02 96 39 75 40 (TO)	152	419	●	●	
ERQUY (22430)	02 96 72 30 12 (TO)	207	422	●	●	
FRÉHEL (22240)	02 96 41 53 81 (TO)	204	423	●	●	
LANTIC (22410)	02 96 71 95 67 (TH)	217			●	
LÉHON (22100)	02 96 39 07 19 (TH)	157			●	
LOGUIVY-DE-LA-MER (22620)	02 96 55 80 36 (TH)	221			●	
MÛR-DE-BRETAGNE (22530)	02 96 28 51 41 (SI)	229	424		●	
PAIMPOL (22500)	02 96 20 83 16 (TH)	220	424	●	●	
PERROS-GUIREC (22700)	02 96 23 21 15 (TO)	223	425	●	●	
PLEUDIHEN-SUR-RANCE (22690)	02 96 83 20 20 (TH)	159	422	●		
PLÉNEUF-VAL-ANDRÉ (22370)	02 96 72 20 55 (TO)	208	423			
PLOUGRESCANT (22820)	02 96 92 51 18 (TO)	223	425		●	
PLOUHA (22580)	02 96 20 24 73 (TH)	216	425		●	
PLOUMANAC'H (22700)	02 96 91 40 61 (SI)	223			●	
PLOUMILLIAU (22300)	02 96 35 45 09 (TH)	224	425		●	
QUINTIN (22800)	02 96 74 01 51 (TO)	226	425	●	● ◆	
SABLE-D'OR-LES-PINS (22290)	02 96 72 17 23 (TH)	207				
ST-BRIEUC (22000)	02 96 33 32 50 (TO)	210	423	●	●	
ST-QUAY-PORTRIEUX (22410)	02 96 70 40 64 (TO)	216	425			
TRÉBEURDEN (22560)	02 96 23 51 64 (TO)		426			
TRÉGUIER (22220)	02 96 92 30 19 (TH)	222	426	●	●	
FINISTÈRE						
BATZ (ÎLE-DE) (29253)	02 98 61 75 70 (TO)	259	427		●	●
BÉNODET (29950)	02 98 57 00 14 (TO)	308	432		●	
BREST (29200)	02 98 44 24 96 (TO)	274	429	●	●	
CAMARET-SUR-MER (29570)	02 98 27 93 60 (SI)	289	430	●	●	
CARANTEC (29660)	02 98 67 00 43 (TO)	258	427	●	●	●
CHÂTEAUNEUF-DU-FAOU (29520)	02 98 81 83 90 (SI)	267	427		●	
CONCARNEAU (29900)	02 98 97 01 44 (TO)	308	432	●	●	
COMMANA (29450)	02 98 78 00 13 (TH)	255	427	●	●	
CROZON-MORGAT (29160)	02 98 27 07 92 (TO)	290	430			
DAOULAS (29460)	02 98 25 80 19 (TH)	288	431			
DOUARNENEZ (29100)	02 98 92 13 35 (TO)	293	431	●	●	
GUIMILIAU (29400)	02 98 68 75 06 (TH)	253			●	
LA MARTYRE (29800)	02 98 25 13 19 (TH)	256	427		●	
LANDERNEAU (29800)	02 98 85 13 09 (TO)	257				
LANDIVISIAU (29400)	02 98 68 03 50 (TO)				●	●
LE CONQUET (29217)	02 98 89 11 31 (TO)	264	427	●		
LE GUILVINEC (29730)	02 98 58 29 29 (TH)	306			●	

BEACH ● ■	BOAT TRIPS	SPEED SAIL	SAILING ● DIVING ■	HORSERIDING	CLIMBING	SWIMMING POOL ● TENNIS ■	GOLF	CASINO ● THALASSOTHERAPY ■	AERIAL SPORTS	COUNTRY HOLIDAYS
◆	●		◆			◆				
				●		● ◆				●
	●					● ◆	●	● ◆	●	●
				●		◆	●			●
				●		● ◆				●
				●		◆				●
◆	●		●			◆	●			
			● ◆	●		◆			●	
◆	●	●	● ◆	●		● ◆		● ◆		
◆			●			◆				●
				●		◆				●
						● ◆	●			●
◆			●			◆				
◆	●		●			◆				
				●		● ◆				
◆	●		● ◆	●	●	◆			●	
	●	●	● ◆	●		◆	●			
			●			● ◆	●			
						● ◆				●
◆			●			◆				
				●		◆				●
◆			● ◆	●		● ◆			●	
◆			● ◆	●		◆		◆		
			●	●		◆				●
◆		●	● ◆	●		● ◆	●			
◆	●		●	●	●	◆				
◆		●	●	●		◆				
◆	●		●		●	◆				
				●		◆				●
				●		◆				●
			● ◆	●		◆	●		●	
◆	●	●	● ◆	●		◆			●	
◆			● ◆	●		● ◆	●			
◆	●		● ◆	●	●	◆	●			
			●	●		● ◆				●
◆	●		● ◆	●		● ◆	●	●		
◆	●		● ◆	●		● ◆	●			
◆	●	●	● ◆	●		● ◆				
◆	●	●	● ◆	●		◆				
	●		● ◆				●			
	●					● ◆				●
◆	●					● ◆				
						● ◆				●
◆	●		● ◆	●		◆	●			
						◆				
◆			● ◆		●	● ◆		◆		
						◆				●
										●
				●		● ◆	●			●
				●		● ◆				●
●		●	●			◆				
◆	●		●	●		◆				

415

TOWN	TELEPHONE TO: tourist office SI: syndicat d'initiative TH: town hall	▲ ITINERARY	■ USEFUL ADDRESSES	MUSEUM	PLACE OF INTEREST	SPECIAL
LOCRONAN (29180)	02 98 91 70 14 (TO)	291	431	●	●	●
MORLAIX (29600)	02 98 62 14 94 (TO)	235	426	●	●	●
OUESSANT (ÎLE-D') (29240)	02 98 48 85 83 (TO)	264	431	●	●	●
PENMARC'H (29760)	02 98 58 81 44 (TO)	307		●	●	●
PLOUESCAT (29430)	02 98 69 62 18 (SI)	262	428			●
PLOUGASNOU (29630)	02 98 67 31 88 (TO)				●	●
PLOUGASTEL-DAOULAS (29470)	02 98 40 34 98 (TO)	280	431	●		●
PLOUGUERNEAU (29880)	02 98 04 70 93 (TO)	263	428	●		●
PONT-AVEN (29930)	02 98 06 04 70 (TO)	310	433	●	●	●
PONT-L'ABBÉ (29120)	02 98 82 37 99 (TO)	306	433	●	●	●
QUIMPER (29000)	02 98 53 04 05 (TO)	296	432	●	●	●
RIEC-SUR-BELON (29340)	02 98 06 97 65 (TO)	311	433			●
ROSCOFF (29680)	02 98 61 12 13 (TO)	261	428	●		●
STE-MARINE (29120)	02 98 56 33 14 (TH)	308			●	●
ST-POL-DE-LÉON (29250)	02 98 69 05 69 (TO)	259	428		●	
ST-THÉGONNEC (29410)	02 98 79 61 06 (TH)	252	429		●	●
SEIN (ÎLE-DE) (29990)	02 98 70 90 35 (TH)	304	433		●	●
SIZUN (29450)	02 98 68 88 40 (SI)	256	429	●	●	●
SPÉZET (29540)	02 98 93 91 18 (SI)		429			●
MORBIHAN						
ARZ (ÎLE-D') (56840)	02 97 44 31 14 (TH)	348	437			
AURAY (56400)	02 97 24 09 75 (TO)	339	434	●	●	●
BELLE-ÎLE-EN-MER (56360)	02 97 31 81 93 (TO)	328	434	●	●	●
CAMPÉNÉAC (56800)	02 97 93 40 39 (TH)			●		
CARNAC (56340)	02 97 52 13 52 (TO)	335	434			
GOURIN (56110)	02 97 23 66 33 (SI)	267				●
GROIX (ÎLE-DE) (56590)	02 97 86 54 96 (SI)	322	435	●	●	
JOSSELIN (56120)	02 97 22 36 43 (TO)	230	424	●	●	●
KERNASCLÉDEN (56540)	02 97 51 61 16 (TH)	269	427		●	●
LA TRINITÉ-SUR-MER (56470)	02 97 55 72 21 (TO)	338				●
LE FAOUET (56320)	02 97 23 23 23 (SI)	269		●	●	●
LE GUERNO (56190)	02 97 42 94 76 (TH)	366	437	●		
LOCMARIAQUER (56740)	02 97 57 33 05 (SI)	338	435		●	
LOCMINÉ (56500)	02 97 46 70 72 (TH)				●	●
LORIENT (56100)	02 97 21 07 84 (TO)	320	434	●		●
MALESTROIT (56140)	02 97 75 14 57 (TO)	354	437	●		●
MOINES (ÎLE-AUX) (56780)	02 97 26 32 45 (TO)	349	437			
MUZILLAC (56190)	02 97 41 53 04 (TO)	365	438		●	●
PONTIVY (56300)	02 97 25 04 10 (SI)	228	425	●	●	●
PORT-LOUIS (56290)	02 97 82 52 93 (TO)	319	435	●	●	●
QUESTEMBERT (56230)	02 97 26 56 00 (TO)	353	438			●
QUIBERON (56170)	02 97 50 07 84 (TO)	334	435	●		●
ROCHEFORT-EN-TERRE (56220)	02 97 43 33 57 (SI)	354	438		●	●
ST-CADO (56550)	02 97 55 33 13 (TH)	334			●	●
ST-GILDAS-DE-RHUYS (56730)	02 97 47 23 15 (TH)	365	438		●	●
SÉNÉ (56860)	02 97 66 90 62 (TH)	346		●		
TRÉHORENTEUC (56430)	02 97 93 05 12 (TO)	360	439		●	
VANNES (56000)	02 97 47 24 34 (TO)	341	436	●	●	●
LOIRE-ATLANTIQUE						
BATZ-SUR-MER (44740)	02 40 23 92 36 (TO)	369	436	●	●	●
CHATEAUBRIANT (44110)	02 40 28 20 90 (TO)	382	440	●	●	●
GUÉRANDE (44350)	02 40 24 96 71 (TO)	367	436	●	●	●
HAUTE-GOULAINE (44115)	02 40 06 14 06 (TH)	384	440		●	●
LA BAULE (44500)	02 40 24 34 44 (SI)	370	437			●
LA TURBALLE (44420)	02 40 23 32 01 (TO)	368		●	●	
LE CROISIC (44490)	02 40 23 00 70 (TO)	369		●	●	●
NANTES (44000)	02 40 20 60 00 (TO)	372	439	●	● ◆	●
ST-JOACHIM (44720)	02 40 91 64 22 (TO)	366	438			●
ST-NAZAIRE (44600)	02 40 22 40 65 (TO)	370	439	●	● ◆	●

PORT ● BEACH ■	BOAT TRIPS	SPEED SAIL	SAILING ● DIVING ■	HORSERIDING	CLIMBING	SWIMMING POOL ● TENNIS ■	GOLF	CASINO ● THALASSOTHERAPY ■	AERIAL SPORTS	COUNTRY HOLIDAY
				●						●
●			●			● ◆				
● ◆			● ◆	●		● ◆				
● ◆	●		● ◆	●		◆				
			● ◆		●	◆				
●	●		● ◆	●		◆				●
● ◆				●		◆				●
●				●		◆				●
				●		● ◆				●
●				●		● ◆	●			
● ◆	●		●	●		◆				
● ◆	●		●			◆		◆		●
● ◆				●		◆				
● ◆				●		◆				●
● ◆						◆				●
◆			●	●		● ◆				●
						◆				●
◆	●		●			◆				
●			● ◆			● ◆				
● ◆	●		● ◆	●		◆	●	◆		
◆			●	●		● ◆		◆		
						● ◆			●	●
● ◆	●			●		◆			●	●
										●
● ◆	●		● ◆			● ◆				●
						◆				●
	●			●		◆				●
◆			● ◆			● ◆				
●				●		● ◆				
● ◆	●		●			●				●
				●		◆				
● ◆			●			● ◆			●	●
				●		◆				●
● ◆	●	●	● ◆	●		● ◆		● ◆	●	
● ◆	●		●			◆				
● ◆	●		●	●		◆	●			
● ◆	●				●	◆				
				●		●				●
●	●		●	●	●	● ◆			●	
● ◆			● ◆			● ◆				
				●		● ◆				●
				●		◆				●
						◆				●
● ◆	●		● ◆	●		● ◆	●	● ◆	●	
● ◆	●		● ◆	●		◆				
● ◆	●		● ◆			◆				
●				●		● ◆				●
						◆				●
● ◆	●		● ◆	●	●	● ◆			●	●

417

☆	PANORAMA
☐	CITY CENTER
☐••	SECLUDED
☐	PARKING
☒	SUPERVISED GARAGE
☐	TELEVISION
☆	QUIET
☋	SWIMMING POOL
☐	CREDIT CARDS ACCEPTED
☆	REDUCTIONS FOR CHILDREN
☆	PETS NOT ALLOWED
♫	MUSIC
⊷	LIVE BAND
☆	PARK, GARDENS
☆	FOOD SERVED OUTDOORS
☆	PARK, GARDENS

RENNES

POSTCODE 35000 I5

CULTURAL LIFE

CHURCH OF NOTRE-DAME EN ST-MELAINE
46, rue St-Melaine
Open daily 9am–6pm.
▲144

ECOMUSEUM OF RENNES COUNTY LA BINTINAIS
Route de Chatillon
Tel. 02 99 51 38 15
Open Mon., Wed.–Fri.
9am–noon and Sat.
2–6pm. Closed Tue.,
public holidays and
Jan. 16–31.
▲145

JARDIN DU THABOR
Entrance via St-Melaine
or rue de Paris
Tel. 02 99 28 56 77
(Ext. 4651)
Open daily 7.15am–
6pm or 9pm (depending
on the season).

MUSÉE DE BRETAGNE
20, quai Émile-Zola
Tel. 02 99 28 55 84
Open 10am–noon and
2–6pm. Closed Tue.
and public holidays.
▲145

MUSÉE DES BEAUX ARTS
20, quai Emile-Zola
Tel. 02 99 28 55 85
Open 10am–noon and
2–6pm. Closed Tue.
and public holidays.
▲145

ST-PIERRE CATHEDRAL
Rue de la Monnaie
*Guided tours organized
by the Tourist Office
(Tel. 02 99 79 01 98).*
▲140

RESTAURANTS

AUBERGE ST-SAUVEUR
6, rue St-Sauveur
Tel. 02 99 79 33 89
Closed Sat. and Sun.
*Beautiful wood-paneled
building. Fine traditional
cuisine.*
Menus: 80–165F
☐ ☐

LA CHOPE
3, rue La Chalotais
Tel. 02 99 79 34 54
Open eve. until
midnight.
Very popular brasserie.
Menus: 85–110F
☐

CHOUIN
12, rue d'Isly
Tel. 02 99 30 87 86
Open until 10.30pm.
Closed Sun., Mon. and
Aug. 1–20.
*Specialty: fish and
seafood.*
Menus: 99–129F
☐

L'ESCU DE RUNFAO
11, rue du Chapître
Tel. 02 99 79 13 10
Closed Sat. lunch and
Sun. eve., Jan. 1–7 and
Aug. 1–6.
*Fine 16th-century
building. Sophisticated
cuisine and friendly
service.*
Menus: 125–260F
☐ ☐

LE PALAIS
7, pl. du Parlement
Tel. 02 99 79 45 01
Closed Sun. eve.–Mon.
☐

HOTEL-RESTAURANTS

CENTRAL HOTEL *
6, rue Lanjuinais
Tel. 02 99 79 12 36
Fax. 02 99 79 65 76
*Rooms and suites in a
handsome 19th-century
building near the docks.*
Rooms: 280–360F
Suites: 700F
☐ ☐

ACCOMMODATION

GARDEN HOTEL **
3, rue Duhamel
Tel. 02 99 65 45 06
Fax. 02 99 65 02 62
Private garden.
☐ ☆ ☐

HOTEL MERCURE *
Rue Paul-Louis-Courier
Tel. 02 99 78 32 32
Fax. 02 99 78 33 44
Peaceful surroundings.
☐ ☐

BÉCHEREL

POSTCODE 35190 H4

CULTURAL ATTRACTIONS

CHÂTEAU DE CARADEUC
Tel. 02 99 66 77 76
Open daily 10am–7pm
Apr.–Sep. 15.
Open Sat.–Sun. 2–6pm.
Nov.–Mar.
*Visit of the park and
surroundings.* ▲146

CANCALE

POSTCODE 35260 I3

CULTURAL ATTRACTIONS

MUSÉE DE L'HUÎTRE ET DU COQUILLAGE
Plage de l'Aurore
Tel. 02 99 89 69 93
Guided tours Mon.–Fri.
3pm, Feb. 15–June 15
and Sep. 15–Oct. 15.
Daily tours 11am, 3pm
and 5pm (in French),
2pm and 5pm (in English)
June 15–Sep. 15. ▲184

MUSÉE DES ARTS ET TRADITIONS
Place St.-Méen
Tel. 02 99 89 79 32
Open 10am–12 noon
and 2.30–6.30pm.
Closed Mon. morning
and restricted visiting
times during low season.
▲183

RESTAURANTS

MAISON DE BRICOURT DUGUESCLIN
1, rue Duguesclin
Tel. 02 99 89 64 76
Closed Tue. (high
season), Tue.–Wed.
(low season), and
Dec. 15–Mar. 15
*This restaurant serves
some of the finest
cuisine in France.
Booking essential.*
Menus: 250F
(lunch)–640F
☐ ☆

LE SAINT-CAST
Route de la Corniche
Tel. 02 99 89 66 08
Closed Wed. (high
season), Tue. (low
season), and during
Feb. school vacations.
*Facing the sea and the
bay of Mont-St-Michel.
Imaginative fish and
seafood dishes.*
Menus: 100–200F
☐•• ☆ ☆

HOTEL-RESTAURANTS

L'EMERAUDE**
7, quai Thomas
Tel. 02 99 89 61 76
Fax. 02 99 89 88 21
Closed Nov. 15–Dec. 15.
By the port. Pleasant view overlooking Mont-St-Michel. Regional seafood dishes served on the terrace in the summer.
Rooms: 285–485F
Menus: 100–300F
⚐ ⚲

MAISON DE BRICOURT RIMAINS****
62, rue des Rimains
Tel. 02 99 89 61 22
Closed Jan.–Mar.
Wonderful sea view and quiet surroundings full of charm.
Rooms: 850F
☐•• 🅿 🚗 ⸙

MAISON RICHEUX****
Château Richeux,
Carrefour (crossroads) des Portes-Rouges on the way to Mont St-Michel
Tel. 02 99 89 25 25
Closed Tue. lunch, and Mon. (low season).
Overlooking the bay of Cancale
Rooms: 750–1,350F
Menus: 110–168F
☐•• ⚲ 🅿 ⸙

LA POINTE DU GROUIN**
Pointe du Grouin
Tel. 02 99 89 60 55
Fax. 02 99 89 92 22
Hotel closed Oct.–Mar.
Stunning view over Mont-St-Michel and Landes island.
Rooms: 390–520F
Menus: 115–295F
☐•• ⚲ 🅿 ⸙

TIREL GUÉRIN ***
La Gouesnière station
Tel. 02 99 89 10 46
Fax. 02 99 89 12 62
Closed mid Dec.–mid Jan.
Rooms: 300–340F
Suites: 580–620F
Menus: 130–240F
⚐ ☐•• ⚲ 🛏 🅿 🚗

ACCOMMODATION

CAMPING DE PORT-MER-PLAGE
32, av. de la côte d'Emeraude
Access from D201 traveling toward la

Pointe du Grouin
Tel. 02 99 89 63 17
Closed Sep. 19–Apr. 30
Private beach.
⚐ ⚲

CHAMPEAUX
POSTCODE 50530 **J4–5**

CULTURAL ATTRACTIONS

COLLÉGIALE
Pl. de la Collégiale
Open daily 9am–7pm (summer) and 9am–6pm (low season)
Guided tours in Jul. and Aug. (information available from the town hall). ▲162

CHÂTEAUBOURG
POSTCODE 35220 **J5**

HOTEL-RESTAURANTS

AR MILIN ***
30, rue de Paris
Tel. 02 99 00 30 91
Fax. 02 99 00 37 56
Restaurant closed Sun. eve. Nov.–Mar.
Closed Dec. 23–Jan.4
An old mill.
Rooms: 325–565F
Menus: 85F (lunch), 99–196F
☐ ⚲ 🅿 ⸙ ⸙

CHÂTEAUGIRON
POSTCODE 35430 **I5**

CULTURAL ATTRACTIONS

CHÂTEAU DE CHÂTEAUGIRON
Tel. 02 99 37 41 69 (town hall)
Open daily 10.30am–12 noon, 2.30–5.30pm, Jul.–Aug. Open Sun. am, May–June and Sep.
▲162

RESTAURANT

L'AUBERGADE
2, rue J.-et-P.-Gourdel
Tel. 02 99 37 41 35
In the city center and close to the château. Gourmet cuisine.
Menus: 138–168F

ACCOMMODATION

CAMPING LES GRANDS BOSQUETS **
Tel. 02 99 37 41 69
Fax. 02 99 37 43 55

Closed Nov.–Mar.
On the river bank .
☐••

COMBOURG
POSTCODE 35270 **I3–4**

CULTURAL ATTRACTIONS

CHÂTEAU DE COMBOURG
23, rue des Princes
Tel. 02 99 73 22 95
Closed Dec.
Open daily 2–5.30pm, Easter–Sep.
Park open 9am–12 noon, 2–6pm, Apr.–Sep. and 9am–12.30pm, 2–4.30pm, Oct.
Visit available on request Mar.–Nov.
Immortalized by the writer Chateaubriand, it is one of the best preserved castles in France. ▲150

HOTEL-RESTAURANTS

LE CHÂTEAU**
1, pl. Chateaubriand
Tel. 02 99 73 00 38
Fax. 02 99 73 25 79
Closed Dec. 15–Jan. 15
At the foot of the castle.
Rooms: 250–470F
Menus: 89–270F
⚲ 🅿 🚗 ⸙

LE LAC**
2, pl. Chateaubriand
Tel. 02 99 73 05 65
Fax. 02 99 79 23 34
Closed Feb.
Right on the edge of the lake.
Rooms: 190–330F
Menus: 62–150F
⚲ 🅿 🚗 ⸙

DINAN
POSTCODE 22105 **H3**

CULTURAL ATTRACTIONS

CHÂTEAU AND MUSÉE DE DINAN
Rue du Gal-de-Gaulle
Tel. 02 96 39 45 20
Open daily 10am–5pm, Jun. 1–Oct. 15
Open 10am–noon, 2–5.30pm, Mar. 16–May and Oct. 16–Nov. 15
Open 1.30–5.30pm, Nov 16–Dec. and Feb. 7– Mar. 15.
Closed Tue., Oct 16–May. Closed Jan.–Feb. 6. ▲153

CHURCH OF ST-SAUVEUR
Place St-Sauveur
Open Mon.–Fri. ▲154

CHURCH OF ST-MALO
Grand-Rue
Open Mon.–Sat.
8am–7pm. ▲155

CLOCK TOWER
Rue de l'Horloge
Open daily 2–6pm, Apr.–May, and 10am–7pm, June–Sep. ▲155

COUVENT DES CORDELIERS
Place des Cordeliers
Not open to the public but the grounds can be visited in the summer.
▲156

PRIORY AND ABBEY ST-MAGLOIRE
Léhon
Tel. 02 96 35 14 75
Open daily 9am–7pm Jul.–Aug.
Visits available on request in low season.
▲158

RESTAURANTS

CHEZ LA MÈRE POURCEL
3, pl. des Merciers
Tel. 02 96 39 03 80
Fax. 02 96 87 07 58
Closed Sun. eve.–Mon. in low season.
15th-century house in old town.
Menus: 97–370F

CRÊPERIE DES ARTISANS
Rue du Petit Pont.
Porte du Jerzual.
Tel. 02 96 39 44 10
Closed Mon. Sep.–Jun
Closed Oct. 15–Apr. 1
Situated in a medieval street.
⸙

CRÊPERIE LES JARDINS DU JERZUAL
Rue du Petit Fort
Tel. 02 96 85 28 75
Open daily Jul.–Aug.
Open Sat.–Sun.
Oct.–Easter. Closed Thur., Easter–Sep.
Traditional crêperie in a popular street leading down to the harbor.
Menus: 50–100F
⸙

LE RELAIS DU CORSAIRE
5, rue du Quai, Le Port.

Tel. 02 96 39 40 17
*Closed Sun. in low
season and Jan. 10–
Feb. 15*
Menus: 78–250F
🇨 ⚹ ☂

RESTAURANT DES GRANDS FOSSÉS ***
2, pl. du Maréchal-Leclerc
Tel. 02 96 39 21 50
*Refined and creative
cuisine in a pleasant
house facing the city
walls.*
Menus: 90–285F
🇨 🇵 ☂

HOTEL-RESTAURANT

LE D'AVAUGOUR
1, pl. du Champ-Clos
Tel. 02 96 39 07 49
Fax. 02 96 85 43 04
*Restaurant closed Thur.
Near castle, in old town.*
Rooms: 350–620F
Menus: 120–180F
🇨 ⚹ 🇵 ♨ ☂

ACCOMMODATION

CAMPING MUNICIPAL DE LA HALLERAIS ****
Taden
Tel. 02 96 39 15 93
(town hall)
Fax. 02 96 39 94 64
Closed Nov.–Mar. 15
〰

HOTEL D'ARVOR **
5, rue Auguste-Pavie
Tel. 02 96 39 21 22
Fax. 02 96 39 83 09
*Located in the former
convent of the Jacobins
in the heart of the old
town.*
Rooms: 280–360F
🇨 🇵

MOULIN DE MÉEN YOUTH HOSTEL
Vallée de la Fontaine
des Eaux
Tel. 02 96 39 10 83
Fax. 02 96 39 10 62
*In an old mill. Camping
facilities available.*
🇨➔ 🇵 ♨

DOL-DE-BRETAGNE
POSTCODE 35120   I3

CULTURAL ATTRACTIONS

MUSEUM OF HISTORY
G2, place de la
Trésorerie
Tel. 02 99 48 09 38

Fax 02 99 48 33 46
Open daily 9.30am–4pm.
*Visits available on
request out of season.*
▲181

ST-SAMSON CATHEDRAL
Guided tours organized
daily by the tourist office
Tel. 02 99 48 15 37
in Jul.–Aug. ▲181

HOTEL-RESTAURANT

HOTEL-RESTAURANT DE BRETAGNE
Place Chateaubriand
Tel. 02 99 48 02 03
Fax 02 99 48 25 75
Closed Oct. and Feb.
school vacations.
Traditional hotel.
Rooms: 130–300F
Menus: 65–155F
🇨 ☐ 🗀 ⚹

ACCOMMODATION

CAMPING DES ORMES ****
Épignac (D 795)
Tel. 02 99 73 49 59
*Three heated
swimming pools,
archery, horse-riding,
golf. Bed-and-breakfast
accommodation in the
castle outbuildings.*

FOUGÈRES
POSTCODE 35300   J4

CULTURAL ATTRACTIONS

CASTLE
Place Symon
Tel. 02 99 99 79 59
Open 9am–7pm,
Jun. 15–Sep. 15, and
9.30am–noon, 2–6pm
Sep. 15–30.
*Restricted visiting times
Oct.–Apr.* ▲170

CRISTALLERIE DE HAUTE BRETAGNE
17, rue du Chêne-Vert
Tel. 02 99 94 46 46
Open by appointment,
Mon.–Fri. ▲173

CHURCH OF ST-SULPICE
Rue Le Bouteiller
Tel. 99 99 05 52
Open 8am–7pm. ▲170

HOTEL DANJOU DE LA GARENNE
38, rue Nationale
Not open to the public.
▲172

MUSÉE EMMANUEL-DE-LA-VILLÉON
Rue Nationale
Tel. 02 99 99 19 98
Open 10am–noon,
2–5pm, Jun.–Sep.;
2–5pm Sat., Sun. out of
season. ▲172

PARC FLORAL DE HAUTE-BRETAGNE
Le Chatellier
Tel. 02 99 95 48 32
Open Sat., Sun. 10am–
6pm, Mar. 20–Nov. 11,
and public holidays.

RESTAURANTS

LE HAUTE SÈVE
37, bd Jean-Jaurès.
Tel. 02 99 94 23 39
Closed Sun. eve.–Mon.,
Jan. 1–15, and Jul.
25–Aug. 20.
*Local produce and
original recipes.*
🇨 ⚹

HOTEL-RESTAURANTS

LES VOYAGEURS ***
10, pl. Gambetta
Tel. 02 99 99 08 20
(hotel)
Tel. 02 99 99 14 17
(restaurant)
Fax. 02 99 99 99 04
*Restaurant open daily
during high season,
closed Sat. and Sun.
during low season.
Friendly welcome in one
of the best restaurants
in town.*
Rooms: 230–280F
Menus: 95–210F
🇨 ⚹

HÉDÉ
POSTCODE 35630   I4

HOTEL-RESTAURANT

HOSTELLERIE DU VIEUX MOULIN **
R.N. 137

Tel. 02 99 45 45 70
Fax. 02 99 45 44 86
Closed Sun. eve.–Mon.,
Sep.–Jun.
Closed 20 Dec.–Feb. 1.
*Hotel full of charm
and fine traditional
restaurant.*
Rooms: 250–450F
Menus: 95–240F
🇨➔ ⚹ 🇵 🚗 ♨

LES IFFS
POSTCODE 35630   H4

CULTURAL ATTRACTIONS

CHÂTEAU DE MONTMURAN
Tel. 02 99 45 88 88
Open daily 2–7pm,
Easter–Nov. 1.
Open Sat.–Sun. 2–6pm,
Nov. 1–Easter. Closed
Dec. 25 and Jan. 1.
Guided tours. ▲147

CHURCH OF ST-OUEN-AUX-IFFS
Open Tue.–Sun.
Key held at local bar.
▲148

MONT-ST-MICHEL
POSTCODE 50170   I3

CULTURAL ATTRACTIONS

THE ABBEY
Tel. 02 33 60 14 14
Open daily 9am–5pm,
May–Sep., and
9.30am–4.30pm,
Oct.–Apr. Night show
"Les Imaginaires"
10pm–midnight
June–Sep. ▲179

ARCHÉOSCOPE
Grande-Rue
Tel. 02 33 48 09 37
Open daily 9am–7pm,
Jul.–Aug. and
9am–6pm, low season.
Closed Nov. 15–Feb. 15,
except during the
Christmas holidays.
▲178

MAISON DE LA BAIE
Genêts
Tel. 02 33 70 86 46
Guided tour of the bay.
▲181

MUSÉE MARITIME ET HISTORIQUE
Grande-Rue
Tel. 02 33 60 23 90
Open 8.30am–11pm
Jul. 14–Aug. Restricted

visiting hours during low
season. ▲178

HOTEL-
RESTAURANTS

LA MÈRE POULARD
Grande Rue
Tel. 02 33 60 14 01
Fax. 02 30 60 37 31
Open all year.
*Famous restaurant
serving traditional
cuisine. Expensive
but well worth a visit.*
C ✻ ⚋ ⌂

LE MOTEL VERT **
Route du Mont-St-
Michel
Tel. 02 33 60 09 33
Fax. 02 33 68 22 09
Closed Nov. 11–Feb.
school vacations.
Bicycle hire available.
Rooms: 190–460F
Menus: 59–112F
⊡·· P ♠ ⌷

LE MOUTON BLANC
Rue Principale
Tel. 02 33 60 14 08
Fax. 02 33 60 05 62
Closed Jan. 15–Feb. 15.
15th-century dwelling.
Rooms: 200–500F
Menus: 99–240F
C ✻ ⌷ ⚋

LE RELAIS DU ROY***
Route de Pontorson
Tel. 02 33 60 14 26
Fax. 02 33 60 37 69
Closed Dec.–Mar. 26
Logis de France.
Rooms: 350–440F
Menus: 95–200F
⊡·· ✻ P ⌷

LE SAINT PIERRE***
Rue Principale
Tel. 02 33 60 14 03
Closed Dec. 15–Feb. 15
*15th-century building.
Historic monument.*
Rooms: 450–650F
Menus: 90–290F
C ✻ ⌷

LES TERRASSES DE LA
MÈRE POULARD ***
Rue Principale

Tel. 02 33 60 14 09
Fax. 02 33 60 37 31
Open all year.
Overlooking the bay.
Rooms: 200–900F
Menus: 99–240F
C ⚋ ✻ P

PLEUDIHEN
SUR-RANCE

POSTCODE 22690   H3

CULTURAL
ATTRACTIONS

MUSÉE DU CIDRE
La Ville-Hervy
Tel. 02 96 83 20 78
Open daily 10am–7pm,
June–Aug., and 2–7pm
Apr.–May. ▲160

ACCOMMODATION

CHEZ MADAME
CHENU
Le Val-Hervelin
Tel. 02 96 83 35 61
Fax. 02 96 83 38 43
Open all year
*Gîte de France.
Tennis.*
Rooms: 180–200F
⊡·· P ♠

LE GRAND GUÉ–
MARIE SERVIN
Route de Miniac
Tel. 02 96 83 21 58
Gîte de France.
Rooms: 200–400F
P ♠

PLEUGUENEUC

POSTCODE 35720   H4

CULTURAL
ATTRACTIONS

CHÂTEAU DE LA
BOURBANSAIS
Tel. 02 99 69 40 07
Zoological garden.
Open daily 10am–noon
and 2–6pm.
*Guided tour of the
castle.* ▲151

HOTEL

LA MOTTE
BEAUMANOIR
Plesder – R.N. 137
Tel. 02 99 69 46 01
Fax. 02 99 69 42 40
Restaurant closed
at the end of the
high season,
Christmas–Feb.
*15th–18th-century
castle set in a park.*
Rooms: 700–1,300F
(breakfast included)
✻ ⚓ P 🚗 ♠ ⌷

ST-BRICE-
EN-COGLÈS

POSTCODE 35460   J4

CULTURAL
ATTRACTIONS

CHÂTEAU DU ROCHER-
PORTAIL
Tel. 02 99 98 61 04
(town hall)
*Privately owned,
not open to public.
Courtyard open on
national monument
day in Sep.* ▲176

ST-JOUAN-
DES-GIÉRETS

POSTCODE 35430   H3

CULTURAL
ATTRACTIONS

MALOUINIÈRE DU BOS
Route de la Passagère,
Quelmer
Tel. 02 99 81 40 11
Guided tour at 3.30pm
Jul.–Aug. ▲160

VILLA DU
COMMANDANT CHARCOT
Route de la Passagère,
Quelmer
Not open to the public.
▲161

ACCOMMODATION

LA MALOUINIÈRE DES
LONGS CHAMPS ***
Tel. 02 99 82 74 00
Fax. 02 99 82 74 14
Open all year.
Reservations only.
Rooms: 265–475F or
apartments. Evening
meal must be booked.
✻ ⚓ P 🚗 ♠

ST-SULIAC

POSTCODE 35430   H3

CULTURAL
ATTRACTIONS

MOULIN DU BEAUCHET
*Water mill. Closed to the
public.* ▲203

RESTAURANT

LA GRÈVE
Le port
Tel. 02 98 58 33 83
Closed Sun. eve.–Mon.,
except Jul.–Aug., and
Nov. 15–Mar. 15
*First floor dining room
facing the river Rance.
Meals served on the
terrace in the summer.*

Menus: 95–185F
C ⚋ ✻ ⌷

ACCOMMODATION

LES MOUETTES
Grande-Rue
Tel. 02 99 58 30 41
*Bed-and-breakfast
accommodation in
charming village.*
Rooms: 250–290F

VITRÉ

POSTCODE 35500   J5

CULTURAL
ATTRACTIONS

CHÂTEAU ET MUSÉE
Pl. du Château
Tel. 02 99 75 04 54
Closed Tue., Sat. am
and Sun. am all year.
Open 10am–noon and
2–6.15pm, Jul.–Sep.
Open 10am–noon and
2–5.30pm (closed Mon.
am), Oct.–June. ▲164

CHÂTEAU DES
ROCHERS-SÉVIGNÉ
Rte d'Argentré-du-Plessy
Tel. 02 99 96 76 51
Same opening hours as
Château de Vitré. ▲169

RESTAURANTS

LA BELLE OSEILLE
30, blvd d'En-Bas
Tel. 02 99 74 64 54
Closed Sun. (except
with a reservation).
*Located in a handsome
15th-century town house.*
Menus: 65–150F
✻ P ⌷

TAVERNE DE L'ÉCU
12, rue Beaudrevue
Tel. 02 99 75 11 09
Closed Tue. eve.–Wed.
*Historical house close to
the castle.*
Menus: 77–158F
C

AU VIEUX VITRÉ
1, rue En-Bas
Tel. 02 99 75 02 52
Closed Sun. and May 1.
Crêperie in the old town.
Menus: 40–80F
⌷

ACCOMMODATION

LE MINOTEL **
47, rue de la Poterie
Tel. 02 99 75 11 11
Fax. 02 99 75 81 26
Pedestrian area.
Rooms: 220–360F
C

ST-MALO

POSTCODE 35400 H3

CULTURAL ATTRACTIONS

ROCHERS SCULPTÉS
Chemin des Rochers Sculptés,
Rothéneuf
Tel. 02 99 56 97 64
Open daily 9am–9pm,
Easter–Sept.
Open daily 9.30am–noon and 2–5.30pm
Oct.–Easter. ▲184

FORT NATIONAL
Grande Plage
Opposite the casino
Tel. 02 99 46 91 25
Closed in bad weather.
*Visit at low tide,
Easter–Sept., and upon
appointment during the
low season.* ▲197

GALERIE QUIC-EN-GROIGNE
Château
Tel. 02 99 40 80 26
Open 9.30am–noon and
2–6pm, Jul.–Aug.
Open 9.30–11.30am
and 2–5.30pm,
Easter–June and Sept.
▲191

MUSÉE D'HISTOIRE DE LA VILLE
Château
Tel. 02 99 40 71 57
Open Oct 10am–noon
and 2–60pm. Closed
Mon., public holidays,
Oct.–Mar, May 1.

MUSÉE INTERNATIONAL DES CAP-HORNIERS
Tour Solidor
Saint-Servan
Tel. 02 99 40 71 58
Same opening times as
Musée d'Histoire de la
Ville. ▲195

RESTAURANTS

LE CHALUT
8, rue de la Corne de Cerf
Tel. 02 99 56 71 58
Closed Sun. eve.–Mon.
low season, Mon. high
season and Jan. 15–Feb. 15.
*In the old town.
Specialty: seafood.*
Menus: 95–300F

LE CORPS DE GARDE
3, montée Notre-Dame
Tel. 02 99 40 91 46
Closed Tue. and
Dec.–Jan. (except
Christmas week).
*Crêperie. Terrace on
the ramparts.*
Menus: 60F
🅲 †

LA DUCHESSE ANNE
Place Guy-la-Chambre
Tel. 02 99 40 85 33
Open 12.15–1.45pm
and 7.15–9.45pm.
Closed Wed. and
Dec.–Jan.
*A charming restaurant
within the ramparts at
St-Vincent gate.
Specialties: fish, shellfish
of constant quality.*
Carte: 210–300F
🅲 †

LE FRANKLIN
4, chaussée du Sillon
Tel. 02 99 40 50 93
*Seafood dishes and
splendid view of the
bay of St-Malo and of
the Fort national.*
Menus: 90–160F
🕀 ⚥ 🅿 ♯

HOTEL-RESTAURANTS

GRAND HÔTEL DES THERMES*
100, boulevard Hébert
Tel. 02 99 40 75 75
Closed Jan.
*Modern, comfortable
and well-situated,
facing the bay.
Thalassotherapy center.*
Rooms: 440–1,440F
Suites: 2.105–2,740F
🕀 🅿 🚗

GRAND HÔTEL DE COURTOISVILLE
69, bd Hébert
Tel. 02 99 40 83 83
Closed Nov. 15–Feb. 15
*By the sea,
near institute of
thalassotherapy.*
Rooms: 350–620F
Menus: 120–180F
🅲 ⚥ 🅿 🚗 ♯

HÔTEL CENTRAL
6, Grande Rue
Tel. 02 99 40 87 70
Fax 02 99 40 47 57
*At the heart of the
privateers' quarter.
Very comfortable
hotel with restaurant
La Frégate.*
Rooms: 430–670F
Menus: 199–299F
🅲 ♯ 🚗 ⚥

ACCOMMODATION

CAMPING MUNICIPAL DU NICET *
Av. de la Varde
Tel. 02 99 40 26 32
Fax. 02 99 40 71 73
Closed Sept. 12–Apr. 1
🕀

DINARD

POSTCODE 35800 H3

CULTURAL ATTRACTIONS

AQUARIUM-LABORATOIRE MARITIME
17, av. George-V
Tel. 02 99 46 13 90
Open 10.30am–12.30pm
and 3.30–7.30pm,
Mon.–Sat.,
Open 2.30–7.30pm,
Sun., public holidays,
May 14–Sep. 15
▲201

BRITISH FILM FESTIVAL
Information available
from the Festival
association:
2, blvd Féart
35800 Dinard
Tel. 02 99 88 19 04
Fax. 02 99 46 67 15
*This festival takes place
at the beginning of Oct.,
from Thurs. to Sun.*

MUSÉE DU SITE BALNÉAIRE
Villa Eugénie
12, rue des Français-Libres
Tel. 02 99 46 81 05
Open 10am–noon and
2–6pm, Easter–Nov. 1
Closed Sat. am and
Sun. am all year around.
▲201

RESTAURANTS

LES MARINS
12, av. George-V
Tel. 02 99 46 78 57
Open eves. only.
Closed Mon.
Carte: 120–200F
🅲 ⚥

HOTEL-RESTAURANTS

HÔTEL PRINTANIA*
5, av. George-V
Tel. 02 99 46 13 07
Fax. 02 99 46 26 32
Open Easter–mid-Nov.
*Hotel with typical Breton
décor and view over the
sea. Traditional cuisine.*
Rooms: 250–420F
Menus: 95–135F
🅲 ⚥ †

LE GRAND HÔTEL**
46, av. George-V
Tel. 02 99 88 26 26
Fax. 02 99 88 26 27
Closed Nov.–Mar.
View over the sea.
Rooms: 650–1,800F
Menus: 120–180F
🅲 ⚥ 🌊 🅿

NOVOTEL-THALASSA *
Av. du Château-Hébert
St-Enogat
Tel. 02 99 82 78 10
Fax. 02 99 82 78 29
Closed Dec.
*All rooms have view
over the sea. Direct
access to the thalasso-therapy center.*
Rooms: 560–820F
Menus: 165–255F

ERQUY

POSTCODE 22430 G3

CULTURAL ATTRACTIONS

CHÂTEAU DE BIENASSIS
Rte de Pleneuf
Tel. 02 96 72 22 03
Open 10.30am–12.30pm
and 2–6.30pm, Jul.–Aug.
Open 2–6pm, Sun. and
public holidays, Easter–June. ▲208

HÔTEL-RESTAURANT

HÔTEL DE LA PLAGE*
21, blvd de la Mer
Tel. 02 96 72 30 09
Fax. 02 96 72 16 62
*Facing the beach
and the harbor.*
Rooms: 190–330F

Menus: 70–142F

🅒 ⅍ ▭

FRÉHEL

POSTCODE 22240 **G3**

CULTURAL ATTRACTIONS

CHAPEL OF ST SÉBASTIEN
Tel. 02 96 41 46 96
(Key available from M. Cadoret, at the farm behind the chapel). ▲201

FORT-LA-LATTE
Tel. 02 96 41 40 31
Open 10–12.30pm, 2.30–6.30pm, June–Sep. Open Sat. am and Sun. am, during low season.
Group visits arranged upon request. ▲204

PHARE DU CAP-FRÉHEL (LIGHTHOUSE)
Tel. 02 96 41 40 03
Visit arranged upon request. ▲205

RÉSERVE ORNITHOLOGIQUE
(BIRD SANCTUARY)
Tel. 02 96 41 50 83
Guided tours Tue., Thur. and Sat. 10am– noon, July–Aug.
Sea bird watching organized upon request.
▲206

RESTAURANT

LE VICTORINE
Place de la Mairie
Tel. 02 96 41 55 55
Small, charming restaurant offering quality cuisine.
Menus: 75 (weekdays) 90–240F
🅒 ⅍ 🏛 ⚓

ACCOMMODATION

LE FANAL
Between Plevenon and Cap-Fréhel
Tel. 02 96 41 43 19
Closed Oct.– Mar.
Rooms: 240–330F
▭•• ▭

LA RICHARDAIS

POSTCODE 35780 **G3**

CULTURAL ATTRACTIONS

TIDAL POWER STATION OF THE RANCE
Tel. 02 96 16 37 14

Open daily 8am–8pm
▲200

RESTAURANT

LE CHATEAUBRIAND
Barrage de la Rance
Tel. 02 99 46 44 44
Closed Oct. 10–May 20
Boat excursions in the bay and on the river Rance. Running commentary. Food available on board
Menus: 250–320F
⅍ 🅿 ▭

HOTEL-RESTAURANT

CLIMAT
14, rue des Genêts
Tel. 02 99 46 69 55
Fax 02 99 88 16 16
Small, reasonably-priced hotel on the bank of the river Rance.
Rooms: 350–435F
Menus: 85–150F
⅍ ▭•• 🅿 ▭ ⚓
▭ 🏛

PLANGUENOUAL

POSTCODE 22400 **G3**

HOTEL-RESTAURANT

DOMAINE DU VAL*
Tel. 02 96 32 75 40
Fax. 02 96 32 71 50
Set in a beautiful park, half a mile from the sea. Restaurant.
Rooms: 450–880F
Menus: 140–340F
▭•• ⅍ 🏛 ⚓
🅿 🏛 ⚓

PLÉNEUF-VAL-ANDRÉ

POSTCODE 22370 **G3**

HOTEL-RESTAURANT

GRAND HÔTEL DU VAL-ANDRÉ *
80, rue Amiral-Chaner
Tel. 02 96 72 20 56
Fax. 02 96 63 00 24
Restaurant closed Mon.–Tue. lunchtime and Nov. 15–Mar. 25. Direct access to the beach. Restaurant with panoramic view of the sea.
Rooms: 375–425F
Menus: 90–195F
▭•• ⅍ 🅿 🚗 🏛
⅍

ST-CAST-LE-GUILDO

POSTCODE 22380 **H3**

HOTEL-RESTAURANT

LES ARCADES
15, rue du Duc-d'Aiguillon
Tel. 02 96 41 80 50
Closed Nov.–Mar.
Some rooms overlook the sea.

ST-BRIEUC

POSTCODE 22000 **F3**

CULTURAL ATTRACTIONS

CHAPELLE DU GRAND SÉMINAIRE
Maison St-Yves
24, rue de Genève
Tel. 02 96 33 35 05
Open 10am–noon, 2–6pm. ▲215

MUSÉE D'HISTOIRE
1, rue M.-Chrisostome
Tel. 02 96 33 39 12
Open Tue.–Sun. 9.30–11.45am and 1.30–5.45pm. Closed Mon. and Sun. am.
▲214

ST-ÉTIENNE CATHEDRAL ▲210
Place du Général-de-Gaulle
Open 8.30am–7pm.

RESTAURANTS

L'AMADEUS
22, rue Gouët
Tel. 02 96 33 92 44
Closed Sun.–Mon. lunch.
🅒 ⅍

AUX PESKED
59, rue Légué
Tel. 02 96 33 34 65
Closed Sat. lunch, Sun. eve., Mon., and Feb. school vacations.

Rooms: 295–480F
Menus: 75–158F
🅒 ⅍ ⚓

ACCOMMODATION

CAMPING DU CHÂTELET **
Rue des Nouettes
Tel. 02 96 41 96 33
Fax. 02 96 41 97 99
Closed Sep. 25–Mar.
▭•• ⚓

CHÂTEAU DU VAL D'ARGUENON
Notre-Dame-de-Guildo
Tel. 02 96 41 07 03
Fax 02 96 41 02 67
Bed-and-breakfast accommodation available at the castle.

Refined cuisine, seafood specialties. Impressive wine list.
Menus: 108–495F
🅒 ⅍ 🅿

CRÊPERIE LE PORCHE
9, rue St-Guillaume
Tel. 02 96 61 93 77
Closed Sun.
Menus: 70–78F

LES QUATRE SAISONS *
61, chemin des Courses
Quartier Cesson
Tel. 02 96 33 20 38
Closed Sun. eve. and Mon. eve.
Pleasant décor, warm welcome. Serves very good regional cuisine.
Menus: 98–450F
⅍ 🅿 ⚓

LA VIEILLE TOUR
75, rue de la Tour
Port du Légué-Plérin
Tel. 02 96 33 10 30
Closed Sun. eve.–Mon.
One of the best restaurants in Côtes-d'Armor.
Menus: 130–350F
⅍ 🅿 ⅍

HOTELS

KER IZEL *
20 rue du Gouët
Tel. 02 96 33 46 29
Fax. 02 96 61 86 12
In the old town, close to the cathedral.
Rooms: 225–320F
🅒 🚗 ▭

HÔTEL LE THÉÂTRE
Place de la Poste
Tel. 02 96 33 23 18
Located in the old town.
Rooms: 190–300F.
🅒 ▭

Magnificent park. Reservations are an absolute must in the winter.
Rooms: 450–590F
🖙 ☆ ⚶

BIGNAN

POSTCODE 56500   F5

CULTURAL ATTRACTIONS

DOMAINE DE KERGUÉHENNEC
Tel. 02 97 60 44 44
Open. Tue.–Sun. 10am–7pm, Apr.–Nov.
Exhibition of contemporary art. ▲233

BINIC

POSTCODE 25520   F3

CULTURAL ATTRACTIONS

MUSÉE D'ART ET DE TRADITION POPULAIRE
Square Fichet-des-Grèves
Tel. 02 96 73 76 48
Open 2.30–6pm, Mon., Wed.–Sun., Apr. 15–Sep. 15. Visits arranged on request during the low season.
▲216

COLPO

POSTCODE 56390   F5

CULTURAL ATTRACTIONS

CHÂTEAU AND DOMAINE DE KORN-ER-HOUËT
Tel. 02 97 66 82 08 (admin.)
Not open to the public.

CHURCH OF NOTRE-DAME-DE L'ASSOMPTION
Tel. 02 97 66 82 56
▲234

ÎLE DE BRÉHAT

POSTCODE 22870
▲221

HOTEL-RESTAURANTS

LE BELLEVUE
Le Port Clos
Tel. 02 96 20 00 05
Closed Jan.
Facing the harbor.
Rooms: 190–300F

Menus: 94F (lunch), 115–175F
🖙 ☆ 🍴

LA VIEILLE AUBERGE
Le Bourg
Tel. 02 96 20 00 24
Fax. 02 96 20 05 12
Closed Nov. 2–Easter holidays.
A privateer's house, dating from 1711.
Menus: 90–300F
Half-board: 360F
🖙 ☆ ⚶ 🍴

JOSSELIN

POSTCODE 56120   G5

CULTURAL ATTRACTIONS

BASILICA OF NOTRE-DAME-DU-RONCIER
8, rue des Devins
Open daily 9am–7pm –6.30pm, low season. Belfry key available from the town hall. ▲232

CHÂTEAU
Tel. 02 97 22 22 50
Open daily 10am–6pm Jul.–Aug. and 2–6pm June and Sep.
Group visits arranged upon request all year.

MUSÉE DES POUPÉES
3, rue des Trente
Tel. 02 97 22 36 45
Fax. 02 97 75 68 16
Open daily 2–6pm Jun.–Sep. and 10am–noon and 2–6pm, Jul.–Aug. ▲231

HOTEL-RESTAURANTS

AU RELAIS DE L'OUST
Rte de Pontivy
Tel. 02 97 75 63 06
Fax. 02 97 22 37 39
Rooms: 215–280F
Menus: 70–188.
🖙 ☆ ⚶

LE CHÂTEAU
1, rue du Général-de-Gaulle
Tel. 02 97 22 20 11
Fax. 02 97 22 34 09
Hotel closed Feb.
Situated on the bank of the river opposite the castle.

Rooms: 215–320F
🖙 ⚶ ☆ 🅿 🚗

RESTAURANT

RESTAURANT DES FRÈRES BLOT
9, rue Glatinier
Tel. 02 97 22 22 08
Closed Sun. eve.–Mon. during low season.
Menus: 78–240F
🖙 ☆

MÛR-DE-BRETAGNE

POSTCODE 22530   F4

CULTURAL ATTRACTIONS

BARRAGE DE GUERLEDAN
Power station
Tel. 02 96 28 51 41
Free visit upon request.

BON-REPOS ABBEY
Access from RN 164 past St-Gelven
Information on site.
▲229

HOTEL-RESTAURANTS

AUBERGE GRAND' MAISON
1, rue Léon-Le-Cerf
Tel. 02 96 28 51 10
Fax 02 96 28 52 30
Restaurant closed Sun. eve.–Mon., Oct. and Feb. school vacations.
Rooms: 280–600F
Menus: 170–380F
🖙 ☆

LE BEAU RIVAGE
Caurel
Tel. 02 96 28 52 15
Restaurant closed Mon. eve.–Tue. during low season, Jan.
Located on the shores of lake Guerlédan.
Rooms: 280–600F
Menus: 170–380F
🖙 ☆ 🅿 🍴 ⚶

HOSTELLERIE DE L'ABBAYE DE BON-REPOS
St-Gelven
Tel. 02 96 24 98 38
Restaurant closed Tue. eve.–Wed., during low season.
Located in the outbuildings of the 12th-century Cistercian abbey, near lake Guerlédan. Worth a visit, at least for a meal in the magnificent

banqueting hall.
Rooms: 250–280F
Menus: 50 (weekdays)–210F
🖙 🅿 ⚶ 🍴

ACCOMMODATION

YOUTH HOSTEL
St-Guen
Tel. 02 96 28 54 34
Fax. 02 96 26 01 56
Closed Nov.–May
⚶

CAMPING NAUTIC INTERNATIONAL
Tel. 02 96 28 57 94
Fax. 02 96 26 02 00
Closed Nov.–Mar.
On the shores of the lake. Many leisure activities available.
🖙 🏊

PAIMPOL

POSTCODE 22500   F2

CULTURAL ATTRACTIONS

BEAUPORT ABBEY
Kerity
Tel. 02 96 20 91 07
Open daily 10am–1pm and 2–7pm, Jul.–Aug. Restricted visiting times during low season. ▲217

MUSÉE DE LA MER
Rue de Lalenne
Tel. 02 96 22 02 19
Open 10am–noon and 3–7pm, Easter–Sep. 15.
▲220

RESTAURANT

L'OSTREA
Route de l'Arcouest 3 miles from Paimpol.
Tel. 02 96 20 74 31
Closed Mon. during low season, and Jan. 2–15.
Specialties: seafood and desserts.
Menus: 145–395F
🅿 ⚶ 🍴 🔆

HOTEL-RESTAURANTS

CHÂTEAU DE COATGUELEN
Plehedel
3 miles from Paimpol.
Tel. 02 96 28 54 34
Fax. 02 96 26 01 56
Closed Nov.–May.
Interesting castle set in a park with a golf course.
Rooms: 400–950F
Menus: 150–380F
🖙 ⚶ 🅿 ▭ ▭

Le repère de Kerroc'h*
22, quai Morand
Tel. 02 96 20 50 13
Fax. 02 96 22 07 94
Closed Jan. 5–Feb. 15.
Located in a beautiful privateers' house, opposite the marina.
Rooms: 390–580F
Menus: 69F ("café formula"), 175–315F
🍴 ☒ ▢ ▭

PERROS-GUIREC

Postcode 22700   E2

HOTEL-RESTAURANTS

Le Sphinx*
67, chemin de la Messe
Tel. 02 96 23 25 42
Fax. 02 96 91 26 13
Closed Jan 5–Feb 15
Charming restored manor house, dating from 1900, with a very pleasant garden that leads directly onto the beach.
Rooms: 500–560F
Menus: 125–265F
▢ ☒ ▣ 🚗 ⚑

Les Feux des Îles *
53, bd Clemenceau
Tel. 02 96 23 22 94
Fax. 02 96 91 07 30
Closed Sun. eve.–Mon., Oct.–Easter.
The rooms and the restaurant overlook the sea and the islands.
Rooms: 390–620F
Menus: 125–320F
▢ ☒ ▣ ⊘ ⚓ ⚑

Printania *
12, rue des Bons-Enfants
Tel. 02 96 49 01 10
Fax. 02 96 91 16 36
Large, beautiful hotel dominating the bay.
Rooms: 450–665F
Menus: 120–185F
⚓ ☒ ☒ ▢ ⚐ ▭ ⚑

ACCOMMODATION

Camping Le Ranolien **
Ploumanach
Tel. 02 96 91 43 58
Fax. 02 96 91 41 90
Situated among the rocks of the Pink Granite Coast.
▢ ⚓

PLOUÉZOCH

Postcode 29252   D2

CULTURAL ATTRACTIONS

Cairn de Barnenez
Tel. 02 96 67 24 73
Open 10am–1pm and 2–6pm. ▲225

PLOUGRESCANT

Postcode 22820   E2

CULTURAL ATTRACTIONS

Chapel of St-Gonery
Tel. 02 96 92 50 00
(Contact Mme Richard)
Open all year. ▲223

ACCOMMODATION

Manoir de Kergrec'h
Take the D8 from Plougrescant.
Tel. 02 96 92 56 06
Fax. 02 96 92 51 27
Bed-and-breakfast accommodation in a sumptuous 17th-century mansion set in a park leading down to the sea.
Rooms: 450–550F
▢ ☒ 🚗 ⚑

PLOUHA

Postcode 22580   F2

CULTURAL ATTRACTIONS

Chapel of Kermaria-an-Isquit
Tel. 02 96 20 35 78
(Contact Mme Cojean).
Open May–Sep.
Group visits arranged by appointment (out of season). Guided tours available on request.

PLOUMILLIAU

Postcode 22300   E2

CULTURAL ATTRACTIONS

Church of St-Milliau
Pl. de l'Eglise
Open 2–6pm, Jul.–Aug.

PONTIVY

Postcode 56300   F5

CULTURAL ATTRACTIONS

Château de Pontivy
Rue du Général-de-Gaulle
Tel. 02 97 25 12 93
Open daily 10.30am–7pm, Jun.–Sep. Open Wed.–Sun. 10am–noon and 2–6pm, Oct.–May.
▲234

HOTEL-RESTAURANTS

Le Robic *
2, rue Jean-Jaurès
Tel. 02 97 25 11 80
Fax. 02 97 25 74 10
Simple, friendly and affordable. ½ mile from the banks of the Blavet.
☒ ▣ ⚑

ACCOMMODATION

Le Rohan *
90, rue Nationale
Tel. 02 97 25 02 01
Fax. 02 97 25 02 85
Open all year.
Near the railway station.
Rooms: 295–395F
☒ ▣ ⚑

Youth Hostel
Ile des Récollets
Tel. 02 97 25 58 27
Fax. 02 97 25 12 97
On an small island in the center of town.
☒ ▣

QUINTIN

Postcode 22800   F3

CULTURAL ATTRACTIONS

Basilica of Notre-Dame
Open daily 9am–noon and 2–7pm. Closed Wed. during term time.
▲227

Château de Quintin
Tel. 02 96 74 94 79
Open 10am–7pm, Jun.–Oct.
Open Wed.–Sun 10am–noon and 2–6pm, Mar. 15–May.
Exhibitions. ▲227

HOTEL-RESTAURANT

Le Commerce
2, rue Rochenen

Tel. 02 96 74 94 67
Restaurant closed Sun. eve.–Mon. lunchtime and Dec. 15–Jan. 15
Traditional cuisine.
Rooms: 170–280F
Menus: 59–289F
▢ ☒ ▣

ROHAN

Postcode 56580   F5

CULTURAL ATTRACTIONS

Thimadeuc Abbey
Tel. 02 97 51 50 29
Open 9am–noon and 2–7pm.
▲230

RESTAURANT

L'Eau d'Oust
6, rue du Lac
Tel. 02 97 38 91 86
Closed Sun.eve.–Mon.
Closed 1 week in Feb. and 1 week in Sept.
Restored farm. Barges to rent nearby.
Menus: 75–215F
▢ ☒ ⚑ ⚓

ST-JEAN-DU-DOIGT

Postcode 22630   D2

CULTURAL ATTRACTIONS

Church of St-Jean-du-Doigt
Open daily 9am–6pm.
▲225

ST-QUAY-PORTRIEUX

Postcode 22410   F3

HOTEL-RESTAURANTS

Ker Moor Hotel *
13, rue du Président-le-Sénécal
Tel. 02 96 70 52 22
Fax. 02 96 70 50 49
Around a Moorish villa dominating the beach. View over the sea from all half-board rooms and from the restaurant.
Rooms: 485–530F
Menus: 95–290F
▢ ☒ ▣ ⚓ ⚑

Le Gerbot d'Avoine *
2, blvd du Littoral
Tel. 02 96 70 40 09
Fax. 02 96 70 34 06
Closed Sun. eve.–Mon.

during low season, and Nov. 20–Dec. 11, Jan. 8–31.
Rooms: 200–330F
Menus: 82–275F

ACCOMMODATION

CAMPING BELLEVUE ***
68, bd du Littoral
Tel. 02 96 70 41 84
Closed Sept. 15–Apr.

TONQUÉDEC

POSTCODE 22140 E2

CULTURAL ATTRACTIONS

CHÂTEAU DE TONQUÉDEC
Tel. 02 96 47 18 63
Open 11am–8pm, Jul. –Aug. and 3–6pm, May–Jun. and Sep.
▲224

TRÉBEURDEN

POSTCODE 22560 E2

HOTEL-RESTAURANTS

MANOIR DE LAN-KERELLEC***
Pointe de Kerellec
Allée centrale
Tel. 02 96 23 50 09
Fax. 02 96 23 66 88
Open Nov. 15–mar. 15.
Part of the "Relais et Châteaux" chain. Magnificent site with breathtaking view of the coastline.
Rooms: 600–1,500F
Menus: 140–370F

TI AL LANNEC**
Allée Mezo-Guen
Tel. 02 96 23 57 26
Fax. 02 96 23 62 14
Closed Nov. 11–mar.
Beautiful, comfortable Breton house with view over Tresmeur beach. Specialty: seafood
Rooms: 500–1,050F
Menus: 205–390F

ACCOMMODATION

LE TOENO YOUTH HOSTEL
60, la Corniche
Goas–Treiz
Tel. 02 96 23 52 22
Fax. 02 96 47 44 34

TRÉGASTEL

POSTCODE 22730 E2

HOTEL-RESTAURANTS

HÔTEL BELLEVUE***
20, rue des Calculots
Tel. 02 96 23 88 18
Fax. 02 96 23 89 91
Closed Oct. 15–Easter.
Charming hotel in a garden full of flowers.
Rooms: 280–500F
Menus: 90–250F

TRÉGUIER

POSTCODE 22220 E2

CULTURAL ATTRACTIONS

CATHEDRAL OF ST-TUGDUAL
Pl. du Mantray
Open 10am–noon and 2–6.30pm.
▲222

MUSÉE RENAN
20, rue Ernest-Renan
Tel. 02 96 92 45 63
Open daily 10am–noon and 2–6pm.
Closed Oct.–Easter.
▲222

HOTEL-RESTAURANT

AIGUE-MARINE***
Port de Plaisance (marina)
Tel. 02 96 92 97 00
Closed Jan.
Good location, opposite the river Tréguier. High-quality rooms and cuisine. Specialty: seafood.
Rooms: 358–450F
Menus: 100–195F

◆

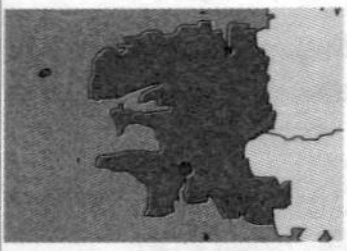

MORLAIX

POSTCODE 29600 D3

CULTURAL ATTRACTIONS

BRASSERIE DES DEUX RIVIÈRES
1, pl. de la Madeleine
Tel. 02 98 63 41 92
Tours Mon.–Wed. at 10.30am, 2pm and 3.30pm, Jul. –Aug. Visit Wed. at 2pm by appointment out of season. ▲242

CHAPEL OF NOTRE-DAME-DE-LA FONTAINE (CARMEL)
9, rue Ste-Marthe
Tel. 02 98 88 05 82
Open daily 8am–6.30pm. ▲242

CHURCH OF ST-MATHIEU
Pl. St-Mathieu
Rue Basse
Tel. 98 88 03 08
Open 9am–noon and 2–7pm. ▲238

CHURCH OF ST-MELAINE
Rampe St-Melaine
Tel. 02 98 88 05 65

MAISON DE LA REINE ANNE
Rue du Mur
(Contact Mme Lahellec)
Tel. 02 98 88 23 26
Open Mon.–Sat. 10.30am–6.30pm and Sun. 2–6pm, Jun.–Aug.
Open Tue.–Sun. 10.30am–noon and 2–6pm, Apr.–May and Sep.
Visits by appointment out of season. ▲238

TOBACCO FACTORY
41, quai de Léon
Tel. 02 98 88 15 32
Open Mon.–Thu. 8am–noon and 1.30–5pm.
Closed Jul. 14–Aug. 21.
Visits by appointment only.
▲243

MUSÉE DES JACOBINS
Pl. des Jacobins
Tel. 02 98 88 68 88
Closed Tue.
Open daily 10am–12.30pm and 2–6.30pm, Jul.–Aug.
Open daily 10am–noon and 2–6pm, Eastern–Jun. and Sep.–Oct.
Open Mon., Wed.–Sun. 10am–noon and 2–5pm, Nov.–Easter. ▲239

RESTAURANTS

BROCÉLIANDE
5, rue des Bouchers
Tel. 02 98 88 73 78
Closed Tue.
Located in the old town.
Menus: 120–150F

LA MARÉE BLEUE
3, rampe Ste-Melaine
Tel. 02 98 63 24 21
Closed Sun. eve.–Mon. low season and 2 weeks in Feb. and Oct.
Located in a small street under the viaduct.
Menus: 75F (weekdays), 98–220F

HOTEL-RESTAURANT

HÔTEL D'EUROPE**
1–3, rue d'Aiguillon
Tel. 02 98 62 11 99
Fax. 02 98 88 83 38
Very comfortable rooms. Gourmet restaurant with an impressive wine list. The wine cellars nearby are open to the public and are well worth a visit.
Rooms: 215–440F
Menus: 130–250F

ACCOMMODATION

HÔTEL DU PORT **
3, quai de Léon
Tel. 02 98 88 07 54
Small, comfortable hotel, opposite the marina.
Rooms: 190–210F

BERNÉ

POSTCODE 56240 E5

CULTURAL ATTRACTIONS

CHÂTEAU DE PONT-CALLEC
Tel. 02 97 34 21 65
Only the park is open.
▲272

CARANTEC

POSTCODE 29660 D2

CULTURAL ATTRACTIONS

CHÂTEAU DU TAUREAU
*Castle in the water.
Access by boat but not open to the public.* ▲259

HOTEL-RESTAURANT

**PORSPOL **
7, Rue Surcouf
Tel. 02 98 67 00 52
Closed Sep. 25–Easter.
Quiet hotel with view over the sea and direct access to the beach.
Rooms: 245–265F
Menus: 89–160F

ACCOMMODATION

CAMPING LES MOUETTES **
Tel. 02 98 67 02 46
Fax. 02 98 78 31 46
Closed Oct.–Apr. 15.

**LA FALAISE **
Tel. 02 98 67 00 53
Closed Oct.–Jan.
Has a nice view of Morlaix bay.
Rooms: 195–275F

CHÂTEAUNEUF-DU-FAOU

POSTCODE 29520 D4

CULTURAL ATTRACTIONS

CHAPEL OF NOTRE-DAME-DES-PORTES
Tel. 02 98 81 70 02

*Open in the summer.
When it is locked, key available from the chapel.* ▲267

HOTEL-RESTAURANT

LE RELAIS DE CORNOUAILLE **
9, rue Paul-Sérurier
Tel. 02 98 81 75 36
Fax. 02 98 81 81 32
Closed Sat., Sun. eve.
Rooms: 180–270F
Menus: 65–180F

COMMANA

POSTCODE 29450 D3

CULTURAL ATTRACTIONS

CHURCH OF ST-DERRIEN
Pl. de l'Eglise
Tel. 02 98 78 00 22
(Mr. Chapalain)
Open all year 9am–7pm.
▲255

GUIMILIAU

POSTCODE 29400 C3

CULTURAL ATTRACTIONS

CHURCH OF ST-MILIAU
Open 9am–6.30pm.
▲253

HUELGOAT

POSTCODE 29690 D3

CULTURAL ATTRACTIONS

CHAOS WINDMILL
Tel. 02 98 99 77 83
(summer) or
02 98 1 90 69 (winter)
Open Tue.–Sun.
1.30–6.30pm, Jul.–Aug.
▲266

HOTEL-RESTAURANTS

AUBERGE DE LA TRUITE
Former railway station
Locmaria
Tel. 02 98 99 73 05

Closed Sun. eve–Mon.
out of season.
In the countryside, near the canal.
Rooms: 125–180F
Menus: 90–325F

HÔTEL DU LAC
Tel. 02 98 99 71 14
Fax 02 98 99 70 91
Closed Nov. 11–Jan. 11
View over the lake.
Rooms: 220–260F
Menus: 68–220F

ÎLE DE BATZ

POSTCODE 29253 C2

HOTEL-RESTAURANTS

KER NOËL
Rupodou
Tel. 02 98 61 79 98
Fax 02 98 61 74 09
Rooms: 120–200F.
Menus: 75–100F

KERNASCLÉDEN

POSTCODE 56540 E5

CULTURAL ATTRACTIONS

CHAPEL OF KERNASCLÉDEN
Open 9am–6pm. ▲272

LA MARTYRE

POSTCODE 29800 C3

CULTURAL ATTRACTIONS

CHURCH OF ST-SALOMON
Open 9am–7pm. ▲256

LAMPAUL-GUIMILIAU

POSTCODE 29400 C3

CULTURAL ATTRACTIONS

CHURCH OF NOTRE-DAME
Open 8am–7pm.
Ossuary open in the summer, and on request out of season (Tel. 02 98 68 76 14, chapel; or

02 98 68 76 67, town hall). ▲254

LANNILIS

POSTCODE 29870 B3

ACCOMMODATION

MANOIR DE TROUZILIT
Tréglonou
Tel. 02 98 04 01 20
Guest rooms (230F) and rural bed-and-breakfast.

CAMPING DES ABERS **
Landeda
Tel. 02 98 04 93 35
Fax 02 98 04 84 35
Closed Oct.–Apr.
Panoramic view.

LE CONQUET

POSTCODE 29217 B3

CULTURAL ATTRACTIONS

MUSÉE D'HISTOIRE LOCALE
Parc de Beauséjour
Tel. 02 98 89 14 41
Open 5–7.30pm,
Wed.–Fri. 5–7.30pm,
Sat.–Sun.
10.30am–noon and
5–7.30pm. ▲264

HOTEL-RESTAURANT

POINTE STE-BARBE**
Tel. 02 98 89 00 26
Fax. 02 98 89 14 81
Restaurant closed
Mon. low season, and
Nov. 11–Dec. 18
*Panoramic view over the islands and the ocean.
Very close to the pier for boat excursions to Ouessant and Molène.*
Rooms: 189–619F
Menus: 96–446F

LE FAOUËT

POSTCODE 56320 E5

CULTURAL ATTRACTIONS

CHAPEL OF ST-FIACRE
Open daily 9am–noon
and 2–7pm, Jun. 15–
Sept. 15. Restricted
visiting times in low
season. ▲270

CHAPEL OF STE-BARBE
Tel. 02 97 23 06 50
Open daily 10am–noon
and 2–7pm, Jun. 15–
Sep. 15. Open Wed.,
Sat.–Sun., Sep. 16–
May 20. ▲271

MUSÉE DES PEINTRES
1, rue de Quimper
Tel. 02 97 23 23 23
Office of tourism.
Open daily 10am–noon
and 2.30–6.30pm,
Jun.–Sep. ▲270

HOTEL-RESTAURANT

LA CROIX D'OR **
9, pl. Bellanger
Tel. 02 97 23 07 33
Fax 02 97 23 06 52
Closed Sun. eve. low
season and Dec. 20–
Jan. 15
Rooms: 225–300F
Menus: 72–230F
C ☆ ⬛

ACCOMMODATION

CAMPING CARAVANNING MUNICIPAL BEG ER ROCH ***
Rte de Lorient
Tel. 02 97 23 15 11
Fax 02 97 23 11 56
Closed Sept. 15–
Feb. 28
Close to the river.
⬛

PLOUESCAT
POSTCODE 29430 C2

HOTEL-RESTAURANT

LA CARAVELLE **
20, rue du Calvaire
Tel. 02 98 69 61 75
Fax. 02 98 61 92 61
Restaurant closed Mon.
Oct–Jun. and Jan. 15–
Feb. 15.
Rooms: 260–1,240F
Menus: 65 (weekdays),
95–185F
C ☆ ⬛ ⬛

PLOUGONVELIN
POSTCODE 29217 B3

CULTURAL ATTRACTIONS

ABBEY OF ST-MATHIEU
Pointe de St-Mathieu
Tel. 02 98 48 35 73
Open site. The museum
of the friends of St

Mathieu is very close
and is open daily
11am–7pm, Jul.–Aug..
Restricted visiting times
out of season. Closed
Dec.–Mar.

HOTEL-RESTAURANT

HOSTELLERIE DE LA POINTE DE ST- MATHIEU ***
Tel. 02 98 89 00 19
Fax. 02 98 89 15 68
Restaurant closed Sun.
eve.in low season and
Jan. 15–Feb. 15.
Rooms: 270–400F
Menus: 98–400F
⬛ ⬛ ☆ ⬛

PLOUGUERNEAU
POSTCODE 29880 B2

CULTURAL ATTRACTIONS

ILIZ KOZ
Direction of Koréjou
beach
Saint Michel
Open Tue.–Sun. 2–6pm,
Jun. 15–Sep. 15,
and Sun. 2.30–5pm,
Sep. 16–Jun. 14. ▲265

MUSÉE DES TRADITIONS MARITIMES
Saint Michel
Open Tue.–Sun. 3–7pm,
Jul.–Aug., Tue.–Sat.
1.30–4.30pm and Sun.
2–6pm, Sep.–Jun. ▲263

ILE VIERGE LIGHTHOUSE
Tel. 02 98 04 78 01 or
02 98 04 74 06
Temporary closed to the
public. ▲264

HOTEL-RESTAURANT

LE CASTEL AC'H **
Kervenny
Tel. 02 98 04 70 11
Fax. 02 98 04 58 43
Overlooking the sea
and close to the Ile
Vierge lighthouse.
Rooms: 180–320F
Menus: 85–205F.
☆ ⬛

ROSCOFF
POSTCODE 29680 D2

CULTURAL ATTRACTIONS

CHURCH OF NOTRE-DAME-DE-KROAZ-BRAZ
Open 9am–noon and
2–6pm. ▲261

HOUSE OF MARY STUART
19, rue Amiral-Réveillère
Closed to the public.
▲261

LIGHTHOUSE
Vieux port
Tel. 02 98 69 70 06
Temporary closed to
the public. ▲262

MAISON DES JOHNNIES
Rue Gambetta
Tel. 02 98 61 12 13
Open Mon., Wed.–Sun.
10am–noon and 3–6pm,
Apr.–Oct. 15. ▲261

MUSÉE OCÉANOGRAPHIQUE AND AQUARIUM
Pl. Georges-Tessier
Tel. 02 98 29 23 25
Open daily 10am–noon
and 1–7pm, Jun.–
Sep. 10. Open daily
1–7pm, Sep. 11–Nov. 1.
▲261

RESTAURANTS

LE TEMPS DE VIVRE
Pl. de l'Eglise
Tel. 02 98 61 27 28
Closed Sun. eve.–Mon.
and Nov. 1 and Feb.
school vacations.
Sophisticated cuisine
served in a charming
setting.
Menus: 165–350F
C

LE YACHTMAN
Bd Ste-Barbe
Tel. 02 98 69 70 78
Closed Mon. lunch and
Nov. 5–Mar. 15.
Restaurant of the
Brittany Hotel. Terrace
and view of the port.
Menus: 98–290F

HOTEL-RESTAURANTS

LE BRITTANY ***
Bd Ste-Barbe
Tel. 02 98 69 70 78
Fax 02 98 61 13 29
Closed Nov. 5–Mar. 15.
18th-century Breton
mansion overlooking the
harbor.
Rooms: 390–690F
Menus: ?
⬛ ☆ ⬛ ⬛ ⬛

LE TALABARDON ***
Place de l'Eglise
Tel. 02 98 61 24 95
Fax 02 98 61 10 54
Closed Nov. 15.–Feb. 15
Traditional hotel by
the sea. High-quality
seafood cuisine.
Rooms: 340–535F
Menus: 93–265F
C ☆ ⬛

ST-GOAZEC
POSTCODE 29520 D4

CULTURAL ATTRACTIONS

CHÂTEAU DE TRÉVAREZ
Tel. 02 98 26 82 79
Open 2–6pm Sat.–Sun.
and school vacations,
Oct.–Mar.
Open 1–6.30pm Mon.,
Wed.–Sun., Apr.–Jun.
and Sep.
Open 11am–7pm,
Jul.–Aug.

ST-POL-DE-LÉON
POSTCODE 29250 D2

CULTURAL ATTRACTIONS

CATHEDRAL
Open daily 9am–noon
and 2–6pm. ▲260

CHURCH OF NOTRE-DAME-DU-KREISKER
Open daily 10am–noon
and 2–6pm, Jul.–Sep. 15.
Visits by appointment
out of season (call the
Tourist office 02 98 69
05 69). ▲260

HOTEL-RESTAURANT

HÔTEL DE FRANCE **
Rue des Minimes
Tel. 02 98 29 14 14
Fax. 02 98 29 10 57
Closed Jan.–Feb.
Beautiful hotel in garden

½ mile from the sea.
Rooms: 250–500F
Menus: 85–250F.
☆ ⌂ ⚲ ☐ ♨

ACCOMMODATION

**CAMPING
ARKLEGUER *****
Tel. 02 98 69 18 81
Open Apr.–Sep.
Close to the sea.
▭•• ↘ ⌇

ST-
THÉGONNEC

POSTCODE 29410   **D3**

CULTURAL
ATTRACTIONS

**CHURCH OF
NOTRE-DAME**
Open 8am–8pm all year.
Ossuary open Easter–
Oct. ▲252

RESTAURANT

CRÊPERIE STEREDENN
6, rue de la Gare
Tel. 02 98 79 43 34
*Offers an impressive
choice of 150 different
crêpes.*
Menus: 46–66F
☐

HOTEL-
RESTAURANT

AR PROSPITAL COZ
18, rue Lidivic
Tel. 02 98 79 45 62
Fax. 02 98 79 48 47
*Rooms and buffet-
supper in the charming
old chapel.*
Rooms: 240–260F
Menus: 85F
☐ ⌂ ⚲ ♨

ST-VOUGAY

POSTCODE 29440   **C3**

CULTURAL
ATTRACTIONS

**CHÂTEAU DE KERJEAN
AND MUSÉE**
Tel. 02 98 69 93 69
Open daily 10am–7pm,
Jul.–Aug. Open
Wed.–Sun. 10am–6pm,
Jun. and Sep. Open for
exhibitions out of season.

SIBIRIL

POSTCODE 29250   **C2**

CULTURAL
ATTRACTIONS

**CHÂTEAU
DE KEROUZÉRÉ**
Tel. 02 98 29 96 05
Guided tours daily at
2.30pm, 4pm and
5.30pm, Jul. 15–Aug.
Restricted visiting hours
out of season. Closed
Nov.–May.
*Visit of the exterior
possible (dogs not
allowed).* ▲262

SIZUN

POSTCODE 29450   **C3**

CULTURAL
ATTRACTIONS

**CHURCH OF
ST-SULIAN**
Open daily 9am–7pm
Museum Open daily
9am–7.30pm May–Sept.
▲256

**MAISON DE LA
RIVIÈRE, DE L'EAU
ET DE LA PÊCHE**
Moulin de Vergraon
Tel. 02 98 68 86 33
Closed Nov.–Feb.
Open daily 10.30am–
7pm, Jul.–Aug.
Open daily 10.30am–
12.30pm and 1.30–
5.30pm, Jun. and Sep.
Restricted visitng times
out of season. ▲256.

MAISON DU LAC
Barrage du Drennec
Tel. 02 98 68 86 33
Open daily 10.30am–
12.30pm and 1.30–6pm,
Jul.–Aug. Open daily
10.30am–12.30pm and
1.30–5.30pm, Jun. and
Sep. ▲256.

**MUSÉE D'ARTS ET
TRADITIONS
POPULAIRES**
10, place Abbé-Broch
Tel. 02 98 68 81 63 or
02 98 68 87 60
Open daily 9am–7.30pm,
May–Sep. ▲256.

HOTEL-
RESTAURANTS

**HÔTEL DES
VOYAGEURS ****
6, rue de l'Argoat
Tel. 02 98 68 80 35
Fax. 02 98 24 11 49
*Restaurant closed Sat.
eve. out of season and
Sep. 10–30.*
*Traditional hotel near the
parish church.*
Rooms: 165–260F
Menus: 68–120F
☐ ☐

**LE CLOS
DES 4 SAISONS ****
2, rue de Brest
Tel. 02 98 68 80 19

BREST

POSTCODE 29200   **B3**

CULTURAL
ATTRACTIONS

ARSENAL
Porte de la Grande-
Rivière
Tel. 02 98 22 11 82
Open 8–11am and
2– 5.30pm, Jun. 15–
Sep. 15. Visits at 10am
and 2.30pm during
school vacations. ▲276

**CONSERVATOIRE
BOTANIQUE NATIONAL**
Vallon de Stangalar
52, allée du Bot
Tel. 02 98 41 88 95
Garden open daily
9am–8pm to the public
during the spring and
summer, 9am–6pm
during the winter.
Greenhouse open
Mon.–Fri. 2–5pm,
Jul.–Aug. ▲277

MÉMORIAL MONBAREY
Fort de Monbarey
Allée Bri-Hakeim
Tel. 02 98 05 39 46
Open 2–6pm. Closed
Sat. from mid-Sep.–
mid.Jun.

MUSÉE DE LA MARINE
Château de Brest
Tel. 02 98 22 12 39
Open daily 9.15am–
noon and 2–6pm.
Closed Tue. ▲275

Fax. 02 98 24 11 93
Closed first week in Sep.
*Charming small hotel
in a garden full of
flowers.*
Rooms: 120–240F
Menus: 59–119F
☐ ⚲ ☐ ♨

SPÉZET

POSTCODE 29540
D4

CULTURAL
ATTRACTIONS

**CHAPEL OF NOTRE-
DAME-DE-CRANN**
Rue du Crann
Open every morning.

**MUSÉE DES
BEAUX ARTS**
22, rue Traverse
Tel. 02 98 00 87 96
Open daily 10–11.45am
and 2–6pm. Closed
Tue., Sun. am.
▲275

OCÉANOPOLIS
Port de Plaisance du
Moulin-Blanc
Tel. 02 98 34 40 40
Open 9.30am–6pm,
Jun. 15–Sep.,
Mon. 2–5pm, Tue.–Fri.
9.30am–5pm and Sat.–
Sun. 9.30am–6pm,
Oct.–Jun. 14
▲277

TOUR MOTTE-TANGUY
Musée du Vieux-Brest
Tel. 02 98 45 05 31
Fax 02 98 00 88 60
Open daily 10am–noon
and 2–7pm, Jun.–Sept.
Open Wed.–Thur.
2–5pm, Sat.–Sun.
2–6pm, Oct.–May.
▲277

RESTAURANTS

**CRÊPERIE LE BLÉ
NOIR**
Vallon de Stangalard
Tel. 02 98 41 84 66
Open all year.
*Restored mill on site of a
botanical conservatory.*
Menus: 50–80F
⚲ ☐ ♨ ⸆

LE NOUVEAU ROSSINI
22, rue du
Commandant-Drogou
Tel. 02 98 47 90 00
Closed Sun. eve.–Mon.
and Aug. 15–Sep. 6
*In the Kerinou area.
Refined cuisine and
impressive menu.*
Menus: 98–340F
⚲ ☐ ♨ ⸆

LE VATEL
23, rue Fautras
Tel. 02 98 44 51 02
Closed Sun., Mon. eve.
and Aug. 1–20
Specialty: seafood
Menus: 95–300F
C

LE FRÈRE-JACQUES
15 bis, rue de Lyon
Tel. 02 98 44 38 65
Closed Sun.
*Charming welcome and
unusual décor. Creative
cuisine.*
Menus: 85–298F

AZENOR
Port de plaisance du
Moulin-Blanc (marina)
Tel. 02 98 41 46 23
*Lunch and dinner cruise.
Visit of Brest harbor.*

HOTEL-RESTAURANTS

MERCURE
CONTINENTAL ***
Square de la Tour-
d'Auvergne
Tel. 02 98 80 50 40
Fax. 02 98 43 17 47
Closed Sat. and Sun.
*Very close to the
popular Rue de Siam.
The 1900s décor of the
hotel, bar and restaurant
is well worth a visit.*
Rooms: 450–620F
Menus: 95F
C ⚲

OCEANIA ***
82, rue de Siam
Tel. 02 98 80 66 66
Fax. 02 98 80 65 50
Closed Sun. eve.
Modern hotel with

AUDIERNE
POSTCODE 29113   B5

HOTEL-RESTAURANTS

AU ROI GRADLON**
1, av. Manu-Brusq
Tel. 02 98 70 04 51
Fax. 02 98 70 14 73
Closed Sun. eve.–Mon.
low season and Jan. 6
–Feb. 21.
Beside the sea.
Rooms: 290–350F
Menus: 85–220F
⚲ P

LE GOYEN***
Pl. Jean-Simon
Tel. 02 98 70 08 88
Fax. 02 98 70 18 77
Closed Mon. low season
Opposite the bay.

---

*personalized rooms.
Traditional restaurant.
bar and nightclub.
Maritime atmosphere.*
Rooms: 460–700F
Menus: 85–190F

LE BELVÉDÈRE ***
Technopole Bres-Iroise
Ste-Anne du Porzic
Tel. 02 98 31 86 00
Fax. 02 98 31 86 39
*The rooms and
restaurant overlook the
entrance to the harbor.
The park leads down to
the Customs Officers'
path that follows the
coastline.*
Rooms: 365–550F
Menus: 88–250F
🛏 ⌂ ▭•• ⚂ ▭ ⚲
🗆 P

ACCOMMODATION

HÔTEL DE LA
CORNICHE ***
1, rue de l'Amiral-Nicol
Tel. 02 98 45 12 42
Fax. 02 98 49 01 53
*Tennis. Near the arsenal,
in a quiet area.*
Rooms: 300–420F
⚲ P 🛏

YOUTH HOSTEL
5, rue de Kerbriant
Port de Plaisance du
Moulin-Blanc (marina)
Tel. 02 98 41 90 41
Fax. 02 98 41 82 66
Open 7am–11pm high
season, 7am–9pm low
season.
*A mile and a half
from the center.
Membership card
essential.*
⚂ 🛏

*Pricey but excellent
regional cuisine.*
Rooms: 350–800F
Menus: 160–450F
⚲ ⇔ P 🍴

CAMARET
POSTCODE 29570   B4

CULTURAL
ATTRACTIONS

TOUR VAUBAN
Le Sillon
Tel. 02 98 27 91 12
*Exhibition center open
during the summer.* ▲289

CHAPEL OF
NOTRE-DAME-DE-
ROCAMADOUR
Le Sillon
Tel. 98 27 90 48
Open all year. ▲289

RESTAURANTS

CRÊPERIE
ROCAMADOUR
11, quai Kléber
Tel. 02 98 27 93 17
Closed Mon. low season
and Nov. 11–Dec. 20
and Jan. 3–Feb. 2.
Menus: 50–70F
C

HOTEL-RESTAURANTS

LE FRANCE ***
19, quai Gustave-
Toudouze
Tel. 02 98 27 93 06
Fax. 02 98 27 88 14
*Restaurant closed
Fri. low season and
Nov.–Easter.
Opposite the harbor
and the Sillon.*
Rooms: 190–420F
Menus: 78–295F
C ⚲ P ⚂

THALASSA ***
Quai du Styvel
Tel. 02 98 27 86 44
Fax. 02 98 27 88 14
Closed Oct.–Mar.
*Comfortable hotel. Well
situated by the harbor.
Heated sea water
swimming pool*
Rooms: 300–550F
Menus: 78–300F
⚂ C 🛏 ▭ 🌊 ▭
⚘ ⚲

CLÉDEN-
CAP-SIZUN
POSTCODE 29113   B4

CULTURAL
ATTRACTIONS

CHAPEL OF ST-THEY-
DE-LA-POINTE-DU-VAN
Take the main route
from Douarnenez,
toward Pointe du Van.
Tel. 02 98 70 33 78
Open 2–6pm
Easter–Sep. ▲294

RESTAURANT

L'ÉTRAVE **
Route de la Pointe-
du-Van
Tel. 02 98 70 66 87
Closed Wed.
*On the clifftops.
Specialty: seafood.*
Menus: 90–245F

HOTEL-RESTAURANT

RELAIS POINTE
DU VAN **
Baie des Trépassés
Tel. 02 98 70 62 79
Fax. 02 98 70 35 20
Open Apr.–Sept.
*In a superb location to
explore on foot.*
Rooms: 252–372F
Menus: 96–210F
▭•• ⚲ P 🛏 🍴

CROZON
MORGAT
POSTCODE 29160   B4

CULTURAL
ATTRACTIONS

CHURCH OF ST-PIERRE
Pl. de-Gaulle
Tel. 02 98 27 05 55
Open daily 8am–7pm.
▲290

HOTEL-RESTAURANTS

HOSTELLERIE
DE LA MER **
Le Fret
Tel. 02 98 27 61 90
Fax. 02 98 27 65 89
Closed Jan.
*Situated right opposite
the sea. Logis de France,
Baladhôtel* ▲395
Rooms: 245–400F
Menus: 105–270F
⚲ P

LA VILLE D'YS **
Port de Morgat
Tel. 02 98 27 06 49
Open Apr.–Sept.
*Terrace overlooking the
small harbor.*
Rooms: 220–340F
Menus: 55–240F
C ⚲ P ⚘ ⚂ 🛏

GRAND HÔTEL
DE LA MER **
Avenue de la Plage
Tel. 02 98 27 02 09
Fax 02 98 27 02 39
Closed Oct. 16–Mar.
*This magnificent Belle
Epoque hotel has just
been restored. Direct
access to the beach.*
Rooms: 345–585F
Menus: 110–200F
⚂ 🛏 P 🗆 ⌂
▭ ⚘

DAOULAS

POSTCODE 29460 C3

CULTURAL ATTRACTIONS

CENTRE CULTUREL DE L'ABBAYE
21, rue de l'Eglise
Tel. 02 98 25 84 39
Open daily 10.30am–
7.30pm, Jun.–Oct.
Open Mon.–Fri.
10am–noon, 1.30–
5.30pm, and Sun.
1.30–5.30pm,
out of season.

DOUARNENEZ

POSTCODE 29100 C4

CULTURAL ATTRACTIONS

PORT-MUSÉE DE PORT-RHU
Pl. de l'Enfer
Tel. 02 98 92 65 20
Open daily 10am–7pm,
during high season.
Open 10am–noon and
2–6pm, low season.
Closed Mon. (except
during school vacations)
▲293

RESTAURANTS

AU GOÛTER BRETON CRÊPERIE TUDAL
36, rue Jean-Jaurès
Tel. 02 98 92 02 74
Closed Sun., 15days in
Jun. and 15 days in Nov.
Open daily during school
vacations.
Menus: 45–60F

LE POURQUOI PAS? ET LE CHARCOT
Tel. 02 98 92 76 13
Fax 02 98 92 90 12
Restaurant closed Sun.
eve.–Mon. low season
and Nov.
Le Pourquoi Pas?
(bar/brasserie) and
Le Charcot (restaurant)
are located opposite the
port museum. A must
for lovers of old ships,
Irish atmosphere and
seafood.
Carte: 80F minimum

LE TRISTAN
25, bis rue du Rosmeur
Tel. 02 98 92 20 17
Closed Wed., Sun. eve.
low season and Nov.
15– Jan. 15
Small restaurant

overlooking the fishing
harbor.
Menus: 99–200F

HOTEL-RESTAURANTS

AUBERGE DE KERVEOC'H
42, route de Kerveoc'h
in the direction of
Quimper
Tel. 02 98 92 07 58
Open Easter–Sept.
Charming country
inn, 1 mile from the
beaches.
Rooms: 265–315F
Menus: 98–250F

THALASSTONIC *
Rue des Professeurs-
Curie
Tel. 02 98 74 45 45
Fax. 02 98 74 36 07
Opposite the
thalassotherapy center.
Rooms: 350–480F
Menus: 96–152F

TY MAD*
Place St-Jean-Treboul
Tel. 02 98 74 00 53
Fax. 02 98 74 15 16
Open Easter–Nov. 1.
Charming 16th-century
Breton chapel. Small
sandy beach and
magnificent view of
the bay.
Rooms: 285–315F
Menus: 65–185F

ÎLE D'OUESSANT

POSTCODE 29240 A3

CULTURAL ATTRACTIONS

ECOMUSÉE DU NIOU–HUELLA
Maison des Traditions
Ouessantes
Tel. 02 98 48 86 37
Open Tue.–Sun.
10.30am–6.30pm,
Jun.–Sep.
Restricted times
during low season.
▲278

MUSÉE DES PHARES ET BALISES
Créac'h lighthouse
Tel. 02 98 48 80 70
Open daily 10.30am
–6.30pm, Jun–Sept.,
school vacations.
Restricted visiting times
during low season.
▲279

PHARE DU STIFF
Tel. 02 98 48 80 21
Temporarily closed to
the public. ▲279

HOTEL-RESTAURANTS

HÔTEL DU FROMVEUR *
Tel. 02 98 48 81 30
Near the small harbor.
Local specialties.
Ancient building.
Half board: 255–320F
Menus: 74–115F

ACCOMMODATION

CAMPING PENN AR BED *
Tel. 02 98 48 84 65
or 02 98 48 80 06 (town
hall)
Open Apr.–Sept.
Just outside market
town of Lampaul. No
caravans on Ouessant.

ÎLE DE MOLÈNE

POSTCODE 29259 A3

RESTAURANT

L'ARCHIPEL
Le Quai
Tel. 02 98 07 38 56
Open Apr.–Sept.
Creative seafood cuisine
Menus: 82–124F

LANDÉVENNEC

POSTCODE 29560 C4

CULTURAL ATTRACTIONS

LANDÉVÉNNEC ABBEY AND MUSEUM
Rue St-Guenolé
Tel. 02 98 27 35 90
Museum open daily
10am–7pm (1–7pm,
public holidays), May–
Sep. Open Sat.–Sun.
2–6pm (daily 2–6pm
school vacations),
Oct.–May. ▲288

LOCRONAN

POSTCODE 29180 C4

CULTURAL ATTRACTIONS

CHURCH OF ST-RENAN
Pl. de l'Eglise
Open 9am–noon and
2–7pm.
Guided tours available.

RESTAURANTS

LA PIERRE DE LUNE
Pl. des Charrettes
Tel. 02 98 91 82 20
Closed Mon.–Tues. out
of season
A former blacksmith
house. Sophisticated
cuisine. Crêpes served
on the terrace in
summer.
Menus: 92–178F

HOTEL-RESTAURANT

MANOIR DE MOILLIEN *
Tel. 02 98 92 50 40
Fax. 02 98 92 55 21
Open Apr.–Dec.
A few miles from
Locronan, toward
Douarnenez. Restaurant
in the superbly restored
manor house. Rooms in
the outbuildings with a
wonderful view of the
surrounding area. Very
tranquil.
Rooms: 360F
Menus: 125–235F

PLOUGASTEL-DAOULAS

POSTCODE 29470 B–C3

CULTURAL ATTRACTIONS

CALVARY
Close to the church.
▲282

CHAPEL OF ST-JEAN
1½ miles from town
toward Landerneau.
Close to the river.

MUSÉE DU PATRIMOINE ET DE LA FRAISE
Rue Louis-Nicolle
Tel. 02 98 40 21 18
Open Tue.–Sun. 2–6pm,
Apr. 15–Jun. 14,
Sept. 15–Oct. Open
Mon.– Sat. 10am–
12.30pm and 2–7pm,

Jun. 15–Sept. 15.
Closed on public
holidays. ▲281

**HOTEL-
RESTAURANTS**

KASTEL ROC'H
Roc'h Kerezen

🏃 ⌂ 🅿 🚗 🚅

QUIMPER

POSTCODE 29000

**CULTURAL
ATTRACTIONS**

**ST-CORENTIN
CATHEDRAL**
Place St-Corentin
Open daily all year
9am–noon and
2–6.30pm. ▲298

FAÏENCERIES
Rue Haute
Tel. 02 98 90 09 36
Open Mon.–Thur.
9–11.15am and 1.30–
4.15pm, Fri. 9–11.15am
and 1.30–3pm.
Exhibitions and shop.
▲303

**MUSÉE DE LA
FAÏENCE**
14, rue Bousquet
Tel. 02 98 90 12 72
Open 10am–6pm,
Apr. 15–Oct. 15.
Closed on Sun. and
public holidays.
*Group visits by
appointment during
low season.* ▲303

**MUSÉE
DÉPARTEMENTAL
BRETON**
1, rue du Roi-Gradlon
Tel. 02 98 95 21 60
Open daily 9am–6pm,
Jun.–Sep.
Open Tue.–Sat.
9am–noon and 2–5pm,
Sun. 9am–noon,
Oct.–May.
▲299

**MUSÉE
DES BEAUX ARTS**
40, place St-Corentin
Tel. 02 98 95 45 20
Open daily 9am–7pm,
Jul.–Aug., 10am–noon
and 2–6pm, Sep.–Jun.
Closed Tue. and public

Tel. 02 98 40 32 00
Fax. 02 98 04 25 40
*Restaurant closed
Sun. eve. during low
season
Close to the calvary.*
Rooms: 250–300F
Menus: 76–150F

🏃 ⌂ 🅿 🚗 🚅

holidays, Sep.–Jun.
▲299

RESTAURANTS

AU VIEUX QUIMPER
20, rue Verdelet
Tel. 02 98 95 31 34
Closed Tue., Sun. lunch
and Jun. 1–15 and
Nov. 15–30.
Typical crêperie.
Meal: around 68F.
🄲

LA PLACE AU BEURRE
2, bis place au Beurre
Tel. 02 98 95 49 88
*Crêperie. On Quimper
square (pedestrianized
area).*
Carte: 50–70F
🄲 🏃 🚅

**LE CAPUCIN
GOURMAND**
19, rue des Réguaires
Tel. 02 98 95 43 12
Closed Sat. lunch, Sun.
*Near the cathedral.
Creative cuisine, with a
high reputation locally.*
Menus: 115–360F
🄲 🏃

LA ROSERAIE
Bel Air (direction
Plomelin-Corniguel)
Tel. 02 98 53 50 80
Closed Sun. eve.–Mon.
*Quiet place full of
charm offering fresh-
produce cuisine.*
Menus: 138–265F
🄳 🏃 🅿 🚅

LA FLEUR DE SEL
1, quai Neuf
Tel. 02 98 55 04 71
Closed Sat. lunch, Sun.
and Dec. 25–Jan. 1.
*On the banks of the
Odet, opposite the
Musée de la Faïence.*
Menus: 80–195F
🄳 ⌂ 🗄

**HOTEL-
RESTAURANT**

**LA TOUR
D'AUVERGNE ***
13, rue des Reguaires
Tel. 02 98 95 08 70
Fax 02 98 95 17 31
Closed Sat. eve–Sun.,
Oct.–Apr. and Sat. lunch,
May–Jul. 15
*In the historic center.
Ideal for walking around
the city. Comfortable.
Traditional cuisine.*
Rooms: 395–550F
Menus: 105–210F
🄳 🗄 🅿 🚗 🚅

ACCOMMODATION

**CAMPING
L'ORANGERIE
DE LANNIRON ****
83, chemin de
Lanniron
Tel. 02 98 90 62 02
Fax 02 98 90 84 31
Closed Sep. 15–Apr.
*1¼ miles from Quimper.
Former Bishops'
residence by the river.*
Restaurant menus:
50F (lunch), 65–96F
🄳

**CHÂTEAU DE
GUILGUIFFIN**
Landudec (direction
Audierne)
Tel. 02 98 91 52 11
Fax 02 98 91 52 52
Closed Nov. 11–Mar.
*Tastefully decorated
guest rooms in a
sumptuous18th-century
castle. Beautiful park.*
Rooms: 400–800F
Suites: 900–1,300F
🄳 🏃 🚗 🚅

HÔTEL GRADLON *
30, rue de Brest
Tel. 02 98 95 04 39
Fax. 02 98 95 61 25
Closed Dec. 20–Jan. 15.
Rooms: 330–480F
Suite: 800F
🄳 🏃 🚗 🚅

BÉNODET

POSTCODE 29950 C5

**HOTEL-
RESTAURANTS**

**HOSTELLERIE
ABBATIALE ***
4, av. de l'Odet
Tel. 02 98 57 05 11
Fax. 02 98 57 14 41
*Former abbey
overlooking the harbor
and the Odet estuary.*
Rooms: 250–500F
Menus: 75–180F
🄳 🏃 🅿 🚅

HÔTEL GWEL-KAER*
Av. de la Plage
Tel. 02 98 57 04 38
Fax. 02 98 66 22 85
Closed Dec. 10–Jan. 20.
By the beach.
Rooms: 250–495F
Menus: 98–380F
🄳 🏃 🅿 🚗 🚅

LE MINARET *
Corniche de l'Estuaire
Tel. 02 98 57 03 13
Closed Oct.–Mar.
*Former Mauresque villa,
with terraces and
gardens on the banks
of the Odet. Various
styles of cuisine.*
Rooms: 280–430F
Menus: 90–210F
⛷ 🅿 🗄 ⌂ 🗄
🚅 🚅

CONCARNEAU

POSTCODE 29900 C5

**CULTURAL
ATTRACTIONS**

MUSÉE DE LA PÊCHE
Rue Vauban
Tel. 02 98 97 10 20
Open daily 9.30am–7pm,
Jun. 15– Sept. 15. Open
9.30am–noon and
2–6pm, Sep. 16–Jun. 14
Within the city walls.
▲310

RESTAURANT

**L'ASSIETTE
DU PÊCHEUR**
12, rue St-Guénolé
B.P. 115
Tel. 02 98 50 75 84

Open daily 12.15–2pm
and 7.15–9.30pm
Closed Oct.–Easter.
Within the city walls.
Meals: 60–95F
C ⊤

HOTEL-RESTAURANTS

LE GALION *
15, rue Guénédé
Tel. 02 98 97 30 16
Fax. 02 98 50 67 88
Closed Sun. eve.–Mon.
during low season and
Nov. 15–Easter.
*Regional food in a
beautiful old house
within the city walls.*
Rooms: 450F
Menus: 130–380F
C ⅄ P

**LES SABLES
BLANCS ***
Rue des Sables-Blancs
Tel. 02 98 97 01 39
Fax. 02 98 50 65 88
Closed Nov.–Feb.
*By the sea, with direct
access to the beach.*
Rooms: 190–340F
Menus: 180F
▭⋯ ⅄ ⅄ ♯ ⊤

ACCOMMODATION

YOUTH HOSTEL
Quai de la Croix
Tel. 02 98 97 03 47
Pedestrianized area.
⅄

HENNEBONT

POSTCODE 56700   E6

HOTEL-RESTAURANTS

**AUBERGE DU
TOUL DOUAR ***
On the old Lorient road
Tel. 02 97 36 24 04
Restaurant closed
Sun. eve.–Mon. Oct.–
May. Closed Feb.
Rooms: 120–150F
Menus: 70–230F
⅄ P ♯ ⊤

**CHÂTEAU DE
LOCGUÉNOLÉ ***
On Port-Louis
Kerivignac road
Tel. 02 97 76 29 04
Fax. 02 97 76 39 47
Restaurant closed Mon.
(except public holidays)
Oct.–Apr. and Jan.2–
Feb. 9
Park bordering the sea.
Rooms: 390–1,350F
Menus: 190–480F
▭⋯ ⅄ ⅄ P ♯ ⊤

ÎLE DE SEIN

POSTCODE 29990   A4

HOTEL-RESTAURANTS

LES 3 DAUPHINS
Quai des Paimpolais
Tel. 02 98 70 92 09
Open all year.
*Opposite the small
harbor.*
Rooms: 180–300F
Meals: around 80F
⅄

LA FORÊT
FOUESNANT

POSTCODE 29940   C5

HOTEL-RESTAURANTS

**MANOIR DU
STANG ****
D 783
Tel. 02 98 56 97 37
Open May–Sep.
*15th-century manor
set in a park.*
Rooms: 160F
Menus: 570–840F
▭⋯ P ♯

PONT-L'ABBÉ

POSTCODE 29120   C5

CULTURAL
ATTRACTIONS

MUSÉE BIGOUDEN
Château de Pont-L'Abbé
Tel. 02 98 66 09 09
Closed Oct.–Easter.
Open Mon.–Sat.,
2–6pm, Easter–May.
Open Mon.–Sat., 9am–
noon and 2–6.30pm,
Jun.–Sep. ▲306

RESTAURANT

**CRÊPERIE
BIGOUDENNE**
33, rue du Gal-de-Gaulle
Tel. 02 98 87 20 41
Closed Sun.–Mon. and
Jan. Open daily during
school vacations.
House built during the

---

reign of Louis XV.
Menus: 50–70F
C

HOTEL-RESTAURANT

**LE CHÂTEAU
KERNUZ ***
Route de Penmarc'h
Tel. 02 98 87 01 59
Fax 02 98 66 02 36
Open Apr.–Sep.
*Located in the 16th-
century castle.*
Rooms: 370–450F
Menu: 150F
▭⋯ ⅄ P ♯

PONT–AVEN

POSTCODE 29930   D5

CULTURAL
ATTRACTIONS

MUSÉE DE PONT-AVEN
Place de l'Hôtel de Ville
Tel. 02 98 06 14 43
Open daily 10am–noon
and 2–6pm Feb.–Dec.
▲311

RESTAURANTS

LA TAUPINIÈRE
Croissant St-André
Tel. 02 98 06 03 12
Fax 02 98 06 16 46
Closed Mon. eve.–Tue.
during low season.
*Reservations
recommended.*
Menus: 260–460F
▭⋯ ⅄ P

HOTEL-RESTAURANT

**LE MOULIN
DE ROSMADEC**
Venelle de Rosnadec
Tel. 02 98 06 00 22
Fax 02 98 06 18 00
Restaurant closed Mon.,
all year; Sun. eve. low
season; Nov. 15–30
and Feb.
Rooms: 400–470F
Menus: 160–398F
C ⅄ ♯ ⊤

QUIMPERLÉ

POSTCODE 29300   D5

RESTAURANT

BISTROT DE LA TOUR
2, rue Dom-Morice
Tel. 02 98 39 29 58
*Original Art Deco décor.
Talented owner-chef.*

▲307
Menus: 99–360F
C

RIEC-SUR-BELON

POSTCODE 29340   D5

RESTAURANT

CHEZ JACKY
Port de Belon
Tel. 02 98 06 90 32
Closed Mon. Oct.–
Easter
*View over the small
harbor of Belon.*
Specialty: seafood
Menus: 100–400F
▭⋯ ⅄

HOTEL-RESTAURANTS

**LES MOULINS
DU DUC ****
Domaine de Kerstinec
Tel. 98 06 42 98
Fax. 98 06 45 38
Closed Jan.–Feb.
*On the banks of the
Belon.*
Rooms: 440–805F
Menus: 140–320F
▭⋯ ⅄ ⅄ ⅄ P
♯ ⊤

ACCOMMODATION

**MANOIR DE
KERTALG ****
Route de Riec-sur-
Belon
Tel. 02 98 39 77 77
Fax. 02 98 39 72 07
Open Apr. 15–Nov. 15.
*Beautiful rooms in a
magnificent domain.
Tea rooms and
exhibitions of paintings.*
Rooms: 490–980F
▭⋯ ⅄ P ♯

ST-JEAN-
TROLIMON

POSTCODE 29120   C5

CULTURAL
ATTRACTIONS

**NOTRE-DAME
DE TRONOËN**
Open 10am–7pm
Jul.–Aug, and 2–5pm
Jun. and Sep.

LORIENT

POSTCODE 56100   E6

CULTURAL ATTRACTIONS

ARSENAL
Arsenal de Lorient
Tel. 02 97 12 12 12
Open 9–11am and 2–5pm May 15–Sept. 15.
▲323

BIBLIOTHÈQUE HISTORIQUE DE LA MARINE
Enclos de la Marine
Tel. 02 97 12 12 12
Open Mon.–Fri.
8.30am–5pm and Sat.
8.30am–noon. ▲323

MEMORIAL
Plâce Alsace-Lorraine
Tel. 02 97 21 07 84
Guided tours at 2pm and 3.30pm
Marine shelter from World War II.

RESTAURANTS

L'AMPHITRYON
127, rue Colonel-Müller
Tel. 02 97 83 34 04
Closed Sat. lunch–Sun.
Original refined recipes.
Impressive wine list.
Menus: 100–350F
ⵛ P

LE PIC
2, bd du Maréchal-Franchet-d'Esperey
Tel. 02 97 21 18 29
Closed Sat. lunch–Sun.

AURAY

POSTCODE 56400   F6

CULTURAL ATTRACTIONS

CHURCH OF ST-GILDAS
Pl. Gabriel-de-Hayes
Open 8am–noon and 2–6.30pm. Closed Sun. am. ▲339

RESTAURANTS

L'ABBAYE
19, pl. St-Sauveur
Tel. 02 97 24 10 85

(except public holidays), and Jan. 2–14.
Menus: 95–195F
ⵛ

LE BISTROT DU YACHTMAN
14, rue Poissonnière
Tel. 02 97 21 31 91
Open until 10pm.
Closed Sun. and Mon. eve. and Aug. 15–31.
Near the marina.
Seafood and fish served in a friendly décor.
Menus: 75–190F

ACCOMMODATION

HÔTEL MERCURE *
31, pl. Jules-Ferry
Tel. 02 97 21 35 73
Fax 02 97 64 48 62
Near the Palais des Congrès. Very good restaurant next to the hotel.
Rooms: 295–445F.
ⵛ

HÔTEL VICTOR-HUGO **
36, rue L.-Carnot
Tel. 02 97 21 16 24
or 02 97 84 95 13
Near the Maison de la Mer and the departure point for boat excursions to island of Groix.
Rooms: 150–260F.

YOUTH HOSTEL
41, rue Victor-Schœldcher
Tel. 02 97 37 11 65
Fax 02 97 87 95 49
Comfortable inn.
Camping facilities in summer. Meals available upon request

Closed Sun. eve.–Mon.
low season, and
Dec. 20–Jan. 25
Listed 17th-century house by the old harbor of St. Goustan.
Menus: 70–150F

LA CLOSERIE DE KERDRAIN
20, rue Louis-Billet
Tel. 02 97 56 61 27
Closed Mon. low season and Jan. 1–15.
16th-century manor.
Gourmet cuisine.
Menus: 100–380F
ⵛ

PILITRINIC
Bois Bas-Penmern
Baden
Tel. 02 97 57 06 85
Fax 02 97 57 22 00
Open noon–2pm and 7–10pm. Closed Sun. eve.–Mon. and Nov. 15–Jan. 15.
In a pine forest with a beautiful view over Moustoir estuary.
Menus: 79–200F

HOTEL-RESTAURANT

LE GAVRINIS *
Toul-Broch
Baden
Tel. 02 97 57 00 82
Fax 02 97 57 09 47
Closed Mon. lunch during low season and Nov. 15–Jan.
Two miles from the sea and near the golf course.
Rooms: 340–454F
Menus: 110–350F

BELLE ÎLE

POSTCODE 56100   E7

CULTURAL ATTRACTIONS

CITADELLE VAUBAN MUSÉE HISTORIQUE DU PALAIS
Tel. 02 97 31 84 17
Open 9am–7pm Jul–Aug, and 9.30am–6pm Apr.–Jun. and Sep.–Oct.
Restricted times during low season. ▲328

LE GRAND-PHARE
Port-Goulphar
Bangor
Tel. 02 97 31 82 08
Open dailyJul–Aug.
Group visits by appointment during low season. ▲331

RESTAURANTS

LE CONTRE-QUAI
Rue St-Nicolas
Sauzon
Tel. 02 97 31 60 60
Fax 02 97 31 66 70
Closed Oct.–Easter.
Old house in the port.
Menus: 135–215F
ⵛ

HOTEL-RESTAURANTS

LE PHARE
Quai Guerveur

Sauzon
Tel. 02 97 31 60 36
Closed Dec.–mid-Mar.
Beautiful view over the small harbor and its lighthouse.
Half-board: 290F
Menus: 85–195F
ⵛ P

CASTEL CLARA **
Port Goulplar
Tel. 02 97 31 84 21
Fax 02 97 31 51 69
Open Feb 15–Nov. 15.
Beside the sea. Linked to the Institute of Thalassotherapy.
Rooms: 1,095–1,390F
Menus: 175–370F

LE MANOIR DE GOULPHAR *
Tel. 02 97 31 80 10
or 02 97 31 56 04
Fax 02 97 31 80 05
Closed Nov.–Mar. 15.
On site of Institute of Thalassotherapy.
Rooms: 630–1,070F
Menus: 140–210F

BELZ

POSTCODE 56550   E6

CULTURAL ATTRACTIONS

CHAPEL OF ST-CADO
Open 9am–6pm. ▲334

CARNAC

POSTCODE 56340   E6

CULTURAL ATTRACTIONS

ARCHÉOSCOPE
Standing stones at Menec
Tel. 02 97 52 07 49
Open daily 10am–6pm Feb. 15–Nov. 12.
Restricted times during low season. ▲338

CHURCH OF ST- CORNÉLY
Open daily 9am–noon and 2–7pm. ▲335

STANDING STONES AT CARNAC
Information:
Tel. 02 97 52 89 99
Visits from 9am–9pm daily Jul.–Aug.
Restricted times during low season. ▲337

MUSÉE PRÉHISTORIQUE
10, pl. de la Chapelle

Tel. 97 52 22 04
Open daily
10am–6.30pm Jul.–Aug.

HOTEL-RESTAURANTS

LE PLANCTON ★★★
12, bd de la Plage
Tel. 02 97 52 13 65
Fax 02 97 52 87 63
Open Mar.–Sep.
Rooms: 550–600F
Menus: 100–210F
🄲 ⚊ ⚡ 🄿 ⚊

LANN ROZ ★★
36, av. de la Poste
Tel. 02 97 52 10 48
Closed Mon. and
Jan.–Feb. 15.
*Pleasant house in a
garden full of flowers.*
Rooms: 370–400F
Menus: 95–185F
🄲 ⚊ ⚡ 🄿 ♠

LE DIANA ★★★★
21, bd de la Plage
Tel. 02 97 52 05 38
Fax. 02 97 52 87 91
Open Easter–Sep.
Restaurant closed Wed.
lunch during low season.
Overlooking the bay.
Rooms: 570–1,170F
Menus: 250–350F
⚊ ⚡ ⚊ 🄿 🚗 ⚊

LE BATEAU IVRE ★★★★
71, bd de la Plage
Tel. 02 97 52 19 55
Closed Jan.
*Away from the main
road and by the sea.
Rooms facing south
with balconies. Heated
swimming pool.*
Rooms: 390–850F
Menus: 150F
⚡ ♠ 🄿 ⚊ ⚊

ÎLE DE GROIX

POSTCODE 56590 D6

CULTURAL ATTRACTIONS

**CHURCH OF
NOTRE-DAME-DE-
PLACEMANEC**
Tel. 02 97 86 53 08
Open all day. ▲327

ECOMUSÉE
Tel. 02 97 86 84 60
Open daily 10am–
12.30pm and 2–5pm,
Apr. 15–May 31.
Open 9.30am–12.30pm
and 3–7pm, Jun–Sept.
Open Tue.–Sun. 10am–
12.30pm and 2–5pm,
Oct.–Apr. 14. ▲325

**RÉSERVE NATURELLE
FRANÇOIS-LE-BAIL**
Open school vacations
and Jul.–Aug.
Information: Maison de
la Réserve, Le Bourg,
near the chapel
(Mme Pichot),
Tel. 02 97 86 55 97,
or Sepnb, Brest,
Tel. 02 98 49 07 18.
Visits upon appointment
during low season.
▲327

HOTEL-RESTAURANTS

LA MARINE ★★
7, rue du Gal-de-Gaulle
Tel. 02 97 86 80 05
Fax 02 97 86 56 37
Closed Jan.
*Beautiful house
surrounded by a closed
garden. Room No 1
faces the sea.*
Rooms: 215–450F
Menus: 80–180F
⚡ ⚊ ♠

TY MAD ★★
Le Port
Tel. 02 97 86 80 19
Closed Jan.–Feb.
*Panoramic view over
the sea.*
Rooms: 250–350F
Menus: 80–160F
⚊ 🄿 ♠ ⚊

ACCOMMODATION

**FORT-MÉNÉ YOUTH
HOSTEL**
Tel. 02 97 86 81 38
Fax 02 97 86 52 43
Closed Oct. 16–Mar.
*Rooms in a former fort.
Camping facilities.
Youth Hostel
Association
membership card
compulsory.*

**GÎTE D'ÉTAPE
LA GOÉLETTERIE**
Port Tudy
Tel. 02 97 86 89 87
Large, original house

*with a view over the sea
and the incoming ships.
Friendly welcome.*
⚊

LOCMARIAQUER

POSTCODE 56740 F6

CULTURAL ATTRACTIONS

**CHURCH OF NOTRE-
DAME-DE-KERDRO**
Pl. de l'Eglise
Open 9am–7pm. ▲339

**MENHIR DE LA TABLE
DES MARCHANDS**
Tel. 02 97 57 37 59
Open daily 10am–7pm
Jun–Sept. Restricted
times during low season.
▲338

PORT-LOUIS

POSTCODE 56290 E6

CULTURAL ATTRACTIONS

**MUSÉE DE LA
COMPAGNIE DES INDES
À PORT-LOUIS**
Fortress
Tel. 02 97 82 19 13
or 02 97 12 10 37
Open daily 10am–7pm
Apr.–Sep. and 1.30–
6pm Oct.–Mar.
Closed Tue., Jan. 1,
May 1, Nov.–Dec. 15
and Dec. 25. ▲333

**MUSÉE DE LA
CITADELLE ET
MUSÉE DE LA MARINE**
Fortress
Tel. 02 97 12 10 37
Open daily 10am–7pm
Apr.–Sep. and 1.30–
6pm Oct.–Mar.
Closed Tue., Jan. 1,
May 1, Nov.–Dec. 15
and Dec. 25. ▲333

HOTEL-RESTAURANTS

**HOTEL-RESTAURANT
DU COMMERCE ★★**
Place du Marché
Tel. 02 97 82 46 05
Fax 02 97 82 11 02
Closed Jan. Restaurant
closed Mon. out of
season.
Close to the fortress.

*Comfortable rooms and
traditional cuisine.*
Rooms: 128–350F
menus: 65–265F
⚊

QUIBERON

POSTCODE 56170 E75

CULTURAL ATTRACTIONS

**MUSÉE DE LA
CHOUANNERIE**
Le Bégo – Plouhamel
Tel. 02 97 52 31 31
Open 10am–noon and
2–6pm. Closed
Oct.–Mar. ▲335

HOTEL-RESTAURANTS

LE BELLEVUE ★★★
Rue Tiviec
Tel. 02 97 50 16 28
Fax 02 97 30 44 34
Open Mar.–Oct. 15
*Near the casino, the
thalassotherapy center,
and the beaches.*
Rooms: 430–700F
Menus: 100–135F
⬜ ⚊ ⚊ ♠ ⚊

**SOFITEL
THALASSA ★★★★**
Pointe de Goulvars
Tel. 02 97 50 20 00
Fax 02 97 30 47 63
Closed Jan. 3–31
*At the tip of the
peninsula in a
breathtaking site.
Linked to the
thalassotherapy
center.*
Rooms: 815–1,630F
Menus: 215–460F
⚊ ⚊ ♠ 🄿 ⚊
⚊ ⚊

STE-ANNE-D'AURAY

POSTCODE 56400 F6

CULTURAL ATTRACTIONS

BASILIQUE STE-ANNE GALERIE D'ART POPULAIRE ET RELIGIEUX, MUSÉE DU COSTUME BRETON
9, rte de Vannes
Tel. 02 97 57 68 80
Basilica open 7am–9.30pm Jul–Aug and 7am–7pm low season.
Grand Pardon de Ste-Anne Jul. 25–26 eve.

VANNES

POSTCODE 56000 F6

CULTURAL ATTRACTIONS

AQUARIUM
Parc du Golfe
Tel. 02 97 40 67 40
Open daily 9am–7pm Jun.–Aug.
Open 9am–noon and 1.30–6.30pm during low season.
▲346

ST-PIERRE CATHEDRAL
Pl. St-Pierre
Tel. 02 97 47 10 88
Chapel open daily 10am–noon and 2–6pm Jun.–Sep.
▲344

CHÂTEAU GAILLARD AND MUSÉE D'ARCHÉOLOGIE DU MORBIHAN
2, rue Noé
Tel. 02 97 42 59 80
Open 9.30am–6pm Jul.–Aug. Closed Sun.,

Gallery and museum open 10am–noon and 2–6pm Mar.–Oct. Closed Sun. am. ▲340

HOTEL-RESTAURANT

LA CROIX BLANCHE ★★
25, rue de Vannes
Tel. 02 97 57 64 44
Closed Sun. eve.–Mon. low season and Feb.
Rooms: 195–365F
Menus: 85–265F
🅲 ⚘ 🅿 🏠 ✝

public holidays and am during low season. *Exhibitions in the summer.* ▲344

MUSÉE DE LA COHUE
9–15 pl. St-Pierre
Tel. 02 97 47 35 86
Open 10am–6pm Jun.–Sep. Restricted times during low season *Beaux-Arts museum.*
▲344

RESTAURANTS

LA MARÉE BLEUE
8, pl. Bir-Hakeim
Tel. 02 97 47 24 29
Closed Sun. eve. in winter and Dec. 20–30.
Menus: 75–290F
🅲 ⚘ 🅿

LE PRESSOIR
7, rue de l'Hôpital-St-André
Tel. 02 97 60 87 63
Open noon–2pm and 7.30–9.30pm
Closed Sun. eve.–Mon., Mar. 1–15, first week in Jul. and Oct. 1–15
Three miles north of town on D 767. Fine cuisine served in a charming setting.
Menus: 135F (lunch), 195–390F
🗆 ⚘ 🅿

ARZON

POSTCODE 56640 F6

CULTURAL ATTRACTIONS

TUMULUS DE TUMIAC
Tel. 02 97 53 81 63
Tourist Office
Just before Arzon on the road from Sarzeau.
▲364

BATZ-SUR-MER

POSTCODE 44740 G6

CULTURAL ATTRACTIONS

MUSÉE DES MARAIS SALANTS
29 bis, rue Pasteur
Tel. 02 40 23 32 79
Open daily 10am–noon and 3–7pm Jun–Sep. Restricted times during low season.
▲369

HOTEL-RESTAURANTS

A L'IMAGE SAINTE-ANNE ★★
8, pl. de la Libération
Tel. 02 97 63 27 36
Fax 02 97 63 97 02
Restaurant closed Sun. eve Nov.–Easter.
Rooms: 250–350F
Menus: 78–230F
🅲 ⚘ 🅿

LE ROOF ★★★
Conleau pensinsula
Rue Daniel Gilard
Tel. 02 97 63 47 47
Fax 02 97 63 48 10
Opposite Goulet de Conleau overlooking the sea or the river.
Rooms: 360–620F
menus: 150–330F
🌣 🅿 🗆 🏠
🗆 ⚘

ACCOMMODATION

AQUARIUM HÔTEL★★★
Parc du Golfe
Rue Daniel-Gilard
Tel. 02 97 40 44 52
Fax 02 97 63 03 20
Near the pier for boat excursions to the isle of Arz.
Rooms: 390–500F
🌣 ⚘ 🅿 🏠

ELVEN

POSTCODE 56250 G6

CULTURAL ATTRACTIONS

FORTERESSE DE LARGOËT
Tel. 02 97 53 35 96
Open daily 8am–8pm, Feb.–Nov. 10.
▲352

GUÉRANDE

POSTCODE 44350 G7

CULTURAL ATTRACTIONS

CHAPEL OF NOTRE-DAME-LA-BLANCHE
Rue de la Prévôté
Tel. 02 40 24 90 68
Chapel. ▲368

COLLÉGIALE ST-AUBIN
Tel. 02 40 24 83 38
Open 10am–noon and 2–6.30pm Jul.–Aug.
Group visits arranged by appointment all year.
▲368

RESTAURANTS

LE VIEUX LOGIS
1, pl. de la Psalette
Tel. 02 40 42 96 46
Closed Mon. eve.–Tue. low season, Jan. and Oct. 8–23
Crêperie in a 17th-century building.
🅲 ⚘ 🏠 ✝

HOTEL-RESTAURANTS

ROC MARIA ★★
1, rue des Halles
Tel. 02 40 24 90 51
Fax. 02 40 62 13 03
Open all year.
15th-century manor house in the medieval town. Crêperie.
Rooms: 260–300F
🅲 🗆

ACCOMMODATION

CAMPING LE PRÉ DU CHÂTEAU DE CAREIL ★★★★
33, rue du Château-de-Careil,
D92
Tel. 02 40 60 22 99
Closed Oct.–Mar.
Quiet, wooded campsite.

HERBIGNAC

POSTCODE 44410 **G7**

CULTURAL ATTRACTIONS

CHÂTEAU DE RANROUËT
From Herbignac, follow the signs for Chapelle-des-Marais.
Tel. 02 40 88 96 17
Open Tue.–Sun.
10am–7pm Jun. 23–Aug.
Open Tue.–Fri. 3–7pm,
Sat.–Sun. and public holidays 10am–1pm and 3–7pm, Apr. 7–Jun. 23 and Sep. 1–15. ▲367

ACCOMMODATION

CHÂTEAU-HÔTEL DE COËTCARET
Tel. 02 40 91 41 20
Fax 02 40 91 37 46
Guest rooms and meal (fixed menu).
Rooms: 400–450F
📧 ※ 🅿 🏨

MAISON DE LA NATURE AND DE LA RANDONNÉE
Le Bignon d'Hoscas
Tel. 02 40 91 33 91
Holiday cottages.
📧 🅿 🏨

ÎLE-AUX-MOINES

POSTCODE 56780 **F6**

CULTURAL ATTRACTIONS

MÉGALITHES
Route de la Pointe-de-Bannec. ▲349

HOTEL-RESTAURANTS

LE SAN FRANCISCO
Rue du Port
Tel. 02 97 26 31 52
Fax 02 97 26 35 59
Restaurant closed Wed. eve.–Thur. Nov.–Easter and Nov. 15–Dec15
Located in a former

convent overlooking the golf course.
Rooms: 315–530F
Menus: 130–235F
※ ※ 🍴

ÎLE D'ARZ

POSTCODE 56840 **F6**

CULTURAL ATTRACTIONS

CHURCH OF NOTRE-DAME
Open 2–6.30pm. ▲350

LA BAULE

POSTCODE 44500 **G8**

RESTAURANTS

LE ROYAL
6, rue Pierre-Loti
Tel. 02 40 11 48 48
Closed Nov. 15–Dec. 15
Menu: 220F
※ 🅿 🏨

LA MARCANDERIE
5, av. d'Agen
Tel. 02 40 24 03 12
Closed Sun. eve.
Menus: 155–285F
🅲 ※ 🅿

HOTEL-RESTAURANTS

LE BELLEVUE ★★★
27, bd de l'Océan
Tel. 02 40 60 28 55
Fax 02 40 60 10 18
Restaurant closed Wed. out of season.
Open 12.30–2pm and 7.30–9.30pm mid-Feb.–mid-Nov.
Set in a beautiful villa, 200 yards from the beach. Specialty: fish and seafood.
Rooms: 490–830F
Menus: 175–260F
🅲 ※ ※ 🅿

LE ROYAL ★★★★
6, rue Pierre-Loti
Tel. 02 40 11 48 48
Fax 02 40 11 48 45
Closed Jan.

By the sea. Linked to thalassotherapy center. Three restaurants.
Rooms: 700–1,640F
※ 🍽 🅿 🚗 🏨

ACCOMMODATION

CAMPING LA ROSERAIE ★★★★
20, av. Jean-Sohier
Tel. 02 40 60 46 66
Open Apr.–Sep.
🅲

LARMOR-BADEN

POSTCODE 56870 **F6**

CULTURAL ATTRACTIONS

CAIRN DE GAVRINIS
Tel. 02 97 57 19 38
Compagnie de Transports Maritimes Sagemor
Open daily 10am–noon and 2–6pm Jun.–Aug; Wed.–Mon. 3–6pm Oct.; Sat.–Sun. and public holidays 10am–noon and 2–6pm, Apr.–May and public holidays.
▲350

LA ROCHE-BERNARD

POSTCODE 56130 **G7**

RESTAURANT

LE CARDINAL
Quai de la Douane
Tel. 02 99 90 79 41
Closed Mon. eve.–Tue. Sep.–Jun.
Overlooks the river Vilaine. Restaurant on the top floor of the former Customs house.
Menus: 90–205F

HOTEL-RESTAURANTS

L'AUBERGE BRETONNE ★★★
2, pl. Duguesclin
Tel. 02 99 90 60 28
Fax 02 99 90 85 00
Restaurant closed Thur.–Fri. lunchtime.
Laid out like a monastery with central vegetable garden.
Rooms: 500–1,500F
Menus: 150–480F
🅲 ※ 🅿 🚗 🏨

MANOIR DU RODOIR ★★★
RN 165 Route de Nantes–Nivillac
Tel. 02 99 90 82 68

Closed Sun. eve.–Mon.
Rooms: 420–490F
menus: 95–235F
🅲 🍽 🅿 🏨

DOMAINE DE BODEUC ★★★
Nivillac
Tel. 02 99 90 89 63
Fax 02 99 90 90 32
Open all year.
By reservation only.
Charming manor house set in a park.
Quiet. restaurant open to residents.
Rooms: 550F
Menu: 170F
🅿 🏨

LE GUERNO

POSTCODE 56190 **G6**

CULTURAL ATTRACTIONS

CHURCH OF ST-JEAN-BAPTISTE-DU-GUERNO
Open all year 8am–8pm.
▲366

PARC ZOOLOGIQUE DE BRANFÉRÉ
Château de Branféré
Tel. 02 97 42 94 66
Open daily 9am–8pm Mar.–Sep. and 1.30–6.30pm Oct.–Feb. Ticket office closes 1 hour before closing time.
Picnic area.
▲366

MALESTROIT

POSTCODE 56140 **G5**

CULTURAL ATTRACTIONS

CHURCH OF ST-GILLES
Open all day. Closes around 7pm. ▲355

ACCOMMODATION

MANOIR DE LA COMBE
Hameau de Pleucadeuc
Tel. 02 97 26 90 65
Fax 02 97 26 94 47

Closed Mon. and Tue.
lunchtime.
*Manor house perched
above the village.*
Rooms: 320F
Menus: 140–220F
⌨•• ☆ 🅿

MUZILLAC

POSTCODE 56190   **G75**

CULTURAL ATTRACTIONS

MOULIN DE PEN-MUR
Take the bypass and
turn off at the sign for
"zone artisanale".
Tel. 02 97 41 43 79
Open 10am–12.30pm
and 2–6pm, Jul.–Sep.
Open Sat.–Sun. and
school vacations during
low season.
▲365

HOTEL-RESTAURANTS

**DOMAINE DE
ROCHEVILAINE**
Pointe de Penn-lann
Billiers
Tel. 02 97 41 61 61
Fax. 02 97 41 44 85
*Manor house
surrounded by small
Breton houses
overlooking the sea.
Refined cuisine.*
Rooms: 495–1,350F
Menus: 220–425F
⌨•• ☆ 🔾 🅿 ♨ ⚓

PAIMPONT

POSTCODE 35380   **H5**

CULTURAL ATTRACTIONS

ABBEY
Tel. 02 99 07 83 20
Mr. Roussel
or 02 99 07 81 37
Presbytery
Church open daily 9am–
7pm, restricted times
during low season.
Sacristy open 10am–
noon and 3–6.30pm
Jul.–Aug., Sat.–Sun. and
public holidays.

CHÂTEAU DE COMPER
Tel. 02 97 22 79 96
Open Mon., Wed.–Sun

10am–7pm Jul.–Sep.,
Mon., Wed.–Thu. and
Sat.–Sun. 10am–7pm
Apr.–Jun. ▲358

HOTEL-RESTAURANTS

**LE RELAIS DE
BROCÉLIANDE ✦✦**
7, rue des Forges
Tel. 02 99 07 81 07
Fax. 02 99 07 80 06
Closed Dec. 15–31.
*On the edge of the
legendary forest.*
Rooms: 180–280F
Menus: 110–280F
🅿 🔾 🔾 🔾 ♨

PLOËRMEL

POSTCODE 56800   **G5**

HOTEL-RESTAURANTS

AU COBH ✦✦✦
10, rue des Forges
Tel. 02 97 74 00 49
*Enjoys a high reputation
locally.*
Rooms: 200–320F
Menus: 58–230F
🇨 ☆ 🅿 ♨

LE ROI ARTHUR ✦✦
Le lac au Duc
Tel. 02 97 73 64 64
Fax 02 97 73 64 50
Restaurant closed
Sun. eve. Nov.–Mar.
*Modern, comfortable
hotel by the lake. Indoor
swimming pool and golf.
Water sports facilities
nearby.*
Rooms: 380–440F
Menus: 110–198F
⚹ ⌨•• 🅿 🔾 🔾
🔾 ⚓ ♨

QUESTEMBERT

POSTCODE 56230   **G6**

CULTURAL ATTRACTIONS

**CHAPEL OF
ST-MICHEL**
Rue St-Michel
Tel. 02 97 26 61 59
At entrance to cemetery.

Ask warden for the key.
▲353

HOTEL-RESTAURANTS

**LE BRETAGNE
ET SA RÉSIDENCE
DES CHÂTEAUX✦✦✦✦**
Tel. 02 97 26 11 12
Fax. 02 97 26 12 37
Restaurant closed
Mon. and Tue. lunchtime
(except Jul.–Aug. and
public holidays).
*One of the best
restaurants in Brittany.*
Rooms: 580–980F
Suites: 1,200–1,400F
Menus: 110–198F
☆ 🅿

ROCHEFORT-EN-TERRE

POSTCODE 56220   **G6**

CULTURAL ATTRACTIONS

**CHURCH OF
NOTRE-DAME-
DE-LA-TRONCHAYE**
Open 9am–noon and
2–6pm/7pm. ▲355

CHÂTEAU
Tel. 02 97 43 31 56
Open 10am–6.30pm,
Jul.–Aug; 10am–noon
and 2–6pm, Jun, Sept;
Sat.– Sun. 10.30am–
noon and 2–6pm
Apr.–May, Oct. ▲354

HOTEL-RESTAURANT

**CHÂTEAU DE
TALHOUËT**
Tel. 02 97 43 34 72
Fax 02 97 43 35 04
Open eves., lunchtime,
reservation only.
*16th–17th-century
castle. Takes overnight
guests.*

Rooms: 600–990F
(breakfast included)
Menus: 230F
⌨•• 🅿 ♨ ♨

ST-GILDAS-DE-RHUYS

POSTCODE 56730   **F7**

CULTURAL ATTRACTIONS

CHURCH OF ST-GILDAS
Open 9am–noon and
2–6pm. ▲365

ST-JOACHIM

POSTCODE 44720   **G7**

CULTURAL ATTRACTIONS

**MAISON DU PARC
RÉGIONAL DE BRIÈRE**
117, île de Fédrun
Tel. 02 40 91 68 68
▲366

**CHAUMIÈRE
BRIÉRONNE**
117, île de Fédrun
Tel. 02 40 66 85 01
Open daily 10.30–1pm
and 2.30–6.30pm Apr.
23–May 8. ▲367

MAISON DE LA MARIÉE
117, île de Fédrun
Tel. 02 40 91 65 91
Open Tue.–Sun.
9am–noon and 2–7pm
Apr.–Sep.
▲367

HOTEL-RESTAURANT

L'AUBERGE DU PARC
162, île de Fédrun
Tel. 02 40 88 53 01
Fax 02 40 91 67 44
Restaurant closed
Sun.–eve. and Mon
(except Jul.–Aug.) and
Jan. 15–Feb.
Hotel open Mar.–Dec 20.
*Situated on the edge
of the marshes amid
canals.*
Rooms: 300F
Menus: 150–195F
🅿 ⚥ ⚙ ✚

Menus: 110–220F
⚥ 🅿 ⚙

ST-LÉRY

POSTCODE 56430   G5

CULTURAL ATTRACTIONS

CHURCH
Open 9am–7pm. ▲*359*

ST-LYPHARD

POSTCODE 44410   G7

HOTEL-RESTAURANT

**AUBERGE
DE KERHINET ***
Kerhinet village
Tel. 02 40 61 91 46
Fax 02 40 61 97 57
Closed Tue. eve.–Wed.
during low season and
Dec. 15–Jan. 15.
Cottage in la Brière.
Rooms: 250–280F

ST-NAZAIRE

POSTCODE 44600   G8

CULTURAL ATTRACTIONS

ÉCOMUSÉE
Rue de Bac-de-Mindin
Tel. 02 40 22 35 33
Open daily 9.30am–
6.30pm Jun.–Sep.
Restricted times during
low season. ▲*370*

ESPADON SUBMARINE
Av. de la Forme–Ecluse
Tel. 02 40 22 35 53
Open daily 9.30am–
6.30pm Jun.–Sep.

Restricted times during
low season. ▲*370*

RESTAURANT

L'AN II
2, rue Villebois-Mareuil
Tel. 02 40 00 95 33
Closed Sun. eve. during
low season.
*large dining-room
overlooking the Loire
estuary. Local
specialties.*
Menus: 110–185F
⚘ ⚥ ⚙ ✚

HOTEL-RESTAURANT

LE BERRY *
1, pl. de la Gare
Tel. 02 40 22 42 61
Fax 02 40 22 45 34
*Very comfortable hotel,
only 10 minutes' walk to
the city center.*
Rooms: 290–435F
Menus: 89–225F
🅶 ⚥ 🅿

SARZEAU

POSTCODE 56370   G5

CULTURAL ATTRACTIONS

**CHÂTEAU DE
SUSCINIO AND
MUSÉE D'HISTOIRE
DE LA BRETAGNE**
Tel. 02 97 41 91 91
Open daily 10am–7pm,
Jul.–Sep.
Reduced times during
low season.
▲*362*

TREHORENTEUC

POSTCODE 56430   G5

ACCOMMODATION

CHURCH
Tel. 02 97 93 05 12
*Information available
from the Tourist
Office.*
▲*360*

NANTES

POSTCODE 44000   H8

CULTURAL ATTRACTIONS

**CATHEDRAL OF
ST-PIERRE AND
ST-PAUL**
Place St-Pierre
Open 8.30am–6pm.
Crypts open 10am–
noon and 2–6pm,
Sun. 2–6.30pm.
Closes at 5pm in
winter.
▲*376*

**CHURCH OF
STE-CROIX**
Place Ste-Croix
Open Mon.–Sat.
8am–noon and
2–6.30pm and Sun.
9.30am–1pm and
2–4pm. ▲*376*

JARDIN DES PLANTES
Rue Gambetta
Tel. 02 40 41 65 02
Open 8am–8pm, May.–
Aug. and 8am–7pm,
Feb.–Apr., Sep.–Oct.
and 8am– 5.30pm,
Nov.–Jan. ▲*378*

**MUSÉE D'HISTOIRE
NATURELLE, MUSÉE
ARCHÉOLOGIQUE**
12, rue Voltaire
Tel. 02 40 41 67 67
Open Tue.–Sat.,
10am–noon and 2–6pm,
Closed Sun.–Mon. and
public holidays.
▲*380*

**MUSÉE DE
L'IMPRIMERIE**
24, quai de la Fosse
Tel. 02 40 73 26 55
Open Tue., Thur.–Fri.
2–6pm, Wed. 10am–
noon and 2–6pm, and
Sat. 10am–noon and
2–5pm. Closed
Sun.–Mon. and public
holidays. ▲*381*

MUSÉE DE LA POSTE
10, blvd A.-Pageot
Tel. 02 51 83 36 04
Open Open Mon.–Fri.
9am–noon and 2–4pm.
▲*381*

**MUSÉE DES BEAUX
ARTS**
10, rue Clemenceau
Tel. 02 40 41 65 65
Open Mon., Wed.–Thu.
and Sat. 10am–6pm,
Fri. 10am–9om and
Sun. 11am–6pm.
▲*378*

**MUSÉE DES
SALORGES**
Château des Ducs
de Bretagne
Place Marc-Elder
Tel. 02 40 41 30 33
Open daily 10am–noon
and 2–6pm.
Closed Tue. Sep.–Jun.
▲*375*

**MUSÉE DOBRÉE
ET MUSÉE
ARCHÉOLOGIQUE**
Pl. Jean-V
Tel. 02 40 71 03 50
Open 10am–noon and
1.30–5.30pm. Closed
Mon. and public
holidays. ▲*380*

MUSÉE JULES-VERNE
3, rue de l'Hermitage
Tel. 02 40 69 72 52
Open 10am–noon and
2–5pm. Closed Tue.,
Sun. am and public
holidays. ▲381

MUSÉE NAVAL MAILLÉ-BRÉZÉ
Quai de la Fosse
Place Marc-Elder
Tel. 02 40 69 56 82
Open 2–6pm Jun.–Sep;
2–5pm Wed., Sat.–Sun
and public holidays
Oct.–May.
Group visits by
appointment all year.
▲381

MUSÉE RÉGIONAL D'ART POPULAIRE
Château des Ducs
de Bretagne
Place Marc-Elder
Tel. 02 40 41 56 56
Open 10am–noon
and 2–6pm.
Closed Tue. Sep.–Jun.
▲375

PLANÉTARIUM
8, rue des Arcadiens
Tel. 02 40 73 99 23
Shows Mon.–Fri. at
10.30am, 2.15pm and
3.45pm; Sun. at 3pm
and 4.30pm. Closed
public holidays. ▲380

RESTAURANTS

LA CIGALE
4, pl. Graslin
Tel. 02 51 84 94 94
Open until midnight
*Brasserie located in a
listed building. Very
pleasant for afternoon
teas as well.*
Menus: 75–150F
☐ ☆

AUBERGE DU CHÂTEAU
5, pl. Duchesse-Anne
Tel. 02 40 74 31 85
Closed Sun.–Mon.
and Aug. 3–25 and
Dec. 24–Jan 2.
Menus: 134–235F
☐ ☆ ☐

HOTEL-RESTAURANTS

LA DUCHESSE ANNE **
3, pl. de la Duchesse-
Anne
Tel. 02 51 86 78 78
Fax. 02 40 74 60 20
Closed Sun. eve– Mon.
lunchtime.
Rooms; 270–420F
Menus: 78–230F
☐ ☆ 🚗

MERCURE ***
Bd Alexandre-Millerand
Tel. 02 40 47 61 03

Fax 02 40 48 23 83
*By the Loire river and
close to the city center.*
Rooms: 470–490F
Menus: 110F
☐·· ☆ ⚓ 🅿 🚗

HOSTELLERIE DU MARAIS D'ORVAULT ****
Chemin Marais-de-Cens
Orvault
Tel. 02 44 76 84 02
Fax 02 40 76 04 21
Open until 10pm.
Closed Mon. lunchtime.
*Beautiful hotel set in a
park.*
Rooms: 530–690F
Menus: 160–350F
☆ 🅿 🚗 ♣

ACCOMMODATION

YOUTH HOSTEL
Cité Universitaire
2, place de la Manu
Tel. 02 40 74 61 86
(CROUS)
or 02 40 20 57 25
(FUAJ)
Open mid-Jun.–mid-Sep.
🅿 ♣

CHÂTEAUBRIANT
POSTCODE 44110 I–J6

CULTURAL ATTRACTIONS

CHÂTEAU
Pl. Charles-de-Gaulle
Tel. 02 40 28 20 90
Open 10am–noon, 3–
7pm, Jun. 15–Sep. 15.
Closed Tue. and Sun.
am. Gardens open to
the public all year.
▲384

CHURCH OF ST-JEAN-DE-BÉRÉ
Tel. 02 40 28 20 90
Open daily 9am–7pm.
Information available
from Châteaubriant
Tourist Office.

RESTAURANT

LE POÊLON D'OR
30 bis, rue du
11-Novembre
Tel. 02 40 81 43 33
Closed Sun. eve.–Mon.
and 10 days in Aug.
Menus: 102–250F
☐ 🅿

HOTEL-RESTAURANT

AUBERGE BRETONNE ***
23, pl. de la Motte
Tel. 02 40 81 03 05
Rooms: 180–380F
Menus: 92–225F
☐ ☆ 🅿

ACCOMMODATION

LE CHÂTEAUBRIANT ***
30, rue du 11-Novembre
Tel. 02 40 28 14 14
Rooms: 200–380F
☐ ☆ 🅿

HAUTE GOULAINE
POSTCODE 44115 I8

CULTURAL ATTRACTIONS

CHÂTEAU DE GOULAINE
Tel. 02 40 54 91 42
Closed Nov. 15–Easter.
Guided tours Wed.–Mon.
2–6pm Jun. 15– Sep. 15.
Restricted times during
low season. ▲384

◆ FOLK MUSIC ◆

◆ ABJEAN (R.): *La Musique bretonne*, Jos Le Doaré, Châteaulin, 1975
◆ *Antologie de la chanson en Bretagne*, L'Harmattan, Paris, 1976
◆ *Celtic Wedding: Music of Brittany played by Irish Musicians* (cassette tape), RCA, 1987
◆ HAMON (A.-G.): *Chantres de toutes les Bretagnes*, Picollec, Paris, 1981
◆ MALRIEUX (P.): *Histoire de la chanson populaire* BRETONNE, Dastum-Skol, Rennes, 1983
◆ MOELO (S.): *Guide de la musique bretonne*, Dastum, Rennes, 1990

◆ FOLKLORE AND RELIGION ◆

◆ ANDREJEWSKI (D.): *Les Abbayes bretonnes*, Fayard, Paris, 1983
◆ CHARDRONNET (J.): *Livre d'or des saints de Bretagne*, Armor, St-Brieuc, 1977
◆ *Dictionnaire des saints bretons*, Sand, Paris, 1986
◆ LE BRAZ (A.): *La Légende de la mort chez les Bretons armoricains*, Lafitte, Marseilles, 1978
◆ LE FLO'CH (M.): *Jeux traditionnels de Bretagne*, Institut culturel de Bretagne, Rennes, 1987
◆ SPENCE (L.): *Legends and Romances in Brittany*, Harrap, London, 1917
◆ RINDER (E.): *Shadow of Arvor: Legendary* ROMANCES AND FOLK-*Tales of Brittany*, Geddes, 1896
◆ ROUDAUT (F.): *Les Chemins du paradis. Taolennou ar* BARADOZ, *le Chasse-*Marée, Douarnenez, 1990
◆ SEBILLOT (P.-Y.): *Le Folklore de Bretagne*, Payot, Paris, 1968

◆ LANGUAGE AND LITERATURE ◆

◆ BALZAC (H. de), trans. M. A. Crawford: *The Chouans*, Penguin, Harmondsworth, 1979
◆ BATES (H.E.): *A Breath of French Air*, London, 1959
◆ CHATEAUBRIAND (F.-B.): *Mémoires d'outre-tombe*, Gallimard/Bibliothèque de la Pléiade, Paris, 1946
◆ COLETTE, trans. P. Mégroz: *The Ripening Seed*, Farrar, Strauss and Cudahy, New York, 1955
◆ CHRÉTIEN DE TROYES: *Le Conte du Graal*
◆ GRACQ (J.): *Au château d'Argol*, José Corti, Paris, 1938
– *Les Eaux étroites*, José Corti, Paris, 1976
◆ FAVEREAU (F.): *Bretagne contemporaine, langue, culture, indentité*, Skol Vreizh, Morlaix, 1993
◆ FLAUBERT (G.): *Par les Champs et par les Grèves*, Groz, Paris, 1988
◆ GOURVILLE (F.): *Langue et Littérature bretonnes*, PUF, Paris, 1976
◆ GUILLOUX (L.): *Le jeu de patience*, Gallimard, Paris, 1969
– *Le sang noir*, Gallimard/Folio, Paris, 1980
–*La maison du peuple*, Grasset/ Les Cahiers rouges, Paris, 1983
◆ GUÉHENNO (J.): *Journal d'un homme de 40 ans*, Grasset, Paris, 1934
– *Changer la vie*, Grasset, Paris, 1964
◆ HÉLIAS (P.), trans. and abr. J. Guicharnaud: *The Horse of Pride: Life in a Breton Village*, Yale, New Haven and London, 1978
∗ HEMON (R.): *Dictionnaire français-breton*, Al Liamm, Brest, 1965
◆ JAMES (H.): *A Little Tour in France*, Home & Van Thal, London, 1949

◆ KEROUAC (J.): *Sartori in Paris*, André Deutsch, London, 1967 ·
_ *Les Grandes Heures littéraires de la Bretagne*, Ouest-France, Rennes, 1978
◆ LOTI (P.), trans. W. P. Baines: *A Tale of Brittany*, 1928
◆ LOTI (P.), trans G. Endore: *An Iceland Fisherman*, Limited Edition Club, New York, 1931
◆ QUÉFFELEC (H.): *Un homme d'Ouessant*, Gallimard/Folio, Paris, 1973
– *Un recteur de l'île de Sein*, Presses de la Cité, Paris, 1982
◆ Richepin (J.): *La Mer*, Gallimard, Paris, 1980
◆ STENDHAL: *Mémoires d'un touriste en Bretagne*, Albatros, Paris, 1986
◆ TROLLOPE (T.A.): *A Summer in Brittany*, Henry Colburn, London, 1840
◆ TUCHMAN (B.): *A Distant Mirror*, 1978

◆ PAINTING ◆

◆ BOYLE-TURNER (C.): *Gauguin and the School of Pont-Aven*, London, 1986
◆ DEBIDOUR (V.-H.): *L'Art de Bretagne*, Arthaud, Paris, 1979.
◆ DELOUCHE (D.): *Eugène Boudin et la Bretagne*, Ursa, Raillé,1987
◆ DERRIEN (P.): *Art gothique en Bretagne*, Ouest-France, Rennes, 1982
◆ *La route des peintres en Cornouaille*, Groupement Touristique de Cornouaille, Quimper, 1990
◆ LE PAUL (J.): *Gauguin and the Impressionists at Pont-Aven*, Abbeville, New York, 1983
◆ GAUGUIN (P.), ed. B. Denvir: *The Search for Paradise: Letters from Brittany and the South Seas*, Collins & Brown, London, 1965
◆ TERRASSE (a.): *Pont-Aven, l'École buissonnière*, Gallimard, Paris, 1992

◆ ARCHITECTURE/ SCULPTURE ◆

◆ AUDIN (P.): *Guide des fontaines guérisseuses, Morbihan, Finistère, Côtes-du-Nord*, Maisonneuve et Larose, Paris, 1983
◆ DEBIDOUR (V.-H.): *La Sculpture bretonne*, Ouest-France, Rennes, 1985
◆ RENOUARD (M.): *Art roman en Bretagne*, Ouest-France, Rennes, 1985
◆ ROYER (É): *Nouveau guide des calvaires bretons*, Ouest-France, Rennes, 1985

◆ GUIDEBOOKS ◆

◆ BELL (B.), ed: *Brittany*, Insight Guides, APA, 1992
◆ *Brittany*, Michelin, 1987
◆ *Brittany and Normandy, the Rough Guide*, Rough Guides, 1992
◆ DAVIES (F.V.): *Brittany in a Week*, Hodder & Stoughton, London, 1993
◆ EPERON (A.): *Brittany*, Pan, London 1990
◆ *Fodor's Brittany and Normandy*, Fodor, 1993
◆ SALE (R.): *Visitor's Guide: Brittany*, Moorland, 1993
◆ SNAILHAM (R.): *Normandy and Brittany: from Le Tréport to St-Nazaire*, Weidenfeld & Nicolson, London 1986

◆ PERIODICALS ◆

_ *Ar men, La Bretagne: Un monde à découvrir* (published bi-monthly) Le Chasse Marée, Douarnenez
_ *Le Chasse-Marée* (published bi-monthly), Douarnenez
_ *Les Cahiers de l'Iroise* (published quarterly since 1954 by the Société d'études de Brest et du Léon; covers heritage, literary and cultural matters), Brest.

443

◆ BIBLIOGRAPHY

GENERAL
◆ READING ◆

◆ DESCHAMPS (M.): Portrait of Brittany, Hale, London, 1980
◆ BARING-GOULD (S.): A Book of Brittany, Methuen, London, 1932
◆ GUILLET (J.), ed: La Batellerie bretonne, Le Chasse-Marée-Estran, Douarnenez, 1988.
◆ HÉLIAS (P.-J.): Images de Bretagne, Jos Le Doaré, Châteaulin 1992
◆ LE NAIL (B.): Bretagne pays de mer, le patrimoine maritime breton, Hachette, Paris 1993
◆ MACDONALD (M.): "We are not French": Language, Culture and Identity in Brittany, 1989.
◆ MEYNIER (A.): La Bretagne, Flammarion, Paris, 1976
◆ SPENCE (K.): Brittany and the Bretons, Gollancz, London 1978

◆ FOOD ◆

◆ BAKER (J.): Cuisine Grandmère from Brittany, Normandy, Picardy and Flanders, Faber, London, 1994
◆ MORAND (S.): La Gastronomie bretonne, Flammarion, Paris, 1972
◆ PAINEAU (G.): Bouquet de Bretagne: Seasonal Recipes from Le Bretagne, Questembert, Pavilion, London, 1993
◆ PERRIN-CHATTARD (B.): The Best Breton Recipes, Ouest-France, Rennes, 1984
◆ RAFFAEL (M.): Brittany (French Regional Cooking), Hamlyn, London, 1990
◆ WILLAN (A.): La France Gastronomique (English text), Pavilion, London, 1991.

NATURAL
◆ HISTORY ◆

◆ Ar vag, voiles au travail en Bretagne atlantique, Estran, Douarnenez, 1984
◆ ARZEL (P.): Les Goémoniers, Le Chasse-Marée, Estran, Douarnenez, 1987
◆ BEAULIEU (F. de), LE MOIGNE: Nature en Bretagne (Ar men-Le Chasse-Marée, Douarnenez, 1991
◆ COUVREUR (G.) and LE GUEN (G.): Bretagne, Masson, Paris, 1990
◆ DARDE (J.-N.): Plages et Côtes de France, Balland, Paris, 1991
◆ DURAND (S.) and LARDEUX (H.): Bretagne, Masson/Guides géologiques régionaux, Paris, 1985
◆ GUERMEUR (Y.) and MONNAT (J.-Y.): Histoire et géographie de oiseaux nicheurs en Bretagne, Ar Vran, 1980
◆ MONNAT (J.-Y.): Bretagne vivante, Éditions SAEP/Animaux et fleurs des régions de France, Colmar-Ingersheim, 1973
◆ VIGHETTI (J.-B.): Le Canaux bretons, Ouest-France, Rennes, 1985

◆ ARCHEOLOGY ◆

◆ AUDREY (B.): Guide des dolmens et des menhirs bretons, Errance, Paris, 1987
◆ BENDER (B.): The Archeology of Brittany, Normandy and the Channel Islands, Faber, London, 1986.
◆ BURL (A.): From Carnac to Callanish: the Prehistoric Stone Rows and Avenues of Brittany, Yale, New Haven and London, 1993
– Megalithic Brittany: a Guide to over 350 Ancient Sites and monuments, Thames and Hudson, London, 1985
◆ CHADWICK (N.): Early Brittany, University of Wales Press, Cardiff, 1969
◆ GIOT (P.): Brittany, Thames and Hudson, London, 1960
◆ GIOT (P.) et al.: Préhistoire de la Bretagne, Ouest-France, Rennes, 1979 – Protohistoire de la Bretagne, Ouest-France, Rennes, 1979.
◆ PATTEN (M.): Statements in Stone: Monuments and Society in Neolithic Brittany, Routledge, London and New York, 1993

◆ HISTORY ◆

◆ CASSARD (J.-C.): Vikings en Bretagne, Skol Vreizh, Morlaix, 1986
◆ CHEDEVILLE (A.) and GUILLOTEL (H.): La Bretagne des Saints et des rois, Ouest-France, Rennes, 1984
◆ CHEDEVILLE (A.) and TONNERRE (N.-Y.): Le Bretagne féodale, XIe-XIIe siècle, Ouest-France, Rennes, 1987
◆ CROIX (A.): L'âge d'or de la Bretagne, 1532–1675, Ouest-France, Rennes, 1993
◆ DIGOU (S.): Châteaux en Bretagne, Jos Le Doaré Châteaulin, 1988
◆ FREGNAC (C.): La Bretagne des châteaux, Hachette, Paris, 1976
◆ FRELAUT (B.): Les Nationalistes bretons de 1939 à 1945, Beltan, Brasparts, 1985
◆ GALLOW (P.) and JONES (M.): The Bretons, Blackwell, Oxford (UK) and Cambridge (USA), 1991
– Histoire littéraire et culturelle de le Bretagne, 3 vols, Champion-Slatkine, Paris/Geneva, 1987
◆ JONES (M.): The Creation of Brittany, Hambleden Press, London and Ronceverte, 1988
◆ LANDS (N.): History, People and Places in Brittany, Spurbooks, 1979.
_ Le Manoir en Bretagne 1380-1600, Cahiers de l'inventaire, Imprimerie Nationale, Paris, 1993
◆ LE SCOUEZEC (G.): Pierres sacrées de Bretagne: Calvaires et enclos paroissaux (vol. 1); Croix et santuaires (vol. 2), Le Seuil, Paris, 1982
_ Les Premiers Bretons, la Bretagne du Ve siècle à l'an mil Jos le Doaré, Châteaulin, 1988
◆ SUTHERLAND (D.): The Chouans, Clarendon Press, Oxford, 1982

ARTS AND
◆ CRAFTS ◆

◆ BONDHUS (S.): Quimper Pottery: a French folk art faience, 1981.
◆ Coiffes de Bretagne, Costumes, Danses, Savoir-vivre, Traditions bretonnes, 5 vols, Jos Le Doaré, Châteaulin
◆ CRESTON (R.-Y.): Le Costume breton, Tchou, Paris, 1974
◆ CUISENIER (J.): French Folk Art, Kodansha, Tokyo, New York and San Francisco, 1977
◆ DANNENBERG (L.): Pierre Deux's Brittany: A French Country Style and Source Book, Phaidon, Oxford, 1990
◆ HÉLIAS (P.-J.): Coiffes et Costumes de Bretagne, Jos Le Doaré, Châteaulin, 1986
◆ JEANNEAU (G.): Meubles bretons, Hachette, Paris, 1973
◆ LE ROUX-PAUGAM (M.): Le Mobilier breton, Ouest-France, Rennes, 1985.
◆ LE ROUX-PAUGAM (M.): Les Coffres paysans du Léon et de Haute-Cornouaille, Quimper, 1976.
◆ MOINE (M.P.): French Country Crafts, Cassell, London, 1993
◆ SOLON (M.L.): A History and Description of the Old French Faience, Cassell, London, 1903

Appendices

◆ LIST OF ILLUSTRATIONS

We should like to thank the following people for their help:
M. Jean Aubert (conservateur du musée des Beaux-Arts de Rennes), M. Pascal Aumasson (conservateur du musée d'Art et d'Histoire de Saint-Brieuc), Banque de données Joconde et Carrare, Mme Martine Bécus, (documentaliste musées de Vitré), Mme François Bercé (conservateur de la bibl. du patrimoine, Paris), M. René Le Bihan (conservateur du musée des Beaux-Arts, Brest), M. Jean-Pierre Bihr, M. Robert
Boulthier (Dastum, Rennes), M. Gildas Buron (conservateur au musée des Marais Salants, Batz-sur-Mer), Mme Cadiou, M. capitaine (DDE, Brest, subdivision des Phares et Balises), M. André Cariou (conservateur du musée des Beaux-Arts, Quimper), M. Christain Carlet (musée des Plans-Reliefs, Paris), Mme Alyson Clark (conservateur de l'écomusée de la Bintinais), Mme Coïc (bibl. de Morlaix), Mme Christian Collet (Archives dépt. du Finistère, Quimper), M. Pierrick Cordonnier (association La Bouëze), M. Coroller, M. Yves Cosson (conservateur du Patrimoine), Mme Françoise Daniel (conservateur du musée des Jacobins, Morlaix), Mme Claire Denis, M. Dominique Denis, Mme Derveaux (Association des amis des bisquines et du vieux Cancale), M. Dominique Le Doaré, Mme Colette Dréan (centre de documentation du patrimoine, Rennes), M. Jean-Claude Le Dro, M. Alain Droguet (conservateur des archives dépt. des Côtes-d'Armor, Saint-Brieuc), M. Jacques Duchemin, M. Louis-Claude Duchêne, Mme Thérèse Dumont (documentaliste, écomusée de Saint-Nazaire), Mme Dunod (conservateur du musée de la duchesse Anne, Dinan), Mme Jacqueline Duroc, M. Claude Duthuit, Mme Catherine Elkar (directrice du FRAC de Bretagne), M. Henri Fermin, M. le chanoine Le Floc'h (Evêché de Quimper), M. Patrice Forget (conservateur des musées de Vitré), M. Roland Gestin, M. Jean-Pierre Gestin (conservateur du Parc d'Armorique), Mme Claudine Glot, Mme Hélène Guéné, Mme Yvonne Jean-Haffen, M. Jean-Jacques Hénaff, M. S. Josefowitz, Mme Marie-Hélène Jouzeau (conservateur des musées du château des ducs de Bretagne, Nantes), M. Jean-Paul Lelu, M. François Loyer, M. Hubert Maheux (Inventaire général, Nantes), Mme Gaby Marcon (conservateur de l'écomusée de Montfort), M. Mauger (archives dépt. d'Ille et Vilaine), Melle Josèphe Mottais, M. Daniel de La Motte Rouge, Mme Geneviève Noufflard, M. Nougaret (archives dép. de Nantes), M. Georges Pellequer, M. Philippe Petout (conservateur du musée de St-Malo), M. Julien Pétry, M. Potier, Mme Pouillas (conservateur de la bibl. municipale de Rennes), Mme Laurence Prod'Homme (conservateur du musée de
Bretagne, Rennes), M. Dominique Provost, Mme Catherine Puget (conservateur du musée de Pont-Aven), Mme Roudotte (conservateur du château de Kerjean), M. Vincent Rousseau (conservateur du musée des Beaux-Arts de Nantes), M. Le Servoisier (conservateur de la bibl. d'Avranches), M. Daniel Sicard (conservateur de l'écomusée de Saint-Nazaire), Mme Michaële Simonin (conservateur au musée des Marais Salants, Batz-sur-mer), M. Philippe Le Stum (conservateur du musée dépt., Quimper),

INDEX

◆ INDEX

THEMATIC INDEX

◆ Thematic index

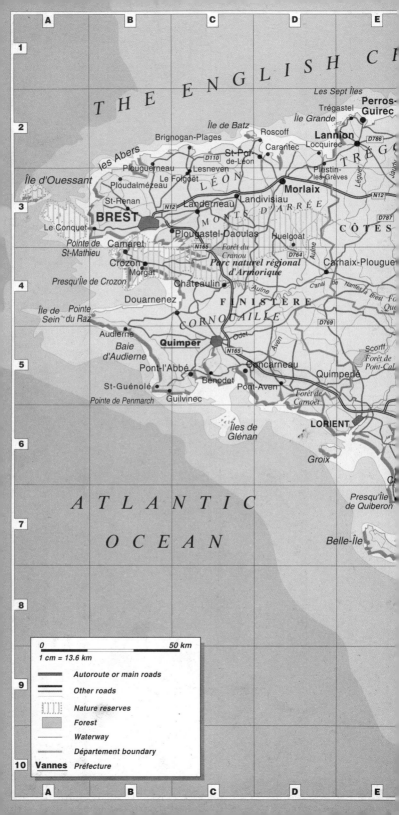